THE QUMRAN RULE TEXTS
IN CONTEXT

TEXTS AND STUDIES IN ANCIENT JUDAISM
TEXTE UND STUDIEN ZUM ANTIKEN JUDENTUM

Edited by
Peter Schäfer
Annette Y. Reed
Seth Schwartz
Azzan Yadin-Israel

Number 154

THE QUMRAN RULE TEXTS IN CONTEXT
Collected Studies

by
Charlotte Hempel

Atlanta

Copyright © 2013 by Mohr Siebeck, Tübingen, Germany

This edition is published under license from Mohr Siebeck, Tübingen, Germany, by SBL Press.

All rights reserved. No part of this work may be reproduced or transmitted in any form or by any means, electronic or mechanical, including photocopying and recording, or by means of any information storage or retrieval system, except as may be expressly permitted by the 1976 Copyright Act or in writing from the publisher. Requests for permission should be addressed in writing to the Rights and Permissions Department, Mohr Siebeck, Tübingen, Germany.

Library of Congress Control Number: 2019951683

Printed on acid-free paper.

For Charles and Imogen

Acknowledgments

The studies collected in this volume span a period of seventeen years, and it is a great pleasure to express my thanks to many friends and colleagues for their support. I will begin by thanking the editors of previous volumes that included my work who have added elegance and clarity where it was lacking in my manuscript. I only came to fully appreciate their efforts while going over the text again!

I am particularly grateful to my colleagues at the University of Birmingham who have supported me in numerous different ways over the years, especially Helen Beebee (now Manchester), Andrew Davies, Ken Dowden, Deryn Guest, Hugh Houghton, Jagbir Jhutti-Johal, Christina Kreinecker, Rosalind MacLachlan, David Parker, Martin Stringer, Karen Wenell, Heather Widdows, and Isabel Wollaston who are all close colleagues in the School Philosophy, Theology, and Religion. I also gratefully acknowledge a teaching buy-out in 2011–2012 supported the College of Arts and Law and its Head, Prof. Michael Whitby, and expertly delivered by Drew Longacre. Finally, and not least, I appreciate the many insightful contributions by my students in Birmingham.

Beyond Birmingham I am blessed to count the following outstanding scholars among my friends, all of whom are credited in the standard fashion in various footnotes, but are singled out here to thank them for their collegiality and friendship stretching over many years: Al Baumgarten, Moshe Bernstein, Joseph Blenkinsopp, George Brooke, John Collins, David Chalcraft, Esther Chazon, Philip Davies, Esther Eshel, Heinz-Josef Fabry, Daniel Falk, Steven Fraade, Florentino García Martínez, Matthew Goff, Martin Goodman, Maxine Grossman, Jutta Jokiranta, Menahem Kister, Michael Knibb, Reinhard Kratz, Amy-Jill Levine, Judy Lieu, Jodi Magness, Sarianna Metso, Hindy Najman, Judy Newman, Carol Newsom, Vered Noam, Sarah Pearce, Mladen Popović, Gary Rendsburg, Larry Schiffman, Eileen Schuller, Aharon Shemesh, Rudolf Smend, Sacha Stern, Annette Steudel, Michael E. Stone, Joan E. Taylor, Eibert Tigchelaar, Emanuel Tov, Gene Ulrich, Jim VanderKam, Geza Vermes, Hanne von Weissenberg, and Sidnie White Crawford.

It was Prof. Jörg Frey who first suggested I publish a volume of Collected Essays with Mohr Siebeck. I am grateful to him and to the editors of the series *Texts and Studies in Ancient Judaism* – Profs. Peter Schäfer, Annette Y. Reed, Seth Schwartz, and Azzan Yadin – for accepting the volume into this prestigious series. It has been a singular pleasure to work with Dr. Henning Ziebritzki and his team who have been a steady source of support.

Finally, I dedicate this book to my children Charles and Imogen Cave and thank them for making me laugh, cook, bake, swim, walk, talk, listen, shout, and proud as well as entertaining me with recorders, piano, guitars, and song. It is thanks to you that I was able to live what can almost pass for a normal life while working on this volume. My husband Dick has been there for me every part of the way as always – thank you!

Birmingham, January 2013   Charlotte Hempel

Table of Contents

Acknowledgments VII
Publication Details of Previously Published Chapters XVII
Abbreviations Including Frequently Cited Sources XIX

Chapter One: Introduction 1

1. The Nature of the Communities 2
2. Beginnings 4
   2.1 The Teacher: From John Wayne to the Wizard of Oz 4
   2.2 Looking for Beginnings in Unexpected Places 6
3. The Community Rule Traditions 8
4. Close Encounters: The Community Rule and the Damascus Document 9
5. Rules in the Context of Wisdom and Law 10
6. Priesthood in the Rule Texts and Beyond 14
7. The Scrolls and the Emerging Scriptures 15
8. Does 4Q Equal Qumran? The Character of Cave 4 Reconsidered 19
9. Concluding Reflections 20

Part I
The Nature of the Communities

Chapter Two: Community Structures and Organization 25

1. Introduction 25
2. Admission Process 28
3. Organization 31
   3.1 Property 31
   3.2 Meetings 32
   3.3 Leadership and Authority Structures 36
   3.4 Communal Meals 40
   3.5 Family Life and Celibacy 42
4. Disciplinary and Judicial Procedures 44
5. Conclusion 45

Chapter Three: The Damascus Document and 1QSa	47
1. Introduction	47
2. 1QSa 1:6–2:11a and Its Present Context	47
3. 1QSa 1:6–2:11a and the Laws of the Damascus Document	53
3.1 'All-Israel' Terminology	54
3.2 Family Life	55
3.3 עדה Terminology	59
3.4 The Book of Hagi	60
3.5 Exclusion from the Congregation	60
4. Conclusion	62

Part II
Beginnings

Chapter Four: The Damascus Document and Community Origins	65
1. Introduction	65
2. Discussion of the Texts	68
2.1 CD 1:3–11a: A First Account of Community Origins in the Damascus Document	68
2.2 CD 2:8b–13: A Second Account of Community Origins in the Damascus Document	70
2.3 CD 3:12b–4:12a: A Third Account of Community Origins in the Damascus Document	73
2.4 CD 5:20–6:11a: A Fourth Account of Community Origins in the Damascus Document	75
3. Analysis of All Four Accounts of Community Origins in the Damascus Document	76
Chapter Five: Emerging Communities in the Serekh	79
1. Introduction	79
2. The Evidence of the S Manuscripts	79
3. Emerging Communal Life in 1QS 6	80
4. An Emerging Community Ideology in 1QS 8	84
5. Expiation Restricted to the Community (1QS 5//4Q256 [4QS^b] and 4Q258 [4QS^d])	92
6. The Evidence of 4Q265	92
7. The Evidence of the Damascus Document	94
8. Conclusions and Outlook	95

Chapter Six: Small Beginnings or Geographical Diversity 97

1. Introduction 97
2. Texts, Communities, and the Site of Qumran 98
3. Yaḥad(s) Before and Outside of Qumran 99
4. 1QS 6:1c–8a: The Under-Studied Enters the Limelight 101
5. CD 13:2b–3a: A Council-Free Version of 1QS 6:3 103
6. Conclusion 105

Part III
The Community Rule Traditions

Chapter Seven: Shifting Paradigms Concerning the Literary Development
of the Serekh 109

1. Introduction and History of Research 109
2. Continuity Alongside Difference Between 1QS and 4QS 114
3. Diversity within 4Q258 (4QS^d) 115
4. The Many in 1QS 116
5. The Council of the Community in S 117
6. Conclusion 119

Part IV
Close Encounters:
The Community Rule and the Damascus Document

Chapter Eight: CD 19–20 and the Community Rule 123

1. Introduction 123
2. CD 20:1–8 and the Community Rule 127
3. The Texts (CD 20:1b–8a and 1QS 8:16b–9:2; 9:8–11a//4Q258 (4QS^d)
   6 8b.11–12; 7 1–3.7–9) 129
4. Analysis 132
5. Conclusion 135

Chapter Nine: Rewritten Rule Texts 137

1. Introduction 137
2. Points of Contact Between S and D 139
   2.1 The Penal Code 144
   2.2 Gatherings of Ten 145
   2.3 Admission into the Community by Swearing an Oath 145

Table of Contents

2.4 Maskil Headings 146
2.5 The Self Designation "The People of Perfect Holiness" 147
2.6 Liturgical Framework 147
3. Analysis and Conclusions 148

Part V
Rules in the Context of Wisdom and Law

Chapter Ten: The Rule Books and the Qumran Wisdom Texts 153

1. Introduction 153
2. The Questions 154
3. Three Qumran Sapiential Works 155
   3.1 The Book of Mysteries 155
   3.2 Instruction 157
   3.3 4QWays of Righteousness 159
4. Wisdom Elements in the Rule Books 160
   4.1 Raz Nihyeh 160
   4.2 The Book of Hagi 161
   4.3 The Maskil 162
      4.3.1 Maskil in Instruction 163
      4.3.2 Maskil in 4QWays of Righteousness 164
      4.3.3 Maskil in the Damascus Document 164
      4.3.4 Maskil in the Community Rule 165
      4.3.5 Maskil in 4Q298 (Address of the Maskil to the Sons of Dawn) 169
5. Conclusion 171

Chapter Eleven: The Damascus Document and MMT 173

1. Introduction 173
2. 4QMMT and Communal Legislation in the Damascus Document (D) 174
3. 4QMMT and Halakhah in D 176
   3.1 General Observations 177
   3.2 Specific Texts 178
      3.2.1 The 4QD Material on the Disqualification of Priests ... 178
      3.2.2 The 4QD Material on Skin Disease, Flux and Childbirth . 180
      3.2.3 4QD Halakhah Dealing with Agricultural Matters 181
      3.2.4 Texts Expressing Concern about Defilement through Contact
             with Gentiles 182
      3.2.5 The Catalogue of Transgressions in 4Q270 (4QD^e) 183
4. Conclusion 185

Chapter Twelve: The Damascus Document and 4QOrdinances[a] (4Q159) ... 187

1. Introduction ... 187
2. Shared Content ... 188
3. Correspondences in Matters of Sequence ... 189
4. Shared Scriptural Basis ... 190
5. Shared Formal Features ... 191
6. Conclusion ... 191

Part VI
Priesthood in the Rule Texts and Beyond

Chapter Thirteen: The Sons of Aaron ... 195

1. Introduction ... 195
2. The Damascus Document (D) ... 197
3. The Community Rule (S) ... 199
4. 4Q286 Berakhot[a] ... 201
5. 4Q279 (4QFour Lots; olim 4QTohorot D) ... 202
6. 4Q265 Miscellaneous Rules olim Serekh Damascus ... 203
7. The Rule of the Congregation ... 204
8. The War Scroll (M) ... 204
9. 4QMMT ... 205
10. Temple Scroll ... 206
11. 4Q174 Florilegium ... 207
12. 4Q390 Apocryphon of Jeremiah C[e] ... 207
13. 4Q513 Ordinances[b] ... 208
14. Conclusion ... 208

Chapter Fourteen: Consider Ourselves in Charge:
Self-Assertion Sons of Zadok Style ... 211

1. Introduction ... 211
2. The Damascus Document ... 213
3. The Community Rule ... 222
4. The Rule of the Congregation ... 224
5. The Rule of Blessings ... 225
6. 4Qpesher Isaiah[c] ... 226
7. 4QFlorilegium ... 226
8. Conclusion ... 226

Part VII
The Scrolls and the Emerging Scriptures

Chapter Fifteen: The Community Rule and the Book of Daniel 231

1. Setting the Scene 231
   1.1 A Shared Bilingual Milieu 232
   1.2 The Book of Daniel and the Scrolls as Tradents of Danielic
       Traditions 233
   1.3 A Claim to Exilic Roots 234
   1.4 A Learned Scribal Context 235
   1.5 The Significance of Mystery and Interpretation 235
   1.6 Consciousness of Proximity with the Angelic Realm 236
2. The Maskilim in Daniel 11–12 237
3. Maskil and Rabbim in the Community Rule 239
   3.1 The Restored Title of the Rule of the Community 241
   3.2 The Introduction to the Teaching on the Two Spirits 1QS 3:13–4:26 242
   3.3 The Introduction to 1QS 5//4Q256 (4QS^b) 9//4Q258 (4QS^d) 1 243
   3.4 The Statutes for the Maskil 1QS 9:12–25//4Q256 (4QS^b) 18:1–7//
       4Q258 (4QS^d) 8:1–9//4Q259 (4QS^e) 3:6–4:8//4Q260 (4QS^f) 1:1–2 244
4. Conclusion 251

Chapter Sixteen: The Damascus Document and Ezra-Nehemiah 253

1. Introduction 253
2. Ezra-Nehemiah and the Damascus Document: Some Common Ground 255
   2.1 Location 256
   2.2 Community 257
   2.3 Issues 259
3. Family and Household Structures in Ezra-Nehemiah and D 259
   3.1 The Authority of the Father in Arranging Marriages
       According to the Damascus Document 265
   3.2 The Overseer Encroaches on the Father's Role 267
   3.3 A Comparative Analysis of the Stipulations Dealing with the
       Arrangement of Marriages in the Damascus Document 267
4. Conclusion 269

Chapter Seventeen: The Serekh Tradition in Light of Post-Qumran
Perspectives on the Emerging Bible 271

1. Introduction 271
2. The Literary Panorama of the Rule Manuscripts 272
3. The Authority of Changing Texts: The Emerging Bible and the Serekh 278

4. The Emerging Bible and the S Tradition: Inconsistencies Welcome! ... 279
5. A Farewell to the End-Serekh 283
6. Conclusion 283

Chapter Eighteen: The Emerging Bible and the Dead Sea Scrolls:
A Common Milieu 285

1. Introduction 285
2. The Scrolls as Case Studies of the Ancient Jewish Literary Craft 287
3. The Scrolls and the Emergence of Jewish Sectarianism in the Persian
   Period 288
4. The Shared Scribal Milieu Behind the Emerging Scriptures and the
   Scrolls 289
5. Tracing Trajectories from Emerging Sectarianism in the Hebrew Bible
   to Incipient Communal Life Attested in the Scrolls 290
6. The Scrolls and Recent Research on the Development of the Psalter .. 291
7. A Life Dedicated to Torah Scholarship: Ps 1:2, Josh 1:8
   and 1QS 6:6b–7a 293
8. Conclusion 298

Part VIII
Does 4Q Equal Qumran?
The Character of Cave 4 Reconsidered

Chapter Nineteen: 'Haskalah' at Qumran:
The Eclectic Character of Qumran Cave 4 303

1. Introduction 303
2. The Qumran Scroll Caves 304
3. Qumran Cave 4 306
4. The Profile of the Caves 308
5. Distinctive Elements in the Profile of Qumran Cave 4 311
   5.1 Texts Written in Cryptic Script 312
   5.2 The Maskil and Cave 4 317
   5.3 Technical Learning: The Calendar Texts 319
   5.4 Multiple Attestation 329
   5.5 4Q477 – The Overseer's Bookkeeping 331
   5.6 The 'Workaday Quality' of a Number of Cave 4 Texts 332
      5.6.1 4Q265 Miscellaneous Rules 332
      5.6.2 Anthologies and Compilations 332
      5.6.3 Raw Data 333

    5.6.4 Serekh and Refinement in Cave 1 334
    5.6.5 A Preponderance of Papyrus in Cave 4
          over against Caves 1 and 11 336
6. Conclusion 336

Cumulative Bibliography 339

Index of References 371
Index of Modern Authors 389

4. The Emerging Bible and the S Tradition: Inconsistencies Welcome! ... 279
5. A Farewell to the End-Serekh 283
6. Conclusion 283

Chapter Eighteen: The Emerging Bible and the Dead Sea Scrolls:
A Common Milieu 285

1. Introduction 285
2. The Scrolls as Case Studies of the Ancient Jewish Literary Craft 287
3. The Scrolls and the Emergence of Jewish Sectarianism in the Persian
   Period 288
4. The Shared Scribal Milieu Behind the Emerging Scriptures and the
   Scrolls 289
5. Tracing Trajectories from Emerging Sectarianism in the Hebrew Bible
   to Incipient Communal Life Attested in the Scrolls 290
6. The Scrolls and Recent Research on the Development of the Psalter .. 291
7. A Life Dedicated to Torah Scholarship: Ps 1:2, Josh 1:8
   and 1QS 6:6b–7a 293
8. Conclusion 298

Part VIII
Does 4Q Equal Qumran?
The Character of Cave 4 Reconsidered

Chapter Nineteen: 'Haskalah' at Qumran:
The Eclectic Character of Qumran Cave 4 303

1. Introduction 303
2. The Qumran Scroll Caves 304
3. Qumran Cave 4 306
4. The Profile of the Caves 308
5. Distinctive Elements in the Profile of Qumran Cave 4 311
   5.1 Texts Written in Cryptic Script 312
   5.2 The Maskil and Cave 4 317
   5.3 Technical Learning: The Calendar Texts 319
   5.4 Multiple Attestation 329
   5.5 4Q477 – The Overseer's Bookkeeping 331
   5.6 The 'Workaday Quality' of a Number of Cave 4 Texts 332
       5.6.1 4Q265 Miscellaneous Rules 332
       5.6.2 Anthologies and Compilations 332
       5.6.3 Raw Data 333

    5.6.4 Serekh and Refinement in Cave 1 334
    5.6.5 A Preponderance of Papyrus in Cave 4
         over against Caves 1 and 11 336
6. Conclusion 336

Cumulative Bibliography 339

Index of References 371
Index of Modern Authors 389

Publication Details of Previously Published Chapters

Chapter 2, 'Community Structures in the Dead Sea Scrolls: Admission, Organization, and Disciplinary Procedures,' in *The Dead Sea Scrolls After Fifty Years* (ed. Peter Flint and James VanderKam; Leiden: Brill, 1999), Vol. II, 67–92

Chapter 3, 'The Earthly Essene Nucleus of 1QSa,' *DSD* 3 (1996): 253–269

Chapter 4, 'Community Origins in the Damascus Document in the Light of Recent Scholarship,' in *The Provo International Conference on the Dead Sea Scrolls: Technological Innovations, New Texts, and Reformulated Issues* (ed. Donald W. Parry and Eugene Ulrich; STDJ 30; Leiden: Brill, 1999), 316–329

Chapter 5, 'Emerging Communal Life and Ideology in the S Tradition,' in *Defining Identities: We, You, and the Other in the Dead Sea Scrolls. Proceedings of the Fifth Meeting of the IOQS in Groningen* (ed. Florentino García Martínez and Mladen Popović; STDJ 70; Leiden: Brill, 2008), 43–61

Chapter 6, '1QS 6:2c–4a – Satellites or Precursors of the Yaḥad?,' in *The Dead Sea Scrolls and Contemporary Culture* (ed. Adolfo Roitman, Larry Schiffman, and Shani Tzoref; STDJ 93; Leiden: Brill, 2011), 31–40

Chapter 7, 'The Literary Development of the S-Tradition: A New Paradigm,' *RQ* 22 (2006): 389–401

Chapter 8, 'CD Manuscript B and the Community Rule – Reflections on a Literary Relationship,' *DSD* 16 (2009): 370–387

Chapter 9, 'Shared Traditions: Points of Contact Between S and D,' in *The Dead Sea Scrolls: Transmission of Traditions and Production of Texts* (ed. Sarianna Metso, Hindy Najman, and Eileen Schuller; STDJ 92; Leiden: Brill, 2010), 115–131

Chapter 10, 'The Qumran Sapiential Texts and the Rule Books,' in *The Wisdom Texts from Qumran and the Development of Sapiential Thought* (ed. Charlotte Hempel, Armin Lange, and Hermann Lichtenberger; BETL 159; Leuven: Peeters, 2002), 277–295

Chapter 11, 'The Damascus Document and 4QMMT,' in *The Damascus Document: A Centennial of Discovery. Proceedings of the Third International Symposium of the Orion Center for the Study of the Dead Sea Scrolls and Associated Literature, 4–8 February, 1998* (ed. Joseph Baumgarten, Esther Chazon, and Avital Pinnick; STDJ 34; Leiden: Brill, 2000), 69–84

Chapter 12, '4QOrd^a (4Q159) and the Laws of the Damascus Document,' in *The Dead Sea Scrolls Fifty Years After Their Discovery* (ed. Lawrence H. Schiffman, Emanuel Tov, and James C. VanderKam; Jerusalem: IES, 2000), 372–376

Chapter 13, 'The Sons of Aaron in the Dead Sea Scrolls,' in *Flores Florentino: Dead Sea Scrolls and Other Early Jewish Studies in Honour of Florentino García Martínez* (ed. Anthony Hilhorst, Émile Puech, and Eibert Tigchelaar; JSJSup 122; Leiden: Brill, 2007), 207–224

Chapter 14, 'Do the Scrolls Suggest Rivalry Between the Sons of Aaron and the Sons of Zadok and If So was it Mutual,' *RQ* 24 (2009): 135–153

Chapter 15, 'Maskil(im) and Rabbim: From Daniel to Qumran,' in *Biblical Traditions in Transmission: Essays in Honour of Michael A. Knibb* (ed. Charlotte Hempel and Judith M. Lieu; JSJSup 111; Leiden: Brill, 2006), 133–156

Chapter 16, 'Family Values in the Second Temple Period,' in *Ethical and Unethical in the Old Testament: God and Humans in Dialogue* (ed. Katherine Dell; LHBOTS 528; London: T & T Clark, 2010), 211–230

Chapter 17, 'Pluralism and Authoritativeness – The Case of the S Tradition,' in *Authoritative Scriptures in Ancient Judaism* (ed. Mladen Popović; JSJSup 141; Leiden: Brill, 2010), 193–208

Chapter 18, 'The Social Matrix that Shaped the Hebrew Bible and Gave us the Dead Sea Scrolls,' in *Studies on the Text and Versions of the Hebrew Bible in Honour of Robert Gordon* (ed. Geoffrey Khan and Diana Lipton; VTSup 149; Leiden: Brill, 2012), 221–237

I am grateful to all the publishers above for their permission to include these studies here.

Abbreviations Including Frequently Cited Sources

ATANT	Abhandlungen zur Theologie des Alten und Neuen Testaments
ATSAT	Arbeiten zu Text und Sprache im Alten Testament
AYBC	Anchor Yale Bible Commentary
BA	*Biblical Archaeologist*
BASOR	*Bulletin of the American Schools of Oriental Research*
BASORSup	Bulletin of the American Schools of Oriental Research: Supplement Series
BETL	Bibliotheca Ephemeridum Theologicarum Lovaniensium
BIS	Biblical Interpretation Series
BJS	Brown Judaic Studies
BKAT	Biblischer Kommentar zum Alten Testament
BZAW	Beihefte zur Zeitschrift für die alttestamentliche Wissenschaft
CBA	Catholic Biblical Association
CBC	Cambridge Bible Commentary
CBQ	*Catholic Biblical Quarterly*
CBQMS	Catholic Biblical Quarterly Monograph Series
ConBNT	Coniectanea Biblica: New Testament Series
CRINT	Compendia Rerum Iudaicarum ad Novum Testamentum
CUP	Cambridge University Press
DAWBSSA	Deutsche Akademie der Wissenschaften zu Berlin, Schriften der Sektion für Altertumswissenschaft
DBSup	Dictionnnaire de la Bible: Supplément
DJD 1	Dominique Barthélemy and Józef T. Milik *Qumran Cave 1* (DJD 1; Oxford: Clarendon, 1955)
DJD 3	Dominique Barthélemy, Józef T. Milik, and Roland de Vaux *Les 'Petites Grottes' de Qumrân* (DJD 3; Oxford: Clarendon, 1962)
DJD 4	James A. Sanders, *The Psalms Scroll of Qumrân Cave 11 (11QPsalms^a)* (DJD 4; Oxford: Clarendon, 1965)
DJD 5	John Marco Allegro and A. A. Anderson *Qumrân Cave 4.1 (4Q158–4Q186)* (DJD 5; Oxford: Clarendon, 1968)
DJD 6	Roland de Vaux and Józef T. Milik *Qumrân Cave 4.2: I. Archéologie, II. Tefilllin, Mezuzot et Targums (4Q128–4Q157)* (DJD 6; Oxford: Clarendon, 1977)
DJD 7	Maurice Baillet *Qumrân Grotte 4.3 (4Q482–4Q520)* (DJD 7; Oxford: Clarendon, 1982)
DJD 10	Elisha Qimron and John Strugnell *Qumran Cave 4.5: Miqṣat Ma'aśe ha-Torah* (DJD 10; Oxford: Clarendon, 1994)

DJD 18	Joseph M. Baumgarten *Qumran Cave 4.13: The Damascus Document (4Q266–4Q273)* (DJD 18; Oxford: Clarendon, 1996)
DJD 20	Torleif Elgvin et al. *Qumran Cave 4.15: Sapiential Texts, Part 1* (DJD 20; Oxford: Clarendon, 1997)
DJD 21	Shemaryahu Talmon, Jonathan Ben-Dov, and Uwe Glessmer *Qumran Cave 4.16: Calendrical Texts* (DJD 21, Oxford: Clarendon, 2001)
DJD 22	George J. Brooke et al. *Qumran Cave 4.27: Parabiblical Texts, Part 3* (DJD 22; Oxford: Clarendon, 1996)
DJD 23	Florentino García Martínez, Eibert J. C. Tigchelaar, and Adam S. van der Woude *Qumran Cave 11.2: 11Q2–18, 11Q20–31* (DJD 23; Oxford: Clarendon, 1998)
DJD 26	Philip S. Alexander and Geza Vermes *Qumran Cave 4.19: Serekh Ha-Yaḥad and Two Related Texts* (DJD 26; Oxford: Clarendon, 1998)
DJD 28	Douglas M. Gropp and Moshe Bernstein et al. *Wadi Daliyeh II: The Samaria Papyri from Wadi Daliyeh and Qumran Cave 4.28: Miscellanea, Part 2* (DJD 28; Oxford: Clarendon, 2001)
DJD 35	Joseph M. Baumgarten *Qumran Cave 4.25: Halakhic Texts* (DJD 35; Oxford: Clarendon, 1999)
DJD 36	Stephen J. Pfann and Philip S. Alexander et al. *Qumran Cave 4.26: Cryptic Texts and Miscellanea, Part 1* (DJD 36; Oxford: Clarendon, 2000)
DJD 39	Emanuel Tov (ed.) *The Texts from the Judaean Desert: Indices and an Introduction to the Discoveries in the Judaean Desert Series* (DJD 39; Oxford: Clarendon, 2000)
DJD 40	Carol Newsom, Hartmut Stegemann, and Eileen Schuller *Qumran Cave 1.3: 1QHodayot^a, with Incorporation of 4QHodayot^{a-f} and 1QHodayot^b* (DJD 40; Oxford: Clarendon, 2009)
DSD	*Dead Sea Discoveries*
DSS	Dead Sea Scrolls
DSSEL	Emanuel Tov *The Dead Sea Scrolls Electronic Library* (Leiden: Brill, 2007)
DSSR 1	Donald W. Parry and Emanuel Tov (eds) *The Dead Sea Scrolls Reader, Part 1: Texts Concerned with Religious Law* (Leiden: Brill, 2004)
DSSR 4	Donald W. Parry and Emanuel Tov (eds) *The Dead Sea Scrolls Reader, Part 4: Calendrical and Sapiential Texts* (Leiden: Brill, 2004)
DSSSE	Florentino García Martínez and Eibert J. C. Tigchelaar *The Dead Sea Scrolls Study Edition* (2 vols; Leiden: Brill, 1998)
ECDSS	Eerdmans Commentaries on the Dead Sea Scrolls

EDEJ	John Collins and Dan Harlow (eds) *The Eerdmans Dictionary of Early Judaism* (Grand Rapids, Mich.: Eerdmans, 2010)
EdF	Erträge der Forschung
EDSS	Lawrence H. Schiffman and James C. VanderKam (eds) *Encyclopedia of the Dead Sea Scrolls* (New York: OUP, 2000)
EJL	Early Judaism and Its Literature
ExpTim	The Expository Times
FAT	Forschungen zum Alten Testament
HAR	Hebrew Annual Review
HAT	Handbuch zum Alten Testament
HdO	Handbook of Oriental Studies
HeyJ	The Heythrop Journal
HSM	Harvard Semitic Monographs
HTR	Harvard Theological Review
IAA	Israel Antiquities Authority
ICC	International Critical Commentary
IEJ	Israel Exploration Journal
IES	Israel Exploration Society
JBL	Journal of Biblical Literature
JJS	Journal of Jewish Studies
JANES	Journal of the Ancient Near Eastern Society
JAOS	Journal of the American Oriental Society
JNES	Journal of Near Eastern Studies
JPS	Jewish Publication Society
JQR	Jewish Quarterly Review
JSJ	*Journal for the Study of Judaism in the Persian, Hellenistic, and Roman Periods*
JSJSup	Journal for the Study of Judaism in the Persian, Hellenistic, and Roman Periods: Supplement Series
JSOT	Journal for the Study of the Old Testament
JSOTSup	Journal for the Study of the Old Testament: Supplement Series
JSP	*Journal for the Study of the Pseudepigrapha*
JSQ	Jewish Studies Quarterly
KBW	Katholisches Bibelwerk
LHBOTS	Library of Hebrew Bible/Old Testament Studies
LSTS	Library of Second Temple Studies
NCB	New Century Bible
NRSV	New Revised Standard Version
N. S.	New Series
NTL	New Testament Library
NTOASA	Novum Testamentum et Orbis Antiquus: Series Archaeologica
NTS	New Testament Studies
OED	Oxford English Dictionary
OTL	Old Testament Library
OUP	Oxford University Press
PTSDSSP 1	James H. Charlesworth et al. (eds) *The Dead Sea Scrolls: Hebrew, Aramaic, and Greek Texts with English*

	Translations, Volume 1 Rule of the Community and Related Documents (Princeton Theological Seminary Dead Sea Scrolls Project 1; Louisville, Ky.: Westminster John Knox Press; Tübingen: Mohr Siebeck, 1994)
PTSDSSP 2	James H. Charlesworth et al. (eds) *The Dead Sea Scrolls: Hebrew, Aramaic, and Greek Texts with English Translations, Volume 2 Damascus Document, War Scroll and Related Documents* (Princeton Theological Seminary Dead Sea Scrolls Project 2; Louisville, Ky.: Westminster John Knox Press; Tübingen: Mohr Siebeck, 1995)
PTSDSSP 3	James H. Charlesworth et al. (eds) *The Dead Sea Scrolls: Hebrew, Aramaic, and Greek Texts with English Translations, Volume 3 Damascus Document II, Some Works of the Torah and Related Documents* (Princeton Theological Seminary Dead Sea Scrolls Project 3; Louisville, Ky.: Westminster John Knox Press; Tübingen: Mohr Siebeck, 2006)
PTSDSSP 4B	James H. Charlesworth et al. (eds) *The Dead Sea Scrolls: Hebrew, Aramaic, and Greek Texts with English Translations, Volume 4b Angelic Liturgy: Songs of the Sabbath Sacrifice* (Princeton Theological Seminary Dead Sea Scrolls Project 4B; Louisville, Ky.: Westminster John Knox Press; Tübingen: Mohr Siebeck, 1999)
PTSDSSP 6B	James H. Charlesworth et al. (eds) *The Dead Sea Scrolls: Hebrew, Aramaic, and Greek Texts with English Translations, Volume 6b Pesharim, Other Commentaries and Related Documents* (Princeton Theological Seminary Dead Sea Scrolls Project 6B; Louisville, Ky.: Westminster John Knox Press; Tübingen: Mohr Siebeck, 2002)
RB	*Revue Biblique*
REB	Revised English Bible
RechBib	Recherches Bibliques
Revised Schürer 2	Emil Schürer *The History of the Jewish People in the Age of Jesus Christ, Volume II* (ed. and rev. Geza Vermes, Fergus Millar, and Matthew Black; Edinburgh: T & T Clark, 1979)
Revised Schürer 3.1	Emil Schürer *The History of the Jewish People in the Age of Jesus Christ, Volume III.1* (ed. and rev. Geza Vermes, Fergus Millar, and Martin Goodman; Edinburgh: T & T Clark, 1986)
RQ	*Revue de Qumran*
SBL	Society of Biblical Literature
SBLMS	Society of Biblical Literature Monograph Series
SBM	Stuttgarter biblische Monographien
SJLA	Studies in Judaism in Late Antiquity
SNTSMS	Society for New Testament Studies Monograph Series
STDJ	Studies on the Texts of the Desert of Judah
SUNT	Studien zur Umwelt des Neuen Testaments
ThR	*Theologische Rundschau*
TLZ	*Theologische Literaturzeitung*

TSAJ	Texte und Studien zum Antiken Judentum
TTZ	*Trierer Theologische Zeitschrift*
TZ	*Theologische Zeitschrift*
UTB	Uni-Taschenbücher
VT	*Vetus Testamentum*
VTSup	Vetus Testamentum: Supplements
WBC	Word Biblical Commentary
WUNT	Wissenschaftliche Untersuchungen zum Neuen Testament
ZTK	*Zeitschrift für Theologie und Kirche*
{ }	scribal deletion

Chapter One

Introduction

This volume brings together seventeen studies on the Qumran Rule texts that appeared in print in a variety of journals and volumes between 1996 and 2012 alongside a substantial final Chapter 19 ('"Haskalah" at Qumran? The Eclectic Character of Qumran Cave 4') which is published here for the first time. The previously published studies have been lightly reworked in the process when I felt a turn of phrase needed to be sharper and sometimes bolder than originally printed. I added additional key bibliographical information and updated references to primary texts where appropriate. Since the chapters gathered here offer a cumulative body of research on the Rule texts in their wider context, bibliographies of chapters published more recently frequently update what was not possible to include in some of the earlier studies. Sections 1–8 of the Introduction correspond to Parts I–VIII of the volume.

The first methodological issue to be addressed here is the somewhat problematic category of Rule texts itself.[1] A great deal has changed in the space of over sixty years since the first scrolls from Qumran Cave 1, including the Community Rule (1QS), were deciphered. Just as the notion of the family and the traditional roles of its members are now considerably removed from the 1950s so 'the Modern Family of Rule Texts' has also undergone dramatic changes. Core members of the family as conceived for the purposes of this volume can be easily identified as the Community Rule (S), the Rule of the Congregation (1QSa), the Damascus Document (D), and 4Q265 (Miscellaneous Rules). Various family members share a common history, genetic legacy, overlapping narratives, alongside fiercely individual and distinctive elements. The latter testify to independent journeys pursued while 'keeping in touch' to varying degrees.

The term 'Qumran' also warrants a health warning since when talking about Qumran Rule texts this terminology is employed here primarily as a heuristic shorthand to refer to the site where most of the texts dealt with in this book were found rather than the home of a single, unified 'Qumran community.'

---

[1] See Charlotte Hempel, 'Rules,' in *The T & T Clark Companion to the Dead Sea Scrolls* (ed. George Brooke and Charlotte Hempel; London: T & T Clark, forthcoming) and eadem, 'סרך,' in *Theologisches Wörterbuch zu den Qumrantexten* (ThWQ) (ed. Heinz-Josef Fabry et al.; Stuttgart: Kohlhammer, forthcoming).

1. The Nature of the Communities

Most of the texts treated in this volume refer at some point to (an) organized group(s) set apart, to a greater or lesser degree, from outsiders and deal with issues such as admission, community organization, leadership, discipline, with some also narrating shared histories. Chapter 2 ('Community Structures and Organization') reviews some of these central organizational matters and suggests a degree of complexity and development across and within individual texts.[2] The main scholarly contribution of this chapter is the close reading of the regulations on admission into the community in 1QS 6, 1QS 5, and CD 15. In particular, by looking beyond the customary boundaries of documents, the chapter demonstrates that a comparable admissions procedure centred on swearing an oath to return to the law of Moses attested in CD 15:5b–10a forms the background to 1QS 5:7c–9a//4Q256 (4QS^b)//4Q258 (4QS^d). Both accounts differ markedly from the elaborate admission process prescribed in 1QS 6:13b–23 that has been at the forefront of scholars' attention and imagination. My reading of the admission texts has since been accepted by John Collins and Stephen Hultgren.[3] This chapter's brief overview on meetings already hints at the complexity of the evidence in both the Damascus Document and the Community Rule that will occupy my attention again and more fully in Chapters 5 and 6. Moreover, the discussion of the array of leadership figures offered here forms a useful basis for subsequent studies on the place of priestly leadership in the Scrolls represented by Chapter 13 and 14.

Most recently Florentino García Martínez suggested we move beyond the quest of trying to identify a core of 'sectarian' texts within the larger corpus of the Scrolls and speak instead of 'clusters of text.'[4] To a large degree the studies

---

[2] The discussion on meals at Qumran is taken forward outside of this volume in Charlotte Hempel, 'Who is Making Dinner at Qumran?,' *JTS* 63 (2012): 49–65.

[3] John J. Collins, *Beyond the Qumran Community: The Sectarian Movement of the Dead Sea Scrolls* (Grand Rapids, Mich.: Eerdmans, 2010), 56–57 and Stephen Hultgren, *From the Damascus Covenant to the Covenant of the Community: Literary, Historical, and Theological Studies in the Dead Sea Scrolls* (STDJ 66; Leiden: Brill, 2007), 234–235. A different view is upheld by James C. VanderKam, 'The Oath and the Community,' *DSD* 16 (2009): 416–432 who prefers to read the various statements on admission into the community as relating to a single process.

[4] Florentino García Martínez, '¿Sectario, no-sectario, o qué? Problemas de una taxonomía correcta de los textos qumránicos,' *RQ* 23 (2008): 383–394. For previous attempts to arrive at criteria for identifying a core group of sectarian texts see, e. g., Esther Chazon, 'Is Divrei Ha-Me'orot a Sectarian Prayer?,' in *The Dead Sea Scrolls: Forty Years of Research* (ed. Devorah Dimant and Uriel Rappaport; STDJ 10; Leiden: Brill, 1992), 3–17; Devorah Dimant, 'The Qumran Manuscripts: Contents and Significance,' in *Time to Prepare the Way in the Wilderness: Papers on the Qumran Scrolls by Fellows of the Institute for Advanced Studies of The Hebrew University, Jerusalem, 1989–1990* (ed. Devorah Dimant and Lawrence H. Schiffman; STDJ 16; Leiden: Brill, 1995), 23–58; Charlotte Hempel, 'Kriterien zur Bestimmung "essenischer Verfasserschaft" von Qumrantexten,' in *Qumran Kontrovers: Beiträge zu den Textfunden vom*

in this volume reveal clusters of texts within larger compositions, and not infrequently a cluster from D shares more with S than other parts of D. This theme runs across much of this volume but is particularly developed in Chapters 8 and 9. A particularly important recurring observation is that our understanding of individual documents frequently benefits from casting our nets wider. Just as earlier attempts at delineating a sub-corpus of sectarian literature are now perceived as too rigid, so the boundaries of individual documents are often porous when it comes to the development of the literature we are studying.

Several studies in this volume are concerned with a careful analysis of the complex relationships between various core members of the family of Rule texts. Chapter 3 ('The Damascus Document and 1QSa') makes the case that the regulations for communal life in the central portions of 1QSa are much more closely related to the Damascus Document than to the Rule of the Community to which the text was physically attached. In particular, attention is drawn to shared characteristics such as,

– an all-Israel perspective;
– the presupposition of family life;
– a proliferation of congregation (עדה) terminology in both 1QSa and D in contrast to the Community Rule;
– references to the Book of Hagi;
– and prescriptions for exclusion from the congregation of members with physical or mental disabilities.

I conclude that 1QSa 1:6–2:11a comprises communal legislation that originated with the parent movement of the Yaḥad – also attested in the communal legislation in the Damascus Document – which was secondarily inserted into its present eschatological context.

Toten Meer (ed. Jörg Frey and Hartmut Stegemann; Einblicke; Paderborn: Bonifatius, 2003), 71–78; Armin Lange, 'Kriterien essenischer Texte,' ibidem, 59–69; and Carol Newsom, '"Sectually Explicit" Literature from Qumran,' in *The Hebrew Bible and Its Interpreters* (ed. Baruch Halpern and David Freedman; Winona Lake, Ind.: Eisenbrauns, 1990), 167–187. Reference should also be made to several studies dealing with sectarianism that have recently appeared, cf. David Chalcraft (ed.), *Sectarianism in Early Judaism* (London: Equinox, 2007); Eyal Regev, *Sectarianism in Qumran: A Cross-Cultural Perspective* (Religion and Society 45; Berlin: de Gruyter, 2007); and Sacha Stern (ed.), *Sects and Sectarianism in Jewish History* (IJS Studies in Judaica 12; Leiden: Brill, 2011). Further also John Collins, 'Sectarian Communities in the Dead Sea Scrolls,' in *The Oxford Handbook of the Dead Sea Scrolls* (ed. Timothy H. Lim and John J. Collins; Oxford: OUP, 2010), 151–172 and Jutta Jokiranta, 'Sociological Approaches to Qumran Sectarianism,' ibidem, 200–231. The history of scholarship on the sectarian scrolls is now also comprehensively covered in several contributions in Devorah Dimant (ed.), *The Dead Sea Scrolls in Scholarly Perspective* (STDJ 99; Leiden: Brill, 2012).

2. Beginnings

The three chapters that follow all relate to the emergence of communal life and offer a fresh reading of counter narratives of 'beginnings.'

2.1 The Teacher: From John Wayne to the Wizard of Oz

The accounts of community origins in the Damascus Document, and CD 1 in particular, were for a long time read with a great deal of confidence in the general outline of events if not the precise dates and details offered.[5] Chapter 4 ('The Damascus Document and Community Origins') queries this account and notes the rhetorical force of writing off the original reform movement that gave rise to the Teacher community as blind and groping for the way. I suggest, instead, that the early reform movement was far from blind but confidently claimed to be the recipient of divine hope and grace at a crunch point in Jewish history. Traces of teacher-free accounts of community origins remain in CD 2:8b–9a.11–13, *Jubilees* (e. g. *Jub.* 21:24) and *1 Enoch* (e. g. *1 Enoch* 93:10), and arguable also in CD 1:3–9a and CD 3:12b–17a. In the Damascus Document all but one of the teacher-free accounts (the exception being CD 2:8b–9a.11–13) were subsequently expanded to represent multi-tiered origin accounts.

Since its original publication in 1999 this chapter can fruitfully be related to several important recent studies that reflect an increased scepticism about the heroic portrait of the teacher of righteousness in the Scrolls.[6] The argument

---

[5] For a recent treatment see James C. VanderKam, 'The Pre-History of the Qumran Community with a Reassessment of CD 1:5–11,' in *The Dead Sea Scrolls and Contemporary Culture* (ed. Adolfo Roitman, Larry Schiffman, and Shani Tzoref; STDJ 93; Leiden: Brill, 2011), 59–76 and further literature referred to there.

[6] Cf. George J. Brooke, 'The "Apocalyptic" Community, the Matrix of the Teacher and Rewriting Scripture,' in *Authoritative Scriptures in Ancient Judaism* (ed. Mladen Popović; JSJSup 141; Leiden: Brill, 2010), 37–53; Steven Fraade, *Legal Fictions: Studies of Law and Narrative in the Discursive Worlds of Ancient Jewish Sectarians and Sages* (JSJSup 147; Leiden: Brill, 2011), 38–42; Florentino García Martínez, 'Beyond the Sectarian Divide: The "Voice of the Teacher" as an Authority-Conferring Strategy in Some Qumran Texts,' in *The Dead Sea Scrolls: Transmission of Traditions and Production of Texts* (ed. Sarianna Metso, Hindy Najman, and Eileen Schuller; STDJ 92; Leiden: Brill, 2010), 227–244; Maxine Grossman, 'Roland Barthes and the Teacher of Righteousness: The Death of the Author of the Dead Sea Scrolls,' in *The Oxford Handbook of the Dead Sea Scrolls* (ed. Lim and Collins), 709–722; Angela Kim Harkins, 'Who is the Teacher of the Teacher Hymns? Re-Examining the Teacher Hymns Hypothesis Fifty Years Later,' in *A Teacher for All Generations: Essays in Honor of James C. VanderKam* (ed. Eric Mason et al.; JSJSup 153; Leiden: Brill, 2012), Vol. I, 449–467; Jutta Jokiranta, 'Qumran – The Prototypical Teacher in the Qumran Pesharim: A Social-Identity Approach,' in *Ancient Israel: The Old Testament in Its Social Context* (ed. Philip F. Esler; Minneapolis, Minn.: Fortress, 2006), 254–263; Michael A. Knibb, 'Teacher of Righteousness,' in EDSS 2:918–921; Loren T. Stuckenbruck, 'The Legacy of the Teacher of Righteousness in the Dead Sea Scrolls,' in *New Perspectives on Old Texts: Proceedings of the Tenth International Symposium of the Orion*

developed in this chapter further illuminates the influential work by Hindy Najman on founder figures which are frequently pseudepigraphically linked to a foundation narrative comprising law and history both in the Hebrew Bible and in early Jewish literature.[7] The Teacher of Righteousness as portrayed in CD 1 can likewise be conceived as a pseudepigraphic founder figure whose 'name' is not drawn from among venerable individuals of the long distant past but rather the result of 'biblical' interpretation.[8] Finally, most recently Angela Kim Harkins has mounted a compelling challenge against reading the Hodayot as offering access to the innermost thoughts and personal struggles of a historical personality.[9] The combined force of this scholarly trajectory leaves us with a Teacher figure who resembles the character of the shady Wizard of Oz more closely than John Wayne of old coming to rescue a community in distress.

Alongside the teacher of righteousness several other established truths of the first several decades of Qumran research appear somewhat diminished by the full corpus of texts such as the dualism of light and darkness,[10] the Masoretic text,[11] and the calendar.[12] At the same time as reservations are expressed about our ability to say very much at all about the historical teacher of righteousness,[13] my own work has looked at a number of previously neglected passages that seem to paint a different picture of beginnings.

Center for the Study of the Dead Sea Scrolls and Associated Literature, 9–11 January, 2005 (ed. Esther G. Chazon, Betsy Halpern-Amaru, and Ruth A. Clements; STDJ 88; Leiden: Brill, 2010), 23–49; idem, 'The Teacher of Righteousness Remembered: From Fragmentary Sources to Collective Memory in the Dead Sea Scrolls,' in *Memory in the Bible and Antiquity: The Fifth Durham-Tübingen Research Symposium (Durham, September 2004)* (ed. Stephen Barton, Loren Stuckenbruck, and Benjamin Wold; WUNT 212; Tübingen: Mohr Siebeck, 2007), 75–94.

[7] Hindy Najman, *Seconding Sinai: The Development of Mosaic Discourse in Second Temple Judaism* (JSJSup 77; Leiden: Brill, 2003; pb. ed. Atlanta, Ga.: SBL, 2009).

[8] See Brooke, 'The "Apocalyptic" Community' and García Martínez, 'Beyond the Sectarian Divide.'

[9] *Reading with an "I" to the Heavens: Looking at the Qumran Hodayot through the Lens of Visionary Traditions* (Ekstasis 3; Berlin: de Gruyter, 2012); see also Carol Newsom, *The Self as Symbolic Space: Constructing Identity and Community at Qumran* (STDJ 52; Leiden: Brill, 2004), 287–351.

[10] See Charlotte Hempel, 'The Teaching on the Two Spirits and the Literary Development of the Rule of the Community,' in *Dualism in Qumran* (ed. Geza Xeravits; LSTS 76; London: T & T Clark International, 2010), 102–120.

[11] See, e. g., Eugene Ulrich, 'The Evolutionary Production and Transmission of the Scriptural Books,' in *The Dead Sea Scrolls: Transmission of Traditions and Production of Texts* (ed. Sarianna Metso, Hindy Najman, and Eileen Schuller; STDJ 92; Leiden: Brill, 2010), 209–225, esp. 210 and further literature cited there and idem, 'Biblical Scrolls Scholarship in North America,' in *The Dead Sea Scrolls in Scholarly Perspective* (ed. Dimant), 49–74, 63 and 65 where he provocatively labels the mid 20th century approach to the MT as "pre-Copernican."

[12] See Sacha Stern, 'The "Sectarian" Calendar of Qumran,' in *Sects and Sectarianism in Jewish History* (ed. Stern), 39–62 and Chapter 19 below.

[13] See also, Collins, *Beyond the Qumran Community*, 90–91.

2.2 Looking for Beginnings in Unexpected Places

In the context of a museological study Eileen Hooper-Greenhill offers an account of master narratives that is reminiscent of the work of first generation Qumran researchers,

> Master narratives are created by presenting a large-scale picture, by eliminating complicating and contradictory details [...] and those things that would have shown a different interpretation of events are excluded.[14]

The material referring to small fellowship groups in different dwelling places in the opening lines of 1QS 6//4QS offers a series of complicating details that remained largely unexplored in the early Qumran master narratives. The opening of access to the Qumran manuscripts in their entirety (such as it is, given the fragmentary state of preservation of many individual texts as well as the corpus as a whole)[15] resulted in a democratisation of the scholarly community. It also brought with it a levelling of primary texts with intriguing contrary pieces of evidence beginning to take centre stage in some quarters of the scholarly narrative and my own work in particular. Chapters 5 and 6 ('Emerging Communities in the Serekh' and 'Small Beginnings or Geographical Diversity?') reconstruct a very basic level of social interaction and fellowship in a part of the Community Rule that was until recently greatly under researched.[16]

Chapter 5 argues that both 1QS 6:2c–4a[17] and the more well known description of the council of the community made up of twelve lay persons and three priests in 1QS 8:1–7 share,

– council of the community language exclusively (i. e., without הרבים)
– a small scale setting
– a concern for the ratio of lay members to priests

---

[14] Eileen Hooper-Greenhill, *Museums and the Interpretation of Visual Culture* (London: Routledge, 2000), 4. I owe this quotation to Kate Gerrard's doctoral dissertation, "A Contemporary Look at the Jewish Past in Poland: Traces of Memory and the Galicia Jewish Museum, Kraków (2004–2011)" (Ph.D. diss., University of Birmingham, 2013), 118.

[15] The latter limitation has recently been stressed by Michael E. Stone, 'The Dead Sea Scrolls and the Literary Landscape of Second Temple Judaism,' in *The Dead Sea Scrolls: Texts and Context* (ed. Charlotte Hempel; STDJ 90; Leiden: Brill, 2010), 15–30 and Joan E. Taylor, 'Buried Manuscripts and Empty Tombs: The Qumran Genizah Theory Revisited,' in *'Go Out and Study the Land' (Judges 18:2): Archaeological, Historical and Textual Studies in Honor of Hanan Eshel* (ed. Aren M. Maeir, Jodi Magness, and Lawrence H. Schiffman; JSJSup 148; Leiden: Brill, 2011), 269–315 as noted in Chapter 19 below.

[16] The ideas developed in Chapters 5 and 6 were first explored in a study that is not included in this collection, see Charlotte Hempel, 'Interpretative Authority in the Community Rule Tradition,' *DSD* 10 (2003): 59–80, esp. 61–68.

[17] Which according to my own translation reads, "And together they shall eat, and together they all pray, and together they shall exchange counsel. And in every place where there are found ten people from the council of the community a priest shall be present."

– a lack of concern for the genealogical background of the priestly component (over against a preference elsewhere for designations such as the sons of Zadok or the sons of Aaron).

Notable differences are the pronounced theological and ideological nature of the account in 1QS 8:1–7a. Thus, despite the fact that the opening lines of 1QS 8 have for a long time been related to community origins,[18] 1QS 6:2–4 offers a more credible historical scenario of emerging communal life on a small scale without presupposing a larger umbrella organization.[19]

I return to this complex of questions in Chapter 6 to engage with the important observation put forward by colleagues that my interpretation of 1QS 6:2–4 needs to account for the larger pool from which the small number of ten people is taken, i. e. "from the council of the community." In other words, the preposition מן (here "from") suggests that the council of the community is already sizeable.[20] This important issue is here further illuminated by a comparative study of 1QS 6:3 and CD 13:2–3 where a 'parallel' statement occurs that lacks the reference to the council of the community altogether. The evidence of CD 13:2–3 sheds important light on the literary development of 1QS 6:2–4 and suggests an original account of small scale social fellowship groups was subsequently associated with the council of the community in 1QS 6 but not in CD 13.

While not yet having reached the dimensions of a 'place of ten' (1QS 6:3) I have been fortunate to be able to conduct my own explorations of this awkward and promising patch of S in conversation with John Collins, Sarianna Metso, Eyal Regev, and Alison Schofield.[21]

---

[18] See Edmund F. Sutcliffe, 'The First Fifteen Members of the Qumran Community: A Note on 1QS 8:1 ff.,' *JSS* 4 (1959): 134–138 and Jerome Murphy-O'Connor, 'La genèse littéraire de la Règle de la Communauté,' *RB* 76 (1969): 528–549.

[19] For the latter term and concept see Collins, *Beyond the Qumran Community*.

[20] Sarianna Metso stresses that the presence of the preposition in 1QS 6, and only here in S, is one of several factors that marks the material as an interpolation, cf. 'Whom Does the Term Yaḥad Identify?,' in *Biblical Traditions in Transmission: Essays in Honour of Michael A. Knibb* (ed. Charlotte Hempel and Judith Lieu; JSJSup 111; Leiden: Brill, 2006), 213–235, 218.

[21] See John. J. Collins, 'The Yaḥad and "The Qumran Community,"' in *Biblical Traditions in Transmission* (ed. Hempel and Lieu), 81–96; idem, 'Forms of Community in the Dead Sea Scrolls,' in *Emanuel: Studies in Hebrew Bible, Septuagint, and the Dead Sea Scrolls in Honor of Emanuel Tov* (ed. Shalom M. Paul et al.; VTSup 94; Leiden: Brill, 2003), 97–111; idem, 'Sectarian Consciousness in the Dead Sea Scrolls,' in *Interpretation, Identity and Tradition in Ancient Judaism* (ed. Lynn LiDonnici and Andrea Lieber; JSJSup 199; Leiden: Brill, 2007), 177–192; Sarianna Metso, 'Whom Does the Term Yaḥad Identify?,' 213–235; Regev, *Sectarianism in Qumran*, chapter 4; and Alison Schofield, 'Rereading S: A New Model of Textual Development in Light of the Cave 4 *Serekh* Copies,' *DSD* 15 (2008): 96–120.

3. The Community Rule Traditions

Not unlike the stimulating intellectual rollercoaster ride that is post-Qumran textual criticism the study of the Rule texts has been enriched by the full publication of the Scrolls. The publication of ten additional and at times radically different manuscripts of the Community Rule was certainly a watershed in the scholarly perception of what Rule texts are and do.[22] Whereas pioneering studies of the Community Rule approached this material almost as if it were a candid camera producing 'reality literature,' recent scholarship is increasingly aware of the significance of these manuscripts as complex literary artefacts whose own claims need to be treated with caution.[23]

In a trajectory mirroring the scholarly study of the Bible, the study of the Dead Sea Scrolls is moving away from a reading of texts as offering unmediated access to personalities, history, and the day-to-day life of a community resident at the site of Qumran. Compare, for instance, the scholarly trajectory in Hebrew Bible research on the prophetic books sketched by Reinhard Kratz, where he outlines scholarly developments beginning in the 1970s that testify to, "Abschied von der Person des Propheten und die Hinwendung zur prophetischen Literatur."[24] Some of the earlier studies gathered in this volume are more confident about accessing real-life communities than the developing appreciation of the literary character of the Rule texts in the most recently published pieces.[25] Thus, the earliest study included here in Chapter 3 opens in footnote 2 by very confidently associating particular texts with a single "Qumran community" and proclaims adherence to the Groningen Hypothesis of Qumran Origins.[26]

---

[22] The notion of reflecting on what texts 'do' is borrowed from Carol Newsom's rhetorical analysis of the Hodayot, cf. Newsom, *Self as Symbolic Space*, 191–286; see also Fraade, *Legal Fictions*, 4.

[23] See Maxine Grossman, *Reading for History in the Damascus Document: A Methodological Study* (STDJ 45; Leiden: Brill, 2002); eadem, 'Roland Barthes and the Teacher of Righteousness;' and most recently Moshe Bernstein, '4Q159: Nomenclature, Text, Exegesis, Genre,' in *The Mermaid and the Partridge: Essays from the Copenhagen Conference on Revising Texts from Cave Four* (ed. George J. Brooke and Jesper Høgenhaven; STDJ 96; Leiden: Brill, 2012), 33–55, 51. Fraade's nuanced studies remind us to avoid neat dichotomies, and his coinage of "imagined as real" is but one of many stimulating insights he develops in this rich collection of studies, see *Legal Fictions*, 15.

[24] See Reinhard G. Kratz, *Prophetenstudien* (FAT 75; Tübingen: Mohr Siebeck, 2011), 4.

[25] See the recent cautionary remarks about applying conclusions arrived at on literary grounds to social realities by Reinhard G. Kratz, 'Der *Penal Code* und das Verhältnis von *Serekh ha-Yachad* (S) und Damaskusschrift (D),' *RQ* 25 (2011): 199–227, 203; also Sarianna Metso, 'Methodological Problems in Reconstructing History from Rule Texts Found at Qumran,' *DSD* 11 (2004): 315–335; and eadem, 'Problems in Reconstructing the Organizational Chart of the Essenes,' *DSD* 16 (2009): 388–415.

[26] See Florentino García Martínez, 'Qumran Origins and Early History: A Groningen Hypothesis,' *Folia Orientalia* 25 (1988): 113–136 (reprinted in García Martínez, *Qumranica Minora I: Qumran Origins and Apocalypticism* [ed. Eibert J. C. Tigchelaar; STDJ 63; Leiden: Brill, 2007], 3–29); for a sympathetic critique see Charlotte Hempel, 'The Groningen Hypoth-

To a significant degree the studies gathered here shed light on issues of text and reality from a number of angles. While chapters 17–19 rightly stress the scribal and learned concerns behind the production and creative transmission of the Rule literature, the picture is certainly not entirely black and white since parts of the penal code and 4Q477 (The Overseer's Record of Rebuke) do seem to reflect some kind of reality as noted in the closing sentence of Chapter 2.[27]

However, the differences between the various manuscripts of the Community Rule are indeed so substantial that they preserve a time capsule of textual birth and development comprising composition, editing, and shaping. Chapter 7 ('Shifting Paradigms Concerning the Literary Development of the Serekh') redirects the scholarly gaze towards acknowledging stunning correspondences alongside headline grabbing differences between the Rule manuscripts. This chapter takes another look at the much debated question of the literary development of the S tradition. Rather than focusing on variants between the different manuscripts, which have been the focus of previous studies, I suggest that it is the striking elements of continuity between manuscripts coupled with remarkable instances of discontinuity within individual manuscripts that shed important light on this question. In a radical departure from previous vantage points that focused predominantly on trying to 'rank' individual manuscripts in terms of textual priority, I propose that the earliest forms of the tradition are to be found in the shared material that runs across several manuscripts.

4. Close Encounters: The Community Rule and the Damascus Document

One of the most important and debated literary relationships in the corpus of the Dead Sea Scrolls is that between the Damascus Document (D) and the Community Rule (S). Chapter 8 ('CD 19–20 and the Community Rule') begins by drawing attention to the fact that of all the texts to come out of Qumran, D and S display the largest number of inter-textual encounters. A close point of literary contact between D and S that is the focus of this chapter is the distinctive use of the self-designation 'the people of perfect holiness' (אנשי תמים הקדש; with some variation concerning the definite article) as a communal self-designation frequently in CD 20 and also in 1QS 8:20. Interestingly, the particular terminological frame of reference shared between 1QS 8:20 and CD 20:1b–8a is not found elsewhere in the Serekh. Moreover, alongside this common terminology 1QS 8–9 also employs self-designations that predominate elsewhere in S such as rabbim and yaḥad (see esp. 1QS 5–7). On the basis of 4Q259 (4QS^e), which lacks the equivalent of 1QS 8:15b–9:11 altogether, and the curious variations

---

esis: Strengths and Weaknesses,' in *Enoch and Qumran Origins: New Light on a Forgotten Connection* (ed. Gabriele Boccaccini; Grand Rapids, Mich.: Eerdmans, 2005), 249–255.

[27] See again Kratz, 'Der *Penal Code*' and Metso, 'Methodological Problems.'

in the level of correctional activity in different parts of 1QS 8 we have strong evidence pointing towards a complex literary history behind 1QS 8–9.[28] The close comparison offered here illustrates that CD 20:1b–8a is closely related to one of the strands in the textual mosaic that is 1QS 8–9.

Chapter 9 ('Rewritten Rule Texts') supplements the particular focus of Chapter 8 by drawing up a profile of points of contact between S and D. Key areas that establish a close relationship between both documents (sometimes in conjunction with other texts such as 4Q265 [Miscellaneous Rules]) are the penal codes,[29] the gatherings of ten (cf. Chapters 5 and 6), admission into the community by means of an oath (cf. Chapter 2), Maskil headings, the self-designation '(the) people of perfect holiness' (cf. Chapter 8), and a shared liturgical frame (cf. the covenant renewal in 1QS 1:16–3:12//4QS and the reference to an expulsion ritual in 4Q266 [4QD^a] 11//4Q270 [4QD^e] 7).[30] In evaluating this list of correspondences the relationship between S and D appears to be based on two types of contact: the use of similar sources – as is probable in the case of the prescriptions on the quorum of ten and some of the penal code traditions – alongside points of contact at a late stage in the growth of both compositions. Examples of the latter kind are the people of perfect holiness in CD 20 and 1QS 8–9 as well as the liturgical framework. In both cases Cave 4 manuscripts of S attest a situation before this particular connection was established. Thus, the passage referring to the people of perfect holiness in 1QS 8:20 is not included (as opposed to not preserved) in 4Q259 (4QS^e) and the covenant ceremony of 1QS 1:16–3:12 is not attested in 4Q258 (4QS^d). The evidence of 4QS lends support to considering the liturgical framework and the self-designation people of perfect holiness to a late stage in the growth of S. This chapter ends by arguing that the intricate relationship between different Rule texts mirrors the kinds of processes scholars have identified in rewritten scripture texts.[31] This important conclusion points forward towards the discussion in Chapters 17–18 which explore the shared practices, sensibilities, and social milieu behind the Rule texts and the emerging Bible further.

5. Rules in the Context of Wisdom and Law

Having explored a variety of Rule texts the following three chapters examine the context of Rule texts in relation to a series of sapiential and legal works. In

---

[28] So also Kratz, 'Der *Penal Code*,' 219.

[29] In addition to the secondary literature referred to in Chapter 9 see now also Kratz, 'Der *Penal Code*.'

[30] For a comprehensive discussion see Daniel Falk, 'Liturgical Texts,' in *The T & T Clark Companion to the Dead Sea Scrolls* (ed. Brooke and Hempel), forthcoming.

[31] See now Molly Zahn, *Rethinking Rewritten Scripture: Composition and Exegesis in the 4QReworked Pentateuch Manuscripts* (STDJ 95; Leiden: Brill, 2011). Such an analogy is developed also by Kratz, 'Der *Penal Code*,' 220–221.

the case of legal works the focus in chapters 11 and 12 will shift to the halakhic portions of the Damascus Document. These portions of the Laws of D are presented side by side with communal rules.[32] I am well aware that the category of legal texts is ambiguous since it has been used to refer to halakhic material as well as communal rules.[33] For want of a clear alternative I reluctantly continue to use the terminology halakhah/halakhic even though I am aware of the danger of anachronism. I do so in order to allow myself to distinguish legal texts that do not presuppose a particular community from those that do.[34]

Beginning with the recognition that it is not always possible to allocate whole documents to a particular social background, Chapter 10 ('The Rule Books and the Wisdom Texts') examines the evidence for sectarian elements in the Qumran wisdom texts as well as considering a selection of sapiential concepts in the Rule books.[35] After reflecting on what can be said about the provenance of Mysteries, Instruction, and 4QWays of Righteousness (4Q420–421), the bulk of the chapter examines wisdom elements in the Rule books. Key concepts singled out are the mystery to be, the Book/Vision of Hagi, and the Maskil. Overall the analysis suggests a complex relationship between both groups of texts. Of particular interest is the presence of a number of overlapping terms and ideas in the material that describes organizational matters in the Rules and the sapiential texts. In this context the occurrence of the expression רז נהיה "the mystery to be" in the Community Rule (1QS 11:3–4) emerges as an important piece of evidence. Even though the expression is found in the Community Rule there are indications to suggest that the final hymn, where the expression occurs, originated independently before its incorporation into some manuscripts of the Community Rule.[36] While the concept of the mystery was clearly known and used by the compiler and readers of the Rule, it is likely an inherited concept. It is further argued that in the Rules the Book/Vision of Hagi appears to contain legal instructions.[37] In Instruction (4Q417 2 i 15–16), on the other hand, the association of the vision

---

[32] See Charlotte Hempel, *The Laws of the Damascus Document: Sources, Traditions, and Redaction* (STDJ 29; Leiden: Brill, 1998; pb. ed. Atlanta, Ga.: SBL, 2006).

[33] See, e. g., DJD 39:132 (Lange and Mittmann-Richert) where the generic classification of 'Texts Concerned with Religious Law' may qualify as 'legal' even though the great majority of texts in this category fall into the sub-classification of 'Community Rules.'

[34] On this issue of terminology see also Hempel, *Laws of the Damascus Document*, 25.

[35] See now also Reinhard G. Kratz, 'Laws of Wisdom: Sapiential Traits in the *Rule of the Community* (1QS V–IX),' in *Hebrew in the Second Temple Period: The Hebrew of the Dead Sea Scrolls and of Other Contemporary Sources. Proceedings of the Twelfth Orion Symposium* (STDJ; Leiden: Brill, forthcoming).

[36] Note that it is lacking from 4Q259 (4QS^e), cf. DJD 26:152 (Alexander and Vermes) and Sarianna Metso, *The Textual Development of the Qumran Community Rule* (STDJ 21; Leiden: Brill, 1997), 144.

[37] The expression is found in CD 10:6//4QD; CD 13:2//4QD; and 1QSa 1:7. This noteworthy confluenece between the Laws of the Damascus Document and 1QSa is explored further in Chapter 3. Significantly, the book of Hagi never occurs in the Serekh.

of Hagi with a Book of Remembrance points to a heavenly account of human actions (cf. Mal 3:16–18). The presence of partly overlapping terminology in both sets of literature is nevertheless significant. As far as the wide-spread use of Maskil in both Rules and wisdom texts is concerned, it proved difficult to establish clear-cut instances where the participle refers to a particular office in the wisdom texts as is frequently the case in the Rules.

As far as the confluence of law and rules is concerned the prime example is the Damascus Document. Chapters 11 and 12 build on the distinction between 'general halakhah' and communal rules which I first proposed in a previous monograph.[38] Whereas a number of chapters in this volume probe the relationship of the communal rules found in D to other Rule texts (Rule texts in the context of Rule texts), the following two studies investigate the halakhic material that forms part of the immediate context of the communal rules both in D and 4Q265 (Miscellaneous Rules).

Chapter 11 ('The Damascus Document and MMT') begins by commenting on several broad areas of correspondence between both documents such as,
– a national, all-Israel frame of reference with a particular concern for the responsibilities of the priesthood;
– camp terminology which is however employed distinctively in each text, as an organizational unit in D over against the Jerusalem-centric usage in MMT;
– and the use of the preposition על 'concerning' to introduce smaller collections of legal stipulations also attested in 4Q159 (Ordinances[a]) 1 ii 6 and 4Q251 (Halakhah A) 17 1.

Having established three broad areas that point to some kind of relationship between the Laws of D and 4QMMT the chapter examines four particular texts in more detail. Relating to the priestly context reflected in both texts I note a shared concern with the shortcomings of some members of the priesthood in the material on priestly disqualifications in D and in 4QMMT. Secondly, a comparable position on matters of purity comes to the fore in the 4QD material on skin disease, flux and childbirth and MMT in as far as both documents are explicit in their concern about the purity of the sanctuary and express corresponding positions on the question of the *ṭevul yom*, i. e. noting the need to wait until sunset after immersion before purity is restored. Thirdly, on matters of agricultural halakhah I begin by rejecting the suggestion that D reflects an agricultural milieu.[39] The stipulations relating to the harvest focus on contributions to the sanctuary and the priests and further demonstrate the priestly outlook that characterises the halakhic sections of D. Finally, the largest number of thematic correspondences

---

[38] *Laws of the Damascus Document*.
[39] See Francis D. Weinert, '*4Q159*: Legislation for an Essene Community Outside of Qumran?,' *JSJ* 5 (1974): 179–207.

between the Laws of D and 4QMMT can be traced to the catalogue of transgressions attested in 4Q270 (4QD^e) 2 i 9–ii 21 and relate to the fourth year produce, the tithe of cattle and sheep, skin disease, and the slaughter of pregnant animals.

By way of conclusion I suggest that the substantial number of concrete points of contact between the Laws of the Damascus Document and 4QMMT suggest that earlier collections of halakhot were incorporated into both documents.

Since the original publication of this chapter, several scholars including myself have paid particular attention to the epilogue of 4QMMT, offering increasingly nuanced assessments of 4QMMT and the epilogue in particular.[40] Thus, Hanne von Weissenberg has paid close attention to the study of individual manuscripts and the use of scripture in the epilogue and stressed the centrality of Jerusalem as the only legitimate cultic place in 4QMMT.[41] A further thorough examination of the place of scripture in the epilogue has been offered by Reinhard Kratz.[42] I myself have reflected on the brief history of scholarship on 4QMMT which initially produced what I have called a 'comfortable theory' of the document's significance and provenance. In particular I argue that early assessments were concerned to fit 4QMMT into the script of a narrative of hostility between the heroic Teacher of Righteousness and the villainous Wicked Priest which has little basis in the text of MMT itself.[43] I end by bolstering the doubts beginning to emerge against the view that 4QMMT refers to the origin of a community in the famous passage supposedly referring to a separation from the people on the part of the author(s) in 4Q397 14–21 7 by noting,

– the uncertainty of reading the word 'people' at all;[44]
– as well as the overwhelmingly positive portrayal of the people in 4QMMT. The concerns expressed in the document relate to poor leadership on the part of misguided priests. Rather than reflecting any degree of hostility to the people, both the legal section and the epilogue of MMT reflect a protectionist attitude towards them. I close by suggesting that rather than witnessing a rift

---

[40] See especially Steven Fraade, 'Rhetoric and Hermeneutics in *Miqsat Ma'aśe Ha-Torah* (4QMMT): The Case of the Blessings and Curses,' *DSD* 10 (2003): 150–161 and Maxine Grossman, 'Reading 4QMMT: Genre and History,' *RQ* 20 (2001): 3–22.

[41] Hanne von Weissenberg, *4QMMT: Reevaluating the Text, the Function, and the Meaning of the Epilogue* (STDJ 82; Leiden: Brill, 2009); and eadem, 'The Centrality of the Temple in 4QMMT,' in *The Dead Sea Scrolls: Texts and Context* (ed. Hempel), 293–305.

[42] Reinhard G. Kratz, 'Mose und die Prophetie: Zur Interpretation von 4QMMT C,' in *From 4QMMT to Resurrection: Mélanges qumraniens en hommage à Émile Puech* (ed. Florentino García Martínez, Annette Steudel, and Eibert Tigchelaar; STDJ 61; Leiden: Brill, 2006), 151–176.

[43] Charlotte Hempel, 'The Context of 4QMMT and Comfortable Theories,' in *The Dead Sea Scrolls: Texts and Context* (ed. Hempel), 275–292.

[44] My own reservations expressed in the course of a paper presented at Yale about the fragmentary reading of the 'separation passage' were developed into a thorough philological investigation of this important passage by Elitzur A. Bar-Asher Siegal, see 'Who Separated from Whom and Why? A Philological Study of 4QMMT,' *RQ* 98 (2011): 229–256.

associated with community origins, 4QMMT is an important Second Temple testament to the kind of halakhic debate we find in much more stylised form in later rabbinic literature.

Chapter 12 ('The Damascus Document and 4QOrdinances^a') proposes that 4Q159 (Ordinances^a) preserves precisely the kind of collection of halakhot that was incorporated into D and MMT. A close relationship between D and 4Q159 is further suggested by,
– correspondences in content (gleanings and the poor, standardization of measures, impoverished Israelites, transvestism, and marriage arrangement);
– overlap in sequence (i. e. moving from an exposition of Lev 25 to Deut 22 in both collections);
– treatment of the same scriptural passages (esp. Lev 25 and Deut 22);
– and formal correspondences (headings of the type 'concerning x' followed by prohibitions using the jussive).

I conclude that the evidence is best explained if the redactor/compiler responsible for the Laws of the Damascus Document in their present form drew upon a collection of traditional legal material not dissimilar from 4QOrdinances^a. Since the original publication of this chapter an international team of scholars has started to work towards a re-edition of 4Q159 and the remainder of texts first published in DJD 5. A preliminary progress report by the now expanded team working on the revision of DJD 5 has just appeared.[45] This volume includes a cautious assessment of 4Q159 by Moshe Bernstein.[46]

6. Priesthood in the Rule Texts and Beyond

Based on the vocal endorsement of the sons of Zadok in 1QS 5, the latter group was for a long time considered as the community leaders par excellence. In the wake of the full publication of the corpus and careful study of all the relevant texts this same group emerges as a bunch of noisy back-seat drivers.

Chapter 13 ('The Sons of Aaron')[47] examines all the references to the sons of Aaron in the corpus of the Scrolls and identifies a trajectory of priestly authority

---

[45] Brooke and Høgenhaven (eds), *The Mermaid and the Partridge*.

[46] Moshe Bernstein, '4Q159: Nomenclature, Text, Exegesis, Genre.' Bernstein's tentatively proposed rearrangement of the fragments of 4Q159 has no substantial impact on the argument proposed in Chapter 12. See now also idem, 'The Re-Presentation of 'Biblical' Legal Material at Qumran: Three Cases from 4Q159 (Ordinances^a),' in *Shoshannat Yaakov: Jewish and Iranian Studies in Honor of Yaakov Elman* (ed. Shai Secunda and Steven Fine; Brill Reference Library of Judaism 35; Leiden: Brill, 2012), 1–20.

[47] See now also Charlotte Hempel, 'אהרון,' in *Theologisches Wörterbuch zu den Qumrantexten* (ThWQ) (ed. Heinz-Josef Fabry et al.; Stuttgart: Kohlhammer, 2010), columns 76–81.

beginning with the sons of Aaron in a national/non-community-specific context (D), to the sons of Aaron as priestly authorities within the community (S), to the sons of *Zadok* as priestly authorities within the community in a different literary stage of S.

Chapter 14 ('Consider Ourselves in Charge: Self-Assertion by the Sons of Zadok') forcefully demonstrates that references to the sons of Zadok are now heavily outnumbered by a very large number of references to the sons of Aaron especially in the more recently published manuscripts from Cave 4. After a survey of all the occurrences of the designation the sons of Zadok in the non-biblical Scrolls it is argued that the sons of Zadok are found in two rather specific contexts: in exegetical contexts referring to the community as a whole and to refer to community leaders in the Scroll made up of 1QS–1QSa–1QSb. In the wake of a very successful Second Temple public relations campaign, the elevated claims made on behalf of the sons of Zadok in a limited number of places have successfully obscured the localized profile of references to this group in the texts at large.

7. The Scrolls and the Emerging Scriptures

Scholars have for a long time attempted to pinpoint the roots of Jewish sectarianism in the corpus of what were at the time still the emerging scriptures. Chapters 15 and 16 explore the basis of such claims with particular reference to the Books of Daniel and Ezra-Nehemiah.

Chapter 15 ('The Community Rule and the Book of Daniel') is inspired by the widely shared conviction that we need to allow for a relationship of some kind between the circles behind Daniel and the groups behind the Dead Sea Scrolls. Attention is drawn, in particular, to the shared bi-lingual milieu, the transmission of Danielic traditions by both communities, the claim to exilic roots of some kind, a shared learned, scribal background, a pre-occupation with mystery and privileged access to interpretation, as well as an awareness of proximity to the angelic realm. Cumulatively these considerations suggest a common milieu behind the Book of Daniel and the Dead Sea Scrolls. Attention is drawn to the curious fact that while the Maskilim of Daniel were teachers of eschatological speculation it is noteworthy that the term Maskil does not occur in most of the eschatological documents from Qumran. Thus, Maskil is not found in the War Scroll, 4QSerekh ha-Milḥama (4Q285 and 11Q14), the Rule of the Congregation (1QSa), 1QpHab, or 11QMelchizedek. The remainder of this Chapter critically examines the evidence for the prominent view that the terminology Maskil and rabbim employed in the Community Rule represents an institutionalisation of the frame of reference attested in Dan 11–12. Close scrutiny exposes several cracks in this particular association. Whereas Maskil and the designation ha-rabbim appear frequently in the Community Rule, the two terms are rarely linked to one another. By contrast, the Maskil is associated with designations other than ha-rabbim such as children of light, children of righteousness, children of truth in the Teaching on the Two Spirits or children of righteousness (4Q259 [4QS^e])/ Zadok (1QS),[48] chosen ones of the time, the chosen of the way (4Q258 [4QS^d])/ those who have chosen the way (1QS) in the long section spelling out the duties of the Maskil in 1QS 9:12 ff. When we consider that rabbim occurs no less than thirty four times in the Community Rule this picture is significant and warns against a close association of the role of the Maskil with the rabbim. While the evidence is complex, close attention to shared features suggests considerable similarity between both groups beyond the Maskil/rabbim terminology.

Chapter 16 ('The Damascus Document and Ezra-Nehemiah') begins with an overview over those areas where correlations between Ezra-Nehemiah and the Damascus Document can been identified such as,
– a geographical presence in Palestine with 'exilic' roots of some kind (as noted also for the Book of Daniel above);
– communities made up of a network of households who consider themselves to be the true representatives of God's people;
– a penchant for genealogical claims;
– and communities tied together by oaths.

This is followed by a closer examination of the place of the family and household in Ezra-Nehemiah and the Damascus Document. In particular, a detailed analysis of two passages on marriage arrangments in the Laws of the Damascus Document reflects a significant shift in the role of the father as head of the family in different parts of this text.

Whereas the father is entrusted with arranging a suitable marriage for his daughter according to 4Q267 (4QD^b) 7//4Q269 (4QD^d) 9//4Q270 (4QD^e) 5// 4Q271 (4QD^f) 3, his place is diminished in the related piece of legislation that has the overseer intrude in the process (cf. CD 13:7b,15b–19//4Q266 [4QD^a] 9 iii). I conclude by emphasizing the importance of the multifaceted evidence of the Damascus Document for our understanding of the role of the family in Second Temple Judaism. I would now add, that whereas both Ezra-Nehemiah and D reflect a family-based movement we also observe the introduction of an additional administrative layer dominated by the overseer in other parts of D that go beyond anything we find in Ezra-Nehemiah. To be in a position to observe this kind of development in a single ancient primary document is remarkable.

---

[48] On this variant see Robert A. Kugler, 'A Note on 1QS 9:14: the Sons of Righteousness or the Sons of Zadok?,' *DSD* 3 (1996): 315–320 and the discussion *ad loc.* in section 3 of Chapter 14 above.

Clear evidence of development within the Damascus Document is significant and must not be downplayed.

The study and conceptualisation of the rich new evidence relating to the Community Rule traditions explored in Chapters 5–9 sheds light not only on the finer points of the literary development of the Community Rule, but preserves a fossil collection, so to speak, from the late Second Temple period. The Serekh tradition preserves ancient case studies that illustrate the processes presupposed by biblical exegetes such as text criticism, composition history, source criticism and redaction criticism.[49] Most recently scholarship dealing with the Hebrew Bible and Qumran has recognized the enormous value of the Qumran manuscripts for our understanding of the scribal craft in the late Second Temple period.[50] As is well known after the loss of nationhood, king, and temple it was literature, texts, and their study and the debates that ensued from this study that allowed Judaism to emerge, survive, and thrive against the odds. Qumran allows us to observe late Second Temple scribal crafting in tremendous fullness.

The evidence of the Rule texts is particularly rich in this regard.[51] The textual picture we now have is much 'messier' and arguably more interesting.[52] Whereas the task of mapping these texts to actual communities has become more difficult,[53] the new evidence exposes how ancient scribes practised their craft.

Chapter 17 ('The Serekh Tradition in Light of Post-Qumran Perspectives on the Emerging Bible') takes the narrowing gap between the Hebrew Bible and the Qumran materials as its starting point both in terms of dating[54] as well as the

---

[49] See Charlotte Hempel, 'Sources and Redaction in the Dead Sea Scrolls – The Growth of Ancient Texts,' in *Rediscovering the Dead Sea Scrolls: An Assessment of Old and New Approaches and Methods* (ed. Maxine Grossman; Grand Rapids, Mich.: Eerdmans, 2010), 162–181 and Reinhard G. Kratz, 'Biblical Scholarship and Qumran Studies,' in *The T & T Clark Companion to the Dead Sea Scrolls* (ed. George J. Brooke and Charlotte Hempel; London: T & T Clark, forthcoming).

[50] See, e. g., George J. Brooke, 'The Qumran Scrolls and the Demise of the Distinction Between Higher and Lower Criticism,' in *New Directions in Qumran Studies* (ed. Jonathan G. Campbell, William J. Lyons, and Lloyd K. Pietersen; LSTS 52; London: T & T Clark, 2005), 26–42; David M. Carr, *Writing on the Tablet of the Heart: Origins of Scripture and Literature* (Oxford: OUP, 2005); Martin Jaffe, *Torah in the Mouth: Writing and Oral Tradition in Palestinian Judaism, 200 BCE–400 CE* (Oxford: OUP, 2001); Kratz, 'Biblical Scholarship and Qumran Studies;' Karel van der Toorn, *Scribal Culture and the Making of the Hebrew Bible* (Cambridge: Harvard University Press, 2007); and Emanuel Tov, *Scribal Practices and Approaches Reflected in the Texts Found in the Judean Desert* (STDJ 54; Leiden: Brill, 2004).

[51] For a concise and judicious overview over the evidence, see Sarianna Metso, *The Serekh Texts* (CQS 9/LSTS 62; London: T & T Clark, 2007).

[52] See Chapter 7 in this volume and Alison Schofield, *From Qumran to the Yaḥad: A New Paradigm of Textual Development for the Community Rule* (STDJ 77; Leiden: Brill, 2009).

[53] See Collins, *Beyond the Qumran Community* and Kratz, 'Der *Penal Code*.'

[54] Carol Newsom, 'A Response to George Nickelsburg's "Currents in Qumran Scholarship: The Interplay of Data, Agendas and Methodology,"' in *The Dead Sea Scrolls at Fifty: Proceedings of the 1997 Society of Biblical Literature Qumran Section Meetings* (ed. Robert A. Kugler and Eileen M. Schuller; Atlanta, Ga.: Scholars Press, 1999), 115–121.

recognition that both collections testify to complex literary developments that can illuminate one another.⁵⁵

The chapter sets out to stimulate more intellectual dialogue and less *Apartheid* between the scholarly debates on the emerging Bible and the textual fluidity of the S manuscripts. Both literatures witness a comparable attitude towards a pluriform and complex textual landscape which was apparently taken for granted and indicates that some – maybe all? – Jews in the late Second Temple period who had the leisure to engage with their literary heritage were accustomed to pluralities of texts.

Chapter 18 ('The Emerging Bible and the Dead Sea Scrolls: A Common Milieu') builds on the arguments developed in earlier chapters, especially the immediately preceding Chapter 17 as well as Chapter 9 ('Rewritten Rule Texts') by reflecting further on the common approach to handling written traditions witnessed by the emerging scriptures and the Rule texts. In the wake of the full publication of the Scrolls, the importance of the Qumran manuscripts for our understanding of Second Temple Judaism beyond the confines of a small sectarian community is now beyond doubt.⁵⁶ Vocal disagreements on matters of scriptural interpretation and legal practice have for a long time been considered the best basis for circumscribing the characteristics of the groups reflected in the Scrolls. In order to be equipped to engage in high levels of scribal activity, scriptural interpretation, and halakhic dispute with others the groups behind the Scrolls shared more with the remainder of the Second Temple learned elite than they may have been prepared to admit, even where disagreement was heated. Once this is realised the Scrolls emerge as a goldmine of evidence that allows us to get close and personal with learned scribal, priestly and legal scholars of the Second Temple period.

Against this background Chapter 18 explores some intriguing points of contact between embryonic sectarianism as identified in Chapters 5 and 6 with emerging sectarianism in the Hebrew Bible. In particular, I suggest that the small fellowship groups that ultimately gave rise to the Qumran milieu are the heirs

---

⁵⁵ See already Peter von der Osten-Sacken, *Gott und Belial: Traditionsgeschichtliche Untersuchungen zum Dualismus in den Texten aus Qumran* (Göttingen: Vandenhoek & Ruprecht, 1969), 11. More recently these phenomena are authoritatively dealt with by Brooke, 'New Perspectives on the Bible and Its Interpretation' and Reinhard G. Kratz, 'Friend of God, Brother of Sarah, and Father of Isaac: Abraham in the Hebrew Bible and in Qumran,' in *The Dynamics of Language and Exegesis at Qumran* (ed. Devorah Dimant and Reinhard G. Kratz; FAT 35; Tübingen: Mohr Siebeck, 2009), 19–37, 79–105; idem, *Das Judentum im Zeitalter des Zweiten Tempels* (FAT 42; Tübingen: Mohr Siebeck, 2004), 123–156; and idem, 'Biblical Scholarship and Qumran Studies.'

⁵⁶ See already Charlotte Hempel, 'Qumran Communities: Beyond the Fringes of Second Temple Society,' in *The Scrolls and the Scriptures: Qumran Fifty Years After* (ed. Stanley Porter and Craig Evans; JSPSup 26; Sheffield: Sheffield Academic Press, 2003), 43–53 and eadem, 'Texts, Scribes and Scholars: Reflections on a Busy Decade in Dead Sea Scrolls Research,' *ExpTim* 120/6 (2009): 272–276.

of the Torah-disciples identified by Alexander Rofé as lying behind the shaping of the Hebrew Bible.[57] My particular focus is again a passage from the opening lines of 1QS 6 (1QS 6:6b–7a), but this time read side by side with Josh 1:8 and Ps 1:2. This approach offers opportunities to bridge the gap between the circles that shaped the final stages of parts of the Hebrew Bible and incipient communal life as described in 1QS 6:6b–7a.

8. Does 4Q Equal Qumran? The Character of Cave 4 Reconsidered

To a very great extent the contents of Cave 4 have been the engine that has driven all of my research since I started doctoral work in 1991. This material has also inspired most of the innovative re-evaluation of the texts in current Qumran Studies. The final chapter published here for the first time offers a reconsideration of the nature of Cave 4.

Chapter 19 ('"Haskalah" at Qumran: The Eclectic Character of Qumran Cave 4') begins with an overview over recent scholarly endeavours to come to terms with the profile of the Qumran Scrolls and the characteristics of particular scroll caves. While acknowledging well rehearsed intrinsic connections between the contents of this cave and the remainder of the Qumran Scrolls,[58] an impressive list of distinctive features is nevertheless identified. In particular I draw attention to,
- the presence of texts written in cryptic script almost exclusively in Cave 4;
- the prominence of the figure of the Maskil and spheres of learning particularly associated with this figure;
- technical learning manifest especially in a sizeable component of calendrical literature;
- literature that constitutes 'raw data' rather than finessed compositions;
- and a large number of compositions attested in five or more copies.

After assessing these and other traits of Cave 4, I conclude that the contents of this particular cave constitute a particularly eclectic and scholarly collection that invites further re-directing our efforts beyond reflecting on the applicability of

---

[57] Alexander Rofé, 'The Piety of the Torah-Disciples at the Winding-Up of the Hebrew Bible: Josh. 1:8; Ps. 1:2; Isa. 59:21,' in *Bibel in jüdischer und christlicher Tradition: Festschrift für Johann Maier zum 60. Geburtstag* (ed. Helmut Merklein, Karlheinz Müller, and Günter Stemberger; Frankfurt a. M.: Hain, 1993), 78–85.

[58] Cf. Dimant, 'The Qumran Manuscripts,' 23–24; see also eadem, 'The Library of Qumran: Its Content and Character,' in *The Dead Sea Scrolls Fifty Years After Their Discovery 1947–1997* (ed. Lawrence H. Schiffman, Emanuel Tov, and James C. VanderKam; Jerusalem: IES, 2000), 170–176; and Sidnie White Crawford, 'Qumran: Caves, Scrolls, and Buildings,' in *A Teacher for All Generations* (ed. Mason et al.), 253–273, 267.

multiple texts in favour of appreciating the learned and eclectic aspects of the material.

9. Concluding Reflections

After the full publication of the Scrolls one might have legitimately expected that the full spread of evidence in front of us would present us with most of the answers that we have been looking for. However, the full corpus of texts has many holes in it – sometimes more holes than preserved text – and even where plenty of text is preserved it is fair to say that we are now still short of just as many answers and often even reformulating the questions. Almost every chapter gathered in this volume emphasizes the creative and fluid processes of composing, shaping, transmitting, and reworking texts that often span across individual manuscripts, compositions as well as the anachronistic dividing lines between biblical and non-biblical Qumran literature. In two recent studies George Brooke perceptively teases out the symbiotic nature of the relationship between the scriptural source text and its interpretation as witnessed in the Scrolls.[59] Symbiosis is defined in the OED as "any intimate association of two or more different organisms."[60] This terminology eloquently captures the textual intimacy identified between several of the Rule texts in the studies that follow.[61] Symbiotic relationships presuppose familiarity as well as proximity between different texts and literary practitioners.

An overall trajectory to emerge from the scholarly journey I have embarked upon in a symbiotic relationship with fellow travellers is moving towards realising the power of the word over and above our ability to grasp social reality.

In the course of the last fifteen years – the Cave 4 era – scholars have increasingly recognized the significance of the Scrolls as a rich text world – from a period when texts, traditions, study, interpretation, and scholarship laid the foundations of western civilisation. Rather than perceiving the complexity of the texts and the archaeological remains as if they are somewhat faulty by failing to fulfil our initial desire for direct access to the social worlds of the people behind the texts, we are beginning to appreciate the richness of the same material from a textual, literary, and scribal point of view.[62]

---

[59] George J. Brooke, 'New Perspectives on the Bible and Its Interpretation,' 19–37, 37 and idem, 'Some Comments on Commentary,' *DSD* 19 (2012): 249–266.

[60] 'Symbiosis, n.,' in OED Online accessed January 05, 2013. http://www.oed.com/view/Entry/196194?redirectedFrom=symbiosis.

[61] See esp. Chapters 8 and 9.

[62] For the distinction between text world and social world see Jutta Jokiranta, 'Social-Scientific Approaches to the Dead Sea Scrolls,' in *Rediscovering the Dead Sea Scrolls* (ed. Grossman), 246–263, 246.

Thus, not every scrap of calendric learning was practised,⁶³ not every copy of MMT was lost in the Second Temple postal system,⁶⁴ not every copy of the Serekh is a manual applied in outlying communities.⁶⁵

Recent scholarship is increasingly aware of the significance of the finds from Qumran as complex literary artefacts whose own claims need to be treated with caution. Thus Lapin advocates a "hermeneutic of suspicion to help keep us from reproducing what our texts claim as our sole knowledge about them."⁶⁶ Such a hermeneutic of suspicion is emerging especially with reference to our ability to fathom the persona and oeuvre of the Teacher of Righteousness.⁶⁷ The *Wiederentdeckung* of Qumran literature *qua* literature with all the ideological and literary complexity of other Second Temple texts is having a considerable impact on the field.

While the literary, scribal, and textual aspects reflected in the Rule texts are becoming clearer, the social and community realities and personalities are becoming ever fuzzier, almost a mirage. Ultimately the Scrolls present us with a complex and sophisticated collection of literature rather than a window into the intricate reality of a group, let alone particular individuals.

Moshe Bernstein recently advocated we allow for a pluriform tradition of legal literature alongside the pluriformity of the emerging scriptures based on the failure of "the most distinguished scholars of Qumran halakhah" to arrive at a generic classifications for compositions such as 4Q265 and 4Q159.⁶⁸ Contemporary scholars, trained to appreciate orderly and carefully construed texts, are compelled to look for handrails of structure and order in a rather messy ancient textual environment. Rather like learning to swim, the security of the floor and the sides are what stops us letting go and experiencing the freedom of swimming in deep water. Once we are there, what appeared to be a threat at first turns into pleasure. It is time to ditch the buoyancy aids and enjoy the kaleidoscopic vision of interrelated Rule texts that reveal complex and shifting scenes.

---

⁶³ See Stern, 'The "Sectarian" Calendar,' Fraade, *Legal Fictions*, 282 and the discussion in Chapter 19 below.

⁶⁴ Grossman, 'Reading 4QMMT;' Fraade, 'Rhetoric and Hermeneutics;' and Hempel, 'MMT and Comfortable Theories.'

⁶⁵ Pace Schofield, *From Qumran to the Yaḥad*.

⁶⁶ Hayim Lapin, 'Dead Sea Scrolls and the Historiography of Ancient Judaism,' in *Rediscovering the Dead Sea Scrolls* (ed. Grossman), 108–127, 127.

⁶⁷ See notes 6 and 9 above.

⁶⁸ See Moshe Bernstein, '4Q159: Nomenclature, Text, Exegesis, Genre,' 53–55. The distinguished scholars of Qumran halakhah he is referring to are, of course, Lawrence Schiffman and the late Joseph Baumgarten.

Part I

The Nature of the Communities

Chapter Two

Community Structures and Organization[1]

1. Introduction

This chapter will examine the organization of the communities reflected in the Scrolls.[2] I employ the plural 'communities' since it is becoming increasingly clear that the Scrolls reflect more than one community. Various models have been suggested to explain the interrelationship of these communities.[3] The erstwhile dominant model, heavily influenced by the reference to two types of Essenes in the writings of Josephus, envisages two life forms practised by members of the same larger movement. This relationship is sometimes described as that of a monastic group to a wider lay movement.[4]

More recently, a growing number of scholars prefer to use sociological categories and speak of a parent movement from which a sect or a splinter group emerged.[5] Moreover, because of the complex literary developments that key

---

[1] This chapter was originally published as 'Community Structures in the Dead Sea Scrolls: Admission, Organization, and Disciplinary Procedures,' in *The Dead Sea Scrolls After Fifty Years* (ed. Peter Flint and James VanderKam; Leiden: Brill, 1999), Vol. II, 2, 67–92.

[2] For earlier treatments of this broad topic see, e. g., Millar Burrows, *The Dead Sea Scrolls* (London: Secker & Warburg, 1956), 355–362; Lawrence H. Schiffman, *Reclaiming the Dead Sea Scrolls: The History of Judaism, the Background to Christianity, the Lost Library of Qumran* (Philadelphia, Pa.: JPS, 1994), 97–143; Geza Vermes, *The Complete Dead Sea Scrolls in English* (London: Allen Lane, 1997), 26–45; Geza Vermes and Martin Goodman, *The Essenes According to the Classical Sources* (Oxford Centre Textbooks 1; Sheffield: JSOT Press, 1989), 7–10.

[3] See most recently John J. Collins, *Beyond the Qumran Community: The Sectarian Movement of the Dead Sea Scrolls* (Grand Rapids, Mich.: Eerdmans, 2010); Alison Schofield, *From Qumran to the Yaḥad: A New Paradigm of Textual Development for the Community Rule* (STDJ 77; Leiden: Brill, 2009); as well as Chapters 3–9 in this volume.

[4] Cf., for example, Albert-Marie Denis, 'Évolution de structures dans la secte de Qumrân,' in *Aux origines de l'église* (RechBib 7; Bruges: Desclée de Brouwer, 1965), 23–49, esp. 49; more recently Vermes, *Complete Dead Sea Scrolls in English*, 26; for a critique of the use of monastic terminology with reference to pre-Christian Jewish groups see Philip R. Davies, *Sects and Scrolls: Essays on Qumran and Related Topics* (South Florida Studies in the History of Judaism 134; Atlanta, Ga.: Scholars Press, 1996), 82–83.

[5] Cf., e. g., Esther Chazon, 'Is *Divrei Ha-Me'orot* a Sectarian Prayer?,' in *The Dead Sea Scrolls: Forty Years of Research* (ed. Devorah Dimant and Uriel Rappaport; STDJ 10; Leiden: Brill, 1992), 3–17; Philip R. Davies, *The Damascus Covenant: An Interpretation of the "Damascus Document"* (JSOTSup25; Sheffield: JSOT Press, 1983), 173–197; Florentino García Martínez, 'Qumran Origins and Early History: A Groningen Hypothesis,' *Folia Orientalia* 25

documents have undergone a single document can contain rules on the organization of different communities or stages in the life of the same community. In what follows I will endeavour to focus primarily on the primary evidence of the Scrolls themselves with only occasional references to the accounts of the classical authors and parallels with Greco-Roman associations.[6]

A central issue for the questions at hand is the interrelationship of the Community Rule and the Damascus Document. Joseph Fitzmyer's statement of 1970 still holds true today,

> This [the relationship of the Serekh to the Damascus Document] is probably the most difficult question to handle in the discussion of Qumran literature today; it complicates the identification of the Jewish group from which the documents have come.[7]

(1988): 113–136 (reprinted in García Martínez, *Qumranica Minora I: Qumran Origins and Apocalypticism* [ed. Eibert J. C. Tigchelaar; STDJ 63; Leiden: Brill, 2007], 3–29); Charlotte Hempel, 'Community Origins in the *Damascus Document* in the Light of Recent Scholarship,' in *The Provo International Conference on the Dead Sea Scrolls: Technological Innovations, New Texts, & Reformulated Issues* (ed. Donald W. Parry and Eugene Ulrich; STDJ 30; Leiden: Brill, 1999), 316–329, reprinted as Chapter 4 in this volume; and Michael A. Knibb, 'The Place of the Damascus Document,' in *Methods of Investigation of the Dead Sea Scrolls and the Khirbet Qumran Site: Present Realities and Future Prospects* (ed. Michael O. Wise et al.; Annals of the New York Academy of Sciences 722; New York: New York Academy of Sciences, 1994), 149–162.

[6] For an emphasis on the central importance of the primary evidence of the Scrolls over and above secondary accounts see Shemaryahu Talmon, 'The Essential "Community of the Renewed Covenant:" How Should Qumran Studies Proceed?,' in *Geschichte – Tradition – Reflexion: Festschrift für Martin Hengel zum 70. Geburtstag* (ed. Hubert Cancik, Hermann Lichtenberger and Peter Schäfer; Tübingen: Mohr Siebeck, 1996), Vol. I, 323–351, 329, 351–352; on the evidence of the classical authors cf. Todd S. Beall, *Josephus' Description of the Essenes Illustrated by the Dead Sea Scrolls* (SNTSMS 58; Cambridge: CUP, 1988); Roland Bergmeier, *Die Essenerberichte des Flavius Josephus: Quellenstudien zu den Essenertexten im Werk des Jüdischen Historiographen* (Kampen: Kok Pharos, 1993); Tessa Rajak, 'Ciò Che Flavio Guiseppe Vide: Josephus and the Essenes,' in *Josephus and the History of the Greco-Roman Period: Essays in Memory of Morton Smith* (ed. Fausto Parente and Joseph Sievers; StPB 41; Leiden: Brill, 1994), 141–160; Vermes and Goodman, *The Essenes According to the Classical Sources*. On parallels with Greco-Roman associations see Hans Bardtke, 'Die Rechtsstellung der Qumrangemeinde,' *TLZ* 86 (1961): 93–104; Martin Hengel, 'Qumran und der Hellenismus,' in *Qumrân: Sa piété, sa théologie et son milieu* (ed. Mathias Delcor; BETL 46; Paris-Gembloux: Duculot; Leuven: University Press, 1978), 333–372, 348–352; Moshe Weinfeld, *The Organizational Pattern and the Penal Code of the Qumran Sect: A Comparison with Guilds and Religious Associations of the Hellenistic-Roman Period* (NTOA 2; Göttingen: Vandenhoeck & Ruprecht; Fribourg: Éditions Universitaires, 1986); see also Matthias Klinghardt, 'The Manual of Discipline in the Light of Statutes of Hellenistic Associations,' in *Methods of Investigation of the Dead Sea Scrolls* (ed. Wise et al.), 251–270 whose attempt to go beyond Weinfeld's conclusions by suggesting that 1QS not only resembles the codes of Hellenistic associations but represents such a code may be slightly overstating the case. For a comprehensive treatment on the Scrolls and Greco-Roman associations see most recently Yonder Moynihan Gillihan, *Civic Ideology, Organization, and Law in the Rule Scrolls: A Comparative Study of the Covenanters' Sect and Contemporary Voluntary Associations in Political Context* (STDJ 97; Leiden: Brill, 2011).

[7] Joseph A. Fitzmyer, *Prolegomenon* to the Reprint of Solomon Schechter, *Documents of Jewish Sectaries. Vol. I: Fragments of a Zadokite Work* (New York: Ktav, 1970), 9–37, 16.

In addition to the Community Rule (1QS, 4QS) and the Damascus Document (CD, 4QD) the following documents will be considered: the Rule of the Congregation or "Messianic Rule" (1QSa), Miscellaneous Rules (4Q265; *olim* Serekh Damascus), the Overseer's Record of Rebukes (4Q477), the so-called Yaḥad Ostracon, Words of the Sage to the Sons of Dawn (4Q298) and the Rule 5Q13. With the exception of the fragment 6QD (6Q15) 5 the remains of 5QD (5Q12) and 6QD largely present material parallel to CD and are here mentioned only for the sake of completeness. Nor will the fragmentary remains of 5QS (5Q11) be considered in what follows. As far as the Damascus Document and the Community Rule are concerned we will be concerned predominantly with those sections that describe community structures rather than the historical and admonitory material. Thus, the discussion of the issue of authority and leadership in the community will not include the Teacher of Righteousness since this individual belongs to the *history* of the communities, or to the future as it appears from CD 6:10–11a, rather than their present organizational structure.[8] A thorough early examination of the relationship between the Damascus Document and the Community Rule and other scrolls was offered by Harold H. Rowley.[9] Along with most scholars of the first generation Rowley was keen to highlight the numerous and impressive similarities between the Damascus Document and the Qumran Scrolls. At the time Rowley was writing it was important to establish the place of the Damascus Document as part of the Qumran corpus, and it is thus understandable and proper that he emphasized similarities and connections. Subsequent generations of scholars are re-examining the relationships of various text to one another in the light of new evidence and methodological advances acknowledging both extensive similarities as well as significant differences. Across a variety of areas in Qumran studies a more complex picture is emerging. Whereas Qumran scholarship tended to gather all the evidence found in the Scrolls to be presented as contributing to the overall picture of 'the sect' it is a key concern of current scholarship to distinguish material that goes back to different forms of social organization.

The following discussion falls into three main sections dealing with the issues of admission into the community, communal organization and disciplinary procedures.

---

[8] For a different approach see Schiffman, *Reclaiming the Dead Sea Scrolls*, 113–126.

[9] Harold H. Rowley, *The Zadokite Fragments and the Dead Sea Scrolls* (Oxford: Blackwell, 1952).

2. Admission Process

Various descriptions of the process of admission into the community are found in the Scrolls.[10] The two most substantial passages are CD 15:5b–16:1a and 1QS 6:13b–23.

The central feature of the admission process as it emerges from CD 15:5b–16:1a consists of swearing an oath to return to the law of Moses and contrasts sharply with the detailed and elaborate process of admission described in 1QS 6. The procedure laid down in 1QS 6:13b–23 reflects a degree of institutionalization that is not paralleled in the rules on joining the movement as laid down in CD. The differences between these two accounts on the admission of new members have frequently been noted.[11] Chaim Rabin argues that CD 15:7–11 refers to the first stage of admission as described in 1QS 6:13–23.[12] Such an interpretation is the result of a harmonizing approach to the differences between the Damascus Document and the Community Rule. By contrast, I would stress that the admission process as described in CD 15 makes no reference to a novitiate and such a concept should not be read into the account on the basis of 1QS 6. The comments introducing CD 15:6b–17 as "an excursion on the procedure for becoming a member of the Yahad" in the translation by E. Cook also gloss over these differences.[13] Not only is the procedure laid down here radically different from the procedure of admission into the Yaḥad in 1QS 6:13b–23 but the term yaḥad never occurs in the laws of the Damascus Document. Finally, Stegemann's

---

[10] See Göran Forkman, *The Limits of the Religious Community: Expulsion from the Religious Community Within the Qumran Sect, Within Rabbinic Judaism, and Within Primitive Christianity* (ConBNT 5; Lund: CWK Gleerup, 1972); Florentino García Martínez and Julio Trebolle Barrera, *The People of the Dead Sea Scrolls: Their Writings, Beliefs and Practices* (Leiden: Brill, 1995), 36–38, 58–59; Sarianna Metso, *The Textual Development of the Qumran Community Rule* (STDJ 21; Leiden: Brill, 1997), 129–133; Józef T. Milik, *Ten Years of Discovery in the Wilderness of Judaea* (trans. John Strugnell; SBT 26; London: SCM, 1959), 101–103; Schiffman, *Reclaiming the Dead Sea Scrolls*, 97–105; Hartmut Stegemann, 'The Qumran Essenes – Local Members of the Main Jewish Union in Late Second Temple Times,' in *The Madrid Qumran Congress: Proceedings of the International Congress on the Dead Sea Scrolls, Madrid, 18–21 March 1991* (ed. Julio Trebolle Barrera and Luis Vegas Montaner; STDJ 11; Leiden: Brill, 1992), Vol. I, 83–166, 112–114. Further, Philip S. Alexander, 'Physiognomy, Initiation, and Rank in the Qumran Community,' in *Geschichte – Tradition – Reflexion* (ed. Cancik, Lichtenberger and Schäfer), Vol. I, 385–394, 391–392 where he makes the interesting suggestion that physiognomy might have been applied in the process of admission at least "by some people some of the time" (392). For a discussion of parallels between the admission process in the Scrolls and Hellenistic cultic associations, esp. the Iobacchi community, see Weinfeld, *Organizational Pattern*, 21–23, 43–44 and most recently also Gillihan, *Civic Ideology*.

[11] Cf. Philip R. Davies, 'Who Can Join the "Damascus Covenant"?,' *JJS* 46 (1995): 134–142; Forkman, *Limits of the Religious Community*, 52–70; Schiffman, *Reclaiming the Dead Sea Scrolls*, 97–101.

[12] Chaim Rabin, *Qumran Studies* (Oxford: OUP, 1957), 4.

[13] Michael Wise, Martin Abegg, and Edward Cook, *The Dead Sea Scrolls: A New Translation* (London: Harper Collins, 1996), 65.

recent description of the admission process as derived from the Community Rule and the Damascus Document fails to pay sufficient attention to the significant differences between CD 15–16 and 1QS 6 when he states, "1QS and the Damascus Document postulate that *full* membership in their related communities was reached only after three years, perhaps four years, of initiation with different stages of admission."[14]

What has been overlooked and not received the attention it deserves is another passage in 1QS that is rather closer to CD's legislation. That is, a comparable procedure to what is laid down in CD 15:5b–10a seems to form the background to 1QS 5:7c–9a. We should note that several variants exist between 1QS 5:7c–9a and the parallel passages preserved in 4Q256 (4QS^b) and 4Q258 (4QS^d). However, none of the variants impinge on the basic thesis to be argued for here.[15] Both passages focus on the act of swearing an oath (... בשבועת ... קום על) to return to the law of Moses לשוב אל תורת משה with all one's heart and all one's soul (בכול לב ובכול נפש) using remarkably similar terms to describe this oath. In addition to these striking parallels it is noteworthy that the simple procedure of admission by swearing an oath described in 1QS 5:7c–9a contrasts with the elaborate prescriptions on the admission of new members in 1QS 6:13b–23. The admission of new members in 1QS 6 is characterized by several stages involving periods of probation and examinations so that full membership is only acquired after a process lasting several years. J. Murphy-O'Connor and J. Pouilly assign both sections on the admission of new members to the same stage in the literary growth of 1QS.[16] What is more, most scholars understand the relationship of the two passages under consideration as forming a single description of a gradual process of admission.

Thus, Pouilly argues,

> Dans un premier temps, nous avons vu que tout 'volontaire' devait s'engager par un serment (V,7–13). Mais son admission définitive dans la Communauté n'est pas immédiate (VI,13–23).[17]

It seems much more likely to me that the two descriptions, rather than referring to different stages in a gradual admission process, are an indication of a development in the community organization behind 1QS. Furthermore, the much

---

[14] Stegemann, 'The Qumran Essenes,' 112.
[15] For the text of 4Q256 and 4Q258 see PTSDSSP 1:62, 72 (Qimron); see also Metso, *Textual Development*, 79–80.
[16] Jerome Murphy-O'Connor, 'La genèse littéraire de la Règle de la Communauté,' *RB* 76 (1969): 528–549, 533–537 and Jean Pouilly, *La Règle de la Communauté de Qumrân: Son évolution littéraire* (Cahiers de la Revue Biblique 17; Paris: Gabalda, 1976), 43.
[17] Pouilly, *La Règle de la Communauté*, 59; cf. also Michael A. Knibb, *The Qumran Community* (Cambridge Commentaries on Writings of the Jewish and Christian World 200 BC to AD 200 2; Cambridge: CUP, 1987), 108–109 and Vermes, *Complete Dead Sea Scrolls in English*, 32–34 for a similar view.

simpler procedure prescribed in 1QS 5 probably predates the more developed process we find in 1QS 6. Such an interpretation, which is already indicated by the *internal* evidence from 1QS alone, is further corroborated by CD 15:5b–10a which shows numerous links to 1QS 5. I am, therefore, suggesting that in 1QS 5:7c–9a we have a case of an earlier piece of communal legislation having been preserved in 1QS alongside the later and more elaborate procedure described in 1QS 6:13b–23. Moreover, this piece of communal legislation seems to describe the same community, probably the group from which the Yaḥad emerged, as the one behind the legislation in CD 15–16, a movement to which admission was gained by swearing an oath.

A series of further texts deals with the topic of admission. 1QSa 1 describes the education of children within the community and refers to a formal process of admission as they become of age, cf. 1QSa 1:6b–9a.[18] Such a procedure is also referred to in CD 15:5–6. 1QS 1:16–2:25a constitutes another text that refers to the admission of new members at an annual covenant ceremony that also involved the reaffirmation of their pledges to the covenant on the part of existing members, cf. 1QS 2:19. It does not seem necessary, however, to suppose that the admission of new members occurred only once year across the board. An annual admission of new members may well have been the practice at some point in the development of the community. However, there is certainly no indication of an annual event in the legislation on the admission process in CD 15, in 1QS 5:7c–9a, or in 1QS 6:13b–23. Further distinctive characteristics of the material in 1QS 1–2 are its pronounced dualistic orientation, cf. the frequent references to the reign of Belial and his lot, as well its liturgical setting. This pronounced liturgical character has led Metso to include 1QS 1:16–2:25 as part of her category 'Sections concerning the cult of the community' and not in her section 'Procedures for the admission of new members.'[19] The material shares characteristics with both categories and might have been included in both sections as is the case with 4Q258 (4QS^d) 1 i in Metso's outline. Finally, 1QS 5:20b–24a contains yet a further reference to the admission and examination of new members in the Community Rule. This material shares with 1QS 1:16–2:25a the coupling of admission of *new* members into the covenant with a re-assessment of *existing* members as well as the reference to an annual assessment although the emphasis in 1QS 5:20b–24a is distinctly hierarchical.[20]

---

[18] On 1QSa cf. Lawrence H. Schiffman, *The Eschatological Community of the Dead Sea Scrolls* (SBLMS 38; Atlanta, Ga.: Scholars Press, 1989); Hartmut Stegemann, 'Some Remarks to *1QSa*, to *1QSb*, and to Qumran Messianism,' *RQ* 17 (1996): 479–505; and Charlotte Hempel, 'The Earthly Essene Nucleus of 1QSa,' *DSD* 3 (1996): 253–269, reprinted as Chapter 3 in this volume.

[19] Metso, *Textual Development*, 119–120.

[20] On the hierarchical emphasis in 1QS 5:20b–24a see Murphy O'Connor, 'La genèse littéraire,' 536 and Metso, *Textual Development*, 130.

It is noteworthy in this context that Josephus (*J. W.* 2.137–138) makes reference to a gradual admission process reminiscent of 1QS 6:13b–23 in his description of the Essenes. He does not appear to be aware of the simpler admission process described in CD 15–16 and also underlying 1QS 5:7c–9a. This picture conforms with the results of Todd S. Beall's study on Josephus' descriptions of the Essenes.[21] Beall concludes that an examination of the passages on the Essenes in Josephus' works in comparison to the literature from Qumran indicates that Josephus and 1QS have more in common than Josephus and the Damascus Document.

3. Organization

3.1 Property[22]

With regard to the practice of ownership the Scrolls provide a complex picture.[23] Broadly speaking, the Community Rule envisages the communal ownership of property in a number of passages, cf. 1QS 1:11b; 3:2; 5:2; 6:17, 19–20, 22 whereas the Damascus Document presupposes the private ownership of goods in its communal legislation, cf. especially CD 9:10b–16a; 13:15–16; 14:12–13.[24] There are, however, a number of statements in the Community Rule that seem to allow for a certain amount of private ownership, cf. 1QS 7:6–8, 24–25.[25] It

---

[21] Beall, *Josephus' Description of the Essenes*.

[22] Several important studies have appeared recently offering a comprehensive analysis and innovative further discussion on this topic, see Catherine Murphy, *Wealth In the Dead Sea Scrolls and in the Qumran Community* (STDJ 40; Leiden: Brill, 2002) and Joan E. Taylor, 'Women, Children, and Celibate Men in the Serekh Texts,' *HTR* 104 (2011): 171–190 which includes an extended discussion of the possibility that women and families were included among the property of men. Finally, see James C. VanderKam, 'The Common Ownership of Property in Essene Communities,' in *'Go Out and Study the Land' (Judges 18:2): Archaeological, Historical and Textual Studies in Honor of Hanan Eshel* (ed. Maeir N. Aren, Jodi Magness, and Lawrence H. Schiffman; JSJSup 148; Leiden: Brill, 2011), 359–375 for a thorough assessment of the issue in the classical authors, the Damascus Document and the Serekh.

[23] Cf. Frank More Cross, *The Ancient Library of Qumran* (3d ed.; Sheffield: Sheffield Academic Press; Minneapolis, Minn.: Fortress, 1995), 73–74; Hans-Josef Klauck, 'Gütergemeinschaft in der Klassischen Antike, in Qumran und im Neuen Testament,' *RQ* 11 (1982): 47–79; David L. Mealand, 'Community of Goods at Qumran,' *TZ* 31 (1975): 129–139; Rabin, *Qumran Studies*, 22–36; Schiffman, *Reclaiming the Dead Sea Scrolls*, 106–110; Stegemann, 'The Qumran Essenes,' 112–114; idem, *The Library of Qumran: On the Essenes, Qumran, John the Baptist, and Jesus* (Grand Rapids, Mich.: Eerdmans, 1998), 176–190; and James C. VanderKam, *The Dead Sea Scrolls Today* (London: SPCK, 1994), 82–86.

[24] For a different view see Rabin, *Qumran Studies*, 24–31 and Klinghardt, 'Manual of Discipline,' 255, both of whom deny the practice of communal ownership at Qumran; see also Stegemann, 'The Qumran Essenes,' 113.

[25] Cf. Knibb, *Qumran Community*, 126; Rabin, *Qumran Studies*, 24–25; and VanderKam, *Dead Sea Scrolls Today*, 83.

is probable that the Community Rule incorporates remnants of legislation from various periods. Finally, both Josephus (*J. W.* 2.122–123; *Ant.* 18.20) and Philo (*Prob.* 84, 91) attribute the practice of communal ownership to the Essenes.

The editors of the recently published so-called 'Yaḥad ostracon' have proposed that the ostracon constitutes a deed of gift, or perhaps a draft deed, where a certain Honi transfers his estate as well as his slave to an individual named Elazar.[26] The editors go on to suggest on the basis of a reference to "fulfilling (an oath) to the community (יחד)" the ostracon is best taken to describe the handing over of the property of a member who is in an advanced stage of joining the community, and that the individual named Elazar is probably a community official such as the Mebaqqer or the Paqid. While the identification of the ostracon as a deed of gift exchanged by the individuals named in the text seems correct the detailed scenario suggested to connect this deed with the administration of common ownership in the community is no more than a possibility. Regrettably the fragmentary ostracon tells us much less then we could wish for. It is equally possible, for example, that Elazar is simply a private individual. Since the original publication of this chapter the renowned epigrapher Ada Yardeni has proposed a formidable alternative transcription of the ostracon which suggests we are dealing with a draft deed that does not refer to the communal property of the Yaḥad at all.[27]

3.2 Meetings

Both the Damascus Document and the Community Rule contain several descriptions of meetings. According to CD 12:22b–13:2 a priest is required for every meeting of ten.[28] This prescription is followed by a note on the organization of the members of the camps into thousands, hundreds, fifties, and tens, cf. Num 31:14, 48, 52.[29] CD 13:2 displays close terminological overlap with 1QS 6:3b–4a as has frequently been noted. It has been suggested that CD is here cross

---

[26] Frank More Cross and Esther Eshel, 'Ostraca from Khirbet Qumrân,' *IEJ* 47 (1997): 17–28; and now also DJD 36:497–507 (Cross and Eshel).

[27] See Ada Yardeni, 'A Draft of a Deed on an Ostracon from Khirbet Qumrân,' *IEJ* 47 (1997): 233–237. For a convenient summary see also Collins, *Beyond the Qumran Community*, 194–196.

[28] This material is discussed in more detail in Chapters 5 and 6 below.

[29] On this division see also 1QS 2:21–22; 1QSa 1:14–15; 1:29–2:1; for discussion see Yigael Yadin, *The Scroll of the War of the Sons of Light Against the Sons of Darkness* (Oxford: OUP, 1962), 59–61 and Nathan Jastram, 'Hierarchy at Qumran,' in *Legal Texts and Legal Issues: Proceedings of the Second Meeting of the International Organization for Qumran Studies Published in Honour of Joseph M. Baumgarten* (ed. Moshe Bernstein, Florentino García Martínez, and John Kampen; STDJ 23; Leiden: Brill, 1997), 349–376, 352–353.

referring to 1QS.³⁰ However, the overlap between both documents may equally be explained as both collections independently drawing upon earlier traditions.

Whereas CD 12:22b–13:2 deals with individual camps CD 14:3–6 describes the make-up of the meeting of *all* the camps as comprising priests, Levites, Israelites and proselytes. 4Q267 (4QD^b) 9 v 8 lacks the first reference to the proselytes found in CD 14:4 but clearly preserves the second reference (CD 14:6) in 4Q267 9 v 10. Moreover, CD 14:8b–12a stipulates that the overseer was to preside over the deliberations of the congregation at the meeting of all the camps. Every member of the congregation was assigned a fixed position. These passages have often been compared with the description of the meeting of the many in 1QS 6:8b–10a.³¹ In comparing both accounts a number of striking similarities may be noted. Thus, both passages employ the term מושב 'meeting' and both are introduced by a similar heading, cf. CD 14:3 (וסרך מושב כל המחנות) and 1QS 6:8 (הזה הסרך למושב הרבים) . Furthermore, in each case the heading is followed by a listing of groups that make up the respective communities and of instructions on the order in which these groups shall sit and be consulted. Even the verbs used in both passages (ישב and שאל *niphal*) are the same. Finally, it is prescribed in CD 14:11b–12a that every participant at the meetings of all the camps who has anything to say regarding any dispute or judgment shall speak to the overseer.

The suggestion by Ralph Marcus that 1QS 6:11–13 stipulates that even the overseer requires the consent of the many before addressing the meeting has not found wide acceptance.³² The recent proposal by Alexander Rofé to read יכיל for וכול in 1QS 6:12 has been adopted in Charlesworth's translation³³ and seems to underlie the translation of García Martínez.³⁴ The kind of procedure envisaged here is comparable to what is said about the meeting of the many in 1QS 6:8b–13a. An important difference between the two accounts is the terminology. Whereas 1QS 6 uses much of the terminology so typical of the Community Rule,

---

³⁰ Édouard Cothenet, 'Le Document de Damas,' in *Les Textes de Qumrân: Traduits et Annotés* (Paris: Letouzey et Ané, 1963), Vol. II, 129–204, 199.

³¹ Cf. Chaim Rabin, *The Zadokite Documents: I. The Admonition II. The Laws* (Oxford: Clarendon, 1954), 68 *ad loc.*; André Dupont-Sommer, *The Essene Writings from Qumran* (trans. Geza Vermes; Oxford: Blackwell, 1961), 159 n. 1; see also Cothenet, 'Document de Damas,' 203 n. 5. Metso suggests that 4Q258 (4QS^d) contained a briefer version of the material, cf. Metso, *Textual* Development, 84.

³² Ralph Marcus, '*Mebaqqer* and *Rabbim* in the Manual of Discipline vi.11–13,' *JBL* 75 (1956): 298–302; cf., however, Burrows, *Dead Sea Scrolls*, 379 and Johann Maier, *Die Qumran-Essener: Die Texte vom Toten Meer* (UTB; München: Reinhardt, 1995), Vol. I, 182.

³³ See Alexander Rofé, 'A Neglected Meaning of the Verb כול and the Text of 1QS vi:11–13,' in *"Sha'arei Talmon:" Studies in the Bible, Qumran, and the Ancient Near East Presented to Shemaryahu Talmon* (ed. Michael A. Fishbane and Emanuel Tov; Winona Lake, Ind.: Eisenbrauns, 1992), 315–321 and PTSDSSP 1:29 and n. 153 (Qimron); see also n. 177 which accompanies Qimron's edition of 1QS in the same volume, 28.

³⁴ Florentino García Martínez, *The Dead Sea Scrolls Translated: The Qumran Texts in English* (Leiden: Brill, 1994), 10.

the present passage in CD 14 expresses a similar procedure, yet it lacks expressions like 'the council of the community' (עצת היחד) or 'the many' (הרבים). In addition to these terminological differences 1QS 6:8b–13a also reflects a more elaborate procedure.

Despite these impressive similarities there are also important differences between both passages. Firstly, as briefly noted already, the terminology used to refer to the community is different in each account. Whereas CD 14 speaks of 'all the camps' (כל המחנות), the communal frame of reference in 1QS 6 are 'the many' (הרבים) and 'the community' (היחד). This terminological difference is characteristic not only of these particular passages, but of the communal terminology employed in the respective documents as a whole. Camp terminology predominates in the Laws of the Damascus Document although the expression 'the many' is also found in a number of passages. I have argued elsewhere that the references to the many in the Laws of the Damascus Document form part of a redactional layer in the Laws intended to bring them into line with 1QS.[35] Secondly, as has often been noted, the Community Rule knows of three groups of members (priests, elders, and the rest of all the people).[36] A different threefold division into priests, Levites and all the people is attested in 1QS 2:19–22. It seems that 1QS reflects a certain amount of development with regard to the division of the membership. The Damascus Document, on the other hand, divides the members of all the camps into four groups. Only in CD 14 are proselytes included into the movement. Philip Davies has argued that here the term 'proselyte' (גר) refers to someone who is not yet a full community member but who has begun the process of initiation.[37] However, in contrast to 1QS 6:13b–23 and Josephus' description of the Essenes the admission process as described at some length in the Damascus Document (CD 15:5b–16:6a) does not mention a prolonged procedure of admission involving various stages. It seems preferable to me to take this reference to proselytes as indicating the presence of converts to the Jewish religion in the movement described in the Laws of the Damascus Document, see also CD 12:10–11.[38] CD 14:3b–6b appears to reflect a more open attitude towards the outside world in as much as proselytes are included in the movement.

The evidence as it stands which comprises remarkable similarities as well as significant differences between CD 14:3–6.8b–12a and 1QS 6:8b–10a is best accounted for by arguing that the author responsible for 1QS 6:8b–10a drew upon a piece of communal legislation along the lines of CD 14:3b–6b and adapted it to

---

[35] Charlotte Hempel, *The Laws of the Damascus Document: Sources, Traditions, and Redaction* (STDJ 29; Leiden: Brill, 1998; Paperback edition Atlanta, Ga.: SBL, 2006).

[36] On the term 'elders' see Alfred R. C. Leaney, *The Rule of Qumran and Its Meaning* (NTL; London: SCM, 1966), 186–188.

[37] Davies, *Sects and Scrolls*, 163–177.

[38] For such a view see, for example, Leaney, *Rule of Qumran*, 135.

the particular needs within his own community, up-dating in particular the self-designation for the community. I have proposed a comparable process of reformulation of an earlier piece of legislation with reference to the 'murmuring offence' in the penal codes of the Community Rule and the Damascus Document.[39]

Strict hierarchical ranking of members, particularly during meetings, is expressed in a wide variety of texts, cf. 1QS 2:19–23; 5:23–24; 6:2b, 4, 8–10, 22, 26; 8:19; 9:2; CD 14:9b–10a, see also 1QSa 1:18; 2:15–17, 21.[40] The hierarchical structure of the Essenes is referred to by Josephus, cf. *J. W.* 2.150. Hierarchical seating was also practised in Greco-Roman associations.[41]

We should also mention the reference to the council of the community comprising twelve men and three priests in 1QS 8:1–4a and in 4Q265 (Miscellaneous Rules) 2 ii 7–8.[42] The problem with the view espoused by some that this passage singles out an inner council of leading members[43] is the use of the expression 'council of the community' with reference to the whole community elsewhere in 1QS. It is therefore more likely that the passage in question refers to a period before the establishment of the community and lays down the required number of members.[44] We should further note that 1QS 6:7b prescribes nightly meetings to study the law and the provision in 1QSa 1:25b–2:11a that allows those who were excluded from the congregation on account of physical defects to put their views forward in private outside of meetings. Finally, a considerable number of offences mentioned in the penal codes are set in the context of community

---

[39] Charlotte Hempel, 'The Penal Code Reconsidered,' in *Legal Texts and Legal Issues* (ed. Bernstein, García Martínez, and Kampen), 337–348.

[40] Cf. Jastram, 'Hierarchy at Qumran;' Stegemann, 'The Qumran Essenes,' 111–112; on the material dealing with meetings in 1QS 6 cf. Metso, *Textual Development*, 133–135; for a list of variant readings of 1QS 5:23–24 in 4Q258 (4QS^d) see ibidem, 83. See also Alexander, 'Physiognomy, Initiation, and Rank,' 392–393, where he explores the potential role of physiognomy in the determination of rank.

[41] Cf. Weinfeld, *Organizational Pattern*, 28–29.

[42] Cf. García Martínez, *Dead Sea Scrolls Translated*, 72 and Maier, *Qumran-Essener*, Vol. II, 215. Vermes, *Complete Dead Sea Scrolls in English*, 155 numbers this fragment frg. 7. This material is analysed in more depth in Chapter 5 below.

[43] So Joseph M. Baumgarten, 'The Duodecimal Courts of Qumran, Revelation, and the Sanhedrin,' *JBL* 95 (1976): 59–78; Cross, *Ancient Library of Qumran*, 167; Milik, *Ten Years of Discovery*, 100; Rabin, *Zadokite Documents*, 21; Stegemann, *Library of Qumran*, 111; Weinfeld, *Organizational Pattern*, 16, and most recently Eibert J. C. Tigchelaar, 'The Dead Sea Scrolls,' in EDEJ: 163–180, 177–178.

[44] Cf. Christoph Dohmen, 'Zur Gründung der Gemeinde von Qumran,' *RQ* 11 (1982): 82–96; Knibb, *Qumran Community*, 129; Leaney, *Rule of Qumran*, 211 and 212 where the otherwise sober tone of Leaney's commentary is interrupted by the outburst, "Remarkable nonsense has been talked about these men;" Metso, *Textual Development*, 80; Murphy-O'Connor, 'La genèse littéraire;' Lawrence H. Schiffman, *Sectarian Law in the Dead Sea Scrolls: Courts, Testimony and the Penal Code* (BJS 33; Chico, Calif.: Scholars Press, 1983), 25; Edmund F. Sutcliffe, 'The First Fifteen Members of the Qumran Community: A Note on 1QS 8:1 ff.,' *JSS* 4 (1959): 134–138; and Preben Wernberg-Møller, *The Manual of Discipline* (STDJ 1; Leiden: Brill, 1957), 122–123.

meetings, e. g. absenting oneself up to three times in one meeting, spitting, falling asleep, interrupting someone else's speech to name but a few. An emphasis on orderly conduct in meetings is also referred to by Josephus (*J. W.* 2.132). Moreover, the codes of Greco-Roman cultic associations paid particular attention to appropriate conduct in meetings.[45]

In sum, the Scrolls deal at some length with the proper conduct of meetings, and passages from various periods are preserved alongside each other.

3.3 Leadership and Authority Structures

The following individuals or groups are assigned a role in the leadership of the communities: the priest (הכהן), the Paqid (האיש הפקיד), the Mebaqqer (המבקר), the Maskil (המשכיל), the judges (השופטים), the sons of Zadok (בני צדוק), the sons of Aaron (בני אהרון), and the Levites (הלוים). The larger topic of leadership in the Dead Sea Scrolls has received a considerable amount of scholarly attention.[46]

On the priest's role in the community compare CD 9:13; 13:2, 5; 14:6; 4Q270 (4QD^e) 7 i 16; 4Q266 (4QD^a) 11 8; 1QS 6:4, 5; and 1QSa 2:19. This list is restricted to those occurrences where an individual priest is assigned a role in the organizational structure of a particular community. We are not concerned here with those passages that mention 'the priests' in the plural as a component in the membership of the community. Leading priests are charged with pronouncing blessings before meals and with administering the law of disease, if necessary advised by the Mebaqqer. The impression gained from key documents such as the Damascus Document and the Community Rule is that this traditional scriptural figure of authority seems to recede behind the leading role of specific functionaries such as Maskil and Mebaqqer.[47] An association of the communal office simply referred to as 'priest' with the early phase of the communities' existence is confirmed by passages like 1QS 6:4 and CD 13:2 where a priest is required to be present in all gatherings of ten members. It seems likely that these simple stipulations dealing with such small numbers preserved both in the Damascus Document and the Community Rule comprise an early tradition. A specification of the office of the priest is evident in the two priestly offices 'the priest who

---

[45] Weinfeld, *Organizational Pattern*, 26.
[46] Cf. Matthias Delcor, 'Qumran: La Règle de la Communauté,' *DBSup* 9 (1979): 851–857, 854–857; Jastram, 'Hierarchy at Qumran,' 356–360; Colin G. Kruse, 'Community Functionaries in the Rule of the Community and the Damascus Document: A Test of Chronological Relationships,' *RQ* 10 (1981): 543–551; Milik, *Ten Years of Discovery*, 99–101; Schiffman, *Reclaiming the Dead Sea Scrolls*, 113–126. For parallels in the authority structures of Hellenistic associations see Weinfeld, *Organizational Pattern*, 19–21, 73.
[47] For the view that the former was a priest see Metso, *Textual Development*, 136.

musters the many' (אשר הכהן יפקד ברואש הרבים) in CD 14:6–7 and 'the priest in charge over the many' (הכהן המופקד על הרבים) in 4Q270 7 i 16 and 4Q266 11 8.[48]

The Community Rule includes a single reference to an official with the title Paqid in 1QS 6:14. John F. Priest ambitiously attempts to correlate the messianic expectations expressed in the Scrolls with an originally bipartite model of leadership comprising of the priestly Paqid and the lay Mebaqqer.[49] The picture that derives from the Scrolls about both topics, i. e. messianism and communal leadership, is far too complex to allow a profitable synthesis at this stage.[50] 4Q289 (Berakhot[d]) 1 4 leaves little doubt about the Paqid's identification as a priestly figure by speaking in a liturgical context of "the priest [who is app]ointed (הכוהן הפ[קיד]) at the head of [...]"[51] The same officer is probably referred to in CD 14:6–8 and parallels as "the priest who musters at the head of the many" referred to above. Some have argued that the Paqid is to be identified with the Mebaqqer whereas others, like Priest referred to above, prefer to think of two distinct offices.[52] According to 1QS 6:14 the role of the Paqid was the examination of potential new members.

Of all the officers that play a leading role in the organization of the communities the Mebaqqer is referred to most frequently, cf. 4Q266 (4QD[a]) 5 i 14; 4Q271 (4QD[f]) 3 14; 4Q266 7 iii 3; CD 15:8, 11, 14; 9:18, 19, 22; 13:6, 7, 13, 16; 14:8–9, 11–12, 13; 4Q266 11 16; 1QS 6:12, 20; 5Q13 (Rule) 4 1; 4Q265 (Miscellaneous Rules) 1 ii 6. This official is most frequently associated with the camps (cf. 4Q266 [4QD[a]] 7 iii 3; CD 15:14; 13:7b, 13, 16; 14:8–9),[53] but also features as an authority in the organization of 'the many' (הרבים), cf. CD 15:8; 1QS 6:12, 20; 4Q265 (Miscellaneous Rules) 1 ii 6. The role of this official covers a host of areas, all in the realm of the practical organization of community life. His duties concentrate particularly on three areas: admission into the community (cf. 4Q266 [4QD[a]] 5 i 14; CD 13:13; 15:8, 11, 14), the administration of finances and supervision of trade (cf. 1QS 6:20; CD 13:16; 14:13), judicial proceedings (cf. CD 9:18, 19, 22; 14:11–12; 4Q266 [4QD[a]] 11 16; see also 4Q477 [The Overseer's Record of Rebukes]).

---

[48] The reading ברואש follows Rabin, *Zadokite Documents*, 69 and has been confirmed by 4Q267 (4QD[b]) 9 v 11, cf. DJD 18:109 (Baumgarten).

[49] John F. Priest, 'Mebaqqer, Paqid, and the Messiah,' *JBL* 81 (1962): 55–61.

[50] For an exposition of messianic expectations in the Scrolls see John J. Collins, *Apocalypticism in the Dead Sea Scrolls* (The Literature of the Dead Sea Scrolls; London: Routledge, 1997), 71–90.

[51] See DSSEL (Nitzan) and DJD 11:67–71 (Nitzan), both of these editions appeared too late for inclusion in the original publication of this chapter.

[52] Amongst those who have suggested that Mebaqqer and Paqid represent the same office are Cross, *Ancient Library of Qumran*, 167; Leaney, *Rule of Qumran*, 195–196; and Metso, *Textual Development*, 77, 136–137 n. 92.

[53] On the Overseer see Milik, *Ten Years of Discovery*, 99; Priest, 'Mebaqqer, Paqid, and the Messiah;' and Stegemann, 'The Qumran Essenes,' 90.

Another figure to occur widely in the Qumran Scrolls is the Maskil.[54] Apart from references to this title in the documents that deal with the organization of the communities (cf. 1QS 3:13; 4Q258 [4QS^d] 1 i 1; 4Q256 [4QS^b] 5 1]; 1QS 9:12, 21; CD 12:21; 13:22), the term Maskil occurs in a number of liturgical texts from Qumran such as 4QShirShabb, 1QSb, the Hodayot, 4Q510–511 (Songs of the Maskil), and 4Q298 (The Maskil's Address to the Son of Dawn).[55] The references to the Maskil in 4Q256 (4QS^b) and 4Q258 (4QS^d) are absent from 1QS 5 on which more will be said below. A further occurrence of Maskil has been proposed as a restoration for the title of the work in 1QS 1:1.[56]

The duties of the Maskil fall into the realm of instruction, compare 1QS 3:13; 9:18. This figure is often linked to calendrical issues[57] and portrayed as someone who enjoys access to esoteric knowledge, see, for example, 1QS 9:12–14, 18, 23. Moreover, Carol Newsom has drawn attention to the Maskil's role in the hierarchical ranking of community members according to 1QS 9:14, 16.[58] A number of scholars hold that the Maskil should be identified with the figure referred to as the Mebaqqer,[59] but in view of the different roles attributed to both figures in the Scrolls this identification seems unlikely. Whereas the former's role belongs into the realm of instruction in calendrical and esoterical matters,[60] the Mebaqqer is much more concerned with the day-to-day practical matters of organization.

The judges are referred to as an authoritative group within in the community in CD 15:4; 16:19 parallel in 4Q270 (4QD^e) 6 iv 13; CD 9:10; 10:1,4–7a; 14:13.[61] Note, however, that in 1QSa 1:15, 24, 29 the judges appear in a list of members of the congregation rather than as a leading group. The judges' role in the Damascus Document focuses on the areas of administration of justice and finance, partly executed in conjunction with the Mebaqqer.

---

[54] For an overview covering the Hebrew Bible, the Dead Sea Scrolls, and the Karaites cf. Hans Kosmala, 'Maśkîl,' *JANES* 5 (1973): 235–241 (reprinted in idem, *Studies, Essays and Reviews* [Leiden: Brill, 1978], Vol. I, 149–155); further Carol Newsom, 'The Sage in the Literature of Qumran: The Functions of the Maskil,' in *The Sage in Israel and the Ancient Near East* (ed. James G. Gammie and Leo G. Perdue; Winona Lake, Ind.: Eisenbrauns, 1990), 373–382; also Metso, *Textual Development*, 135–140.

[55] See Stephen Pfann, '4Q298: The Maskil's Address to All Sons of Dawn,' *JQR* 85 (1994): 203–235 and Menahem Kister, 'Commentary to 4Q298,' *JQR* 85 (1994): 237–249.

[56] Cf. Jean Carmignac, 'Conjecture sur la première ligne de la Règle de la Communauté,' *RQ* 2 (1959): 85–87.

[57] So already Denis, 'Évolution de structures,' 44–45.

[58] Newsom, 'The Sage in the Literature of Qumran,' 376; see also Schiffman, *Reclaiming the Dead Sea Scrolls*, 124.

[59] Newsom, 'The Sage in the Literature of Qumran,' 375; García Martínez and Trebolle Barrera, *People of the Dead Sea Scrolls*, 55–58; VanderKam, *Dead Sea Scrolls Today*, 112; and Vermes, *Complete Dead Sea Scrolls in English*, 29.

[60] On these spheres of influence of the Maskil see further Chapter 19 below, especially section 5.2.

[61] For a detailed discussion see Schiffman, *Sectarian Law in the Dead Sea Scrolls*, 23–54; for a critique of Schiffman's approach see Weinfeld, *Organizational Pattern*, 73.

Leadership functions are further attributed to the sons of Zadok and the sons of Aaron.⁶² Both groups, as well as both personal names, occur frequently in the Qumran Scrolls. I will consider here only those passages where these groups are given a leadership role in the communities. The Community Rule and the Rule of the Congregation contain passages that assign a leading role to the sons of Zadok (cf. 1QS 5:2, 9; 1QSa 1:2, 24; 2:3) in juxtaposition to passages that assign a key role to the sons of Aaron in the community leadership (cf. 1QS 5:21–22; 9:7; 1QSa 1:15–16, 23). Recently interest has increased in both references to the authoritative role of the sons of Zadok in 1QS 5, since these are absent in two Cave 4 manuscripts of the Community Rule (4Q256 [4QS^b] and 4Q258 [4QS^d]).⁶³ Both of the 4QS scrolls completely lack the references to the sons of Zadok and have a shorter text which has 'the many' (הרבים) in charge. To be precise, in 4Q256 and 4Q258 'the many' replaces 'the sons of Zadok, the priests who keep the covenant and […] the multitude of the men of the community who hold fast to the covenant' (1QS 5:2–3). The most likely interpretation seems to me the view first espoused by J. T. Milik and subsequently elaborated by Geza Vermes and others that the shorter version of 4QS is the more original and to think of 1QS 5 as evidence for a Zadokite recension.⁶⁴ Moreover, I have suggested elsewhere that a similar Zadokite recension can be identified in 1QSa.⁶⁵ 1QS 9:14 reads 'the sons of Zadok' (בני הצדוק) where 4Q259 (4QS^e) 1 iii 10 has 'the sons of righteousness' (בני הצדק). Metso plays down the actual significance of the variants in 4Q256 (4QS^b) and 4Q258 (4QS^d) and argues,

---

⁶² See Jacob Liver, 'The "Sons of Zadok the Priests" in the Dead Sea Sect,' *RQ* 6 (1967): 3–30; and Jastram, 'Hierarchy at Qumran,' 364–365. For detailed treatments of the evidence on priestly leadership in the Scrolls see Chapters 13 and 14 below and further literature referred to there.

⁶³ Cf. Philip S. Alexander, 'Redaction History of *Serek ha-Yaḥad*: a Proposal,' *RQ* 17 (1996): 437–453; Albert I. Baumgarten, 'The Zadokite Priests at Qumran,' *DSD* 4 (1997): 137–156; James H. Charlesworth and Brent A. Strawn, 'Reflections on the Text of *Serek ha-Yaḥad* Found in Cave IV,' *RQ* 17 (1996): 403–435; Davies, *Sects and Scrolls*, 154–156; Paul Garnet, 'Cave 4 Ms Parallels to 1QS 5.1–7: Towards a *Serek* Text History,' *JSP* 15 (1997): 67–78; Charlotte Hempel, 'Comments on the Translation of 4QS^d I,1,' *JJS* 44 (1993): 127–128; Metso, *Textual Development*, 27–28, 41–42, 74–90, 122–123; Józef T. Milik, 'Le travail d'édition des fragments manuscrits de Qumrân,' *RB* 63 (1956): 49–67, 61; Geza Vermes, 'Preliminary Remarks on Unpublished Fragments of the Community Rule from Qumran Cave 4,' *JJS* 42 (1991): 250–255; idem, 'The Leadership of the Qumran Community: Sons of Zadok-Priests-Congregation,' in *Geschichte – Tradition – Reflexion* (ed. Cancik, Lichtenberger and Schäfer), Vol. I, 375–384 as well as Chapter 7 below.

⁶⁴ For bibliographical details see note 63 above.

⁶⁵ Hempel, 'The Earthly Essene Nucleus,' reprinted as Chapter 3 in this volume; see also Robert A. Kugler, 'A Note on 1QS 9:14: The Sons of Righteousness or the Sons of Zadok,' *DSD* 3 (1996): 315–320 who argues that 1QS 9:14 represents a further example of a Zadokite recension in 1QS.

There cannot be any decisive difference in the denotation of the two expressions, for the rabbim includes both priests and (lay)men.[66]

The position advocated by Metso may be compared to Rabin's interpretation of 1QS 5.[67] By contrast, there seem to me a number of important differences. Thus, in the 1QS 5 tradition it was clearly felt necessary to define the priestly leadership in a particular way as 'the sons of Zadok'. Moreover, although 1QS 5 does mention both the sons of Zadok the priests as well as the multitude of the men who keep the covenant, it seems rather unlikely that both groups are considered equal with regard to their authority. Rather, I am inclined to concur with the statement by Leaney that the sons of Zadok are here portrayed as "an honoured and privileged group within the sect."[68] One may further ask whether the rather convoluted statements in 1QS 5 do not reflect a certain amount of development and a late stage where the positions advocating democratic leadership and those advocating Zadokite leadership have become merged. A comparable picture emerges from 1QSa 1:22b–25 where authority is attributed in a similarly convoluted fashion to the sons of Aaron in line 23 and the sons of Zadok in line 24.

Finally, CD 13:3–4 rules that a Levite may take charge in the community if the priest is inexperienced. This passage may either reflect a set of particular historical circumstances or, more probably, rivalry between various priestly groups.[69]

In sum, with respect to the leadership of the community neither the evidence of the Scrolls themselves nor scholarly evaluations of this evidence present a uniform picture.

3.4 Communal Meals

A number of texts describe the practice of eating communally, cf. 1QS 6:2; 6:4b–6a.[70] Furthermore in 1QSa 2:17b–22 the communal meals of the community in

---

[66] Metso, *Textual Development*, 122.

[67] Rabin, *Qumran Studies*, 105.

[68] Leaney, *Rule of Qumran*, 105.

[69] George J. Brooke, *The Dead Sea Scrolls and the New Testament* (Minneapolis, Minn.: Fortress, 2005), 115–139.

[70] See Friedrich Avemarie, '"Tohorat Ha-Rabbim" and "Mashqeh Ha-Rabbim:" Jacob Licht Reconsidered,' in *Legal Texts and Legal Issues* (ed. Bernstein, García Martínez, and Kampen), 215–229; Cross, *Ancient Library of Qumran*, 75–78; García Martínez and Trebolle Barrera, *People of the Dead Sea Scrolls*, 60–61; Leaney, *Rule of Qumran*, 183–184; Milik, *Ten Years of Discovery*, 105–107; Johan P. M. van der Ploeg, 'The Meals of the Essenes,' *JSS* 2 (1957): 163–175; Schiffman, 'Communal Meals at Qumran,' *RQ* 10 (1979): 45–56; Schiffman, *Sectarian Law in the Dead Sea Scrolls*, 191–210; idem, *Eschatological Community of the Dead Sea Scrolls*, 65–67; Stegemann, *Library of Qumran*, 190–193; idem, 'The Qumran Essenes,' 108–110; Edmund F. Sutcliffe, 'Sacred Meals at Qumran?,' *HeyJ* 1 (1960): 48–65. For a recent contribution on meals in the Community Rule with further bibliography see Charlotte Hempel, 'Who is Making Dinner at Qumran?,' *JTS* 63 (2012): 49–65.

the present are considered a foretaste of the eschatological meal in the presence of the messiahs (cf. especially 1QSa 2:21–22; Stegemann suggests that the meal in 1QSa 2 is presided over by the local priest rather than the priestly messiah).[71] According to both 1QS 6:4b–6a and 1QSa 2:17b–22 the priest/priest-messiah is to pronounce blessings and prayers before the meal. The gradual admission process described in 1QS 6:13b–23 stresses the phased admission of new members, first to the food and then to the drink. Stricter rules pertained with regard to sharing the drink of the community because of the halakhic principle that liquids are more susceptible to defilement. The penal code contains a number of penalties that refer to a reduction of one's food ration (cf. 1QS 6:25; 4Q265 [Miscellaneous Rules] 1 i) and to the exclusion from the *tohorah* (טהרה), a term that most probably refers to the ritually clean food of the community.[72] Friedrich Avemarie proposed with reference to the penal code and the admission legislation that the term refers more broadly to a member's purity that may be violated by any personal contact with a penitent or novice.[73] Moreover, it appears from 1QS 5:13 that a ritual bath preceded the meals. Such a bath is also mentioned in Josephus' account (*J. W.* 2. 129) and corroborated by the presence of *miqvaot* in the excavated settlement of Khirbet Qumran. It is interesting to note that 4Q256 (4QS[b]) and 4Q258 (4QS[d]) lack 1QS 5:13's reference to 'the waters of purity,' merely referring to the touching of 'the purity'. Metso summarizes the evidence as follows,

> In 1QS the premises of conversion and thus of touching 'the waters of purity' are stated explicitly in the text of 1QS, but are lacking in 4QS[b,d].[74]

However, the passage in 1QS 5:13 does not in fact refer to *touching* the waters of purity as paraphrased by Metso, but to *entering* the waters in order to touch the purity. It seems more likely, moreover, that the passage refers to ritual washing before meals rather than conversion.

Some have tried to argue that the communal meals described in the Scrolls are of a cultic or sacred character.[75] Others have made a good case for the non-sacral character of the communal meal as it emerges from the texts.[76] Thus, Schiffman notes,

---

[71] Stegemann, 'Some Remarks.'
[72] Cf. Saul Lieberman, 'The Discipline in the So-Called Dead Sea Manual of Discipline,' *JBL* 71 (1952): 199–206 and Hempel, 'Dinner at Qumran.'
[73] Avemarie, '"Tohorat Ha-Rabbim."'
[74] Metso, *Textual Development*, 81.
[75] So, e. g., Stegemann, *Library of Qumran*, 190–193; see also Jean-Baptiste Humbert, 'L'espace sacré à Qumrân,' *RB* 101 (1994): 161–214. Humbert's thesis has been challenged by Jodi Magness, 'The Chronology of the Settlement at Qumran in the Herodian Period,' *DSD* 2 (1995): 58–65, 60 n. 10.
[76] Van der Ploeg, 'Meals of the Essenes;' Schiffman, 'Communal Meals at Qumran;' Schiffman, *Sectarian Law in the Dead Sea Scrolls*, 191–210; Schiffman, *Eschatological Community of the Dead Sea Scrolls*, 56–67; Sutcliffe, 'Sacred Meals at Qumran.'

All the motifs – purity, benedictions, bread and wine, and the role of the priest – can be explained against the background of contemporary Jewish ceremonial and ritual practice.[77]

In addition to the literary evidence of the Qumran scrolls a number of archaeological finds testify to the communal meals of the group that inhabited the Qumran site. These include a dining room adjacent to a storage chamber containing around a thousand neatly arranged pottery vessels, the excavation of a kitchen with five fireplaces, and the discovery of a large number of animal bones with remnants of pottery buried in between the buildings and outside the perimeter of the buildings.[78]

3.5 Family Life and Celibacy

The evidence that is pertinent to this issue falls into three categories: the literary evidence of the Scrolls; the archaeological evidence of the cemeteries; and the accounts of Philo, Josephus, and Pliny. All three of the classical authors describe the Essenes as celibate, although Josephus goes on to mention 'another order of Essenes' that promoted a married lifestyle (cf. Philo, *Apol.* II.14–17; Pliny, *Nat.* 5.73; Josephus, *J. W.* 2.120–121; *Ant.* 18.21 and *J. W.* 2.160–161). The excavated graves in the cemeteries at Qumran similarly point in two directions. Although the great majority of the excavated skeletons are male a number of graves further from the centre of the graveyard have revealed the remains of women and children. Finally, the literary evidence of the Scrolls is once again not clear-cut. On the one hand, the Damascus Document and the Rule of the Congregation abound with references to women and family life in the context of communal organization, see CD 7: 6b–9a (CD 19:2b–5a); 4Q266 (4QD^a) 6 ii and parallels;[79] 4Q270 (4QD^e) 4 and parallels; 4Q270 5 14–21 and parallels; CD 15:5b–6a; 16:10–12; 11:11; 12:1b–2a; 13:16;[80] 14:12c–16a; 4Q270 7 i 12–15; 1QSa 1:4–5, 9–11. In addition to these documents other texts that do not refer to the life of a particular community such as the Temple Scroll, the War Scroll, the halakhic part of 4QMMT, or the wisdom corpus contain references to women. These texts fall outside the scope of this chapter.

The Community Rule, on the other hand, never mentions women in its communal legislation. Neither the Hebrew idiom 'one born of a woman' in 1QS

---

[77] Schiffman, *Sectarian Law in the Dead Sea Scrolls*, 193–194.
[78] See Schiffman, *Sectarian Law in the Dead Sea Scrolls*, 200–201.
[79] For the text of 4QD see DJD 18 (Baumgarten); for further discussion see Chapter 16 below.
[80] Cf. Elisha Qimron, 'The Text of CDC,' in *The Damascus Document Reconsidered* (ed. Magen Broshi; Jerusalem: IES, 1992), 9–49, 35 where he reads and reconstructs, [וכן] ל[כ]ל לו[ק]ח א[ש]ה.

11:21 nor the promise of 'fruitfulness of seed' (פרות זרע) in 1QS 4:7 which forms part of a blessing and employs traditional language associated with a blessed existence such as peace, eternal life, a crown of glory and a robe of honour[81] constitute references to the presence of women in the community. However, this silence in 1QS/4QS cannot be used as *conclusive* evidence to argue that the Community Rule describes a celibate community. The evidence on the question of celibacy is open to several interpretations, and scholars are divided on this question.[82] Although we cannot confidently claim that the Community Rule attests a celibate lifestyle it is clear that women were less visible in the organizational structure described in that document than is the case in the Damascus Document or the Rule of the Congregation.

---

[81] Cf. Knibb, *Qumran Community*, 100.

[82] Cf., e. g., Joseph M. Baumgarten, 'The Qumran-Essene Restraints on Marriage,' in *Archaeology and History in the Dead Sea Scrolls: The New York University Conference in Memory of Yigael Yadin* (ed. Lawrence H. Schiffman; JSPSup 8; Sheffield: JSOT Press, 1990), 13–24; Philip R. Davies and Joan E. Taylor, 'On the Testimony of Women in 1QSa,' *DSD* 3 (1996): 223–235; Hempel, 'Earthly Essene Nucleus,' 262–266, reprinted as Chapter 3 below; Hempel, 'Penal Code Reconsidered;' Elisha Qimron, 'Celibacy in the Dead Sea Scrolls and the Two Kinds of Sectarians,' in *The Madrid Qumran Congress* (ed. Trebolle Barrera and Vegas Montaner), Vol. I, 287–294; Schiffman, *Reclaiming the Dead Sea Scrolls*, 127–143; Eileen M. Schuller, 'Women in the Dead Sea Scrolls,' in *Methods of Investigation of the Dead Sea Scrolls* (ed. Wise et al.), 115–131; Stegemann, 'The Qumran Essenes,' 126–134; Stegemann, *Library of Qumran*, 193–198; John Strugnell, 'More on Wives and Marriage in the Dead Sea Scrolls: (4Q416 2 ii 21 [Cf. *1 Thess* 4:4] and *4QMMT* §B),' *RQ* 17 (1996): 537–547; Shemaryahu Talmon, 'The Community of the Renewed Covenant: Between Judaism and Christianity,' in *The Community of the Renewed Covenant: The Notre Dame Symposium on the Dead Sea Scrolls* (ed. Eugene Ulrich and James VanderKam; Christianity and Judaism In Antiquity 10, Notre Dame: University of Notre Dame Press, 1994), 3–24; idem, 'Qumran Studies: Past, Present, and Future,' *JQR* 85 (1994): 1–31. Since the original publication of this chapter this debate has continued apace, cf., e. g., Eileen Schuller, 'Women in the Dead Sea Scrolls,' in *The Dead Sea Scrolls After Fifty Years: A Comprehensive Assessment* (ed. Peter Flint and James VanderKam; Leiden: Brill, 2000), Vol. II, 117–144; eadem, 'Women in the Dead Sea Scrolls: Research in the Past Decade and Future Directions,' in *The Dead Sea Scrolls and Contemporary Culture* (ed. Adolfo Roitman, Larry Schiffman, and Shani Tzoref; STDJ 93; Leiden: Brill, 2011), 571–588; Maxine Grossman, 'Reading for Gender in the Damascus Document,' *DSD* 11 (2004): 212–239; eadem, 'Women and Men in the Rule of the Congregation: A Feminist Critical Assessment,' in *Rediscovering the Dead Sea Scrolls: An Assessment of Old and New Approaches and Methods* (ed. Maxine Grossman; Grand Rapids, Mich.: Eerdmans, 2010), 229–245; eadem, 'Rethinking Gender in the Community Rule: An Experiment in Sociology,' in *The Dead Sea Scrolls and Contemporary Culture* (ed. Roitman, Schiffman, and Tzoref), 497–512; Tal Ilan, 'Women in Qumran and the Dead Sea Scrolls,' in *The Oxford Handbook of the Dead Sea Scrolls* (ed. Timothy Lim and John Collins; Oxford: OUP, 2010), 123–147; Robert Kugler and Esther Chazon, 'Women at Qumran: Introducing the Essays,' *DSD* 11 (2004):167–173; Taylor, 'Women, Children, and Celibate Men;' Cecilia Wassen, *Women in the Damascus Document* (Academia Biblica 21; Atlanta, Ga.: SBL, 2005); and Sidnie White Crawford, 'Not According to Rule: Women, the Dead Sea Scrolls and Qumran,' in *Emanuel: Studies in Hebrew Bible, Septuagint, and Dead Sea Scrolls in Honor of Emanuel Tov* (ed. Shalom Paul et al.; VTSup 94; Leiden: Brill, 2003), 127–150.

4. Disciplinary and Judicial Procedures

A host of passages describe the judicial and disciplinary procedures of the communities, cf. 1QS 5:6b–7a; 5:24b–6:1a; 6:24–7:25; 8:16–9:2; CD 9:2–8a; 9:16b–10:10a;[83] 14:20; 4Q266 (4QD^a) 10–11; 4Q267 (4QD^b) 9 vi; 4Q270 (4QD^e) 7 i; 4Q477 (The Overseer's Record of Rebukes); 1QSa 1:11, 20.[84] Penal codes are now attested in three documents (4Q266 [4QD^a]; 4Q267 [4QD^b]; 4Q270 [4QD^e]; 4Q265 [Miscellaneous Rules]; 1QS), and scholars have recently turned their attention to study the different versions of the code.[85] In the Cave 4 manuscripts of the Community Rule penal code material is preserved in 4Q256 (4QS^b), 4Q259 (4QS^e), and 4Q261 (4QS^g).[86] Further penal code material is preserved in 11Q29 (Fragment Related to *Serekh ha-Yaḥad*) which may constitute another copy of the Community Rule from Cave 11 as proposed by E. J. C. Tigchelaar.[87] A number of studies have been devoted to the different versions of the penal code.[88] Further penal legislation of a more general application is found in 1QS 8:16–9:2. The latter section is paralleled in 4Q258 (4QS^d) but forms part of the block of material missing from 4Q259 (4QS^e). The presence of penal code material in 4QD that parallels 1QS 6:24–7:25 is of paramount importance for the question of the relationship between both documents, and thus also for our understanding of the communities reflected in the Scrolls, yet again testifying to the complexity of the interrelationship of both texts. Following on from the penal code the end of the Damascus Document (as preserved in 4Q266 [4D^a] 11 and 4Q270 [4QD^e] 7) contains remnants of an expulsion ceremony. The exact relationship of this ceremony to the penal code is not entirely clear. I have proposed elsewhere that the expulsion ceremony applies to the fundamental case of anyone who "despises these judgments" (כול המואס במשפטים האלה, cf. 4Q266 [4QD^a] 11 5–6 and parallels) rather than to any of the specific – and often much less severe – individual offences listed in the penal code.[89] A host of passages admonish the practice of

---

[83] See Schiffman, *Sectarian Law in the Dead Sea Scrolls*, 55–88.

[84] On 1QSa 1:11 see Davies and Taylor, 'Testimony of Women,' for detailed discussion and bibliography.

[85] Cf. Avemarie, "'Tohorat Ha-Rabbim,'" 228–229; Schiffman, *Sectarian Law in the Dead Sea Scrolls*, 155–190; Schiffman, *Reclaiming the Dead Sea Scrolls*, 108–110; for an instructive comparison with penal codes of Greco-Roman cultic associations see Weinfeld, *Organizational Pattern*, 23–43. More recently see also, Reinhard G. Kratz, 'Der *Penal Code* und das Verhältnis von *Serekh ha-Yachad* (S) und Damaskusschrift (D),' *RQ* 25 (2011): 199–227.

[86] Cf. Metso, *Textual Development*, 119.

[87] Eibert J. C. Tigchelaar, 'A Newly Identified 11QSerekh ha-Yaḥad Fragment (11Q29)?,' in *The Dead Sea Scrolls Fifty Years After Their Discovery 1947–1997* (ed. Lawrence H. Schiffman, Emanuel Tov, and James C. VanderKam; Jerusalem: IES, 2000), 285–292.

[88] Cf. Joseph M. Baumgarten, 'The Cave 4 Versions of the Qumran Penal Code,' *JJS* 43 (1992): 268–276; Hempel, 'Penal Code Reconsidered;' see further Metso, *Textual Development*, 124–128.

[89] See Hempel, *Laws of the Damascus Document*, 180.

rebuke as laid down in Lev 19:17–18, cf. CD 7:2; 9:2–8, 17–23; 1QS 5:24–6:1; 7:8–9; 9:16–18.[90] Moreover, 4Q477 contains a record of rebukes that have been brought against community members.[91]

5. Conclusion

The pivotal importance of the relationship between the Community Rule and the Damascus Document is still a central issue in Qumran research and in need of a great deal of attention in the years to come in light of the vital and extensive Cave 4 evidence pertaining to both texts. However difficult it is to be sure about the real-life application of all the communal legislation attested in the Scrolls a number of texts – some of them published only recently – are almost alive with the actions of real people, in particular the penal codes, the so-called Yaḥad Ostracon, and 4Q477.

---

[90] See Bilhah Nitzan, 'The Laws of Reproof in 4QBerakhot (4Q286–290) in Light of their Parallels in the Damascus Document and Other Texts from Qumran,' in *Legal Texts and Legal Issues* (ed. Bernstein, García Martínez, and Kampen), 149–165; Forkman, *Limits of the Religious Community*, 47–50; Schiffman, *Sectarian Law in the Dead Sea Scrolls*, 89–109; and Weinfeld, *Organizational Pattern*, 74–76.

[91] See Esther Eshel, '4Q477: The Rebukes by the Overseer,' *JJS* 45 (1994): 111–122; Charlotte Hempel, 'Who Rebukes in 4Q477?,' *RQ* 16 (1995): 655–656; and Stephen A. Reed, 'Genre, Setting and Title of 4Q477,' *JJS* 47 (1996): 147–148.

Chapter Three

The Damascus Document and 1QSa[1]

1. Introduction

The Rule of the Congregation or Messianic Rule (1QSa) is one of the two annexes to the Community Rule from Cave 1. 1QSa begins in 1:1 with the title וזה הסרך לכול עדת ישראל באחרית הימים ("And this is the rule for all the congregation of Israel in the last days"). This title gave rise to the widely held view that 1QSa is a document containing prescriptions for the life of a community – here frequently referred to as "the congregation of Israel" – in the Messianic age. It is further often argued that these regulations, although explicitly related to the last days, nevertheless reflect the life and organization of an existing community from which the document emerged.

In what follows I would like to focus particularly on 1QSa 1:6–2:11a and its relationship to the Laws of the Damascus Document.

2. 1QSa 1:6–2:11a and Its Present Context

It seems legitimate to isolate 1QSa 1:6–2:11a from its present context for the purposes of this analysis. A new heading, an indentation, and a paragraph sign in the margin in 1:6 introduce this section. This second heading – unlike 1QSa 1:1 – contains no reference to "the last days".

1QSa 1:6 reads,

וזה הסרך לכול צבאות העדה לכול האזרח בישראל

And this is the rule for all the hosts of the congregation for all who are native Israelites.

The material that follows deals with the education and offices of community members (1QSa 1:6b–25a) and the admission to community meetings (1QSa 1:25b–2:11a). It is the material in these two sections in 1QSa which most strongly conveys the impression that we are dealing with rules on the organization of an existing community. The remainder of 1QSa, i. e. 1QSa 2:11b–22, describes what appears to be a banquet in the Messianic age and lays down in detail its

---

[1] This chapter was originally published as 'The Earthly Essene Nucleus of 1QSa,' *DSD* 3 (1996): 253–269.

procedure. This last part of 1QSa will not be our main concern. Its subject matter sets it apart to some degree from what precedes. This final section may also have been introduced by a new heading, although because of the damage to the manuscript in 2:11 this is hard to tell.

Most commentators on 1QSa would agree that this so-called Messianic Rule reflects the life of an existing earthly community. The prevailing opinion on 1QSa is that we have in front of us a messianic or eschatological Rule which describes the life and conduct of the Qumran community in the messianic age.[2] Lawrence Schiffman's monograph is the fullest expression of this view to date.[3] Compare, for example, the following statement by Schiffman,

> The events predicted in this text [i. e. 1QSa] actually constitute a kind of mirror image of the society described in the *Manual of Discipline*.[4]

An assessment of 1QSa along these lines has gone almost unchallenged in Qumran studies over a considerable period.[5] In fact, until fairly recently not a great deal of scholarly attention was being devoted to the Rule of the Congregation. This state of affairs is reflected in Adam S. van der Woude's review of Qumran scholarship between 1974 and 1988 where he introduces the discussion of contributions on 1QSa with the words,

> Nur wenige Arbeiten sind in der Berichtsperiode der Gemeinschaftsregel gewidmet worden.[6]

Most recently something of a resurgence of interest in the Rule of the Congregation can be noted. Apart from Schiffman's monograph on 1QSa mentioned above Hartmut Stegemann has proposed a new approach to 1QSa. Stegemann has presented his argument on 1QSa most fully in his paper 'Some Remarks

---

[2] With the term 'Qumran community' I refer to the social organization that is reflected in 1QS in its final form. The relationship of this community to the forms of social organization reflected in the Laws of the Damascus Document is best perceived as that of a sect to its parent movement. Here my views are influenced by a number of elements of the Groningen Hypothesis, cf. Florentino García Martínez, 'Qumran Origins and Early History: A Groningen Hypothesis,' *Folia Orientalia* 25 (1988): 113–36 (reprinted in García Martínez, *Qumranica Minora I: Qumran Origins and Apocalypticism* [ed. Eibert J. C. Tigchelaar; STDJ 63; Leiden: Brill, 2007], 3–29) and Florentino García Martínez and Adam S. van der Woude, 'A "Groningen" Hypothesis of Qumran Origins and Early History,' *RQ* 56 (1990): 521–41. See also note 10 below.

[3] *The Eschatological Community of the Dead Sea Scrolls* (SBLMS 38; Atlanta, Ga.: Scholars Press, 1989).

[4] *Eschatological Community*, 9.

[5] Something of an exception is the following judgement of Albert-Marie Denis on 1QSa 1:1, "L'expression du titre: «aux derniers jours» ne doit pas faire illusion. Il n'y a rien d'eschatologique dans ce document, c'est une simple clause de style." 'Évolution de structures dans la secte de Qumrân,' in *Aux origines de l'église* (ed. J. Giblet et al.; RechBib 7; Louvain: Desclée de Brouwer, 1965), 23–49, 47.

[6] 'Fünfzehn Jahre Qumranforschung (1974–1988): III. Studien zu früher veröffentlichten Handschriften,' *ThR* 57 (1992): 1–57, 11.

to 1QSa, to 1QSb, and to Qumran Messianism'.[7] Furthermore, he summarizes his position again in his monograph *The Library of Qumran: On the Essenes, Qumran, John the Baptist, and Jesus*.[8] According to Stegemann 1QSa does not describe the vision of a community in the messianic age but constitutes the oldest rule book of the Yaḥad for the present time. In Stegemann's view this rule book is older than both 1QS 5–11 and the Damascus Document. Furthermore, in his view the expression באחרית הימים in 1QSa 1:1 – often translated as "in the last days" – refers not to the messianic age but to the last period of history in which the community behind this document believed itself to be living which would culminate in God's final visitation.[9] Finally, Stegemann proposes a new interpretation of 1QSa 1:11b–22 and emphasizes that the meal described in these lines is presided over by the priest of local communities and not, as often thought, by the priestly messiah.

Although I do not agree with a number of aspects of Stegemann's reconstruction, for example his outline of the chronological relationship between 1QSa, 1QS 5–11, and the Damascus Document – space does not permit me to go into any detail here[10] – he deserves credit for re-opening the important question of how eschatological this so-called eschatological Rule really is.

In this chapter a crucial concern is to emphasize that an association of the communal rules contained in 1QSa 1:6–2:11a with the Qumran community as described in 1QS is quite misleading. It is likely that this prevailing view is based on the introductory lines to 1QSa (1:1–3), on the one hand, and the fact that 1QSa is found on the same scroll immediately after the Community Rule (1QS).

It is often argued that the author of the Rule of the Congregation was preoccupied with the messianic age, and only subconsciously and unwittingly did his account become coloured by his own earthly community background. Although this is admittedly the impression one gains from 1QSa in its present form, it fails to do justice to 1QSa 1:6–2:11a which constitutes well over half of the text of 1QSa (thirty five out of fifty two lines).

Interpretations of 1QSa that have hitherto been proposed have hinged to a great extent on the first three lines.

1QSa 1:1–3 reads,

וזה הסרך לכול עדת ישראל באחרית הימים בה<א>ספם [ליחד להתה]לך על פי משפט בני צדוק הכוהנים
ואנושי בריתם אשר סר[ו] מלכת ב[דרך העם המה אנושי עצתו אשר שמרו בריתו בתוך רשעה לכ]פר
בעד ה[ארץ

---

[7] *RQ* 17 (1996): 479–505.

[8] (Grand Rapids, Mich.: Eerdmans, 1998).

[9] On this expression in the Qumran literature cf. also Annette Steudel, 'אחרית הימים in the Texts from Qumran,' *RQ* 16 (1993): 225–246. As far as 1QSa in particular is concerned Steudel follows Stegemann, cf. especially 230.

[10] Chapters 6, 8, 9, and 18 in this volume offer pertinent analyses on this complex set of issues.

> This is the rule for the whole congregation of Israel in the last days when they assemble [as a community to wa]lk <u>according to the authority of the sons of Zadok the priests and the men of their covenant</u> who have depar[ted from walking in] the way of the people. These are the men of his council <u>who have kept his covenant</u> in the midst of wickedness in order to ato[ne for the la]nd.[11]

These few lines as well as the description of a banquet in the messianic age in 1QSa 2:11b–22 have dominated and, indeed, overshadowed the interpretation of 1QSa 1:6–2:11a.

In addition to being introduced by a new heading that lacks reference to the last days this section –taken by itself– contains nothing that would associate the material with the messianic age. I, therefore, suggest that 1QSa 1:6–2:11a comprises traditional Essene communal legislation, with some evidence for a Qumranic recension towards the end of the section, which was later incorporated into its present eschatological setting.[12] What is more, the picture of the community behind this communal legislation corresponds closely to the picture that emerges from the communal rules in the Laws of the Damascus Document. It seems likely, therefore, that both the communal rules of the Damascus Document and 1QSa 1:6–2:11a emerged from a similar – if not identical – social situation.[13]

The introduction to 1QSa in 1:1–3, by contrast, shows remarkable terminological links with the Community Rule, especially 1QS 5:1–3. We now know from two manuscripts of the Community Rule from Cave 4 that 1QS 5:1–3 represents a particular recension of the Serekh that attributes a central role to the sons of Zadok in the authority structure of the community. In light of this new evidence the place of the sons of Zadok at Qumran will have to be re-evaluated. So far the debate on the leading position of the sons of Zadok in the light of 4QS has focused on 1QS 5 and 4Q258 (4QS^d) and 4Q256 (4QS^b). As I hope to show here, 1QSa 1:1–3 is a further text that is central to that debate.[14]

---

[11] The underlined words occur also in 1QS 5 to be discussed below.

[12] On the distinction between the Qumran community and the Essene movement cf. García Martínez, 'Qumran Origins.' For my own most recent thinking about the literary and communal realities reflected in the Scrolls see especically Chapters 7 and 18 below.

[13] In the course of the discussion of her New York paper entitled 'Women in the Dead Sea Scrolls' Eileen Schuller expresses a similar view, cf. 'Women in the Dead Sea Scrolls,' in *Methods of Investigation of the Dead Sea Scrolls and the Khirbet Qumran Site: Present Realities and Future Prospects* (ed. Michael Wise et al.; Annals of the New York Academy of Sciences 722; New York: New York Academy of Sciences, 1994), 115–131 especially 129. Schuller does not elaborate on the relationship between the Damascus Document and 1QSa however.

[14] In this context it is important to distinguish between material in the Scrolls that attributes particular authority to a group labelled "the sons of Zadok" (1QS 5 and 1QSa 1:1–3) and the Ezekiel Midrash in CD 3:20–4:4. In the latter passage "the sons of Zadok" is used to refer to the *whole community*. In the material at issue here, by contrast, the label "the sons of Zadok" refers to *a particular group of leading priests within the community*. For a critical assessment of the sons of Zadok in the scrolls cf. Philip R. Davies, *Behind the Essenes: History and Ideology in the Dead Sea Scrolls* (BJS 94; Atlanta, Ga.: Scholars Press, 1987), 51–72, especially 52–55. Davies' discussion was written before the evidence of the 4QS manuscripts was widely avail-

1QS 5:1–3a reads,

וזה הסרך לאנשי היחד המתנדבים לשוב מכול רע להחזיק בכול אשר צוה לרצונו להבדל מעדת אנשי
העול להיות ליחד בתורה ובהון ומשיבים <u>על פי בני צדוק הכוהנים שומרי הברית</u> ועל פי רוב אנשי היחד
המחזקים בברית

This is the rule for the men of the community who have volunteered to turn back from all evil, to hold fast to all that he has commanded according to his will, to keep separate from the congregation of the men of injustice, and to form a community with regard to Torah and wealth. They shall obey <u>the authority of the sons of Zadok the priests who keep the covenant</u> and the multitude of the men of the community who hold fast to the covenant.

I have underlined the words that are found both in 1QSa 1:1–3 and 1QS 5. Fascinatingly, the words that correspond exactly between 1QSa 1:1–3 and 1QS 5 are not found in two manuscripts of the Community Rule from Cave 4, 4Q258 (4QS^d) and 4Q256 (4QS^b). That is to say, the phrase "the sons of Zadok the priests who keep the covenant" is not found in 4QS^d and 4QS^b which have instead "the many" (הרבים) in the position of prominent authority.[15] Most recently this state of affairs has been noted by Geza Vermes in his introduction to the translation of 1QSa in the revised fourth edition of *The Dead Sea Scrolls in English*.[16]

The situation is similar when we turn to the second occurrence of this phrase in 1QS 5 in lines 8b–10,

ויקם על נפשו בשבועת אסר לשוב אל תורת מושה ככול אשר צוה בכול לב ובכול נפש לכול הנגלה ממנו
<u>לבני צדוק הכוהנים שומרי הברית</u> ודורשי רצונו ולרוב <u>אנשי בריתם</u> המתנדבים יחד לאמתו ולהתהלך
כרצונו

And he shall take upon himself a binding oath to return to the law of Moses according to all that he has commanded with all (his) heart and all (his) soul, to all that has been revealed of it to <u>the sons of Zadok the priests who keep the covenant</u> and seek his will and to the multitude of <u>the men of their covenant</u> who have volunteered together for his truth and to walk according to his will.

Apart from the phrase "the sons of Zadok the priests who keep the covenant" the latter passage also mentions "the men of their covenant" of 1QSa 1:2. This designation occurs one more time in 1QS in 6:19, again following a reference to the authority of the priests. The most likely antecedent of the third person masculine plural suffix is "the priests".

---

able to scholars and deserves renewed attention in the light of the new evidence. For my own analyses which take full account of the evidence from Cave 4 see Chapters 13 and 14 below.

[15] Cf. Geza Vermes, 'Preliminary Remarks on Unpublished Fragments of the Community Rule from Qumran Cave 4,' *JJS* 42 (1991): 250–255; see also idem, 'Qumran Forum Miscellanea I,' *JJS* 43 (1992): 299–305.

[16] *The Dead Sea Scrolls in English* (rev. and enl. 4th ed.; Harmondsworth: Penguin, 1995), 119.

A careful analysis of the differences between the Cave 4 manuscripts of the Community Rule and 1QS is one of the tasks that will occupy Qumran scholars in the foreseeable future.[17] One of the scholars entrusted with the official edition of 4QS, Geza Vermes, has proposed a preliminary interpretation of the divergences between 4Q258 (4QS^d) 1 and 1QS 5,

> ... the most likely hypothesis is that 1QS in its final form is a composite document and that the 'Congregation' tradition of 4QSd and b corresponds to one of its components, probably the earlier one, and the 'sons of Zadok' tradition to another.[18]

Whatever the direction of the development was, it seems clear that we find in 1QSa 1:1–3 an expression that goes back to the same tradition – perhaps even the same author – as 1QS 5. If Vermes's tentative suggestion is right, i. e. that 4QS^d represents an earlier tradition than "the sons of Zadok" tradition in 1QS 5, then this could have important implications for the interpretation of 1QSa. It seems likely to me that 1QSa is also a composite work, and that the introduction, especially 1:1–3, promotes a different picture of the community behind 1QSa from the bulk of the document in 1QSa 1:6–2:11a. Now, if whoever was responsible for 1QS 5 was reworking the Community Rule in favour of "the sons of Zadok" tradition, it is quite likely that the same person inserted references to that tradition into 1QSa on the same scroll. Furthermore, the same "sons of Zadok" tradition that is attested in the redactional 1QSa 1:1–3 can also be detected in a number of redactional phrases in 1QSa 1:6–2:11a, i. e. 1:24 and 2:3. I will proceed by discussing each passage in its context.

1QSa 1:22b–25a reads,

ובני לוי יעמודו איש במעמדו על פי בני אהרון להביא ולהוציא את כול העדה איש בסרכו על יד ראשי א[בות העדה לשרים ולשופטים ולשוטרים למספר כול צבאותם על פי בני צדוק הכוהנים [וכול ר]אשי אבות העדה[19]

> And the sons of Levi shall serve each in his place <u>under the authority of the sons of Aaron</u> to bring in and lead out the whole congregation, everyone in their position, <u>under the instruction of the heads of the fathers of the congregation</u>, the commanders, the judges and the officers according to the number of all their hosts <u>under the authority of the sons of Zadok [and all the h]eads of the fathers of the congregation.</u>

The authority structure pronounced by this passage seems clear. The levites are to be responsible for bringing in and leading out the congregation, but they are to obey the ultimate authority of the priests and the heads of the fathers of the congregation. Two factors lead me to believe that the last phrase in this passage goes back to a recension of 1QSa in favour of the tradition reflected in 1QS 5 – one may call it a 'Zadokite recension.'

---

[17] See now Chapter 7 in this volume for my own most recent contribution on this question.

[18] 'Preliminary Remarks,' 255. By "'Congregation' tradition" Vermes refers to הרבים of 4QS^d which he rather curiously translates with 'the Congregation.'

[19] Text and reconstructions are taken from DJD 1:110 (Barthélemy).

Firstly, the last phrase, i. e. 1QSa 1:24b–25a, is clearly redundant. Both the authority of the priests as well as the authority of the heads of the fathers of the congregation have already been mentioned.

Secondly, rather than being a straightforward repetition of the expressions used earlier in the passage, "the sons of Zadok" are here used to describe the priests instead of the earlier "the sons of Aaron." Whereas repetition as such may have been understood as a simple literary device, this change in terminology seems to have a different purpose. What is more, I have shown earlier that it is the "sons of Zadok" tradition that has entered 1QSa at a redactional level. It, therefore, seems probable that we have here evidence of a recension which is trying to enhance the authority of the sons of Zadok and which should be seen as related to both, 1QSa 1:1–3 and 1QS 5.

A second interpolation can be identified in 1QSa 1:27b–2:3a which reads,

אלה ה‹א›נשים הנקראים לעצת היחד מבן עש כול ח[כמי] העדה והנבונים והידעים תמימי הדרך ואנושי החיל עם [שרי השב]טים וכול שופטיהם ושוטריהם ושרי האלפים ושרי [למאות] ולחמשים ולעשרות והלויים בתו[ך מחל]קת עבודתו אלה אנושי השם קיראי מועד הנועדים לעצת היחד בישראל לפני בני צדוק הכוהנים[20]

These are the men called for the council of the community from the age of tw(enty). All the w[ise] of the congregation and those who have insight and knowledge, the perfect of way and men of valour together with [the commanders of the tri]bes and all their judges and their officers and the commanders of thousands, the commanders [of hundreds] and fifties and tens, and the levites (everyone) in the mid[st of the divi]sion of his service. These are the men of renown who have been called for the assembly of the council of the community in Israel before the sons of Zadok the priests.

As in the preceding passage, here "the sons of Zadok" have again been appended at the end of this regulation. Furthermore, we have another case of a repetition. The phrase "these are the men ..." occurs at the beginning of the passage as well as in 2:1b–2a. Only in the second formulation, which repeats the first, have "the sons of Zadok" been introduced. It, therefore, seems likely that the insertion of "the sons of Zadok" at the end of this passage goes back to the same recension attested in 1:24 above.

3. 1QSa 1:6–2:11a and the Laws of the Damascus Document

In order to support my claim that the community reflected in 1QSa 1:6–2:11a should be associated with the community behind the Laws of the Damascus Document I will focus on a number of aspects shared by both collections.

---

[20] Text and reconstructions are again from DJD 1:110 (Barthélemy).

3.1 'All-Israel' Terminology

Both the communal rules in the Laws of the Damascus Document and 1QSa 1:6–2:11a reflect a community that refers to itself using 'all-Israel' terminology.[21] The boundaries between insiders and outsiders in both texts correspond to the boundaries between Israel and the nations.

I will begin by referring to a number of prescriptions that reflect an all-Israel ideology in the communal legislation of the Laws of the Damascus Document. Such an ideology is reflected in several passages of the communal rules as preserved in the mediaeval text of the Damascus Document.

Thus, CD 15:5 refers to a new member about to enter the community as "the one who enters the covenant for all Israel" (הבא בברית לכל ישראל). Further on in this same section on the admission of new members we find in CD 15:8–9 a reference to "the covenant which Moses made with Israel" (הברית אשר כרת משה עם ישראל). Towards the end of the section on the admission of new members CD 16:1 begins, moreover, with the words "with you a covenant and with all Israel" (עמכם ברית ועם כל ישראל).

Two further important passages that reveal the national self-understanding of the community described in the communal legislation of the CD Laws are found in the section on the meeting of all the camps (CD 14:3–18a). Firstly, the members of the meeting of all the camps are described in 14:3–6a as made up of priests, levites, Israelites and proselytes (גר). Finally, one of the categories of people to be cared for with the money collected and deposited with the overseer and the judges according to CD 14:12b–16a is "the one who has been taken captive by a foreign people" (אשר ישבה לגוי נכר).

In these passages those addressed are depicted as a national entity. It may well be that this all-Israel terminology is used because the movement addressed thought of itself as the 'true Israel.' Nevertheless, the point I would like to emphasize is that these passages lack the hostility against the majority of Israel that characterizes, for example, the Community Rule (see, for example, 1QS 5:1–3a).

In 1QSa 1:6–2:11a the following two passages clearly illustrate a similar self-understanding of the community behind the text. 1QSa 1:6, the heading that introduces this part of 1QSa reads,

וזה הסרך לכול צבאות העדה לכול האזרח בישראל

This is the rule for all the hosts of the congregation, for all native Israelites.

Moreover, 1QSa 1:19b–22a is a section that provides for simpleminded people and their role in the community. They are to be excluded from a number of communal roles and play a restricted part in the community's life. One of the

---

[21] There are a few exceptions within the Laws of the Damascus Document, and this incoherence is due to the composite nature of the Laws.

activities from which these people are to be excluded is the war against the nations in 1:21,

ולהתיצב במלחמה להכניע גוים

(not) ... to take part in the war to crush the nations.

Again, this all-Israel perspective could be caused by a self-understanding of the community behind 1QSa 1:6–2:11a as the 'true Israel.' On the other hand, it seems equally possible that the author(s) of this text addressed – at least in theory – all Israel.

Whatever the case may be, I would like to stress the positive and unpolemical nature of the references to Israel in this text. Furthermore, this portrayal of Israel at large contrasts sharply with the Community Rule and even the first lines of the Rule of the Congregation.

Cf. especially 1QSa 1:2–3,

... ואנושי בריתם אשר סר[ו מלכת ב]דרך העם המה אנושי עצתו אשר שמרו בריתו בתוך רשעה ...

... and the men of their covenant who have depar[ted from walking in] the way of the people. These are the men of his council who have kept his covenant in the midst of wickedness ...

In 1QSa 1:1–3 the boundaries between the community and those outside are clearly drawn within Israel itself. The distinction that is emphasized in 1QS and in 1QSa 1:1–3 is the distinction between that part of Israel that has renounced wickedness and the great majority who have not.

3.2 Family Life

Another important point of similarity between the communal legislation of the Damascus Document and 1QSa is the fact that both works presuppose family life, i. e. marriage and children, in contrast to 1QS.

1QSa 1:8b–11 contains sufficient illustration of the fact that family life is presupposed in 1QSa 1:6–2:11a. In this instance my task is less to show that the Damascus Document and 1QSa share this feature, since no one would dispute this. Disagreement enters, however, when it comes to explaining this communality and the lack of references to women in the communal legislation of 1QS 5–9.

References to women and legislation on relations between the sexes are found frequently in the mediaeval text of the Laws of the Damascus Document as well as in the Cave 4 manuscripts. It has long been noted that the Damascus Document presupposes family life and the evidence is briefly recapitulated here mainly for the sake of introducing our discussion of this issue.

There are five passages in the mediaeval text of the Laws of the Damascus Document which contain references to women or children.

– CD 16:10–12 contains a section of halakhah dealing with women's oaths.
– CD 11:11 forms part of the Sabbath Code and reads,

אל ישא האומן את היונק לצ את ולבוא בשבת

The childminder shall not carry a child (whilst) going and coming on the sabbath.

– CD 15:5b–6a introduces the legislation on the admission of new members:

והבא בברית לכל ישראל לחוק עולם את בניהם אשר יגיעו לעבור על הפקודים בשבועות הברית יקימו עליהם

And he who enters the covenant for all Israel it shall be an eternal statute, together with their children who reach the age to pass over to the mustered, they shall bind themselves with the oath of the covenant.

– CD 14:12c–16a legislates on the provision for the needy:

שכר שני ימים לכל חדש לממעיט ונתנו על יד המבקר והשופטים ממנו יתנו [...] ולבתולה אשר [אי]ן לה ג[וא]ל [ו]לע.²² [א]שר אין לו דורש ...

The wages of at least two days each month they shall give to the overseer and the judges. From it they shall give to [...] the virgin who [has] no re[la]tives, and the [boy w]ho has no one to take care of him ...

What is more, if we accept the restoration suggested recently by Elisha Qimron for CD 13:16 the mediaeval text of the Laws might include yet another reference to the presence of women, i. e. וכן [כ]ל לו[וק]ח אש[ה "for everyone who takes a wife."²³

– Finally, CD 12:1b–2a prohibits sexual relations in the city of Jerusalem:

אל ישכב איש עם אשה בעיר המקדש לטמא את עיר המקדש בנדתם

No one shall lie with a woman in the city of the sanctuary so as to defile the city of the sanctuary with their uncleanness.

Thus, references to women and family life occur widely in the mediaeval text of the Laws. This impression is further reinforced by the evidence from the 4Q fragments of the Laws of the Damascus Document.

---

²² 4Q266 (4QDᵃ) 18 iii 9 reads ולנער, cf. Elisha Qimron, 'The Text of CDC,' in *The Damascus Document Reconsidered* (ed. Magen Broshi; Jerusalem: IES, 1991), 9–49, 36 n. 21 and my translation follows this reading. Rabin reads ול[למה א]שר אין לה דורש and translates "and for the virgin who has no one to seek her *in marriage*," cf. Chaim Rabin, *The Zadokite Documents: I. The Admonition, II. The Laws* (Oxford: Clarendon Press, 1954), 70–71. However, the photograph given in Qimron's edition clearly supports the reading לו rather than לה. The reading ולנער in 4Q266 (4QDᵃ) 18 in conjunction with the masculine suffix make a good case for reconstructing ולנער in CD as well.

²³ Qimron, 'Text of CDC,' 35.

From Joseph Baumgarten's preliminary description of the contents of the Cave 4 manuscripts it emerges that a number of additional pieces of legislation dealing with the subject of women and marriage are found in 4QD that are not preserved in CD.[24] In particular Baumgarten mentions a passage that deals with the case of a wife accused of unfaithfulness (cf. Num 5)[25] and a passage that lays down rules to be followed when marriages are arranged within the community.[26]

Finally, the 4QD Penal Code preserves two offences that mention women (see especially 4Q270 [4QD^e] 7 i 12–13 and 7 i 14–15).

In contrast to this, women and family life are not mentioned in 1QS, nor does it include any regulations on relations between the sexes.[27] Yet, this silence in 1QS cannot be used as *conclusive* evidence to maintain either that the members of the 1QS community were celibate or to maintain that they practised marriage. Both the internal literary evidence of the Scrolls as well as the archaeological evidence are open to several interpretations, and scholars are divided on the question whether or not 1QS 5–9 contains the regulations for a celibate community. A whole host of scholars have discussed this issue from the time soon after the discovery of the Scrolls until very recently when the celibacy debate has been revived.[28] It would be unnecessarily repetitive to outline again all the

---

[24] 'The Laws of the *Damascus Document* in Current Research,' in *The Damascus Document Reconsidered* (ed. Magen Broshi; Jerusalem: The IES, 1992), 51–62, here 53–54. See now the official edition of 4QD in DJD 18 (Baumgarten).

[25] Cf. 4Q270 (4QD^e) 8 1–19.

[26] Cf. 4Q270 (4QD^e) 5 14–21; 4Q272 (4QD^f) 1 i 4–15 (lines 1–3 are very fragmentary); and 4Q269 (4QD^d) 9 1–7.

[27] For the sake of completeness it is worth mentioning that 1QS 11:21 makes use of the Hebrew idiom "one born of a woman" which cannot, however, be taken as a reference to women in the description of the community in 1QS.

[28] The following bibliographical list does not purport to be complete: Joseph M. Baumgarten, 'The Qumran-Essene Restraints on Marriage,' in *Archaeology and History in the Dead Sea Scrolls: The New York University Conference in Memory of Yigael Yadin* (ed. Lawrence H. Schiffman; JSPSup 8; Sheffield: JSOT Press, 1990), 13–24; Herbert Braun, *Spätjüdisch-häretischer und frühchristlicher Radikalismus: Jesus von Nazareth und die essenische Qumransekte* (Tübingen: Mohr Siebeck, 1957), 40; idem, *Qumran und das Neue Testament* (Tübingen: Mohr Siebeck, 1966), Vol. I, 40–41 and 192–193; Joseph Coppens, 'Le célibat essénien,' in *Qumrân: Sa pieté, sa théologie et son milieu* (ed. Mathias Delcor et al.; Paris: Gembloux; Leuven: Leuven University Press, 1978), 295–303; Antoine Guillaumont, 'A propos du célibat des esséniens,' in *Hommages à André Dupont-Sommer* (ed. André Caquot and Marc Philonenko; Paris: Libraire Adrien-Maisonneuve, 1971), 395–404; Hans Hübner, 'Zölibat in Qumran?,' *NTS* 17 (1970–71): 153–167; Abel Isaakson, *Marriage and Ministry in the New Temple* (ASNU 24; Lund: Gleerup, 1965), especially 45–65; Elisha Qimron, 'Review of Philip R. Davies *The Damascus Covenant*,' *JQR* 77 (1986–87): 84–87; idem, 'Celibacy in the Dead Sea Scrolls and the Two Kinds of Sectarians,' in *The Madrid Qumran Congress: Proceedings of the International Congress on the Dead Sea Scrolls Madrid 18–21 March 1991* (ed. Julio Trebolle Barrera and Luis Vegas Montaner; STDJ 11; Leiden: Brill, 1992), Vol. I, 287–294; Lawrence H. Schiffman, *Sectarian Law in the Dead Sea Scrolls: Courts, Testimony and the Penal Code* (BJS 33; Chico, Calif.: Scholars Press, 1983), 214–215; idem, *Eschatological Community*, 69; Eileen M. Schuller, 'Women in the Dead Sea Scrolls;' Hartmut Stegemann,

arguments that have been put forward for or against the view that 1QS reflects a celibate community. Rather, I will limit myself to stating the key arguments that have led me to believe that 1QS 5–9 in its final form seems to describe a community in which women played no role in contrast to the Laws of the Damascus Document and 1QSa 1:6–2:11a.

Whether or not the members of the community described in 1QS 5–9 in its present form were married cannot, as we saw, be decided on the basis of the literary evidence. However, what can be said with confidence – and what has been emphasized frequently by those scholars who fall into the pro-celibacy camp of Qumran studies – is that women are not mentioned in the communal legislation of 1QS. Thus, even if the members of the community behind 1QS 5–9 were married it seems that the role of women was marginal indeed in that community.

A passage that seems to suggest that some Jews in the Essene milieu did refrain from marriage is CD 7:6b–9a. Whether or not this passage has been inserted into its present context at a secondary stage,[29] the protasis of this statement clearly presupposes that an alternative lifestyle from the one in camps with wives and children did exist. Thus, compare especially CD 7:6b–7a: 'And if they live in camps according to the rule of the land and take wives and beget children ...' (ואם מחנות ישבו כסרך הארץ ולקחו נשים והולידו בנים).

As far as the reasoning behind a celibate lifestyle among pious Jews of the Second Temple period is concerned it has been noted frequently that such a position is taking the rigid requirements for ritual purity echoed in many texts from the Dead Sea Scrolls one step further, cf. esp. CD 12:1b–2a and the laws on the purity of Jerusalem in columns 45–47 of the Temple Scroll. Furthermore, Antoine Guillaumont has demonstrated that traditions on sexual abstinence in particular situations are reflected in non-Essene Jewish sources as well as in the Hebrew Bible itself, cf. Exod 19: 14–15. (Moses came down from the mountain

---

'The Qumran Essenes – Local Members of the Main Jewish Union in Late Second Temple Times,' in *The Madrid Qumran Congress* (ed. Trebolle Barrera and Vegas Montaner), Vol. I, 83–166; James C. VanderKam, *The Dead Sea Scrolls Today* (Grand Rapids, Mich.: Eerdmans; London: SPCK), 90–91.

[29] Cf. Philip R. Davies, *The Damascus Covenant: An Interpretation of the "Damascus Document"* (JSOTSup25; Sheffield: JSOT Press, 1983), 142 for a brief outline of the position that this passage is secondary. Davies himself disagrees although he does not disregard the latter position as a possibility. Both Baumgarten ('Qumran-Essene Restraints,' especially 18–19) and Qimron ('Celibacy,' especially 289–292) have recently offered an interpretation of CD 7:6b–9a as an integral part of its present context. One may wonder whether the blessing that precedes this passage in CD 7:4b–6a, especially line 6a (לחיותם אלף דור), should necessarily be taken as literally as both scholars suggest. It may, alternatively, be a traditional concept associated with a blessed life, and perhaps one should not read too much into it. Similarly, I would understand the much debated expression פרות זרע in 1QS 4:7 as a traditional concept associated with a blessed existence, cf. Michael A. Knibb, *The Qumran Community* (Cambridge Commentaries on Writings of the Jewish and Christian World 200 BC to AD 200 2; Cambridge: CUP, 1987), 100, for an interpretation of 1QS 4:6b–8 along such lines.

to the people. He hallowed them and they washed their clothes. He said, "Be ready by the third day; do not go near a woman." [REB]).

To sum up, it seems likely to me in the light of the considerations outlined above that the community reflected in 1QS 5–9 either lacked women altogether or attributes an extremely peripheral place to women and family life in relation to the Yaḥad.

The main implication for the purposes of the present argument is to note that the presupposition of family life constitutes a further aspect shared by the community described in 1QSa 1:6–2:11a and the communal legislation of the Damascus Document. The position of women emerges here as by no means equal to that of the male members of the community, but they certainly constitute a visible presence in the community behind both texts.

3.3 עדה Terminology

The editor of 1QSa Barthélemy noted long ago that the term עדה ("congregation") occurs abundantly in 1QSa, and this terminological characteristic led him to designate the document 'Règle de la Congrégation.'[30]

It seems noteworthy that over against one occurrence of עדה in 1QS in a context where it designates the community behind the document (1QS 5:20), the term occurs no less than seven times in the Laws of the Damascus Document as they have come down to us in the Genizah text, cf. CD 10:4,5,8; 13:10–11,13; 14:10. The situation is much the same when we take the Cave 4 evidence into account.[31] The term עדה occurs once in 4Q256 (4QS^b) and 4Q258 (4QS^d) respectively (4Q256 9 2; 4Q258 1 2) and in both instances parallels 1QS 5:1–2 where it designates not the community behind the text but "the congregation of the men of injustice" (עדת אנשי העול). As far as the Cave 4 manuscripts of the Damascus Document are concerned עדה occurs thirteen times altogether. Two occurrences are from the Admonition and need not concern us here (4Q266 [4QD^a] 2 ii 1 and 4Q269 [4QD^d] 2 3). Seven occurrences of עדה in the Cave 4 manuscripts parallel the mediaeval text of the Laws where, as we saw, the term is used frequently to designate the community behind the text (4Q266 8 iii 4 [x 2]; 10 i 3; 4Q267 [4QD^b] 9 iv 10; 4Q270 [4QD^e] 6 iv 15,16,18). Apart from these nine occurrences

---

[30] DJD 1:108 (Barthélemy) who refers to nineteen occurrences though the total reaches twenty.

[31] The figures cited in the original 1996 publication of this chapter were based on John Strugnell et al. (eds), *A Preliminary Concordance to the Hebrew and Aramaic Fragments from Qumran Caves II–X*, Printed from a card index prepared by Raymond E. Brown et al., Prepared and arranged for printing by Hans-Peter Richter (5 volumes; Göttingen: Privately published, 1988). For the purposes of the republication of the article in this volume the data and references above have been updated on the basis of DJD 18 (Baumgarten) and Martin G. Abegg, *The Dead Sea Scrolls Concordance: The Non-Biblical Texts from Qumran* (Leiden: Brill, 2003).

of עדה that cover text that is paralleled in the mediaeval text of the Laws, the Cave 4 manuscripts revealed a further four occurrences which have no parallel in the Genizah text of the Laws (4Q266 [4QD^a] 8 i 9; 10 i 4; 4Q267 [4QD^b] 5 iii 6; 4Q270 [4QD^e] 7 i 14). All in all, the term occurs eleven times in the Laws of the Damascus Document from Cairo and Qumran excluding the seven instances where 4QD preserves a parallel to CD.

From this brief survey it becomes clear that the term עדה so characteristic of the Rule of the Congregation is also unusually widely attested in the Laws of the Damascus Document.[32]

3.4 The Book of Hagi

The enigmatic Book of Hagi (ספר ההגי) which occurs twice in the Laws of the Damascus Document (CD 10:6; 13:2) is mentioned only in 1QSa 1:7 outside of CD. Furthermore, the book seems to have the same function in both documents. It appears to have been a book that was used for the instruction of community members, officials, and priests.

According to the CD Laws the judges of the congregation (10:4 – note the use of 'congregation,' Hebrew עדה) and the priest presiding over any gathering of ten community members (13:2) are required to be well versed (מבונן) in the ספר ההגי. On the other hand, every native Israelite is to be taught (למד) in the Book of Hagi according to 1QSa 1:7. It seems likely to me that these regulations on the Book of Hagi in the Laws of the Damascus Document and 1QSa are compatible, and that the use of בין and למד respectively indicates that different members of the community were expected to show different degrees of familiarity with and knowledge of the Book of Hagi, and that every new member had to acquire some knowledge of its contents.

3.5 Exclusion from the Congregation

Finally, the regulations of 1QSa 2:5b–9a on the exclusion of physically disabled and debilitated people from the congregation are paralleled in 4Q266 (4QD^a) 8 i

---

[32] The expression עצת (ה)יחד ("the council of [the] community") occurs three times in 1QSa 1:6–2:11a, and a variant form עצת הקודש ("the council of holiness") is found once in this material. The term is familiar from the Community Rule where it frequently occurs, cf. 1QS 3:2; 5:7; 6:3,10,12–13,14,16; 7:2,22,24; 8:1,5,22; 11:8. In 1QS the term is used to refer to the body of full community members, and it is used interchangeably with הרבים ("the many") in column 6. It seems to me that the occurrences of the expression עצת היחד in 1QSa warrant further study. Moreover, an examination of all these cases would have to go hand in hand with an examination of the use and meaning of the expression in the different manuscripts of the Community Rule.

6b–9 and 4Q270 (4QD^e) 6 ii.³³ The text of 4Q266 continues that of column 15 of the Genizah text (CD 15:15–17) and rules that mentally and physically disabled people are to be excluded from the congregation because of the presence of the מלאכי הקודש, "the holy angels." The relevant passage from 4Q266 (4QD^a) reads as follows,

וכול היותו אויל
[ומ]שוגע אל יבו וכול פתי ושוגה וכה עינים לבלתי ראות
[ו]חגר או פסח או חרש או נער זעטוט א[ל יבו] איש [מ]אלה אל
תוך העדה כי מלאכ[י] הקוד[ש בתוכם

And no fool [or im]becile shall enter. And no one who is a simpleton or misguided, no one with dimmed eyes unable to see, [n]o one who limps, is lame or deaf, no young boy – no[ne of] these [shall enter] the midst of the congregation for the angel[s of] holine[ss are in their midst.]³⁴

The comparable passage in 1QSa 2:5b–9a reads,

וכול מנוגע בבשרו נכאה רגלים או
ידים פסח או עור או חרש או אלם או מום מנוגע בבשרו
לראות עינים או איש זקן כושל לבלתי התחזק בתוך העדה
אל יב[ואו] אלה להתיצב [ב]תוך עדת א[נ]ושי השם כיא מלאכי
קודש [בעד]תם³⁵

No one physically afflicted, either struck with deformed feet or hands, lame, or blind, or deaf, or dumb, or physically afflicted with any defect that can be seen, or an old man who is tottering and unable to keep still in the midst of the congregation, none of these shall en[ter] to stand [in] the midst of the congregation of the m[e]n of renown, for holy angels are [in] their [congrega]tion.³⁶

In the recent new edition of 1QSa by James H. Charlesworth and Loren T. Stuckenbruck the restoration כי מלאכי קודש [בעצ]תם has been suggested for 1QSa

---

³³ For a detailed discussion of the different categories of people that are excluded in 1QSa 2 see Lawrence H. Schiffman, 'Purity and Perfection: Exclusion from the Council of the Community in the *Serekh Ha-ʿEdah*,' in *Biblical Archaeology Today: Proceedings of the International Congress on Biblical Archaeology, Jerusalem, April 1984* (ed. Janet Amitai; Jerusalem: IES, 1985), 373–389.

³⁴ The Hebrew text cited in the original article was based on the preliminary publication in Joseph Baumgarten, 'The Laws of the *Damascus Document* in Current Research,' in *The Damascus Document Reconsidered* (ed. Magen Broshi; Jerusalem: IES, 1991), 51–62, 58. For the republication of the article here the text of 4Q266 has been supplemented in light of Baumgarten's official edition of 4Q266 in DJD 18 (DJD 18:63; see also 4Q270 6 ii in DJD 18:56–57 [Baumgarten]). The English translation has also been updated, cf. Charlotte Hempel, *The Laws of the Damascus Document: Sources, Traditions, and Redaction* (STDJ 29; Leiden: Brill, 1998; Paperback edition Atlanta, Ga.: SBL, 2006), 75.

³⁵ The Hebrew text is taken from DJD 1:110 (Barthélemy).

³⁶ Cf. also 1QM 7:4; 4QFlor 1 3b–5a and 4QMMT B 39–54 of the composite text in DJD 10:50–53 (Qimron and Strugnell). The belief that angels are in the midst of the congregation articulated in 1QSa and 1QM has frequently been attributed to the messianic contents of those writings. This interpretation will have to be refined in the light of the evidence of 4Q266.

2:8–9.³⁷ Such a reconstruction seems less likely to me because of the occurrence of עדה immediately preceding in 1QSa 2:4b–5a which reads,

וכול איש מנוגע באלה לבלתי החזיק מעמד בתוך חעדה

> No one afflicted by any of these shall be authorized to take up his position in the midst of the congregation.

4. Conclusion

In light of these comparative observations it seems likely that the core of the Rule of the Congregation consists of a piece of communal legislation that goes back to the Essene parent movement of the Qumran community. This material is found in 1QSa 1:6–2:11a and may originally have existed independently as the presence of a second heading in 1QSa 1:6 suggests. In terms of its size the section in 1QSa 1:6–2:11a is the largest in 1QSa and our results are, therefore, of crucial importance for one's perception of the whole document. The communal legislation preserved in this section displays, furthermore, a number of important features in common with the communal legislation in the Laws of the Damascus Document pointing to a similar social setting.³⁸ Apart from having been embedded into its present Messianic setting 1QSa 1:6–2:11a underwent a 'Zadokite recension' which resulted in the addition of a number of redactional passages that reflect the social background of 1QS 5.

---

³⁷ PTSDSSP 1:116–117 (Charlesworth and Stuckenbruck, following Licht). Curiously at 1QSa 2:10 they restore עדה.

³⁸ I have restricted myself to a discussion of the relationship between the Laws of the Damascus Document and the Rule of the Congregation in this chapter. It seems likely that an investigation of the relationship of the Rule of the Congregation to other works from the Qumran corpus such as 1QM/4QM would further our knowledge of the complexity of the literary developments reflected in the Scrolls.

Part II

Beginnings

Chapter Four

The Damascus Document and Community Origins[1]

1. Introduction

This chapter offers a re-examination of the various descriptions of the emergence of a movement contained in the Admonition of the Damascus Document. A great deal of scholarly attention has been devoted to the Admonition of the Damascus Document not least because of these descriptions contained within it. It has rightly been pointed out that focus on the Admonition has led to a neglect of the Laws of the Damascus Document. This document is, as we now know from the additional legal material preserved in the manuscripts from Cave 4, primarily a legal work.[2] I nevertheless chose to talk about the Admonition on this occasion. The Admonition introduces us to the Laws of the Damascus Document and is, therefore, vital in determining how those Laws were intended to be read – at least at one stage in the compositional history of the document. Thus even if it is quantitatively shorter than the legal part of the document the Admonition will probably remain a focus of attention hopefully, however, alongside rather than over and above the Laws.

An increasing number of scholars have come to view the non-biblical literature from Qumran as associated with more than one form of social organization. Scholars could for a long time speak of the non-biblical Qumran corpus as neatly divided into pseudepigrapha and 'sectarian literature' and understand the sectarian literature to go back – more or less in its entirety – to the Qumran community. Such a view has become questioned in recent years, and for very good reasons it seems to me. A great many scholars no longer regard the Qumran community as the sole form of social organization reflected in the non-biblical Qumran literature. As far as the dissatisfaction with the old paradigm is concerned some – if not universal – agreement can be identified. Differences of opinion prevail, however, with regard to a new paradigm. The picture to be derived from the evidence of the Scrolls has been recognized as a much more

---

[1] This chapter was originally published as 'Community Origins in the Damascus Document in the Light of Recent Scholarship,' in *The Provo International Conference on the Dead Sea Scrolls: Technological Innovations, New Texts, & Reformulated Issues* (ed. Donald W. Parry and Eugene Ulrich; STDJ 30; Leiden: Brill, 1999), 316–329.

[2] For a description of the Cave 4 manuscripts of the Damascus Document see PTSDSSP 2:59–63 (Baumgarten and Davis).

complex one, and one wonders whether a consensus comparable to the former consensus view will ever be reached again.

Let me briefly mention a number of positions. The long-held and still influential consensus view advocated *inter alia* by Hartmut Stegemann in his early publications argues for an identity of the Essenes with the Qumran community, the origins of which he sees among the Hasidim.[3] In more recent publications Stegemann stands by the view that the Essenes originated among the Hasidim. Rather than identifying the Essenes with the Qumran community, however, Stegemann now prefers to speak of the 'main Jewish Union of Second Temple times' or 'die Essenische Union.'[4] Devorah Dimant believes the works describing the history and organization of communities at Qumran to go back to the Qumran community the roots of which can be traced back to the third century BCE.[5] Shemaryahu Talmon still essentially seems to conceive of a single form of social organization being described in what he calls 'foundation documents' of the 'community of the renewed covenant' albeit one that has undergone development.[6] According to Talmon the Qumran settlement was a centre kept by the community where male members spent limited periods in celibacy preparing for the expected eschatological battle. Philip Davies speaks of the Damascus sect and the Yaḥad.[7] Florentino García Martínez has in mind an Essene parent movement distinct from the Qumran community and emphasizes the importance

---

[3] See Hartmut Stegemann, *Die Entstehung der Qumrangemeinde* (Bonn: Privately Published, 1971).

[4] Hartmut Stegemann, 'The Qumran Essenes – Local Members of the Main Jewish Union in Late Second Temple Times,' in *The Madrid Qumran Congress: Proceedings of the International Congress on the Dead Sea Scrolls, Madrid, 18–21 March 1991* (ed. Julio Trebolle Barrera and Luis Vegas Montaner; STDJ 11; Leiden: Brill, 1992), Vol. I, 83–166; also idem, *The Library of Qumran: On the Essenes, Qumran, John the Baptist, and Jesus* (Grand Rapids, Mich.: Eerdmans, 1998).

[5] Devorah Dimant, 'Qumran Sectarian Literature,' in *Jewish Writings of the Second Temple Period: Apocrypha, Pseudepigrapha, Qumran Sectarian Writings, Philo, Josephus* (ed. Michael E. Stone; CRINT 2.2; Philadelphia, Pa.: Fortress, 1984), 483–550 and eadem, 'The Qumran Manuscripts: Contents and Significance' in *Time to Prepare the Way in the Wilderness: Papers on the Qumran Scrolls by Fellows of the Institute for Advanced Studies of The Hebrew University, Jerusalem, 1989–1990* (ed. Devorah Dimant and Lawrence H. Schiffman; STDJ 16; Leiden: Brill, 1995), 23–58.

[6] Shemaryahu Talmon, 'The Community of the Renewed Covenant: Between Judaism and Christianity,' in *The Community of the Renewed Covenant: The Notre Dame Symposium on the Dead Sea Scrolls* (ed. Eugene Ulrich and James VanderKam; Christianity and Judaism in Antiquity 10; Notre Dame: University of Notre Dame Press, 1994), 3–24; and idem, 'Qumran Studies: Past, Present, and Future,' *JQR* 85 (1994): 1–31.

[7] Philip R. Davies, 'The "Damascus" Sect and Judaism,' in *Pursuing the Text: Studies in Honor of Ben Zion Wacholder* (ed. John Reeves and John Kampen; JSOTSup 184; Sheffield: Sheffield Academic Press), 70–84 (reprinted in idem, *Sects and Scrolls: Essays on Qumran and Related Topics* [South Florida Studies in the History of Judaism 134; Atlanta, Ga.: Scholars Press, 1996], 163–177); and idem, 'Who Can Join the "Damascus Covenant"?,' *JJS* 46 (1995): 134–142.

of the formative period in which the particular character of the Qumran community developed.[8] Jerome Murphy-O'Connor also distinguishes the Essenes and the Qumran community and has argued for Essene origins in Babylon.[9] Michael Knibb has argued that whereas the Admonition of the Damascus Document in its final form presupposes the death of the teacher, the legal part of the document goes back to a pre-teacher community.[10] Esther Chazon has argued that we should allow for the presence of the literary remains of a parent movement alongside those of the Yaḥad or for cross-fertilization from contemporary groups.[11] Finally, I have argued elsewhere that the bulk of the Rule of the Congregation as well as the communal rules in the Laws of the Damascus Document seem to reflect the parent community of the Yaḥad.[12]

The Yaḥad in turn has emerged as a community that has undergone substantial changes and developments in light of new texts from Qumran Cave 4. In particular the important variants of 1QS 5 attested in 4Q258 (4QS^d) may be mentioned here.[13] Whereas it is probably still correct to think of a single Yaḥad community, the authority structure in that community seems to have evolved considerably at least at one point in its history.

Whichever of the above suggestions for a new paradigm one finds more convincing, it seems evident to me that the descriptions of the emergence of a movement in the Damascus Document will have to be re-examined in view of the paradigm shift. If more than one form of social organization is reflected in the non-biblical Qumran corpus, then the claim to be the true heir to the original movement would be a crucial one in the processes of the self-definition of various groups. The establishment of such a claim is an important function of the descriptions of the emergence of a pious movement in the Admonition.

---

[8] Florentino García Martínez and Julio Trebolle Barrera, *The People of the Dead Sea Scrolls: Their Writings, Beliefs and Practices* (Leiden: Brill, 1995), 77–96. For Florentino García Martínez's most recent scholarship see '¿Sectario, no-sectario, o qué? Problemas de una taxonomía correcta de los textos qumránicos,' *RQ* 23 (2008): 383–394 and the discussion in the Introduction to this volume.

[9] Jerome Murphy-O'Connor, 'The Essenes and their History,' *RB* 81 (1974): 215–244.

[10] Michael A Knibb, 'The Place of the Damascus Document,' in *Methods of Investigation of the Dead Sea Scrolls and the Khirbet Qumran Site: Present Realities and Future Prospects* (ed. Michael O. Wise *et a l.*; Annals of the New York Academy of Sciences 722; New York: New York Academy of Sciences, 1994), 149–162.

[11] Esther Chazon, 'Is *Divrei Ha-Me'orot* a Sectarian Prayer?,' in *The Dead Sea Scrolls: Forty Years of Research* (ed. Devorah Dimant and Uriel Rappaport; STDJ 10; Leiden: Brill, 1992), 3–17, 14, 17.

[12] Charlotte Hempel, 'The Earthly Essene Nucleus of 1QSa,' *DSD* 3 (1996): 253–269, reprinted as Chapter 3 in this volume.

[13] Geza Vermes, 'Preliminary Remarks on Unpublished Fragments of the Community Rule from Qumran Cave 4,' *JJS* 42 (1991): 250–255; idem, 'Qumran Forum Miscellanea I,' *JJS* 43 (1992): 300–301; also Charlotte Hempel, 'Comments on the Translation of 4QS^d I,1,' *JJS* 44 (1993): 127–128.

In the light of these considerations it seems desirable to reconsider those passages in the Admonition that give an account of the origins of a movement. There are four such descriptions in the Admonition. Three of these accounts are usually cited in the literature. The second of the descriptions to be discussed below is brief and not regularly referred to in the literature for reasons that will become clear shortly.

The interpretation of these passages from the Admonition has literally filled volumes. Constraints of time and space allow me only to outline a few characteristics that seem to appear in a new light when brought into line with some more recent developments in Qumran scholarship.[14] Specific mention should be made of the contribution to the questions addressed below by John Collins in the *Festschrift* for Prof. Joseph Fitzmyer.[15] I will be asking some questions very similar to those addressed by Collins but arrive at somewhat different conclusions.

2. Discussion of the Texts

2.1 CD 1:3–11a: A First Account of Community Origins in the Damascus Document

1:3	כי במועלם אשר עזבוהו הסתיר פניו מישראל וממקדשו
1:4	ויתנם לחרב ובזכרו ברית ראשנים השאיר שארית
1:5	לישראל ולא נתנם לכלה ובקץ חרון שנים שלוש מאות
1:6	ותשעים לתיתו אותם ביד נבוכדנאצר מלך בבל
1:7	פקדם ויצמח מישראל ומאהרן שורש מטעת לירוש
1:8	את ארצו ולדשן בטוב אדמתו ויבינו בעונם וידעו כי

---

[14] For earlier bibliography on the Damascus Document see Florentino García Martínez, 'Damascus Document: A Bibliography of Studies 1970–1989,' in *The Damascus Document Reconsidered* (ed. Magen Broshi; Jerusalem: IES, 1992), 63–83 and Charlotte Hempel, *The Damascus Texts* (CQS 1; Sheffield: Sheffield Academic Press, 2000). Joseph A. Fitzmyer, *A Guide to the Dead Sea Scrolls and Related Literature* (rev. and enl. ed.; Grand Rapids, Mich.: Eerdmans, 2008), esp. 189–196 includes more recent bibliography. On the particular texts discussed here see also Jonathan Campbell, 'Qumran-Essene Origins in the Exile: A Scriptural Basis?,' *JJS* 46 (1995): 144–156; Antti Laato, 'The Chronology of the *Damascus Document* of Qumran,' *RQ* 15 (1992): 605–607; and most recently James C. VanderKam, 'The Pre-History of the Qumran Community with a Reassessment of CD 1:5–11,' in *The Dead Sea Scrolls and Contemporary Culture* (ed. Adolfo Roitman, Larry Schiffman, and Shani Tzoref; STDJ 93; Leiden: Brill, 2011), 59–76 and further literature referred to there.

[15] John J. Collins, 'The Origin of the Qumran Community: A Review of the Evidence,' in *To Touch the Text: Biblical and Related Studies in Honor of Joseph A. Fitzmyer* (ed. Maurya P. Horgan and Paul J. Kobelski; New York: Crossroad, 1989), 159–178.

1:9	{אנשים}אשימים הם ויהיו כעורים וכימגששים דרך
1:10	שנים עשרים ויבן אל אל מעשיהם כי בלב שלם דרשוהו
1:11a	ויקם להם מורה צדק להדריכם בדרך לבו

Notes

1:4 ראשנים
Qimron transcribes ראשונים. The photograph reproduced on the opposite page of his transcription clearly lacks the *waw*, however.[16]

1:9 אשימים הם
4Q266 (4QDª) 2 i 13 reads אשמים המה.[17]

Translation

1:3 For when they acted unfaithfully in that they forsook him he hid his face from Israel and from his sanctuary 1:4 and gave them over to the sword. But when he remembered the covenant with the ancestors he left a remnant 1:5 for Israel and did not give them over to annihilation. And in the time of wrath – three hundred 1:6 and ninety years after he had given them into the hand of Nebuchadnezzar, king of Babylon – 1:7 he visited them and caused a root of planting to grow from Israel and from Aaron to take possession of 1:8 his land and to grow fat on the goodness of his soil. They considered their sin and knew that 1:9 they were guilty. But they were like the blind and like those who grope for the way 1:10 for twenty years. And God considered their deeds for they sought him with a whole heart. 1:11a And he raised for them a teacher of righteousness to lead them in the way of his heart.

This famous passage from the first page of the Damascus Document as known from the Cairo manuscripts is referred to and often quoted in most publications on the Qumran community and its history. For the present purposes I would like to emphasize one feature in this account and proceed to spell out its significance for the issues outlined above.

The origins of the community are depicted in this account as a two-stage process. CD 1:3–9a describe the emergence of a pious movement three hundred and ninety years after the fall of Jerusalem. CD 1:9b–11a describe a second phase in the community's earliest history. These last lines make the appearance of an individual, the teacher of righteousness, a pivotal moment in the community's emergence.

So much is universally agreed. What seems worth stressing, however, is the vantage point from which this piece is written. It seems to me that this passage – in its present form – is clearly written from the point of view of those who ac-

---

[16] Elisha Qimron, 'The Text of CDC,' in *The Damascus Document Reconsidered* (ed. Magen Broshi; Jerusalem: IES, 1992), 9–49, 10–11.

[17] Qimron, 'Text of CDC,' 11 n. 3–3.

cepted the teacher's authority. Lines 9b–11a in particular can be seen almost as a piece of propaganda: community origins as his followers saw it.

One may wonder whether all the members of the original movement would have accepted the description of themselves as 'blind' and 'groping for the way'? In other words, is it not somewhat naive to take the reference to the initial phase of blindness and lack of orientation as a confessional statement by the new community? Furthermore, common sense and experience suggest that the arrival of a new figure who 'sorts things out' in an existing community rarely passes without tension. It seems to me that what we have here – particularly in lines 9b–11 – is a whitewashed version of events.

Before suggesting possible solutions to a number of these questions in the light of recent scholarly trends concerning community developments reflected in the Scrolls let me discuss three other texts from the Admonition.

2.2 CD 2:8b–13: A Second Account of Community Origins in the Damascus Document

2:8b   ויסתר את פניו מן הארץ

2:9   מי עד תומם וידע את שני מעמד ומספר ופרוש קציהם לכל

2:10   הוי עולמים ונהיית עד מה יבוא בקציהם לכל שני עולם

2:11   ובכולם הקים לו קריאי שם למען התיר פליטה לארץ ולמלא

2:12   פני תבל מזרעם vacat ויודיעם ביד משיחו רוח קדשו וחוזי

2:13   אמת ובפרוש שמו שמותיהם ואת אשר שנא התעה

Notes

2:10 ונהיית
Here we should read ונהיות.[18]

2:11 קריאי שם
4Q266 (4QD^a) has קריאים in the absolute state.[19]

2:12 משיחו
Read משיחי in analogy with וחוזי at the end of the line.[20]

2:13 אמת ובפרוש שמו שמותיהם
Qimron suggests an improved reading on the basis of 4Q266 (4QD^a) which I follow in my translation: אמתו בפרוש שמותיהם.[21]

---

[18] Cf. Qimron, 'The Text of CDC,' 13 n. 7.
[19] Cf. Qimron, 'The Text of CDC,' 13 n. 8–8.
[20] Cf. Qimron, 'The Text of CDC,'13 n. 10.
[21] Qimron, 'The Text of CDC,' 13 n. 11–11; see also PTSDSSP 2:15 n. 9 (Baumgarten and Schwartz). 4Q266 2 ii 13 reads [בפרוש שמותי]הם.

Translation

2:8b *And he hid his face from the land* 2:9 from (. . .) until their end. He knew the years of their existence and the number and the exact determination of their times for all 2:10 happenings of eternity and events throughout all time, what will come to be in their times for all the years of eternity. 2:11 *And amongst all of them he raised for himself renowned ones in order to leave a remnant of survivors for the land and to fill 2:12 the face of the earth with their descendants.* Vacat And he made known to them through those anointed with his holy spirit and seers of 2:13 his truth with exactness their names. But those whom he hated he led astray.

This passage forms part of a long predestinarian section describing the fate of the wicked. A very brief description of community origins is buried within this discourse. Since the main concerns of the section are God's dealings with the wicked this passage rarely features in scholarly discussions of community origins.

CD 2:2–13 shows remarkable similarities to the teaching on the two spirits in 1QS 3:13–4:26 as has often been pointed out.[22] The description of the origins of a movement fits awkwardly into its present context as if an originally independent account of community origins has been inserted into this predestinarian discourse.[23]

I have highlighted the words that seem to me to form part of this description in the text and in my translation. The text at the beginning of CD 2:9 is corrupt. Most unfortunately 4Q266 (4QD^a) which has preserved parts of this passage is of no help for the beginning of this line. What seems clear, however, is that we have moved from a reference to the exile in 2:8b to a predestinarian statement in 2:9b–10. Since 2:9a speaks of 'their end' it seems likely that lines 9b–10 deal with the wicked.

Crucial for our present purposes is the question of the antecedent of ובכולם at the beginning of line 10. The majority of commentators take 'the years of eternity' at the end of line 9 to be the antecedent which leaves us with the rather odd statement that God raises renowned ones and leaves a remnant constantly throughout history. It seems to me that the present text of CD 2:8b–13 is the result of conflating predestinarian statements with an account of community origins. In the process of combining the two elements – and not helped by the corrupt beginning of line 9, the original antecedent of 'and in/amongst all of them' was lost.

---

[22] Philip R. Davies, *The Damascus Covenant: An Interpretation of the "Damascus Document"* (JSOTSup 25; Sheffield: JSOT Press, 1983), 72–73; Armin Lange, *Weisheit und Prädestination: Weisheitliche Urordnung und Prädestination in den Textfunden von Qumran* (STDJ 18; Leiden: Brill, 1995), 233–270.

[23] See also Lange, *Weisheit und Prädestination*, 251 n. 76 who notes with reference to CD 2:11–13, "Der Unterabschnitt hebt sich inhaltlich vom vorhergehenden Kontext ab."

Moreover, it seems much more likely to me that the antecedent of 'and in/amongst all of them' is a group of survivors who have survived the exile – the moment of God's hiding his face from the land referred to in line 8b. As has frequently been noted, the reference to God's hiding his face in 2:8b is reminiscent of CD 1:3 and is best taken to refer to the exile. Thus, CD 2:8b establishes a particular point in time for the emergence of the group described in line 11, i. e. the exile in line with other accounts of community origins in the Admonition. It therefore makes no sense to take the first word of line 11 in a temporal sense. Our passage cannot be locating the emergence of a group of renowned ones to the time of the exile *as well as* in all periods of eternity.

The solution suggested by Michael Knibb with reference to this passage is indicative of the problem I am at pains to point out,

> Although the author is speaking in general terms about the preservation by God of a remnant throughout history, the underlying thought is that the Essene movement formed the remnant in what was for the author the end of the exile (lines 8b–9a) and the climax of history.[24]

Instead, I suggest a partitive understanding of the preposition and translate 'and amongst all of them'. Taking the beginning of line 11 thus, it is possible to make sense of this particular passage as well as making sense in terms of the notions about community origins expressed elsewhere in the document.

Finally, it is worth noting that in the short passage under discussion (CD 2:8b–13) six further third person masculine plural suffixes occur aside from ובכולם at the beginning of line 11. In all the other six cases the suffixes refer to a group of people – either the wicked or, towards the end of the section, the righteous remnant. It seems likely to me that the suffix refers to a group of people at the beginning of line 11 also.

Although it is impossible to prove in the absence of positive evidence, the translation I have chosen seems to me to produce a more meaningful and less contradictory statement than the alternative discussed.

In short, I suggest that embedded in the discourse on the fate of the wicked we have a second account of community origins which places the emergence of a righteous remnant at the time of the exile. It is important to note that this second account describes the emergence of the movement in one stage only.

---

[24] Michael A. Knibb, *The Qumran Community* (Cambridge Commentaries on Writings of the Jewish and Christian World 200 BC to AD 200 2; Cambridge: CUP, 1987), 27.

2.3 CD 3:12b–4:12a: A Third Account of Community Origins in the Damascus Document

3:12b	ובמחזיקים במצות אל
3:13	אשר נותרו מהם הקים אל את בריתו לישראל עד עולם לגלות
3:14	להם נסתרות אשר תעו בם כל ישראל *vacat* שבתות קדשו ומועדי
3:15	כבודו עידות צדקו ודרכי אמתו וחפצי רצונו אשר יעשה
3:16	האדם וחיה בהם *vacat* פתח לפניהם ויחפרו באר למים רבים
3:17	ומואסיהם לא יחיה והם התגוללו בפשע אנוש ובדרכי נדה
3:18	ויאמרו כי לנו היא ואל ברזי פלאו כפר בעד עונם וישא לפשעם
3:19	ויבן להם בית נאמן בישראל אשר לא עמד כמהו למלפנים ועד
3:20	הנה המחזיקים בו לחיי נצח וכל כבוד אדם להם הוא כאשר
3:21	הקים אל להם ביד יחזקאל הנביא לאמר הכהנים והלוים ובני
4:1	צדוק אשר שמרו את משמרת מקדשי בתעות בני ישראל
4:2	מעליהם יגישו לי חלב ודם *vacat* הכהנים הם שבי ישראל
4:3	היוצאים מארץ יהודה והנלוים עמהם *vacat* ובני צדוק הם בחירי
4:4	ישראל קריאי השם העמדים באחרית הימים הנה פרוש
4:5	שמותיהם לתולדותם וקץ מעמדם ומספר צרותיהם ושני
4:6	התגוררם ופירוש מעשיהם *vacat* הקודש שונים אשר כפר
4:7	אל בעדם ויצדיקו צדיק וירשיעו רשע וכל הבאים אחריהם
4:8	לעשות כפרוש התורה אשר התוסרו בו הראשונים עד שלים
4:9	הקץ השנים האלה כברית אשר הקים אל לראשנים לכפר
4:10	על עונותיהם כן יכפר אל בעדם ובשלום הקץ למספר השנים
4:11	האלה אין עוד להשתפח לבית יהודה כי אם לעמוד איש על
4:12a	מצודו נבנתה הגדר רחק החיק

Notes

4:2 מעליהם
My translation follows the reading מעלי הם suggested by Qimron.[25]

4:6 הקודש שונים
CD's reading of the first two words after the vacat appears to be corrupt. The translation is based on conjectural improvements made to CD's reading demanded by the context.

---

[25] 'Text of CDC,' 17 n. 1.

Translation

3:12b But with those who held fast to the commandments of God 3:13 who were left over from them God established his covenant with Israel forever in order to reveal 3:14 to them the hidden things in which all Israel had gone astray: vacat his holy sabbaths and his glorious 3:15 feasts, his righteous testimonies and his true ways, and the desires of his will which humanity 3:16 must do so that they may live through them. Vacat He opened before them and they dug a well with plentiful water. 3:17 Those who reject it shall not live. But they defiled themselves with human transgression and abominable ways 3:18 and said: 'This is ours'. But God in his wonderful mysteries forgave them their sin and pardoned their transgression. 3:19 And he built for them a sure house in Israel the like of which has not stood from former times until 3:20 now. Those who hold fast to it shall have eternal life and all the glory of Adam shall be theirs. As 3:21 God determined for them through Ezekiel the prophet saying, "The priests and the Levites and the sons of 4:1 Zadok who kept charge of my sanctuary when the children of Israel went astray 4:2 from me, they shall offer to me fat and blood." Vacat The priests are the converts of Israel 4:3 who went out from the land of Judah. (And the Levites are) those who joined them. Vacat And the sons of Zadok are the chosen ones of 4:4 Israel, renowned ones who shall arise at the end of days. Here is an exact list 4:5 of their names according to their generations, the appointed time when they lived, the number of their troubles, the years of 4:6 their sojourn and an exact list of their deeds. Vacat The (f)irst holy (ones) whom God 4:7 forgave. And they declared the righteous righteous and the wicked wicked. And all who came after them 4:8 are to act according to the exact interpretation of the law in which the first ones were instructed until the completion of 4:9 the appointed time of these years. Like the covenant which God established with the first ones to forgive 4:10 them their sins, so God will forgive them. And at the completion of the appointed time according to the number of these 4:11 years there shall be no more joining the house of Judah but everyone shall stand on 4:12a his watchtower. The wall is built, the boundary is far away.

This third account of community origins may be divided into four sections. CD 3:12b–17a describes the establishment of an everlasting covenant with the faithful at the time of the exile, comparable to the reference to the land becoming desolate in 3:10. CD 3:17b–20b refers to divine expiation and the establishment of a 'sure house' for the new movement. CD 3:20c–4:4a contain the famous midrash on Ezek 44:15. Finally CD 4:4b–12a announces a list now lost and continues with an exhortation to join the movement before it is too late.

For our present purposes it is crucial to observe that in 3:12b–17a the emergence of a movement is described in a single stage in terms of re-establishing the covenant with Israel forever. Furthermore, the issue of the calendar is placed at the heart of the emergence of the movement.

By contrast the Ezekiel Midrash in 3:20c–4:4a very explicitly reviews the emergence of the community from a vantage point that is far removed from its beginnings. The midrash is full of references to various stages in the history of the community. Whereas we saw two stages in the development of the community depicted in CD 1, the Ezekiel Midrash seems to talk about three stages in the history of the movement.

2.4 CD 5:20–6:11a: A Fourth Account of Community Origins in the Damascus Document

5:20	ובקץ חרבן הארץ עמדו מסיגי הגבול ויתעו את ישראל
5:21	ותישם הארץ כי דברו סרה על מצות אל ביד משה וגם
6:1	במשיחו הקודש וינבאו שקר להשיב את ישראל מאחר
6:2	אל ויזכר אל ברית ראשנים *vacat* ויקם מאהרן נבונים ומישראל
6:3	חכמים וישמיעם ויחפורו את הבאר באר חפרוה שרים כרוה
6:4	נדיבי העם במחוקק הבאר היא התורה וחופריה *vacat* הם
6:5	שבי ישראל היוצאים מארץ יהודה ויגורו בארץ דמשק
6:6	אשר קרא אל את כולם שרים כי דרשוהו ולא הושבה
6:7	פארתם בפי אחד *vacat* והמחוקק הוא דורש התורה אשר
6:8	אמר ישעיה מוציא כלי למעשיהו *vacat* ונדיבי העם הם
6:9	הבאים לכרות את הבאר במחוקקות אשר חקק המחוקק
6:10	להתהלך במה בכל קץ הרשיע וזולתם לא ישיגו עד עמד
6:11a	יורה הצדק באחרית הימים

Notes

5:20 מסיגי הגבול
4Q266 (4QDᵃ) 3 ii 7 reads מסגי גבול.[26]

6:1 במשיחו
Read במשיחי.[27]

6:1 מאחר
4Q267 (4QDᵇ) 2 7 reads מאחרי אל.

6:3 4Q266 (4QDᵃ) and 4Q267 (4QDᵇ) include the introductory formula אשר אמר מושה here.

6:6 4Q267 (4QDᵇ) attests the slightly longer reading דרשוהו כול[ם כיא שרי]ם כ.

6:7 פארתם
The translation follows the reading תפארתם suggested by Rabin.[28]

---

[26] Cf. Qimron, 'Text of CDC,' 19 n. 11–11.
[27] Cf. 4Q267 (4QDᵇ) 2 6 and Qimron, 'Text of CDC,' 21 n. 1.
[28] Chaim Rabin, *The Zadokite Documents: I. The Admonition II. The Laws* (Oxford: Clarendon, 1954), 23.

Translation

5:20 And in the time of the desolation of the land the removers of the boundary arose and led Israel astray. 5:21 And the land became desolate for they spoke rebellion against the commandments of God (given) through Moses and also 6:1 through the holy anointed ones. And they prophesied lies to turn Israel away from following 6:2 God. But God remembered the covenant with the ancestors. Vacat And he raised from Aaron understanding ones and from Israel 6:3 wise ones and made them hear. And they dug the well, "The well which the princes dug, which 6:4 the nobles of the people delved with the staff". The well is the law and those who dug it are 6:5 the converts of Israel who went out from the land of Judah and sojourned in the land of Damascus 6:6 whom God called, all of them, princes for they sought him and their (re)putation 6:7 was not diminished by anyone. And the staff is the interpreter of the law about whom 6:8 Isaiah said, "He brings forth a tool for his work." Vacat And the nobles of the people are those 6:9 who came to dig the well with the staffs which the ruler set up 6:10 to walk in them during all the time of wickedness without which they will achieve nothing until it arises 6:11a one who will teach righteousness at the end of days.

The fourth account of community origins begins again with the time of the exile. This passage describes the early stages of the emergence of a movement but differs remarkably from other descriptions of the same events (contrast CD 1:3–9a; 2:8b–9a.11–13; 3:12b–17a). Whereas elsewhere we had Israel at large being guilty – or at least the great majority of Israel – and bringing about the exile because of their disobedience, here a particular group ("the removers of the boundary") is introduced who prophesied lies and turned Israel away from God. This group is mentioned elsewhere in the Admonition (cf. CD 1:16; 19:16), but the present passage is the only instance where they are introduced with reference to the time of the emergence of the movement. Israel is here pictured as the passive victim of the propaganda of a particular group at the time of the exile. Present rivalries are probably being read into the past. Distinctively among the accounts of the early period in the new movement's history the present description introduces a polemical edge.

Finally, the Well midrash doubtlessly describes community origins in several stages as well as introducing an individual – the interpreter of the law – at a pivotal stage in the community's development.

3. Analysis of All Four Accounts of Community Origins in the Damascus Document

Having discussed the texts let me conclude by trying to bring together the evidence of the four accounts as well as relating it to recent Qumran scholarship as outlined in the introduction.

Clearly different levels of complexity can be identified in the various accounts. Some descriptions or elements of descriptions are brief and describe the emergence of a pious movement after the exile as a single process (CD 1:3–9a; 2:8b–9a.11–13; 3:12b–17a). Such 'one stage' descriptions are found side by side – and in two cases within – more complex descriptions. This group of complex accounts describes the emergence of a movement in several stages (CD 1:9b–11a; 3:20c–4:4a; 5:20–6:11a). Some descriptions make the appearance of an individual the crucial moment in the development of the movement. Others do not refer to an individual but nevertheless clearly perceive the emergence of the movement as consisting of several stages. Furthermore, these 'complex descriptions' convey a sense of temporal distance and remoteness of the writer(s) from the beginnings of the movement. One gains the impression that the writer(s) of these passages no longer identify with the beginnings of the movement but are very conscious of a considerable period of time having elapsed.

This picture is best explained if we allow that present accounts of community origins incorporate a number of earlier, more primitive accounts that were elaborated in various ways. The simple one-stage descriptions that now function as historical introductions looking back briefly to the remote past may well have existed independently at some stage. This point is a crucial one. If we were to assume that the one-stage descriptions go back to the same writers and the same time as the more complex descriptions, my distinction between both types would be of little real value. One could argue that the same group of people chose to talk only briefly about the community's early history in its origin narrative and to spell out more recent events in some detail. By contrast, I want to argue that the one-stage descriptions originated independently at a different time and in a different community from the complex ones. This is indicated by the presence of a simple one-stage description of the origin of a community of pious Jews after the exile in CD 2 that is not followed by the account of later developments. It seems probable to me that one-stage descriptions like the one in CD 2 originated with the parent movement of the community that lies behind more complex descriptions elsewhere in the Admonition. Moreover, having been alerted to the existence of one-stage descriptions as independent units by CD 2:8b–9a.11–13, it seems to me that a reasonable case can be made for CD 1:3–9a and CD 3:12b–17a having at one time existed independently.

Put very simply, I am arguing that those parts of the Admonition that describe the inception of a movement after the exile are not merely *about* that early movement but were composed *by* members of that movement. George W. Nickelsburg comes to a comparable conclusion in a study on *1 Enoch* and Qumran Origins where he observes,

> The writers of the Scrolls had inherited historical traditions about the founding of the community from circles responsible for the composition of large parts of 1Enoch.[29]

---

[29] George W. Nickelsburg, '*1 Enoch* and Qumran Origins: The State of the Question and

Apart from classifying the evidence of the emergence of a movement into different types, my conclusions shed new light on the history of the communities behind the Admonition. Once we allow for a number of simple one-stage descriptions having emerged with an earlier movement we are in a position to draw upon these one-stage descriptions as more or less first-hand accounts of its origins by the earlier group rather than flashbacks of a later group to its earliest past.

The lengthy debate on how to interpret the claim to exilic origins of the community in the Admonition of the Damascus Document would have to take into account that this claim, rather than applying to the off-shoot community, would already have been made by the parent movement.[30]

If I am correct – and the Admonition indeed incorporates accounts of the emergence of a parent movement alongside of accounts of the emergence of its off-shoot community – we should look at accounts of the emergence of a pious movement in the pseudepigrapha in a new light. A number of scholars have drawn attention to the relevance of the pseudepigrapha, in particular *Jubilees* and *1 Enoch*, for the study of the passages discussed in this chapter.[31] As has frequently been noted, for instance, CD 1 shares the imagery of planting to describe the inception of a pious movement with *Jubilees* (e. g. *Jub.* 21:24) and *1 Enoch* (e. g. *1 Enoch* 93:10). This common imagery may not merely be a traditional form of expression taken over by the off-shoot community of an earlier movement, but the correspondence may have emerged because members of the same movement were responsible for the use of the phrase in question in all three cases. It has frequently been pointed out that where the Damascus Document is talking about the Qumran community's earliest history it is most probably referring to the same pious movement the emergence of which is mentioned in the pseudepigrapha. One can deduce from my discussion above that those parts of the Damascus Document are not only talking about the same pious movement but were also composed by the same movement.

Some Prospects for Answers,' in *Society of Biblical Literature Seminar Papers* (ed. Kent H. Richards; Atlanta, Ga.: Scholars Press, 1986), 341–360, 354.

[30] On this issue see Campbell, 'Qumran-Essene Origins in the Exile;' Davies, *The Damascus Covenant*; Michael A. Knibb, 'The Exile in the Literature of the Intertestamental Period,' *HeyJ* 17 (1976): 249–272; idem, 'Exile in the Damascus Document,' *JSOT* 25 (1983): 99–117; Jerome Murphy-O'Connor, 'An Essene Missionary Document? CD II,14–VI,1,' *RB* 77 (1970): 201–229; idem, 'The Essenes and their History.'

[31] Cf. Philip R. Davies, *Behind the Essenes: History and Ideology in the Dead Sea Scrolls* (BJS 94; Atlanta, Ga.: Scholars Press, 1987), 107–134; idem, 'The Prehistory of the Qumran Community,' in *The Dead Sea Scrolls: Forty Years of Research* (ed. Devorah Dimant and Uriel Rappaport; STDJ 10; Leiden: Brill, 1992), 116–125; Dimant, 'Qumran Sectarian Literature,' 544; García Martínez and Trebolle Barrera, *People of the Dead Sea Scrolls*, 88, 245 n. 114; Michael A. Knibb, *Jubilees and the Origins of the Qumran Community: An Inaugural Lecture Delivered on 17 January 1989* (London: King's College London, 1989), 3–20; and Nickelsburg, '*1 Enoch* and Qumran Origins.'

Chapter Five

Emerging Communities in the Serekh[1]

1. Introduction

The Community Rule (S) is a key text in any quest for identity in the Dead Sea Scrolls. However, the picture of community painted by this text is exceedingly complex chiefly because of the complex literary development and multiple attestations of the S tradition. What I would like to do today is dissemble those parts of the S tradition that deal with the council of the community (עצת היחד) as described in 1QS 6:2c–4a//4Q258 (4QS^d) 2 7–8//4Q263 (4QS^i) lines 3b–5a and 1QS 8:1–7a//4Q258 6 1–2//4Q259 (4QS^e) 2 9–16 as well as a number of stray elements of that tradition elsewhere in S, in 4Q265 (Miscellaneous Rules), and in the Damascus Document.

2. The Evidence of the S Manuscripts[2]

In the course of a study on diversity and development in the S tradition,[3] I was struck by the way in which council of the community terminology is used in S. On the one hand it is used frequently alongside and apparently synonymously with the rabbim, whereas at other times the language occurs by itself without references to the many. This has often been noted in discussions of the question whether the council in 1QS 8 refers to an elite group or to the community as a

---

[1] This chapter was originally presented at the Fifth Meeting of the *International Organization for Qumran Studies* (IOQS) held in Groningen, NL, in 2004 and published as 'Emerging Communal Life and Ideology in the S Tradition,' in *Defining Identities: We, You, and the Other in the Dead Sea Scrolls. Proceedings of the Fifth Meeting of the IOQS in Groningen* (ed. Florentino García Martínez and Mladen Popović; STDJ 70; Leiden: Brill, 2008), 43–61. I would like to use this opportunity to reiterate here my thanks to Prof. Florentino García Martínez who stepped down as Secretary from IOQS in 2004 for his vision in bringing this thriving international organization to life and for heading it with his inimitable and effective style of leadership, a powerful cocktail of charm and firm handedness.

[2] In what follows I have relied on the editions of the Hebrew text by Elisha Qimron for the text of 1QS in PTSDSSP 1:6–50 (Qimron) and the editions in DJD 26 (Alexander and Vermes) for the text of the 4QS manuscripts. English translations are my own.

[3] Charlotte Hempel, 'The Literary Development of the S-Tradition. A New Paradigm,' *RQ* 22 (2006): 389–401, reprinted as Chapter 7 in this volume.

whole.⁴ It struck me as worthwhile to have a closer look at those passages in S that speak exclusively of the council of the community in the hope of teasing out characteristics of this exclusive usage that might distinguish it from the usage alongside ha-rabbim. It seems likely, furthermore, that the exclusive usage of one set of terms is traditio-historically earlier than the merging of the two, a suspicion that is confirmed by the highly developed communal organization reflected in the merged terminology over against the relatively primitive communal set-up reflected in the exclusive use of עצת היחד.⁵

3. Emerging Communal Life in 1QS 6

In column 6 of 1QS we find a number of miscellaneous pieces of communal rules. This material has been the focus of a number of scholarly investigations in recent years. Thus, John Collins argues that the term יחד, even in passages like 1QS 6:2–4, refers to an "umbrella organization."⁶ His view represents a much more restrained version of the somewhat extreme suggestion by Hartmut Stegemann that יחד is a designation for "the main Jewish union in late Second Temple times" or "a confederation of all existing Jewish groups."⁷ Both share a desire to move away from a narrow understanding of the term יחד.⁸ Eyal Regev has recently suggested an interpretation of 1QS 6 that is rather similar to the position put forward by Collins: local councils of the community form part of a larger organization, the meeting of the rabbim.⁹ Sarianna Metso proposes that 1QS 6:1c–8a is an interpolation that was included into the Serekh to provide

---

⁴ More is to be said on this debate below. For bibliographical references see note 27 below.

⁵ For a different assessment of the relationship between both terms see Eyal Regev, 'The *Yaḥad* and the *Damascus Covenant*: Structure, Organization and Relationship,' *RQ* 21 (2003): 233–262. On reading Regev's analysis one is left wondering whether the texts that speak of the council of the community and the rabbim ostensibly as synonyms (an observations shared by Regev though qualified with "at first glance," see 239) paint the picture he describes or are made to fit an admittedly neat and ingenious synthesis. Despite our differences of interpretation I greatly appreciate his close and careful readings of the texts at hand.

⁶ John J. Collins, 'Forms of Community in the Dead Sea Scrolls,' in *Emanuel: Studies in Hebrew Bible, Septuagint, and the Dead Sea Scrolls in Honor of Emanuel Tov* (ed. Shalom M. Paul et al.; VTSup 94; Leiden: Brill, 2003), 97–111, esp. 99. See also idem, 'The Yaḥad and "The Qumran Community,"' in *Biblical Traditions in Transmission: Essays in Honour of Michael A. Knibb* (ed. Charlotte Hempel and Judith M. Lieu; JSJSup 111; Leiden: Brill, 2006), 81–96.

⁷ Hartmut Stegemann, 'The Qumran Essenes – Local Members of the Main Jewish Union of Late Second Temple Times,' in *The Madrid Qumran Congress: Proceedings of the International Congress on the Dead Sea Scrolls, Madrid 18–21 March 1991* (ed. Julio Trebolle Barrera and Luis Vegas Montaner; STDJ 11; Leiden: Brill, 1992), Vol. I, 83–166, quotations from 138 and 155 respectively.

⁸ See also Frank M. Cross, *The Ancient Library of Qumran* (3d ed.; Sheffield: Sheffield Academic Press, 1995), 70–71.

⁹ Regev, '*Yaḥad* and the *Damascus Covenant*.'

guidance to travelling members of the community while they are visiting outlying settlements, possibly the camps as described in the Damascus Document.[10] Like Collins, and unlike the view proposed here with reference to 1QS 6:2–4 in particular, Metso presupposes a larger and more developed organization that forms the framework behind the primitive scenario outlined here.

As I have spelt out more fully elsewhere,[11] I regard 1QS 6:2c–4a//4Q258 (4QS^d) 2 7–8//4Q263 (4QS^i) lines 3b–5a as the most primitive communal set-up described in S:

> And together (יחד) they shall eat, and together (יחד) they all pray, and together (יחד) they shall exchange counsel (√ עצה). And in every place where there are found ten people from the council of the community (מעצת החיד [=היחד]) a priest shall be present. (1QS 6:2c–4a)

What is described here is a very basic level of social interaction between like-minded Jews. I see no need to presuppose that the highly developed communal structure described elsewhere in S co-existed with the primitive scenario outlined here. Instead, it seems more likely to me that some very early and primitive material continued to be handed on and cherished by the tradents of S. The influence of this primitive material on the development of the tradition is indicated by the fact that all of the activities mentioned here are the cornerstones, and seeds, of much of the detailed and elaborate procedures found elsewhere in S such as sharing food and exchanging counsel.[12] Thus, access to the טהרת הרבים is an important step towards full membership according to the protracted admission process laid down in 1QS 6:13b–23//4Q256 (4QS^b) 11 8,11–13//4Q261 (4QS^g) 3 1. Moreover, making one's counsel (עצה) available to the community is the culmination of the same process (cf. 1QS 6:23//4Q261 3 1). However, in 1QS 6:2c–4a we do not yet have rabbim terminology or any concept of the pure food and drink of the community. We can imagine quite well how this kind of primitive set-up might have given rise to the more sophisticated procedures over time. Strikingly however, we already have in 1QS 6:2c–4a the repeated

---

[10] Sarianna Metso, 'Whom Does the Term Yaḥad Identify?,' in *Biblical Traditions in Transmission* (ed. Hempel and Lieu), 213–235. See also eadem, 'Methodological Problems in Reconstructing History from Rule Texts Found at Qumran,' *DSD* 11 (2004): 315–335, esp. 322–325.

[11] Charlotte Hempel, 'Interpretative Authority in the Community Rule Tradition,' *DSD* 10 (2003): 59–80, esp. 61–68.

[12] The centrality of the activities mentioned in 1QS 6:2–4 for much of the remainder of S has also been recognized by Matthias Klinghardt, *Gemeinschaftsmahl und Mahlgemeinschaft: Soziologie und Liturgie christlicher Mahlfeiern* (Tübingen: Francke, 1996), 229. However, Klinghardt's analysis goes much further than I am prepared to go in making the meal and subsequent symposium the focal point of the Communal Rule. His analysis of the Rule as a collection of statutes of one or more religious associations is illuminating, although he seems at times to read too much into the text of S. For instance, there is nothing in the text that suggests the communal meeting described in 1QS 6:8b–13a took place after a meal or in 1QS 7:10 that the offence of lying down to sleep during the meeting occurred in the context of a *"Gelagesituation,"* 233.

adverbial use of יחד and even an occurrence of עצת היחד. I therefore propose not only that the small scale practicalities outlined here go back to a primitive stage in the development of communal identity in S, but that this material also preserves the roots of the emerging עצת היחד terminology.[13] The reference to the council of the community in the context of such a small scale context as a place of ten is noteworthy.[14] Moreover, both 1QS 6:2c–4a and the classic account of the council of the community in 1QS 8:1–7a//4Q258 (4QS^d) 6 1–2//4Q259 (4QS^e) 2 9–16 share,

- the exclusive use of council of the community language (without הרבים);
- the small scale setting;
- an interest in the ratio of lay members and priests;
- as well as a lack of concern for the genealogical background of the priestly component (cf. a priest/three priests over against a preference elsewhere for designations such as sons of Zadok or sons of Aaron).

An important difference is, of course, the idealistic, cultic, and theologically charged concerns that come to the fore in 1QS 8 over against the more down to earth realism that characterizes 1QS 6:2c–4a.

This hypothesis of a close relationship between the earliest layer of 1QS 6 and the earliest layer of 1QS 8 as complimentary pieces of evidence that shed light on the earliest periods of communal life might gain support from the intriguing remains in 4Q265 (Miscellaneous Rules) 7 6.[15] There, after the Sabbath rules and immediately preceding the council of the community material, we come across the fragmentarily preserved expression אל ימ[. In 1962 Milik tentatively proposed to restore the verb: (?) אל ימ[וש.[16] In his *editio princeps* of this text of 1999, Baumgarten takes up Milik's restoration without the question mark and supplements the text further as follows: אל ימ[וש כהן מבונן בספר ההגי במקום עשר].[17] In his notes on the restoration Baumgarten refers to CD 13:2, although comparable phrases occur also in 1QS 6:3–4 and 1QS 6:6. If Milik's tentatively proposed restoration were correct, not to mention Baumgarten's much more extensive restoration, this passage would add welcome grist to my mill in as much as it

---

[13] On the question of the significance of עצת היחד terminology in 1QSa see now the astute remarks by Collins, 'Forms of Community,' 109.

[14] Both Metso ('Whom Does the Term Yaḥad Identify?') and Collins ('The Yaḥad and "The Qumran Community"') draw attention to the partitive *min* in the statement (מעצת היחיד [=היחד]). This does indicate that the overall membership of the community was larger, but the figure of ten still indicates a small scale setting. For further discussion see Chapter 6 in this volume.

[15] I am grateful to Dr. Lutz Doering (Durham), Prof. Larry Schiffman (New York) and the late Prof. Joseph Baumgarten (Baltimore) for sharing their insights – and in Lutz' case also a number of bibliographical references – with me in the course of our discussions of this intriguing and fragmentary passage and its immediate context.

[16] DJD 3:188 (Milik). I owe this reference to Lutz Doering.

[17] DJD 35:69 (Baumgarten).

would provide us with an ancient witness that offers an explicit link between the two passages on the council of the community in 1QS 6 and 1QS 8. However, despite the obvious attractiveness of Milik's restoration for my hypothesis and its endorsement by Doering,[18] I would like to offer a cautious note. Since the immediately preceding statement (i. e. the reference to a distance of thirty *ris* from the sanctuary in 4Q265 7 6) may still belong to the sabbath rules,[19] the phrase in question in the second half of this line may constitute yet another formally coherent אל plus jussive clause which could equally be reconstructed along the lines אל ימ[רא (CD 11:12)//אל ימ]ר (4Q271 [4QD^f] 5 i 7), a prohibition that occurs in the Damascus Document as part of the sabbath code and forbids driving on one's servants on the sabbath.[20]

In sum, it seems advisable to be somewhat cautious as far as the restoration of 4Q265 7 6 is concerned. There is one consideration, however, that might offer some support for Milik's and Baumgarten's restoration of the text. The crux in discussions of 4Q265 has always been its heterogeneous character and the intriguing way in which this text strings together a wide variety of *topoi*. These features are nowhere so clearly laid bare as in fragment 7, and Baumgarten has highlighted "the difficulty of finding the connecting thread" here.[21] On having looked at this material again it seems possible that the red thread that runs through the last two thirds of this fragment is the topic of quantities and numbers. Such a concern can be identified as follows,

4Q265 7 5 two thousand cubits
4Q265 7 6a thirty stades
4Q265 7 6b [ten (members of the community)]
4Q265 7 7 fift[een men]
4Q265 7 11 fir[st] week
4Q265 7 13 [eighty days]
4Q265 7 15a seven days
4Q265 7 15b th[irty three days].

---

[18] Lutz Doering, *Schabbat: Sabbathalacha und –Praxis im antiken Judentum und Urchristentum* (TSAJ 78; Tübingen: Mohr Siebeck, 1999), 220.
[19] So Lawrence H. Schiffman, 'Some Laws Pertaining to Animals in Temple Scroll Column 52,' in *Legal Texts and Legal Issues: Proceedings of the Second Meeting of the International Organization of Qumran Studies, Published in Honour of Joseph M. Baumgarten* (ed. Moshe Bernstein, Florentino García Martínez, and John Kampen; STDJ 23; Leiden: Brill, 1997), 167–178, esp. 176–177.
[20] For a full discussion of the textual evidence and the meaning of the prohibition see Doering, *Schabbat*, 190–193. For a different translation of 4Q271's text see DJD 18:180–183 where Baumgarten translates "do not contend (?) with his slave ..." and suggests that we are dealing with a prohibition of "secular confrontations on the Sabbath."
[21] 'Scripture and Law in 4Q265,' in *Biblical Perspectives: Early Use and Interpretation of the Bible in Light of the Dead Sea Scrolls* (ed. Michael E. Stone and Esther G. Chazon; STDJ 28; Leiden: Brill, 1998), 25–33, here 28.

I have marked the restored part of the passage in question in italics above. Thus, altough it is wise not to build too much on the fragmentary remains of line 6b, the suggestion that quantities and measures of some kind are the red thread, the associative[22] link, in the bulk of this fragment offers some support for Baumgarten's reconstruction of the reference to the groups of ten.

4. An Emerging Community Ideology in 1QS 8

A number of features that characterize the various manuscripts of S that preserve material from 1QS 8 strongly point in the direction of a gradual expansion and reworking:[23] we note particularly the high level of activity by Scribe B especially in lines 8–10 of 1QS 8[24] and the absence of the sizeable chunk of text – the equivalent of 1QS 8:15–9:11 – from 4Q259 (4QS^e).[25] As far as the latter is concerned I am convinced by Metso's case to consider the shorter version of 4QS^e as the more original.[26]

I share the view of those scholars who have emphasized that because of the usage of the expression council of the community elsewhere in S, it is best taken here to refer to the community in an incipient stage rather than an inner council.[27] On my reading of the evidence, 1QS 8:1–7a constitutes the original

---

[22] The term 'associative' is helpfully applied to the Laws of the Damascus Document by Baumgarten in his introduction to his *editio princeps* where he refers to the 'Topical and Associative Arrangement of Laws,' DJD 18:14.

[23] For a synchronic reading and an analysis of the rhetorical movement of 1QS 8:1–9:11 see now Carol Newsom, *The Self as Symbolic Space: Constructing Identity and Community at Qumran* (STDJ 52; Leiden: Brill, 2004), 152–165. See also Collins' discussion of this material in 'Forms of Community,' 105–107.

[24] Cf. the helpful summary and bibliography in Sarianna Metso, *The Textual Development of the Qumran Community Rule* (STDJ 21; Leiden: Brill, 1997), 7 and her own analysis 95–105. Note also the recent remarks by Eibert J. C. Tigchelaar in 'The Scribe of 1QS,' in *Emanuel* (ed. Paul et al.), 439–452, esp. 451.

[25] The evidence of 4QS^e led Claus-Hunno Hunzinger to speak of a "lockere Verankerung dieses Abschnittes innerhalb der Sektenschrift," 'Beobachtungen zur Entwicklung der Disziplinarordnung der Gemeinde von Qumrān,' in *Qumran-Probleme* (ed. Hans Bardtke; DAWB-SSA 42; Berlin: Akademie-Verlag, 1963), 231–247, 244.

[26] See Sarianna Metso, 'The Primary Results of the Reconstruction of 4QS^e,' *JJS* 44 (1993): 303–308. For details on the views of those who prefer to think of the longer text of 1QS as the more original see ibidem 304. See also Metso, *Textual Development*, 72.

[27] For the latter view see, e. g., Joseph M. Baumgarten, 'The Duodecimal Courts of Qumran, Revelation and the Sanhedrin,' *JBL* 95 (1976): 59–78 (reprinted in idem, *Studies in Qumran Law* [SJLA 24; Leiden: Brill, 1977], 145–171); Józef T. Milik, *Ten Years of Discovery in the Wilderness of Judaea* (SBT 26; London: SCM, 1959), 100. The former position was first outlined by Edmund F. Sutcliffe, 'The First Fifteen Members of the Qumran Community: A Note on 1QS 8:1 ff.,' *JSS* 4 (1959): 134–138 followed by many subsequent scholars. See, e. g., Johann Maier, 'Zum Begriff יחד in den Texten von Qumran,' *ZAW* 31 (1960): 148–166, esp. 149; Preben Wernberg Møller, *The Manual of Discipline: Translated and Annotated with an*

core of the council of the community passus in 1QS 8–9.[28] I have arrived at this judgment on the basis of a number of considerations. On a very basic literary level the line of argument made by this text is smooth and comes to a logical climax with the reference to the judgment of the wicked in line 7. What follows in lines 7b–8a introduces the new metaphor of the fortified city (based on Isa 28:16[29]) after an identification of the council with the temple in previous lines. This subtle change of metaphors was noted by Georg Klinzing in his fine study of this material from the early 1970s entitled *Die Umdeutung des Kultus in der Qumrangemeinde und im Neuen Testament*[30] which we will have cause to mention again below. Finally, as was noted already by Brownlee, the passage employing the metaphor of the fortified city is set apart from its context on either side by a significant amount of empty space in both lines 7 and 8.[31] After 1QS 8:8b we begin to observe a pattern of formally repetitive statements about the council with a significant heightening of the cultic rhetoric as well as a number of widely recognized interpolations that presuppose a rather well-established community.[32] This pattern of repetition and gradual expansion that I suggest on the level of three passages (i. e. 1QS 8:1–7a; 8:8b–10a and 9:3–6[33]) is already

---

Introduction (STDJ 1; Leiden: Brill, 1957), 122–123; and Alfred R. C. Leaney, *The Rule of Qumran and Its Meaning* (London: SCM, 1966), 211–212. Jean Pouilly, slightly differently, takes עצת היחד to mean "le programme de la Communauté," *La Règle de la Communauté de Qumrân: Son évolution littéraire* (Cahiers de la Revue Bibliques 17; Paris: Gabalda, 1976), 20–21.

[28] The classic and influential study of the literary growth of the Community Rule by Jerome Murphy-O'Connor attributed 1QS 8:1–16 and 9:3–8 to the earliest layer or Manifesto of the document, cf. J 'La genèse littéraire de la Règle de la Communauté,' *RB* 76 (1969): 528–549. This was revised by Pouilly who argued for the secondary character of 1QS 8:10–12, cf. Pouilly, *Règle de la Communauté*. In this assessment of 1QS 8:10–12 Pouilly followed Albert-Marie Denis, 'Évolution de structures dans la secte de Qumrân,' in *Aux origines de l'église* (ed. Jean Giblet; RechBib 7; Louvain: Desclée de Brouwer, 1965), 23–49. Pouilly's revised form of Murphy-O'Connor's analysis has been accepted by many. In a detailed study of the earliest layer of the Community Rule Christoph Dohmen proposed that the original manifesto comprised 1QS 8:1–7a.12b–15a and 9:16b–21, cf. 'Zur Gründung der Gemeinde von Qumran (1QS VIII–IX),' *RQ* 11 (1982): 81–96. More recently Metso has argued on the basis of the evidence of 4Q258 (4QS^d) and 4Q259 (4QS^e) that, "The earliest form of the introduction of 1QS column VIII thus consisted of 1QS VIII, 1–13a+15a," see Metso, *Textual Development*, 118 and Metso, 'Primary Results,' 304–305.

[29] Cf. William H. Brownlee, *The Dead Sea Manual of Discipline* (BASORSup 10–12; New Haven: ASOR, 1951), 33.

[30] (SUNT 7; Göttingen: Vandenhoeck and Ruprecht, 1971).

[31] Brownlee, *Dead Sea Manual of Discipline*, 33.

[32] The repetitive and secondary character of 1QS 8:7b–10a and 9:3–11 is highlighted also by Dohmen, 'Gründung der Gemeinde,' 85–86, 89–91. He perceptively describes 9:3–11 as a "Nachbildung" with a pronounced cultic *Tendenz* (90).

[33] 1QS 8:16b–9:2 is commonly recognized as secondary, see Metso, *Textual Development*, 72 and the earlier literature referred to there. With reference to 1QS 9:3–11 Metso has also observed that it "appears to be a duplicate of the beginning of column VIII," *Textual Development*, 72 and 'Primary Results,' 304–305. My own view is that there is a clear difference between the

apparent in the development of the formula "when these exist in Israel".[34] As clearly illustrated by the synoptic table of the different attestations of the formula in DJD 26, and as argued convincingly by Alexander and Vermes, the original formula was "When these exist in Israel" which was subsequently supplemented to read "When these exist as a community in Israel" or "When these exist *as a community* in Israel **according to all these rules**."[35] The additions do not always occur together, and I have highlighted in various ways the different elements the longer formulae may include. The original form of the formula which presupposes the emergence of a group in Israel with no reference to previous rules is found in the passage here identified as the earliest version of the council of the community statement. Thus, we observe a movement towards expansion in these formulae just as we observe successive elaboration of the passages as a whole. A further new element in a number of later passages from 1QS 8–9 is a repeated emphasis on separation, cf. 1QS 8:11,13; 9:5,9.[36]

Perhaps the strongest support for taking 1QS 8:1–7a as the nucleus of this column is the presence of a formally compatible structure elsewhere in the Community Rule as well as in 4Q265. One of the chief conclusions to emerge from Klinzing's traditio-historical analysis is the identification of a shared tradition in 1QS 8:4–8; 8:8–10; 9:3–6 and 5:4–7.[37] My own argument differs from Klinzing in a number of respects and also incorporates the evidence of 4Q265 which was not available to him.[38] A key difference in our analyses concerns the close relationship I perceive between 1QS 8:1–4a and 8:4b–8a over against Klinzing's distinction between both passages. He notes that the former contains organizational matters as well as general ethical admonitions.[39] The evidence

---

idealistic tenor of 1QS 9:3–6 and the more realistic flavour of 1QS 9:7–11. For a discussion of 1QS 9:7–11//4Q258 (S^d) see Charlotte Hempel, 'The Community and Its Rivals According to the Community Rule from Caves 1 and 4,' *RQ* 21 (2003): 47–81, esp. 61–63.

[34] For a discussion of the significance of the development of this formula for our understanding of the development of the text see Metso, 'Primary Results,' 305. On the successive growth of the formula see also Dohmen, 'Gründung der Gemeinde,' 83.

[35] Cf. DJD 26:113 (Alexander and Vermes). The inclusion of ליחד in 1QS 9:3 is, however, in error.

[36] See also Georg Klinzing, *Die Umdeutung des Kultus in der Qumrangemeinde und im Neuen Testament* (Göttingen: Vandenhoeck and Ruprecht, 1971), 53. The readings of the 4QS manuscripts which attest these references to separation (i.e. 4Q258 [4QS^d] and 4Q259 [4QS^e]) differ only once from the text of 1QS, cf. 1QS 9:5//4Q258 [4QS^d] 7 6 where the former has an unexpected hi. or a full spelling of the ni. imperfect יבדילו and the latter reads an unambiguous ni. imperfect יבדלו. For discussions of the reading of 1QS 9:5 see Brownlee, *Dead Sea Manual of Discipline*, 35 n. 9; Elisha Qimron, *The Hebrew of the Dead Sea Scrolls* (HSS 29; Atlanta, Ga.: Scholars Press, 1986), 19; and Wernberg Møller, *Manual of Discipline*, 133.

[37] Klinzing, *Umdeutung des Kultus*, 50–93 which also includes a helpful synoptic table, see 70.

[38] For the edition of 4Q265 see DJD 35:57–78 (Baumgarten); see also Charlotte Hempel, *The Damascus Texts* (CQS 1; Sheffield: Sheffield Academic Press, 2000), 89–104.

[39] Klinzing, *Umdeutung des Kultus*, 52. Although he takes 1QS 8:2–4 and 1QS 8:4 to have

of 4Q265 provides further support for a close connection between the council of the community issue with the temple imagery and the atoning function. This argument holds only, of course, if we consider the evidence of 4Q265 as that of an independent witness. I believe it is and will say a little more on this below.

Moreover, the bulk of what Klinzing calls general ethical guidelines is firmly based on Micah 6:8. A glance at the context of this verse in Micah 6:6–8 reveals that the verse quoted in 1QS is the culmination of an extended passage dealing with the importance of these ethical guidelines over and above the cult,

> With what shall I come before the Lord ... Will the LORD be pleased with thousands of rams, with tens of thousands of rivers of oil? ... What does the LORD require of you but to do justice, and to love kindness, and to walk humbly with your God. (Micah 6:7–8, NRSV)[40]

Similarly, the reference to a 'broken spirit' is taken from Ps 51:19 (Hebrew).[41] Again, it is extremely illuminating to take into account the immediate context of this allusion in vv. 18–19 (Hebrew, English vv. 16–17), which are rendered by the NRSV as follows,

> For you have no delight in sacrifice; if I were to give a burnt offering, you would not be pleased. The sacrifice acceptable to God is a broken spirit ...

And it is this intrinsic link between the quotation from Micah 6:8 and the allusion to Psalm 51:19 and the subsequent attribution of an atoning function to the council that would explain why both the quotation from Micah 6:8 and a variation of the atonement motif are found again in close proximity to one another in 1QS 5, and in even closer proximity in the shorter and probably more original version attested by 4Q256 (4QS^h) and 4Q258 (4QS^d). The following table provides an overview over the main elements of the evolving tradition on the emerging community on my reading of the evidence.

---

originated separately, he allows for the possibility that they may have been combined prior to their combination here as the parallel structure in 1QS 5 indicates.

[40] As recognized by Catherine Murphy, *Wealth in the Dead Sea Scrolls and in the Qumran Community* (STDJ 40; Leiden: Brill, 2002), 42.

[41] So Brownlee, *Dead Sea Manual of Discipline*, 31. The phrase occurs again in 1QS 11:1 and 4Q393 (Communal Confession) 1–2 ii 7.

Table: Glimpses of an Evolving Tradition[42]

	1QS 5:3b–7// 4QS$^{d/b}$	1QS 8:1–7a// 4QS^d//4QS^e	1QS 8:8b– 10a//4QS^d//4QS^e	4Q265 7:7–10
Make-up of the Council of the Community		x		x
Quotation of Micah 6:8[43]	x	x		
Council or community established	x	x		x
Plant imagery[44]		x (not S^e)[45]		[x] ?[46]
Israel and Aaron motif	x	x	x (var.)[47]	?
Expiation[48]	x (not S$^{d/b}$)	x	x (not S^e)	x
Judgment[49]	x (not S$^{d/b}$)	x	x (not S^e)	x

---

[42] Some elements of this evolving tradition have also been incorporated into the final psalm in 1QS 11:7–9 which includes references to an emerging council of the community, a holy building, and an eternal plant, cf. Klinzing, *Umdeutung des Kultus*, 74–75. Echoes of this tradition are further present in 1QSa 1:3 where we have references to his council, wickedness, atonement, and the land.

[43] Micah 6:8 is also a crucial text in the Teaching on the Two Spirits and offers a tangible connection between the Treatise and the remainder of the Community Rule, see further Charlotte Hempel, 'The Teaching on the Two Spirits and the Literary Development of the Rule of the Community,' in *Dualism in Qumran* (ed. Geza Xeravits; LSTS 76; London: T & T Clark International, 2010), 102–120.

[44] On this imagery see Patrick Tiller, 'The Eternal Planting in the Dead Sea Scrolls,' *DSD* 4 (1997): 312–335 and George J. Brooke, 'Miqdash Adam, Eden, and the Qumran Community,' in *Gemeinde ohne Tempel* (ed. Beate Ego, Armin Lange, and Peter Pilhofer; WUNT 118; Tübingen: Mohr Siebeck, 1999), 285–301, esp. 291–293. Note Brooke's apposite closing statement, "The cultic connection is part of the very woop and warf of the tapestry of images which are held together around the metaphor of planting." 293.

[45] 4Q259 (4QS^e) reads "eternal [j]udgment." Alexander and Vermes draw attention to the superlinear correction of the same word in 1QS 8:5 and plausibly suggest the possibility of a misreading caused by an attempt to copy an imperfect manuscript, DJD 26:143.

[46] The editor restores a reference to the eternal plant in 4Q265 7 8, cf. DJD 35:70 (Baumgarten). Not much can be built on the restoration, except perhaps to note that the presence of a number of shared elements of the council tradition in 4Q265 with 1QS 8:1–7 make it appear plausible.

[47] 1QS and 4Q258 (4QS^d) refer to "a most holy dwelling for Aaron," whereas 4Q259 (4QS^e) has "a m[o]st holy refuge," cf. DJD 26:144 (Alexander and Vermes).

[48] For a discussion of atonement in the Dead Sea Scrolls see Ed P. Sanders, *Paul and Palestinian Judaism* (St. Albans: SCM, 1977), 298–305.

[49] In 1QS 5 the judgment is here and now ("they shall declare guilty all those who transgress the statutes") whereas both in 1QS 8 and in 4Q265 7 the eschatological judgment of the wicked is referred to.

Having established the earliest core of the council of the community tradition in 1QS 8:1–7a we can now identify the key concerns expressed in this passage.

Firstly, as far as the make-up of the council is concerned we note a shift away from the pragmatic stance of 1QS 6:2–4 where it is required that a gathering of ten[50] must include a priest. This is replaced by the theologically motivated figures of twelve laypeople (representing the twelve tribes) and three priests (representing the three tribes descended from Levi, cf. Num 3:17).[51] Whereas the set-up in 1QS 6 has a pragmatic ring to it, the present passage is theologically motivated,[52] and rather than describing events as they were at the time seems to give us an author's view of how things should have been.[53] We also observe a lack of concern for the genealogical background of the priests, an issue that receives considerable stress elsewhere in 1QS//4QS.[54]

Both 1QS 6:3–4//4QS and 1QS 8:1//4QS testify to a time when those innerpriestly disputes were not an issue yet, an observation that corresponds well with Kugler's persuasive assessment of priesthood at Qumran.[55]

---

[50] The traditional quorum for a congregation is also attested in *m. Sanh.* 1:6.

[51] So already Milik, *Ten Years of Discovery*, 100.

[52] On the theological character of the description of the community in 1QS 8:1–10 see Denis, 'Évolution de structures,' 41 and Sarianna Metso, 'Whom Does the Term Yaḥad Identify?.' Regev's doubts about the feasibility of restricting the numbers of an emerging community in such a way are laid to rest if one recognizes the theological character of this account, cf. '*Yaḥad* and the *Damascus Covenant*,' 237 n. 10.

[53] Dohmen's description of the incipient group as a symbolic group points in the right direction. He notes the predominance of symbolism, while still thinking in terms of real events, however, "Vielleicht handelte es sich am Anfang um eine kleine symbolische Gruppe, die stellvertretend für die ganze Bewegung diese harte Lebensweise übernehmen sollte," 'Gründung der Gemeinde,' 83. See also Metso, *Textual Development*, 123.

[54] Cf., for instance, 1QS 5:2–3, 9 and 1QS 5:21; 9:7. On the significance of the textual differences between 1QS and 4Q256 (4QS^b)//4Q258 (4QS^d) on this issue see Philip S. Alexander, 'The Redaction-History of *Serekh ha-Yaḥad*: A Proposal,' *RQ* 17 (1996): 437–453; Albert I. Baumgarten, 'The Zadokite Priests at Qumran: A Reconsideration,' *DSD* 4 (1997): 137–156; Markus Bockmuehl, 'Redaction and Ideology in the Rule of the Community (1QS/4QS),' *RQ* 18 (1998): 541–560; James H. Charlesworth and Brent A. Strawn, 'Reflections on the Text of Serek ha-Yaḥad Found in Cave IV,' *RQ* 17 (1996): 403–435; Paul Garnet, 'Cave 4 MS Parallels to 1QS 5:1–7: Towards a *Serek* Text History,' *JSP* 15 (1997): 67–78; Charlotte Hempel, 'Comments on the Translation of 4QSd I,1,' *JJS* 44 (1993): 127–128; eadem, 'The Earthly Essene Nucleus of 1QSa,' *DSD* 3 (1996): 253–269, reprinted as Chapter 3 in this volume; eadem, 'Interpretative Authority;' Michael A. Knibb, 'Rule of the Community,' in EDSS 2:793–797; Robert Kugler, 'A Note on 1QS 9:14: the Sons of Righteousness or the Sons of Zadok?,' *DSD* 3 (1996): 315–320; Metso, *Textual Development*, 74–90, 143–149; Geza Vermes, 'Preliminary Remarks on Unpublished Fragments of the Community Rule from Qumran Cave 4,' *JJS* 42 (1991): 250–255; idem, 'The Leadership of the Qumran Community: Sons of Zadok-Priests-Congregation,' in *Geschichte – Tradition – Reflexion: Festschrift für Martin Hengel zum 70. Geburtstag* (ed. Hubert Cancik, Hermann Lichtenberger, and Peter Schäfer; Tübingen: Mohr, 1996), Vol. I, 375–384.

[55] Robert Kugler, 'Priesthood at Qumran,' in *The Dead Sea Scrolls After Fifty Years: A Comprehensive Assessment* (ed. Peter W. Flint and James C. VanderKam; Leiden: Brill, 1999), Vol. II, 93–116. For my own contributions dealing with the complex evidence on priesthood in the

Secondly we note the emphatic statement about adhering perfectly to all that has been revealed from all of the Torah. The implied concern of this statement seems to be the degree of adherence rather than limited access to a set of revelations.[56]

This is followed by the quotation from Micah 6:8. As I have argued above, the context of this quotation in Micah 6:6–8 already contains a strong cult critical statement. This is elaborated upon with a number of comparable ethical statements partly derived from Isa 26:3 and Ps 51:19. As noted earlier, the latter allusion also refers to a cult-critical passage from Ps 51. Finally, the reference in 1QS 8:3b//4Q259 (4QS^e) to "making up for trespasses by practicing justice" (ולרצת עוון בעושי משפט) adds an explicitly cult-critical note to the implicit allusions identified above in previous lines. The notion of the council of the community replacing the cult is developed further in 1QS 8:4b–7a//4Q259 (4QS^d)//4Q259 (4QS^e).[57] However, the language used is rather mild and inclusive. Note, for instance, the reference to remaining faithful in the land (1QS 8:3a) and the council's function of making expiation for the land (1QS 8:6). These statements do not reflect a group that had withdrawn – or indeed considered it desirable to withdraw – from society at large.[58] Remarkable also is the universalistic tone of 1QS 8:4 which refers to conduct with everyone (להתהלך עם כול) and the rule of time (תכון העת), both notions close to the Maskil material in 1QS 9:12 ff. – so close in fact that they strike me as almost out of place here.[59] I am not sure I would agree with Metso that the material at hand is part of an introduction to the Maskil material in 1QS 9:12 ff.[60] Instead, I prefer to think – on the basis of a number of distinct emphases – of both blocks of material having emerged independently. Put very briefly, the cultic language of the council of the com-

---

Dead Sea Scrolls see Charlotte Hempel, 'The Sons of Aaron in the Dead Sea Scrolls,' in *Flores Florentino: Dead Sea Scrolls and Other Early Jewish Studies in Honour of Florentino García Martínez* (ed. Anthony Hilhorst, Émile Puech, and Eibert Tigchelaar; JSJSup 122; Leiden: Brill, 2007), 207–224 and eadem, 'Do the Scrolls Suggest Rivalry Between the Sons of Aaron and the Sons of Zadok and If So was it Mutual?,' *RQ* 24 (2009): 135–153 reprinted as Chapters 13 and 14 in this volume.

[56] I noted a similar concern expressed with reference to the people of injustice and their lack of commitment to the hidden things in 1QS 5:11–12, cf. Hempel, 'Community and Its Rivals,' 57.

[57] For two recent discussions of the community without a temple see Brooke, 'Miqdash Adam' and in the same volume Lawrence H. Schiffman, 'Community Without Temple: The Qumran Community's Withdrawal from the Jerusalem Temple,' in *Gemeinde ohne Tempel* (ed. Ego, Lange, Pilhofer), 267–84 (reprinted in Lawrence H. Schiffman, *Qumran and Jerusalem: Studies in the Dead Sea Scrolls and the History of Judaism* [Grand Rapids, Mich.: Eerdmans, 2010], 81–97).

[58] On claims to the land in the Damascus Document see Maxine L. Grossman, *Reading for History in the Damascus Document: A Methodological Study* (STDJ 45; Leiden: Brill, 2002), 179.

[59] Note 1QS 9:12: אלה החוקים למשכיל להתהלך בם עם כול חי לתכון עת ועת.

[60] Metso, *Textual Development*, 123, 144.

munity tradition seems to give way to a more sapiential tone in the statutes for the Maskil. I am however quite prepared to acknowledge refinements to this broad thesis as suggested by 1QS 8:4 where we see a clear connection between both blocks of material.

The tenor of 1QS 8:1–7a is by and large biblical, and the ideal envisaged is an ideal Israel.[61] "The wicked" (הרשעים) are present in this ideal world (1QS 8:7) and will be judged, but we have no reference to a particular group of opponents or any form of advocated separation. In short, I would be loath to connect this earliest statement on the council of the community in 1QS 8:1–7a to any pre-conceived notions about the Teacher of Righteousness and various macro-political events that have often been seen to lie behind this material.[62]

The formally repetitive passages about the council in 1QS 8:8b–10a and 1QS 9:3–6[63] gradually become more explicit about the rejection of the temple, even though an element of this notion is already present in the earliest layer.[64]

In essence, 1QS 8:1–7a testifies to an emerging ideology, a vision of a community characterized by strong idealism and cultic concerns. It seems unlikely that it ever matched a historical reality that just happened to consist of the theologically conducive number of twelve plus three. A much more realistic scenario of a small-scale council of the community as it may have started to emerge in practice is described in 1QS 6:2–4.[65] As far as 1QS 8:1–7a is concerned, the cultic frame of reference, which has often been noted,[66] and the cult-critical tenor of the passage point in the direction of a dissident priestly movement although suggestions of political rivalries or competing claims to high priestly office are conspicuously absent. This dissident priestly movement perceived itself as representing the land and its people. This group probably constituted the forebears of the group that is more narrowly defined and segregated elsewhere in S. The former position is not that far removed from some of the strongest criticism of

---

[61] On this issue see John J. Collins, 'The Construction of Israel in the Sectarian Rule Books,' in *Judaism in Late Antiquity Part 5: The Judaism of Qumran. A Systemic Reading of the Dead Sea Scrolls* (ed. Alan J. Avery-Peck, Jacob Neusner, and Bruce D. Chilton; HdO 57; Leiden: Brill, 2001), Vol. I, 25–42.

[62] So already Sutcliffe, 'First Fifteen Members,' 138. See also Murphy-O'Connor, 'Genèse littéraire,' 531. The Teacher is mentioned in connection with the council of the community in some of the *pesharim* where we also find a strong element of polemic and threats against the council. The situation described in the *pesharim* seems, therefore, quite removed from the optimism and idealistic tone in the present passage.

[63] The latter passage is part of the long section missing from 4Q259 (4QS^e), cf. Metso, 'Primary Results;' eadem, *Textual Development*, 71–73. Note Newsom's reference to 1QS 9:3–11 as a "recapitulation" of 1QS 8:1 ff. and her list of overlapping terminology, *Self as Symbolic Space*, 164–165. John Collins also speaks of 1QS 9:3–11 in terms of a "reformulation" and duplication of 1QS 8:4b–10, 'The Yaḥad and "The Qumran Community,"' 89.

[64] This observation seems to be shared by Newsom when she notes "references to sacrificial terminology [...] are elaborated [..] in 9:4–5," *Self as Symbolic Space*, 165.

[65] This line of interpretation is developed further in Chapter 6 of this volume.

[66] Cf. Murphy-O'Connor, 'Genèse littéraire,' 529. See also Maier, 'Zum Begriff יחד,' 165.

the wrong kind of cult in the Bible, cf. esp. Isaiah 1:10 ff., Amos 5:21–24, and Micah 6:6–8. An important new development attested here is an association of the emphasis on ethical virtues over and against cultic obedience with a particular group within the land. This development is taken even further in 1QS 5 where atonement is made possible by a particular group on behalf of a particular community within the land which leads me to my next section.

5. Expiation Restricted to the Community (1QS 5//4Q256 [4QS^b] and 4Q258 [4QS^d])

As noted already by Klinzing, parts of 1QS 5 resemble the earliest layer of 1QS 8 with some significant modification. To this we may now add that 4Q256 and 4Q258 testify to a shorter text that narrows the gap attested in 1QS 5 between the quotation from Micah 6:8 and the Aaron and Israel motif. Curiously, however, the latter manuscripts also lack the references to atonement and judgment that are otherwise widely attested in compatible texts. A noteworthy difference between 1QS 5 and 8, that has been pointed out by Murphy-O'Connor and others, is that whereas both passages speak of expiation, the former restricts those granted expiation to community members whereas the latter passage speaks in biblical and more inclusive terms of expiation for the land.[67]

6. The Evidence of 4Q265

The presence in 4Q265 of a self-contained passage on the council of the community indicates that we are dealing with an independent tradition that found its way into several compositions. Questions of the literary nature and genre of 4Q265 are still very much unresolved although it is fairly clear that the text preserves independent traditions of some familiar material. Note for instance the only occurrence of the combination המבקר על היחד in 4Q265 4 ii 6.[68] The evidence of 4Q265 with regard to the council of the community tradition is complex, and because of the text's fragmentary character difficult to interpret. However, a number of observations can be made with a degree of confidence.

---

[67] Cf. Murphy-O'Connor, 'Genèse littéraire,' 535. See also Dohmen, 'Gründung der Gemeinde,' 83; Michael A. Knibb, *The Qumran Community* (Cambridge Commentaries on Writings of the Jewish and Christian World 200 BC to AD 200 2; Cambridge: CUP, 1987), 131. Bertil Gärtner notes the difference briefly (27), but subsequently focuses exclusively on the resemblances between both passages, *The Temple and the Community in Qumran and the New Testament* (SNTSMS 1; Cambridge: CUP, 1965), 30.

[68] Note that just two lines after this unusual designation the fragment attests the more familiar title המבקר על הרבים.

Firstly, 4Q265 mirrors the evidence of S by using the terminology council of the community both synonymously with ha-rabbim in 4 ii 3–4 in the context of admission into the community, as well as by itself (exclusive usage) in the context of setting out the make-up and purpose of this council of the community in idealistic and cultic terms in fragment 7. As is indicated by the evidence of S, it seems likely that the council of the community terminology originated independently of the rabbim terminology, and that the two subsequently became merged. Rabbim terminology is found in very developed texts, as far as the complexity of the organization is concerned, whereas the exclusive use of council of the community language in S and 4Q265 is found in small scale, less rigidly organized, idealistic, and cultic contexts.

Secondly, as far as scope is concerned, the material on the council of the community in 4Q265 resembles the section in 1QS 8:1–7a identified above as the earliest representation of the council of the community tradition. Both passages start off with a description of the make-up of the council consisting of fifteen members and end with a reference to judgment. However, because of its fragmentary nature we cannot be certain whether the missing part of 4Q265 7 84 included either the plant imagery or the Aaron and Israel motif or something altogether different. Given the constancy of the Aaron and Israel motif across the board, see the Table "Glimpses of an Evolving Tradition" above, a restoration along these lines seems reasonable, however.[69]

Thirdly, 4Q265 rather curiously combines terminological elements from 1QS 8:1–7a (the council of the community shall be established; will of God; to atone for the land) with features known only from 1QS 8:8b–10a (cf. the references to the sweet odour and an end of injustice).[70] Interestingly, and further attesting the fluidity of the traditions, the reference to the end of injustice is lacking both from Scribe A in 1QS 8:10 and probably also from 4Q259 (4QS^e) 3 1.[71]

On the basis of this complex picture it seems likely that 4Q265 constitutes a literarily dependent yet more developed version of the original council of the community tradition from the one preserved in 1QS 8:1–7a. Some of its developments are, moreover, also found in the second and more developed form of the tradition preserved in 1QS 8:8b–10a.

---

[69] See also n. 46 above.
[70] 1QS 8:10 reads ואין עולה. 4Q265 7 10 has וסופה במשפט קצי עולה.
[71] Cf. the notes on the readings of this line in DJD 26:145 (Alexander and Vermes); on the superlinear additions in 1QS 8:10 and 1QS 8:12–13 as "additions-glosses" over against smaller corrections that may have followed a manuscript, possibly 4QS^e, see Émile Puech, 'Remarques sur l'écriture de 1QS VII–VIII,' *RQ* 10 (1979): 35–43, esp. 42–43.

7. The Evidence of the Damascus Document

We come across rudiments of a similar tradition to the one attested in 1QS 8:1–7a in the Damascus Document (CD 1:7–8//4Q266 [4QD^a] 2 i 11–12// 4Q268 [4QD^c] 1 14–15). We note the following correspondences of topics and terminology:
- the early period of an emerging movement
- plant imagery
- the Israel and Aaron motif [72]
- the land (ארץ, cf. 1QS 8:3,6//4Q259 [4QS^e] 2 11,15 and CD 1:8//4Q266 [4QD^a] 2 i 12//4Q268 [4QD^c] 1 15])
- iniquity (עוון, cf. 1QS 8:3//4Q259 2 11 and CD 1:8//4Q266 2 i 12//4Q268 1 15).[73]

These shared linguistic features point to a common milieu. I have argued elsewhere that the first stage of community origins in CD 1 goes back to and describes the emergence of the pre-Teacher group.[74] An interesting difference between both passages is the lack of reference to expiation in this part of the Damascus Document. This lack of references to atonement in CD 1 is more than made up for in CD 3–4 where we find an intriguing series of references to atonement by God in the context of the community's origins or founding members. The relevance of CD 3–4 in discussions of 1QS 8 was again already picked up by Klinzing.[75] Especially revealing in its relationship to 1QS 8 is CD 4:6–7 "<the fir>st holy <ones> for whom God made expiation, who declared the righteous righteous and the wicked wicked."[76] An obvious and fascinating difference between what is said about atonement in CD 3–4 and 1QS 5 and 8 is the named responsible party: God in the former versus the council of the community in the

---

[72] Two separate studies of the poetry of CD 1 have, however, both argued that the original text lacked the reference to Aaron in CD 1:7, cf. Mark Boyce, 'The Poetry of the *Damascus Document* and Its Bearing on the Origin of the Qumran Sect,' *RQ* 14 (1990): 615–628 and Philip R. Davies, *The Damascus Covenant: An Interpretation of the "Damascus Document"* (JSOTSup 25; Sheffield: Sheffield Academic Press, 1983), 232–233. For a discussion of this material see also Grossman, *History in the Damascus Document*, 146–147. If the reconstruction of the original text by Boyce and Davies is correct, then the overlapping motif of Israel and Aaron would be present only in the final stage of this text. The Israel and Aaron motif occurs again in a context of community foundation in CD 6:2–3.

[73] The term recurs again in the context of community origins in CD 3:18.

[74] See Charlotte Hempel, 'Community Origins in the Damascus Document in the Light of Recent Scholarship,' in *The Provo International Conference on the Dead Sea Scrolls: Technological Innovations, New Texts and Reformulated Issues* (ed. Donald W. Parry and Eugene Ulrich; STDJ 30; Leiden: Brill, 1999), 316–329, reprinted as Chapter 4 in this volume.

[75] See *Umdeutung des Kultus*, 75–80.

[76] See also CD 3:18 and 4:9–10. I am inclined to agree with Davies, *Damascus Covenant*, 99, that the first ones here are "the founder members of the community covenant."

latter. Even if God would have been considered the ultimate source of atonement even in 1QS 5 and 8, theologically speaking, the difference in expressing things is noteworthy.

8. Conclusions and Outlook

Some of the primitive and small scale communal scenarios described in 1QS 6 deserve to be read without presuppositions derived from the overwhelming majority of communal rules in S that describe a much more evolved and complex level of organization. On my reading of these isolated statements they originated independently of S and reflect the life of the forebears of the Yaḥad. Those forebears were, furthermore, not concerned with separation and the establishment of rigid boundaries between themselves and Israel at large. The only visible element of separation was the small-scale gathering of some like-minded people to eat, pray and exchange counsel. It is quite possible that this was the kind of thing one did in middle class Second Temple Judaism, and this scenario might, therefore, describe only one group of many that engaged in these kinds of gatherings.[77] To some degree my position overlaps with the views recently expressed by Collins, Metso, and Regev.[78] A big difference is that all three, admittedly in very different ways, presuppose the existence of a framework, a central organization, to have existed alongside these small groups.

I argued for some kind of a relationship between the material in 1QS 6:2–4 and 1QS 8:1–7a based on several overlapping traits (such as exclusive use of council of the community language, small numbers, concern with the ratio of priests and lay persons). I emphasized the recognizable shift towards the theological, cultic and ideological in the latter material. 1QS 6:2–4 offers a more credible historical scenario of emerging communal life. Finally, I advocated the identification of a moderately dissident priestly group behind the particular development of prophetic critiques of the cult in 1QS 8:1–7a while stressing the lack of references in the text to any high priestly rivalries. Finally the repeated references to atonement by God in CD 3–4 in a community emergence context may point to the presence of a recognizable cultic/theological layer in D and S that deserves further investigation. An exceedingly interesting avenue for further investigation is the relationship of the material discussed here to 4QMMT which is conciliatory and low-key on polemics and of course also priestly and cultic in outlook. 4QMMT does contain a famous reference to separation but no indica-

---

[77] See the reflections of Johann Maier who asked already in 1960, "ob das Wort יחד nicht schon vor der Qumrangemeinde irgendwo einen festen 'Sitz im Leben' gehabt hat" even referring in this context, though rather too tentatively, to 1QS 6:2, 'Zum Begriff יחד,' 165.

[78] See notes 5, 6 and 10 above.

tion of replacing the cult with ethical virtues along the lines of Micah 6 – in fact, quite the opposite is true. In 4QMMT, it is the finer points of cultic halakhah that are the issues at hand.

Chapter Six

Small Beginnings or Geographical Diversity[1]

1. Introduction

This chapter arose in response to an invitation to offer some reflections on the most recent scholarly developments on the question of the identity and history of the Qumran Community. The recent scholarship I have been asked to comment on has, in fact, made the term 'Qumran community' exceedingly problematic. Thus, John Collins went as far as stating in a recent *Festschrift* for Michael Knibb,

> We have [..] reached a point where it is no longer helpful to characterize any part of the textual evidence as describing 'the Qumran community.'[2]

There has, of course, never been any doubt that the non-biblical Scrolls describe more than one type of community. Prior to the full publication of the evidence from Cave 4 our picture of the organization of the communities reflected in the Scrolls drew chiefly on the regulations on the camps as known from the legal part of the Damascus Document (D) and the Yaḥad as described in the Community Rule (S).[3] The differences witnessed by both texts were often accounted for by referring to Josephus's reference to two types of Essenes, one married and one

---

[1] This chapter originated in the context of an international conference celebrating the sixtieth anniversary of the discovery of the Dead Sea Scrolls in the wonderful surroundings of the Israel Museum in Jerusalem and was originally published as '1QS 6:2c–4a – Satellites or Precursors of the Yaḥad?,' in *The Dead Sea Scrolls and Contemporary Culture* (ed. Adolfo Roitman, Larry Schiffman, and Shani Tzoref; STDJ 93; Leiden: Brill, 2011), 31–40. I would like to thank the organizers of the Jerusalem meeting, esp. Adolfo Roitman and Judith Amselem, for their invitation and hospitality. I am also grateful to a number of colleagues for engaging with my arguments in various forms, esp. Profs. Al Baumgarten, John Collins, and Michael Stone. I subsequently presented a version of this paper to the Senior Qumran Seminar at the University of Helsinki chaired by Prof. Raija Sollamo and at a Day Conference in honour of Dr. Jenny Dines at Heythrop College London. I would like to thank Prof. Sollamo for the warm Finnish hospitality I enjoyed and the participants at both events, esp. Drs. Jutta Jokiranta, Hanne von Weissenberg, Profs. Judith Lieu and David Chalcraft for their stimulating contributions.
[2] John. J. Collins, 'The Yaḥad and "The Qumran Community,"' in *Biblical Traditions in Transmission: Essays in Honour of Michael A. Knibb* (ed. Charlotte Hempel and Judith Lieu; JSJSup 111; Leiden: Brill, 2006), 81–96, here 96.
[3] Cf. Sarianna Metso, 'Whom Does the Term Yaḥad Identify?,' in *Biblical Traditions in Transmission* (ed. Hempel and Lieu), 213–235.

celibate (cf. *J. W.* 2.120–121, 160).[4] Rather than clarifying this existing picture the full publication of all the fragmentary manuscripts from Cave 4 has muddied the waters considerably in a number of respects.[5]

Let me restrict myself to mentioning just three examples of new material that challenged our existing thinking on the relationship of the Damascus Document and the Community Rule:[6]

- A large amount of additional penal code material that displays striking overlaps with S is attested in Cave manuscripts of D.
- Some of the Cave 4 manuscripts of the Community Rule attest a radically different text from 1QS.
- 4Q265 Miscellaneous Rules comprises traditions that resemble D and S as well as material different from either of the two.

In what follows I will turn to a number of particular challenges posed by these complexities and the richness of our evidence before returning in closing to the wider significance of this material for enhancing our understanding of Second Temple Judaism more broadly.

2. Texts, Communities, and the Site of Qumran

A number of key issues emerging or re-emerging succinctly in recent debates are,
- How many communities are reflected in the Scrolls?
- Which one resided at Qumran?
- Where were they before they settled at Qumran?
- How do the communities relate to one another?
- How do the communities relate to the rest of Jewish society?

---

[4] Cf. Eileen Schuller, *The Dead Sea Scrolls: What Have We Learned 50 Years On* (London: SCM, 2006), 80–81. For a recent discussion of the classical evidence on the celibacy question see Joan E. Taylor, 'Philo of Alexandria on the Essenes: A Case Study on the Use of Classical Sources in Discussions of the Qumran-Essene Hypothesis,' *Studia Philonica Annual* 19 (2007): 1–28, esp. 20–26 and further literature referred to there. See also Sidnie White Crawford, 'Not According to Rule: Women, the Dead Sea Scrolls and Qumran,' in *Emanuel: Studies in the Hebrew Bible, Septuagint, and Dead Sea Scrolls in Honor of Emanuel Tov* (ed. Shalom M. Paul et al.; VTSup 94; Leiden: Brill, 2003), 127–150.

[5] See recently John J. Collins, 'Sectarian Consciousness in the Dead Sea Scrolls,' in *Interpretation, Identity and Tradition in Ancient Judaism* (ed. Lynn LiDonnici and Andrea Lieber; JSJSup 199; Leiden: Brill, 2007), 177–192 and Alison Schofield, 'Rereading S: A New Model of Textual Development in Light of the Cave 4 *Serekh* Copies,' *DSD* 15 (2008): 96–120.

[6] For further literature on both texts see conveniently Charlotte Hempel, *The Damascus Texts* (CQS 1; Sheffield: Sheffield Academic Press, 2000) and Sarianna Metso, *The Serekh Texts* (CQS 9/LSTS 62; London: T & T Clark, 2007).

It seems fruitful to reflect on these lines of scholarly investigation in analogy with the work of biographers. It is perhaps not too far fetched to describe the task at hand and the efforts of previous scholars as attempts to write a biography of the Yaḥad. In the Introduction to his intellectual biography of Elias Bickerman, Albert Baumgarten provocatively asks himself and his readers: "Why Bickerman?".[7] Part of the answer he supplies stresses the extent to which a good biography will not only illuminate the life of its immediate subject, but rather – as in Bickerman's case – can shed light on the history of a century played out in various countries. I think the same applies to our efforts at refining the biography of the Yaḥad. Since the Scrolls were first discovered, and the Community Rule in particular began to be interpreted, scholarship has tended to write a biography of the Yaḥad that privileged the subject. It was as if we looked at a school photograph with a very dear relative in the photo. Our eyes are drawn to the one person we are most interested in. Admittedly, scholars have always looked beyond the Yaḥad, as any biographer would, to talk about the family and the background into which the subject was born. However, there has been something of a shift in perspective in recent studies that has enhanced our awareness of the huge amount of light the Scrolls can shed on the wider background of our subject, the Yaḥad.[8] More recently this trend has accumulated momentum.

3. Yaḥad(s) Before and Outside of Qumran

The influx of a considerable amount of new and challenging texts over the last two decades or so has stimulated research on the Scrolls, including the Rule texts, immensely.[9] The ripples of the challenges posed by incorporating the new evidence into our perceptions of the social realities behind the texts have not left our reading of long known passages untouched. One of those current ripples of scholarly investigation that is gradually gaining in size and becoming a fully-fledged wave will be the focus of what follows. In particular, the remainder of this chapter will offer some reflections on the work of a number of scholars who have recently argued that the Rule of the Community, a document that is customarily considered the Yaḥad's handbook, if you like, should be associated

---

[7] Albert I. Baumgarten, *Elias Bickerman as a Historian of the Jews* (TSAJ 131; Tübingen: Mohr Siebeck, 2010), 1.

[8] See recently, for instance, Philip R. Davies, 'Sect Formation in Early Judaism,' in *Sectarianism in Early Judaism: Sociological Advances* (ed. David J. Chalcraft; London: Equinox, 2007), 132–155 and Michael E. Stone, 'The Dead Sea Scrolls and the Literary Landscape of Second Temple Judaism,' in *The Dead Sea Scrolls: Texts and Context* (ed. Charlotte Hempel; STDJ 90; Leiden: Brill, 2010), 15–30.

[9] See Charlotte Hempel, 'Texts, Scribes, Caves and Scholars: Reflections on a Busy Decade in Dead Sea Scrolls Research,' *ExposTim* 120/6 (2009): 272–276.

also with a geographically much broader phenomenon.[10] To put it differently, scholars have gone beyond looking at non- or proto-sectarian texts in their search for life outside Qumran.

An early and rather extreme advocate of such a view was the late Hartmut Stegemann who identified the Qumran establishment as inhabited by "local members of the main Jewish union of Second Temple times" – almost a pan-Yaḥad hypothesis.[11] More recently John Collins has made a strong case for the presence of "a variety of community forms" behind the texts in a number of publications.[12] He prefers to speak of the Yaḥad as an "umbrella organization" not an individual community based at Qumran, although he considers the Qumran branch as an "elite offshoot" of this broader movement.[13] In the wake of Collins' publications, Sarianna Metso has offered a sober assessment of his hypothesis as well as suggesting an alternative line of interpretation on which I will say more below.[14] Eyal Regev has argued that the rabbim of the Community Rule were the precursors of the much more spread-out camp organization of the Damascus Document.[15] Devorah Dimant allows for the antiquity of some of the sources eventually incorporated into the Community Rule by a skilful compiler, some of which "may have been produced well before the Qumran community appeared on the historical scene."[16] Torleif Elgvin and Alison Schofield both stress the difficulties posed by Jodi Magness' re-dating of the communal occupation of the site for traditional readings of the Community Rule as offering a vision and realization of the group's foundation in the wilderness.[17]

---

[10] Already in 1960 Johann Maier tentatively asked whether the term Yaḥad had a 'Sitz im Leben' in the days prior to the Qumran Community, see 'Zum Begriff יחד in den Texten von Qumran,' *ZAW* 31 (1960): 148–166, esp. 165.

[11] 'The Qumran Essenes – Local Members of the Main Jewish Union of Late Second Temple Times,' in *The Madrid Qumran Congress: Proceedings of the International Congress on the Dead Sea Scrolls, Madrid 18–21 March 1991* (ed. Julio Trebolle Barrera and Luis Vegas Montaner; STDJ 11; Leiden: Brill, 1992), Vol. I, 83–166. See also Sidnie White Crawford 'Not According to Rule,' 148–150. In their introduction to the translation of the Community Rule Michael Wise, Martin Abegg and Edward Cook rightly stress the significance of the reference to the existence of "local chapters" (as they call it) throughout Palestine in the composition. Cf. Michael O. Wise, Martin G. Abegg and Edward M. Cook, *The Dead Sea Scrolls: A New Translation* (London: HarperCollins, 1996), 123–143.

[12] Cf. 'The Yaḥad and "The Qumran Community;"' 'Sectarian Consciousness in the Dead Sea Scrolls;' and 'Forms of Community in the Dead Sea Scrolls,' in *Emanuel* (ed. Paul et al.), 97–111.

[13] Cf. his references to "[A]n extensive sectarian movement with multiple places of residence scattered through the land," 'Sectarian Consciousness in the Dead Sea Scrolls,' 181, see also 179–180 and 'The Yaḥad and "The Qumran Community."'

[14] 'Whom Does the Term Yaḥad Identify?.'

[15] *Sectarianism in Qumran: A Cross-Cultural Perspective* (Religion and Society 45; Berlin: de Gruyter, 2007), esp. 163–196.

[16] 'The Composite Character of the Qumran Sectarian Literature as an Indication of Its Date and Provenance,' *RQ* 22 (2006): 615–630, here 622.

[17] Cf. Alison Schofield, 'Rereading S' and Torleif Elgvin, 'The *Yaḥad* is More than Qumran,'

4. 1QS 6:1c–8a: The Under-Studied Enters the Limelight

Finally, in a recently published paper I identified a passage in 1QS 6:2c–4a that seems to me to give us a flavour of how communal life may have emerged long before the fully-fledged Yaḥad was born and settled at the site of Qumran.[18] More particularly I argued that the small-scale gatherings described in the opening lines of 1QS 6 have a more pragmatic, less theologically charged flavour than what we learn about the council of the community in 1QS 8. With regard to 1QS 8 it has, of course, been suggested long ago that this part of the Community Rule reflects an early phase in the emergence of a community.[19] Where I hope my own observations have added a new element to the discussion is by encouraging us to look at the opening lines of 1QS 6 for a more convincing picture of how things may have started.

At the same time as I was first thinking about this material I was delighted to read the work of Sarianna Metso, John Collins, and Eyal Regev[20] on this same and previously rather neglected part of the Community Rule in 1QS 6. Here I would like to draw on the wonderful notion developed by Maxine Grossman, I am told, in conversation with Albert Baumgarten, of "orphaned passages." This phrase, as I understand it, denotes passages that are deprived of their full impact because they do not chime with existing scholarly currents. In the case of 1QS 6:1c–8a we may speak of a set of passages that was for a time orphaned – orphaned may even be too strong a term here and we should rather think of neglected children – and these children seem to have been adopted into a very lively family of scholars who are finally lavishing attention and care on this part of the Community Rule. In any case, the renewed interest in this material seems indicative of the current climate in Scrolls studies that is increasingly less Yaḥad- and Qumran centric.

In a nutshell, my own position on this material is that it reflects some very primitive forms of social interaction among Second Temple Jews such as communal prayer, meals, and deliberation. I describe 1QS 6:2c–4a as portraying "a very basic level of social interaction between likeminded Jews."[21] I translate the passage in question as follows,

---

in *Enoch and Qumran Origins: New Light on a Forgotten Connection* (ed. Gabriele Boccaccini et al.; Grand Rapids, Mich.: Eerdmans, 2005), 273–279.

[18] Cf. Charlotte Hempel, 'Emerging Communal Life and Ideology in the S Tradition,' in *Defining Identities: We, You, and the Other in the Dead Sea Scrolls. Proceedings of the Fifth Meeting of the IOQS in Groningen* (ed. Florentino García Martínez and Mladen Popović; STDJ 70; Leiden: Brill, 2008), 43–61, reprinted as Chapter 5 in this volume.

[19] See already Edmund F. Sutcliffe, 'The First Fifteen Members of the Qumran Community: A Note on 1QS 8:1 ff.,' *JSS* 4 (1959): 134–138 and Jerome Murphy-O'Connor, 'La genèse littéraire de la Règle de la Communauté,' *RB* 76 (1969): 528–549.

[20] See esp. *Sectarianism in Qumran*, chapter 4.

[21] Cf. Hempel, 'Emerging Communal Life and Ideology,' 45. My analysis of 1QS 6:2c–4a ties in well with Wassen and Jokiranta's low tension spectrum, see Cecilia Wassen and Jutta

And together (יחד) they shall eat, and together (יחד) they all pray, and together (יחד) they shall exchange counsel (√ עצה). And in every place where there are found ten people from the council of the community (מעצת החיד [=היחד]) a priest shall be present. (1QS 6:2c–4a)

My sociologically trained colleague David Chalcraft has convinced me since that the term "primitive" is problematic and I would do better to speak in terms of an embryonic state of affairs.[22] John Collins has recently applied the term "fossil" to this line of interpretation.[23] I suggest labelling the alternative favoured by Collins and others the "sprout" or "satellite" view. A variant of both is Sarianna Metso's proposal which may be labelled a "sprouting fossil." On the one hand she is a strong supporter of the view that 1QS 6:1c–8a contains material distinct in origin from the remainder of 1QS 5–7 that was subsequently incorporated in its present context.[24] On the other hand, she suggests that one of the reasons for its inclusion into S was to accommodate travelling Yaḥadists.[25]

This debate (fossil versus sprouts/satellites) is highly relevant for the historical evaluation of the Dead Sea Scrolls. If small-scale gatherings of like-minded Jews that pre-date the highly developed Yaḥad structure are attested in parts of the Community Rule, then such activities (fellowship) may well mirror similar gatherings of like-minded Jews in Second Temple times (cf. the reference to a quorum of 10 in *m. Sanh.* 1:6). My reading of this particular passage in the Rule supports the plausible recent proposal by Martin Goodman that "attachment to a group of like-minded enthusiasts within the Jewish community" attested by the Scrolls and the New Testament (Goodman refers to Acts 4:32 in particular) may not have been all that unusual.[26]

Jokiranta, 'Groups in Tension: Sectarianism in the Damascus Document and the Community Rule,' in *Sectarianism in Early Judaism* (ed. Chalcraft), 205–245.

[22] I am grateful to David Chalcraft for these comments in a personal communication.

[23] Cf. John J. Collins, 'The Nature and Aims of the Sect Known from the Dead Sea Scrolls,' in *Flores Florentino: Dead Sea Scrolls and Other Early Jewish Studies in Honour of Florentino García Martínez* (ed. Anthony Hilhorst, Emile Puech, and Eibert Tigchelaar; JSJSup 122; Leiden: Brill, 2007), 31–52, here 43.

[24] Thus Metso, following Leaney and Knibb, notes, "… an argument can be made that the passage may have originated in a different setting, described that which happened somewhere else than in the community behind the Serek, and then may have been secondarily borrowed and inserted into the Serek." ('Whom Does the Term Yaḥad Identify?,' 218–219). See also Alfred R. C. Leaney, *The Rule of Qumran and Its Meaning* (NTL; London: SCM, 1966), 180 and Michael A. Knibb, *The Qumran Community* (Cambridge Commentaries on Writings of the Jewish and Christian World 200 BC to AD 200 2; Cambridge: CUP, 1987), 115.

[25] See Metso, 'Whom Does the Term Yaḥad Identify?,' 225 and eadem, *The Textual Development of the Qumran Community Rule* (STDJ 21; Leiden: Brill, 1997), 135. She is tempted to speculate that the places visited by the Yaḥadists were camps, which may account for the similarities between 1QS 6 and CD 12:22 ff., 'Whom Does the Term Yaḥad Identify?,' 226–227.

[26] *Rome and Jerusalem: A Clash of Ancient Civilizations* (London: Allen Lane, 2007), esp. 239–242. It is interesting to note the strong similarities and differences between the direction taken by John Collins, Alison Schofield and myself. We share a less Qumran-centric vision, but

5. CD 13:2b–3a: A Council-Free Version of 1QS 6:3

The material describing small-scale gatherings legislated upon in the opening lines of column 6 of the Community Rule from Cave 1 and its parallels in Cave 4 has been at the centre of some of the recent debates outlined briefly above. In the remainder of this chapter I would like to focus on one tiny but important detail rightly highlighted by two of my colleagues. Both Metso and Collins have astutely pointed out that when 1QS 6:3 refers to a gathering of ten – the small-scale aspect of which is a linchpin of my own interpretation – the ten are said to be "from the council of the community." In other words, the preposition מן (here "from") seems to indicate that the organization as a whole – of which these ten form a part– is much larger.[27] The significance of the preposition מן deserves more thought than I devoted to it in a footnote in my aforementioned article.[28] The impasse which the מן may bring about with regard to my theory can be breached however. The clues are found in one of the exciting passages of inter-textual intimacy that we come across between the Rule and the Damascus Document.[29] As is well known, a remarkably similar statement to the one in 1QS 6:3 is attested also in CD 13:2–3.

The close literary relationship between both texts at other points, especially in the penal codes, makes reference to the Damascus Document in the search for the earliest form of a shared passage methodologically acceptable here.[30]

---

in my case the focus is temporal on the pre-Yaḥad situation, the fossil approach. In their case the arguments seem to focus more on the geographically spread-out reality of the phenomenon. Both hypotheses share a broader perspective which is sure to stimulate further fruitful debate in the next decade. In a provocative article Robert Kugler, interestingly, has just moved in the opposite direction and argues for traces of sectarian redaction in works generally considered non-sectarian referring to them as "hitherto unrecognized 'sectarian' compositions," cf. Robert A. Kugler, 'Whose Scripture? Whose Community? Reflections on the Dead Sea Scrolls Then and Now, By Way of Aramaic Levi,' *DSD* 15 (2008): 5–23. Beyond the level of the reception history of these texts, i. e. how they might have been read and received by members of the Yaḥad, I remain unconvinced of his case.

[27] Metso stresses that the presence of the preposition in 1QS 6, and only here in S, is one of several factors that marks the material as an interpolation, cf. 'Whom Does the Term Yaḥad Identify?,' 218. See also Collins, 'Nature and Aims of the Sect,' 42 and idem, 'The Yaḥad and the "Qumran Community,"' 88–89.

[28] Cf. Hempel, 'Emerging Communal Life and Ideology,' 46 n. 14, see now Chapter 5 above, esp. n. 14.

[29] On the importance of similarities alongside differences between D and S see now John Collins, 'Sectarian Consciousness in the Dead Sea Scrolls,' 183.

[30] See Steven D. Fraade, 'Ancient Jewish Law and Narrative in Comparative Perspective: The Damascus Document and the Mishnah,' in *Diné Israel: An Annual of Jewish Law* 24 (2007): 65–99 (reprinted in idem, *Legal Fictions: Studies of Law and Narrative in the Discoursive Worlds of Ancient Jewish Sectarians and Sages* [JSJS 147; Leiden: Brill, 2011], 227–254) and Charlotte Hempel, 'CD Manuscript B and the Community Rule: Reflections on a Literary Relationship,' *DSD* 16 (2009): 370–387, reprinted as Chapter 8 in this volume.

The key texts are as follows,

1QS 6:2c–4a//4Q258 (4QS^d)//4Q261 (4QS^g)//4Q263 (S^i)[31]

ויחד יואכלו ויחד יברכו ויחד יועצו
ובכול מקום אשר יהיה שם עשרה
אנשים מעצת היחד אל ימש מאתם איש
כוהן

And together they shall eat, together they shall pray, and together they shall exchange counsel. And in every place where there are found ten people from the council of the community a priest shall be present.

CD 13:2b–3a (not preserved in 4QD)[32]

ובמקום עשרה אל ימש איש כהן מבונן
בספר ההגי על פיהו ישקו כולם

And in a place of ten there shall not be lacking a priest learned in the Book of Hagi. All of them shall obey him.

In light of the evidence of the Damascus Document there is no doubt in my mind that we have to allow for a stage in the circulation of this passage that lacked any association with the council of the community – a council-free version of the passage. In its present context in CD, the passage containing the reference to the quorum of ten is attached to the previous statement (the division of the camp community into thousands, hundreds, fifties and tens) on the basis of the catchword "ten" and forms part of a piece of legislation on the organization of the camps.[33] It is noteworthy that the statement on a quorum of ten is rather loosely connected to the macro-structures of the camps in the Damascus Document. The related passage in the Community Rule is similarly loosely connected to its context since it is found in a passage that contains a diverse collection of regulations in 1QS 6:1c–8a. If we consider further the very fact that the same item of legislation is attested in both D and S, all of these indications taken together give the impression of a tradition that pre-dates both compositions. It is likely that such an independent tradition was incorporated into two rather different contexts in D and S where it evolved in different ways.[34] As far as S is concerned the passage falls within my own category of early S strata that run across the manuscript spectrum before the manuscripts went their separate ways, so to speak.[35] Whether we follow the Geza Vermes/Sarianna Metso line[36] that

---

[31] The Hebrew text is taken from the edition by Martin Abegg, in *The Dead Sea Scrolls Electronic Library* (ed. Emanuel Tov; Leiden: Brill, revised edition 2006), henceforth *DSSEL*.

[32] The Hebrew text is taken from *DSSEL* (Abegg); see also 1QS 6:6b–7a and 1QSa 2:21–22.

[33] Cf. Charlotte Hempel, *The Laws of the Damascus Document: Sources, Traditions and Redaction* (STDJ 29; Leiden: Brill, 1990; Paperback edition Atlanta, Ga.: SBL, 2006), 107–114.

[34] Cf. Hempel, *Laws of the Damascus Document*, 111.

[35] See Charlotte Hempel, 'The Literary Development of the S Tradition – A New Paradigm,' *RQ* 22 (2006): 389–401, reprinted as Chapter 7 below; cf. also Schofield, 'Rereading S,' 87–88.

[36] See Metso, *Textual Development*, 89–90 and Geza Vermes, 'Preliminary Remarks on Unpublished Fragments of the Community Rule from Cave 4,' *JJS* 42 (1991): 250–255.

1QS is expansive over against 4Q258 (4QS^d) or Philip Alexander's position[37] that 1QS was abbreviated in 4QS^d, the material in common between 1QS/4QS^d must predate the parting of the ways between 1QS and 4QS.

To bring my discussion of this particular example to a close: the full impact of the preposition מן in the 1QS 6 passage deserves due acknowledgment and consideration. It is equally short-sighted, however, to read the 1QS 6 passage in isolation from the occurrence of a sister passage in an entirely different context in CD 13. In the end, taking both of these considerations seriously seems to indicate that both the fossil and the sprout hypothesis encapsulate parts of the truth: what started as a fossil eventually sprouted – at least literarily through the addition of "from the council of the community" in 1QS 6:3.[38] I am thus left, like Metso, with a sprouting fossil view although I remain unconvinced about her travelling Yaḥadists theory.

6. Conclusion

To conclude, it is a commonplace to refer to Qumran as offering a unique window into Second Temple Judaism.[39] What I tried to reflect upon in this chapter is, in essence, the question what sort of a view we get out of that window. Because it is in the nature of windows that they do not allow us to scan the entire horizon, it is possible that some of the landscape we see in the texts may span across a much wider area.[40]

---

[37] See Philip Alexander, 'The Redaction-History of *Serekh ha-Yaḥad*: A Proposal,' *RQ* 17 (1996): 437–453.

[38] My own conclusion comes close to Metso's view when she astutely observes, "Since the passages are often thematically very similar, we may suspect that they have undergone redaction in light of each other, perhaps changing the details of the settings from which they originated, and also to have undergone reworking in the contexts in which they were inserted." ('Whom Does the Term Yaḥad Identify?,' 215). Metso is to be commended for studying the references to gatherings of ten in 1QS 6 from a broad perspective that incorporates CD and other texts beyond. See further Stephen J. Hultgren, *From the Damascus Covenant to the Covenant of the Community: Literary, Historical, and Theological Studies in the Dead Sea Scrolls* (STDJ 66; Leiden: Brill, 2007), 215–216 and Lawrence H. Schiffman, *Sectarian Law in the Dead Sea Scrolls: Courts, Testimony and the Penal Code* (BJS 33; Chico: Scholars Press, 1983), 84–85.

[39] See recently Schuller, *Dead Sea Scrolls*, 22.

[40] For nuanced reflections on such questions see Michael Stone, 'The Dead Sea Scrolls and the Literary Landscape.'

Part III

The Community Rule Traditions

Chapter Seven

Shifting Paradigms Concerning the Literary Development of the Serekh[1]

1. Introduction and History of Research

This chapter addresses the much-debated question of the literary growth of the Community Rule tradition. This issue has attracted a considerable amount of scholarly interest. In the days prior to the publication of the Cave 4 manuscripts the groundbreaking analysis of the 'genèse littéraire' of 1QS offered by Murphy O'Connor and its acceptance with some modifications by Pouilly were the dominant contributions on this topic.[2] Since the announcement of important variants in a number of 4QS manuscripts by Józef Milik in 1960[3] and the subsequent disclosure of one of the most important cases by Geza Vermes in 1991,[4] scholars have naturally shifted their attention to analyses of the new and revealing textual witnesses. In the years that followed the divergences between 1QS and 4Q256 (4QS^b) and 4Q258 (4QS^d), in particular, became the subject of a large number of articles[5] as well as a seminal and influential monograph.[6]

---

[1] This chapter was originally published as 'The Literary Development of the S-Tradition: A New Paradigm,' *RQ* 22 (2006): 389–401. I benefited greatly from being able to present versions of this chapter in a number of learned seminars and would like to take this opportunity to thank those present at these events for their comments, especially the respective chairs Profs. Geza Vermes (Oxford), Prof. William Horbury (Cambridge), Prof. Moshe Bernstein (New York), Prof. Marty Abegg (Trinity Western), and Prof. David Parker (Birmingham).

[2] Cf. Jerome Murphy-O'Connor, 'La genèse littéraire de la Règle de la Communauté,' *RB* 76 (1969): 528–549 and Jean Pouilly, *La Règle de la Communauté de Qumrân: Son évolution littéraire* (Cahiers de la Revue Biblique 17; Paris: Gabalda, 1976).

[3] Józef T. Milik, 'Textes des variantes des dix manuscrits de la Règle de la Communauté trouves de la Grotte 4: Recension de P. Wernberg Møller, The Manual of Discipline,' *RB* 67 (1960): 410–416.

[4] Geza Vermes, 'Preliminary Remarks on Unpublished Fragments of the Community Rule from Qumran Cave 4,' *JJS* 42 (1991): 250–255.

[5] See, e. g., Philip S. Alexander, 'The Redaction-History of *Serekh ha-Yaḥad*: A Proposal,' *RQ* 17 (1996): 437–453; Albert I. Baumgarten, 'The Zadokite Priests at Qumran: A Reconsideration,' *DSD* 4 (1997): 137–156; Markus Bockmuehl, 'Redaction and Ideology in the Rule of the Community (1QS/4QS),' *RQ* 18 (1998): 541–560; James H. Charlesworth and Brent A. Strawn, 'Reflections on the Text of Serek ha-Yaḥad Found in Cave IV,' *RQ* 17 (1996): 403–435; Paul Garnet, 'Cave 4 MS Parallels to 1QS 5:1–7: Towards a *Serek* Text History,' *JSP* 15 (1997): 67–78; Charlotte Hempel, 'Comments on the Translation of 4QSd I,1,' *JJS* 44 (1993): 127–128; and Michael A. Knibb, 'Rule of the Community,' in EDSS 2:793–797.

[6] Cf. Sarianna Metso, *The Textual Development of the Qumran Community Rule* (STDJ 21;

The particular textual issues highlighted by Vermes were the striking differences between the opening words of 1QS 5 and 4Q258 (4QS^d) 1 and 4Q256 (4QS^b) 9. It is probably no exaggeration to say that these differences have become a linchpin in one's assessment of the relationship of the various manuscript traditions of S to one another and the related matter of the literary development of the S tradition. The key passages in translation read as follows,[7]

1QS	4Q258 (4QS^b) and 4Q256 (4QS^d) – Composite Text
5^1 *And this is the rule for* **the people of the community** who eagerly volunteer to turn back from all evil and to hold fast to all that He has commanded *as His wish.* They shall keep separate from the congregation of ^{2}the **people of injustice** to form a community with regard to law and wealth. They shall be accountable to **the sons of Zadok, the priests who keep the covenant and to the multitude of the people of** ^{3}**the community who hold fast to the covenant.** *On their authority decisions shall be taken* regarding any matter pertaining to law, wealth …	b^1/d^1 *Midrash for the* **Maskil** *over (or: concerning)* **the people of the law** who eagerly volunteer to turn back from all evil and to hold fast to all] ^{b2}that He has commanded. ^{d2}They shall keep separate from the congregation of the **people of injustice** to form a community with regard to la[w] and wealth. They shall be accountable ^{b3}to **the many** regarding any matter ^{d3}pertaining to law and wealth …

The key issue raised by this material, as is immediately obvious, is the lack of the lengthy sons of Zadok passage in 4Q256 and 4Q258 which have instead "the many" (הרבים) in a position of authority. This difference has led Vermes, convincingly in my view, to propose that 4Q258 (4QS^d) offers the more original text which was reworked in favour of the Zadokites in 1QS. The sons of Zadok are placed in authority alongside the multitude of the people of the community (רוב אנשי היחד), though the way in which the former group is singled out leaves little doubt in the reader's mind as to their prominence in the coalition.[8] There

---

Leiden: Brill, 1997). See also Catherine Murphy, *Wealth in the Dead Sea Scrolls and in the Qumran Community* (STDJ 40; Leiden: Brill, 2002), 103–117 for an admirably clear exposition of the evidence.

[7] Here and throughout this chapter I have relied on the editions of the Hebrew text by Elisha Qimron (PTSDSSP 1:6–50) for 1QS and Philip S. Alexander and Geza Vermes (DJD 26) for the 4QS manuscripts. English translations are my own.

[8] For an overview over leadership in the Scrolls with further bibliography see Charlotte Hempel, 'Community Structures in the Dead Sea Scrolls: Admission, Organization, Disciplinary Procedures,' in *The Dead Sea Scrolls After Fifty Years: A Comprehensive Assessment*

is a case to be made for this Zadokite redaction having left its mark all across the scroll including the two appendices to the Community Rule in the Cave 1 manuscript, 1QSa and 1QSb. I have tried to make such a case with reference to 1QSa elsewhere,[9] and Vermes himself has frequently noted the presence of Zadokite endorsements in all three compositions, though our conclusions differ considerably.[10] Vermes's hypothesis on the development reflected in 1QS 5 and 4Q256 (4QS^b) and 4Q258 (4QS^d) was subsequently confirmed in more detail by Metso's study.[11]

In general, Vermes's initial analysis has found almost universal support. The biggest challenge was voiced by Philip Alexander who in essence pointed out that since the copy of 1QS is palaeographically earlier than 4Q256 (4QS^b) and 4Q258 (4QS^d) we should allow very seriously for the possibility that the earlier copy also offers the more original text.[12] Although I have aligned myself with Vermes and Metso rather than Alexander on this question, the argument put forward in what follows stands independently of either position.

Since 1998 we are, furthermore, in the fortunate position of having Alexander and Vermes's *editio princeps* of the 4QS manuscripts available.[13] With this scholarly tool at our fingertips, it seems to me that this is a good time to look at a number of the issues raised by the evidence of the 4QS manuscripts again and to reconsider our initial assessment of this material. The editors of DJD 26 identify four recensions of S:

A (1QS)
B (4QS^b and 4QS^d) which is subdivided into B^1 (4QS^b) and B^2 (4QS^d)
C (4QS^e)
D (4QS^g).[14]

(ed. Peter W. Flint and James C. VanderKam; Leiden: Brill, 1999), vol. II, 67–92, esp. 79–84, reprinted as Chapter 2 in this volume.

[9] Charlotte Hempel, 'The Earthly Essene Nucleus of 1QSa,' *DSD* 3 (1996): 253–267, reprinted as Chapter 3 in the present volume.

[10] Geza Vermes, 'The Leadership of the Qumran Community: Sons of Zadok – Priests – Congregation,' in *Geschichte – Tradition – Reflexion: Festschrift für Martin Hengel zum 70. Geburtstag* (ed. Hubert Cancik, Hermann Lichtenberger, and Peter Schäfer; Tübingen: Mohr Siebeck, 1996), Vol. I, 375–384. See also Robert Kugler, 'A Note on 1QS 9:14: The Sons of Righteousness or the Sons of Zadok,' *DSD* 3 (1996): 315–320. A close relationship between 1QS, 1QSa and 1QSb is further proposed in DJD 26:10 (Alexander and Vermes).

[11] For bibliographical references see notes 4–6 above. More recent supporters of Vermes's initial assessment include John Collins, 'Forms of Community in the Dead Sea Scrolls,' in *Emanuel: Studies in Hebrew Bible, Septuagint, and the Dead Sea Scrolls in Honor of Emanuel Tov* (ed. Shalom M. Paul et al.; VTSup 94; Leiden: Brill, 2003), 97–111 and in the same volume Eibert J. C. Tigchelaar, 'The Scribe of 1QS,' 439–452.

[12] See Alexander, 'Redaction-History' and table 7 in DJD 26:24 (Alexander and Vermes).

[13] DJD 26.

[14] See DJD 26:12 (Alexander and Vermes).

Finally, with an important monograph on the textual development of the Community Rule and a good number of scholarly papers and articles she has published since Sarianna Metso has made a substantial contribution to this debate.[15]

The discussion to date has, in short, focused on attempts to find agreement about the recensional sequence of the manuscripts. More particularly one of the cruxes of the debate has been whether or not the palaeographically earlier 1QS recension represents a more developed form of the Rule.

The direction which my own assessment of the evidence is moving towards is a more complex and less rigid assessment of the manuscripts. On looking at the evidence closely it strikes me as sensible to move away from considering the growth of the S tradition *exclusively* in terms of the number of preserved manuscripts or manuscript families. In my view the manuscripts clearly testify to complex literary developments and interrelationships, and these developments are not confined to the boundaries of any of the preserved manuscripts. To be fair, in principle Metso already allowed for a significant amount of complexity. Thus, in her introduction to chapter 3 on the literary development of the Community Rule she observes,

> It is unlikely that every individual stage of the redactional process of the Community Rule can be detected on the basis of the twelve preserved manuscripts.[16]

More recently Metso has made a related point very succinctly when she argues, "There is no reason to presume that 4QS^d would have preserved the very *Urtext* of the Serek."[17] These remarks are most welcome and touch on the issues I am concerned with here.

However, as far as 4QS is concerned scholarship to date has tended *in practice* to read the evidence of the primary manuscripts as though they represent something akin to solid building blocks in the growth of the tradition. This seems to be the underlying view of Vermes when he wrote in 1992 that columns 5 onwards of 1QS are "faithfully represented by 4QS^d."[18] As far as Metso's careful and detailed analysis of the textual growth is concerned,[19] I do not think I am misrepresenting her by highlighting the way in which complexity has entered her analysis somewhat one-sidedly, that is on the side of 1QS over against 4QS.[20]

---

[15] See especially Metso, *Textual Development* and, e. g., eadem, 'In Search of the Sitz im Leben of the Community Rule,' in *The Provo International Conference on the Dead Sea Scrolls: Technological Innovations, New Texts and Reformulated Issues* (ed. Donald W. Parry and Eugene Ulrich; STDJ 30; Leiden: Brill, 1999), 306–315.

[16] *Textual Development*, 107.

[17] Sarianna Metso, 'Whom Does the Term Yaḥad Identify?,' in *Biblical Traditions in Transmission: Essays in Honour of Michael A. Knibb* (ed. Charlotte Hempel and Judith M. Lieu; JSJSup 111; Leiden: Brill, 2006), 213–235, here 220.

[18] Geza Vermes, 'Qumran Forum Miscellanea I,' *JJS* 43 (1992): 299–305, 301.

[19] This is clearly summarized in a stemma in *Textual Development*, 147.

[20] An exception is 4Q259 (4QS^e) which looks as if it inspired not only the primitive stage O of her stemma but also A, cf. *Textual Development*, 147.

Let me say a few words about the relevance in this context of what we may call *The Manchester Hypothesis*. We recall that Philip Alexander's view does allow for development on the part of the tradents/editors/authors of the 4QS manuscripts of S by proposing a shortening of 1QS's longer text. Crucially, however, his proposal does not deal with developments within the preserved parts of the text of 4QS, and the redactional activity envisaged by him is restricted to parts of the text of 4QS that differ from 1QS. Thus, in effect, Alexander treats the preserved text of the 4QS witnesses in much the same way as the otherwise opposing views of Vermes and Metso.

It is this influential principle that has dominated the debate in practice – i. e. that 4Q256 (4QS^b) and 4Q258 (4QS^d) constitute more or less solid stages in the history of the growth of the S tradition – that I would like to challenge both on the basis of a number of general considerations as well as on the basis of my reading of a number of key texts. It is easy to imagine how the excitement about finally having a host of different manuscripts of the text of S in front of us that were not available to the scholarly public for decades would initially result in a frantic focus on the variants between these new manuscripts and 1QS. And this endeavor has produced some very significant and important results that I do not wish to underestimate. It seems timely now to try and build on this initial phase of studies and maybe move beyond it in certain respects.

The bulk of the material preserved in 4Q258 (4QS^d) is made up of what one may call the constitutional core of S represented by 1QS 5–9//4QS. And for this material we have a considerable amount of manuscript evidence for change and redaction as manifest in the textual variants attested mainly by 1QS, 4Q256 (4QS^b), 4Q258 (4QS^d), and 4Q259 (4QS^e). It is more than likely that this kind of material evolved and developed also where there is no clear-cut manuscript evidence other than inconsistencies within individual manuscripts. Firstly, the evidence of the manuscripts leaves us in little doubt about the fluidity and adaptability of this type of material. And secondly, there are no sound reasons for supposing the preserved manuscripts of S provide us with the full spectrum of witnesses on the growth of this text. In this context it is worth noting the multiple attestation of a number of traditions found in S also in two other texts, i. e. the penal code in the Damascus Document and several types of material (some penal) in 4Q265 (4QMiscellaneous Rules *olim* Serekh Damascus).[21] Such multiple,

---

[21] On the complex development of the penal codes see Joseph M. Baumgarten, 'The Cave 4 Versions of the Qumran Penal Code,' *JJS* 43 (1992): 268–276; Charlotte Hempel, 'The Penal Code Reconsidered,' in *Legal Texts and Legal Issues: Proceedings of the Second Meeting of the International Organization for Qumran Studies, Published in Honour of Joseph M. Baumgarten* (ed. Moshe Bernstein, Florentino García Martínez, and John Kampen; STDJ 23; Leiden: Brill, 1997), 337–348; and Sarianna Metso, 'The Relationship Between the Damascus Document and the Community Rule,' in *The Damascus Document: A Centennial of Discovery. Proceedings of the Third International Symposium of the Orion Center, 4–8*

yet independent attestations of shared tradition complexes – neither the penal material in the Damascus Document nor 4Q265 are simply copies or extracts of S – further underlines the likelihood that the material now found in the various recensions of S had a complex history.

2. Continuity Alongside Difference Between 1QS and 4QS

One area which I have recently published on strongly points in the direction outlined above. In an article that appeared in *Revue de Qumran* in 2003 I was able to show that despite the well-known variants between 1QS and 4Q256 (4QS^b)// 4Q258 (4QS^d), some equally stunning elements of continuity can be found such as the presence of references to the people of injustice.[22] This continuity between 1QS and 4QS is clearly evident even in the very same passage where we have the major disagreement on the sons of Zadok versus the many as it clearly emerges from the synoptic translation above.[23]

I do not wish to imply that others have not been aware of such elements of continuity, but it does seem worthwhile to try and incorporate this evidence more prominently and explicitly in our thinking. These shared features almost certainly go back to a very early common stratum in the growth of the tradition. It is theoretically possible to argue that they derive from a later redaction but the following considerations make this appear much less likely. Firstly, an early date for this material is indicated by the phenomenon that the people of injustice are regularly associated with the emerging community, at "defining moments".[24] Secondly, the "sons of Aaron" terminology unites manuscripts where other terms differ, giving the impression that these references have been left untouched by later differences. Thirdly, council of the community (עצת היחד) language, where it occurs exclusively (that is, not alongside the rabbim), is found in small scale

---

February 1998 (ed. Joseph M. Baumgarten, Esther G. Chazon, and Avital Pinnick; STDJ 34; Leiden: Brill, 2000), 85–93. On 4Q265 see DJD 35:57–78 (Baumgarten) and Charlotte Hempel, *The Damascus Texts* (CQS 1; Sheffield: Sheffield Academic Press, 2000), 89–104 and further literature referred to there.

[22] Charlotte Hempel, 'The Community and Its Rivals According to the Community Rule from Caves 1 and 4,' *RQ* 21 (2003): 47–81. The pronounced emphasis on separation from the people of injustice is also noted by John Collins recently, cf. 'Forms of Community in the Dead Sea Scrolls,' esp. 102.

[23] To this we may add another perhaps surprising element of continuity between 1QS and 4Q258 (4QS^d) which constitutes at the same time an element of discontinuity within the manuscripts of 1QS and 4Q258 (4QS^d) themselves: the alternative combination of the sons of *Aaron* and with the multitude of Israel is attested both in 1QS 5:21–22 and 4Q258 (4QS^d) 2 1–2. I have addressed these issues in Charlotte Hempel, 'Interpretative Authority in the Community Rule Tradition,' *DSD* 10 (2003): 59–80, esp. 76–79.

[24] Cf. Hempel, 'Community and Its Rivals,' 52.

contexts.²⁵ Finally, there is little evidence for a final redaction across the manuscripts, but rather the evidence indicates that the different manuscripts eventually went their separate ways. The common elements between them leave us with hints of what the tradition looked like before 'the parting of the ways.'

Applied to the text in 1QS 5//4Q258 (4QSᵈ) this would mean that preserved cases of continuity give us a taste of the earliest form of the traditions. To put it slightly differently, it seems to me worthwhile to look for the answer on the earliest form of the material beyond the question of which variant is the most original and to allow for the possibility that the common ground between the variants might hold a further important key to this question.

3. Diversity within 4Q258 (4QSᵈ)

One of the characteristics of 4Q258 that tells against considering this manuscript as representing a monolithic stage in the growth of S is a strong element of diversity within it. Thus, whereas "the many" are a key figure in 4Q258 1 1–3, another passage a little further on in 4Q258 1 5–7 does not mention the rabbim and refers instead to the council of the community (עצת היחד) with particular authority in the hands of the council of the people of the community (עצת אנש[י] [ה]יחד). The latter body appears here over against a further reference to the sons of Zadok in the 1QS text (1QS 5:9). We also note the complete absence in this passage of the term rabbim in both 1QS as well as 4Q256 (4QSᵇ) and 4Q258 (4QSᵈ) in favour of the council of the community.²⁶

Another telling example of diversity within 4Q258 is the endorsement of the authority of the sons of *Aaron* and the multitude of Israel in both 1QS 5:20–22 and the equivalent in 4Q258 mentioned earlier. In this passage both the sons of Zadok and the rabbim are conspicuously absent. This diversity within 1QS and 4Q258 (4QSᵈ) 2 1–2 over against earlier statements in each manuscript is telling. It is even more significant that both texts, despite being greatly at odds elsewhere, are fully in agreement here. This is again indicative of an early stratum in the growth of the S tradition as a whole as well as pointing in the direction of some form of literary history and complexity within 4Q258 (4QSᵈ).

---

²⁵ I have elaborated on this in Charlotte Hempel, 'Emerging Communal Life and Ideology in the S Tradition,' in *Defining Identities: We, You, and the Other in the Dead Sea Scrolls. Proceedings of the Fifth Meeting of the IOQS in Groningen* (ed. Florentino García Martínez and Mladen Popović; STDJ 70; Leiden: Brill, 2008), 43–61, reprinted as Chapter 5 in this volume.
²⁶ See also Hempel, 'Community and Its Rivals,' 48–52.

4. The Many in 1QS[27]

Since the authoritative role allotted to the many (ha-rabbim) in 4Q256 (4QS[b]) and 4Q258 (4QS[d]) which distinguished that tradition from the 'Zadokite rant' of 1QS 5 is one of the hotspots in the debate about their recensional relationship, it makes good sense to have a closer look at this term in 1QS. A glance at the old Kuhn *Konkordanz* sheds revealing light on the occurrence of the term in 1QS.[28] The term is absent from 1QS 1–5. Its absence from the first four columns is hardly surprising because of the different content of these columns which is broadly liturgical and theological over against the primarily constitutional content of 1QS 5–9. More importantly, a number of 4QS manuscripts (4Q258 [4QS[d]] and probably also 4Q259 ([4QS[e]][29]) seem to lack the equivalent of 1QS 1–4 altogether which suggests that there was a stage in the growth of the tradition when 1QS 5 onwards formed the beginning of the text as is indeed the case with 4Q258 (4QS[d]).[30] In short, the absence of an important constitutional term such a ha-rabbim in 1QS 1–4 is entirely plausible. Its absence in 1QS 5, even without the evidence of the 4QS[d/b] variants is rather astonishing especially when we contemplate the frequency of the term in 1QS 6–7.[31] It seems convincing to me to argue with Vermes that its presence in 4QS[b/d] over against 1QS 5 points to a Zadokite recension[32] in 1QS, but it is highly remarkable that this recension left rabbim terminology untouched once we reach 1QS 6 onwards. Turning to the evidence of 1QS 8, where rabbim occurs much more sporadically, we do however have a significant instance in 1QS 8:26 where 1QS preserves a reference to the authority of the rabbim (רבים[ה פי] ל[ע])[33] that is absent from the parallel in 4Q258 (4QS[d]) 7 1! This brief survey makes it clear that the rabbim tradition of 4QS[d/b] fame is extremely well established and strong in 1QS 6 onwards, in one case going over and above what is said in 4QS[d].

To sum up my discussion of the term rabbim in S, it appears that the evidence is rather complex. The terminology appears at times in 4QS[d] over against other terms in 1QS. Elsewhere the term is almost omnipresent in 1QS, especially in 1QS 6–7.

---

[27] On this term and further literature see Sarianna Metso, 'Qumran Community Structure and Terminology as Theological Statement,' *RQ* 20 (2002): 429–444, esp. 440–441. See also eadem, *Textual Development*, 77 n. 56.

[28] Cf. Karl Georg Kuhn, *Konkordanz zu den Qumrantexten* (Göttingen: Vandenhoeck & Ruprecht, 1960), 198–199.

[29] So Metso, *Textual Development*, 51.

[30] See DJD 26:85 (Alexander and Vermes) and Metso, *Textual Development*, 107.

[31] This is noted also by Vermes, 'Leadership of the Qumran Community,' 380.

[32] Vermes, 'Preliminary Remarks.'

[33] As read by Kuhn, *Konkordanz*, 199; see also PTSDSSP 1:38 (Qimron). The reading is certain despite the damage to the manuscript at this point, cf. DJD 26:112 where Alexander and Vermes note, "the tops of most of the missing letters have survived."

5. The Council of the Community in S[34]

On reading 1QS 6 onwards with a particular eye on the term rabbim I was struck by a clear conflation of this term with another expression, council of the community (עצת היחד), in a number of texts such as the rules on communal meetings (1QS 6:8b–13a//4Q256 [4QS^b] 11 5–8//4Q258 [4QS^d] 3 1–3) and in detailed prescriptions on admission into the community (1QS 6:13b–23//4Q256 [4QS^b] 11 8,11–13//4Q261 [4QS^g] 3 1). As we saw, both terms are attested also in 4Q258 (4QS^d, cf. 4QS^d 1 2 for rabbim and 4QS^d 1 5–7 for "council of the community"). Having noticed this striking conflation of both sets of terminology in 1QS, I began to look out for passages where each term appears in this manuscript without the other. The key passage on the council of the community is, of course, found in the opening lines of 1QS 8. It is noteworthy that in this passage the rabbim are never mentioned. The presence of passages that attest exclusively one set of terms indicates that the conflation is probably secondary.

Another example is the prescription on joining the community by swearing an oath in 1QS 5:7–10. I have written on this elsewhere emphasizing the differences between this simple admission procedure over against a more drawn out procedure laid down in 1QS 6:13–23 and their implications for the relationship of the Community Rule and the Damascus Document.[35] My chief concern then was to demonstrate that the earlier 1QS passage shares the simple procedure of swearing an oath of admission with CD 15. Here I would like to look at the two admission passages in 1QS 5 and 1QS 6 again within the context of 1QS alone. It is interesting how both passages, despite important differences, begin with a heading that has the council of the community as its central designation. In the latter and longer passage this terminology is rather awkwardly synonymous with rabbim in the body of the legislation. Noteworthy is that the 1QS 5 passage which describes the more primitive state of affairs on my reading of it, does not include a single reference to the rabbim either in 1QS or in 4QS$^{d/b}$. This is particularly striking in 1QS 5:9 where 1QS again has the sons of Zadok and the people of their covenant in charge over against 4Q256 (4QS^b) 9 8//4Q258 (4QS^d) 1 7–8 – manuscripts which previously focused on "the many" but now endorse the council of the people of the community.

To summarize the discussion of passages that speak exclusively of the council of the community the following observations can be made. In evaluating the evidence I tried to uncover clues of the distinctiveness of each tradition that emerged before they became conflated and their distinctiveness blurred.

---

[34] On this term and further literature see Sarianna Metso, 'Qumran Community Structure and Terminology as Theological Statement,' *RQ* 20 (2002): 429–444, esp. 440–441. See also eadem, *Textual Development*, 77 n. 56.

[35] Hempel, 'Community Structures,' 70–73.

Whereas rabbim is an administrative term[36] that occurs in highly structured and evolved, pragmatic communal rules, the council of the community terminology *by itself* usually occurs in more primitive, small scale settings,[37] often alongside lofty, ideological language and at times in a cultic setting, cf. the famous material on the community replacing the cult in 1QS 8.[38] The rabbim are led by a mebaqqer and a paqid, officials with specific titles who may or may not be identical with one another or be priests.[39] The council of the community, by contrast, is led by priests, in 1QS 6:3 by *a* priest and in 1QS 8:2 by three priests opposite twelve lay members. It seems likely, therefore, that the terms rabbim and "council of the community" emerged in distinct literary – and probably also communal – settings and were eventually conflated in parts of the S tradition.

This initial conclusion based on the evidence of S can draw further support from a wider body of texts that point in the same direction. Thus, 4Q265 at times attests the same conflation of terminology we observed in S (cf. 4Q265 4 ii). Elsewhere in the short but revealing passage on the council of the community in 4Q265 7 7–10 the council of the community is described as a small scale event with no reference to the rabbim. In the Damascus Document, by contrast, we find occasional references to the rabbim but none to the council of the community. Finally, and perhaps most fascinatingly, in 1QSa – on the same scroll as 1QS – we find four references to the council of the community in this relatively short composition but none to the rabbim.

In sum, we identified a small number of passages in both 1QS and 4QS[d] which employ "council of the community" language with no reference to the rabbim. What seems to have happened in the growth of the S tradition is a merging of previously independent traditions that resulted in the blurring of their distinc-

---

[36] Cf. Metso, *Textual Development*, 77 where she notes the "administrative connotation" of the term ha-rabbim.

[37] The opening lines of 1QS 6 have recently aroused a great deal of scholarly interest. I have argued elsewhere that 1QS 6 represents a hotchpotch of relatively primitive pieces of communal legislation. Moreover, I identify 1QS 6:3–4 as the most primitive communal set-up in S. Both there and in 1QS 8:1 ff., which speaks of a small scale context of fifteen members, we have council of the community terminology and a notable absence of rabbim, cf. Hempel, 'Emerging Communal Life' and 'Interpretative Authority.' 61–68. For a different assessment see Metso, 'Whom Does the Term Yaḥad Indentify?;' Collins, 'Forms of Community;' idem, 'The Yaḥad and the "Qumran Community,"' in *Biblical Traditions in Transmission* (ed. Hempel and Lieu), 81–95; and Eyal Regev, 'The *Yaḥad* and the *Damascus Covenant*: Structure, Organization and Relationship,' *RQ* 21 (2003): 233–262.

[38] See also Johann Maier, 'Purity at Qumran: Cultic and Domestic,' in *Judaism in Late Antiquity. Part V: The Judaism of Qumran. A Systemic Reading of the Dead Sea Scrolls* (ed. Alan J. Avery-Peck, Jacob Neusner, and Bruce D. Chilton; HdO 57; Leiden: Brill, 2001), 91–124, esp. 109. The terminology "council of the community" is curiously also prominent in the *pesharim*. The polemical tone of the latter seems to suggest, however, that they go back to a different period in the history of the community. This terminological congruence is nevertheless noteworthy and deserves further study.

[39] See Metso, *Textual Development*, 77 and Hempel, 'Community Structures,' 79–84.

tiveness. The evidence points to a rabbim take-over in the S tradition (literary or otherwise) which occurred at some point before the Zadokite coup in evidence in 1QS 5.[40]

6. Conclusion

To conclude, 4QS, and 4Q256 (4QS^b) 9 8 // 4Q258 (4QS^d) 1 7–8 in particular, shed a vast amount of new light on the complex growth and redaction of the S tradition by providing invaluable firsthand physical evidence. What I have tried to emphasize is that there is no need to assume that this high level of redaction and complex growth left individual manuscripts, especially also the Cave 4 manuscripts, untouched. In making my case I paid particular attention to internal discrepancies within individual manuscripts. This was, of course, all we had to go on in our study of the S tradition before the publication of 4QS. Now the 4QS evidence is fully available it is necessary to look beyond the admittedly important discrepancies between manuscripts and to appreciate the complete picture of discrepancies between and within manuscripts, as well as continuity between manuscripts. Spreading our scholarly nets wider in the way outlined above will not diminish the important witness of the new evidence, but rather lead to fuller appreciation of it. My concrete conclusions point towards the presence of smaller, inter-related layers of material across the manuscript spectrum, such as the people of injustice stratum,[41] the material allotting pivotal authority to the sons of *Aaron* in both 1QS and 4QS^d, and finally a group of passages that speak exclusively in terms of the council of the community attested both in 1QS and 4QS^d. An avenue for future study is to take the evidence of relevant portions of the Damascus Document and especially also 4Q265 more fully into account when we are dealing with the relevant portion of the S tradition touched upon in these external sources. I have noted some intriguing evidence on the council of the community and the rabbim outside of S which proved illuminating.

In thinking about these issues I have benefited a great deal from William McKane's insights on the growth of the book of the Jeremiah, and his work offers a suitable analogy in some respects.[42] I find it helpful to adopt his term "rolling corpus" for the growth of S (maybe adapted slightly to "rolling corpora") and prefer to think of the growth of the S tradition as a complex and evolving process, or more accurately several complex and evolving processes. The extant manuscripts of S provide no more and no less than snapshots of this process, stills in a moving picture.

---

[40] For evidence of a pre-Zadokite struggle with the people of injustice see 'Community and Its Rivals,' 55.
[41] See Hempel, 'Community and Its Rivals.'
[42] See Willam McKane, *Jeremiah* (ICC; Edinburgh: T & T Clark, 1986).

Part IV

Close Encounters:
The Community Rule and the Damascus Document

Chapter Eight

CD 19–20 and the Community Rule[1]

1. Introduction

One of the most important and debated literary relationships in the corpus of the Dead Sea Scrolls is that between the Damascus Document (D) and the Community Rule (S).[2] The relationship between both compositions to one another has been a central issue in Scrolls scholarship ever since it became clear that the Cairo Damascus Document shares the same provenance as those new texts soon after the discovery of the first Scrolls. The publication of eight Cave 4 manuscripts of the Damascus Document and ten Cave 4 manuscripts of the Community Rule has inaugurated a new phase in this enquiry.[3]

Both in the Community Rule and in the Damascus Document, legal material is often embedded in a non-legal framework such as admonitory and narrative material in the Damascus Document and admonitory material in the Community Rule. As far as the Damascus Document is concerned Steven Fraade has offered a thorough discussion of the relationship of its narrative and legal components suggesting that the document as a whole is best seen as "an anthology that was drawn upon so as to provide performative "scripts" [...] for the annual covenant renewal ceremony ...". [4] The issue of a connection between law, discipline, and obedience on the one hand, and communal liturgy on the other hand is also evident in both documents. Thus, the final section of the Damascus Document as now attested in the Cave 4 manuscripts contains an explicit reference to a gathering of the inhabitants of the camps in the third month (4Q266 [4QD^a] 11

---

[1] This chapter was originally published as 'CD Manuscript B and the Community Rule – Reflections on a Literary Relationship,' *DSD* 16 (2009): 370–387.

[2] A sizeable body of literature has been devoted to this issue. For some recent treatments which include earlier bibliography see Hilary Evans Kapfer, 'The Relationship Between the Damascus Document and the Community Rule: Attitudes Toward the Temple as a Test Case,' *DSD* 14 (2007): 152–177 and the succinct and valuable discussion in Alison Schofield, *From Qumran to the Yaḥad: A New Paradigm of Textual Development for the Community Rule* (STDJ 77; Leiden: Brill, 2009), 163–173.

[3] For an overview see Charlotte Hempel, 'Texts, Scribes and Scholars: Reflections on a Busy Decade in Dead Sea Scrolls Research,' *ExpTim* 120 (2009): 272–276.

[4] Steven D. Fraade, 'Ancient Jewish Law and Narrative in Comparative Perspective: The Damascus Document and the Mishnah,' *Diné Israel: An Annual of Jewish Law* 24 (2007): 65–99 (reprinted in idem, *Legal Fictions: Studies of Law and Narrative in the Discoursive Worlds of Ancient Jewish Sectarians and Sages* [JSJSup 147; Leiden: Brill, 2011]), here 87 [245].

1–20//4Q269 [4QD^d] 16//4Q270 [4QD^e] 7 i–ii), often thought to be a community internal covenant renewal ceremony.[5] In the Community Rule as attested by 1QS, 4Q255 (papS^a), 4Q256 (4QS^b), 4Q257 (papS^c), and 4Q262 (4QS^h) communal legislation and disciplinary issues are also presented in a broader liturgical context as witnessed by the inclusion of a covenant ceremony (or fragments thereof) in these manuscripts.[6] This liturgical bridge between some of the S manuscripts and D has also been noted by Ben Zion Wacholder when he observes, "… the author of the Rule of the Community begins his composition with MTA's [i. e. D's, C. H.] finale."[7]

The presence of significant overlap as well as differences between various parts of both documents has regularly occupied scholars. Chief among the overlapping texts are versions of the penal code in the Community Rule (1QS 6:24–7:25//4Q258 [4QS^d] 5 1//4Q259 (4QS^e) 1 4–15; 2 3–8//4Q261 (4QS^g) 3 2–4; 4a–b 1–7; 5a–c 1–9; 6a–e 1–5), the Damascus Document (CD 14:18b–22// 4Q266 [4QD^a] 10 i–ii//4Q267 [4QD^b] 9 vi//4Q269 [4QD^d] 11 i–ii; 4Q270 [4QD^e] 7 i), and also in 4Q265 (Miscellaneous Rules *olim* Serekh Damascus; 4Q265 4 i 2–ii 2), and 11Q29 (Fragment Related to Serekh ha-Yaḥad).[8] Although most extensively attested, the penal code is only one of several passages indicative of a close and complex literary relationship between the Community Rule

---

[5] See DJD 18:76–78, 162–167 (Baumgarten) and Charlotte Hempel, *The Laws of the Damascus Document: Sources, Traditions and Redaction* (STDJ 29; Leiden: Brill, 1990; pb. ed. Atlanta, Ga.: SBL, 2006), esp. 175–185; Hartmut Stegemann, 'More Identified Fragments of 4QD^d (4Q269),' *RQ* 18 (1998): 497–509, esp. 503–509; and Schofield, *From Qumran to the Yaḥad*, 165.

[6] For an overview see Table 1 in DJD 26:1–2 (Alexander and Vermes) and Sarianna Metso, *The Serekh Texts* (CQS 9/LSTS 62; London: T & T Clark, 2007).

[7] Cf. Ben Zion Wacholder, *The New Damascus Document: The Midrash on the Eschatological Torah of the Dead Sea Scrolls. Reconstruction, Translation and Commentary* (STDJ 56; Leiden: Brill, 2007), 367. Wacholder does not note the presence of S manuscripts such as 4Q258 (4QS^d) that lack the liturgical material found in 1QS 1–4. Thus, although his observation is illuminating, the overall picture to be drawn from the full spectrum of S manuscripts is more nuanced.

[8] See Joseph M. Baumgarten, 'The Cave 4 Versions of the Qumran Penal Code,' *JJS* 43 (1992): 268–276; Charlotte Hempel, 'The Penal Code Reconsidered,' in *Legal Texts and Legal Issues: Proceedings of the Second Meeting of the International Organization for Qumran Studies Published in Honour of Joseph M. Baumgarten* (ed. Moshe Bernstein, Florentino García Martínez, and John Kampen; STDJ 23; Leiden: Brill, 1997), 337–348; Jutta Jokiranta, 'Social Identity in the Qumran Movement: The Case of the Penal Code,' in *Explaining Christian Origins and Early Judaism: Contributions from Cognitive and Social Science* (ed. Petri Luomanen, Ilkka Pyysiäinen, and Risto Uro; BIS 89; Leiden: Brill, 2007), 277–298; Sarianna Metso, 'The Relationship Between the Damascus Document and the Community Rule,' in *The Damascus Document: A Centennial of Discovery. Proceedings of the Third International Symposium of the Orion Center, 4–8 February 1998* (ed. Joseph M. Baumgarten, Esther G. Chazon, and Avital Pinnick; STDJ 34; Leiden: Brill, 2000), 85–93; Aharon Shemesh, 'The Scriptural Background of the Penal Code in the *Rule of the Community* and *Damascus Document*,' *DSD* 15 (2008): 191–224; and Carol Newsom, *The Self as Symbolic Space: Constructing Identity and Community at Qumran* (STDJ 52; Leiden: Brill, 2004), 148–152.

and the Damascus Document. We may refer also to the intriguing overlapping requirement that a priest must be present in a place of ten. Sarianna Metso, John Collins, Eyal Regev, and myself have written on the latter topic recently.[9] Another very complicated area is the presence of rabbim terminology in both documents.[10]

Metso recently referred to this type of evidence as "inter-textual."[11] Schofield's assessment of the relationship between S and D as reflecting a "constant dialogic exchange" also captures the phenomena well.[12] The most pertinent evidence of this kind is collected in Eibert Tigchelaar's 'Annotated List of Overlaps and Parallels in the Non-biblical Texts from Qumran and Masada' in DJD 39.[13] The terminology Tigchelaar employs differs slightly from the one I have used above in as far as he refers to 'overlaps' in the context of various copies of the same composition and otherwise employs the term 'parallels' when referring to material from different compositions. The material he has collected is based chiefly on the indications of such evidence provided by various editors in the DJD Series supplemented by some of his own examples.[14] There is a lack of consistency, however, between the terminology employed in Tigchelaar's table and individual DJD volumes with DJD 26 – the 4QS volume edited by Philip Alexander and Geza Vermes – identifying both parallel manuscripts of the Community Rule and overlaps with other documents under the same heading as 'Parallels.'[15] This is also the practice in Joseph Baumgarten's edition of the Cave

---

[9] See John Collins, 'The Yaḥad and "The Qumran Community,"' in *Biblical Traditions in Transmission: Essays in Honour of Michael A. Knibb* (ed. Charlotte Hempel and Judith M. Lieu; JSJSup 111; Leiden: Brill, 2006), 81–96; Charlotte Hempel, 'Emerging Communal Life and Ideology in the S Tradition,' in *Defining Identities: We, You, and the Other in the Dead Sea Scrolls. Proceedings of the Fifth Meeting of the IOQS in Groningen* (ed. Florentino García Martínez and Mladen Popović; STDJ 70; Leiden: Brill, 2008), 43–61, reprinted as Chapter 5 in this volume; eadem, '1QS 6:2c–4a – Satellites or Precursors of the Yaḥad?,' in *The Dead Sea Scrolls and Contemporary Culture* (ed. Adolfo Roitman, Larry Schiffman, and Shani Tzoref; STDJ 93; Leiden: Brill, 2011), 31–40, reprinted as Chapter 6 in this volume; Sarianna Metso, 'Whom Does the Term Yaḥad Identify?,' in *Biblical Traditions in Transmission* (ed. Hempel and Lieu), 213–235; Eyal Regev, *Sectarianism in Qumran: A Cross-Cultural Perspective* (Religion and Society 45; Berlin: de Gruyter, 2007), 163–196. Further, Alison Schofield, 'Rereading S: A New Model of Textual Development in Light of the Cave 4 *Serekh* Copies,' *DSD* 15 (2008): 96–120.

[10] On this question see Regev, *Sectarianism in Qumran*, 163–196 and 269–300. See also Hempel, *Laws of the Damascus Document*, 81–85, 122–123, 135–136, 138–139, 178, 190; eadem, *The Damascus Texts* (CQS 1; Sheffield: Sheffield University Press, 2000), 51–52; and Schofield, *From Qumran to the Yaḥad*, 172–173.

[11] Cf. Sarianna Metso, 'Methodological Problems in Reconstructing History from Rule Texts Found at Qumran,' *DSD* 11 (2004): 315–335, esp. 330.

[12] Schofield, *From Qumran to the Yaḥad*, 164, see also 166.

[13] Eibert J. C. Tigchelaar, 'Annotated List of Overlaps and Parallels in the Non-biblical Texts from Qumran and Masada,' DJD 39:285–322, esp. 319–320.

[14] 'Annotated List of Overlaps and Parallels,' 287.

[15] See DJD 26:139 (Alexander and Vermes).

4 manuscripts of the Damascus Document in DJD 18.[16] To designate two such radically different pieces of evidence with the same term is both imprecise and revealing. Tigchelaar's efforts to list both types of correspondences separately are certainly a move in the right direction. Fraade coined the phrase 'synoptic 'intersections' in a recent comparative study of the Damascus Document and the Mishnah.[17] A close analysis of such overlaps sheds important light on a number of enquiries,

- The literary resemblances and differences between portions of text, such as the penal code, in a number of compositions can be drawn upon to try and map out the ways in which the material evolved.
- The presence of shared blocks of material in texts that are otherwise different in important ways indicates that these blocks originated independently of their place in the final documents in at least one of the texts and conceivably in both. It is hard to imagine, for instance, that two different authors composed the same list of offences often in the same sequence in both the Damascus Document and the Community Rule.
- Because the Damascus Document and the Community Rule deal with matters of communal life, those passages where the texts differ and those where they overlap will inevitably be crucial in discussions of the communities that are portrayed in those texts, be those portrayals historically accurate or not.[18]

An interesting further question we might want to raise is whether we are able to draw up a *profile of intersections*.[19] It emerges, first of all, very clearly from Tigchelaar's tables that the *Serekh* and the Damascus Document together with 4Q265 (Miscellaneous Rules *olim* Serekh Damascus) are the hub of what Fraade calls synoptic intersections in the non-biblical scrolls, attesting by far the largest number of instances.[20] In other words, the Community Rule and the Damascus Document are – for one reason or another – more closely related inter-textually than other Qumran texts. Moreover, my impression is that we find a proliferation of such inter-textual evidence in the area of community discipline, cf. the penal

---

[16] See DJD 18:62 (Baumgarten).

[17] Cf. Fraade, 'Damascus Document and Mishnah,' 93.

[18] On the latter question see the seminal study by Philip R. Davies, 'Redaction and Sectarianism in the Qumran Scrolls,' in *The Scriptures and the Scrolls: Studies in Honour of A. S. van der Woude on the Occasion of his 65th Birthday* (ed. Florentino García Martínez, Anthony Hilhorst, and Casper J. Labuschagne; VTSup 49; Leiden: Brill, 1992), 152–163; Sarianna Metso, 'In Search of the Sitz im Leben of the Community Rule,' in *The Provo International Conference on the Dead Sea Scrolls: Technological Innovations, New Texts, and Reformulated Issues* (ed. Donald W. Parry and Eugene Ulrich; STDJ 30; Leiden: Brill, 1999), 306–315; eadem, 'Methodological Problems;' and Maxine L. Grossman, *Reading for History in the Damascus Document: A Methodological* Study (STDJ 45; Leiden: Brill, 2002).

[19] The idea of a profile of inter-textual connections between S and D is explored more fully in Chapter 9 below.

[20] Cf. Tigchelaar, 'Annotated List of Overlaps and Parallels,' 319–320.

codes as well as the less formally cohesive penal material in CD 20 and 1QS 8 to be dealt with in more detail below. In other words, the texts are closest and more elaborate when it comes to the stick rather than the carrot. Also interesting to note is the presence of penal material both at the end of the Admonition and near the end of the Damascus Document as a whole as now preserved in 4Q266 (4QD^a) 11, 4Q269 (4QD^d) 16, and 4Q270 (4QD^e) 7. It needs to be acknowledged, however, that we are no longer in a position to say categorically that CD 20 preserves the end of the Admonition without at least noting the fluid to and fro between law and admonitory material in the document as it now emerges.[21] It suffices to quote one of the more recent statements on this issue by Ben Zion Wacholder who rightly notes, "the two themes [i. e. legal and admonitory] are constantly interwoven".[22] What we can say with some justification, it seems to me, is that when the Damascus Document was redacted and reached its final form discipline and penal material ('the stick') was clearly a major issue.[23] Such matters play a large role in the Community Rule also where they are found repeatedly in the central columns of the manuscripts. In short, disciplinary material plays a major role at three levels,
– in the Community Rule
– in the Damascus Document
– and where both texts intersect when they intersect.

This seems to indicate that the issue of discipline and commitment was particularly crucial when the Damascus Document was completed and when the Community Rule was compiled.[24]

2. CD 20:1–8 and the Community Rule

It is exactly another such passage which has often been noted as exemplifying a close relationship between the Community Rule and the Damascus Document that I would like to deal with in more detail here. I am referring to CD 20:1b–8a

---

[21] See Hartmut Stegemann, 'Towards Physical Reconstructions of the Qumran Damascus Document Scrolls,' in *The Damascus Document* (ed. Baumgarten, Chazon, and Pinnick), 177–200.

[22] Wacholder, *The New Damascus Document*, 12.

[23] Cf. Carol Newsom's description of the community that emerges from her reading of the Serekh ha-Yaḥad in light of the work of Michel Foucault as a 'disciplinary institution,' cf. Newsom, *The Self as Symbolic Space*, esp. 95–101.

[24] Alison Schofield is correct when she also emphasizes that the inter-textual encounters appear to be located near or at the point of the Damascus Document's final redaction. Cf. "In the history of ideas, these two texts parallel each other in many ways, and the final redactor(s) of D, at least, must have been familiar with the other (S) tradition," *From Qumran to the Yaḥad*, 165, see also 167–168.

and its relationship to 1QS 8–9. In 1972 Jerome Murphy-O'Connor pointedly observed,

> Had CD XX,1c–8a been found as an isolated fragment it would have been presumed that it belonged to the Rule ...[25]

In 1987 Michael Knibb noted in his comments on CD 20 that CD 20:1b–8a,

> stands apart from the rest of the passage. It deals with the temporary expulsion of erring members and is similar in character to 1QS 8:16b–9:2.[26]

In 1991 Philip Davies wrote,

> I shall consider here what I regard as the strongest individual case of direct correspondence between CD and 1QS, namely sections of the material in each document which overlap both literarily and, it would seem, also historically: CD XIX,33b–XX,34 and 1QS VIII–IX.[27]

Davies concluded his 1991 article with the statement,

> ... one could argue [...] that the group reflected in CD XX and 1QS IX are one and the same, and indeed, at more or less the same moment.[28]

The purpose of this study is to revisit this fascinating discussion in light of the texts published since the earlier studies by Murphy-O'Connor, Knibb, and Davies, in particular the Cave 4 manuscripts of the Community Rule.[29] One of the most striking developments we can now trace, but could not then, is the fact that the material with the closest overlap between 1QS 8–9 and CD 20 is absent from 4Q259 (4QS^e, see 4Q259 3 esp. line 6).[30] Metso has explained 4Q259's considerably shorter text as a witness to a more original stage in the growth of S.[31] Others prefer to explain the evidence of 4Q259 (4QS^e) as a secondarily shortened text, either shortened deliberately (so Philip Alexander)[32] or accidentally (so Émile Puech and James VanderKam).[33] Metso's hypothesis seems more

---

[25] Murphy-O'Connor, 'A Literary Analysis of Damascus Document XIX,33–XX,34,' *RB* 79 (1972): 544–564, 554–555.

[26] Michael A. Knibb, *The Qumran Community* (Cambridge Commentaries on Writings of the Jewish and Christian World 200 BC to AD 200 2; Cambridge: CUP, 1987), 71, cf. also 72.

[27] Philip R. Davies, 'Communities at Qumran and the Case of the Missing "Teacher,"' *RQ* 15 (1991): 275–286 (reprinted in idem, *Sects and Scrolls: Essays on Qumran and Related Topics* [South Florida Studies in the History of Judaism 134; Atlanta, Ga.: Scholars Press, 1996], 139–150], here 276 [139–140]. Cf. 1QS 9:9–10 and CD 20:31–32.

[28] 'Communities at Qumran and the Case of the Missing "Teacher,"' 283.

[29] See esp. DJD 26 (Alexander and Vermes).

[30] Cf. DJD 26:144–149 (Alexander and Vermes).

[31] See Sarianna Metso, 'The Primary Results of the Reconstruction of 4QS^e,' *JJS* 44 (1993): 303–308.

[32] Philip S. Alexander, 'The Redaction-History of Serekh ha-Yaḥad: A Proposal,' *RQ* 17 (1996): 437–453.

[33] Cf. Émile Puech, 'Recension: J. Pouilly, La Règle de la Communauté de Qumrân. Son evolution littéraire,' *RQ* 10 (1979): 103–111 and James C. VanderKam, 'Messianism in the

likely to me.³⁴ This is important because it might indicate that the close relationship between 1QS 8–9 and CD 20 outlined by Davies and others is essentially confined to a particular block of material in 1QS that may be secondary.

It deserves mentioning that this particular part of the Damascus Document has provoked a great deal of interest because the two mediaeval Cairo manuscripts attest radically different though related readings just before our passage sets in. Unfortunately CD manuscript A breaks off just before the passage we are looking at. It would have been fascinating to be able to read its version of these lines, if they existed. Alas, the evidence of the 4QD manuscripts offers no parallel for the first half of CD 20.³⁵ Most recently a monograph by Stephen Hultgren and studies by Menahem Kister and Liora Goldman have moved this debate further.³⁶

3. The Texts (CD 20:1b–8a and 1QS 8:16b–9:2; 9:8–11a//4Q258 (4QSᵈ) 6 8b.11–12; 7 1–3.7–9)³⁷

Before presenting the texts, let me briefly explain my system of visual enhancement which also summarizes the key points I would like to make. I left out of consideration the material found in 1QS 9:3–7 because these lines have little in common with the otherwise closely related passage in CD 20. Moreover, a number of scholars have recently drawn attention to the way in which 1QS 9:3–6 takes up earlier statements from 1QS 8:1–7a in a repetitive manner.³⁸ The statement assigning a pivotal role to the sons of Aaron in matters of justice and wealth (1QS 9:7) was joined to the preceding lines on the basis of the catchword

---

Scrolls,' in *The Community of the Renewed Covenant: The Notre Dame Symposium on the Dead Sea Scrolls* (ed. Eugene Ulrich and James C. VanderKam; Christianity and Judaism in Antiquity 10; Notre Dame, Ind.: University of Notre Dame Press, 1994), 211–234, here 213 where VanderKam argues that a mechanical error may have resulted in 4Q259's shorter text.

[34] For a further recent endorsements of Metso's line of argument see Eibert J. C. Tigchelaar, 'The Scribe of 1QS,' in *Emanuel: Studies in Hebrew Bible, Septuagint, and the Dead Sea Scrolls in Honor of Emanuel Tov* (ed. Shalom M. Paul et al.; VTSup 94; Leiden: Brill, 2003), 439–452, esp. 452 and Schofield, *From Qumran to the Yaḥad*, 108.

[35] Cf. DJD 18:3 (Baumgarten); for a recent analysis see Schofield, *From Qumran to the Yaḥad*, 102–103.

[36] See Stephen Hultgren, *From the Damascus Covenant to the Covenant of the Community: Literary, Historical, and Theological Studies in the Dead Sea Scrolls* (STDJ 66; Leiden: Brill, 2007), esp. 5–76; Menahem Kister, 'The Development of the Early Recensions of the Damascus Document,' *DSD* 14 (2007): 61–76; and Liora Goldman, 'A Comparison of the Genizah Manuscripts A and B of the Damascus Document in Light of Their Pesher Units,' in *Meghillot: Studies in the Dead Sea Scrolls IV* (ed. Moshe Bar-Asher and Devorah Dimant; Jerusalem: University of Haifa/Bialik Institute, 2006), XIV, 169–189 [Hebrew with English abstract].

[37] For the text of 4Q258 (4QSᵈ) 6–7 see DJD 26:105–114 (Alexander and Vermes).

[38] See John J. Collins, 'The Yaḥad and "The Qumran Community,"' 89 and Newsom, *Self as Symbolic Space*, 164–165, both of whom note how 1QS 9:3–11 recapitulates parts of 1QS 8. See also Hempel, 'Emerging Communal Life and Ideology in the S Tradition,' esp. 56, reprinted as Chapter 5 in this volume.

'Aaron' and to the following statement through the catchword 'wealth' (הון),[39] and is otherwise only very loosely connected to the surrounding material.

Table: Visual Enhancement of Key Features in CD 20 and 1QS 8–9

Grey background	Material shared by CD 20 and 1QS, chiefly the self-designation "people of perfect holiness"
Italics	Language reminiscent of the shared terminology but not part of a self-designation (e. g. perfect conduct)
Bold italics	Material distinctive in CD 20:1b–8a (e. g. "men of knowledge," "upright ones," "disciples of God")
Bold underlined	Language familiar from the organization of the communities in the Damascus Document and/or the Community Rule (e. g. rabbim, yaḥad, reproof, tohorah)
Grey background, bold, and underlined	Language found in the shared material and familiar from organizational texts (e. g. wealth)
Double underlined	An expression unique in the non-biblical Dead Sea Scrolls (i. e. community of holiness – יחד קודש)
Dotted underlined	'Context hooks' i. e. transitional statements found just before the beginning (S) and at the end of the passage in question (D), i. e. CD 20:1 and 1QS 9:11, where both passages make reference to a messianic turning point.[40]
[…]	Text not quoted here

CD 20:1b–8a

(Translation by Michael A. Knibb with minor changes)[41]

(20:1b) Such shall be the case (2) for everyone who enters/is a member of the congregation of the men of perfect holiness (כל באי עדת אנשי תמים הקדש), but shrinks from carrying out the precepts of *the upright* (ישרים). (3) He is the man who is melted in a furnace. When his deeds become apparent, he shall be sent away from *the congregation* (מעדה) (4) like one whose lot had never fallen among ***the disciples of God*** (למודי אל). According to his unfaithfulness ***the men of knowledge*** (אנשי דעות) shall **reprove him** (יוכיחוהו) (5)

---

[39] The connection through the catchword הון is particularly clear in the shorter text of 4Q258 (4QS^d) 7 7, cf. DJD 26:110, 114 (Alexander and Vermes).

[40] Cf. the references in CD 20:1 "until the messiah of Aaron and Israel arises" and 1QS 9:11 "until the coming of the prophet and the messiahs of Aaron and Israel."

[41] See Knibb, *The Qumran Community*, 70–71. For the Hebrew text of CD see Elisha Qimron, 'The Text of CDC,' in *The Damascus Document Reconsidered* (ed. Magen Broshi; Jerusalem: IES, 1992), 9–49.

until the day he again stands in the place (במעמד) of the men of perfect holiness (אנשי תמים קודש). (6) But when his deeds become apparent, according to the interpretation of the law (מדרש התורה) (cf. מדרש התורה [42] היאה in 1QS 8:15//4Q258 [4QS^d] 6 7//4Q259 [4QS^e] 3 6) in which the men of perfect holiness (אנשי תמים הקדש) walk (7) let no man make any agreement with him in regard to property (הון) or work (עבודה), (8) because all the holy ones of the most high have cursed him.

1QS 8:16–9:2; 9:8–11a[43]
(Translation my own)[44]

(8:16b) No person from among **the people of the community, the covenant of** (17) **the community** (איש מאנשי היחד ברית היחד), who fails to observe any of the commandments deliberately shall touch the **purity** (בטהרת) of the people of holiness (אנשי הקודש), (18) nor shall he have knowledge of any of **their counsel** (עצתם) until his actions have been cleansed from any injustice and *he conducts himself perfectly* (להלך בתמים דרך). Then they shall allow him to approach (19) **the council on the authority of the many** (בעצה על פי הרבים) and afterwards he shall be **enrolled** (יכתב) **according to his rank** (בתכונו). This law shall apply to **everyone who joins the community** (כול הנוסף ליחד). (20) These are the rules according to which the people of perfect holiness (אנשי התמים קודש) shall conduct themselves each one with his neighbour. (21) Every one who enters/is a member of the council of holiness (made up of) those whose conduct is perfect (כול הבא בעצת הקודש ההולכים בתמים דרך) according to that which He has commanded, every person from among them (22) who has deliberately or inadvertently transgressed any part of the law of Moses **they shall send him away** from **the council of the community** (23) (מעצת היחד) **never to return again**. And no person from among **the people of holiness** (איש מאנשי הקודש) shall share **his property** or **his counsel** (עצתו) regarding any (24) matter. And if he has acted inadvertently **he shall be excluded from the purity and from (exchanging) counsel** (מן הטהרה ומן העצה) and they shall resort to the rule (25) which (states): He shall not judge or be consulted concerning any **counsel** (עצה) **for two years**. (This applies) on condition that *his conduct is perfect* (אם תתם דרכו) (26) **in meetings** (במושב), in study (במדרש), and **in counsel** (ובעצה) **[accor]ding to the many** ([ע]ל [פי] הרבים). If he does not commit a further inadvertent sin **until he has completed the two** (27) **years** – (9:1) for it was on account of one inadvertent sin that he was punished for two (years) – but the one who has acted deliberately **shall never return again**. Only the one who has sinned inadvertently (2) shall be tested for two years *with regard to the perfection of his conduct* (לתמים דרכו) and **his counsel** (ועצתו) **according to the many** (על פי הרבים) and afterwards he shall be **enrolled according to his rank** in the community of holiness (ליחד קודש). *Vacat*. [...] (8) And the property of the people of holiness whose conduct is perfect (הון אנשי הקודש ההולכים בתמים) shall not be mixed with **their property**, (that is) with the **property** of the people of deceit who (9) have not cleansed their conduct to keep away from injustice and to *conduct themselves perfectly* (וללכת בתמים דרך). They shall not deviate from any counsel

---

[42] 4Q259 (4QS^e) 3 6 reads the masculine form of the pronoun (הואה), cf. DJD 26:144, 146 (Alexander and Vermes).

[43] Only 4Q258 (4QS^d) 6–7 offers some corresponding material from 4QS, cf. DJD 26:105–114 (Alexander and Vermes).

[44] For an edition of the Hebrew text of 1QS see PTSDSSP 1:6–50 (Qimron).

of the law so as to walk (10) in all the hardness of their heart, but they shall be judged by the first rules (cf. CD 20:31–32) according to which **the people of the community** (אנשי היחד) began to be instructed (11) until the coming of the prophet and the messiahs of Aaron and Israel (cf. CD 20:1).

4. Analysis

Both passages share a great deal of terminology while at the same time also preserving a fair number of distinctive features. What is particularly striking is the very distinctive use of the self-designation 'the people of perfect holiness' as a communal self-designation frequently in CD 20 and also in 1QS 8:20. This self-designation is not found anywhere else in the Scrolls.[45] Carol Newsom coined the apt phrase "rhetoric of perfection" with reference to the Community Rule and noted also that the Damascus Document is the only other text that shares this rhetoric.[46] We noted earlier, moreover, that the shared material, here as elsewhere, is devoted to the larger topos of discipline.

On the other hand, there are clear differences too. The most striking feature is the internal evidence of the S passage. We seem to be looking at two sets of terminology side by side. One set of terms is very familiar from other parts of S (cf. rabbim, yaḥad) whereas the other self-designation ("the people of perfect holiness") does not occur elsewhere in S and is the one that resembles CD 20. Moreover, the more familiar S language (rabbim and yaḥad) is entirely lacking from the CD 20 passage. Particularly striking is the switch between both sets of terms in 1QS 8:19b–21,

---

[45] On this terminology see DJD 26:107–108 (Alexander and Vermes); see also Cecilia Wassen, *Women in the Damascus Document* (Academia Biblica 21; Atlanta, Ga.: SBL, 2005), 122–128 where she shows clearly that the contrast drawn in CD 7:4–6 is between those who walk in perfect holiness (obeying the rules of the small law code just preceding this reference) and those who despise. See also Albert-Marie Denis, *Les thèmes de connaissance dans le Document de Damas* (Studia Hellenistica 15; Louvain: Publications Universitaires, 1967), 135–138. Wassen's interpretation has been endorsed by Eyal Regev, 'Cherchez les femmes: Were the Yaḥad Celibates?,' *DSD* 15 (2008): 253–284, esp. 255–259. Much was made by previous scholars of a supposed dichotomy between those (implied: celibate individuals) who walk in perfect holiness and those who live in camps and marry and have children, see, e. g., Elisha Qimron, 'Celibacy in the Dead Sea Scrolls and the Two Kinds of Sectarians,' in *The Madrid Qumran Congress: Proceedings of the International Congress on the Dead Sea Scrolls, Madrid 18 -21 March 1991* (ed. Julio Trebolle Barrera and Luis Vegas Montaner; STDJ 11; Leiden: Brill, 1992), Vol. I, 286–294; and more recently Schofield, *From Qumran to the Yaḥad*, 165, see also 171. If Wassen is right, and I think her case is persuasive, then this passage could well speak of a similar conflict or crisis situation to the one that left its mark on CD 20:1b–8a. Wassen herself suggests that, "the writer of XX,1b–8a may have used the language of CD VII 4–5 to highlight the desirable qualities of all the members," *Women in the Damascus Document*, 124–125 n. 51.

[46] Newsom, *Self as Symbolic Space*, 159–160.

This law shall apply to everyone who joins the community [יחד]. These are the rules according to which the people of perfect holiness shall conduct themselves each one with his neighbour. Every one who enters/is a member of the council of holiness (made up of) those whose conduct is perfect ...

Also curious is the unique self-designation "community (yaḥad) of holiness" found only in 1QS 9:2 in the corpus of non-biblical scrolls. Given that this expression is a compound phrase which contains elements from both sets of terminology attested in the S passage, it seems plausible to speculate that it represents an attempt to bridge the terminological chasm that characterizes our passage in the Community Rule. What we have here is an extremely interesting scenario: we have inter-textual evidence, to adopt Metso's terminology, whereby the inter-textual connections between CD 20 and 1QS 8–9 at this point are such that the particular terminological connections bring the two passages from different compositions closer to each other than either passage is to the rest of the document they are found in. Having read between the texts in this way, we also read between the lines in each text. The terminological shifts in the choice of self-designations in the S text indicate that the inter-textual connections dominate only one strand in the material. The same is true for the internal evidence of CD 20 which also includes, alongside the shared terms, some distinctive terminology such as "men of knowledge" (a hapax in the non-biblical Dead Sea Scrolls) and "disciples of God" (another hapax in the non-biblical Scrolls), and "the upright" (a designation not infrequent in the Dead Sea Scrolls and amply attested in the Hebrew Bible esp. in the wisdom literature). The distinctive terms used in CD 20:1b–8a alongside the people of perfect holiness terminology are not found in administrative/constitutional contexts and all have a sapiential flavour (the upright, knowledge, learning/discipleship).[47] In short, what we have in front of us is a very interesting web of interlocking traditions. Add to this that one of the S manuscripts (4Q259 [4QSᵉ]) is lacking virtually all of this material we plainly witness the fluidity with which this material evolved in front of our eyes. The problem that remains, if what I say is convincing, is to reconstruct convincingly how this web of interlocking traditions originated. Here conclusive answers are hard to come by. Given that CD 20 incorporates "people of perfect holiness" terminology without amalgamating it into a yaḥad/rabbim frame of reference – as is the case in S – or, indeed, any other dominant framework characteristic of the Damascus Document such as the camp/s, the returnees of Israel, or the (new) covenant, it may be that these shared strands of material have been imported into the dominant narratives of both CD and 1QS. We seem to have some

---

[47] On the close connection between wisdom literature and language and the Community Rule see Reinhard G. Kratz, 'Laws of Wisdom: Sapiential Traits in the *Rule of the Community* (1QS V–IX),' in *Hebrew in the Second Temple Period: The Hebrew of the Dead Sea Scrolls and of Other Contemporary Sources. Proceedings of the Twelfth Orion Symposium* (STDJ; Leiden: Brill, forthcoming).

evidence suggesting the secondary reinforcement of the rabbim framework in 1QS 8:26 which includes a reference to the rabbim that is clearly not yet present in 4Q258 (4QS^d) 7 1.[48] It is also worth noting that whereas the self-designation "people of perfect holiness" or similar self-portrayals are extremely limited in the Dead Sea Scrolls, the virtues of holiness and perfection as modes of conduct are endorsed more widely.[49] It may be that after some time a segment of the community began to add to the general aspiration to perfection of conduct and holiness the ideological claim: some of us are attaining this and others are not, leading eventually to the self-designation "people of perfect holiness." In other words, it is possible to envisage how the self-designation grew out of an initial desire to achieve perfect conduct. It is striking, for instance, how both elements (holiness and perfection) form the central pillars in the description of the community in what is often seen as cultic terms in 1QS 8–9.[50]

Furthermore, the fact that 4Q259 (4QS^e) lacks all of this material coupled with Eibert Tigchelaar's curious and revealing observation that parts of this section in 1QS display noticeable differences in the quantity of scribal corrections[51] all further point towards a staggered growth of the Community Rule at this point.[52] Are we right in thinking, then, that at exactly one juncture in the evolving literary growth of 1QS its textual tradition shows signs of an inter-textual relationship with CD manuscript B? Considered together with the fact that the passage in CD 20 we looked at is also almost certainly a late and somewhat extraneous development in CD/D, is it conceivable that both documents were worked on by the same group at one point? In other words rather than speaking of inter-textual links involving entire documents we seem to be dealing with inter-textual redactional layers. If Metso is correct and the much shorter text preserved in 4Q259 (4QS^e) offers the more original text, then the latter manuscript may now present us with the sort of text the redactor responsible for 1QS worked with. If the same individual or school of thought lies behind CD 20:1b–8a onwards,

---

[48] Cf. DJD 26:112 (Alexander and Vermes); Charlotte Hempel, 'The Literary Development of the S Tradition – A New Paradigm,' *RQ* 22 (2006): 389–401, reprinted as Chapter 7 in this volume; and Schofield, *From Qumran to the Yaḥad*, 102–103.

[49] On the sapiential roots of this language see recently Hultgren, *From the Damascus Covenant to the Covenant of the Community*, 357–358 n. 86.

[50] On the unusual term "house of perfection" that occurs in the latter context see Marc Philonenko's contribution to a *Festschrift* for Émile Puech, noting some connections with Mandaean sources, cf. 'Sur les expressions "Maison fidèle en Israël," "Maison de vérité en Israël," "Maison de perfection et de vérité en Israël,"' in *From 4QMMT to Resurrection: Mélanges qumraniens en hommage à Émile Puech* (ed. Florentino García Martínez, Annette Steudel, and Eibert Tigchelaar; STDJ 61; Leiden: Brill, 2006), 243–246.

[51] Cf. Tigchelaar, 'The Scribe of 1QS.'

[52] On these issues see also Charlotte Hempel, 'Sources and Redaction in the Dead Sea Scrolls – The Growth of Ancient Texts,' in *Rediscovering the Dead Sea Scrolls: An Assessment of Old and New Approaches and Methods* (ed. Maxine Grossman; Grand Rapids, Mich.: Eerdmans, 2010), 162–181.

it is worth noting the reference to the messiah of Aaron and Israel in CD 20:1a (identified graphically above as a 'context hook' [dotted underlined] which resembles the reference to a messianic turning point in 1QS 9:11 [until the coming of the prophet and the messiahs of Aaron and Israel].[53] If both documents were adapted by the same circles – 'a perfect holinessist crowd' – then they may either have been inspired by CD 20:1a in drafting 1QS 9:11 or even been responsible for both.

5. Conclusion

The full corpus of the ancient manuscripts of the Community Rule and the Damascus Document was published just over a decade ago. It is therefore inevitable that scholars are still noticing finer points of overlap and difference and are struggling to make sense of an immensely complex, challenging and exciting body of evidence. We began by noting the preponderance of inter-textual passages in D and S, relating in particular to disciplinary issues, and suggested that the communities seemed to have struggled with 'commitment issues' at the time when passages like the penal code, CD 20:1b–8 and 1QS 8:16–9:11 were composed. Although the penal codes frequently refer to what may be described as rather mundane infringements such as falling asleep during a meeting, it is worth stressing that they also make reference to some very serious offences that strike at the heart of the community's survival, see, e. g., 1QS 7:17–19. In revisiting the close and curious inter-textual relationship between CD 20:1b–8a and 1QS 8:16–9:2; 9:8–11a//4Q258 (4QS^d) 6–7 we were able to reflect not only on the relationship between both documents to one another but also tried to evaluate the internal complexities of each text. This internal complexity emerged as particularly evident in the Community Rule where four rather different types of evidence were drawn upon,

- 1QS 8:16–9:2; 9:8–11a//4Q258 (4QS^d) 6–7 shares a particular terminological frame of reference with CD 20:1b–8a that is not found elsewhere in the Serekh.
- Alongside the language shared with CD 20, 1QS 8–9 also employs communal self-designations and organizational terminology that predominate in the central columns of 1QS (esp. 1QS 5–7) such as rabbim and yaḥad.
- A complex literary history behind 1QS 8–9 is further suggested by the evidence of 4Q259 (4QS^e) which lacks the equivalent of 1QS 8:15b–9:11 altogether. It seems commendable, essential even, to relate the scholarly dis-

---

[53] Hultgren argues the CD 20:1 is an introduction to a now lost section, cf. *From the Damascus Covenant to the Covenant of the Community*, 67–76.

cussion on the shorter text of 4Q259 vis-à-vis 1QS to the close relationship between the longer 1QS text and CD 20:1b–8a.
– Furthermore, both Tigchelaar and Newsom have drawn attention to the significance of the pattern of scribal corrections in 1QS 8. Tigchelaar rightly draws our attention to the variations in the level of correctional activity in different parts of 1QS 8, noting especially the small number of corrections in 1QS 8:15–9:11 – exactly the same portion of text missing from 4Q259. He correctly observes that, "the accumulation of errors and corrections in specific sections may reflect a complicated textual tradition."[54] Newsom's observations point in the same direction,

> The extensive interlinear corrections of 1QS 8 also lend an impression of considerable scribal activity, although the actual history of the development may never be resolved. The result, however, is a mosaic-like effect of thematically related but verbally distinguishable units.[55]

Newsom is surely right when she notes that we can never retrace the literary history behind 1QS 8–9 with a degree of precision. What I hope to have shown is that a careful comparison between 1QS 8–9 and CD 20 provides us with additional vital evidence to consider when we contemplate the textual mosaic of 1QS 8–9.

---

[54] Tigchelaar, 'The Scribe of 1QS,' 451.
[55] *Self as Symbolic Space*, 152.

Chapter Nine

Rewritten Rule Texts[1]

1. Introduction

The theme chosen by the organizers of the 2009 Toronto Dead Sea Scrolls conference *The Transmission of Traditions and the Production of Texts as They Emerge from the Dead Sea Scrolls* was well chosen in as much as these ancient manuscripts provide us with firm ancient, and one would like to say first-hand, evidence of such processes. One of the texts that has received a great deal of attention in terms of its textual history is the Community Rule (S) as attested particularly in the well preserved copy from Cave 1 and the more recently published ten Cave 4 manuscripts of the text.[2] There are good reasons why the Rule texts are a particularly fruitful field to harvest to illuminate the complex transmission of texts. Whereas scholars are frequently at pains to draw attention to small but significant differences between different copies of the same work attested at Qumran such as the War Scroll from Caves 1 and 4[3] and most recently also the manuscripts of MMT,[4] the evidence of the Rule manuscripts has swamped us with evidence since the early 1990s. In the particular case of the Rule of the Community the differences between 1QS and the various 4QS manuscripts are substantial and varied and allow us, therefore, first-hand glimpses at the transmission and production of a complex web of ancient traditions and texts. Though

---

[1] This chapter originated as a contribution to the proceedings of an international conference ('Shared Traditions: Points of Contact Between S and D,' in *The Dead Sea Scrolls: Transmission of Traditions and Production of Texts* [ed. Sarianna Metso, Hindy Najman, and Eileen Schuller; STDJ 92; Leiden: Brill, 2010], 115–131) hosted by the editors. An earlier version of the chapter was presented at a Workshop hosted by Prof. Reinhard Kratz and Prof. Annette Steudel of the University of Göttingen in February 2009. I am grateful to them and to the organizers of the Toronto Conference in the same year for the opportunity to explore these issues in a congenial and stimulating environment.

[2] See, e.g., Charlotte Hempel, 'The Literary Development of the S Tradition – A New Paradigm,' *RQ* 22 (2006): 389–401, reprinted as Chapter 7 in this volume; Sarianna Metso, *The Serekh Texts* (CQS 9/LSTS 62; London: T & T Clark, 2007); and Alison Schofield, *From Qumran to the Yaḥad: A New Paradigm of Textual Development for the Community Rule* (STDJ 77; Leiden: Brill, 2009).

[3] On the war texts see Jean Duhaime, *The War Texts: 1QM and Related Manuscripts* (CQS 6; London: T & T Clark, 2004) and Brian Schultz, *Conquering the World: The War Scroll (1QM) Reconsidered* (STDJ 76; Leiden: Brill, 2009) and earlier literature cited there.

[4] See Hanne von Weissenberg, *4QMMT: Reevaluating the Text, Function, and the Meaning of the Epilogue* (STDJ 82; Leiden: Brill, 2009).

it is impossible to deny that the S tradition evolved and did so in complex ways scholars are still debating the direction in which the developments we witness took shape: from earlier manuscripts to later ones (the position of Alexander who stresses palaeography as a key criterion followed by Tov and Dimant),[5] from short to long (Vermes, Metso, and others),[6] from "the many" to "the sons of Zadok" in 1QS 5 par. or *vice versa*. Overall, a great deal of the initial discussion of the intriguing relationship between 1QS and 4QS focused on differences and on exploring how to account for these differences in as cogent an argument as possible. In my own most recent contribution to this discussion I emphasized the fruitfulness of noting equally remarkable similarities and overlaps between S manuscripts that diverge radically in other places. In an article that appeared in *Revue de Qumran* in 2006 I suggested that our initial excitement about finally having access to significant new variants in 4QS partially blinded us for a time from noting the importance of overlapping material in other places. Whereas much of the early scholarly debate about the literary growth of S was chiefly concerned with determining which manuscripts or family of manuscripts represents the earlier text,[7] I proposed that the quest for the beginning of the growth of this textual tradition is to be found in the shared material found across the manuscript spectrum.[8] Such a more balanced approach is now also advocated by Schofield.[9]

In particular, I identified important common ground between different S manuscripts in the material mandating a careful separation from the people of injustice (אנשי העול) shared by 1QS 5, 4Q256 (4QS^b), and 4Q258 (4QS^d) in spite of major differences in the surrounding material.[10] Another example is the shared reference to the sons of Aaron and the multitude of Israel in 1QS 5:20–22 and 4Q258 (4QS^d) 2 1–2. Both manuscripts allot a key role to the sons of Aaron here in remarkable contrast to the language they employ elsewhere esp. in 1QS 5:2–3 ("the sons of Zadok, the priests who keep the covenant and the multitude of the men of the community") and 4Q258 1 2 ("the many").[11]

---

[5] Cf. Philip S. Alexander, 'The Redaction-History of Serekh ha-Yaḥad: A Proposal,' *RQ* 17 (1996): 437–453; Emanuel Tov, *Scribal Practices and Approaches Reflected in the Texts Found in the Judean Desert* (STDJ 54; Leiden: Brill, 2004), 27; and Devorah Dimant, 'The Composite Character of the Qumran Sectarian Literature as an Indication of Its Date and Provenance,' *RQ* 22 (2006): 615–630, 619.

[6] See Geza Vermes, 'Preliminary Remarks on Unpublished Fragments of the Community Rule from Qumran Cave 4,' *JJS* 42 (1991): 250–255 and Sarianna Metso, *The Textual Development of the Qumran Community Rule* (STDJ 21; Leiden: Brill, 1997).

[7] Note, for instance, Metso's now famous and helpful stemma where the guiding criteria at the time were differences between manuscripts, see Metso, *Textual Development*, 147.

[8] Hempel, 'Literary Development.'

[9] Cf. *From Qumran to the Yaḥad*, 137.

[10] On this material see Charlotte Hempel, 'The Community and Its Rivals According to the Community Rule from Qumran Caves 1 and 4,' *RQ* 21 (2003): 47–81.

[11] See Heinz-Josef Fabry, 'Zadokiden und Aaroniden in Qumran,' in *Das Manna fällt auch heute noch: Beiträge zur Geschichte und Theologie des Alten, Ersten Testaments. Festschrift für Erich Zenger* (ed. Frank Lothar Hossfeld and Ludger Schwienhorst-Schönberger; Herders

2. Points of Contact Between S and D

I would like to develop this approach further and beyond the data presented by individual S manuscripts to include also the evidence of the Damascus Document (D) in as much as it relates directly to the literary development of the Community Rule. Here again a similar scholarly trajectory can be traced. Whereas prior to the publication of the Cave 4 manuscripts of the Damascus Document by the late Joseph Baumgarten[12] scholars were occupied by and large with accounting for the differences between the community attested in the Laws of the Damascus Document (the organization of families in camps presided over by a *Mebaqqer* in particular) and the Rule of the Community which never refers to families (explicitly) or camps but was for a long time associated with a celibate lifestyle. The overwhelming impression of differences between organizational matters laid down in the Rule and the Damascus Document was often accounted for on the basis of the evidence of Josephus who speaks of two types of Essenes, one married and one celibate (cf. *J. W.* 2:120–121, 160; the latter passage introduces 'another class of Essenes' ἕτερον Ἐσσηνῶν τάγμα).[13] The overwhelming impression of distinctiveness between what is laid down in the Damascus Document and what we find in the Rule was, then, for a long time employed to create two mental boxes for these texts: a married branch and a somewhat superior celibate bunch of people, the former living spread out in camps whereas the latter resided at Qumran.

Most recently this rather comfortable picture the texts seemed to present to us has suffered disruption from a variety of fronts. Firstly, scholars are today much more wary in their interpretation of the texts and the other archaeological remains as reflecting a celibate community.[14] Secondly, the umbilical cord between the site of Qumran and the emergence of the Yaḥad has been severely damaged by a

---

biblische Studien 44; Freiburg: Herder, 2004), 201–217; Charlotte Hempel, 'The Sons of Aaron in the Dead Sea Scrolls,' in *Flores Florentino: Dead Sea Scrolls and Other Early Jewish Studies in Honour of Florentino García Martínez* (ed. Anthony Hilhorst, Émile Puech, and Eibert Tigchelaar; JSJSup 122; Leiden: Brill, 2008), 207–224, reprinted as Chapter 13 in this volume; and eadem, 'Do the Scrolls Suggest Rivalry Between the Sons of Aaron and the Sons of Zadok and If So was it Mutual?,' *RQ* 24 (2009): 135–153, reprinted as Chapter 14 in this volume.

[12] DJD 18 (Baumgarten).

[13] Cf. Eileen Schuller, *The Dead Sea Scrolls: What Have We Learned 50 Years On* (London: SCM, 2006), 80–81. For a recent discussion of the classical evidence on the celibacy question see Joan E. Taylor, 'Philo of Alexandria on the Essenes: A Case Study on the Use of Classical Sources in Discussions of the Qumran-Essene Hypothesis,' *Studia Philonica Annual* 19 (2007): 1–28, esp. 20–26 and further literature referred to there. See also Sidnie White Crawford, 'Not According to Rule: Women, the Dead Sea Scrolls and Qumran,' in *Emanuel: Studies in the Hebrew Bible, Septuagint, and Dead Sea Scrolls in Honor of Emanuel Tov* (ed. Shalom M. Paul et al.; VTSup 94; Leiden: Brill, 2003), 127–150.

[14] See the seminal study by Eileen Schuller, 'Women in the Dead Sea Scrolls,' in *The Dead Sea Scrolls After Fifty Years: A Comprehensive Assessment* (ed. Peter Flint and James VanderKam; Leiden: Brill, 1999), Vol. II: 117–144, and White Crawford, 'Not According to Rule.'

re-dating of the incipient phase of communal occupation of the site to the early decades of the first century BCE.[15] In short, both the neat geographical divide (Qumran versus *Hinterland*) and the neat divide of lifestyles (married versus celibate) have both been challenged considerably by recent scholarly developments. To this we may add the gradual demolition of the uniqueness of a number of crucial archaeological features attested by the Qumran site. I am thinking here particularly of the mushrooming of Qumran type burials in a number of other places (such as Khirbet Qazone, Ein Ghuweir, Beit Zafafa) to an extent that makes it problematic to speak of the burial practice attested at Qumran as a distinctive Qumran type.[16] Equally intriguing is the discovery of large numbers of individual dining dishes in Hasmonean Jericho.[17] In light of these developments Alison Schofield quite properly devoted a chapter to the significance of the broader archaeological picture for our understanding of what was going on at Qumran in her recent monograph on the Community Rule and the Yaḥad.[18] Thirdly, a number of scholars have recently challenged the exclusive association of the Yaḥad, as it emerges from the Community Rule, with Qumran. Thus, John Collins now speaks of the Yaḥad as an umbrella organization,[19] and Alison Schofield conceives of a Jerusalemite provenance for the earliest stages of the Community Rule, a text that was eventually revised at Qumran and in outlying related communities.[20] In short, we witness a broadening of the borders and horizons from a number of fronts.

---

[15] See Jodi Magness, *The Archaeology of Qumran and the Dead Sea Scrolls* (Grand Rapids, Mich.: Eerdmans, 2002), 47–72; John J. Collins, *Beyond the Qumran Community: The Sectarian Movement of the Dead Sea Scrolls* (Grand Rapids, Mich.: Eerdmans, 2009), 166–208; Torleif Elgvin, 'The Yaḥad is More than Qumran,' in *Enoch and Qumran Origins: New Light on a Forgotten Connection* (ed. Gabriele Boccaccini; Grand Rapids, Mich.: Eerdmans, 2005), 273–279.

[16] See, e. g., Pesah Bar-Adon, 'Another Settlement of the Judean Desert Sect at 'Ain el-Guweir on the Dead Sea,' *BASOR* 225 (1977): 2–25; Magness, *Archaeology of Qumran*, 210–225; Rachel Hachlili, 'The Qumran Cemetery: A Reconsideration,' in *The Dead Sea Scrolls Fifty Years After Their Discovery 1947–1997* (ed. Lawrence H. Schiffman, Emanuel Tov, and James C. VanderKam; Jerusalem: IES, Shrine of the Book, Israel Museum, 2000), 661–672; Konstantinos D. Politis, 'The Discovery and Excavation of the Khirbet Qazone Cemetery and Its Significance Relative to Qumran,' in *The Site of the Dead Sea Scrolls: Archaeological Interpretations and Debates* (ed. Katharina Galor, Jean-Baptiste Humbert, and Jürgen Zangenberg; STDJ 57; Leiden: Brill, 2006), 213–219; and Boas Zissu, 'Odd Tomb Out: Has Jerusalem's Essene Cemetery Been Found?,' *BAR* 25 (1999): 50–55, 62.

[17] See Rachel Bar-Nathan, 'Qumran and the Hasmonaean and Herodian Winter Palaces of Jericho: The Implication of the Pottery Finds for the Interpretation of the Settlement at Qumran,' in *The Site of the Dead Sea Scrolls* (ed. Galor, Humbert, and Zangenberg), 263–277.

[18] Schofield, *From Qumran to the Yaḥad*, 220–271.

[19] See now Collins, *Beyond the Qumran Community* and earlier literature referred to there.

[20] Schofield, *From Qumran to the Yaḥad*. See also Charlotte Hempel, '1QS 6: 2c–4a – Satellites or Precursors of the Yaḥad?,' in *The Dead Sea Scrolls and Contemporary Culture* (ed. Adolfo Roitman, Larry Schiffman, and Shani Tzoref; STDJ 93; Leiden: Brill, 2011), 31–40, reprinted as Chapter 6 in this volume.

Finally, most recently scholarship on the question of how to identify and distinguish between sectarian and non-sectarian texts is also moving in the direction of noting fluidity and complexity. During the first decades of Qumran research it was taken for granted that we should endeavour to identify a core group of sectarian texts to be associated with a single sectarian community who resided at Qumran. Things are no longer that straightforward. Today many scholars shy away from speaking of a neat divide between sectarian and non-sectarian material and acknowledge instead more gradated phenomena (cf. concepts such as 'pre-sectarian,' 'proto-sectarian,' 'parent-movement,' and the Groningen Hypothesis's[21] 'formative period'). Inaugurating the latest phase in these scholarly developments Brooke now advocates distinguishing between 'incipient' sectarianism as distinct from 'nascent,' 'full-blown,' and 'rejuvenated' sectarianism;[22] and Florentino García Martínez has proposed abandoning the distinction between sectarian and non-sectarian texts altogether and speaks instead of 'clusters' of texts that share particular characteristics.[23] In sum, I perceive an intellectual climate in our approach to the texts, the social trajectories that produced them and recent archaeological analyses that produces a much more challenging and complex picture of the Qumran finds. Speaking rather broadly we note again and again that emerging *rapprochements* continue to gnaw away at the distinctiveness of what was once confidently called 'the Qumran Community.' Increasing numbers of pieces of evidence are nibbling away at the pedestal of uniqueness that the Qumran community once occupied with considerable pride. Should this worry us? Does it make our corner of antiquity and our scholarly niche any less important? I think not. By contrast, the broadening of the horizons we witness enhances the wider relevance of the texts and the people we are studying.

Another invasion of data that has been biting large chunks out of the particularity of the Community Rule is the penal code material. This legislation was formerly closely associated with the S community but is now attested much more fully also in the Cave 4 manuscripts of the Damascus Document, 4Q265 (Miscellaneous Rules) and 11QFragment Related to Serekh ha-Yaḥad.[24] There is no

---

[21] See Florentino García Martínez, 'Qumran Origins and Early History: A Groningen Hypothesis,' *Folia Orientalia* 25 (1988): 113–136 (reprinted in idem, *Qumranica Minora I: Qumran Origins and Apocalypticism* [ed. Eibert Tigchelaar; STDJ 63; Leiden: Brill, 2007], 31–52).

[22] George J. Brooke, 'From Jesus to the Early Christian Communities: Trajectories Towards Sectarianism in the Light of the Dead Sea Scrolls,' in *The Dead Sea Scrolls and Contemporary Culture* (ed. Roitman, Schiffman, and Tzoref), 413–434.

[23] Cf. Florentino García Martínez, '¿Sectario, no-sectario, o qué? Problemas de una taxonomía correcta de los textos qumránicos,' *RQ* 23 (2008): 383–394.

[24] Cf. 1QS 6:24–7:25 // 4Q258 (4QS^d) 5 1 // 4Q259 (4QS^e) 1 4–15, 2 3–8 // 4Q261 (4QS^g) 3 2–4; 4a–b 1–7; 5a–c 1–9; 6a–e 1–5 in the Community Rule and CD 14:18b–22 // 4Q266 (4QD^a) 10 i–ii // 4Q267 (4QD^b) 9 vi // 4Q269 (4QD^d) 11 i–ii; 4Q270 (4QD^e) 7 i in the Damascus Document. See also 4Q265 (Miscellaneous Rules) 4 i 2–ii 2 and 11Q29 (Fragment Related to Serekh ha-Yaḥad). For scholarly discussions see, *inter alia*, Joseph M. Baumgarten, 'The Cave 4 Versions of the Qumran Penal Code,' *JJS* 43 (1992): 268–276; Charlotte Hempel, 'The Penal

doubt in my mind that the points of contact between S and D are crucial pieces of evidence in our search for the production of these particular texts. Moreover, the insights gained from the full evidence available for D and S are likely to testify to ways in which ancient Jewish texts grew, developed and related in other cases too.[25] I noted already in the opening paragraphs of this chapter that I have been stimulated by the discovery of overlap and common ground between otherwise heavily diverging manuscripts of the Community Rule. A related area of investigation that scholars have explored over recent years is the significance of shared traditions and points of contact between the Rule and the Damascus Document.

The relationship between the Damascus Document and the Community Rule has always been a topic of great interest to scholars of the Dead Sea Scrolls ever since the Qumran discoveries provided an ancient home for the mediaeval manuscripts of the Damascus Document – a text that was something of a cuckoo in its mediaeval nest. Thus, most recently Schofield has rightly noted that, "the D material illuminates the transmission history of S."[26] However, I think she goes somewhat too far when she identifies "our categories of 'S' and 'D'" as "themselves scholarly constructs."[27] Whereas some have argued for a development from S to D (so, e. g., Kruse and Regev)[28] most scholars are in favour of a model that presumes the community structures reflected in S are a further development of the camp structure of D (e. g. recently Evans Kapfer and Schofield).[29]

Code Reconsidered,' in *Legal Texts and Legal Issues: Proceedings of the Second Meeting of the International Organization for Qumran Studies Published in Honour of Joseph M. Baumgarten* (ed. Moshe Bernstein, Florentino García Martínez, and John Kampen; STDJ 23; Leiden: Brill, 1997), 337–348; Jutta Jokiranta, 'Social Identity in the Qumran Movement: The Case of the Penal Code,' in *Explaining Christian Origins and Early Judaism: Contributions from Cognitive and Social Science* (ed. Petri Luomanen, Ilkka Pyysiäinen, and Risto Uro; BIS 89; Leiden: Brill, 2007), 277–298; Sarianna Metso, 'The Relationship Between the Damascus Document and the Community Rule,' in *The Damascus Document: A Centennial of Discovery. Proceedings of the Third International Symposium of the Orion Center, 4–8 February 1998* (ed. Joseph M. Baumgarten, Esther G. Chazon, and Avital Pinnick; STDJ 34; Leiden: Brill, 2000), 85–93; and most recently also Reinhard G. Kratz, 'Der *Penal Code* und das Verhältnis von *Serekh ha-Yachad* (S) und Damaskusschrift (D),' *RQ* 25 (2011): 199–227.

[25] See Charlotte Hempel, 'Sources and Redaction in the Dead Sea Scrolls – The Growth of Ancient Texts,' in *Rediscovering the Dead Sea Scrolls: An Assessment of Old and New Approaches and Methods* (Grand Rapids, Mich.: Eerdmans, 2010), 162–181.

[26] *From Qumran to the Yaḥad*, 171.

[27] *From Qumran to the Yaḥad*, 189.

[28] See Colin G. Kruse, 'Community Functionaries in the Rule of the Community and the Damascus Document (A Test of Chronological Relationships),' *RQ* 40 (1981): 543–551; Eyal Regev, *Sectarianism in Qumran: A Cross-Cultural Perspective* (Religion and Society 45; Berlin: de Gruyter, 2007); and idem, 'Between Two Sects: Differentiating the Yaḥad and the Damascus Covenant,' in *The Dead Sea Scrolls: Texts and Context* (ed. Charlotte Hempel; STDJ 90; Leiden: Brill, 2010), 431–449.

[29] Hilary Evans Kapfer, 'The Relationship Between the Damascus Document and the Community Rule: Attitudes Toward the Temple as a Test Case,' *DSD* 14 (2007): 152–177 and Schofield, *From Qumran to the Yaḥad*.

The full publication of the manuscripts has provided a wealth of new data and stimuli to this long-standing debate. I have already mentioned the most extensive point of contact between both texts, i. e. the penal code. In what follows I would like to stand back from particular areas of textual intimacy between S and D and from particular texts in favour of trying to draw up a preliminary list of points of contact. In this endeavour I am able to draw initially on Eibert Tigchelaar's 'Annotated List of Overlaps and Parallels in the Non-biblical Texts from Qumran and Masada' in the final volume in the DJD Series. The data collected by Tigchelaar is drawn from indications of textual overlap provided by various editors in the DJD Series though he also added some of his own examples.[30] I observed elsewhere that the Community Rule and the Damascus Document clearly emerge as the frontrunners as far as Tigchelaar's entries on parallels in different non-biblical compositions are concerned.[31] Thus, despite huge and well known differences between D and S these two textual traditions overlap and interlink more often than any other non-biblical Scrolls.

There are, however, a number of further instances of textual intimacy or intertextual contact between the S and D traditions that are not accounted for in tables of this nature or the comparable data gathered by Alexander and Vermes drawn on by Tigchelaar as well as Schofield.[32] In the course of my work on both texts I have written on several inter-textual meeting points between S and D, and for the purposes of this chapter I would like to draw a selection of these together. I have no doubt other items can be added to my list. I am also fully aware that other texts should be included in the web of shared traditions or features that emerges from D and S, such as 4Q265 (Miscellaneous Rules) and 1QSa to name but two obvious examples.

A further complication ought perhaps to be at least mentioned. Although we might be quick to speak of the relationship of different manuscripts of S to one another and to other compositions, there are frequently some important variables to take account of. Thus, Alexander and Vermes noted the possibility that two of the Cave 4 manuscripts (4Q262 [4QS^h] and 4Q264 [4QS^j]) are not complete copies of the Rule but may constitute the remains of collections that also include excerpts from S.[33] In a similar vein Metso has observed a close connection between 4Q262 (4QS^h) and 5Q13, a text citing parts of the Rule but clearly not a copy of S.[34] Finally, the suspected possible copy of S from Cave 11 published

---

[30] Cf. Eibert Tigchelaar, 'Annotated List of Overlaps and Parallels in the Non-biblical Texts from Qumran and Masada,' DJD 39:285–322, here 287.

[31] Cf. Tigchelaar, 'Annotated List of Overlaps and Parallels,' 319 and Charlotte Hempel, 'CD Manuscript B and the Community Rule – Reflections on a Literary Relationship,' *DSD* 16 (2009): 370–387, esp. 372–376, reprinted as Chapter 8 in the present volume.

[32] See DJD 26:3 (Alexander and Vermes) and Schofield, *From Qumran to the Yaḥad*, 179.

[33] DJD 26:190, 201 (Alexander und Vermes).

[34] Metso, *Serekh Texts*, 62 where she observes, "One has even to reckon with the possibility

by García Martínez, Tigchelaar and van der Woude may just as likely be a Penal Code text rather than anything resembling a more comprehensive manuscript of S.[35] Similar caution has been advocated by George Brooke with reference to the identification of Psalms scrolls from Qumran.[36] A particularly interesting specific example is the long noted close relationship between 4Q502 (papRitMar) 16 1–4 which Eibert Tigchelaar has recently identified as a possible fragment belonging to 4Q257 (papS^c).[37]

The following areas of close contact between D and S are particularly noteworthy.

2.1 The Penal Code[38]

It is again fascinating to observe that initial explorations of the relationship between this code in D and S focused on differences. Thus, two of the first studies by the late Prof. Joseph Baumgarten and myself immediately turned to differences of various kinds to try and trace a development. Baumgarten focused particularly on the nature of the punishments stipulated to ask whether a development could be traced towards more leniency or stringency.[39] I attempted to make a case for a development between the S penal code and the D penal code on the basis of differences in the list of infringements.[40] In this context I paid particular attention to the five infringements present in D but lacking in S,

– Despising the judgment of the many
– Taking someone's food against the law
– Fornication with one's wife
– Murmuring against the fathers
– Murmuring against the mothers

The key point to make in the present context is the remarkable degree of *similarity* and close inter-textual relationship between the penal codes now preserved in D and S. This closeness extends from matters of genre and form, to content, sequence, and terminology.

---

that the scant remains of 4QS^h would represent a copy of 5Q13 with which it bears uncanny resemblance."

[35] See DJD 23:433–434 (García Martínez, Tigchelaar, and van der Woude).

[36] Cf. George Brooke, 'The Psalms in Early Jewish Literature in the Light of the Dead Sea Scrolls,' in *The Psalms in the New Testament* (ed. Steve Moyise and Maarten J. J. Menken; The New Testament and the Scriptures of Israel; London: T & T Clark, 2004), 5–24.

[37] Eibert J. C. Tigchelaar, "'These are the names of the spirits of ...:" A Preliminary Edition of *4QCatalogue of Spirits (4Q230)* and New Manuscript Evidence for the *Two Spirits Treatise (4Q257 and 1Q29a)*,' *RQ* 84 (2004): 529–547, here 538.

[38] For references and selective bibliography see note 24 above.

[39] Baumgarten, 'The Cave 4 Versions of the Qumran Penal Code.'

[40] Hempel, 'Penal Code Reconsidered.'

2.2 Gatherings of Ten[41]

Alongside the otherwise dominant paradigm of camps led by a series of overseers in the Damascus Document and the well known yaḥad/rabbim organization described in S both traditions also contain a reference to gatherings of ten individuals to be led by a priest (Cf. 1QS 6:2c–4a//4Q258 (4QS^d)//4Q263 (4QS^i); CD 13:2b–3a). Whether one is inclined to suggest that these gatherings are remnants of an embryonic stage of social interaction (Hempel) or rather reflect a broader Yaḥad organization with outlying communities (Collins and Schofield) or legislate for travelling members of the Yaḥad meeting on a journey (Metso) – the important emphasis to note for our present purposes is the close point of contact between otherwise rather different organizations in this case. Whichever interpretation one favours it is curious to find this correspondence between D and S both in terms of content and terminology.

2.3 Admission into the Community by Swearing an Oath

In a previous study I was keen to stress the close similarity between the requirement to swear an oath to return to the law of Moses with all one's heart and all one's soul found both in D and S (cf. CD 15:5b–3//4Q266 [4QD^a] 8 i//4Q270 [4QD^e] 6 ii and 1QS 5:7c–10a//4Q256 [4QS^b]//4Q259 [4QS^d]).[42] This simple procedure contrasts sharply with a much more complex admission process laid down in 1QS 6: 13b–23. What does this point of contact between S and D indicate? In my view it is most likely an early, embryonic way of expressing a common purpose practiced by Second Temple Period Jews. Metso rightly notes the close relationship of the oath attested in S and D to Neh 10:28–29. It appears there is broader evidence for such an oath in the late Second Period. She takes the

---

[41] See 1QS 6:6b–8a (cf. 4Q258 [S^d] 2 10b) and 1QSa 2:21–22; further *m. Sanh.* 1:6. For some recent discussions see John. J. Collins, 'The Yaḥad and "The Qumran Community,"' in *Biblical Traditions in Transmission: Essays in Honour of Michael A. Knibb* (ed. Charlotte Hempel and Judith Lieu; JSJSup 111; Leiden: Brill, 2006), 81–96; idem, *Beyond the Qumran Community*; Charlotte Hempel, '1QS 6:2c–4a – Satellites or Precursors of the Yaḥad?;' eadem, 'Interpretative Authority in the Community Rule Tradition,' *DSD* 10 (2003): 59–80; eadem, 'Emerging Communal Life and Ideology in the S Tradition,' in *Defining Identities: We, You, and the Other in the Dead Sea Scrolls. Proceedings of the Fifth Meeting of the IOQS in Groningen* (ed. Florentino García Martínez and Mladen Popović; STDJ 70; Leiden: Brill, 2008), 43–61, reprinted as Chapter 5 in this volume; Sarianna Metso, 'Whom Does the Term Yaḥad Identify?,' in *Biblical Traditions in Transmission* (ed. Hempel and Lieu), 213–235; and Schofield, *From Qumran to the Yaḥad*.

[42] Charlotte Hempel, 'Community Structures in the Dead Sea Scrolls: Admission, Organization, Disciplinary Procedures,' in *The Dead Sea Scrolls After Fifty Years: A Comprehensive Assessment* (ed. Peter W. Flint and James C. VanderKam; Leiden: Brill, 1999), Vol. II, 67–92, esp. 70–73, reprinted as Chapter 2 in this volume.

lack of explicit reference in S and D to the covenant of Neh 10 as an indication that Nehemiah may not have been transmitted as scriptural at Qumran.[43] A different way of looking at the triangle S, D, and Nehemiah is to suggest a comparable social development that is attested in Nehemiah and our texts.[44] The central point to be stressed again is the close contact between D and S on this matter. James VanderKam has addressed this issue at some length in favour of the alternative view which considers various statements on admission into the community (attested in D, S, and Josephus) to relate to a single procedure.[45] Moreover, in his estimation the entrance vow took place in the course of the annual covenant ceremony. While VanderKam arrives at a different conclusion from my own, I welcome the debate of this question which seems to me not to have been given the attention it deserves.

2.4 Maskil Headings[46]

Whereas brief Maskil headings occur in a large number of texts from the corpus of the Scrolls and in the Psalms, both D and S share a more elaborate heading announcing the statutes for the Maskil to walk in them with all the living according to the rule for each time (D: למשפט עת ועת //S: לתכון עת ועת). A series of rules addressing the dealings of the Maskil with others follow this heading in S, and I have elsewhere identified the scant remains of Maskil traditions in D.[47] The almost *verbatim* correspondence between D and S as far as the Maskil headings are concerned presents further striking and crucial evidence in our quest to trace the transmission of traditions in S and D.

---

[43] Sarianna Metso, 'Creating Communal Halakhah,' in *Studies in the Hebrew Bible, Qumran, and the Septuagint Presented to Eugene Ulrich* (ed. Peter W. Flint, Emanuel Tov, and James C. VanderKam; VTSup 101; Leiden: Brill, 2006), 279–301, here 297.

[44] See already Morton Smith, 'The Dead Sea Scrolls in Relation to Ancient Judaism,' *NTS* 7 (1960): 347–360, esp. 255–357 and, more recently, Stephen Hultgren, *From the Damascus Covenant to the Covenant of the Community: Literary, Historical, and Theological Studies in the Dead Sea Scrolls* (STDJ 66; Leiden: Brill, 2007) and Joseph Blenkinsopp, *Judaism the First Phase: The Place of Ezra and Nehemiah in the Origins of Judaism* (Grand Rapids, Mich.: Eerdmans, 2009), esp. 189–227.

[45] James C. VanderKam, 'The Oath and the Community,' *DSD* 16 (2009): 416–432.

[46] Cf. CD 12:20b–22a//4Q266 (D^a) 9 ii 7–8 and 1QS 9:12//4Q259 (4QS^e).

[47] See Charlotte Hempel, *The Laws of the Damascus Document: Sources, Traditions and Redaction* (STDJ 29; Leiden: Brill, 1998), 105–106, 114–121, 189; and eadem, '*Maskil(im)* and *Rabbim*: From Daniel to Qumran,' in *Biblical Traditions in Transmission* (ed. Hempel and Lieu), 133–156, reprinted as Chapter 15 in this volume, and further literature referred to there.

2.5 The Self Designation "The People of Perfect Holiness"

CD 20:1b–8a deals with the temporary expulsion of disobedient members, and its close relationship to 1QS 8–9 is evident in the distinctive use of the self-designation "the people of perfect holiness" (אנשי תמים הקדש) frequently in CD 20 and also in 1QS 8:20. In addition to the close resemblance between CD 20:1–8 and S, we also note that the self-designation "the people of perfect holiness" is not found anywhere else in the Scrolls even if the ambition to attain perfection and holiness are expressed more frequently in our texts. I have dealt with this material in more detail elsewhere and noted that the close relationship between 1QS 8–9 and CD 20 is particularly prominent in a section of 1QS that is lacking from 4Q259 (4QS^e) and, following Metso, may be part of a secondary expansion.[48]

2.6 Liturgical Framework

A number of scholars have noted the shared liturgical framework present in the Damascus Document and some of the Rule manuscripts. Thus, the Damascus Document as now attested more fully by the Cave 4 manuscripts (see esp. 4Q266 [4QD^a] 11 and 4Q270 [4QD^e] 7) ends with the description of a covenant renewal event at an annual ceremony. Similarly 1QS and some 4QS copies preserve a substantial account of a covenant ceremony in their opening columns. Vermes suggests both events are identical.[49] Ben Zion Wacholder and Alison Schofield have also commented on the literary connection.[50] Significantly, we have again cause to note further complexity in parts of the S tradition since manuscripts such as 4Q258 (4QS^d) lack the liturgical material found in 1QS 1–4. In other words, we come across a further point of contact between in S and D that is more prominent in the longer form of the S tradition as represented by 1QS// 4Q255–257 (4QS^{a-c}) and 4Q262 (4QS^h).

In this connection Steven Fraade has recently addressed the intriguing relationship of the narrative and legal elements in the Damascus Document and proposed considering the document as a whole as "an anthology that was drawn upon so as to provide performative 'scripts' [...] for the annual covenant renewal

---

[48] Hempel, 'CD Manuscript B and the Rule of the Community,' reprinted as Chapter 8 above. The bibliographical references in this section have been curtailed for the sake of avoiding repetition of the discussion in Chapter 8. For the view that the longer text of 1QS is secondarily expanded over against the shorter text of 4Q259 (4QS^e) at this juncture, see Sarianna Metso, 'The Primary Results of the Reconstruction of 4QS^e,' *JJS* 44 (1993): 303–308.

[49] Geza Vermes, *The Dead Sea Scrolls: Qumran in Perspective* (3d rev. ed.; London: SCM, 1994), 94.

[50] Cf. Ben Zion Wacholder, *The New Damascus Document: The Midrash on the Eschatological Torah of the Dead Sea Scrolls. Reconstruction, Translation and Commentary* (STDJ 56; Leiden: Brill, 2007), 367 and Schofield, *From Qumran to the Yaḥad*, 165.

ceremony ..."[51] Several, though not all, manuscripts of the Community Rule (cf. 1QS, 4Q255 [papS^a], 4Q256 [4QS^b], 4Q257 [papS^c] and 4Q262 [4QS^h]) also include a covenant ceremony and may have functioned in a similar 'performative' manner.[52]

3. Analysis and Conclusions

In the remainder of this chapter I would like to offer an attempt at sketching the larger picture painted by these various pieces of inter-textual contact between S and D. First of all it seems noteworthy to me that we have come across inter-textual data in a variety of shapes and sizes. It seems very likely to me that some of the connections are based on the fact that the authors/compilers of both complex corpora drew on similar source material as is likely the case with the legislation on a quorum of ten and some of the penal code traditions. On the other end of the spectrum we also note some close points of contact that must go back to a later stage in the shaping of the traditions. We may argue about whether this general distinction holds water and where to locate a particular instance of literary contact. The strongest examples of literary contact that go back to a late stage in the growth of the traditions we discussed are the sections on the people of perfect holiness in CD 20 and 1QS 8–9 as well as the liturgical framework shared by some manuscripts of S and D. In each case the evidence of the Cave 4 manuscripts of S can be interpreted to attest a situation before this particular connection was established. Thus, we have a covenant ceremony in some S manuscripts and 4QD but not in all of the S manuscripts. Similarly we have identified a close relationship between CD 20:1–8 and a part of 1QS that is lacking in 4Q259 (4QS^e). In this respect Alison Schofield's recent observation noting that the inter-textual points of contact between S and D appear to be located near or at the point of the Damascus Document's final redaction is convincing.[53] At other times she is not quite as nuanced in her comments, however. Thus, in offering some reflections on the relationship of S to non-S texts she rightly notes, "in addition to utilizing similar theology and terminology, D and S shared similar literary sources and, by extension, a close relationship between their authoring communities."[54] She also maintains – in commenting on

---

[51] Steven D. Fraade, 'Ancient Jewish Law and Narrative in Comparative Perspective: The Damascus Document and the Mishnah,' *Diné Israel: An Annual of Jewish Law* 24 (2007): 65–99 (reprinted in idem, *Legal Fictions: Studies of Law and Narrative in the Discoursive Worlds of Ancient Jewish Sectarians and Sages* [JSJS 147; Leiden: Brill, 2011], 227–254), here 87 [245].

[52] For an overview of what is preserved in the different manuscripts of the Community Rule see Table 1 in DJD 26:1–2 (Alexander and Vermes) and Metso, *Serekh Texts*.

[53] Cf. Schofield, *From Qumran to the Yaḥad*, 165, see also 167–168.

[54] Schofield, *From Qumran to the Yaḥad*, 179.

the table of eighteen 'parallels' between S and other texts – that "S was widely known and influential."[55] Given that out of the eighteen 'parallels' listed ten are from D and two from 4Q265, by and large made up of penal code material, it is doubtful where the overarching influence of S is the best way to account for the points of contact. Two further 'parallels' occur in 5Q11 which may constitute a further copy of the Rule from Cave 5.[56] We further already noted the possible identification of 4Q502 16 as part of 4Q257 (4QS^c).[57] In short, it seems just as likely – if not more so – that the reasons we witness so-called parallels between S and other compositions, chiefly D and 4Q265, is that all of these compositions made use of some of the same source material. Alongside such developmental connections we also found some evidence for links at the seams that gave the material its final form. In this connection Karel van der Toorn speaks of evolving ancient texts in terms of pearls on a string.[58] Our overview over a number of prominent points of contact between S and D has uncovered shared pearls as well as shared types of string between both corpora.

Having talked and reflected on the points of contact between S and D on the level of the texts we may want to ask whether it is possible to make the leap from textual contact to people or social contact? Two options present themselves here. Firstly, it is conceivable that most of the complex literary creations are products of scribal activity, and it is quite likely that the scribes responsible for the complex texts we are working with took an active part in shaping the traditions at their disposal often influenced by the work of their colleagues. Secondly, this is not to say that we do not have representations of something resembling real events on the level of sources or building blocks that entered the final literary structures. It may be possible, for instance, to connect García Martínez's recent suggestion of looking for clusters of texts that reflect similar provenance[59] with clusters of groups that would have given rise to the textual clusters. One conceivable example of the latter development is the material describing small gatherings of ten led by a priest in authority. Finally, in light of the date of a complex work like 1QS (100–75 BCE) and the date of the communal occupation of the site (early first century BCE), a great deal of the material that eventually comprised S originated outside of Qumran. Is it conceivable that some of the traditions contained within S correspond to similar data elsewhere?

Most recently Alison Schofield has proposed that the different manuscripts of S ultimately originated in Jerusalem where a core of the S tradition emerged. A master copy in the shape of 1QS was further promulgated first in Jerusalem and

---

[55] Ibidem.
[56] Cf. Metso, *Serekh Texts*, 6.
[57] See note 37 above.
[58] Karel van der Toorn, *Scribal Culture and the Making of the Hebrew Bible* (Cambridge: Harvard University Press, 2007).
[59] García Martínez, '¿Sectario, no-sectario, o qué?.'

then at Qumran. Thus, she notes, "It may be that 1QS was the authoritative text of Qumran, the product of the activity of the hierarchical and exegetical center of the movement."[60] This particular part of her theory results in a neat divide between the Qumran centre (almost a *politburo*) and outlying communities. This reconstruction seems to me to imply a level of control not supported by the large number of different manuscripts of S attested at Qumran. Schofield further proposes that the Cave 4 manuscripts of the Rule are depositories of blocks of the S traditions that were transmitted and evolved in a number of communities outside of Qumran. I see no need to assign only 1QS to an educated elite, an ancient Jewish equivalent of Oxbridge, if you like.[61] Rather, anyone involved in the active scribal transmission of any S manuscript, be it 1QS or 4QS, would by definition have belonged to the educated elite. Someone from outside the confines of the educated elite would not have been able to read let alone compile and shape this kind of material. It may be preferable, therefore, to think of an ivy *league* of communities if we wanted to go along this route – which I am not sure I do.

There is no need in my view to place 1QS on a pedestal and allot to it a priority that is reminiscent of the now waning star of the Masoretic text in text-critical research. Instead, the texts seem to paint a rather fluid picture of literary activity with influences and material shared in some remarkable ways between D and S as well as other compositions. These amply attested literary relationships illuminate our understanding of how texts emerged, grew, developed, used older sources, and cross-fertilized more broadly. In light of the evident literary creativity witnessed by the Damascus Document and the Community Rule it would be worthwhile to encourage more dialogue with the current debates on the phenomena often referred to with the term 'rewritten scripture.'[62] Different ancient Jewish texts are fluid and influencing each other, and as scholars we are caught in the difficult position of trying to trace how the influence operated. It seems certain that comparable processes and activities can be witnessed in the realm of D, S and 4Q265 and the literature dubbed 'rewritten scripture.' This should not be unexpected since the constituency of people performing such complex learned processes are almost certainly genetically related to one another. If we think of the community or at least its scribal component as learned and engaged in sophisticated dealings with texts and traditions, it is unlikely that they would have made a conscious distinction in their approach to re-writing scripture and re-writing Serekh or D-type-traditions when going about their business.

---

[60] *From Qumran to the Yaḥad*, 279.

[61] See *From Qumran to the Yaḥad*, 190 for the notion of "the movement's hierarchical center," further 275.

[62] For a valuable overview see Sidnie White Crawford, *Rewriting Scripture in Second Temple Times* (Studies in the Dead Sea Scrolls and Related Literature; Grand Rapids, Mich.: Eerdmans, 2008).

Part V

Rules in the Context of Wisdom and Law

Chapter Ten

The Rule Books and the Qumran Wisdom Texts[1]

1. Introduction

It will be useful to preface my observations with a few sentences on the question of communities behind the Scrolls especially as reflected in key texts such as the Damascus Document, the Community Rule, and the Rule of the Congregation. I share the conviction of those scholars who have argued that the Qumran texts reflect the life and thought of more than one community and find it useful to think of these in terms of a parent movement and an off-shoot community. I further hold that both groups have left behind communal legislation, that is, rules dealing with matters of community organization and authority. Thus, in my view, the bulk of the communal legislation in the Laws of the Damascus Document and the communal legislation preserved in 1QSa refer to the parent group whereas most of the Community Rule describes the Yaḥad, an off-shoot of the parent group. However, the situation is more complex and it is, in fact, impossible to allocate each document *in toto* to a particular background. Very frequently the Yaḥad or the S-tradents have left their mark on the final form of documents that contain a great deal of pre-Qumranic material.[2] Conversely, although the bulk of the Community Rule contains material that describes the organization of the Yaḥad it also contains remnants of communal rules that go back to its parent group. An important example of the latter kind are the rules on entering the community by swearing an oath in 1QS 5:7–9 which envisage a much simpler procedure than that found in 1QS 6:13–23. Moreover, this simpler procedure of admission mirrors the practice described in the Damascus

---

[1] This chapter was originally published as 'The Qumran Sapiential Texts and the Rule Books,' in *The Wisdom Texts from Qumran and the Development of Sapiential Thought* (ed. Charlotte Hempel, Armin Lange, and Hermann Lichtenberger; BETL 159; Leuven: Peeters, 2002), 277–295. It originated as a contribution to an international colloquium hosted by Profs Armin Lange and Hermann Lichtenberger, and I gratefully acknowledge their generous hospitality.

[2] Cf. Charlotte Hempel, 'The Earthly Essene Nucleus of 1QSa,' *DSD* 3 (1996): 253–269, reprinted as Chapter 3 in this volume, where I argue for the presence of a number of redactional passages in 1QSa such as 1QSa 1:1–3. See further my identification of a Serekh-redaction in the Laws of the Damascus Document in Charlotte Hempel, *The Laws of the Damascus Document: Sources, Traditions and Redaction* (STDJ 29; Leiden: Brill, 1990; pb. ed. Atlanta, Ga.: SBL, 2006).

Document in CD 15:5–10.³ I have further argued elsewhere, that aside from the communal legislation the Laws of the Damascus Document contain a stratum of halakhic traditions that do not reflect any organized community and go back to priestly circles in the Second Temple Period.⁴

The specific question I would like to address in this chapter is the relationship of the Qumran wisdom texts to the Rule books. I will begin by raising a number of questions we need to ask in order to clarify the topic at hand. It is much more difficult to find answers to most of these questions at this point. Moreover, in view of the fragmentary state of preservation of many of the wisdom texts a good number of questions will, I fear, remain unanswered.

When dealing with the Rule books I will pay particular attention to those parts of these works that deal with communal legislation, or the rules proper contained within them. I set this emphasis because those sections take us closest to the communities reflected in the texts.

2. The Questions

A question that is frequently being raised is: are the Qumran wisdom texts sectarian? Thus, John Collins identifies the following as "one of the most persistent problems in the study of the sapiential materials in the Dead Sea Scrolls,"

> Should they be regarded as products of the community, or communities, responsible for hiding them in the caves, or should they be viewed as part of the general heritage of Judaism around the turn of the era?[5]

I would prefer to reformulate the question and ask: are there any sectarian elements in the wisdom texts? Or, do they display any signs of redactional activity?

---

[3] For a fuller discussion see Charlotte Hempel, 'Community Structures in the Dead Sea Scrolls: Admission, Organization, Disciplinary Procedures,' in *The Dead Sea Scrolls After Fifty Years: A Comprehensive Assessment* (ed. Peter W. Flint and James C. VanderKam; Leiden: Brill, 1999), Vol. II, 67–92, esp. 70–73, reprinted as Chapter 2 in this volume.

[4] Hempel, *Laws of the Damascus Document*.

[5] John J. Collins, *Jewish Wisdom in the Hellenistic Age* (Edinburgh: T & T Clark, 1998), 113. On this question see further Devorah Dimant, 'The Qumran Manuscripts: Contents and Significance,' in *Time to Prepare a Way in the Wilderness: Papers on the Qumran Scrolls by Fellows of the Institute for Advanced Studies of the Hebrew University, Jerusalem, 1989–1990* (ed. Devorah Dimant and Lawrence H. Schiffman; STDJ 16; Leiden: Brill, 1995), 23–58; Daniel J. Harrington, *Wisdom Texts from Qumran* (The Literature of the Dead Sea Scrolls; London: Routledge, 1996), 75–80; W. Lowndes Lipscomb and James A. Sanders, 'Wisdom at Qumran,' in *Israelite Wisdom: Theological and Literary Essays in Honor of Samuel Terrien* (ed. John G. Gammie et al.; Missoula, Mont.: Scholars Press, 1978) 277–285; Hartmut Stegemann, *The Library of Qumran: On the Essenes, Qumran, John the Baptist, and Jesus* (Leiden: Brill, 1998), 100; and Adam S. van der Woude, 'Wisdom at Qumran,' in *Wisdom in Ancient Israel: Essays in Honour of John A. Emerton* (ed. John Day, Robert P. Gordon, and Hugh G. M. Williamson; Cambridge: CUP, 1995), 244–256, esp. 254–255.

That is, are there any indications that the Qumran tradents of these texts have left their mark on the material? One of the characteristics of the Qumran wisdom texts that unites them as a category is, of course, their wisdom component. That is, they display sapiential terminology, forms and concerns. A great deal of the material that displays these characteristics does not seem to exhibit sectarian features. It may be helpful, therefore, to allow for the possibility that what is presented by Collins as alternatives, sectarian or inherited traditions, may well both be present alongside one another in this material. And a scenario along such lines has been proposed by Torleif Elgvin with reference to 4QWays of Righteousness.[6] In the context of this debate Daniel Harrington has drawn attention to the presence of copies of both Instruction and Mysteries in Cave 1, the cave from which many of the key sectarian texts were recovered.[7] This is noteworthy but I am not sure it is a decisive consideration as the presence of a clearly pre-Qumranic work like the Genesis Apocryphon in Cave 1 may illustrate.[8] So much on formulating the bigger questions.

3. Three Qumran Sapiential Works

In what follows I will consider three of the Qumran sapiential texts (Mysteries, Instruction and Ways of Righteousness) and the question of their provenance.

3.1 The Book of Mysteries

This work is preserved in a number of fragmentary copies, and I will here consider only the question of whether it displays any signs of a Qumranic redaction. Collins has drawn attention to 4Q299 (Mysteries) 8 6 and argued on the basis of the statement "with great insight he opened our ears" (ברוב שכל גלה אוזננו),

> The appeal to special revelation suggests strongly that the Book of Mysteries originated in a sectarian milieu.[9]

---

[6] Elgvin argues that 4Q420–421 comprise early sapiential traditions alongside later sectarian editing, cf. DJD 20:173–202, 202.

[7] See Harrington, *Wisdom Texts from Qumran*, 75.

[8] For a different assessment of the Genesis Apocryphon see John C. Reeves, 'What Does Noah Offer in 1QapGen X,15?,' *RQ* 12 (1986): 415–419. On the basis of halakhic parallels between 1QapGen 10:15, Jubilees, and the Temple Scroll Reeves argues that the Genesis Apocryphon may be a sectarian work. Since I would consider neither Jubilees nor the Temple Scroll as of sectarian origin I am not convinced by his case. Note, however, Reeves' more cautious final sentence where he argues, "that *Genesis Apocryphon* was a sectarian *or proto-sectarian* (emphasis mine) product," ibidem, 418.

[9] Collins, *Jewish Wisdom*, 128.

The statement in question is rather general, however, and I would be reluctant to build a case for sectarian provenance on this rather slender piece of evidence. 4Q299 8 6 seems to refer to the divine origin of enlightenment that is revealed to those who devote themselves to the study of wisdom, a notion that is not uncommon in the wisdom tradition and not exclusively sectarian.[10] A statement referring to special revelation is sectarian only if the revelation is linked to a particular group as is the case, for instance, in the famous Well Midrash in Admonition of the Damascus Document in CD 3:12 ff. By contrast, the national terms of reference employed in 4Q299 6 ii 8; 10; 60 4 suggest a non-sectarian provenance for this work as has been convincingly argued by Armin Lange.[11] More particularly Lange has proposed, on the basis of a considerable number of cultic references present in the work, that Mysteries emerged from priestly circles.[12] The all-Israel perspective of Mysteries is particularly pronounced in 4Q299 10. It is interesting to note the use of the term 'judges' (שופטים) in a clearly non-community specific context in lines 5 and 7 of this fragment. The sphere in which the judges operate according to this fragment seems to be Israel and the nations, cf. the references to "all the nations" (כול גואים) and 'Israel' ([ל]ישרא) in line 3. In the Laws of the Damascus Document and 1QSa, by contrast, the biblical terminology 'judges' is applied to refer to a group within the community, cf. CD 15:4; 16:19//4Q270 (Dᵉ) 6 iv 13; CD 9:10; 10:1,4–7a; 14:13; 1QSa 1:15,24,29.

Ambiguous is the partially preserved reference to "those who have turned from transgression" (שבי פשע) in 4Q299 71 1. This expression is applied to the particular circumstances of a movement in the Damascus Document (CD 2:5// 4Q266 [4QDᵃ] 2 ii 5; CD 20:17) and occurs further also in 1QS 10:20//4Q260 (4QSᶠ) 4 10. Since the expression is scripturally based (cf. Isa 59:20) there is no need to assume it has a sectarian connotation in Mysteries.[13] The expression "all the fathers of the congregation" (כול אבות העדה) in 4Q299 76 3 is similarly based on scripture (cf. Num 31:26) but also occurs in a community specific sense in 1QSa and perhaps also in the War Scroll.[14] Finally, the occurrence of the expression "time of wickedness" (קץ רשעה) in 4Q301 3a–b 8 has lead Schiffman

---

[10] Cf. also the reference to a sealed vision in terms reminiscent of Daniel in 4Q299 3 c// 4Q300 1 a ii – b, cf. DJD 20:43–44, 102–103 (Schiffman) and Collins, *Jewish Wisdom*, 128.

[11] See Lange, 'Physiognomie oder Gotteslob? 4Q301 3,' *DSD* 4 (1997): 282–296, esp. 284–286.

[12] Lange, 'Physiognomie oder Gotteslob,' 286 where he concludes, "Myst. wurde somit in weisheitlichen Kreisen verfaßt, deren kultisches Interesse auf eine Nähe zum Tempel deutet." He further argues that Mysteries goes back to "einer am Tempel beheimateten weisheitlichen Gruppe," 287.

[13] Cf. DJD 20:83 (Schiffman); see also DJD 26:165 on 4Q260 4 10 (Alexander and Vermes). The editors conclude, "In Qumran Hebrew שבי פשע is virtually a title of the Community." (165). For a similar view see Dimant, 'Qumran Manuscripts,' 41 n. 45. However, since שבי פשע is a scripturally derived expression I would be inclined to allow for the possibility of different shades of meaning in different Qumran contexts.

[14] Cf. DJD 20:86 (Schiffman).

to observe, "This usage certainly places the document as a 'sectarian' work."[15] It is equally likely that we have here a redactional phrase that was appended at the end of a hymnic section. The four lines of text that precede the line in question contain poetic material in praise of God that displays no signs of sectarian provenance. This is followed in line 8 by a partially preserved reference to the time of wickedness which follows on somewhat uneasily from the preceding hymn of praise. In sum, the bulk of Mysteries seems to contain traditional sapiential material interspersed with a small number of ambiguous terms attested both in the Bible and sectarian contexts and one apparently sectarian turn of phrase.

3.2 Instruction

Geza Vermes has argued that Instruction is "unquestionably sectarian and displays a terminology akin to the Community Rule, the Damascus Document and the Thanksgiving Hymns."[16] By contrast Armin Lange, Patrick Tiller, and John Strugnell have argued that it is a pre-Qumranic composition which does not presuppose a particular community setting.[17] Daniel Harrington has formulated his position on 4QInstruction along the following lines,

> Some of the language in the more theological parts of the work can be found in the so-called sectarian writings from Qumran (Community Rule, Thanksgiving Hymns, Damascus Document, etc.). But the work presupposes a secular or non-"monastic" setting.[18]

Elsewhere he seems to single out Instruction and Mysteries as shedding some light on a broad Second Temple movement and tentatively associates them with the movement described in the Damascus Document.[19] The absence of institu-

---

[15] DJD 20:119.
[16] Geza Vermes, *The Complete Dead Sea Scrolls in English* (London: Penguin, 1997), 402.
[17] See Lange, *Weisheit und Prädestination: Weisheitliche Urordnung und Prädestination in den Textfunden von Qumran* (STDJ 18; Leiden: Brill, 1995), 45–92 where his treatment of 4QSapiential Work A is presented under the heading "nichtessenische und protoessenische Texte;" Tiller, 'The "Eternal Planting" in the Dead Sea Scrolls,' *DSD* 4 (1997): 312–335, here 324–325; Strugnell, 'More on Wives and Marriage in the Dead Sea Scrolls (4Q416 2 ii 21 [cf. 1 Thess 4:4] and 4QMMT § B,' *RQ* 17 (1996): 537–547, 546 where he notes, "*4Q415 ff.* has nothing characteristically sectarian in it, in matter or language;" and idem, 'The Sapiential Work 4Q415ff and Pre-Qumranic Works from Qumran: Lexical Considerations,' in *The Provo International Conference on the Dead Sea Scrolls: Technological Innovations, New Texts, and Reformulated Issues* (ed. Donald W. Parry and Eugene Ulrich; STDJ 30; Leiden: Brill, 1999), 595–608.
[18] Harrington, *Wisdom Texts from Qumran*, 40–41. See also idem, 'Two Early Jewish Approaches to Wisdom: Sirach and Qumran Sapiential Work A,' *JSP* 16 (1997): 25–38, here 36–37.
[19] Harrington, 'Ten Reasons Why the Qumran Wisdom Texts are Important,' *DSD* 4 (1997): 246–265, 253 where he observes, "To assume that the Qumran wisdom texts are merely 'library books' seems unlikely. Rather, at least some of them such as Sapiential Work A and the Book of

tions and officials such as the camp (מחנה) and the overseer (מבקר) in 4QInstruction speaks against an association with the communal situation reflected in the Laws of the Damascus Document. The similarities between both works are confined rather to general features such a married life-style and the private ownership of property. It is often noted by scholars that a work like Instruction deals with traditional wisdom themes such as advising caution in financial matters and marital advice and thus clearly presupposes family life and private property. It is not impossible to explain this, as Harrington seems to favour, as indicating the provenance of these instructions from a community that lived an integrated life in society at large. A much simpler explanation, however, is to suppose that the material is traditional wisdom which originated from a non-community specific background and reflects wisdom traditions that were cherished in society at large. To introduce an intermediary entity of a movement that very much resembled society at large behind such instructions should only be done on the basis of positive evidence. In the absence of positive evidence the former kind of reasoning resembles the argument that if we were to be presented with the photograph of a polar bear to say that it is, in fact, not a polar bear but a person dressed up in a very convincing polar bear outfit. This is a provocative way of putting it but I hope it clarifies my point. Harrington's singling out above of "the more theological parts of the work" is interesting and might well hold the key to these questions. It seems conceivable that Instruction is a composite work and that large parts of it comprise a collection of traditional sapiential material whereas other portions may have originated with a particular strand of Second Temple Judaism, though not the Yaḥad, but perhaps its forerunners.[20] In light of its fragmentary character it may not be possible to unravel the literary growth of Instruction with confidence. We can, however, endorse Harrington's basic distinction between the pragmatic instruction material and the more abstract or theological elements. As has been noted by Harrington and others this mixture of behavioural guidelines interspersed with theological passages is known also from Ben Sira.[21] Along similar lines Torleif Elgvin has highlighted the potential significance of distinguishing various layers in Instruction.[22] In 4Q416 2 iii we

---

Mysteries (both in Cave 1 – 1Q26 and 1Q27) probably represented the distinctive intellectual and religious heritage of a larger movement within Second Temple Judaism." See further idem, *Wisdom at Qumran*, 151–152.

[20] Cf. DJD 34:12 (Strugnell and Harrington) for a similar assessment.

[21] Harrington, *Wisdom Texts from Qumran*, 40. See also Collins, *Jewish Wisdom*, 118. On Ben Sira and Sapiential Work A see further James K. Aitken, 'Apocalyptic, Revelation and Early Jewish Wisdom Literature,' in *New Heaven and New Earth: Prophecy and the Millennium* (ed. C. T. Robert Hayward and Peter J. Harland; VTSup 77; Leiden: Brill, 1999), 181–193.

[22] Elgvin, 'The Reconstruction of Sapiential Work A,' *RQ* 16 (1993–1995): 559–580, 560–562. See also idem, 'The Mystery to Come: Early Essene Theology of Revelation,' in *Qumran Between the Old and New Testaments* (ed. Fred H. Cryer and Thomas L. Thompson; Copenhagen International Seminar 6/JSOTSup 290; Sheffield: Sheffield Academic Press, 1998), 113–150, esp. 115 n. 10 where he comments, "The discourses have more 'sectarian terminology'

seem to have one of the "more theological passages", to use Harrington's terms, alongside practical instructions.[23] It is noteworthy that the theological admonitions are here linked to the more worldly instructions in two cases. Thus, as has been noted by Strugnell and Harrington, the instructions to honour father and mother as well as relations between husband and wife are intrinsically linked with the instruction to devote oneself to the study of the mystery to be. This has been clearly spelt out by Strugnell and Harrington,

> This Qumran text is furthermore distinctive in that it links family obligations and interactions to the 'mystery that is to come' – the maven should honour his parents because they uncovered his ear to 'the mystery that is to come' (4Q416 2 iii 18), and, while 'keeping company with' his wife, he should take care not to be distracted from 'the mystery that is to come' (4Q416 2 iii 20–21).[24]

This close link between practical instruction and theological concerns is intriguing and may indicate that both aspects of the text cannot be neatly separated across the board. A redactor responsible for combining the theological parts of the work with the practical advice is a likely contender for intertwining both in these two cases. In any case, the two passages that establish a close connection between practical advice and theological reflection seem to me an important crux in the evaluation of this text.

3.3 4QWays of Righteousness

This text has been published by Elgvin who describes it as a composite wisdom text that contains sectarian organization and halakhic material alongside traditional wisdom elements.[25] In a subsequent study Eibert Tigchelaar convincingly shows, however, that 4Q420–421 (Ways of Righteousness) is best understood as a Rule rather than a sapiential text.[26] Tigchelaar offers improved readings and restorations of a number of fragments and notes textual overlap with the work Halakhah B (4Q264a).[27] 4QWays of Righteousness is fascinating because of the way in which it combines sapiential elements, communal organization, and halakhic material.

---

than the sections with wisdom sayings. The wisdom sayings might reflect an older tradition, to which a writer close to the early Essene community added discourses of his own."

[23] Cf. Harrington, *Wisdom Texts from Qumran*, 45.

[24] DJD 34:35 (Strugnell and Harrington). Note, however, that the editors' comments quoted above presuppose an emendation of a 3rd m. sg. to the 3rd m. pl. of the verb גלה in 4Q416 2 iii 18, see DJD 34:122; see further Harrington, 'Two Early Jewish Approaches.'

[25] See DJD 20:173 (Elgvin); further idem, 'Wisdom in the Yaḥad: 4QWays of Righteousness,' *RQ* 17 (1996): 205–232.

[26] Tigchelaar, 'Sabbath Halakha and Worship in 4QWays of Righteousness: 4Q421 11 and 13+2+8 Par 4Q264a 1–2,' *RQ* 18 (1998): 359–372.

[27] See DJD 35:53–56 (Baumgarten).

160   Chapter Ten

4. Wisdom Elements in the Rule Books

The question of whether there are any wisdom elements in the Rule Books is much easier to answer than the reverse which has been my concern thus far. Wisdom elements in the Rule Books are clearly present, and this has frequently been emphasized.[28] I will deal with this aspect of the debate by focusing on three specific issues that shed light on the relationship of the Rule Books to the Qumran sapiential texts: the mystery to be, the Book/Vision of Hagi, and the Maskil.

4.1 Raz Nihyeh

Of all the passages in the Rule books that display wisdom features one is particularly noteworthy, and that is the occurrence of the expression רז נהיה "the mystery to be" in the Community Rule (1QS 11:3–4). It is of particular interest because this expression is characteristic of a number of sapiential works from Qumran such as Instruction and Mysteries, and its meaning in the sapiential corpus has been the subject of considerable scholarly debate.[29] One could argue that the presence of this expression, which is so characteristic of key Qumran sapiential texts, in the community text *par excellence* indicates a close connection between works like Mysteries or Instruction and the Yaḥad. However, things are more complex than that. The expression רז נהיה occurs in the context of the hymn that makes up the final portion of 1QS, and this hymn is missing from one of the Cave 4 manuscripts of the Community Rule. Thus, 4Q259 (4QS^e) has the calendric text Otot after the section on the Maskil in 1QS 9:26 in place of the short calendric section and the final hymn found in 1QS.[30] In any case, it seems likely that the hymn originally existed independently before its incorporation into some versions of the Community Rule.[31] Thus, the presence of the expres-

---

[28] Thus, van der Woude aptly observes, "wisdom terminology also abounds in non-sapiential writings found among the Dead Sea Scrolls," 'Wisdom at Qumran,' 256. Cf. also Raymond C. van Leeuwen, 'Scribal Wisdom and a Biblical Proverb at Qumran,' *DSD* 4 (1997): 255–264 and Lange, *Weisheit und Prädestination*.

[29] See, for instance, Collins, *Jewish Wisdom*, 123; Elgvin, 'Mystery to Come,' 131–139; Harrington, *Wisdom Texts from Qumran*, 78; idem, 'The RĀZ NIHYEH in a Qumran Wisdom Text (1Q26, 4Q415–418, 423),' *RQ* 17 (1996): 549–553; idem, 'Two Early Jewish Approaches to Wisdom,' 34–35; Lange, *Weisheit und Prädestination*, 45 ff.; DJD 20:31 (Schiffman); and Lawrence H. Schiffman, *Reclaiming the Dead Sea Scrolls: The History of Judaism, the Background to Christianity, the Lost Library of Qumran* (Philadelphia and Jerusalem: JPS, 1994), 206.

[30] Cf. DJD 26:129–152 (Alexander and Vermes); Uwe Glessmer, 'Der 364-Tage Kalender und die Sabbatstruktur seiner Schaltungen in ihrer Bedeutung für den Kult,' in *Ernten was man sät: Festschrift für Kaus Koch zu seinem 65. Geburtstag* (ed. Dwight R. Daniels, Uwe Glessmer and Martin Rösel; Neukirchen-Vluyn: Neukirchener Verlag, 1991), 379–398; Sarianna Metso, 'The Primary Results of the Reconstruction of 4QS^e,' *JJS* 44 (1993): 303–308; and eadem, *The Textual Development of the Qumran Community Rule* (STDJ 21; Leiden: Brill, 1997), 48–54.

[31] Cf. DJD 26:152 (Alexander and Vermes) and Metso, *Textual Development*, 144.

sion רז נהיה in 1QS 11, whilst significant, does not provide a decisive clue to the relationship between the Rule Books and the Qumran wisdom works. Its presence in the final hymn of 1QS can be reconciled with the view that the mystery is a pre-sectarian concept.

4.2 The Book of Hagi

Another major link between the Rule Books and Instruction is the occurrence in both of the term Hagi (הגי). In this case we are on firmer ground in the sense that in the Rule Books the Book of Hagi (ספר ההגי) is referred to in contexts that are clearly describing matters of communal organization rather than blocks of material that may have been combined with communal legislation at a secondary stage such as 1QS's final hymn. In other words, in the Laws of the Damascus Document and in 1QSa the Book of Hagi is firmly rooted in the structure of a community (cf. CD 10:6//4Q266 [4QD^a] 8 iii 5 and 4Q270 [4QD^e] 6 iv 17; CD 13:2; 14:8//4Q267 [4QD^b] 9 v 12; and 1QSa 1:7). As I have argued elsewhere, the community behind the communal legislation in both the Laws of the Damascus Document and 1QSa is best identified with the parent group of the Yaḥad.[32] The passages in question require that both ordinary community members and leading figures are to be familiar with the contents of the Book of Hagi. It is interesting that the expression 'the Book of Hagi' is confined to communal legislation texts that go back to the parent movement and is entirely absent from the Community Rule. This absence from the Community Rule is particularly striking in the case of 1QS 6:3–4 (cf. 4Q258 [4QS^d] 2 7–8; 4Q261 [4QS^g] 2a–c 2–3; 4Q263 [4QS^i] 1 4–5) where virtually the same statement occurs as in CD 13:2 though significantly without the reference to the Book of Hagi. Thus, CD 13:2 reads,

ובמקום עשרה אל ימש איש כהן מבונן בספר ההגי על פיהו ישקו כולם

> And in a place of ten there shall not be lacking a priest who is learned in the Book of Hagi. All of them shall obey him.

1QS 6:3–4//4QS, on the other hand, lacks the reference to the Book of Hagi and reads,

ובכול מקום אשר יהיה שם עשרה אנשים מעצת היחד אל ימש מאתם איש כוהן

> And in any place where there are ten men from the council of the community there shall not be lacking among them a priest.

The only other occurrence of the term Hagi usually rendered 'meditation' occurs in Instruction where we find a reference to 'the vision of Hagi' (חזון ההגי) in

---

[32] See Charlotte Hempel, 'Earthly Essene Nucleus of 1QSa,' and eadem, *Laws of the Damascus Document*, esp. 149–151.

4Q417 2 i 15–16, cf. also 4Q417 2 i 17.³³ Apart from being struck by the significance of this overlap between the Laws of the Damascus Document, 1QSa and Instruction it is exceedingly difficult to be sure what this book/vision contained because the references in the Damascus Document and 1QSa tell us nothing about its contents and the reference to it in Instruction is both fragmentary and difficult. Taking up an earlier suggestion by Louis Ginzberg, Lange has argued that the term should be rendered "Buch bzw. Vision der Erklärung" and that its contents were of a halakhic nature.³⁴ This seems plausible with reference to the Damascus Document and 1QSa. I am not convinced, however, that the character of the vision in Instruction is best perceived as halakhic. In 4QInstruction 2 the vision of Hagi is identified with the Book of Remembrance. Thus, if the vision were understood in halakhic terms the same would apply to the Book of Remembrance. It seems more likely, however, that the Book of Remembrance is referring to a heavenly record of human conduct, cf. Mal 3:16–18.³⁵

4.3 The Maskil³⁶

The participle Maskil is clearly a sapiential term which is further associated with duties of a sapiential nature in some of the Rule Books. It also occurs in some of the Qumran sapiential texts. Moreover, the term Maskil has a pervasive presence in the Scrolls also outside of the Rule Books and the sapiential texts. Thus, it occurs frequently in the liturgical Scrolls such as the Songs of the Sabbath Sacrifice, the Rule of Blessings, and the Songs of the Maskil.³⁷ On this

---

³³ Cf. Harrington, 'Ten Reasons,' 253; idem, *Wisdom Texts from Qumran*, 55–56; see also John J. Collins, 'In the Likeness of the Holy Ones: The Creation of Humankind in a Wisdom Text from Qumran,' in *The Provo International Conference on the Dead Sea Scrolls* (ed. Parry and Ulrich), 609–618.

³⁴ Cf. Lange, *Weisheit und Prädestination*, 84–85. See also Louis Ginzberg, *An Unknown Jewish Sect* (New York: Jewish Theological Seminary of America, 1976), 49–51. Further, Hermann Lichtenberger, *Studien zum Menschenbild in Texten der Qumrangemeinde* (SUNT 15; Göttingen: Vandenhoeck & Ruprecht, 1980), 27–28 where he remarks with reference to the Book of Hagi in CD and 1QSa, "es ist wohl ein Gesetzeswerk."

³⁵ See George J. Brooke, 'Biblical Interpretation in the Wisdom Texts from Qumran,' in *The Wisdom Texts from Qumran* (ed. Hempel, Lange, and Lichtenberger), 201–220; Collins, 'Likeness of the Holy Ones,' 609 n. 2; and Elgvin, 'Mystery to Come,' 139–147.

³⁶ See John Kampen, 'The Diverse Aspects of Wisdom in the Qumran Texts,' in *The Dead Sea Scrolls After Fifty Years* (ed. Flint and VanderKam), Vol. I, 211–243; Lange, *Weisheit und Prädestination*, 144–164; Hans Kosmala, 'Maśkîl,' *JANES* 5 (1973): 235–241 (reprinted in idem, *Studies, Essays and Reviews* [Leiden: Brill, 1978], Vol. I, 149–155); and Carol Newsom, 'The Sage in the Literature of Qumran: The Functions of the Maskil,' in *The Sage in Israel and the Ancient Near East* (ed. James G. Gammie and Leo G. Perdue; Winona Lake, Ind.: Eisenbrauns, 1990), 373–382.

³⁷ Cf. Newsom, 'The Sage in the Literature of Qumran,' who is able to show that some of the issues raised in the liturgical material overlap with the areas of instruction entrusted to the Maskil elsewhere.

occasion I will pay particular attention to the material that refers to the Maskil as the instructor or those passages that describe the role of the Maskil as part of a social group. As we will see, Maskil occurs frequently in the Rule Books in the latter sense but much more rarely so in the wisdom texts. The term is absent from what remains of Mysteries. In what follows I will limit myself to the following texts: Instruction, 4QWays of Righteousness, the Damascus Document, the Community Rule, and 4Q298 Address of the Maskil to the Sons of Dawn.

4.3.1 Maskil in Instruction

The participle maskil occurs in a number of copies of Instruction as follows: once in triple attestation at 4Q416 (2 ii 15)//4Q418 8 15//4Q418a (19 2); once in 4Q417 (1 i 25 [*olim* 2 i 25]; and two more times in 4Q418 (81+81a 17; 238 1).[38] In one instances (4Q418 238 1) the relevant fragment is so small and the context is so fragmentary that it is impossible to make much of it.[39] In the three remaining passages that preserve a sufficient amount of text to permit a relatively informed judgment the term does not refer to a particular office. Thus, in 4Q416 (2 ii 15)//4Q418 (8 15)//4Q418a (19 2) the addressee is admonished to resemble a wise servant (עבד משכיל). In 4Q417 1 i 25 (*olim* 2 i 25) the participle maskil occurs in a formally coherent unit that comprises participles (frequently 'understanding one' בן מבין or מבין, and in this case בן משכיל 'wise one') followed by an imperative and an object to which a second person singular suffix may be appended (cf. 4Q417 1 i 13–14 and the present passage 1 i 25; a similar construction without the suffix occurs in 1 i 18 – in the latter case the phrase is interrupted by an intriguingly positioned *vacat* which may suggest a degree of hesitation on the part of the scribe[40]). It is clear that in 4Q417 1 i maskil is used synonymously with mebin. Finally, in 4Q418 81+81a 17 the construction "all your wise teachers" (כול משכילכה) makes it clear that this passage does not refer to an office held by an individual either. In sum, there is no clear-cut case in Instruction where the participle refers to a particular office.

---

[38] The figures and references cited in the original 2002 publication of this chapter were based on Ben Zion Wacholder and Martin G. Abegg, *A Preliminary Edition of the Unpublished Dead Sea Scrolls: The Hebrew and Aramaic Texts from Cave 4*. Fascicle 4: *Concordance of Fascicles 1–3* (Washington, D. C.: Biblical Archaeology Society, 1996), 251. For the purposes of the republication of the article in this volume the data and discussion have been updated on the basis of DJD 34.

[39] See DJD 34:447–448 (Strugnell and Harrington).

[40] See DJD 34:151–169 and Plate 8.

4.3.2 Maskil in 4QWays of Righteousness

In 4Q421 the term maskil occurs twice. Scholars are in disagreement on how to understand the participle, and the context of both occurrences is fragmentary.[41] In the first case it occurs alongside another participle נבון 'discerning' and seems to have the meaning 'wise one' (4Q421 1a ii-b 10). The second occurrence in 4Q421 1a ii-b 12 may refer to the office of the maskil in connection with reproof although it is difficult to be sure. It is noteworthy that the topic of rebuke is dealt with in the Community Rule (1QS 5:24–6:1//4QS), the Damascus Document (CD 9:2–8.16–20//4QD) and 4Q477, but in none of these passages is the Maskil involved in the process.

4.3.3 Maskil in the Damascus Document

Baumgarten has tentatively proposed restoring a reference to the Maskil as part of the title of this work in 4Q266 (4QD^a).[42] No strong case can be built on such an entirely hypothetical restoration. In fact, the complete lack of references to this figure in the Admonition might even speak against it. We will see below, however, that 4Q298 (Address of the Maskil to the Sons of Dawn) may provide some support for Baumgarten's proposal. CD 12:20b–22a//4Q266 (4QD^a) 9 ii 7–8 announces rules for the wise leader with the words,

ואלה החקים למשכיל להתהלך בם עם כול חי למשפט עת ועת

And these are the statutes by which the Maskil shall deal with all the living according to the rule appropriate for every time.

This announcement is almost identical to the heading that introduces the section on the Maskil in 1QS 9:12//4Q259 (4QS^e) 3 6–8[43] which reads,

אלה החוקים למשכיל להתהלך בם עם כול חי לתכון עת ועת למשקל איש ואיש

These are the statutes by which the Maskil shall deal with all the living according to the rule appropriate for every time and according to the weight of each man ...

---

[41] Cf. Elgvin, 'Wisdom in the Yaḥad;' 215; Kampen, 'Diverse Aspects of Wisdom,' 233 and n. 99; Johann Maier, *Die Qumran-Essener: Die Texte vom Toten Meer* (UTB 1863; München: Reinhardt, 1995), Vol. II, 489; Tigchelaar, 'Sabbath Halakha,' 370; Michael Wise, Martin Abegg, and Edward Cook, *The Dead Sea Scrolls: A New Translation* (London: Harper Collins, 1996), 390.

[42] DJD 18:31–32 (Baumgarten). Similar restorations that include a reference to the Maskil in the opening lines of a work have been proposed also for the War Scroll and the Community Rule, cf., for instance, Johan van der Ploeg, *Le rouleau de la guerre* (STDJ 2; Leiden: Brill, 1959), 54–55 and Jean Carmignac, 'Conjecture sur la première ligne de la Règle de la Communauté,' *RQ* 2 (1959): 85–87.

[43] Immediately preceding this heading the sizeable block of material attested by 1QS 8:15–9:11 is lacking from 4Q259 (4QS^e), cf. DJD 26:148 (Alexander and Vermes) and Metso, 'Primary Results.'

Unlike in 1QS where this heading introduces a section of rules describing the role of the Maskil no such rules follow in the Laws of the Damascus Document. As far as the Damascus Document is concerned I have argued elsewhere that this heading forms part of remnants of traditions dealing with the Maskil that have been overshadowed by the figure of the overseer (מבקר) in the Laws in their present form.[44] The tradition complex dealing with the Maskil in the Damascus Document is made up of the present heading and CD 13:22//4QD where we have the fragmentary remains of a concluding statement, "[And] these are the ordi[nan]ces for the wise leader" (אלה המש[פט]ים למשכיל[)]. I have further assigned CD 13:7c–8 and CD 13:14–15a to this complex of traditions.[45]

4.3.4 Maskil in the Community Rule

The term Maskil occurs in a number of places in the Community Rule and, as is the case in the Damascus Document, chiefly in headings. Carmignac followed by others suggested reconstructing למשכיל in 1QS 1:1 as part of the title of the Community Rule.[46] The introduction to the teaching of the two spirits makes reference to the Maskil in 1QS 3:13. Furthermore, 4Q256 (4QS^b) 9 1//4Q258 (4QS^d) 1 1 begin the section parallel to 1QS 5:1 with the words מדרש למשכיל which are significantly absent in the parallel text of 1QS 5.[47] Finally, 1QS 9 comprises two further headings that refer to the Maskil in 1QS 9:12//4Q259 (4QS^e) 3 6–7 and 1QS 9:21//[4Q256 (4QS^b) 18 4–5, largely reconstructed]// 4Q258 (4QS^d) 8 5–6//4Q259 (4QS^e) 4 2–3.

Of all these passages 1QS 9:12–26//4QS is the most instructive in informing us about the role of the Maskil, and in what follows I shall focus on this material.

---

[44] Cf. Hempel, *Laws of the Damascus Document*, 105–106, 118–121, 123–125, 150, 189.

[45] A further possible reference to the Maskil is partially preserved in 4Q266 (4QD^a) 5 i 17. This passage uniquely combines terminology characteristic of the Admonition and the Laws and probably belongs to a transitional passage that links both parts of the work, cf. further Hempel, *Laws of the Damascus Document*, 171–174.

[46] Cf. Carmignac, 'Première ligne;' André Dupont-Sommer, *The Essene Writings from Qumran* (Oxford: Blackwell, 1961), 72 n. 3. More recently a reconstruction along these lines has been accepted by Metso, *Textual Development*, 111–112 and with reference to 4Q257 (4QS^c) by Alexander and Vermes, cf. DJD 26:70, see also 32.

[47] See DJD 26:96 (Alexander and Vermes); Charlotte Hempel, 'Comments on the Translation of 4QS^d I,1,' *JJS* 44 (1993): 127–128; Metso, *Textual Development*, 135–136. On the differences between 1QS 5 and 4QS see also Philip Alexander, 'The Redaction-History of *Serekh ha-Yaḥad*: A Proposal,' *RQ* 17 (1996): 437–453; Markus Bockmuehl, 'Redaction and Ideology in the Rule of the Community (1QS/4QS),' *RQ* 18 (1998): 541–560; Geza Vermes, 'Preliminary Remarks on Unpublished Fragments of the Community Rule from Qumran Cave 4,' *JJS* 42 (1991): 250–255; and idem, 'The Leadership of the Qumran Community: Sons of Zadok – Priests – Congregation,' in *Geschichte – Tradition – Reflexion: Festschrift für Martin Hengel zum 70. Geburtstag* (ed. Hubert Cancik, Hermann Lichtenberger, and Peter Schäfer; Tübingen: Mohr Siebeck, 1996), Vol. I, 375–384.

By delineating this section on the Maskil to run until 1QS 9:26 I follow Michael Knibb.⁴⁸ It seems clear that after the lacuna in 1QS 9:26 we have the beginning of a new section that eventually leads to the hymn in 1QS 10:9 ff. The only other passage that seemingly goes into detail about the content of the Maskil's teaching is the Instruction on the Two Spirits in 1QS 3:13–4:26//4QS. This part of 1QS is absent from 4Q258 (4QSᵈ) and 4Q259 (4QSᵉ), and I am convinced by the arguments of those who have proposed that it constitutes an originally independent section that was secondarily associated with the Community Rule and the Maskil.⁴⁹

Let me return, therefore, to 1QS 9:12–26. Whereas several passages are associated with the Maskil in the title or heading, this passage is followed by a series of statements that are specifically describing his role.⁵⁰ Preben Wernberg-Møller has suggested, by contrast, that in 1QS 9:12 ff.

> ... the ensuing injunctions are most naturally taken as applying to the community as a whole, and not only to the teacher of the society.⁵¹

Hence he translates Maskil as 'wise man.'⁵² Admittedly, some of the statements in 1QS 9:12 ff. are ambiguous. In the majority of cases it seems quite clear, however, that the injunctions refer to a leader. Note, for example, the frequent third person plural suffixes ("them") which express the interaction between the individual figure of the Maskil who is entrusted with guiding, instructing or weighing those in his charge. What is more, community members are unambiguously referred to in this section with a range of terms other than Maskil such as "sons of Zadok/righteousness" (בני הצדוק/הצדק),⁵³ "chosen of the time" (בחירי העת), or "those who choose/the chosen of the way" (בוחרי/בחירי דרך).⁵⁴

---

⁴⁸ Cf. Knibb, *The Qumran Community* (Cambridge Commentaries on Writings of the Jewish and Christian World 200 BC to AD 200 2; Cambridge: CUP, 1987), 141–144. This delineation has also been adopted by Metso, *Textual Development*, 118–119. For the view that the section on the Maskil runs until 1QS 10:5 see Newsom, 'The Sage in the Literature of Qumran,' 374. See further Alexander, 'Redaction-History,' 441–442.

⁴⁹ Cf. Jörg Frey, 'Different Patterns of Dualistic Thought in the Qumran Library: Reflections on their Background and History,' in *Legal Texts and Legal Issues: Proceedings of the Second Meeting of the International Organization for Qumran Studies Published in Honour of Joseph M. Baumgarten* (ed. Moshe Bernstein, Florentino García Martínez, and John Kampen; STDJ 23; Leiden: Brill, 1997), 275–335, 289–307; Lange, *Weisheit und Prädestination*, 127–128; Metso, *Textual Development*, 139–140; Hartmut Stegemann, 'Zu Textbestand und Grundgedanken von 1QS III,13–IV,26,' *RQ* 13 (1988): 95–113; and idem, *Library of Qumran*, 110.

⁵⁰ Cf. Metso, *Textual Development*, 145.

⁵¹ Preben Wernberg-Møller, *The Manual of Discipline: Translated and Annotated with an Introduction* (STDJ 1; Leiden: Brill, 1957), 66.

⁵² Cf., e. g., *Manual of Discipline*, 35. So also Elgvin, 'Wisdom in the Yaḥad,' 215.

⁵³ 1QS 9:14 reads "the sons of Zadok" (בני הצדוק) whereas 4Q259 (4QSᵉ) 3 10 has "the sons of righteousness" (בני הצדק). Even prior to the availability of the variant in 4Q259 a number of scholars had proposed emending 1QS's text to read "the sons of righteousness." For a recent discussion of this passage which argues against emending 1QS see Robert Kugler, 'A Note on 1QS 9:14: The Sons of Righteousness or the Sons of Zadok,' *DSD* 3 (1996): 316–320.

It seems likely to me that 1QS 9:12–26 comprises pre-sectarian traditions associated with the Maskil. Remnants of this complex of traditions are also found in the Laws of the Damascus Document, as I suggested above. The community situation that emerges from 1QS 9:12–26 resembles neither the bulk of the Community Rule nor the Laws of the Damascus Document precisely. Metso seems right when she notes that, "... the passages addressed to the *maskil* in IX,12–26 can easily be interpreted as referring to an already existing communal life."[55] However, the terms used to refer to this group are distinct from the terminology of 'yahad' (יחד) and 'rabbim' (רבים) that were to become the standard self-designations in the Community Rule in its final form. Nor do we find any 'camp' (מחנה) or 'congregation' (עדה) terminology familiar from the communal legislation in the Damascus Document. The one occurrence of yahad in 1QS 9:18–19 seems disruptive and is likely to be secondary. Thus, right in the middle of a statement outlining the Maskil's role of guiding and instructing "those who choose/the chosen of the way" (1QS 9:16b–19a//4Q258 [4QS^d] 8 2 and 4Q259 [4QS^e] 3 16) 1QS 9:18–19 appends "among the men of the Yahad" (בתוך אנשי היחד). The text as it stands implies a sub-group of "those who choose/the chosen of the way" among the larger entity of the men of the Yahad. It seems likely that the self-designation "those who choose/the chosen of the way" which – particularly on the reading attested in 4Q258 (4QS^d) and 4Q259 (4QS^e) – mirrors the earlier expression "chosen of the time" (1QS 9:14) is original and that the terminology "the men of the Yahad" (אנשי היחד) was inserted at a later time. We have positive manuscript evidence that this kind of editorial process did occur in 1QS 9:5–6 where the expression "the men of the Yahad" occurs but is absent from the parallel in 4Q258 (4QS^d) 7 6.[56]

The evidence of 4Q259 (4QS^e) can easily be reconciled with the suggestion that the long section on the duties of the wise leader originated independently. The text of 4Q259 (4QS^e) 3 6 moves directly from the equivalent of 1QS 8:15 to the equivalent of 1QS 9:12.[57] Thus, the text of 4Q259 (S^e) resumes with the heading announcing the duties of the Maskil in 1QS 9:12 which might suggest that the latter material circulated as an independent unit before being incorporated into the S tradition.

As has often been noted, 1QS 9:15–16 seems to allot a role to the Maskil in the admission process of new members.[58] However, in the detailed legislation on

---

[54] Whereas 1QS 9:17–18 reads "those who choose the way" (בוחרי דרך), 4Q258 (4QS^d) 8 2 and probably also 4Q259 (4QS^e) 3 16 read "the chosen of the way" (בחירי דרך), cf. DJD 26:118 (Alexander and Vermes).

[55] *Textual Development*, 144.

[56] DJD 26:113–114 (Alexander and Vermes) and Metso, *Textual Development*, 44–45. See also Alexander, 'Redaction-History,' 441 n. 7.

[57] Cf. DJD 26:148 (Alexander and Vermes) and Metso, 'Primary Results.'

[58] Cf., for instance, Newsom, 'The Sage in the Literature of Qumran,' 376.

the admission into the community in 1QS 6:13 ff. it is the Paqid who is in charge of the process and in CD 15 it is the overseer. It seems that the legislation and procedure underwent development in the course of time, and that some elements of the Maskil tradition became subsumed in the duties of other functionaries. The Maskil's role appears to build on his particular gifts of insight that allow him to judge the spiritual makeup of individuals rather than focusing on administrative duties.[59] It is for this reason that the Maskil and the overseer have distinct roles and should not be identified in my view.[60]

The evidence on the Maskil in the Community Rule seems to point in two directions. On the one hand, Maskil traditions appear to comprise traditional material that pre-dates the Yaḥad as in 1QS 9. On the other hand, references to this individual are found at key junctures in 1QS in its final form which goes back to the time of the Yaḥad. Matters are further complicated by the evidence of the heading in 1QS 5:1 where the Maskil is absent over against the parallels in 4QS (cf. 4Q256 [4QS^b] 9 1 and 4Q258 [4QS^d] 1 1). A comparable conclusion has been reached by Metso who detects early and late Maskil material in the Community Rule. She seems to me on the right track when she advocates Maskil material as part of an early source as well as references to this figure that were introduced at a later stage "for editorial purposes."[61] More detailed work may need to be done to isolate further early traditions associated with the Maskil in the Scrolls. Metso suggests 4Q258 (4QS^d) 1 1ff//4Q256 (4QS^b) 9 1 ff., and I would want to argue for an incorporation of the remnants of a Maskil tradition in the Damascus Document into the larger picture.[62]

---

[59] Cf. Newsom, 'The Sage in the Literature of Qumran,' 382 where she observes with reference to the Maskil, "he also had insight into character, into the "spirits" of individuals, a knowledge he used very directly to form the membership of the sect." See further Philip S. Alexander, 'Physiognomy, Initiation, and Rank in the Qumran Community,' in *Geschichte – Tradition – Reflexion* (ed. Cancik, Lichtenberger, and Schäfer), Vol. I, 385–394, esp. 391, who suggests that the Maskil might have employed physiognomy in order to assess the merits of community members.

[60] For the view that the Maskil and the overseer are titles referring to one and the same official see Knibb, *Qumran Community*, 121; Newsom, 'The Sage in the Literature of Qumran,' 375; and Vermes, *Complete Dead Sea Scrolls in English*, 29. For my own position see Hempel, 'Community Structures in the Dead Sea Scrolls,' 81–82.

[61] Metso, *Textual Development*, 145.

[62] Cf. Metso, *Textual Development*, 145 where she notes, "It may be asked whether the sections addressed to the *maskil* in 4QS^b 5,1 ff./4QS^d 1 I,1 ff. (par. 1QS V,1 ff.) and in 1QS IX,12–16 originate from a common source, from some kind of handbook addressed to the leader of the Essene communities." Note that Metso's numeration of the columns of the 4QS manuscripts above predates the system eventually adopted in DJD 26. The latter is used in this chapter. See further Metso, *Textual Development*, 139 n. 106. For my views on the place of the Maskil in the Damascus Document see section 4.3.3 and n. 44 above.

4.3.5 Maskil in 4Q298 (Address of the Maskil to the Sons of Dawn)

Finally the figure of the Maskil occurs in the title of 4Q298.[63] The editors argue that the work comprises an address by the Maskil to novices in the process of joining the community and describe the function and content of the work as follows,

> Since this composition seems to be an introductory address, it is probable that he [the Maskil] is speaking to novices and that the term 'Sons of Dawn' implies that these individuals are 'dawning' out of the darkness and into the light, and are thus on the verge of becoming 'Sons of Light.'[64]

The editors further propose connecting this text with the admission process as described in 1QS 6:13 ff. Their basic contention has been accepted by John Collins,[65] John Kampen,[66] and considered plausible by Daniel Harrington.[67] Despite such wide-ranging support in favour of the editors' reconstruction of the document's function the evidence on which this hypothesis is based is very slender indeed. The main arguments brought forward are the text's introductory character and the assumption that the term "sons of dawn" designates novices. Let me deal with each one in turn. Firstly, the character of the document as an introductory address is nowhere substantiated by the editors, and I am not sure what they mean by it. I suspect what is meant is that the text was material taught to novices which presupposes rather than establishes the argument they are trying to make. We are left with the term "sons of dawn" (בני שחר) as the only and vital clue, and there is no indication anywhere in the Scrolls that this term designates novices. In particular the texts describing the admission process in some detail in both the Damascus Document and the Community Rule never use the term. In fact, they do not use light and darkness imagery either. Moreover, where the imagery of light and darkness does occur it is assumed that individuals are born with a particular portion of light and darkness, and the notion that one's light-darkness-ratio can be improved through teaching and instruction is nowhere expressed.[68] It seems much more likely to me that the term "sons of dawn" is no more than a synonym for "sons of light."[69] At most the interpreta-

---

[63] See DJD 20:1–30 (Pfann and Kister).
[64] See DJD 20:17 (Pfann and Kister); see also Menahem Kister, 'Commentary to 4Q298,' *JQR* 85 (1994): 237–249, 238; and Stephen Pfann, '4Q298: The Maskîl's Address to All Sons of Dawn,' *JQR* 85 (1994): 203–235, 225.
[65] Collins, *Jewish Wisdom*, 128.
[66] Kampen, 'Diverse Aspects of Wisdom,' 233.
[67] Harrington, 'Review of T. Elgvin et al. DJD 20,' *DSD* 4 (1997): 357–360, esp. 357 and idem, *Wisdom Texts from Qumran*, 65.
[68] Cf., for instance, Stegemann, 'Textbestand und Grundgedanken,' 117–121.
[69] The self-designation "sons of dawn" also occurs in CD 13:14–15 following the reading of Solomon Schechter (*Documents of Jewish Sectaries. Vol. 1: Fragments of a Zadokite Work* [Cambridge: CUP, 1910], 13) and Joseph M. Baumgarten ('The "Sons of Dawn" in CDC

tion put forward by the editors is one of many possibilities, and it is certainly not warranted to read the entire text from the outset with this very thinly supported hypothesis in mind.[70]

Also rather far-fetched is the tentatively proposed idea that the partially preserved expression "[those who pur]sue righteousness" (ורוד[פי צדק]) in 4Q298 1–2 i 2, which is based on Isa 51:1 as noted in the commentary, might refer to 'catechumens.'[71] Here the editors propose the idea of a progression from pursuers of righteousness to those who know righteousness. It is again preferable to think of both terms as synonyms.[72]

Of great interest are the close terminological parallels between the Community Rule and 4Q298 in what the editors label a "list of Essene virtues."[73] There is, however, no indication in these virtues to suggest that they originated with the Essenes or the Qumran sect. By contrast, the editors themselves quite correctly note a dependence on biblical precedents, especially Micah 6:8 and Zeph 2:3. The parallels with Micah extend beyond terminology to overlaps in sequence.

As far as the use of the term Maskil in 4Q298 is concerned the editors' interpretation of the participle as referring to the office of the wise leader seems convincing to me. The designation "sons of dawn" does seem to refer to a particular group placed under his guidance. It seems appropriate, therefore, to add this fascinating new text to the growing body of Maskil traditions in the Scrolls. Finally, in support of his proposed restoration of a reference to the Maskil in 4Q266 (4QD[a]) 1 Joseph Baumgarten refers to the occurrence of the term Maskil in the title of 4Q298.[74] One may add to this that the formal similarity between the body of 4Q298 and the early portions of the Admonition of the Damascus Document, such as the repeated calls to hearken (cf. 4Q298 3–4 ii 3–4 and 4Q266 [4QD[a]] 1 a–b 5; CD 1:1; 2:2,14)[75] may provide some additional support for Baumgarten's restoration.

13:14–15 and the Ban on Commerce among the Essenes,' *IEJ* 33 [1983]: 81–85). The collaborative DJD edition of 4Q298 is contradictory with regard to the reading of CD 13:14–15, cf. DJD 20:16 n. 28 and 21.

[70] A commendably cautious note has entered the edition of 4Q298 at one point but that is the exception, cf. DJD 20:21 where the hypothesis that the expression "sons of dawn" refers to catechumens is specified as "tentative."

[71] DJD 20:22 (Pfann and Kister).

[72] Cf. 4Q299 8 7 for the comparable term "those who pursue knowledge" (רודפי דעת), cf. DJD 20:50 (Schiffman); also 4Q424 3 2, cf. Gershon Brin, 'Wisdom Issues in Qumran: The Types and Status of the Figures in 4Q424 and the Phrases of Rationale in the Document,' *DSD* 4 (1997): 297–311, 298 where he lists the expression "those who pursue knowledge" as a standard wisdom expression. See further Gershon Brin, 'Studies in 4Q424, Fragment 3,' *VT* 46 (1996): 271–295, 277.

[73] Cf. DJD 20:16 (Pfann and Kister).

[74] Cf. DJD 18:32.

[75] A further call to hearken occurs in 4Q270 (4QD[e]) 2 ii 19. On this passage see Hempel, *Laws of the Damascus Document*, 163–170 and eadem, 'The Laws of the Damascus Document and 4QMMT,' in *The Damascus Document: A Centennial of Discovery. Proceedings of*

5. Conclusion

To conclude, it emerges from the discussion offered above that the relationship between the Qumran sapiential texts and the Rule Books is a complex one, and the topic is sure to arouse a great deal of further discussion. The most interesting and fascinating result of the discussion offered above, to my mind, is the presence of a number of overlapping terms and ideas in the material that describes organizational matters in the Rules and the sapiential texts as was the case particularly with the Book/Vision of Hagi. As far the Maskil is concerned we noted the presence of a sizeable tradition complex in the Laws of the Damascus Document, the Community Rule, and 4Q298. More texts could be added to these that fall outside the scope of this paper. In the course of the literary growth of the Laws of the Damascus Document and the Community Rule the role seems to have become merged with other traditions. In the Qumran sapiential texts the participle maskil occurs, but with the notable exception of 4Q298 it proved difficult to establish clear-cut cases where it refers to a particular office in the Qumran wisdom texts.

---

the Third International Symposium of the Orion Center (ed. Joseph M. Baumgarten, Esther G. Chazon, and Avital Pinnick; STDJ 34; Leiden: Brill, 2000), 69–84, reprinted as Chapter 11 in this volume.

Chapter Eleven

The Damascus Document and MMT[1]

למשכיל
For Michael Knibb

1. Introduction

In light of the publication of the Cave 4 manuscripts of the Damascus Document the balance of admonitory material vis-à-vis Laws has changed considerably in favour of its legal components. Whereas the first hundred years or so of research on the Damascus Document have focused primarily though not exclusively on the Admonition it is foreseeable that the next centenary celebration will look back on a substantial increase of studies dealing with the legal part of the document. In this chapter I will attempt a preliminary comparative study of the Laws of the Damascus Document and the halakhic portion of 4QMMT, a question that has been addressed by Lawrence Schiffman in a paper entitled 'The Place of 4QMMT in the Corpus of Qumran Manuscripts' and, more briefly, by Philip Callaway.[2]

Before addressing the particular issues at stake I will begin by briefly outlining my approach. In my book on the Laws of the Damascus Document I proposed a

---

[1] This chapter was published originally as 'The Damascus Document and 4QMMT,' in *The Damascus Document: A Centennial of Discovery. Proceedings of the Third International Symposium of the Orion Center for the Study of the Dead Sea Scrolls and Associated Literature, 4–8 February 1998* (ed. Joseph Baumgarten, Esther Chazon, and Avital Pinnick; STDJ 34; Leiden: Brill, 2000), 69–84. It is a pleasure to express my thanks again to the organizers, participants, and editors of that project and to retain the original dedication to my teacher Michael Knibb to whom I owe a great deal, not least my first encounters with the Scrolls in 1989.

[2] Cf. Lawrence H. Schiffman, 'The Place of 4QMMT in the Corpus of Qumran Manuscripts,' in *Reading 4QMMT: New Perspectives on Qumran Law and History* (ed. John Kampen and Moshe J. Bernstein; SBL Symposium Series 2; Atlanta, Ga.: Scholars Press, 1996), 81–98 (reprinted in idem, *Qumran and Jerusalem* [Grand Rapids, Mich.: Eerdmans, 2010], 123–139), esp. 90–94 [131–135] and Philip R. Callaway, '4QMMT and Recent Hypotheses on the Origin of the Qumran Community,' in *Mogilany 1993: Papers on the Dead Sea Scrolls* (ed. Zdzislaw J. Kapera; Kraków: Enigma, 1996), 15–29, esp. 26. See also John Strugnell, 'MMT: Second Thoughts on a Forthcoming Edition,' in *The Community of the Renewed Covenant: The Notre Dame Symposium on the Dead Sea Scrolls* (ed. Eugene Ulrich and James C. VanderKam; Christianity and Judaism in Antiquity 10; Notre Dame: University of Notre Dame Press, 1994), 57–73, 68.

source- and redaction critical analysis of this corpus.[3] In the wake of my source critical work on the Laws I have undertaken a number of comparative studies to which this chapter may now be added.[4] I have come to the view that since the Laws of the Damascus Document comprise a disparate collection of material some of its components may be fruitfully compared with the Community Rule whereas other portions of this collection have a great deal more in common with a work such as 4QOrdinances[a] or the halakhic part of 4QMMT.

Apart from a number of miscellaneous traditions and traces of redactional activity I distinguish two main literary strata in the Laws of the Damascus Document: a stratum of halakhah and a stratum of community organization. I am well aware that some are uncomfortable with the use of the term halakhah in the context of the Dead Sea Scrolls.[5] I retain the terminology because it expresses the distinction I am trying to make very well. The alternative of speaking simply of 'laws' with lower case 'l' seems unsatisfactory to me because that term is customarily used with upper case 'L' to refer to the part of the Damascus Document that is distinguished from the Admonition.

2. 4QMMT and Communal Legislation in the Damascus Document (D)

Turning now to the specific question at hand it seems that when it comes to establishing the relationship between the Laws of D and 4QMMT we can safely exclude the communal legislation stratum. There is nothing in MMT that refers to matters pertaining to the organization and authority structure of a particular community.[6] By contrast the point of reference is Israel at large with particular emphasis on the distinctive position of the priesthood vis-à-vis the laity.

---

[3] Charlotte Hempel, *The Laws of the Damascus Document: Sources, Traditions and Redaction* (STDJ 29; Leiden: Brill, 1990; pb. ed. Atlanta, Ga.: SBL, 2006).

[4] See Charlotte Hempel, 'The Earthly Essene Nucleus of 1QSa,' *DSD* 3 (1996): 253–267, reprinted as Chapter 3 in this volume; eadem, 'The Penal Code Reconsidered,' in *Legal Texts and Legal Issues: Proceedings of the Second Meeting of the International Organization for Qumran Studies Published in Honour of Joseph M. Baumgarten* (ed. Moshe Bernstein, Florentino García Martínez, and John Kampen; STDJ 23; Leiden: Brill, 1997), 337–348; and eadem, '4QOrd[a] (4Q159) and the Laws of the Damascus Document,' in *The Dead Sea Scrolls Fifty Years After Their Discovery 1947–1997* (ed. Lawrence H. Schiffman, Emanuel Tov, and James C. VanderKam; Jerusalem: IES, Shrine of the Book, Israel Museum, 2000), 372–376, reprinted as Chapter 12 in this volume.

[5] Cf. John Strugnell, 'Second Thoughts,' 65–66; also idem, 'More on Wives and Marriage in the Dead Sea Scrolls: (*4Q416* 2 ii [Cf. *1 Thess* 4:4] and *4QMMT* §B),' *RQ* 17 (1996): 537–547, esp. 541 n. 7. Prof. Shemaryahu Talmon has expressed similar reservations in a discussion at the Hebrew University's Orion Centre in April 1996.

[6] This has frequently been noted, cf. Yaakov Sussman, 'The History of the Halakhah and the Dead Sea Scrolls: Preliminary Talmudic Observations on *Miqṣat Ma'aśe ha-Torah* (4QMMT),' DJD 10:179–200, 186; also DJD 10:113, 121 (Qimron and Strugnell); and Stugnell, 'Second Thoughts,' 68.

It is worth noting that the Laws of the Damascus Document are virtually unique among the Qumran documents as well as the wider body of early Jewish literature in combining almost seamlessly communal legislation with halakhic material that lacks reference to a particular organized community. Thus, we have the Community Rule and the Rule of the Congregation[7] as the two main representatives besides the Damascus Document that preserve communal legislation on the one hand, and a host of writings that preserve halakhic traditions on the other hand. Almost uniquely the Laws of the Damascus Document preserve both elements side by side. I say *almost* uniquely because the curious text 4Q265 (Miscellaneous Rules) comprises the only further example that I can think of.[8]

A further feature that deserves to be mentioned here is the shared employment of camp-terminology in MMT and in the communal legislation of D.[9] It seems to me that the use and meaning of the terminology is quite distinct in both documents. In the Damascus Document the term camp (מחנה) appears as a unit in the organization of the movement described in the communal legislation. The terminology is used in this sense very unselfconsciously in this text and no need was felt, it seems, to offer a definition. In 4QMMT camp-terminology occurs in two passages.[10] In the section dealing with the place of slaughter (4Q394 3–7 ii 14b–19 and parallels) the references to the camp occur in an exegetical context.[11] The passage in question, though fragmentary, constitutes a piece of halakhic exegesis based on Lev 17:3–4 as noted by Qimron.[12] The scriptural base text includes a reference to the camp which is identified with Jerusalem in the

---

[7] For the view that the bulk of 1QSa constitutes communal legislation see Hempel, 'Earthly Essene Nucleus.'

[8] On 4Q265 see DJD 35:57–78 (Baumgarten) and Charlotte Hempel, *The Damascus Texts* (CQS 1; Sheffield: Sheffield Academic Press, 2000), 89–104 and further literature referred to there.

[9] This feature has been discussed previously by Hartmut Stegemann, 'The Qumran Essenes – Local Members of the Main Jewish Union of Late Second Temple Times,' in *The Madrid Qumran Congress: Proceedings of the International Congress on the Dead Sea Scrolls, Madrid 18–21 March 1991* (ed. Julio Trebolle Barrera and Luis Vegas Montaner; STDJ 11; Leiden: Brill, 1992), Vol. I, 83–166, esp. 134–137.

[10] Cf. Lawrence H. Schiffman, 'The Temple Scroll and the Systems of Jewish Law of the Second Temple Period,' in *Temple Scroll Studies* (ed. George J. Brooke; JSPSup 7; Sheffield: JSOT Press, 1989), 239–255, esp. 248–249.

[11] See Lawrence H. Schiffman, 'Sacral and Non-Sacral Slaughter According to the *Temple Scroll*,' in *Time to Prepare the Way in the Wilderness: Papers on the Qumran Scrolls by Fellows of the Institute for Advanced Studies of the Hebrew University, Jerusalem, 1989–1990* (ed. Devorah Dimant and Lawrence H. Schiffman; STDJ 16; Leiden: Brill, 1995), 69–84 (reprinted in idem, *The Courtyards of the House of the Lord: Studies on the Temple Scroll* [ed. Florentino García Martínez; STDJ 75; Leiden: Brill: 2008], 297–313). Further, Esther Eshel, '4QLev^d: A Possible Source for the Temple Scroll and *Miqṣat Ma'aśe ha-Torah*,' *DSD* 2 (1995): 1–13.

[12] Cf. DJD 10:156–157 (Qimron). For a discussion of the scriptural background see Moshe J. Bernstein, 'The Employment and Interpretation of Scripture in 4QMMT: Preliminary Observations,' in *Reading 4QMMT* (ed. Kampen and Bernstein), 29–51, esp. 39–40; George J. Brooke, 'The Explicit Presentation of Scripture in 4QMMT,' in *Legal Texts and Legal Issues*

interpretation offered subsequently. The exegetical context of the references to the camp are accentuated by the technical term כָּתוּב[13] introducing the reference to Lev 17 as well as the multiple occurrences of the third person singular pronoun in the technical sense attested frequently in exegetical texts from Qumran. The second section that employs camp terminology is found in 4Q394 8 iv 8b–12a and parallels and begins with the prohibition of dogs entering Jerusalem.[14] Although the original prohibition is not scriptural the subsequent justification beginning with כי is written in the same exegetical style as the previous section on camps. That is, an element of the prohibition, 'the camp of holiness' (מחנה הקודש), is identified with Jerusalem, and the third person singular pronoun is used repeatedly. It seems possible that the term 'the camp of holiness' and the exegetical leap to identify this with Jerusalem are based on Deut 23:15 where the notion of the holiness of the camp is developed. Finally, it is worth noting that in both sections of MMT that employ camp terminology Jerusalem is identified as the camp, and that this identification is followed in both cases by an affirmation in Deuteronomic style of the election of Jerusalem as 'the place which He has chosen from all the tribes of Israel.'[15] In sum, the Laws of the Damascus Document and MMT employ camp-terminology in a distinct manner. In the Laws of D camp-terminology is used to refer to what appear to be well-established administrative and organizational units whereas in MMT camp-terminology occurs in two passages in an exegetical/definitional context characterized by a Jerusalem-centric perspective.[16]

3. 4QMMT and Halakhah in D

Let me now turn to the halakhah stratum of the Damascus Document and its relationship to the halakhic section of MMT. Here correspondences can be observed

---

(ed. Bernstein, García Martínez, and Kampen), 67–88, 72. Brooke shows that on closer inspection Lev 17:3 has been reordered here rather than paraphrased – a term that implies rewording.

[13] On the use of כתוב in MMT see Brooke, 'Explicit Presentation of Scripture in 4QMMT,' 71.

[14] Elisha Qimron has recently identified a fragment of a third copy of the Temple Scroll (11QT^c) that includes a prohibition of rearing chickens in Jerusalem and noted its affinity to the attitude about dogs in Jerusalem in 4QMMT, cf. Elisha Qimron, 'Chickens in the Temple Scroll (11QT^c),' *Tarbiz* 64 (1995) 473–476 [Hebrew] and Elisha Qimron, *The Temple Scroll: A Critical Edition with Extensive Reconstructions. Bibliography by F. García Martínez* (Beer Sheva: Ben-Gurion University of the Negev Press; Jerusalem: Israel Exploration Society, 1996), 69. See also Joseph M. Baumgarten, 'The "Halakhah" in *Miqṣat Ma'aśe ha-Torah* (MMT),' *JAOS* 116 (1996): 512–516, 514 where he argues that the halakhic concern articulated in MMT about dogs may have a bearing on the practice of burying animal bones attested at Qumran.

[15] The latter phrase is partly restored in the Composite Text (B 32–33) based on 4Q394 3–7 ii 19//4Q397 3 5 (see DJD 10:48–51 [Qimron and Strugnell]). Since the opening words of such a statement are clearly preserved in 4Q394 3–7 ii 19 (היא המקום אשר) the editors' restoration seems plausible.

[16] For discussion see DJD 10:143–145 (Qimron).

on a number of levels. I will begin with three observations of a general kind and then turn to a number of specific texts.

3.1 General Observations

Firstly, the halakhah stratum of the Laws of D shares with the halakhic section of MMT a lack of reference to a particular community that defines itself in distinction from society at large.

Second, on a formal level both the halakhah stratum of the Laws of D and the halakhic section of MMT frequently employ headings introduced by the preposition על 'concerning.'[17] This preposition seems to have been the standard way of compiling strings of halakhic statements or expositions in the late Second Temple period. Baumgarten has drawn attention to the historical significance of this phenomenon.[18] Outside of D and MMT it is found also in 4Q159 (Ordinances[a]) 1 ii 6 and 4Q251 (Halakhah A) 17 1.[19]

Third, a particular sub-category of halakhah in D deals with matters pertaining to the priesthood. I have chosen the term *torot* to identify this sub-category, a term derived from Jacob Milgrom's analysis of Lev 1–16 where he defines *torot* as "the special lore of the priesthood."[20] Moreover, in a paper on the origins of the Temple Scroll Hartmut Stegemann applied the term *torot* to the laws contained in the Temple Scroll.[21] I have assigned the two sizeable blocks of additional legal material from 4QD that deal with the disqualification of certain categories of priests[22] and the section dealing with the diagnosis of skin

---

[17] The late Professor Joseph Baumgarten has drawn my attention to the difference in length of the blocks of material introduced by על headings in D and MMT respectively. On closer inspection great variety in the length of the blocks of material thus introduced exists already within D itself. One need only compare the brief sections on women's oaths (CD 16:10–12) or oaths (CD 9:8b–10a) to the long treatment of the sabbath (CD 10:14–11:18b).

[18] Cf. DJD 18:14–15 and idem, 'The Laws of the Damascus Document–Between Bible and Mishnah,' in *The Damascus Document* (ed. Baumgarten, Chazon, and Pinnick), 17–26.

[19] Since the original publication of this chapter the official edition of 4Q251 (Halakha A) has appeared, cf. DJD 35:25–51 (Larson, Lehmann, and Schiffman), and commenting on 17 1 the editors observe, "This is a title, such as those found throughout the Damascus Document. Such titles come before collections of laws on a specific topic," DJD 35:45. 4Q159 is dealt with more fully in Chapter 12 below.

[20] Jacob Milgrom, *Leviticus 1–16: A New Translation with Introduction and Commentary* (New York: Doubleday, 1991), 2.

[21] Cf. Hartmut Stegemann, 'The Origins of the Temple Scroll,' in *Congress Volume: Jerusalem 1986* (ed. John A. Emerton; VTSup 40; Leiden: Brill, 1988), 235–256, esp. 255 where he describes the laws of the Temple Scroll as "... old *tôrôt* originating among the priests at the temple in Jerusalem."

[22] Cf. Joseph M. Baumgarten, 'The Disqualifications of Priests in 4Q Fragments of the "Damascus Document," a Specimen of the Recovery of pre-Rabbinic Halakha,' in *The Madrid Qumran Congress* (ed. Trebolle Barrera and Vegas Montaner), Vol. II, 503–513.

disease[23] to this category. As I will argue below a great deal of the additional legal material in 4QD reflects priestly concerns. However, what seems to set apart the sections on priestly disqualifications and skin disease is that whereas much of 4QD gives the impression of having been written *by priests* these particular sections seem to have been written *by priests* as well as *for priests* and, one might add, *about priests*. It is of course well known that priestly concerns lie at the heart of the halakhot in MMT also.

3.2 Specific Texts

3.2.1 The 4QD Material on the Disqualification of Priests

As noted above, the material on the disqualification of certain categories of priests preserved in 4Q266 (4QD^a) 5 ii 1–16; 4Q267 (4QD^b) 5 iii 1–8; 4Q273 (4QD^h) 2 1–2; 4 i 5–11 shares an explicit focus on priestly concerns with the halakhic portion of MMT. This hardly needs spelling out for the disqualification material and is equally beyond dispute regarding MMT. In the latter case one need only look at the refrain "For the priests shall take heed concerning x so as not to cause the people to bear sin" which occurs three times in MMT (4Q394 [MMT^a] 3–7 i 14–16; 3–7 i 19–ii 1a; 3–7 ii 13–14)[24] and is based on Lev 22:16.[25] Related to this priestly flavour is a concern with the purity of the sanctuary and the offerings expressed in both texts. Furthermore, both texts include statements that describe the conduct of some priests as falling short of the expected standard, cf. 4Q266 (4QD^a) 5 ii 10–11 which refers to a priest who has caused his name to fall from the truth and the critique of intermarriage with Israelites (on Qimron's interpretation)[26] or with gentiles (on Baumgarten's interpretation)[27] practised by some priests according to 4Q396 (MMT^c) 1–2 iv 4–11. Whatever interpretation

---

[23] Cf. Joseph M. Baumgarten, 'The 4QZadokite Fragments on Skin Disease,' *JJS* 41 (1990): 153–165 and Elisha Qimron, 'Notes on the 4QZadokite Fragments on Skin Disease,' *JJS* 42 (1991): 256–259.

[24] The textual remains of this phrase are substantially preserved in both the first and third instance. 4Q394 3–7 i 19–ii 1a may contain the remnants of a further occurrence of the same refrain.

[25] Cf. DJD 10:48 (Qimron and Strugnell); see also Bernstein, 'Employment and Interpretation of Scripture in 4QMMT,' 36.

[26] Cf. DJD 10:171–175 (Qimron and Strugnell).

[27] Baumgarten's position is spelt out by Qimron in DJD 10:55, 171 n. 178a, and Baumgarten has argued his case in 'The "Halakhah" in *Miqṣat Ma'aśe ha-Torah*,' 515–16. Grabbe has recently expressed his support for Baumgarten's interpretation, cf. Lester L. Grabbe, '4QMMT and Second Temple Jewish Society,' in *Legal Texts and Legal Issues* (ed. Bernstein, García Martínez, and Kampen, 89–108,103 n. 53. See also Robert A. Kugler, 'Halakic Interpretative Strategies at Qumran: A Case Study,' in *Legal Texts and Legal Issues*, 131–140, esp. 135–136, who concludes his analysis "… we are left with an ambiguous passage, at least with respect to precisely whom priests may not marry," 136.

one favours for the latter fragmentary passage it seems clear from 4Q396 1–2 iv 9–11 that some priests are being criticized for their nuptial practices. To be sure, the shortfall in the behaviour of priests criticized in each document is of a different kind, and there is nothing to indicate in 4Q266 (4QD^a) 5 ii that priestly marital practices are an issue in D. It is nevertheless noteworthy that both texts seem to contain material commenting on priestly misconduct of some kind. This overlap, though general, suggests that both texts reflect inner-priestly disputes. It has already been suggested convincingly by Schiffman that inner-priestly disputes form the background to 4QMMT.[28] I would like to add to this that these particular sections of the Laws of D point in a similar direction. It is not possible to attach any more precise labels to these priestly groups since the debates about the names to be given to the Qumran groups, legitimate though they may be, should not dominate the discussion of the issues raised by their writings.[29] Finally, the theological rationale given for the disqualification of priests with imperfect pronunciation from reading the torah in 4Q266 (4QD^a) 5 ii 1–3 reflects a broadly equivalent approach to physical defects as is expressed with regard to the blind and the deaf in 4QMMT (4Q394 [MMT^a 8 iii 19–iv 4). According to 4QD priests with defective pronunciation are barred from reading the torah in case they mislead in a capital matter. 4QMMT seems to criticize the presence of blind and deaf people in the vicinity of the purity of the temple because the deaf are unable to hear the commandments and the blind may inadvertently fail to act according to the laws on mixtures.[30] Thus, in all three cases the theological concern is obedience to the torah which may be put in jeopardy by physical imperfections.[31] A rather different rationale for excluding the blind and the deaf from the congregation is expressed in CD 15:15b–17a//4Q266 (4QD^a) 8 i 6–7 and 1QSa 2:4b–9. Both texts include the blind and the deaf in lists of persons to

---

[28] Cf. Lawrence H. Schiffman, 'The New Halakhic Letter (4QMMT) and the Origins of the Dead Sea Sect,' *BA* 53 (1990): 64–73 [reprinted in idem, *Qumran and Jerusalem*, 112–122].

[29] A similar sentiment is expressed by Strugnell, 'Second Thoughts,' 65. See also Joseph Baumgarten's cautious assessment of this issue in 'Sadducean Elements in Qumran Law,' in *The Community of the Renewed Covenant* (ed. Ulrich and VanderKam, 27–36 and the balanced and cautious argumentation by Yaakov Sussman, 'History of the Halakhah,' 192–196, 200. Further, Grabbe, '4QMMT and Second Temple Jewish Society;' Lawrence H. Schiffman, 'The Sadducean Origins of the Dead Sea Scroll Sect,' in *Understanding the Dead Sea Scrolls* (ed. Hershel Shanks; London: SPCK, 1993), 35–49; idem, 'New Halakhic Texts from Qumran,' *Hebrew Studies* 34 (1993): 21–33; James C. VanderKam, 'The People of the Dead Sea Scrolls: Essenes or Sadducees,' in *Understanding the Dead Sea Scrolls* (ed. Shanks), 50–62. See also Albert I. Baumgarten, 'Rabbinic Literature as a Source for the History of Jewish Sectarianism in the Second Temple Period,' *DSD* 2 (1995): 14–57, esp. 22–30.

[30] The Hebrew term used is תערבת; for linguistic comments see DJD 10:96 (Qimron).

[31] Cf. DJD 10:160 where Qimron observes with reference to the blind and the deaf in 4QMMT, "… none of them are able to act in accordance with the laws of purity." See also Aharon Shemesh, '"The Holy Angels are in their Council:" The Exclusion of Deformed Persons from Holy Places in Qumranic and Rabbinic Literature,' *DSD* 4 (1997): 179–206, 201 n. 60.

be excluded from the congregation because of the presence of angels.[32] On my analysis of the Laws of D the exclusion passage in CD 15//4QD[a] occurs in the context of a piece of communal legislation on the admission into the covenant community. It suffices to stress here that the theological emphases reflected in the material on the disqualification of priests and the exclusion of the blind and the deaf in 4QMMT overlap.

3.2.2 The 4QD Material on Skin Disease, Flux[33] and Childbirth

A similar relationship exists between the block of material dealing with skin disease, flux, and childbirth in 4Q266 (4QD[a]) 6 i–iii; 4Q269 (4QD[d]) 7; 4Q272 (4QD[g]) 1 i–ii; 4Q273 (4QD[h]) 4 ii and the halakhic portion of MMT. This part of the Laws of D is heavily based on Lev 12–15 and, as noted above, the portion dealing with skin disease in particular has a pronounced and explicit priestly character. A concern for the purity of the sanctuary, a dominant theme in MMT, is reflected also in 4Q266 (4QD[a]) 6 ii 4 where women with a discharge are prohibited from entering the sanctuary. As noted by Baumgarten such a prohibition is not scriptural and was probably derived in analogy to the legislation on childbirth in Lev 12:4.[34] Finally, 4Q266 (4QD[a]) 6 ii 4 reflects the same halakhic position on the question of purification that is expressed in MMT as has been noted already by Schiffman.[35] Thus, both 4Q266 (4QD[a]) 6 ii 4 and 4Q396 1–2 iv 1a insist that an impure person (a woman with a discharge in the case of D

---

[32] See also the material in 4Q396 1–2 i 5–6 and 4Q394 8 iii 12b–19a which is critical of various categories of people entering the assembly and marrying Israelites. Cf. further 1QM 7:4b–6a, 4Q174 (Florilegium) 1 3b–5a and 11QT[a] 45:12–14. For scholarly discussions see Joseph M. Baumgarten, *Studies in Qumran Law* (SJLA 24; Leiden: Brill, 1977), 75–87; George J. Brooke, *Exegesis at Qumran: 4QFlorilegium in Its Jewish Context* (JSOTSup 29; Sheffield: JSOT Press, 1985), 178–183; Maxwell J. Davidson, *Angels at Qumran: A Comparative Study of 1Enoch 1–36, 72–108 and Sectarian Writings from Qumran* (JSPSup 11; Sheffield: Sheffield Academic Press, 1992), 185–186; DJD 10:145–147 (Qimron and Strugnell); Lawrence H. Schiffman, 'Exclusion from the Sanctuary and the City of the Sanctuary in the Temple Scroll,' *HAR* 9 (1985) 301–320 (reprinted in idem, *Courtyards of the House of the Lord*, 381–401); idem, 'Purity and Perfection: Exclusion from the Council of the Community in the *Serekh Ha-'Edah*,' in *Biblical Archaeology Today* (ed. Janet Amitai; Jerusalem: IES, 1985), 373–389; idem, *The Eschatological Community of the Dead Sea Scrolls: A Study of the Rule of the Congregation* (SBLMS; Atlanta, Ga.: Scholars Press, 1989), 47–48; Shemesh, '"The Holy Angels are in their Council;"' and Yigael Yadin, *The Temple Scroll* (Jerusalem: IES, 1983), Vol. I, 289–291.

[33] Cf. Joseph M. Baumgarten, 'The Laws about Fluxes in 4QTohora[a] (4Q274),' in *Time to Prepare the Way in the Wilderness* (ed. Dimant and Schiffman), 1–8 and idem, 'Zab Impurity in Qumran and Rabbinic Law,' *JJS* 45 (1994): 273–277. See also Jacob Milgrom, '4QTohora[a]: An Unpublished Qumran Text on Purities,' in *Time to Prepare the Way in the Wilderness* (ed. Dimant and Schiffman), 59–68. Whereas Baumgarten argues that 4Q274 1 1–4a deals with *zab* impurity Milgrom is of the opinion that the same lines pertain to skin disease.

[34] DJD 18:56.

[35] See Schiffman, 'Place of 4QMMT,' 90.

and a person with leprosy in the case of MMT) remains so until sunset on the eighth day.[36] The same halakhic position comes to the fore in 4Q269 (4QD^d) 8 ii 3b–6 which deals with the topic of purification after contracting corpse impurity and the passage laying down the requirements for those preparing the red cow in MMT (4Q394 3–7 i 16b–ii 1a). Both passages insist on the sprinkler waiting for sundown.[37] Finally, Avi Solomon has recently argued that CD 11:21–12:1 is best understood against the background of the *ṭevul yom* debate.[38]

3.2.3 4QD Halakhah Dealing with Agricultural Matters

Legal questions relating to the agricultural sphere, particularly the harvest, make up a large proportion of the additional legal material from Cave 4 in D (cf. 4Q266 [4QD^a] 6 iii a; 4Q270 [4QD^e] 3 i; 4Q266 [4QD^a] 6 iii//4Q267 [4QD^b] 6// 4Q270 [4QD^e] 3 ii;[39] 4Q266 [4QD^a] 6 iv; 4Q271 [4QD^f] 2 1–5//4Q270 [4QD^e] 3 iii 13–15). In an article on 4Q159 (Ordinances^a) Francis Weinert suggested some years ago that the agricultural questions dealt with in 4Q159, particularly the material on the rights of the poor to gather grapes and grain in 4Q159 1 ii 2–5, suggest an agricultural milieu. Thus, he argued, "*4Q159* would seem to presume an agricultural situation where poverty lies in the background."[40] Should the same be said about D? I think not. Rather, it seems to me that the agricultural issues raised in D are dealt with from the particular point of view of the priesthood. The key issue is the harvest and the appropriate contributions to the priests

---

[36] Cf. Joseph Baumgarten, 'Pharisaic-Sadducean Controversies about Purity,' *JJS* 31 (1980): 157–170; DJD 10:166–170 (Qimron and Strugnell); Lawrence H. Schiffman, '*Miqṣat Ma'aśe ha-Torah* and the Temple Scroll,' *RQ* 14 (1990): 435–457, esp. 438–42 (reprinted in idem, *Courtyards of the House of the Lord*, 123–147); and idem, 'Pharisaic and Sadducean Halakhah in the Light of the Dead Sea Scrolls: The Case of the Tebul Yom,' *DSD* 1 (1994): 285–299 (reprinted in idem, *Courtyards of the House of the Lord*, 425–439).

[37] Cf. DJD 18:130–132 (Baumgarten); DJD 10:152–154 (Qimron and Strugnell), and the articles by Baumgarten and Schiffman cited in the immediately preceding note. Cf. also Magen Broshi, 'Anti-Qumranic Polemics in the Talmud,' in *The Madrid Qumran Congress* (ed. Trebolle Barrera and Vegas Montaner), Vol. II, 589–600, esp. 591–592. The same halakhic position is expressed also in 4Q277 (Tohorot B^b) 1 ii 5, cf. DJD 35:115–119 (Baumgarten) and Joseph M. Baumgarten, 'The Red Cow Purification Rites in Qumran Texts,' *JJS* 46 (1995): 112–119. Since its original publication this chapter has been updated to include the reference to the official edition of 4Q277 in DJD 35.

[38] See Avi Solomon, 'The Prohibition Against *ṭevul yom* and Defilement of the Daily Whole Offering in the Jerusalem Temple in CD 11:21–12:1: A New Understanding,' *DSD* 4 (1997): 1–20.

[39] On this text and its parallels in 4Q266 (4QD^a) and 4Q267 (4QD^b), cf. Joseph M. Baumgarten, 'A Qumran Text with Agrarian Halakhah,' *JQR* 86 (1995): 1–8. Note that the numeration of fragments has changed since this chapter was first published, and I have adopted the numeration as it appears in Baumgarten's editio princeps of the 4QD manuscripts.

[40] Francis D. Weinert, '*4Q159*: Legislation for an Essene Community Outside of Qumran?,' *JSJ* 5 (1974): 179–207, 206.

and the sanctuary. Thus, this very substantial portion of 4QD shares the priestly character of the halakhic portion of MMT. Nor do I agree with Weinert's assessment of the situation behind 4Q159 as indicative of poverty and agriculture since the topic of gleanings addressed there is based on scripture (cf. Deut 23:25–26), and the writer's concern is exegetical rather than a social comment.

A specific topic that is addressed both in 4Q266 (4QD^a) 6 iv 4 and 4Q396 1–2 iii 2b–3a is the fourth year produce.[41] Although the legislation in 4QMMT does not explicitly refer to the fourth year, Qimron has shown that 4QMMT is closely based on Lev 19:23–24, the biblical text on the produce of the fourth year.[42] According to Lev 19:23–25 the fourth year produce from the fruit trees is to be offered to the Lord. In addition to 4QD and 4QMMT a host of post-biblical sources interpret this law to mean that the fourth year produce belongs to the priests, cf. *Jub.* 7:35–37, 11QT^a 60:3–4; 1QapGen 12:13–15.[43] As far as this study is concerned it is of interest that the position advanced with regard to the fourth year produce is shared by 4QMMT and D.

3.2.4 Texts Expressing Concern about Defilement through Contact with Gentiles

Concern to avoid defilement through contact with gentiles, particularly the pagan cult, is voiced in a number of passages in the Laws of D.[44] CD 12:6b–11 provides a series of restrictions in dealings with gentiles[45] which includes a prohibition of selling clean animals or birds to the gentiles lest they sacrifice them as well as a prohibition of selling untithed produce to the gentiles (following the interpretation of Ginzberg and Schiffman of CD 12:9b–10a).[46] In the additional legal material from Cave 4 4Q266 (4QD^a) 5 ii 5–6 seems to refer to the impurity of priests taken captive by the gentiles.[47] Finally 4Q269 (4QD^d) 8 ii 1–3 refers to the dangers of defilement through gentile sacrifices, if we accept Baumgarten's

---

[41] Cf. Schiffman, 'Place of 4QMMT,' 90–91.

[42] Cf. DJD 10:164–165 (Qimron and Strugnell).

[43] For a comprehensive discussion see Joseph M. Baumgarten, 'The Laws of 'Orlah and First Fruits in the Light of Jubilees, the Qumran Writings, and Targum Ps. Jonathan,' *JJS* 38 (1987): 195–202; Menahem Kister, 'Some Aspects of Qumranic Halakhah,' in *The Madrid Qumran Congress* (ed. Trebolle Barrera and Vegas Montaner), Vol. II, 571–588, esp. 575–588; and Schiffman, '*Miqṣat Ma'aśe ha-Torah* and the Temple Scroll,' 452–456.

[44] See Schiffman, 'Place of 4QMMT,' 92.

[45] Cf. Lawrence H. Schiffman, 'Legislation Concerning Relations with Non-Jews in the *Zadokite Fragments* and in Tannaitic Literature,' *RQ* 11 (1989): 379–389.

[46] See Louis Ginzberg, *An Unknown Jewish Sect* (New York City: Jewish Theological Seminary of America, 1976), 77–78 and Schiffman, 'Legislation Concerning Relations with Non-Jews,' 387–388.

[47] Following the interpretation proposed in DJD 18:51 (Baumgarten).

interpretation of the third person m. pl. suffix in line 1,[48] as well as metals that have been used in pagan cults. As far as 4QMMT is concerned, as restored in the *editio princeps* 4Q394 3–7 i 6b–8a prohibits bringing gentile wheat into the temple. However, too little text is preserved to allow us even to be certain about the subject matter addressed, and in a review article of DJD 10 Baumgarten has rightly drawn attention to the textual uncertainties of this ruling.[49] We are on slightly firmer ground in 4Q394 3–7 i 11b–12a which deals with the sacrifices of gentiles. Whatever the exact scenario envisaged here it is clear that this part of 4QMMT as well as a number of passages from the Laws of D address the danger of defilement through contact with gentiles.

3.2.5 The Catalogue of Transgressions in 4Q270 (4QD^e)

A fragmentary catalogue of transgressions preserved in 4Q270 (4QD^e) 2 i 9–ii 21 is particularly instructive for an analysis of the relationship between the Laws of the Damascus Document and the halakhic portion of MMT.[50] It is instructive to distinguish between the body of the catalogue, the actual list of transgressions, and the conclusion found at the end of the catalogue. The conclusion to the catalogue in the form of a warning against transgressors of the consequences of provoking the divine wrath is found in 4Q270 (4QD^e) 2 ii 17b–18. Immediately following on from this conclusion lines 19–21 begin with a call to hearken reminiscent of similar calls in the Admonition and read, "And now listen to me all who know righteousness" (ועתה שמעו לי כל יודעי צדק). In particular, this call to hearken may be compared to 4Q266 (D^a) 1 a-b 5; CD 1:1; 2:2,14.[51] In his outline of the contents of the Damascus Document Baumgarten placed the fragments containing this catalogue at the end of the Admonition rather than taking it as part of the legal portion of D, and I believe he was following Milik's placement here. It seems likely that the presence of the call to hearken influenced this editorial decision. Furthermore, in an outline of the contents of 4QD that appeared some years before his official edition Baumgarten notes in his description of the catalogue of transgressions, "The author *concludes* (emphasis mine) with an appeal to the יודעי צדק to choose between the 'ways of life' and the 'paths of perdition.'"[52] Rather

---

[48] Cf. DJD 18:131.

[49] Cf. Joseph M. Baumgarten, 'The "Halakhah" in *Miqṣat Ma'aśe ha-Torah*,' 512.

[50] Cf. DJD 18:142–146 (Baumgarten).

[51] See also 4Q298 which attests similar calls to attention, cf. Stephen Pfann, '4Q298: The Maskîl's Address to All Sons of Dawn,' *JQR* 85 (1994): 203–235 and Menahem Kister, 'Commentary to 4Q298,' *JQR* 85 (1994): 237–249, and DJD 20:1–30 (Pfann and Kister). See also 4Q185, cf. Armin Lange, *Weisheit und Prädestination: Weisheitliche Urordnung und Prädestination in den Textfunden von Qumran* (STDJ 18; Leiden: Brill, 1995), 253 n. 83.

[52] Joseph M. Baumgarten, 'The Laws of the *Damascus Document* in Current Research,' in *The Damascus Document Reconsidered* (ed. Magen Broshi; Jerusalem: IES, 1992), 51–62, 53.

than taking this call to hearken and the subsequent admonition to follow the ways of life and to avoid the paths of destruction as a conclusion to the preceding catalogue of transgressions, it seems preferable to understand the call to hearken as an introduction to what follows as is indeed the case in all the other instances where a similar call to attention occurs in the Admonition of the Damascus Document.[53] An initial understanding of this call to attention as a conclusion can be accounted for by the fragmentary nature of the material. Because of accidents of preservation virtually everything that followed the call to hearken has been lost so that as the fragments now stand it looks at first sight as if this call concludes the preceding list of transgressions.

For our present purposes it is most instructive to focus on the fragmentary list of transgressions preserved in 4Q270 (4QD^e) 2 i 9–ii 17a. This list includes a number of issues that are developed in more detail elsewhere in the Laws of D, and, what is more, several of the topics addressed in the catalogue are included in the halakhic portion of 4QMMT as well as in 11QT. This overlap between 4QD, 4QMMT, and 11QT has been noted by a number of scholars.[54] It is noteworthy, furthermore, that the catalogue does not raise any topic dealt with in the communal legislation stratum of the Laws and that the overlap is restricted to the halakhah stratum. That is to say, there is nothing in the list of transgressions that speaks in terms of a particular organized community. Baumgarten takes the reference to 'those anointed with the holy spirit' in 4Q270 (4QD^e) 2 ii 14 as a reference to "inspired teachers of the community."[55] It seems more likely to me, however, that this expression refers to the prophets as is the case in CD 2:12–13. Such an identification is suggested by a number of biblical passages, esp. Ps 105:15.[56] Moreover, the reference to the offence of revealing a secret of his people to the nations in 4Q270 (4QD^e) 2 ii 13 clearly reflects a national perspective.[57] As far as the literary growth of the Laws of the Damascus Document is concerned two alternatives seem possible. Either this list was a pre-existent

---

[53] See also Hartmut Stegemann, 'Towards Physical Reconstructions of the Qumran Damascus Document Scrolls,' in *The Damascus Document* (ed. Baumgarten, Chazon, and Pinnick), 177–200.

[54] Cf. DJD 18:145–146 (Baumgarten); Otto Betz, 'The Qumran Halakhah Text *Miqṣat Ma'aśe ha-Torah* (4QMMT) and Sadducean, Essene, and Early Pharisaic Tradition,' in *The Aramaic Bible: Targums in Their Historical Context* (ed. Derek R. G. Beattie and Martin J. McNamara; JSOTSup 166; Sheffield: JSOT Press, 1994), 176–202; and Schiffman, 'Place of 4QMMT.'

[55] DJD 18:146.

[56] Cf. Michael A. Knibb, *The Qumran Community* (Cambridge Commentaries on Writings of the Jewish and Christian World 200 BC to AD 200 2; Cambridge: CUP, 1987), 27.

[57] A similar offence is found in 11QT^a 64:6–9 and the En Gedi inscription, see DJD 18:146 (Baumgarten) and Moshe Weinfeld, *The Organizational Pattern and the Penal Code of the Qumran Sect: A Comparison with Guilds and Religious Associations of the Hellenistic-Roman Period* (NTOA 2; Göttingen: Vandenhoeck & Ruprecht/Fribourg: Éditions Universitaires, 1986), 25.

document that was incorporated into the Laws, and a number of issues were spelt out in more detail subsequently; or the list of transgressions is a kind of summary of the topics dealt with in the halakhic stratum of the Laws of D. The former seems more likely to me. It seems less likely that we are dealing with a summary of halakhic points that was composed at a late stage in the development of the halakhah stratum since not all the material mentioned in the catalogue is dealt with elsewhere, although because of the fragmentary nature of both the catalogue and the rest of the Laws it is difficult to be sure.

If the catalogue of transgressions pre-dates the rest of the Laws it could be of central importance for our understanding of the growth of the Laws, or at least for the literary growth of the halakhic component of the Laws. It may have served as a skeleton parts of which were subsequently fleshed out. Moreover, the largest number of thematic correspondences between the Laws of D and the halakhic portion of 4QMMT can be traced to this catalogue of transgressions:[58]

a. 4Q270 (4QD^e) 2 ii 6 as read and partly restored by Baumgarten deals with the fourth year produce. This topic is dealt with again in 4Q266 (D^a) 6 iv 4 and in 4Q396 1–2 iii 2b–3a, and both passages were briefly dealt with above.
b. 4Q270 (4QD^e) 2 ii 7–8 is partially preserved and as plausibly completed by Baumgarten deals with the tithe of cattle and sheep, an issue referred to also in 4Q396 1–2 iii 3b–4a.
c. Skin disease is mentioned in the catalogue in 4Q270 (4QD^e) 2 ii 12, taken up in the body of the Laws of D in 4Q266 (4QD^a) 6 i as well as in 4Q396 1–2 iii 4b–11; iv 1a.
d. Slaughtering pregnant animals is referred to as a contentious issue in 4Q270 (4QD^e) 2 ii 15 as well as in 4Q396 1–2 i 2–4.[59]

In sum, the relatively small amount of text preserved in 4Q270 (4QD^e) of the list of transgressions deals with four issues that are paralleled in the halakhot in MMT.

4. Conclusion

By way of conclusion let me sum up the results of these comparative remarks as well as offer a number of further reflections. Rather than comparing the Laws of the Damascus Document *in toto* to 4QMMT I have focused on those parts of both documents that resemble each other most closely, i. e. the halakhah stratum of the Laws of D and the halakhic portion of 4QMMT. Correspond-

---

[58] The overlap between the catalogue of transgressions and 4QMMT is noted also by Baumgarten in DJD 18:13.
[59] See also 11QT^a 52:5, cf. Schiffman, '*Miqṣat Ma'aśe ha-Torah* and the Temple Scroll,' 448–451; idem, 'Place of 4QMMT,' 88 and 93. Further, Joseph M. Baumgarten, 'A Fragment on Fetal Life and Pregnancy in 4Q270,' in *Pomegranates and Bells: Studies in Biblical, Jewish, and Near Eastern Ritual, Law, and Literature in Honor of Jacob Milgrom* (ed. David P. Wright, David N. Freedman, and Avi Hurvitz; Winona Lake, Ind.: Eisenbrauns, 1995), 445–448.

ences of various kinds (theological, halakhic, formal, and thematic) between the halakhah stratum in the Laws of D and the halakhic portion of MMT were identified. Priestly concerns were seen to lie behind a substantial portion of the Laws of D and virtually all of the halakhot in MMT. The priestly character of the latter is widely acknowledged,[60] and I hope to have been able to show that a considerable portion of the Laws of D shares such concerns. A concentration of thematic overlap was noted between the halakhot listed in 4QMMT and the catalogue of transgressions in 4Q270 (D^e). On the negative side 4QMMT's focus on Jerusalem and the Temple is more pronounced than in the halakhic parts of D. Moreover, MMT's characteristic references to the practice of opponents result in a presentation of its halakhot that is distinct from the Laws of D.

It seems to me that the close relationship between the halakhah stratum of D, particularly the catalogue of transgressions, and the halakhic portion of MMT is beyond doubt. I would like to end by attempting to relate these results to the literary and compositional history of both documents. As far as the Laws of the Damascus Document are concerned I suggest that the compiler of that corpus made use of a body of halakhic traditions and incorporated these into the Laws as we know them today alongside a variety of other material most notably a sizeable amount of communal legislation. I have argued elsewhere that 4Q159 constitutes an example of the kind of source used by the compiler of the Laws of D.[61] Moreover, I noted above that the list of transgressions fragmentarily preserved in 4Q270 (D^e) may well constitute an important witness to the growth of the halakhah stratum of D. Turning to 4QMMT, the excitement over the initial assessment of it as a letter by the teacher of righteousness to the wicked priest, still held by some[62] and questioned by others,[63] may have prevented us from thinking in terms of a compositional history of 4QMMT. An exception is the much debated question of the relationship of the calendric section to the rest of the work.[64] I see no reasons to suppose that the compositional history of 4QMMT is any less complex than is increasingly taken for granted for other Dead Sea Scrolls. It seems probable to me that its author(s) made use of earlier collections of halakhot of the kind that lie behind the Laws of D.

---

[60] Cf., for example, the observations offered by Sussman in 'History of the Halakhah,' 187.

[61] See Hempel, '4QOrd^a (4Q159) and the Laws of the Damascus Document.'

[62] This position has been restated recently by Hanan Eshel, '4QMMT and the History of the Hasmonean Period,' in *Reading 4QMMT* (ed. Kampen and Bernstein), 53–65.

[63] See, for example, Schiffman, 'New Halakhic Letter' and Strugnell, 'Second Thoughts,' 70–73.

[64] Cf. Florentino García Martínez, 'Dos notas sobre 4QMMT,' *RQ* 16 (2993): 293–297; Schiffman, 'Place of 4QMMT,' 82–86; Strugnell, 'Second Thoughts,' 61–62; J. C. VanderKam, 'The Calendar, 4Q327, and 4Q394,' in *Legal Texts and Legal Issues* (ed. Bernstein, García Martínez, and Kampen), 179–194.

Chapter Twelve

The Damascus Document and 4QOrdinances^a (4Q159)[1]

1. Introduction

This chapter will explore the relationship between the Laws of the Damascus Document and 4Q159 (Ordinances^a). The Laws of the Damascus Document and Ordinances^a display significant similarities, a fact that has not gone unnoticed in Qumran scholarship to date. Thus, Francis Weinert has suggested that 4Q159 should be studied in conjunction with the Damascus Document since it reflects a different background from what he calls 'Qumran proper.'[2] In a later article Weinert attempts to place 4Q159 within the framework of Jerome Murphy-O'Connor's hypothesis which locates the origins of the Essene movement in Babylon.[3] Moreover, Joseph Baumgarten has pointed out that 4Q159 displays close formal similarities to the Laws of the Damascus Document.[4]

The text of 4Q159 was first published by John Allegro in a preliminary form in 1961,[5] and Allegro's edition of the complete text appeared in 1968.[6] Furthermore, a number of studies have included comments on the text and restoration of 4Q159, notably the detailed review article of DJD 5 by John Strugnell.[7] What is more, Lawrence Schiffman has recently produced a new critical edition of 4Q159 that also includes a commentary accompanying his translation.[8]

---

[1] This chapter was published originally under the title, '4QOrd^a (4Q159) and the Laws of the Damascus Document,' in *The Dead Sea Scrolls Fifty Years After Their Discovery* (ed. Lawrence H. Schiffman, Emanuel Tov, and James C. VanderKam; Jerusalem: IES, 2000), 372–376.

[2] Francis D. Weinert, '*4Q159*: Legislation for an Essene Community Outside of Qumran?,' *JSJ* 5 (1974): 179–207, 206.

[3] 'A Note on 4Q159 and a New Theory of Essene Origins,' *RQ* 9 (1977–1978): 223–230.

[4] 'The Laws of the *Damascus Document* in Current Research,' in *The Damascus Document Reconsidered* (ed. Magen Broshi; Jerusalem: IES, 1992), 51–62.

[5] John M. Allegro, 'An Unpublished Fragment of Essene Halakhah (4QOrdinances),' *JJS* 6 (1961): 71–73.

[6] DJD 5:6–9, Plate II.

[7] Cf. Jacob Liver, 'The Half-Shekel Offering in Biblical and Post-Biblical Literature,' *HTR* 56 (1963): 173–198, esp. 191–98; John Strugnell, 'Notes en marge du volume V des "Discoveries in the Judaean Desert of Jordan,"' *RQ* 7 (1970): 163–276, esp. 175–179; Weinert, '*4Q159*: Legislation;' and Yigael Yadin, 'A Note on 4Q159 (Ordinances),' *IEJ* 18 (1968): 250–252; see also Jean Carmignac, 'Ordonnances,' in *Les Textes de Qumran: Traduits et Annotés* (ed. Jean Carmignac, Édouard Cothenet, and Hubert Lignée; Paris: Letouzey et Ané, 1963), Vol. II, 295–297.

[8] PTSDSSP 1:145–157 (Schiffman).

4Q159 consists of three parts usually referred to as fragment 1, fragments 2–4, and fragment 5. The following examination will include a discussion of fragment 1 and fragments 2–4 only, since Weinert has made a good case for considering fragment 5 as a different text altogether.[9] Weinert is followed by Schiffman whose recent edition treats fragment 5 as a separate composition which he describes as "A Pesher not Related to 4QOrdinances."[10]

Those parts of the text of fragments 1 and 2–4 that are in a reasonable state of preservation deal with seven stipulations:

1. A regulation concerning the rights of the poor to gather grapes and grain at the winepress or threshing-floor or produce in the field (4Q159 1 ii 2–5; cf. Deut 23:25–26);
2. A statute on the half-shekel offering (4Q159 1 ii 6–12; cf. Exod 30:11–16);
3. A reference to the standardization of bath and ephah (4Q159 1 ii 13; cf. Ezek 45:11);
4. A prohibition of selling an Israelite as a slave (4Q159 2–4 1–3a; cf. Lev 25:47–55);
5. A case to be judged in front of a court of twelve (4Q159 2–4 3b–6a; cf. Deut 17:8–13);
6. A prohibition of wearing garments of the other sex (4Q159 2–4 6b–7; cf. Deut 22:5);
7. A stipulation dealing with a husband denying his wife's virginity at marriage (4Q159 2–4 8–10a; cf. Deut 22:13–21).

2. Shared Content

It is remarkable that five out of the seven stipulations preserved in 4Q159 contain material that is also dealt with in the legal material from 4QD,[11]

1. The regulation dealing with the rights of the poor in 4Q159 1 ii 2–5 is closely related to the legislation on gleanings in 4Q266 (4QD^a) 6 iii and parallels;
2. The reference to the standardization of bath and ephah based on Ezek 45:11 occurs both in 4Q159 1 ii 13 and in 4Q271 (4QD^f) 2 and parallels;
3. The prohibition of selling an Israelite as a slave in 4Q159 2–4 1–3a is reminiscent of 4Q271 (4QD^f) 2 and parallels which deals with the case of an impoverished Israelite, and both passages are based on Lev 25;
4. A prohibition of transvestism occurs in 4Q159 2–4 6b–7 and has been partly restored by Baumgarten in 4Q271 (4QD^f) 3 3–4.[12] Baumgarten's restoration seems likely in light of the textual remains. Moreover, the latter part of 4Q271

---

[9] Cf. '4Q159: Legislation,' 180, 203–204.
[10] PTSDSSP 1:156–157 (Schiffman).
[11] See DJD 18 (Baumgarten).
[12] DJD 18:175.

(4QD^f) 3 and parallels draws on the same chapter of Deuteronomy as the present prohibition is derived from, that is Deut 22. The shared connection to Deut 22 in this fragments speaks in favour of Baumgarten's restoration.

5. Finally, both 4Q159 2–4 8–10a and 4Q271 (4QD^f) 3 12–15 and parallels deal with cases where a groom challenges his bride's virginity. Both passages are based on Deut 22:13–21 and both elaborate the biblical account by providing for an examination of the bride by experienced women. Such an examination is clearly described in the text of 4Q271 (4QD^f). As far as 4Q159 is concerned Jeffrey Tigay's suggested restoration along these lines, that is restoring נשים as the last word of line 8 in fragments 2–4, has now been dramatically confirmed by 4Q271 (4QD^f).[13] In 4Q271 this material forms part of a lengthy section dealing with the arrangement of marriages.[14]

This degree of correspondence in two fragmentary compositions is remarkable, and the lost material in both documents might well have provided further overlap.

3. Correspondences in Matters of Sequence

It is noteworthy, furthermore, that the five corresponding passages occur in the same relative sequential order in both documents. Although both 4Q159 and the Damascus Document include material that is not represented in the other collection of laws, the corresponding material occurs in the same relative sequence. Baumgarten has already drawn attention to the correspondence in sequence between 4Q159 and 4Q271 (4QD^f) 3.[15] Both texts move from the subject of impoverished Israelites to the topic of transvestism and the examination of

---

[13] See Jeffrey H. Tigay, 'Examination of the Accused Bride in 4Q159: Forensic Medicine at Qumran,' *JANES* 22 (1993): 129–134.

[14] Note further the recurrence of the expression referring to the priestly redemption money for a life in 4Q270 (4QD^e) 2 ii 9 and 4Q159 1 ii 6 as noted in DJD 18:146 (Baumgarten). The expression is taken from Lev 27 where it denotes the donation of a person's value to the sanctuary. This seems to be the meaning of the phrase in 4Q270 (4QD^e) 2 ii 9. In 4Q159 the expression has been incorporated into the legislation dealing with the half-shekel, cf. PTSDSSP 1:151 n. 9 (Schiffman). What is more, Baumgarten has drawn attention to the comparable halakhic principle that underlies 4Q270 (4QD^e) 3 ii 19–21 and 4Q159 1 ii 6–8, see 'A Qumran Text With Agrarian Halakhah,' *JQR* 86 (1995): 1–8, 7–8. 4Q270 (4QD^e) 3 ii 19–21 requires the holy offering from the bread only once a year. As Baumgarten has noted this regulation differs markedly from rabbinic requirements for the holy offering to be set aside every time dough was kneaded to make bread. This difference is comparable, Baumgarten goes on to say, to the position vis-à-vis the half-shekel payment to the temple which according to 4Q159 1 ii 6–8 was only due once in a person's lifetime rather than once a year as was the practice attested elsewhere, cf. Liver, 'Half-Shekel Offering.' This seems to indicate that even for topics not dealt with in both documents we can see that both come from the same 'school of thought' when it comes to halakhah.

[15] DJD 18:176.

brides. It emerges from the preceding outline of halakhic issues that such a loose correspondence in sequence reaches more widely – at least according to the sequential arrangement of the fragments in DJD 5 and 18.[16] With regard to the subjects of transvestism and the challenge of a bride's virginity both 4Q159 and 4QD follow the sequence of the biblical text on which these passages are based. Deut 22:5 prohibits transvestism and later on in the same chapter Deut 22:13–21 deals with a husband who questions his bride's virginity. More remarkable is the proximity and the relative sequence of the halakhic exposition of the material dealing with the impoverished Israelite in Lev 25 to issues raised in Deut 22 in both 4Q159 and 4QD. In other words both collections of laws move from an exposition of Lev 25 to Deut 22.

4. Shared Scriptural Basis

It is noteworthy that all the stipulations preserved in 4Q159 as well as the corresponding material in 4QD have a firm basis in scripture. The material in front of us comprises halakhic exegesis.

A significant difference in the presentation of the halakhic exegesis in 4Q159 over against the Laws of the the Damascus Document is the presence of a number of passages in 4Q159 that reflect an historical interest. Thus, Schiffman has drawn attention to the calculation of the half-shekel based on the number of adult males resulting from the census of the Israelites in the desert specified in Exod 38:26 and Num 1:46. Schiffman has perceptively noted regarding this material,

> This portion of the text is somewhat strange since it is retrospective, dealing with the first census, and seems out of place in a code for present-day behavior.[17]

A further passage that reflects an historical perspective is found in 4Q159 2–4 3a where the prohibition of selling an Israelite as a slave is justified by a reference to Israel's delivery from slavery out of Egypt. What is more, 4Q159 1 ii 17, though poorly preserved, may well comprise the remains of a further reference to an episode in Israel's history. Schiffman follows Allegro's *editio princeps* and reads, י[שראל שרף מוש]ה "…[I]srael, Mose[s] burnt …" here.[18]

---

[16] Since the original publication of this chapter an alternative arrangement of the fragmentary remains of 4Q159 based on considerations of content has been tentatively proposed by Moshe Bernstein. Bernstein's proposal is broadly compatible to my own argument, particularly as far as the sequence of material based on Deut is concerned, see Bernstein, '4Q159: Nomenclature, Text, Exegesis, Genre,' in *The Mermaid and the Partridge: Essays from the Copenhagen Conference on Revising Texts from Cave Four* (ed. George J. Brooke and Jesper Høgenhaven; STDJ 96; Leiden: Brill, 2011), 33–55.

[17] PTSDSSP 1:146 (Schiffman).

[18] DJD 5:7 (Allegro). For a different reading see Carmignac, 'Ordonnances,' 296–297 and Weinert, '*4Q159*: Legislation,' 182.

In sum, both 4Q159 and the corresponding material in 4QD are firmly based on scripture. Distinctively, 4Q159 includes a number of references to the narrative framework of the Pentateuch that surrounds the legal portions. A large part of the Laws of the Damascus Document contains legal material that is firmly rooted in scripture, but lacks references to the narrative framework of biblical law.

5. Shared Formal Features

One of the specific links between 4Q159 and the Laws of the Damascus Document noted by Baumgarten concerns a question of form. Having drawn attention to the headings of the form 'Concerning x' (על plus x) attested several times in the Laws of D,[19] Baumgarten pointed out that a similar heading is partially preserved in 4Q159 1 ii 6 followed by a reference to Exod 30:12.[20] He further notes the use of clauses of the type אל plus jussive plus איש in both collections. Finally, in the Introduction to his edition of the Cave 4 manuscripts of the Damascus Document Baumgarten remarks on two cases in 4Q159 2–4 6b–7 – the prohibition of transvestism – where biblical לא has been changed to אל.[21] The same is true also for 4Q271 (4QD^f) 3 3 where the formulation אל י[הי]ו recurs. Thus, on a form critical level the regulations of 4Q159 have much in common with a considerable portion of the Laws of the Damascus Document. Moreover, this formal resemblance covers material from the Laws of D over and above the passages that treat topics also dealt with in 4Q159 discussed above.[22]

6. Conclusion

By way of conclusion I would like to relate the foregoing discussion to the results of my source critical work on the Laws of the Damascus Document.[23]

---

[19] Cf. CD 16:10a,13a//4Q271 (4QD^f) 4 ii 12–13; CD 9:8b; 10:10b//4Q270 (4QD^e) 6 iv 20 and CD 10:14a. Baumgarten plausibly suggests a further possible heading of this type in 4Q266 (4QD^a) 6 iii 3–4 (DJD 18:58), and I would like to propose that 4Q270 (4QD^e) 2 ii 1 is another possible instance of such a heading in 4QD. Baumgarten reads the beginning of line 1 על קדון[(DJD 18:144). The material that follows, especially lines 5–9, deals with priestly shares. It seems at least conceivable that line 1 preserves the remains of the rubric [על קדו]שים introducing this material.

[20] 'Laws of the *Damascus Document* in Current Research,' 56.

[21] DJD 18:13.

[22] In contrast to those sections in the Laws of the Damascus Document that formally resemble 4Q159 the latter lacks introductory formulae to introduce explicit references to scripture as noted already by Weinert, 'Note on 4Q159,' 228.

[23] *The Laws of the Damascus Document: Sources, Traditions and Redaction* (STDJ 29; Leiden: Brill, 1990; pb. ed. Atlanta, Ga.: SBL, 2006).

One of the main literary strata that can be identified in the Laws is a stratum of halakhic material that does not refer to a particular organized community, displays a degree of formal cohesion, and is heavily dependent on scripture. On my analysis of the Laws all of the passages from 4QD referred to above as well as the material elsewhere in the Laws that displays formal similarity to 4Q159 have been assigned to the halakhah stratum of the Laws.[24] Moreover, in common with this stratum of the Laws 4Q159 does not reflect a particular organized community and frequently uses all-Israel terminology, cf. 4Q159 1 ii 4; 2–4 2,5,8. There is little evidence in either collection of laws that warrants an association with a community that had separated from society at large. Thus, rather than arguing that 4Q159 is closely related to the Laws of the Damascus Document *as a whole* I propose that it resembles *a particular component* of the Laws. It seems likely to me that the redactor/compiler responsible for the Laws of the Damascus Document in their present form drew upon a collection of traditional legal material not dissimilar to 4QOrdinances[a].

---

[24] For a discussion on the use of the somewhat controversial term 'halakhah' for a strand in the Laws of the Damascus Document see the Introduction to Chapter 11 above.

Part VI

Priesthood in the Rule Texts and Beyond

Chapter Thirteen

The Sons of Aaron[1]

1. Introduction

The evidence of the Dead Sea Scrolls on the priestly designations 'sons of Aaron' and 'sons of Zadok' is one of the areas where the more recently published texts have provided scholars with a significant amount of additional evidence. One thinks here, for instance, of the important textual variants between 1QS 5 and 4Q258 (4QS^d) 1 and 4Q256 (4QS^b) 9.[2] The topic of the priesthood as depicted in the non-biblical scrolls has been one that has been the subject of a number of studies since the earliest decades after the discovery, and has been lavished with even more attention in the last two decades.[3] In what follows I would like to look particularly at the evidence of the Scrolls on the sons of

---

[1] This chapter was originally published as 'The Sons of Aaron in the Dead Sea Scrolls,' in *Flores Florentino: Dead Sea Scrolls and Other Early Jewish Studies in Honour of Florentino García Martínez* (ed. Anthony Hilhorst, Émile Puech, and Eibert Tigchelaar; JSJSup 122; Leiden: Brill, 2007), 207–224. It was a great privilege to write these thoughts in a *Festschrift* for Florentino García Martínez. I first met Florentino at the Meeting of the International Organization of Qumran Studies in Cambridge in 1995 and have benefited tremendously from his boundless generosity, energy and efficiency ever since. He has done an enormous amount for the discipline, and his hard and selfless labour has paved a much smoother path for my own generation of scholars. I should also like to thank Menahem Kister for an informal discussion while writing this paper.

[2] See, e. g., Geza Vermes, 'Preliminary Remarks on Unpublished Fragments of the Community Rule from Qumran Cave 4,' *JJS* 42 (1991): 250–255; Philip S. Alexander, 'The Redaction-History of *Serekh ha-Yaḥad*: A Proposal,' *RQ* 17 (1996): 437–453; Albert I. Baumgarten, 'The Zadokite Priests at Qumran: A Reconsideration,' *DSD* 4 (1997): 137–156; Markus Bockmuehl, 'Redaction and Ideology in the Rule of the Community (1QS/4QS),' *RQ* 18 (1998): 541–560; James H. Charlesworth and Brent A. Strawn, 'Reflections on the Text of Serek ha-Yaḥad Found in Cave IV,' *RQ* 17 (1996): 403–435; Paul Garnet, 'Cave 4 MS Parallels to 1QS 5:1–7: Towards a *Serek* Text History,' *JSP* 15 (1997): 67–78; Charlotte Hempel, 'Comments on the Translation of 4QSd I,1,' *JJS* 44 (1993): 127–128; Michael A. Knibb, 'Rule of the Community,' in EDSS 2:793–797; and Sarianna Metso, *The Textual Development of the Qumran Community Rule* (STDJ 21; Leiden: Brill, 1997).

[3] For an excellent concise overview with ample bibliography see Robert A. Kugler, 'Priests,' in EDSS 2:688–693. See also idem, 'Priesthood at Qumran,' in *The Dead Sea Scrolls After Fifty Years: A Comprehensive Assessment* (ed. Peter Flint and James C. VanderKam; Leiden: Brill, 1999), Vol. II, 93–116 and Geza Vermes, 'The Leadership of the Qumran Community: Sons of Zadok – Priests – Congregation,' in *Geschichte – Tradition – Reflexion: Festschrift für Martin Hengel zum 70. Geburtstag* (ed. Hubert Cancik, Hermann Lichtenberger, and Peter Schäfer; Tübingen: Mohr Siebeck, 1996), Vol. I, 375–384.

Aaron. My impression is that both in some of the primary sources as well as in the secondary literature the sons of Aaron have suffered under the dominant place allotted to the sons of Zadok in a number of places.[4] This situation is recognized also by Geza Vermes when he regretfully observes the way in which "the terminological clash between sons of Zadok and sons of Aaron largely remained untouched for some four decades of Qumran research during which period most scholars [...] happily and simply maintained, without any proviso, that the sect was governed by the sons of Zadok the priests ...".[5] I have always been puzzled by the awkward coexistence of both designations in the Rule texts.[6] I was inspired to reflect more closely on the picture that emerges about the somewhat elusive Aaronides by the excellent article by Heinz-Josef Fabry, 'Zadokiden und Aaroniden in Qumran.'[7] There Fabry offers an overview over and analysis of the complex evidence on the priesthood as it emerges from various strands in the Hebrew Bible from the Deuteronomistic History, the Priestly work, the Book of Ezekiel, the Chronicler to the Greek Bible, Ben Sira and Qumran. With reference to the Scrolls he rightly emphasizes the way in which references to the sons of Aaron the priests vastly outnumber references to the sons of Zadok the priests.[8] I agree with a great deal of what he has to say but wish to add some further nuances to this ongoing debate. In particular, this chapter is intended to respectfully contradict his conviction that,

> Die Regelliteratur lässt uns keine inhaltlichen und konzeptionellen Unterschiede [with respect to Aaronides and Zadokites] mehr wahrnehmen.[9]

---

[4] See, e. g., the seminal article by Jacob Liver, 'The "Sons of Zadok the Priests" in the Dead Sea Sect,' *RQ* 6 (1967): 3–30. For a different point of view see Philip R. Davies, *Behind the Essenes: History and Ideology in the Dead Sea Scrolls* (BJS 94; Atlanta, Ga.: Scholars Press, 1987), 51–72 where he concludes "Scholars of Qumran simply must stop talking Zadokite," 71 and already Georg Klinzing, *Die Umdeutung des Kultus in der Qumrangemeinde und im Neuen Testament* (SUNT 7; Göttingen: Vandenhoeck & Ruprecht, 1971), 136.

[5] 'Leadership of the Qumran Community,' 379.

[6] See, e. g., Charlotte Hempel, 'The Earthly Essene Nucleus of 1QSa,' *DSD* 3 (1996): 253–269, reprinted as Chapter 3 in this volume; eadem, 'Interpretative Authority in the Community Rule Tradition,' *DSD* 10 (2003): 59–80; and eadem, 'The Literary Development of the S-Tradition: A New Paradigm,' *RQ* 22 (2006): 389–401, esp. 395–397, reprinted as Chapter 7 in this volume. See already Liver, 'Sons of Zadok the Priests,' 13 where he notes, "The selfsame texts in the Rule Scroll, wherein mention is made of 'the sons of Zadok the priests,' contain parallel references to 'the sons of Aaron the priests' or to the priests in general."

[7] Heinz-Josef Fabry, 'Zadokiden und Aaroniden in Qumran,' in *Das Manna fällt auch heute noch: Beiträge zur Geschichte und Theologie des Alten, Ersten Testaments. Festschrift für Erich Zenger* (ed. Frank Lothar Hossfeld and Ludger Schwienhorst-Schönberger; Herders biblische Studien 44; Freiburg: Herder, 2004), 201–217.

[8] 'Zadokiden und Aaroniden,' 209.

[9] 'Zadokiden und Aaroniden,' 213. He continues by granting that such differences "müssen aber bestanden haben" on the basis of the terminology in messianic contexts.

In what follows I will argue that despite the fact that both traditions co-exist in some sources, we are in a position to trace a trajectory of development in the rule texts and beyond.

In order to form as full a picture as possible, I have considered all the references to the sons of Aaron and the sons of Zadok in the Scrolls. Before looking at the evidence, it is worth noting that I have left out of consideration the references to a priest or priests that do not specify their genealogical descent. I have argued elsewhere that a number of passages that speak of incipient communal life in a small-scale context lack concern for the genealogical descent of the priest(s), i. e. 1QS 6:2–4 and 1QS 8:1.[10] Both of these passages share with some of the material discussed below an emphasis on priestly authority in the community without any explicit concerns for the kind of priest required.

Finally, a number of scholars have argued – frequently in the days before the complex evidence of the 4QS manuscripts had become available – that there is no issue to debate since 'sons of Zadok' and 'sons of Aaron' are simply synonyms for one and the same entity.[11] This view seems unlikely to me. As we will see, the full range of passages also indicates that there are contexts in which only one of the two sets of terms are employed which points towards a subtle difference in the use of the terminology.[12] In what follows I hope to draw up a profile of the occurrences of both sets of terms.

2. The Damascus Document (D)

The Admonition of the Damascus Document never refers to the sons of Aaron. Noteworthy, however, are repeated references to the people as a whole in terms of 'Aaron and Israel' both in contexts describing communal origins (cf. CD 1:7//4Q266 [4QD^a] 2 i 11//4Q268 [4QD^c] 1 14; CD 6:2//4Q267 [4QD^b] 2 8) as well as in eschatological contexts that refer to a Messiah of Aaron and Israel (cf. CD 19:11; 20:1).

---

[10] 'Emerging Communal Life and Ideology in the S Tradition,' in *Defining Identities: We, You, and the Other in the Dead Sea Scrolls. Proceedings of the Fifth Meeting of the IOQS in Groningen* (ed. Florentino García Martínez and Mladen Popović; STDJ 70; Leiden: Brill, 2008), 43–61, reprinted as Chapter 5 in this volume.

[11] See, e. g., Gary A. Anderson, 'Aaron,' in EDSS 1:1–2; Klinzing, *Umdeutung des Kultus*, 135–136; Michael A. Knibb, *The Qumran Community* (Cambridge Commentaries on Writings of the Jewish and Christian World 200 BC to AD 200 2; Cambridge: CUP, 1987), 105; Alfred R. C. Leaney, *The Rule of Qumran and Its Meaning* (NTL; London: SCM, 1966), 177 who comments with reference to 1QS 5:22, "Sons of Aaron is no more than a variant for sons of Zadok here." Further, Revised Schürer 2:252–253 n. 56 (Vermes).

[12] Note also the point made by Fabry, namely, that we would expect a more even distribution of designations if their employment was more or less random in the Scrolls, see 'Zadokiden und Aaroniden,' 209.

References to the expectation of a Messiah of Aaron and Israel are also interspersed in the legal part of the Damascus Document, cf. CD 12:23; CD 14:19 // 4Q266 (4QD^a) 10 i 12 // 4Q269 (4QD^d) 11 i 2. However, unlike the Admonition the legal part of the Damascus Document contains six references to the sons of Aaron including one in the catalogue of transgressions. Of these, four references are preserved in the material dealing with the disqualification of certain categories of priests.

a. 4Q266 (4QD^a) 5 ii 5 // 4Q267 (4QD^b) 5 iii 8
'[one] of the sons of Aaron who is taken captive by the nations'
b. 4Q266 (4QD^a) 5 ii 8
'one of the sons of Aaron who departs to ser[ve the nations'
c. 4Q266 (4QD^a) 5 ii 9–10
'[one of the sons of] Aaron who causes his name to fall from the truth (corrected to: whose name was thrown from the peoples)'[13]
d. 4Q266 (4QD^a) 5 ii 12
'from Israel, the counsel of the sons of Aaron[14]

Two further references to the sons of Aaron occur in the Laws. One spells out the responsibility of the sons of Aaron to diagnose skin disease, cf. 4Q266 (4QD^a) 6 i 13 // 4Q272 (4QD^g) 1 ii 2.[15] Finally, the catalogue of transgressions lists someone who fails to "[give to] the sons of Aaron [the fourth (year)] planting," cf. 4Q270 (4QD^e) 2 ii 6. Although part of this statement is reconstructed, the preserved text in the lines that follow leaves little doubt that this part of the catalogue deals with priestly dues.[16]

In sum, the Laws of the Damascus Document frequently refer to the sons of Aaron in contexts that are not community specific. The national context (Israel and the nations) is repeatedly in focus in the material on priestly disqualifications. Moreover, the catalogue of transgressions and the skin disease material

---

[13] The text appears to be corrected from "fallen from the truth" to "was thrown from the peoples," cf. DJD 18:51 (Baumgarten). The latter would correspond more closely with the interest of this passage in gentiles. By contrast, the reference to someone who has diverted from the truth is reminiscent of the penal code as noted by Baumgarten, DJD 18:51.

[14] The occurrence of the term counsel/council is interesting here since it is a key term in the Community Rule where it describes one of the central elements of fellowship of community members. However, the reference to "Israel" immediately before the reference to the sons of Aaron seems to indicate that we are still in a national context of Israel and the nations as in earlier references. On this issue see also Florentino García Martínez, 'Priestly Functions in a Community Without Temple,' in *Gemeinde ohne Temple* (ed. Beate Ego, Armin Lange, and Peter Pilhofer; WUNT 118; Tübingen: Mohr Siebeck, 1999), 303–319, 314–315. In contrast to the emphasis placed here, García Martínez examines these laws against a community-internal rather than national backdrop.

[15] We may compare this to CD 13:4–7a which clarifies that it is a priestly duty to diagnose skin disease, even if the priest is a simpleton and needs help and advice from the overseer.

[16] See DJD 18:142–146 (Baumgarten) and Charlotte Hempel, *The Damascus Texts* (CQS 1; Sheffield: Sheffield Academic Press, 2000), 33–34, 42–43, 87–88 and further literature referred to there.

both employ sons of Aaron terminology to refer to traditional priestly duties and privileges rather than as figures of authority in a particular community.

The sons of Aaron play no role in the Admonition, as we saw. However, the Damascus Document does contain a reference to "the so]ns of Zadok the priests" (4Q266 [4QD^a] 5 i 16) in an intriguing passage that includes material reminiscent both of the Admonition and the Laws (4Q266 [4QD^a] 5 i // 4Q267 [4QD^b] 5 ii).[17] By combining references to the "returnees/penitents of Israel" with references to "the sons of Zadok" the former passage is reminiscent of CD 3:20c–4:4a, which comprises a quotation and interpretation of Ezek 44:15 applying it to three phases in the reform movement's development. In the latter well-known passage the sons of Zadok are identified as the elect of Israel at the end of days. It is the 'sons of Zadok' terminology found here in the Admonition that gave rise to the document's earlier title *Fragments of a Zadokite Work*.[18] In any case, it seems clear that both in this 'mixed passage' in 4Q266 (4QD^a) 5 i and in the Admonition 'sons of Zadok' is the preferred terminology. Noteworthy, moreover, is the community specific background of both references. In the 'mixed passage' the references to the overseer and the Maskil in nearby lines make this clear. In CD 3–4 'sons of Zadok' refers not to the priests, in particular, but apparently to the community as a whole.[19] In short, it seems clear that we can observe a distinctive use of the terminology 'sons of Aaron' in the Damascus Document, namely in non-community-specific contexts with reference to traditional priestly duties and rights.

3. The Community Rule (S)

Before turning to the sons of Aaron, it is worth noting that – not unlike the Damascus Document – the Community Rule also refers to the make-up of the community in the present and the future in terms of Aaron and Israel, cf. 1QS 5:6 // 4Q256 (4QS^b) 9 5–6 // 4Q258 (4QS^d) 1 5 and 1QS 8:6 // 4Q259 (4QS^e) 2 14; 1QS 8:8–9 // 4Q258 (4QS^d) 6 2–3 // 4Q259 (4QS^e) 2 17–18; 1QS 9:5–6 // 4Q258 (4QS^d) 7 6–7. Again very reminiscent of the picture painted in the Damascus Document, 1QS 9:11 – but not 4Q259 (4QS^e) – includes a reference to the expectation of "a prophet and messiahs of Aaron and Israel." Of particular interest for the present enquiry are two places in the Community Rule manuscripts

---

[17] See DJD 18:4–5, 47–49 (Baumgarten) and Charlotte Hempel, *The Laws of the Damascus Document: Sources, Traditions and Redaction* (STDJ 29; Leiden: Brill, 1990; pb. ed. Atlanta, Ga.: SBL, 2006), 171–174; eadem, *Damascus Texts*, 34.

[18] Solomon Schechter, *Documents of Jewish Sectaries: Fragments of a Zadokite Work* (Cambridge: CUP, 1910). The earlier title is favourably recalled by Baumgarten in DJD 18:1. For a nuanced treatment see Maxine L. Grossman, *Reading for History in the Damascus Document: A Methodological Study* (STDJ 45; Leiden: Brill, 2002), 185–209.

[19] Cf. Liver, 'Sons of Zadok the Priests,' 10.

where the sons of Aaron are assigned the role of leading authority figures in the community.

The first passage is found in 1QS 5:21//4Q258 (4QS^d) 2 1–2:

1QS	4QS^d
... according to the authority of the sons of Aaron (...) and[20] the authority of the multitude of Israel	according to the authority of the sons of Aaron (...) the authority of the multitude of Israel

The common ground between 1QS and 4QS^d in this particular passage is extremely interesting since it contrasts sharply with the much more widely discussed instance in 1QS 5//4QS^d where both manuscripts differ sharply in their authority structure. I have recently drawn attention to the immense significance of the shared tradition in 1QS 5:21//4Q258 (4QS^d) 2 1–2 and elsewhere in the S manuscripts.[21] In that study I suggest that the earliest elements in the growth of the S tradition are to be found in the common ground between the manuscripts allowing us glimpses of a state of affairs before the manuscripts went their separate ways, so to speak. What is significant for the current enquiry is the presence in the S tradition – and if I am correct in the earliest strands of the S tradition – of an endorsement of the sons of Aaron's leading role in the community. This tradition differs from the strong endorsement of the sons of Zadok in other parts of S, esp. 1QS 5.

A similar picture emerges from the second passage I wish to focus on, namely 1QS 9:7//4Q258 (4QS^d) 7 7 which contains a further endorsement of the authoritative role of the sons of Aaron in both 1QS and 4QS^d.

1QS 9:7//4Q258 (4QS^d) 7 7 read:[22]

1QS	4QS^d
Only the sons of Aaron shall rule with regard to judgment and property *and on their authority decisions shall be taken concerning any rule of the people of the community.*	Only the sons of Aa]ron [shall ru]l[e with regard to] judgment and property. *Vacat.*

The emphatically placed adverb 'only' seems to imply that there was scope for disagreement in some circles.

---

[20] The absence of the conjunction in 4QS^d may be significant, cf. Hempel, 'Interpretative Authority,' 76–79.

[21] 'The Literary Development of the S-Tradition.'

[22] This passage forms part of the section not attested in 4Q259 (4QS^e), cf. DJD 26:11, 144–149 (Alexander and Vermes) and Metso, *Textual Development*, esp. 69–74.

In sum, the Community Rule, which in parts of its textual history is well-known for promoting the authority of the sons of Zadok over against 'the many' (esp. the lines of 1QS 5)[23] also contains two important passages where several manuscripts (1QS 5:21 // 4Q258 [4QS^d] 2 1–2 and 1QS 9:7 // 4Q258 [4QS^d] 7 7) favour the sons of Aaron as authority figures in the community.[24] This is exceedingly interesting in itself and contains, as I tried to argue elsewhere, important clues to the textual development of the S tradition.[25]

It is instructive to reflect on the significant differences in the employment of the terminology 'sons of Aaron' in the Community Rule and the Damascus Document. In the Community Rule the group is clearly priestly but their role falls fairly and squarely within the community rather than within a national frame of reference as was the case in the Damascus Document. It seems likely, therefore, that we can observe a trajectory in the references to priestly authority in the Scrolls beginning with the sons of Aaron in a national/non-community-specific context (D), to the sons of Aaron as priestly authorities within the community (S), to the sons of *Zadok* as priestly authorities within the community in a different literary stage of S.

4. 4Q286 Berakhot^a[26]

A reference to the sons of Aaron in 4QBerakhot^a may appropriately be discussed at this juncture because of its notable resemblance to 1QS 9:7. Thus, 4Q286 17b 1–2 seems to refer to the sons of Aaron as figures of authority in matters of judgment and wealth (משפט והון). This is an exceedingly interesting and curious piece of evidence because of the obvious terminological overlap with 1QS 9:7 which equally singled out "only the sons of Aaron' as in charge of judgment and wealth" (במשפט והון). The overlap is noted by Bilhah Nitzan, the editor of 4QBerakhot.[27] Nitzan relates this statement to "the cultic arrangements of the community for atonement of sins."[28] However, since the language used ('wealth and judgment') occurs frequently in the Community Rule to refer to key areas of communal life and fellowship without necessarily implying a cultic context (cf. e. g. 1QS 5:2–3; 5:16; 6:9), this may also be the case in 4Q286. It is just as

---

[23] See note 2 above.

[24] Cf. in this context the emphatic statement by Fabry, "*Man kommt um die Feststellung nicht herum, dass die ältere Stufe der Gemeinderegel nicht von den Zadokiden spricht!*" [emphasis his], 'Zadokiden und Aaroniden,' 212.

[25] See Hempel, 'Literary Development of the S Tradition.' Fabry also recognizes, "Die fortlaufende Redaktionsgeschichte der S-Literatur zeigt einen Kompetenzgewinn der Zadokiden …," 'Zadokiden und Aaroniden,' 212.

[26] DJD 11:1–74, esp. 38–39 (Nitzan).

[27] DJD 11:38–39.

[28] DJD 11:39.

likely that fragment 17b like fragments 20a,b,13, and 14 deal with matters of communal organization such as reproof and authority.[29] The important point to notice here is the presence of a reference to the sons of Aaron's authority within the community in a text which never mentions the sons of Zadok. In 4Q286 (Berakhot[a]) there is no need, therefore, to emphasize '*only* the sons of Aaron' as in 1QS 9:7. In contrast to this passage we may point to 1QS 5:2–3 (where the sons of Zadok and the multitude of the people of their covenant oversee wealth and judgment) and the corresponding material in 4Q256 (4QS[b]) and 4Q258 (4QS[d]) (where the many are in charge of wealth and torah). Unless significant evidence to the contrary has not been preserved in 4Q286, this little piece of evidence supports the wider picture painted by 1QS/4QS, namely, that an existing sons of Aaron strand in the community structure was subsequently challenged by a sons of Zadok strand. In any case, this passage provides further clear evidence of the authority of the sons of Aaron in the community.

5. 4Q279 (4QFour Lots; olim 4QTohorot D)

This text was published in DJD 26 as an S 'Related Text' and may therefore be suitably discussed at this point.[30] This texts contains a reference to the sons of Aaron in 4Q279 5 4. The editors comment,

> Frg. 5 seems to be eschatological in content, and to refer to the assignment of rewards ('lots') to the priests, the Levites, the Israelites and the proselytes in the messianic age [...]. If this is the case, then we would very tentatively suggest that 4Q279 is the remains of a Messianic Rule.[31]

The fragment begins with a reference to a written hierarchical membership record ("his [f]ellow written down after [him]") familiar from S (cf. 1QS 5:23; 6:22) and D (cf. CD 13:12; 14:4; 4Q270 [4QD[e]] 7 i 10). The presence of proselytes would bring this scenario closer to D than S, cf. esp. CD 14:4,6 where we also have a fourfold community structure: priests, levites, Israelites and proselytes.[32] The first and fourth component correspond in 4Q279 (Four Lots) and D with the noteworthy difference that 4Q279 specifies 'sons of Aaron' rather than speaking more generally of 'the priests' as is the case in D. This reference to the sons of Aaron clearly falls within the community-specific realm (note especially the reference to a written record of the hierarchical make-up of the community). However, rather than employing this language to refer to the role of the sons of

---

[29] On 4Q286 and 4Q288 fragments dealing with reproof, see DJD 11:40 ff. (Nitzan).
[30] See DJD 26:217–223 (Alexander and Vermes).
[31] DJD 26:218 (Alexander and Vermes).
[32] See DJD 26:223, "If our interpretation is correct [...], then the mention of a reward for proselytes in the messianic age is noteworthy."

Aaron as authority figures the present passage is concerned with the make-up of the community in real or ideological terms. Since the sons of Aaron are the first of the four groups referred to here their pre-eminent place in the community is nevertheless evident.

6. 4Q265 Miscellaneous Rules olim Serekh Damascus[33]

4Q265 7 3 prohibits priests, who are referred to as belonging to the seed[34] of Aaron, from sprinkling purifying waters on the sabbath. Apart from the emphasis on the sabbath, the passage explicitly stresses the priestly prerogative of the sprinkling.[35] As pointed out by Baumgarten, 4Q274 Tohorot A 2 i 2 attests a further such prohibition in the Qumran corpus.[36] Moreover, 4Q277 Tohorot B^b 1 ii 5–7 restricts sprinkling in cases of corpse impurity to priests and further prohibits a child from sprinkling the impure.[37] Baumgarten takes the latter to refer to the level of maturity of the priest.[38]

One of the noteworthy characteristics of 4Q265 is that it contains a mixture of general halakhic topics alongside clearly community-internal legislation such as the make-up of the council of the community or the penal code. In certain respects such a broad range of material is reminiscent of the Laws of the Damascus Document. In my view the material devoted to the sabbath both in 4Q265 and in the Damascus Document lacks an explicit basis in the life of the community.[39] These rules were clearly handed on and cherished in the community, but the context lacks references to sectarian organizational structures. Moreover, the reference to the Temple (4Q265 7 6) points to a wider context. The reference to the priestly rite of sprinkling (or rather *not* sprinkling on the sabbath) belongs, then, closer to the priestly duties in the non-community-specific realm which we witnessed in the Laws of the Damascus Document.

---

[33] For text, translation and commentary see DJD 35:69–71 (Baumgarten). See also Hempel, *Damascus Texts*, 89–104 and Lutz Doering, *Schabbat* (TSAJ 78; Tübingen: Mohr Siebeck, 1999), 242–246. For general discussion of the sprinkling ritual see Joseph Baumgarten, DJD 35:83–87 and idem, 'The Red Cow Purification Rites in Qumran Texts,' *JJS* 46 (1995): 112–119.

[34] On this terminology see García Martínez, 'Priestly Functions,' 303.

[35] See, e. g., Baumgarten, 'Red Cow Purification Rites,' 118.

[36] Baumgarten, DJD 35:103–105. For a general discussion of issues of purity see ibidem 79–96 and Hannah K. Harrington, *The Purity Texts* (CQS 5; London: T & T Clark, 2004).

[37] See DJD 35:116–118 (Baumgarten). A possible further attestation of such a prohibition is found in 4QD although the crucial word "sprinkle" is restored in both manuscripts (4Q269 [4QD^d] 8 ii 6//4Q271 [4QD^f] 2 13), see DJD 18:13, 130–132, 173–175 and idem, DJD 35:25, 118.

[38] DJD 35:82–83 (Baumgarten) and idem, 'Red Cow Purification Rites,' 118.

[39] See Hempel, *Laws of the Damascus Document*, 15–72 and eadem, *Damascus Texts*, 96–98, 103–104.

7. The Rule of the Congregation[40]

Much more within the realm of community-internal affairs are two references to the sons of Aaron as figures of authority in 1QSa 1:16//4Q249c pap cryptA Serekh ha-Edah[e41] line 5 and 1QSa 1:23–24. I have argued elsewhere that the large central section of this text is reminiscent of the communal rules contained in the Damascus Document and was only secondarily associated with the messianic age.[42] Moreover, an interesting crux in this text, as in the S tradition, is the awkward endorsement of the sons of Zadok as authority figures alongside the sons of Aaron and often in the same context, cf. 1QSa 1:2, 24; 2:3. Finally, the messianic assembly in the latter part of this text also speaks of the [sons of] Aaron the priests.[43] It is in any case fairly clear that 1QSa is much closer to the end of the spectrum that envisages the sons of Aaron as communal leaders – be it in this age or the age to come – rather than speaking of what one may call their traditional cultic roles in a national context. In sum, the role allocated to the sons of Aaron in 1QSa is reminiscent of the situation in the Community Rule. This resemblance emerges firstly from their role as community leaders rather than cultic officials. Secondly, 1QSa and S both speak of sons of Aaron *and* sons of Zadok with both groups vying (literally in any case) in effect for the same job.

8. The War Scroll (M)[44]

Three kinds of references to Aaron occur in the M tradition,

a. Akin to the Damascus Document, esp. the Admonition, the War Scroll contains a number of references to the people of God as comprising the traditional elements 'Israel' and 'Aaron,' cf. 1QM 3:12–14//4Q496 (4QM^f)[45] 10 4 (the make-up of the people to be written on a banner). A further inscription including the name of the prince of the

---

[40] On the priestly designations in this text see, e. g., Fabry, 'Zadokiden und Aaroniden;' Hempel, 'Earthly Essene Nucleus;' Lawrence H. Schiffman, *The Eschatological Community of the Dead Sea Scrolls* (SBLMS 38; Atlanta, Ga.: Scholars Press, 1989); Hartmut Stegemann, 'Some Remarks to 1QSa, to 1QSb and to Qumran Messianism,' *RQ* 17 (1996): 479–505; and Vermes, 'Leadership of the Qumran Community.'

[41] For the edition of the cryptic manuscripts of the Rule of the Congregation see DJD 36:513–574, here 551 (Pfann).

[42] 'Earthly Essene Nucleus.'

[43] Most scholars take 1QSa 2:11–21a to describe a messianic event. An exception is Stegemann, 'Some Remarks.'

[44] For a new edition of the text of M see DSSR 1:208–243 (Abegg). See also Yigael Yadin, *The Scroll of the War of the Sons of Light Against the Sons of Darkness* (trans. Batya and Chaim Rabin; Oxford: OUP, 1962) and Jean Duhaime, *The War Texts: 1QM and Related Manuscripts* (CQS 6; London: T & T Clark, 2004).

[45] The 4QM^f recension of the War Scroll is similar to 1QM though allotting a more prominent role to the prince of the congregation in the form of two superlinear additions in fragment 10, cf. Duhaime, *War Texts*, 22–23; see also DJD 7:56–68 (Baillet).

congregation refers to 'Israel,' 'Levi,' 'Aaron,' and the names of the twelve tribes is prescribed in 1QM 5:1.[46]

b. 1QM 17:2 contains a historical reference to Aaron's sons Nadab, Abihu, Eleazar and Ithamar (cf. Numbers 3).

c. Finally, the Scroll allocates a crucial role to the sons of Aaron alongside the Levites in guiding the battle, cf. 1QM 7:9–9:9.[47] A comparable scenario emerges from 4Q493 (4QM^c) 1–2, part of a manuscript containing a different recension of the War Scroll from 1QM.[48] Both in 1QM and in 4Q493 (4QM^c) the priests play a leading role in the battle and are identified in the first instance as 'sons of Aaron'.

It is interesting that this text refers to the priests genealogically explicitly as the sons of Aaron while never employing sons of Zadok language.[49] This feature aligns the War Scroll with a sizeable group of texts such as MMT, the legal part of D, and curiously also 4QS.

9. 4QMMT[50]

4QMMT speaks of the sons of Aaron in two passages and never refers to the sons of Zadok at all.[51]

a. 4QMMT B17 (4Q394 3–7 i 19- ii 1//4Q395 1 10–11)
At the end of a section dealing with the red cow ritual the sons of Aaron are admonished to ensure proper conduct in cultic matters ("the sons of Aaron are to take care of"). A similar phrase occurs at other junctures, but only here the genealogically explicit terminology 'the sons of Aaron' is employed for the priests, cf. B11–12 and B25–27. In short, the priests' role is to ensure proper conduct in cultic matters.

b. B79 (4Q396 1–2 iv 8)
A second reference to the sons of Aaron occurs in a passage that forbids unsuitable marital unions. Scholars differ as to whether this passage concerns the condemnation of marriages between priests and laity (so Qimron and Himmelfarb)[52] or Israelites and foreigners (so Baumgarten, Hayes, and Sharpe).[53]

---

[46] According to Yadin, *Scroll of the War*, 278–279 this inscription was to be made on a shield.

[47] For discussion and analysis see Yadin, *Scroll of the War*, 208–228.

[48] Cf. DJD 7:49–53, esp. 50 (Baillet) where he identifies this manuscript as evidence of a "recension différente;" see also Duhaime, *War Texts*, 30, 41.

[49] Cf. also Davies, *Behind the Essenes*, 57; Fabry, 'Zadokiden und Aaroniden,' 210; and Vermes, 'Leadership of the Qumran Community,' 379.

[50] For the text, introduction and analysis of various aspects of this document see DJD 10 (Qimron and Strugnell).

[51] So also Fabry, 'Zadokiden und Aaroniden,' 209–210.

[52] DJD 10:171–175 (Qimron) and Martha Himmelfarb, 'Levi, Phinehas, and the Problem of Intermarriage at the Time of the Maccabean Revolt,' *JSQ* 6 (1999): 1–24.

[53] Cf. DJD 10:171 n. 178a (Qimron and Strugnell); Christine Hayes, *Gentile Impurities and Jewish Identities: Intermarriage and Conversion from the Bible to the Talmud* (Oxford: OUP, 2002), 82–91; and Carolyn J. Sharpe, 'Phinean Zeal and Rhetorical Strategy in 4QMMT,' *RQ* 18 (1997): 207–222.

What is of interest for our present purposes is the use of 'sons of Aaron' to refer to the priestly component of the people. In short, in MMT – akin to the Laws of the Damascus – the sons of Aaron occur in passages relating to their priestly role in society at large rather than an authoritative leadership group within a community.

10. Temple Scroll

The picture is rather similar when we turn to the Temple Scroll. Like MMT this text never refers to the sons of Zadok,[54] and references to the sons of Aaron occur in contexts referring to the cultic role of the priests.

a. 11Q19 22:4–5[55] // 11Q20 5:25[56] refer to the responsibility of the sons of Aaron to sprinkle the sacrificial blood on the altar after the sons of Levi have done the slaughtering. This passage forms part of the 'Festival Calendar,' a part of the scrolls that is widely believed to be an originally independent piece inserted after the description of the altar.[57] The prominent role of the Levites in the Temple Scroll has often been noted.[58] What is of interest for our present enquiry is the cultic and non-community-specific part played by the sons of Aaron in this passage.
b. 11Q19 34:13–14[59] refers to the sons of Aaron's role in burning the sacrifices upon the altar and forms part of the description of the inner court of the Temple, especially the slaughter house.[60]
c. A third reference to the sons of Aaron occurs in the context of the allocation of storerooms in 11Q19 44:5.[61]

In sum, the Temple Scroll falls clearly within the large group of texts that employ sons of Aaron terminology in a non-community-specific sense emphasizing their traditional cultic duties. Again, this text never employs sons of Zadok language.

---

[54] So already Davies, *Behind the Essenes*, 57 and Fabry, 'Zadokiden und Aaroniden,' 209–210.

[55] Cf. Yigael Yadin, *The Temple Scroll II: Text and Commentary* (Jerusalem: IES, 1983) and Elisha Qimron, *The Temple Scroll: A Critical Edition with Extensive Reconstructions* (Beer-Sheva: Ben-Gurion University of the Negev; Jerusalem: IES, 1996).

[56] Cf. DJD 23:357–409 (García Martínez, Tigchelaar and van der Woude). The word "the priests" is added superlinearly in 11Q20, cf. ibidem 378.

[57] Cf. Sidnie White Crawford, *The Temple Scroll and Related Texts* (CQS 2; Sheffield: Sheffield Academic Press, 2000), 49–57 and earlier literature cited there. Further, Florentino García Martínez, 'Temple Scroll,' in EDSS 2:927–933.

[58] Cf. White Crawford, *Temple Scroll*, 56. See also Michael E. Stone, 'Levi,' in EDSS 1:485–486 and further literature cited there. Fabry eloquently speaks of the "Archivierung umfangreicher Materialien aus der Levi-Tradition in Qumran," and asks whether this interest might have been stimulated by a search for the common roots of the two rival priestly traditions, 'Zadokiden und Aaroniden,' 213.

[59] Cf. Yadin, *Temple Scroll*, Vol. II, 147.

[60] See White Crawford, *Temple Scroll*, 36–38.

[61] Cf. Yadin, *Temple Scroll*, Vol. II, 185–186.

11. 4Q174 Florilegium[62]

4Q174 5 2[63] contains a reference to Israel and Aaron in a fragmentary context. Brooke suggests that we have here the remains of a reference to the expected messiah of Israel and Aaron.[64] This interpretation has been questioned by Steudel who thinks of a phrase 'Israel and Aaron' to describe the make-up of the community as attested, e. g., in CD 1.[65] Also reminiscent of D and S is the reference to the sons of *Zadok* in 4Q174 1–2 i 17[66] in a passage interpreting Ezek 37:23.[67] We saw above that Ezek 44 was interpreted in the Damascus Document with reference to various phases in the community's emergence (cf. CD 3:20–4:4). 4QFlorilegium is thus closely aligned with those texts that speak of the make-up of the community both in terms of 'Israel and Aaron' and in terms of the sons of Zadok, the latter inspired by Ezekiel. A particularly close relationship exists between 4QFlorilegium and the Admonition of the Damascus Document with reference to the notions of priestly authority and role.

12. 4Q390 Apocryphon of Jeremiah C^e

4Q390 is one of six manuscripts of 4QApocryphon Jeremiah C published by Devorah Dimant.[68] One of the characteristic features identified by Dimant is that the composition seems to speak of events known from the scriptures in the past tense, whereas non-scriptural Second Temple period events and the eschatological period are referred to in the future tense, as is the case in the passage to be considered below. Dimant proposes a revelation received by Jeremiah as the most likely 'narrative context' of the composition[69] and suggests that the composition is best understood as 'an apocalypse'.[70] As far as the provenance of the work is concerned Dimant proposes to consider the Apocryphon as "a type of intermediate category, related, but not identical, to the sectarian literature" and comparable to Jubilees and the Temple Scroll in this regard.[71]

---

[62] Cf. DJD 5:53–57 (Allegro); see also John Strugnell, 'Notes en marge du volume V des "Discoveries in the Judaean Desert of Jordan,"' *RQ* 7 (1970): 163–276, esp. 220–225.

[63] Reconstructed by Steudel to occur at 4Q174 4 7, see *Der Midrasch zur Eschatologie aus der Qumrangemeinde (4QMidrEschat$^{a.b}$)* (STDJ 13; Leiden: Brill, 1994), 26, 32.

[64] George J. Brooke, *Exegesis at Qumran: 4QFlorilegium in Its Jewish Context* (JSOTSup 29; Sheffield: Sheffield Academic Press, 1985), 160–161.

[65] See Steudel, *Midrasch zur Eschatologie*, 49.

[66] Reconstructed by Steudel to occur at 4Q174 3 17, see *Midrasch zur Eschatologie*, 25, 31–32.

[67] Cf., e. g., Knibb, *Qumran Community*, 261 and Steudel, *Midrasch zur Eschatologie*, 32.

[68] DJD 30.

[69] DJD 30:97–98, 100, 243.

[70] DJD 30:100.

[71] DJD 30:112.

The fragmentary passage that is of immediate relevance for our present concerns occurs in 4Q390 1 2–3 and forms part of an historical overview of the Second Temple period.[72] The period is presented in Deuteronomistic style as a cycle of wrongdoing and punishment referring to a seventy year period of priestly rule.[73] The present passage belongs with those parts of the scriptures and the Scrolls that speak of the sons of Aaron as the legitimate, God-given priesthood. Moreover the preserved text clearly refers to their leading role over Israel. The present passage is fragmentary, and it is somewhat ambiguous whether or not the sons of Aaron or the Israelites are the subject of polemic.[74] A critical attitude towards the priests is a feature that characterizes other parts of this composition.[75] Whatever the case may be, this text clearly offers a further attestation of the sons of Aaron in what appears to be a national (non-community-specific) context.

13. 4Q513 Ordinances[b76]

4Q513 10 ii 8 mentions the sons of Aaron in a fragmentary context. The preceding lines speak of the sanctuary and purity, the issue of mixing and the children of Israel. The context in this particular fragment and in the text as a whole is clearly national and cultic.

The remaining references to Aaron in the Scrolls occur in historical, scriptural, and exegetical contexts and will not need to be considered here.[77]

14. Conclusion

In sum, I hope to have shown that the priestly terminology in the Scrolls, especially the terms sons of Aaron and sons of Zadok, do not appear to be employed entirely randomly and synonymously. Rather, the following line of development has left its mark on the literature,

a. A sizeable group of texts speak of the sons of Aaron in a non-community-specific, national context. These texts usually emphasize the cultic duties of the sons of Aaron[78] and do not refer to the sons of Zadok at all.

---

[72] DJD 30:237–244.
[73] DJD 30:97, 237–238.
[74] DJD 30:239.
[75] DJD 30:112, 116.
[76] See DJD 7:287–295, esp. 291 and Plate 72 (Baillet).
[77] Nor will the remaining isolated reference to the sons of Aaron in a text classified as "non-caractérisé" (i. e. 5Q20 1 2) shed much light, see DJD 3:193–197 (Milik).
[78] Fabry already points in a similar direction when he observes the exclusively liturgical functions and actions of the sons of Aaron in the Temple Scroll, MMT and M, see 'Zadokiden und Aaroniden,' 211. Earlier still Liver rightly highlighted the way in which the sons of Zadok

b. A second group of texts speak of the sons of Aaron with reference to the make-up of the community, in particular its priestly (versus lay) component. Sons of Aaron is never used to refer to the community as a whole as is the case with the sons of Zadok in CD 3–4.[79]
c. A third group of texts refers to Aaron to describe the priestly messiah who is expected alongside a lay or royal messiah.
d. Finally, the sons of Aaron appear as authority figures alongside the sons of Zadok in a number of community-specific texts, esp. the Community Rule and 1QSa. In this context we emphasized the important witness of one element of the tradition that employs sons of Aaron terminology in a community-specific context to the exclusion of the sons of Zadok in several manuscripts, see esp. 1QS 5:21 // 4Q258 (4QS^d) 2 1–2 and 1QS 9:7 // 4Q258 (4QS^d) 7 7. This shared element of common ground between 1QS and 4QS seems to me to go back to an early period in the growth of the S tradition.

The view that the Zadokites played a key role at the very beginning of the community's existence and that priestly rivalries were bringing it about has gradually been losing ground.[80] The results of the comprehensive survey above and the profile that can be derived from it also speak in favour of the sons of Aaron as the earlier strand in the Scrolls even in community-specific contexts.[81] Morevoer, we noted that a number of passages dealing with the earliest forms of communal life lack interest in the geneological background of the priestly leadership altogether (cf. 1QS 6:2–4 and 1QS 8:1).[82]

There has been a considerable amount of scholarly interest in the equally complex portrayal of the sons of Aaron in the Hebrew Bible.[83] I am particularly intrigued by the way in which the evidence of the Scrolls, which goes back to a later period, seems to mirror the complexity of the Hebrew Bible. The impression one gets is that the developments that left their mark on the Bible are com-

---

are allocated "primarily not cultic but didactic functions" and "the lack of allusion to any ritual function of the sons of Zadok the priests in these prefatory phrases is ample evidence that their unique place among the priesthood as a whole, lay not in the cultic sphere," 'Sons of Zadok the Priests,' 6, see also 28–30.

[79] *Pace* Anderson, 'Aaron,' 2, who claims "Aaron and Zadok function as ciphers for the sect as a whole."

[80] See, e. g., Kugler, 'Priesthood at Qumran,' 97–100 and John J. Collins, 'The Origin of the Qumran Community: A Review of the Evidence,' in *To Touch the Text: Biblical and Related Studies in Honor of Joseph A. Fitzmyer, S. J.* (ed. Maurya P. Horgan and Paul J. Kobleski; New York: Crossroad, 1989), 159–178.

[81] Here my own conclusions differ significantly from those reached by Kugler, 'Priesthood at Qumran,' 101.

[82] Cf. chapter 7 above.

[83] See, e. g., Joseph Blenkinsopp, 'The Judaean Priesthood during the Neo-Babylonian and Achaemenid Periods: A Hypothetical Reconstruction,' *CBQ* 60 (1998): 25–43; idem, 'Bethel in the Neo-Babylonian Period;' and Gary N. Knoppers, 'The Relationship of the Priestly Genealogies to the History of the High Priesthood in Jerusalem,' in *Judah and the Judeans in the Neo-Babylonian Period* (ed. Oded Lipschits and Joseph Blenkinsopp; Winona Lake, Ind.: Eisenbrauns, 2003), 93–107 and 109–133 and further literature cited there. Further, George Nickelsburg, 'Aaron,' in *Reallexikon für Antike und Christentum* (Supplement-Band I; Stuttgart: Hiersemann, 2001), cols. 1–11.

ing around in further waves in writings of a later time.[84] I hope to have shown that despite the complexity of the evidence a reasonable trajectory can be traced based on the use of sons of Aaron terminology across a varied spectrum of non-biblical texts from the corpus of the Scrolls.

---

[84] In Fabry's view the post-exilic rivalries simply continued, "Die Konflikte in der nachexilischen Priesterschaft blieben bestehen und wirkten sich offensichtlich bis ins 1.Jh. v. Chr., möglicherweise sogar bis in neutestamentliche Zeit hinein aus," see 'Zadokiden und Aaroniden,' 215.

Chapter Fourteen

Consider Ourselves in Charge: Self-Assertion Sons of Zadok Style[1]

1. Introduction

We have now been in the fortunate position of having the full corpus of non-biblical Dead Sea Scrolls at our disposal for well over a decade. Those who are new to the field will take this situation for granted and allow the rest of us to feel like ancient pioneers. One might have expected that having the full spread of the evidence in front of us would present us with all the answers that we have been looking for. However, the full corpus of texts has many holes in it – sometimes more holes than preserved text – and even where plenty of text is preserved I think it is fair to say that we are now still short of just as many answers and often even reformulating the questions.

Another consequence that arose from beholding the full spectrum of texts is that a number of erstwhile key concepts no longer emerge as dominant as we once thought they were. I have recently noted in a different context that the dualism between light and darkness, for instance, emerges as a much less central concept in the corpus as a whole than it did in the initial phases of Qumran research.[2] In the early decades of Qumran research the notion of dualism between light and darkness was prominent in two major texts: the Community Rule and the War Scroll from Cave 1. More recently a much more limited proportion of the corpus of the Dead Sea Scrolls and not even all the manuscripts of the Rule can be drawn upon to uphold this dominance.[3]

---

[1] This chapter was originally published as 'Do the Scrolls Suggest Rivalry Between the Sons of Aaron and the Sons of Zadok and If So was it Mutual,' *RQ* 24 (2009): 135–153. The research was first presented at a Symposium for members of the Editorial Advisory Board of the *Theologisches Wörterbuch zu den Qumrantexten* hosted at the University of Bonn in November 2008, and I would like to thank Prof. Fabry and his team for the generous hospitality and the members of the Symposium, especially Prof. Florentino García Martínez, for their constructive comments.

[2] Cf. Charlotte Hempel, 'The Teaching on the Two Spirits and the Literary History of the Community Rule,' in *Dualism in Qumran* (ed. Geza Xeravits; LSTS 76; London: T & T Clark, 2010), 102–120.

[3] Thus, 4Q258 (4QS^d) lacks the Treatise on the Two Spirits altogether and begins with the equivalent of 1QS 5:1, cf. DJD 26:90 (Alexander and Vermes).

One of the many aspects of British culture that I have come to admire is the support for the underdog and the perhaps implied resentment of top-dogs. One candidate for top-dogs who have seen their role challenged in the textual picture that emerged in recent years are the sons of Zadok.[4] Already in the late 1980s a debate flared up about whether or not the groups behind the Scrolls were Zadokites or not. I am thinking here of Philip Davies' plea to "stop talking Zadokite."[5] More recently, the full corpus of non-biblical Scrolls has delivered a double blow to this group. Firstly, the following table illustrates the extent to which the new evidence from Cave 4 has revealed many more references to the sons of Aaron than to the sons of Zadok.[6]

Table 1: Distribution of the Designations Sons of Aaron and Sons of Zadok in Caves 1 and 4 as well as CD.[7]

	בני צדוק	בני אהרון
Cave 1	x 6	x 7
CD	x 2	x 0
Cave 4	x 3	x 18

Secondly, the Rule manuscripts mirror this larger development by presenting us with Cave 4 copies that lack key endorsements of the sons of Zadok attested in the opening lines of 1QS 5, most famously in 4Q258 (4QS^d) 1 and 4Q256 (4QS^b) 9. In order to make sense of the plentiful evidence now in front of us, I previously investigated the picture that emerges from the non-biblical Scrolls about the sons of Aaron. In doing so I was inspired by an article published by Heinz-Josef Fabry entitled "Zadokiden und Aaroniden in Qumran."[8] My own

---

[4] See the seminal early treatment by Jacob Liver, 'The "Sons of Zadok the Priests" in the Dead Sea Sect,' *RQ* 6 (1967): 3–30. More recently see Robert A. Kugler, 'Priests,' in EDSS 2:688–693; idem, 'Priesthood at Qumran,' in *The Dead Sea Scrolls After Fifty Years: A Comprehensive Assessment* (ed. Peter Flint and James C. VanderKam; Leiden: Brill, 1999), Vol. II, 93–116; and Geza Vermes, 'The Leadership of the Qumran Community: Sons of Zadok – Priests – Congregation,' in *Geschichte – Tradition – Reflexion: Festschrift für Martin Hengel zum 70. Geburtstag* (ed. Hubert Cancik, Hermann Lichtenberger, and Peter Schäfer; Tübingen: Mohr Siebeck, 1996), Vol. I, 375–384.

[5] Philip R. Davies, *Behind the Essenes: History and Ideology in the Dead Sea Scrolls* (BJS 94; Atlanta, Ga.: Scholars Press, 1987) 51–72, here 71. See also Georg Klinzing, *Die Umdeutung des Kultus in der Qumrangemeinde und im Neuen Testament* (SUNT 7; Göttingen: Vandenhoeck & Ruprecht, 1971), 136. Further, Maxine L. Grossman, *Reading for History in the Damascus Document: A Methodological Study* (STDJ 45; Leiden: Brill, 2002), 185–209.

[6] See also the discussion in Heinz-Josef Fabry, 'Zadokiden und Aaroniden in Qumran,' in *Das Manna fällt auch heute noch: Beiträge zur Geschichte und Theologie des Alten, Ersten Testaments. Festschrift für Erich Zenger* (ed. Frank Lothar Hossfeld and Ludger Schwienhorst-Schönberger; Herders biblische Studien 44; Freiburg: Herder, 2004), 201–217, esp. 209–210.

[7] Cf. Martin G. Abegg, *The Dead Sea Scrolls Concordance. Volume One: The Non-Biblical Texts from Qumran [Parts 1–2]* (Leiden: Brill, 2003), 12 and 631.

[8] See note 6 above.

results appeared in 2007 in the *Festschrift* for Florentino García Martínez.⁹ In this chapter I will endeavour to draw out the implications of my findings with respect to the sons of Aaron by relating them to the evidence of the Scrolls on the sons of Zadok.

In his contribution to a multi-volume *Festschrift* for Martin Hengel, Geza Vermes perceived the importance of this issue when he notes the way in which,

> the terminological clash between sons of Zadok and sons of Aaron largely remained untouched for some four decades of Qumran research during which period most scholars [...] happily and simply maintained, without any proviso, that the sect was governed by the sons of Zadok the priests ...¹⁰

In what follows I will discuss all the texts in the corpus of the non-bibical Scrolls that refer to the sons of Zadok.

2. The Damascus Document

A number of references to the sons of Zadok in this document led Solomon Schechter to publish the mediaeval Cairo manuscripts under the title *Documents of Jewish Sectaries. I. Fragments of a Zadokite Work* in 1910.¹¹ This title still has strong supporters today.¹² However, the number of occurrences of the designation the sons of Zadok in the Damascus Document is actually rather small and dwarfed by references to the sons of Aaron (see Table 1 above).

The first two out of a total of three references to the sons of Zadok in the Damascus Document occur in CD 4 as part of a citation and interpretation of Ezekiel 44:15. Whereas the Masoretic text of Ezek 44:15 speaks of one group ("the levitical priests, the sons of Zadok"), it has frequently been observed that the verse as quoted in the Damascus Document mentions three groups: the priests, the levites, and the sons of Zadok. The subsequent interpretation identifies each group with the members of the new movement in three subsequent phases of its existence. The priests are interpreted as "the converts of Israel who went out from the land of Judah", the levites are identified as those who joined them (in a pun on the verb לוה as already in Num 18:2 and 18:4), and the sons of Zadok as the elect of Israel at the end of days. The following observations point towards

---

⁹ Cf. Charlotte Hempel, 'The Sons of Aaron in the Dead Sea Scrolls,' in *Flores Florentino: Dead Sea Scrolls and Other Early Jewish Studies in Honour of Florentino García Martínez* (ed. Anthony Hilhorst, Émile Puech, and Eibert Tigchelaar; JSJSup, 122; Leiden: Brill, 2007), 207–224, reprinted as Chapter 13 above.
¹⁰ 'Leadership of the Qumran Community,' 379.
¹¹ Solomon Schechter, *Documents of Jewish Sectaries. I: Fragments of a Zadokite Work* (Cambridge: CUP, 1910).
¹² The earlier title is favourably recalled by Joseph M. Baumgarten in DJD 18:1.

a use of the terminology here that is rather distinctive from the references to the sons of Zadok in the Community Rule, for instance,

a. The context and genre is clearly and explicitly exegetical, and Grossman rightly draws attention to its similarity to the *pesher* interpretation.[13]
b. The context is eschatological[14] (although the text apparently envisages a realized eschatology): the sons of Zakok are the chosen ones of Israel who stand up in the last days, an expression referring to "the final period of history" as noted by Steudel.[15] Given the passage continues by announcing a list of their names and deeds (now lost) it seems clear that this latter group has already appeared.
c. Connected to this is the chronological and somewhat hierarchical aspect of the description here as well as elsewhere in the Admonition. The emergence of the community is often described as a multi-tier process[16] with a clear hierarchical pecking order leaving us in little doubt that the final stage is the crowning moment of the development outlined.[17] The implication seems to be that the emergence of the sons of Zadok is a high point. Remarkably this is the case both here and in 1QS 5 where the the sons of Zadok are depicted as community leaders. Despite the important difference that in CD 4 'the sons of Zadok' refers to the whole community rather than the priestly leadership as is the case in 1QS 5, I think we can pick up a common trend characterizing this terminology in both cases. This common trend is an effort to position the sons of Zadok at the front of the line or on top of the pile.[18]
d. We noted already that the designation 'the sons of Zadok' appears to refer to the community as a whole rather than its priestly leadership in the Admonition of the Damascus Document.[19] It is nevertheless interesting that the community is described in sacerdotal language. This choice of language is indicative of Zadokite sympathies. By contrast, more widespread across the corpus of the Scrolls, and importantly also elsewhere in the Damascus Document, the community is conceived of as being made up out of a priestly alongside a lay component (Israel and Aaron, cf., e. g., CD 1:7 // 4Q266 [4QD^a] 2 i 11 // 4Q268 [4QD^c] 1 14; CD 6:2 // 4Q267 [4QD^b] 2 8). This is also true with reference to the messianic future which is said to be inaugurated by the arrival of the Messiah of Aaron and Israel (cf., e. g., CD 19:11; 20:1; CD 12:23; CD 14:19 // 4Q266 [4QD^a] 10 i 12 // 4Q269 [4QD^d] 11 i 2). This larger picture draws our attention to the somewhat distinctive use of language in CD 4, even within the context of the Admonition at large. We may note in this context that an unpublished dissertation submitted to the University of

---

[13] *Reading for History*, 187.

[14] See also Davies, *Behind the Essenes*, 69.

[15] Annette Steudel, 'אחרית הימים in the Texts from Qumran,' *RQ* 16 (1993): 225–246, here 231.

[16] Cf. Charlotte Hempel, 'Community Origins in the Damascus Document in the Light of Recent Scholarship,' in *The Provo International Conference on the Dead Sea Scrolls: Technological Innovations, New Texts, & Reformulated Issues* (ed. Donald W. Parry and Eugene Ulrich; STDJ 30; Leiden: Brill, 1999), 316–329, reprinted as Chapter 4 in this volume.

[17] *Pace* Davies, *Behind the Essenes*, 54, who denies any hierarchical implications here.

[18] Preben Wernberg-Møller even proposed that 1QS 5 contains a clear 'echo' of CD 3–4 and further argued that the references to the sons of Zadok in 1QS 5 are a "late – and misunderstood – version" of CD 3–4, cf. 'צדק, צדיק and צדוק in the Zadokite Fragments (CDC), the Manual of Discipline (DSD) and the Habakkuk-Commentary (DSH),' *VT* 3 (1953): 310–315, here 313 and 314. See also Davies, *Behind the Essenes*, 58.

[19] See Grossman, *Reading for History*, 192–194, 201.

Edinburgh in 1988 by Mark Boyce proposed distinguishing three types of material in the Admonition: poetry, redactional material and midrashic material.[20] Not surprisingly both occurrences of the sons of Zadok in CD 4 fall within Boyce's group of midrashic texts. Boyce's call to distinguish between poetry and midrashic layers in the Admonition of the Damascus Document deserves more exploration.

Fabry has rightly drawn attention to the fact that we need to differentiate carefully between different parts of the Damascus tradition when evaluating the evidence on the designations for the priesthood. In a paper he presented at a conference held at the University of Birmingham in 2007 he distinguishes between CD and 4QD (and even within 4QD) and finds a rather distinctive profile in each group of manuscripts.[21] I am grateful to him for drawing attention to this, and I think this point deserves much further thought. I personally never found any evidence in favour of a Cairo recension – mediaeval or otherwise – of the Damascus Document. With the notable exception of the difficulties posed by the differences between the mediaeval manuscripts A and B,[22] the textual history of the D manuscripts is much more stable than that of the Rule manuscripts. This, to me, is remarkable. Equally noteworthy is the closeness between the penal code traditions in D and the S penal code, and this part of D has received an extraordinary amount of scholarly attention in order to understand and shed light on the literary development of S and D.[23] Thus, the areas where the new Cave 4 manuscripts of the Damascus Document throw light on highly significant textual

---

[20] See Mark Boyce, "The Poetry of the Damascus Document" (PhD diss., University of Edinburgh, 1988).

[21] Cf. Heinz-Josef Fabry, 'Priests at Qumran – a Reassessment,' in *The Dead Sea Scrolls: Texts and Context* (ed. Charlotte Hempel; STDJ 90; Leiden: Brill, 2010), 243–262.

[22] The literature devoted to the divergences between CD Manuscripts A and B is extensive. Reference may be made to a number of recent studies which also contain details of earlier discussions, cf. Liora Goldman, 'A Comparison of the Genizah Manuscripts A and B of the Damascus Document in Light of Their Pesher Units,' in *Meghillot: Studies in the Dead Sea Scrolls IV* (ed. Moshe Bar-Asher and Devorah Dimant; Jerusalem: University of Haifa/Bialik Institute, 2006), 169–189 [Hebrew, English abstract XIV]; Stephen Hultgren, *From the Damascus Covenant to the Covenant of the Community: Literary, Historical and Theological Studies in the Dead Sea Scrolls* (STDJ 66; Leiden: Brill, 2007), esp. 5–76; and Menahem Kister, 'The Development of the Early Recensions of the Damascus Document,' *DSD* 14 (2007): 61–76.

[23] See, e. g., Joseph M. Baumgarten, 'The Cave 4 Versions of the Qumran Penal Code,' *JJS* 43 (1992): 268–276; Charlotte Hempel, 'The Penal Code Reconsidered,' in *Legal Texts and Legal Issues: Proceedings of the Second Meeting of the International Organization for Qumran Studies Published in Honour of Joseph M. Baumgarten* (ed. Moshe Bernstein, Florentino García Martínez, and John Kampen; STDJ 23; Leiden: Brill, 1997), 337–348; Jutta Jokiranta, 'Social Identity in the Qumran Movement: The Case of the Penal Code,' in *Explaining Christian Origins and Early Judaism: Contributions from Cognitive and Social Science* (ed. Petri Luomanen, Ilkka Pyysiäinen, and Risto Uro; BIS 89; Leiden: Brill, 2007), 277–298; Sarianna Metso, 'The Relationship Between the Damascus Document and the Community Rule,' in *The Damascus Document: A Centennial of Discovery. Proceedings of the Third International Symposium of the Orion Center, 4–8 February 1998* (ed. Joseph M. Baumgarten, Esther G. Chazon, and Avital Pinnick; STDJ 34; Leiden: Brill, 2000), 85–93; Aharon Shemesh, 'The Scriptural Background of the Penal Code in the *Rule of the Community* and *Damascus Document*,' *DSD*

inter-relationships is *not* between the ancient Qumran manuscripts of this document and the two mediaeval CD manuscripts but between the Damascus Document and the Community Rule. Going back to Fabry's point, I do not believe, therefore, that associating differences in the use of priestly designations with CD and 4QD respectively tells the whole story. Another way of putting it might be to note that the references to the sons of Zadok are found predominantly in the Admonition and the references to the sons of Aaron are found exclusively in the Laws.

The third and final reference to the sons of Zadok in the Damascus Document is of immense interest. The only reference to the sons of Zadok attested in the Cave 4 manuscripts (4Q266 5 i 16) is part of an intriguing passage that contains material reminiscent of both the Admonition and the Laws (4Q266 [4QD^a] 5 i; cf. also 4Q267 [4QD^b] 5 ii although this manuscript breaks off before the reference to the sons of Zadok).[24] In a table outlining the contents of the Damascus Document in his *editio princeps* of the 4QD manuscripts Joseph Baumgarten refers to this material under the heading, "The overseer, the priests, introduction to laws" and locates it after the catalogue of transgressions and just before the rules on the disqualification of priests.[25] In his reconstruction of the Damascus Document, Hartmut Stegemann places this fragment at the beginning of the Laws and at or near the juncture between the Admonition and the Laws.[26] In my monograph on the Laws of 1998 I dealt with this material in a chapter entitled "Transitional Passage Introducing the Laws."[27]

This 4QD passage uniquely combines references to "the returnees/penitents of Israel" (שבי ישראל) and "the sons of Zadok" (בני צדוק) with references to the figures of the Maskil ([מש]כיל)[28] and Mebaqqer (המבקר) otherwise not familiar from the Admonition.[29] When I first struggled with this passage I was struck by the way in which it appears to offer something of a missing link between the Ad-

---

15 (2008): 191–224; and Carol Newsom, *The Self as Symbolic Space: Constructing Identity and Community at Qumran* (STDJ 52; Leiden: Brill, 2004).

[24] See DJD 18:4–5, 47–49 (Baumgarten); Charlotte Hempel, *The Laws of the Damascus Document: Sources, Traditions and Redaction* (STDJ 29; Leiden: Brill, 1990; pb. ed. Atlanta, Ga.: SBL, 2006), 171–174; eadem, *The Damascus Texts* (CQS 1; Sheffield: Sheffield Academic Press, 2000), 34.

[25] DJD 18:3–5.

[26] Cf. Hartmut Stegemann, 'Towards Physical Reconstructions of the Qumran Damascus Document Scrolls,' in *The Damascus Document* (ed. Baumgarten, Chazon, and Pinnick), 177–200. He is followed by Cecilia Wassen, *Women in the Damascus Document* (Academia Biblica 21; Atlanta, Ga.: SBL, 2005), 34.

[27] See Hempel, *Laws of the Damascus Document*, 171–174.

[28] Baumgarten's partial reconstruction of a reference to the Maskil in 4Q266 5 i 17 is supported by the context which comprises a formula (אלה החקים למשכיל) also found in CD 12:20–21 and 1QS 9:12//4Q259 (4QS^e) 3 6–7, cf. DJD 18:48; on the latter material see Chapter 10 above, especially section 4.3.4.

[29] For the sake of completeness we should note that the editor proposes reconstructing a reference to the Maskil in the Admonition, i. e. in the opening words of the document in his edition

Consider Ourselves in Charge: Self-Assertion Sons of Zadok Style

monition and the Laws. Only when looking at it again in the context of closely studying the references to the sons of Zadok in the Damascus Document did I realize that this 'mixed' or transitional passage is for the most part intriguingly close to the Ezek 44:15 Midrash dealt with above rather than the Admonition as a whole. Only here and in the opening lines of CD 4 do we come across the phrases "the returnees of Israel" and "the sons of Zadok" side by side.

The texts in question read as follows,

CD 3:20b–4:5a[30]	4Q266 5 i 9–19 // 4Q267 5 ii underlined[31]
20b הוא כאשר	9 המחזי]קים בשם קו֯ד֯ו֯שו ה֯ם[32]
21 הקים אל להם ביד יחזקאל הנביא לאמר הכהנים והלוים ובני	10]יה כי ביהודה נ֯מ֯וצא קש֯ר
4:1 צדוק אשר שמרו את משמרת מקדשי בתעות בני ישראל	11 ו֯לש֯ו֯ב על עונת אבותם]לישראל בעומ֯ד֯[ו֯]
2 מעלי הם יגישו לי חלב ודם vacat הכ֯ת֯נים הם שבי ישראל	12]ב֯יושבי ירושלי]ם֯ vac וכו֯ל֯ הנשא֯ו֯רים
3 היוצאים מארץ יהודה והנלוים עמהם vacat ובני צדוק הם בחירי	13 [֯֯ אי֯ש (ל) לפי ד֯ו֯ח֯ו֯ יקר֯ב֯ו
4 ישראל קריאי השם העמדים באחרית הימים הנה פרוש	14]ו֯ח י֯חק}֯{נ֯ו לפי המבקר ו֯כ֯ו֯ל
5 שמותיהם ...	15 יתהל]ל֯כו בם vac כול שבי ישראל]֯
	16 ב]נ֯י צדוק הכהנים הנה המ֯]ה [
	17 מדרש ה]תורה האחרון vac ואלה הח̇ו̇]ק̇ים למש]כיל[
	18]ג֯ם לכול ישראל כ' לויוש]יע אל]ת֯ בל ֯֯]א
	19]ב֯ד֯ר֯כו להתהלך י֯מ֯ים

CD 3:20b–4:5a	4Q266 5 i 9–19 // 4Q267 5 ii underlined[34]
3:20b This was in accordance with what	9 [those who hold] fast to [his] ho[ly] name, th[ey]
21 God had established for them through Ezekiel the prophet: "The priests and the Levites and **the sons**	10] for in **Judah** has been fou[nd conspir]acy [ ]

---

of 4Q266 (4QD[a]) 1 a–b, but that is somewhat conjectural, cf. DJD 18:31–32 (Baumgarten); for further discussion see Chapter 10 above, especially sections 4.3.3, 4.3.4, and 4.3.5.

[30] For the Hebrew text of CD see DSSEL (Abegg).

[31] For the Hebrew text of 4Q266 and 4Q267 see DSSEL (Baumgarten) and DJD 18:47–48, 101, Plates 6 and 19.

[32] 4Q266 5 i 9 reads בשם קוד]שו ה[ם whereas 4Q267 5 ii 1–2 has המה הקו]דש בשם, cf. DJD18:47, 101, Plates 6 and 19. There appear to be faint traces of a letter after *shin* in 4Q267 on Plate 19, however, which Baumgarten tentatively identifies as the remains of a *waw*, cf. DJD 18:101.

[33] The English translation is a slightly adapted form of the translation offered by Michael A. Knibb *The Qumran Community* (Cambridge Commentaries on Writings of the Jewish and Christian World 200 BC to AD 200 2; Cambridge: CUP, 1987), 33.

[34] The English translation is my own.

CD 3:20b–4:5a	4Q266 5 i 9–19//4Q267 5 ii <u>underlined</u>
4:1 of Zadok who remained in charge of my sanctuary when the children of Israel went astray	11 [<u>To return</u> to the sins of their fathers] for **Israel** <u>when it arises</u> [ ]
4:2 from me, they shall offer me fat and blood." **The priests, they are the converts of Israel**	12 [among the inhabitants of Jeru<u>sale</u>]m. *Vacat.* <u>And all</u> those who are le<u>ft o[ver</u>]
4:3 who went out from the land of **Judah**, and <the Levites are> those who joined them, and **the sons of Zadok, they are the chosen ones**	13 *Everyone accor<u>ding to [his] spirit</u> [shall draw] near*
4:4 of **Israel**, the renowned men who shall appear at the end of days. Here is an exact list	14 *[ ] they shall leave according to (the decision of) the overseer and [al]l*
4:5 of their names …	15 *[they shall wa]lk in them. Vacat.* All **the converts of Israel** [ ] 16 [**the s]ons of Zadok the priests behold the[y**] 17] the latter [interpretation of the] law. *Vacat.* And these are the statu[te]s for the wise lea[der] 18 [ ] in them for all Israel for [God] will not sa[ve] all [ ] 19 [ ] in his way to walk perfect[ly

A number of terminological correspondences deserve noting (and are marked in bold in the texts):[35]

a. Both passages speak in terms of Judah and Israel with Judah being the negative entity in both texts (with the key term קשר reliably restored in 4Q266 on the basis of 4Q267);
b. The designation "the returnees of Israel" (שבי ישראל);
c. The references to the sons of Zadok/the priests (by referring to "the sons of Zadok the priests" as one group 4Q266 5 i 16 is closer to the MT of Ezekiel 44:15 than CD 4);
d. The distinctive use of the third person masculine plural pronoun "they" הם. This feature provides a connection between 4Q266 5 i 9–12 and lines 15–16. The former is based on Jeremiah 11:9–11 as noted already by Baumgarten.[36]

The transitional passage attested in 4Q266 5 i//4Q267 5 ii which occurs somewhere between the Admonition and the legal part of the Damascus Document is extremely intriguing, and it is difficult to fathom the connection of the material so reminiscent of CD 3–4 to a brief statement on what looks like the admission process (cf. the use of the verbs קרב 'drawing near' and רחק 'leaving, keeping a distance' at the word of the overseer) in lines 13–15a and printed in italics in the

---

[35] See also Wernberg Møller, 'צדק, צדיק and צדוק.'
[36] Cf. DJD 18:49.

texts above.³⁷ I am still none the wiser now than when I wrote in my 1998 book: "... it is difficult to see how 4QD^a 5 i 13–14,17b relates to the remainder of this passage."³⁸ However, Wassen's recognition of the clear connection between the reference to the latter interpretation of the law both here (4Q266 5 i 17) and at the very end of the Damascus Document (4Q266 11 21) lends further support to my conclusion in 1998 that this material goes back to a late stage in the growth of the Damascus Document and should be attributed to a 'Damascus Redactor' responsible for the shape of the document as a whole.³⁹ Be this as it may, what is extremely interesting for our present purposes is that the part of this transitional passage that I previously described as reminiscent of the Admonition as a whole is especially close to the Ezekiel midrash in CD 3–4. Thus, all three references to the sons of Zadok in the Damascus Document seem to occur in comparable, exegetical-midrashic contexts, and we will come across two more such examples (4Qpesher Isaiah^c and 4QFlorilegium) below. This trend points towards a sizeable strand in the Dead Sea Scrolls where 'the sons of Zadok' occur imbedded in interpretation of scripture, a phenomenon we never witness with the designation 'the sons of Aaron.' The close relationship between CD 3–4 and 4Q266 (4QD^a) 5 i is not the result of a citation or cross-reference. Instead, the fact that – by speaking of "the sons of Zadok the priests" rather than of several different groups – 4Q266 is closer to the MT of Ezekiel 44 than CD suggests, instead, an independent exegetical tradition in 4Q266.

The remainder of the Laws contains six references to the sons of Aaron and none to the sons of Zadok. The catalogue of transgressions mentions someone who neglects to "[give to] the sons of Aaron [the fourth (year)] planting," cf. 4Q270 (4QD^e) 2 ii 6. The fascinating material on priestly disqualifications refers to the sons of Aaron four times. In this context Fabry makes the valuable observation that this particular set of references implies criticism of the sons of Aaron or is, at the very least, not uniformly complimentary but ambiguous.⁴⁰ Again, I think Fabry has put his finger on something that can fruitfully be probed further. There is no doubt that the material on priestly disqualifications in the Damascus Document draws attention to a variety of shortcomings of some of the sons of Aaron. The question is whether this constitutes evidence that this material is somewhat anti-Aaronitic? Or, as seems more likely to me, are those voicing the critique better identified as fellow sons of Aaron who have kept on the straight and narrow? The particular situations outlined in 4QD are:

---

³⁷ Cecilia Wassen also observes the affinity of this part of 4Q266 5 i to the admission process, cf. *Women in the Damascus Document*, 135. See also Hempel, *Laws of the Damascus Document*, 173.

³⁸ *Laws of the Damascus Document*, 174.

³⁹ See Wassen, *Women in the Damascus Document*, 34 and Hempel, *Laws of the Damascus Document*, 174.

⁴⁰ Cf. Fabry, 'Priests at Qumran – A Reassessment.'

a. "[one] of the sons of Aaron who is taken captive by the nations" (4Q266 [4QDᵃ] 5 ii 5 // 4Q267 [4QDᵇ] 5 iii 8).[41] Here it seems beyond doubt that being captured by the nations is hardly the chap's fault.
b. The situation is rather more severe in a second case which speaks of "one of the sons of Aaron who departs to ser[ve the nations" (4Q266 [4QDᵃ] 5 ii 8).[42] Moreover, if the following line is still dealing with this case the same person is accussed of instructing "his people in the foundation/basic principles of the people and also to betray". Despite the severity of the offence, it is worth noting that this still points towards an aberrant individual (איש מבני אהרון) rather than a critique of the sons of Aaron as a group or category.
c. Similarly, an aberrant member of this group seems to be in mind when we read of "[one of the sons of] Aaron who causes his name to fall from the truth (corrected to: whose name was thrown (נפל [hi. > ho.] from the peoples [אֱמֶת < אֱמוֹת])[43] in 4Q266 5 ii 9–10.[44]
d. The final example seems to be either neutral or even positive by using the phrase "from Israel, the counsel of the sons of Aaron" (4Q266 [4QDᵃ] 5 ii 12).[45]

It is instructive to take into account a number of further concerns raised in 4Q266 5 ii and parallels even if the text speaks of priests in general rather than the sons of Aaron. The opening lines on priestly disqualification speak of priests with various types of defective speech, poor eyesight, or being somewhat slow-witted ([אין] ממהר לה[ב]ין) who are excluded from reading the book lest they seriously mislead, cf. 4Q266 (4QDᵃ) 5 ii 1–4 // 4Q267 (4QDᵇ) 5 iii 1–7 // 4Q273 (4QDʰ) 2.[46] The reference to "his brothers the priests" in 4Q266 5 ii 4 makes it clear these individuals are priests. The fragmentary remains of this material do not attest the designation the sons of Aaron but the language used here leaves us with a rather harmonious impression: his brothers, the priests, will step into the breach. In short, it seems to me that what is at issue may be less critical of the sons of Aaron at large but rather a sign of self-awareness: the sons of Aaron themselves are aware that some of their number have shortcomings or have been aberrant, and this material is trying to address this situation. The terminology 'the sons of Aaron' is used here synonymously with the priests. In a personal communication with me some time ago Menahem Kister observed that in his view all the references to the sons of Aaron simply mean the priests. His assessment fits here and in a fair number of cases, but, as I hope we will see, not across the board. An understanding of sons of Aaron as simply the priests corresponds rather well

---

[41] Cf. DJD 18:49–52, 102 (Baumgarten). Note Grossman's pertinent observation, "... a reading of this text at face value undercuts most of the authoritative claims made in texts like Ezra/Nehemiah or Chronicles, by identifying all of the post-exilic priestly leaders as unfit for service." *Reading for History*, 200.

[42] Cf. DJD 18:49–52 (Baumgarten).

[43] The text appears to be corrected from "fallen from the truth" to "was thrown from the peoples," cf. DJD 18:51 (Baumgarten), cf. n. 13 in Chapter 13 above.

[44] Cf. DJD 18:49–52.

[45] Cf. DJD 18:49–52 (Baumgarten).

[46] Cf. DJD 18:49–52, 102, 195 (Baumgarten).

with references to Aaron as the counterpart to Israel in the community make-up. Both with regard to the community's present and in the messianic future, priestly and lay components are expressed in terms of Aaron and Israel. In sum, on my reading of the text the material on priestly disqualifications in 4Q266 (4QD^a) and parallels does not allude to rivalry, or even express an awareness of rivalry, between different priestly groups other than inadequacies in some members of the group – a rather *introspective criticism*, if you like. By contrast, a competitive sense of self-assertion and rivalry is confined to the leadership aspirations of the sons of Zadok.[47]

It is interesting to compare the priestly disqualifications material in 4QD to 4QMMT B 49–54[48] which is referred to by the editors under the heading "The Blind and the Deaf."[49] Put very briefly, MMT mentions difficulties that are encountered if someone blind or deaf is unable to adhere to halakhic requirements. The passage closes by stating that such individuals should not come near טהרת המקדש. Qimron and Strugnell refer to 11QT^a 45:12–14 which bans the blind from the Temple city. As far as I understand Qimron and Strugnell, they are taking MMT B 49–54 to refer to laity or priests and laity. In my view, the material on priestly disqualifications in 4QD has much in common with this part of MMT:

a. Both are concerned with inadvertent halakhic infringements on account of a disability;
b. Both texts include sight (MMT adds hearing whereas 4QD adds mental ability and speech);
c. Both MMT and 4QD are concerned with access to pure/holy food.

It seems at least worth raising the possibility that 4QMMT is also dealing with priests. One detail that may mitigate against this interpretation is that 4QD is concerned with speech (the priest who instructs) whereas MMT is concerned with someone not able to receive instruction (the deaf). In any case, it is certainly fruitful to study both passages alongside each other.

MMT never mentions the sons of Zadok. Moreover, the question of the identity of the sons of Aaron in this text is extremely interesting. Who are the sons of Aaron/the sons of the priests in MMT? As is the case in the Laws of the Damascus Document, I do not think there is a distinction to be made in MMT between the terminology priests and sons of Aaron. What we would like to know is: are the sons of Aaron the same as or part of the infamous 'they-group'? Or are they or some of them part of the 'you plural-group'? We may further ask who would

---

[47] Grossman discusses the possibility that the use of the designation the sons of Aaron "in the legal texts can be read with an ideological overtone: they argue for the view that any descendant of Aaron can have priestly authority in the community, and that special Zadokite status is not important." *Reading for History*, 191.

[48] See already Charlotte Hempel, 'The Damascus Document and 4QMMT,' in *The Damascus Document* (ed. Baumgarten, Chazon, and Pinnick), 69–84, esp. 74–77, reprinted as Chapter 11 in this volume.

[49] Cf. DJD 10:160–161 (Qimron and Strugnell).

be in a position to tell them what to do? Surely the speakers are fellow priests of some kind. In which case, are we dealing with the sons of Aaron bemoaning the shortcoming of some of their number comparable to the scenario we identified in 4QD? Note, for instance, the formulation "some of the priests" (מקצת הכהנים) in the critical statement on priestly unions attested in 4QMMT B 80.[50] One gets the impression that 4QMMT also stresses that some of the sons of Aaron had shortcomings – comparable to the priestly disqualification material in 4QD – but this is not to be equated with a wide-ranging condemnation of the whole group.

Returning to the Damascus Document, the final reference to the sons of Aaron occurs in a closing statement on the procedures laid down for dealing with skin disease and reads, "this is the law of *sara'at* for the sons of Aaron to separate/distinguish" (4Q266 [4QD^a] 6 i 13//4Q272 [4QD^g] 1 ii 2.).[51] Similarly, CD 13:4–7a emphasizes the priestly duty to diagnose skin disease, even if the priest (הכהן) is a simpleton and needs assistance from the overseer.[52]

In short, in the Damascus Document references to the sons of Aaron occur exclusively in non-community specific, often national contexts, frequently denoting nothing more than priests in distinction from the laity. The three occurrences of the sons of Zadok in CD/4QD are all closely related to one another. CD 4 deals with an interpretation of Ezek 44:15, and as we saw this interpretation seems to be reflected also in 4Q266 (4QD^a) 5 i//4Q267 (4QD^b) which may also be based on Ezek 44:15 as well as Jer 11:9–11.[53] The designation 'sons of Zadok' is not used to refer to the priests in the Damascus Document, but apparently refers to the community as a whole. Finally, we noted the absence of any awareness of rivalry on the part of the sons of Aaron. On my proposed reading of the material on priestly disqualifications, this section appears introspectively aware of the odd rotten apple in the group, but there is nothing in the Damascus Document that is anti-Aaronitic. Rather, it appears to be taken for granted in this text that the priests and the sons of Aaron are one and the same thing.

3. The Community Rule

Rather surprisingly perhaps, the number of occurrences of the phrase "the sons of Zadok" is actually rather meagre even in the Community Rule. We are dealing with two, and at most three occurrences, cf. 1QS 5:2; 1QS 5:9 and the possible

---

[50] Cf. DJD 10:56–57 (Qimron and Strugnell).

[51] Cf. DJD 18:52–54, 89–91 (Baumgarten).

[52] Interestingly, this passage is preceded by another scenario with an inadequate priest, who is assisted by an able Levite. See Hempel, *Laws of the Damascus Document*, 111–114 and further literature referred to there.

[53] The latter was noted by Baumgarten, see note 36 above.

third reference in 1QS 9:14.[54] This statistical picture contrasts sharply with the central role attributed to the sons of Zadok in the limited number of references we have. We are faced with a rather small but extremely vocal textual minority. It is well known that the two references to the sons of Zadok the priests as community authorities in 1QS 5 are lacking in 4Q258 (4QS[d]) 1 and 4Q256 (4QS[b]) 9.[55] However, as it emerges from Table 2 included below, *for each and every case where the sons of Zadok occur in 1QS a 'Zadok-free' tradition is also attested in the Cave 4 manuscripts*. In other words, not only are references to the sons of Zadok a vocal minority but the small number of passages strongly endorsing the sons of Zadok are preserved side by side with S manuscripts where they are not mentioned at all. This absence from 4QS speaks perhaps louder even than the vocal minority in 1QS![56]

Table 2: The Sons of Zadok in 1QS but never in 4QS

Cave 1	Cave 4
1QS 5:2 The sons of Zadok and the multitude of the people of the community	4Q256 (4QS[b]) 9 3 // 4Q258 (4QS[d]) 1 2 The many
1QS 5:9 The sons of Zadok the priests and the multitude of the people of their covenant	4Q256 (4QS[b]) 9 7–8 // 4Q258 (4QS[d]) 1 7 The council of the people of the community
1QS 9:14 The Maskil is to separate and to weigh the sons of Zadok (בני הצדוק)	4Q259 3 10 The Maskil is to separate and weigh the sons of righteousness (בני הצדק)

The Rule also contains two significant instances promoting the sons of Aaron as authority figures in the community (1QS 5:21 // 4Q258 [4QS[d]] 2 1–2 and 1QS 9:7 // 4Q258 [4QS[d]] 7 7). *Crucially here two different Cave 4 manuscripts back this up*. I include a table with the bare facts.

---

[54] The latter reference (בני הצדוק) is often emended to read "the sons of righteousness" (בני הצדק) on the basis of 4Q259 (4QS[e]) 3 10, see DJD 26:144–149 (Alexander and Vermes); see also Robert A. Kugler, 'A Note on 1QS 9:14: The Sons of Righteousness or the Sons of Zadok,' *DSD* 3 (1996): 315–320.

[55] See note 10 above.

[56] The significance of the prominence of the Zadokites in the Cave 1 copy of the Community Rule is also rightly stressed by Grossman, *Reading for History*, 207.

Table 3: The Sons of Aaron in 1QS and 4QS

Cave 1	Cave 4
1QS 5:21–22 The sons of Aaron and the multitude of Israel	4Q258 (4QS^d) 2 1–2//4Q261 (4QS^g) 1a–b 1–2 The sons of Aaron and the multitude of Israel
1QS 9:7 Only the sons of Aaron	4Q258 (4QS^d) 7 7 [Only the sons of Aa]ron

I argued elsewhere that this element of continuity between 1QS and 4QS is highly noteworthy and offers us important clues about the textual development of the S tradition.[57] On my reading of the texts (and in particular the manuscript evidence), the sons of Aaron are important communal authorities in the S tradition before the sons of Zadok even had a look in, as I tried to show in my contribution to the *Festschrift* for Florentino García Martínez where I identified the following line of development,

> It seems likely, therefore, that we can observe a certain trajectory in the references to priestly authority in the scrolls beginning with the sons of Aaron in a national/non-community-specific context (D), to the sons of Aaron as priestly authorities within the community (S), to the sons of Zadok as priestly authorities within the community in a different literary stage of S.[58]

4. The Rule of the Congregation

In the Rule of the Congregation (1QSa) the sons of Zadok and the sons of Aaron occur as community authorities side by side, often in one and the same passage. I have suggested elsewhere that the sons of Zadok were added to 1QSa in a very similar and perhaps even the same process as we witness in 1QS on the same scroll.[59]

---

[57] See Hempel, 'Literary Development of the S Tradition.' Fabry also recognizes, "Die fortlaufende Redaktionsgeschichte der S-Literatur zeigt einen Kompetenzgewinn der Zadokiden ...," 'Zadokiden und Aaroniden in Qumran,' 212.

[58] 'Sons of Aaron in the Dead Sea Scrolls,' 214.

[59] See Charlotte Hempel, 'The Earthly Essene Nucleus of 1QSa,' *DSD* 3 (1996): 253–269, reprinted as Chapter 3 in this volume.

Table 4: The Sons of Zadok and the Sons of Aaron Juxtaposed in 1QSa[60]

The sons of Zadok	The sons of Aaron
1QSa 1:2 The sons of Zadok the priests and the people of their covenant (cf. 1QS 5:9)	1QSa 1:15–16 The sons of Aaron the priests and all the heads of the fathers of the congregation
1QSa 1:24–25 The sons of Zadok the priests and all the heads of the fathers of the congregation (context: overseeing the correct position of different groups during assembly)	1QSa 1:23 The sons of Aaron (context: overseeing the correct position of different groups during assembly)
1QSa 2:3 The sons of Zadok the priests	1QSa 2:13 [the sons of] Aaron

5. The Rule of Blessings

A whole section of blessings pronounced by the Maskil in 1QSb is devoted to the sons of Zadok (cf. 1QSb 3:22 ff.). Although no one else is mentioned, the way in which the sons of Zadok are singled out rather emphatically as God's chosen ones gives the impression that a need was felt to stress this status.

It is striking how much of the relatively meagre 'sons of Zadok harvest' in the corpus of the Scrolls is found in this one scroll: six out of eleven occurrences of the designation 'sons of Zadok' in the Dead Sea Scrolls are found in 1QS–1QSa–1QSb.[61] Speaking about the Cave 1 copy of the Community Rule George Brooke observed in the South African *Journal of Semitics* that it is a "thoroughly priestly document" framed by a covenant liturgy and with priests at the helm of the organization.[62] It seems to me that Brooke is correct and, what is more, that we should extend his observations to apply to the collection of documents 1QS–1QSa–1QSb – what we seem to have here is a priestly scroll or a priestly collection of texts.

---

[60] For the Hebrew text of 1QSa see DSSEL (Barthélemy); note that in the 2006 edition of DSSEL the English translation by Michael Wise, Martin Abegg, and Edward Cook with N. Gordon inadvertently translates בני צדוק with "the sons of Aaron" in 1QSa 1:24.

[61] Cf. Grossman, *Reading for History*, 202 where she notes the distinctive emphasis on the sons of Zadok in what she refers to as the "constellation of texts (1QS, 1QSa, 1QSb)."

[62] Cf. George J. Brooke, 'From "Assembly of Supreme Holiness for Aaron" to "Sanctuary of Adam:" The Laicization of Temple Ideology in the Qumran Scrolls and Its Wider Implications," *Journal of Semitics* 8 (1996): 119–145, here 123, cf. also 124.

6. 4Qpesher Isaiah[c]

4Q163 22 3 refers to the sons of Zadok as part of the interpretation of Isa 30:1–5. Unfortunately, very little is preserved of the interpretation beyond the reference to the sons of Zadok. We would very much like to know whether the reference to the sons of Zadok applies here to the community as a whole or to priestly communal authorities.[63]

7. 4QFlorilegium

A further reference to the sons of Zadok and the men of their council is attested in 4Q174 1–2 i 17[64] in a passage interpreting Ezek 37:23.[65] It is not possible to be certain whether 'the sons of Zadok' is applied to the community as a whole (referred to as Yaḥad in the same line) or to a leading group. It is nevertheless clear that like CD 3–4 this passage is exegetical and, more particularly, also draws on Ezekiel.

8. Conclusion

In the Damascus Document and 1QS the sons of Zadok are confined to a limited portion of their respective textual traditions. There may even be a connection between both pockets of Zadokite prominence across these texts, a possibility muted already by Wernberg Møller in an article that appeared in *Vetus Testamentum* in 1953.[66]

In a relatively small number of passages the sons of Aaron compete with the sons of Zadok as figures of communal authority. In the great majority of cases, however, the sons of Aaron perform traditional priestly duties, and the designation is synonymous with the priests. This widespread use of the sons of Aaron for the priests corresponds very well with the use of Aaron and Israel to refer

---

[63] Cf. Maurya Horgan, *Pesharim: Qumran Interpretations of Biblical Books* (CBQMS 8; Washington, D. C.: CBA, 1979), 102, 119.

[64] According to the physical reconstruction proposed by Annette Steudel this reference occurs at 4Q174 3 17, cf. *Der Midrasch zur Eschatologie aus der Qumrangemeinde (4QMidrEschat*[a.b]*): Materielle Rekonstruktion, Textbestand, Gattung und traditionsgeschichtliche Einordnung des durch 4Q174 ("Florilegium") und 4Q177 ("Catena A") repräsentierten Werkes aus den Qumranfunden* (STDJ 13; Leiden: Brill, 1993), 25, 31–32.

[65] Cf., e. g., George J. Brooke, *Exegesis at Qumran: 4QFlorilegium in Its Jewish Context* (JSOTSup 29; Sheffield: Sheffield Academic Press, 1985) 117–119; Knibb, *Qumran Community*, 261; and Steudel, *Midrasch zur Eschatologie*, 32.

[66] See also Wernberg Møller, 'צדק, צדיק and צדוק.' See also Davies, *Behind the Essenes*, 70 who suggests, "for a short period of time only, the term 'sons of Zadok' was used of the priests at Qumran."

to the make-up of the community and the expectations of lay and priestly messianic figures.

On a visit to Helsinki I learnt a great deal from my colleagues Dr. Jutta Jokiranta and Professor David Chalcraft,[67] two scholars who are at the forefront of applying social scientific approaches to the Scrolls. One of the notions that I learnt from them is the insight that if we talk of a sect this notion needs to be *relational* – a group is not a sect in and of itself but *in relation to* another entity.[68] I would like to borrow that concept and apply it – heuristically of course – to the lack of rivalry I perceive in the portrayal of the priests as the sons of Aaron in the Damascus Document. In my view the passages speaking of the sons of Aaron, either as priests or as community functionaries, are not relational with respect to other priestly groups. Put more bluntly, it seems likely that none of the references to the sons of Zakok were there when the references to the sons of Aaron were written down. By contrast, the references to the sons of Zadok in the Damascus Document and the Serekh seem to be relational indeed – whoever included them was aware that he or she was putting things right. In the Damascus Document the relational aspect refers to earlier forms of the community membership who came before the sons of Zadok, such as the returnees of Israel and those who joined them (cf. CD 3:20b–4:5a). In the Community Rule the sons of Aaron appear to have been in place, at least in the literature, when the sons of Zadok either take over or position themselves side by side with this group (see Tables 2 and 3 above). Whereas the sons of Aaron are a quiet presence in several S manuscripts as well as frequently in D, the sons of Zadok are presented as the crowning moment in the chronological development of the community in CD 4 and in the developing authority structure portrayed in 1QS. Thus, even though references to the sons of Zadok are numerically limited, and particularly prominent in the 1QS–1QSa–1QSb Scroll, the exalted claims made on behalf of this group have successfully convinced scholars of the communities' Zadokite leanings. On closer inspection such Zadokite leanings are outweighed by the much broader textual powerbase of the sons of Aaron.

---

[67] Prof. Chalcraft is based at the University of Sheffield (formerly Derby), UK, and was also visiting the University of Helsinki.

[68] I am grateful to Jutta Jokiranta and David Chalcraft for numerous interdisciplinary conversations, see also Cecilia Wassen and Jutta Jokiranta, 'Groups in Tension: Sectarianism in the Damascus Document and the Community Rule,' in *Sectarianism in Early Judaism: Sociological Advances* (ed. David Chalcraft; London: Equinox, 2007), 205–245.

Part VII

The Scrolls and the Emerging Scriptures

Chapter Fifteen

The Community Rule and the Book of Daniel[1]

1. Setting the Scene

The aim of this chapter is to offer a fresh investigation of the much discussed question of the Maskilim in Daniel 11–12 in light of the evidence of the Dead Sea Scrolls. The identity of this elevated group in the final chapters of Daniel has received a vast amount of scholarly attention because it is generally believed that the author(s)/editor(s) of the Book of Daniel belonged to this select circle.[2] It is further taken for granted by most that we must allow for a relationship of some kind between the circles behind Daniel and the communities behind the Scrolls.[3] In light of the rapid developments of all kinds in Scrolls scholarship over the last few years it seems timely to re-examine the relationship of Daniel to the Scrolls afresh.

---

[1] This chapter originated as a contribution to a *Festschrift* in honour of my esteemed teacher Michael Knibb and was originally published as '*Maskil(im)* and *Rabbim*: From Daniel to Qumran,' in *Biblical Traditions in Transmission: Essays in Honour of Michael A Knibb* (ed. Charlotte Hempel and Judith M. Lieu; JSJSup 111; Leiden; Brill, 2006), 133–156. Earlier versions of this material were presented at the Cambridge Old Testament Seminar in November 2004, the King's College London Biblical Studies Research Seminar in February 2005, and the 2005 Summer Meeting of the *Society for Old Testament Study* (SOTS). I am grateful to the chairs of the Cambridge and London seminars, Profs. Robert Gordon and Judith Lieu, as well as the members of the SOTS programme committee for giving me an opportunity to discuss an evolving piece of research and to those present for their insights and comments.

[2] On the social setting of the Book of Daniel see the contributions by Rainer Albertz, 'The Social Setting of the Aramaic and Hebrew Book of Daniel,' in *The Book of Daniel: Composition and Reception* (ed. John J. Collins and Peter W. Flint; VTSup 83.2; Leiden: Brill, 2002), Vol. I, 171–204; Stefan Beyerle, 'The Book of Daniel and Its Social Setting,' in *Book of Daniel* (ed. Collins and Flint), Vol. I, 205–228; Lester L. Grabbe, 'A Dan(iel) for all Seasons: For Whom was Daniel Important?,' in *Book of Daniel* (ed. Collins and Flint), Vol. I, 229–246; and Philip R. Davies, 'The Scribal School of Daniel,' in *Book of Daniel* (ed. Collins and Flint), Vol. I, 247–265 and the further literature referred to there. Further, Klaus Koch, *Das Buch Daniel* (EdF 144; Darmstadt: Wissenschaftliche Buchgesellschaft, 1980), esp. chapter 7 and John J. Collins, 'Daniel and His Social World,' *Interpretation* 39 (1985): 131–143.

[3] On this issue see, *inter alia*, Frederick F. Bruce, 'The Book of Daniel and the Qumran Community,' in *Neotestamentica et Semitica: Studies in Honour of Matthew Black* (ed. E. Earle Ellis and Max Wilcox Edinburgh: T & T Clark, 1968), 221–235; Matthias Henze, *The Madness of King Nebuchadnezzar: The Ancient Near Eastern Origins and Early History of Interpretation of Daniel 4* (JSJSup 61; Leiden: Brill, 1999), 217–243; Koch, *Buch Daniel*, 168–169, and the monograph by Alfred Mertens, *Das Buch Daniel im Lichte der Texte vom Toten Meer* (SBM 12; Stuttgart: Echter KBW, 1971).

Before turning to the specific texts a number of more general observations can be made regarding points of contact between the author(s)/editor(s) of Daniel and the groups behind the scrolls.

1.1 A Shared Bilingual Milieu

We have a bilingual milieu both in the Book of Daniel which famously switches from Hebrew to Aramaic in 2:4 and back to Hebrew at the beginning of chapter 8 as well as in the Scrolls which include Aramaic compositions alongside Hebrew ones.[4] As is well known, the Qumran manuscripts of the Book of Daniel attest the shift from Hebrew to Aramaic in 2:4 and back to Hebrew after 7:28. The rationale or reason behind the dividing line between the material preserved in Hebrew and Aramaic is not clear-cut in either collection. However, it seems fair to say that in both cases the choice of language is not arbitrary. Thus, in Daniel most of the Aramaic material comprises the tales, with the notable exception of chapter 7. In the Scrolls the Aramaic material is confined to non-sectarian texts,[5] and Devorah Dimant has calculated in 1995 that the Aramaic component in the Scrolls is around thirteen per cent.[6] This is borne out by a number of calculations that have been published since the original publication of this chapter.[7] Dimant further describes the contents of the Aramaic works as much more

---

[4] On this issue see John J. Collins, *Daniel* (Hermeneia; Minneapolis, Minn.: Fortress, 1993), 12–24; Koch, *Buch Daniel*, 34–54; Adam S. van der Woude, 'Die Doppelsprachigkeit des Buches Daniel,' in *The Book of Daniel in the Light of New Findings* (ed. Adam S. van der Woude; BETL 106; Leuven: Peeters, 1993), 3–12. Robert R. Wilson, 'From Prophecy to Apocalyptic: Reflections on the Shape of Israelite Religion,' *Semeia* 21 (1981): 79–95, esp. 92–93 suggests that a change in the make-up of the group behind Daniel may explain the change of language. The presence of a compatible bilingualism at Qumran seems to indicate that the group Wilson is referring to may be much larger than the circles behind the Book of Daniel.

[5] So already Stanislav Segert, 'Die Sprachenfrage in der Qumrangemeinschaft,' in *Qumran-Probleme* (ed. Hans Bardtke; DAWBSSA 42; Berlin: Akademie, 1963), 315–339, who suggested, somewhat analogously to Rainer Albertz on Daniel (see note 8 below): "Bei den hebräischen ausserbiblischen Schriften wird es sich, soweit kein Gegenbeweis vorliegt, um essäische Erzeugnisse handeln, während die Schriften fremden Ursprungs eher unter den aramäischen gesucht werden können." 322.

[6] Devorah Dimant, 'The Qumran Manuscripts: Contents and Significance,' in *Time to Prepare a Way in the Wilderness: Papers on the Qumran Scrolls by Fellows of the Institute for Advanced Studies of the Hebrew University, Jerusalem, 1989–1990* (ed. Devorah Dimant and Lawrence H. Schiffman; STDJ 16; Leiden: Brill, 1995), 23–58, 34–35.

[7] Eibert J. C. Tigchelaar, 'The Dead Sea Scrolls,' in EDEJ: 163–180, esp. 165. For a comprehensive list of identified Aramaic texts from Qumran and other sites in the Judaean Desert see DJD 39: 221–226 (Tov). On the difficulties of arriving at accurate figures see now Katell Berthelot and Daniel Stökl Ben Ezra, 'Aramaica Qumranica: Introduction,' in *Aramaica Qumranica: Proceedings of the Conference on the Aramaic Texts from Qumran in Aix-en-Provence 30 June–2 July 2008* (ed. Katell Berthelot and Daniel Stökl Ben Ezra; STDJ 94; Leiden: Brill 2010),1–12, here 1.

uniform and notes, "They contain almost exclusively visionary-pseudepigraphic compositions, testaments and narrative aggadic works."[8] It seems fair to say that both collections, Daniel and the Scrolls, were read, cherished, written, and redacted in circles in which at the very least the elite was completely at home in either language. Moreover, both appear to associate some types of material with Aramaic and other types of texts with Hebrew. And finally, in both cases the Aramaic component goes back to or deals with the community's past, its heritage, whereas the texts or passages dealing most closely with the present are composed in Hebrew.[9]

1.2 The Book of Daniel and the Scrolls as Tradents of Danielic Traditions

Beyond this, both the communities behind the Scrolls and the author(s)/editor(s) of Daniel cherished and preserved some of the same kind of material as manifested by the presence of a wider Daniel-cycle in the Scrolls.[10] Whereas it used to be taken for granted that the Qumran Daniel-cycle presupposes the Book of Daniel,[11] current thinking allows for the possibility that it includes independent traditions related to Daniel.[12] Thus, the Qumran texts testify to a movement which cherished the Book of Daniel, earlier traditions of the kind incorporated in the book such as the Prayer of Nabonidus,[13] as well as other independent traditions. The way this is often put is to say that the Scrolls testify to an interest in Daniel by preserving eight copies of the book as well as texts from a wider Daniel cycle. A better and more nuanced way of looking at this is to note that

---

[8] Dimant, 'Qumran Manuscripts,' 35.

[9] Note that Albertz has recently argued that "the entire Aramaic section of Daniel 2–7 can be interpreted as an older source that was incorporated by a Hebrew-writing editor," 'Social Setting of Daniel,' 178.

[10] On the Daniel cycle at Qumran see George J. Brooke, 'Parabiblical Prophetic Narratives,' in *The Dead Sea Scrolls After Fifty Years: A Comprehensive Assessment* (ed. James C. VanderKam and Peter W. Flint; Leiden: Brill, 1999), Vol. I, 271–301, esp. 290–297; John J. Collins, 'Apocalypticism and Literary Genre in the Dead Sea Scrolls,' in *Dead Sea Scrolls After Fifty Years* (ed. VanderKam and Flint), Vol. II, 403–430, esp. 410–417; John J. Collins, 'Daniel, Book of: Pseudo Daniel,' in EDSS 1: 176–178; Peter Flint, 'The Daniel Tradition at Qumran,' in *Book of Daniel* (ed. Collins and Flint), Vol. II, 329–367; and Michael A. Knibb, 'The Book of Daniel in Its Context,' in *Book of Daniel* (ed. Collins and Flint), Vol. I, 16–35.

[11] Cf. Józef T. Milik, 'Prière de Nabonide et autres écrits d'un cycle de Daniel,' *RB* 63 (1956): 407–415. This was also the earlier view of Collins, *Daniel*, 72, and is still the favoured position of Knibb, cf. 'Book of Daniel in Its Context,' 19–24.

[12] So DJD 22:136 (Collins and Flint); Flint, 'Daniel Tradition at Qumran,' 340. See also Grabbe, 'A Dan(iel) for all Seasons,' 237 and Loren Stuckenbruck, 'Daniel and Early Enoch Traditions in the Dead Sea Scrolls,' in *Book of Daniel* (ed. Collins and Flint), Vol. II, 368–386, esp. 371–377.

[13] Note, however, the stimulating essay by Andrew Steinmann, 'The Chicken and the Egg: A New Proposal for the Relationship Between the *Prayer of Nabonidus* and the *Book of Daniel*,' *RQ* 20 (2002): 558–570, who challenges the order of priority of both works.

both the community behind the Book of Daniel and the communities behind the Scrolls were tradents of Danielic traditions.[14] An important difference is the way in which the Book of Daniel has shaped the material into a coherent composition and that this composition itself is already amply attested at Qumran and quoted from as an authoritative text in a number of places (such as 4Q174 [Florilegium] and 11Q13 [Melchizedek]).[15] But if we imagine ourselves in the period just before the Book of Daniel was completed then we have a community behind Daniel just like the community behind the Scrolls handing on and cherishing the same kind of traditions.[16] There is no need, furthermore, to assume that the further developments of these traditions as represented by the Danielic cycle found at Qumran were an exclusively sectarian endeavour. By contrast, it seems entirely feasible that the same circles who cherished and produced those traditions prior to the composition of the book continued to do so.[17]

1.3 A Claim to Exilic Roots

Both groups, though they emerged in the second century BCE, lay claim to ideological or historical (or conceivably both) roots in the exile (cf., e. g., the setting of the tales and CD 1//4QD).[18] An interesting difference is the popularity of reviews of history culminating in the emergence of a reform movement in the second century BCE in a number of texts such as CD 1//4QD, *1 Enoch* (e. g. 93:10) and *Jubilees* (e. g. 21:24), in contrast to the absence of any such account of the emergence of a reform movement as the legitimate objects of divine favour in Dan 11–12. Whereas in CD 1 the biggest event in the historical overview is the emergence of a pious movement and subsequently its leader the

---

[14] See Florentino García Martínez, *Qumran and Apocalyptic: Studies on the Aramaic Texts from Qumran* (STDJ 9; Leiden: Brill, 1992), 149.

[15] On this issue see the nuanced discussion in Klaus Koch, 'Stages in the Canonization of the Book of Daniel,' in *Book of Daniel* (ed. Collins and Flint), Vol. II, 421–446, esp. 427–432.

[16] See Bruce, 'Book of Daniel and the Qumran Community,' 225.

[17] So also Flint, 'Daniel Tradition at Qumran,' 363–364; see further Esther Eshel, 'Possible Sources of the Book of Daniel,' in *Book of Daniel* (ed. Collins and Flint), Vol. II, 387–394 and Stuckenbruck, 'Daniel and Early Enoch Traditions.'

[18] On the Babylonian diaspora as background to Daniel see Koch, *Buch Daniel*, 170–171. On exile in the Second Temple Period and the Damascus Document in particular see Michael A. Knibb, 'The Exile in the Literature of the Intertestamental Period,' *HeyJ* 17 (1976): 249–272; idem, 'Exile in the Damascus Document,' *JSOT* 25 (1983): 99–117. For a literal interpretation of exile in the Damascus Doucment see Jerome Murphy-O'Connor, 'An Essene Missionary Document? CD II,14–VI,1,' *RB* 77 (1970): 201–229. For an overview of the discussion and further literature see Charlotte Hempel, *The Damascus Texts* (CQS 1; Sheffield: Sheffield Academic Press, 2000), 56–60. On exilic orgins – to use a convenient shorthand – underpinning both Daniel and Qumran see also Davies, 'Scribal School of Daniel,' 259.

Teacher of Righteousness,[19] in the last chapters of Daniel the event in focus is the Antiochene crisis. The favourable portrayal of the wise is mentioned as the most appropriate and exemplary response to the crisis without itself being the main point of the story. We may have a missing link in 4Q245 (pseudo Daniel^c) 2 4 if we follow the interpretation put forward by the editors Collins and Flint that the verb קום refers to the rise of a reform movement[20] over against Florentino García Martínez, Émile Puech, and Michael Knibb who take the term to refer to resurrection.[21]

1.4 A Learned Scribal Context

Both communities attest to a learned environment where the scriptures are studied and applied to the authors' contemporary situation. The learned, scribal character of the Scrolls' communities is evident, and the Habakkuk Pesher is a prime example of the way in which these texts apply the scriptures to events of the authors' own day. As far as Daniel is concerned, Philip Davies has described the situation very well when he notes, "Daniel, then, is a book in which everything significant is done by *writing*."[22]

1.5 The Significance of Mystery and Interpretation

More specifically, both collections give prominence to notions of mystery and interpretation as manifest in the use of *raz* and *pesher/peshar* terminology.[23] Rather than assuming that the Scrolls were influenced by the Book of Daniel it

---

[19] For a close analysis of the accounts of community origins in the Damascus Document see Chapter 4 above.

[20] See DJD 22:153–164, esp. 163 (Collins and Flint) and Collins, 'Apocalypticism and Literary Genre,' 412–413.

[21] See García Martínez, *Qumran and Apocalyptic*, 137–149; Émile Puech, *La croyance des Esséniens en la vie future: Immortalité, resurrection, et vie éternelle* (Paris: Gabalda, 1993), 568–570; Michael A. Knibb, 'Eschatology and Messianism in the Dead Sea Scrolls,' in *The Dead Sea Scrolls After Fifty Years* (ed. VanderKam and Flint), Vol. II, 379–402, esp. 382–384; and Knibb, 'Book of Daniel in Its Context,' 20.

[22] Philip R. Davies, 'Reading Daniel Sociologically,' in *Daniel in the Light of New Findings* (ed. van der Woude), 353. On the learned, scribal character of the circles behind Daniel see further, for instance, Albertz, 'Social Setting,' 201; Davies, 'Scribal School of Daniel,' 255, 257–258; Michael A. Knibb, '"You are Indeed Wiser than Daniel:" Reflections on the Character of the Book of Daniel,' in *Daniel in the Light of New Findings* (ed. van der Woude), 399–411, esp. 404 ff.; and idem, 'Book of Daniel in Its Context,' 16–19.

[23] See Bruce, 'Book of Daniel and the Qumran Community,' 225–229. On 'secret' as an important symbol in Daniel see Davies, 'Reading Daniel Sociologically,' 356–357. On subtle differences in the usage of *pesher* terminology in Daniel and Qumran see Koch, 'Canonization of the Book of Daniel,' 429.

seems wise to allow for the possibility that there was a certain section of Second Temple Jewish society which favoured such preoccupations and shared the same terminology. Collins seems right when he cautiously sums up the evidence, "The Essene understanding of mystery and interpretation may be indebted to Daniel 2 and 4 but can be attributed to the common milieu."[24] As far as *raz* is concerned, we now have a host of new evidence in the form of the substantial wisdom texts Mysteries (1Q27; 4Q299–301) and Instruction (1Q26; 4Q415–418; 418a; 418c; 423).[25] Neither of these texts, interestingly, preserve an occurrence of *pesher* nor do they employ the term Maskil with reference to a particular office or individual.[26] Given the sparsity of our sources it is unwise to assume that the terminology *raz* and *pesher* was not used more widely by Second Temple period Jews. The common usage in Daniel and the Scrolls is best accounted for by the fact that the same groups lie behind some of the traditions in the Scrolls and Daniel.

1.6 Consciousness of Proximity with the Angelic Realm

Finally, both the Scrolls and the Visions of the Book of Daniel alongside other early Jewish texts such as 1 Enoch reflect a self-understanding characterized by a close relationship of some kind with the angelic realm.[27] As far as the Scrolls are concerned obvious examples are the Songs of the Sabbath Sacrifice large parts of which describe the worship of angelic priests in the heavenly temple and the War Scroll. As far as the Visions of Daniel are concerned Collins has drawn attention

---

[24] *Daniel*, 79.

[25] The secondary literature dealing with these texts is extensive. For a discussion of the Qumran wisdom texts in relation to Daniel that includes further bibliographical information see Knibb, 'Book of Daniel in Its Context,' 31–34. Since the publication of Knibb's discussion several major books on the topic have appeared: John J. Collins, Gregory E. Sterling, and Ruth A. Clements (eds), *Sapiential Perspectives: Wisdom Literature in Light of the Dead Sea Scrolls* (STDJ 51; Leiden: Brill, 2004); Matthew J. Goff, *The Worldly and Heavenly Wisdom of 4QInstruction* (STDJ 50; Leiden: Brill, 2003); Charlotte Hempel, Armin Lange, and Hermann Lichtenberger (eds), *The Wisdom Texts from Qumran and the Development of Sapiential Thought* (BETL 159; Leuven: Peeters, 2002); and Eibert J. C. Tigchelaar, *To Increase Learning for the Understanding Ones: Reading and Reconstructing the Early Jewish Sapiential Text 4QInstruction* (STDJ 44; Leiden: Brill, 2001). To this may now be added the excellent commentary by John Kampen which has appeared since the original publication of this chapter, cf. John Kampen, *Wisdom Literature* (ECDSS; Grand Rapids, Mich.: Eerdmans, 2011).

[26] See Charlotte Hempel, 'The Qumran Sapiential Texts and the Rule Books,' in *The Wisdom Texts from Qumran* (ed. Hempel, Lange, and Lichtenberger), 277–295, esp. 287, reprinted as Chapter 10 in this volume. Note, however, Eibert J. C. Tigchelaar, 'Towards a Reconstruction of the Beginning of 4QInstruction,' in *The Wisdom Texts from Qumran* (ed. Hempel, Lange, and Lichtenberger), 99–126, 123.

[27] See Michael Mach, 'Angels,' in EDSS 1:24–27 and further literature referred to there. Also, André Lacocque, 'Socio-Spiritual Formative Milieu of the Daniel Apocalypse,' in *Daniel in the Light of New Findings* (ed. van der Woude), 315–343, esp. 324 and now also Archie T. Wright, 'Angels,' in EDEJ: 328–321.

to the term "people of the holy ones" and the references to "the backdrop of a heavenly battle between Michael, the angelic prince of Israel, and the 'princes' of Persia and Greece."[28] He has further made a good case for seeing communion with the angelic hosts as the primary objective of the maskilim.[29]

Cumulatively the observations above make a strong case for a common milieu between both collections of literature. The remainder of this chapter will deal with the evidence of Dan 11–12 and the Community Rule in turn.

2. The Maskilim in Daniel 11–12

The hi. participle plural Maskilim occurs several times in the last chapters of the Book of Daniel apparently with reference to a particular privileged group within the community. It is widely held that the author(s)/editor(s) of the book are to be found in those circles.[30] When we look at this material it becomes clear very quickly that we are told very little about this group. They are introduced rather abruptly, it seems to me, in Dan 11:33 after the previous verse 32 spoke about the make-up of the people in terms of those who violate the covenant over against the people (עם) who know their God.[31] The text continues in verses 33–35,

> The Maskilim of the people shall instruct the many (רבים), but they will stumble by sword and flame, captivity and plundering for some days. When they fall they will receive a little help, and many (רבים) shall attach themselves to them under false pretences. Some of the Maskilim will stumble in order to refine amongst them and to purify and to make white until the time of the end for this is still at the appointed time.

One way around the sparse amount of detail we are given about this group is to argue, as Collins does for instance, that since they are the group behind the book, the kinds of views expressed in the Book of Daniel also give expression to the ideology of this group. This seems likely, although large parts of the book clearly emerged independently, and it seems to be the framework and the presentation of these earlier components that brings us closest to the voice of the Maskilim. Thus, a good case has been made that in view of the astonishing

---

[28] Collins, 'Daniel and His Social World,' 139; idem, *The Apocalyptic Vision of the Book of Daniel* (HSM 16; Missoula, Mont.: Scholars Press, 1977), 123–147; and idem, 'The Mythology of Holy War in Daniel and the Qumran War Scroll: A Point of Transition in Jewish Apocalyptic,' *VT* 25 (1975): 596–612.

[29] Collins, 'Daniel and His Social World,' 140.

[30] Cf., e. g., Albertz, 'Social Setting of Daniel,' 193 and Collins, *Daniel*, 66–67.

[31] Note that Bernhard Hasslberger refers to the *passus* on the wise in Daniel 11 in terms of an excursus, *Hoffnung in der Bedrängnis: Eine formkritische Untersuchung zu Dan 8 und 10–12* (ATSAT 4; St. Ottilien: Eos, 1977), 267. Koch also argues convincingly that the way in which the term Maskil is used in Daniel 11–12 gives the impression that the term was "an established term for the authors of Daniel […] not their invention," 'Canonization of the Book of Daniel,' 429.

amount of knowledge displayed in Chapter 11 about Greek history we should reckon with the incorporation and adaptation of a history of the Ptolemies and Seleucids in this chapter.[32] In any case, the few passages where the group of the Maskilim comes to the fore and names itself are clearly of particular interest, and there is little doubt that those passages are part of the redactional work of those responsible both for the book as a whole as well as Chapter 11 in particular.

Otto Plöger famously saw in this group and behind the Book of Daniel "the conventicle-spirit of deliberate separatism" and argued for taking this material as referring to membership in a particular group.[33] His views on the opposition between priestly hierarchy and visionary conventicles as the cornerstones of post-exilic society have now been recognized as too simplistic. As far as the present passage is concerned, the boundaries between those who are with us and those who are against us seem to be relatively fluid and low.[34] It is characterized by a degree elitism[35] that is nevertheless willing to admit the right kind of aspirants into the fold. This non-insular generosity is indicated by the fact that this group is said to instruct (יבינו) the many and welcomes those who join them as long as they do so sincerely. Moreover the *hiphil* participle already implies the causative (making someone have insight) which fits the context well.[36] The portrayal of the wise here is best described as advocates of *aspirational elitism*.

It is further generally recognized that both the terms Maskilim and rabbim in this part of Daniel are based on the suffering servant as portrayed in Isa 53:11.[37]

---

[32] So George A. Barton, 'The Composition of the Book of Daniel,' *JBL* 17 (1898): 62–86. More recently see Uriel Rappaport, 'Apocalyptic Vision and Preservation of Historical Memory,' *JSJ* 23 (1992): 217–226 and Paul L. Redditt, 'Daniel 11 and the Sociological Setting of the Book of Daniel,' *CBQ* 60 (1998): 463–474, 470–471. Collins, *Daniel*, 377, notes, however, that "It is clear that Daniel does not simply incorporate a source, because the account exhibits traditional theological patterns and is modeled on Daniel 8 to some degree." A number of possibilities of how a Greek source may have been incorporated are outlined by Rappaport, 'Apocalyptic Vision,' 224 n. 14.

[33] Otto Plöger, *Theocracy and Eschatology* (trans. S. Rudman; Richmond, Va.: John Knox, 1969), 19. For a critique see, e. g., Koch, *Buch Daniel*, 169–170.

[34] I wonder whether, in light of the fluid and low boundaries between the wise and the rest of the people envisaged here, the description of the authors' attitude as "incipient sectarian" is not too strong a term for this material, cf. Collins, 'Mythology of Holy War,' 603.

[35] Here my own position is close to the one outlined by Davies, 'Scribal School of Daniel,' 253, who also speaks of 'elitism' in this context and emphasizes the lack of 'separatism.'

[36] This is also highlighted with reference to Dan 11:33, 35; 12:3 (in contrast to Dan 1:4) by Klaus Koch, *Daniel* (BKAT 22.1; Neukirchen-Vluyn: Neukirchener Verlag, 1986), 18, 20, 44, see also 4. See further Davies, 'Scribal School of Daniel,' 253.

[37] See, e. g., Harold L. Ginsberg, 'The Oldest Interpretation of the Suffering Servant,' *VT* 3 (1953): 400–404 and Mertens, *Buch Daniel*, 70 who admits to simplifying the picture when he sums up his reading of the evidence as follows, "An die Stelle des Ebed Jahwe bei Jesaja sind im Daniel-Buch die 'Weisen' getreten. Im Schrifttum vom Toten Meer aber steht an derselben Stelle der 'Lehrer der Gerechtigkeit'…" Further, Beyerle, 'Daniel and Its Social Setting,' 215 and n. 40; Collins, *Daniel*, 385; Davies, 'Scribal School of Daniel,' 251–252; and Knibb, "'You are Indeed Wiser than Daniel,'" 406–407.

This is particularly clear further on in Dan 12:3 which clearly alludes to Isa 53:11 in its description of the eschaton and the elevated fate of the Maskilim at that time: 'The Maskilim shall shine like the brightness of the sky, and those who bring righteousness to many like the stars for ever and ever.'

3. Maskil and Rabbim in the Community Rule [38]

The Dead Sea Scrolls Concordance lists thirty seven entries for Maskil in the sense of 'Instructor' in the non-biblical Scrolls.[39] A number of those are multiple occurrences in different copies of the same document. The texts that mention this individual or office are the Damascus Document (x3),[40] the Rule of the Community (x4), the Rule of Blessings (x3, 1QSb), the Hodayot (x4), Hodayot-like text (x1, 4Q433a), The Songs of the Sabbath Sacrifice (x7), as a heading in an Address by the Maskil to the sons of Dawn (x1, 4Q298), Songs of the Maskil (x2, 4Q510 and 4Q511), 4QInstruction (x3) and once in 4QWays of Righteousness (4Q421) and 4QNarrative B (4Q461) respectively.

One curiosity, to begin with, is that if the Maskilim of Daniel, as often and rightly thought, were teachers of eschatological speculation it is extremely perplexing that the individual/office Maskil does not occur in most of the eschatological documents from Qumran. Thus, the term is entirely absent from the War Scroll (a text that has been called "a sort of midrash on the end of Dn 11 and the beginning of Dn 12"[41]), 4QSefer ha-Milḥama (4Q285 and 11Q14), the Rule of the Congregation (1QSa), 1QpHabakkuk, and 11Q13 (Melchizedek). The term is present in 1QSb, the Rule of Blessings, as is often noted. Given the well-known close relationship between the Book of Daniel and the War Scroll

---

[38] On the Maskil see Hempel, 'The Sapiential Texts and the Rule Books,' 286–294; John I. Kampen, 'The Diverse Aspects of Wisdom in the Qumran Texts,' in *The Dead Sea Scrolls After Fifty Years* (ed. VanderKam and Flint), Vol. I, 211–243, esp. 238–239; Hans Kosmala, 'Maśkîl,' *JANES* 5 (1973): 235–241 (reprinted in idem, *Studies, Essays and Reviews* [Leiden: Brill, 1978], Vol. I, 149–155); Carol Newsom, 'The Sage in the Literature of Qumran: The Functions of the Maskil,' in *The Sage in Israel and the Ancient Near East* (ed. James G. Gammie and Leo G. Perdue; Winona Lake, Ind.: Eisenbrauns, 1990), 373–382; eadem, 'Apocalyptic and the Discourse of the Qumran Community,' in *JNES* 49 (1990): 135–144; eadem, *The Self as Symbolic Space: Constructing Identity and Community at Qumran* (STDJ 52; Leiden: Brill, 2004), 169–174, 189–190; and Armin Lange, *Weisheit und Prädestination: Weisheitliche Urordnung und Prädestination in den Textfunden von Qumran* (STDJ 18; Leiden: Brill, 1995), 144–164.

[39] Martin G. Abegg, *The Dead Sea Scrolls Concordance. Volume One: The Non-Biblical Texts from Qumran [Part 1]* (Leiden: Brill, 2003), 489.

[40] Here and in the following examples I am not including occurrences of the same passage in different copies of the same work.

[41] Bruce, 'Book of Daniel and the Qumran Community,' 233.

in particular, the absence of the designation in this work certainly deserves to be reflected upon.[42]

We also note the prevalence of the term in liturgical texts which reminds us of the occurrence of Maskil in the heading of a number of Psalms as well as its use in Chronicles with reference to the cultic duties of the Levites.[43] In what follows I would like to focus on the Community Rule, in particular, because this text figures rather prominently in discussions of Daniel and Qumran.[44]

The standard textbook account of the relationship of the Maskilim in Dan 11–12 and the Qumran community runs as follows: the Maskil appears as a key community functionary in the sectarian Scrolls, and the community itself which he leads has adopted the designation ha-rabbim. This represents an institutionalization of the terminology we find in Daniel.[45] In what follows I will suggest that things are not quite as simple as that.

Let me begin this discussion with another curiosity. It is true that we have both the Maskil and the designation ha-rabbim as important terms in the Community Rule, but the two terms are never closely linked to one another with one possible partial exception. By contrast, when the texts introduce the Maskil, which is across the board most often in headings, designations other than ha-rabbim are used. Thus, in the Teaching on the Two Spirits we have a variety of terms to designate 'the good side' (e. g. children of light, children of righteousness, children of truth – never rabbim). The other long section on the Maskil in 1QS 9:12 ff., to be discussed below, never associates this figure with the rabbim, but instead uses other designations such as (children of righteousness [4Q259 S^e]/ Zadok [1QS],[46] chosen ones of the time, the chosen of the way [4Q258 S^d]/ those who have chosen the way [1QS]). There is certainly no shortage of the designation ha-rabbim in the Community Rule. It occurs no less than thirty four times, but not once in the two passages most closely associated with the Maskil which employ other terms. Thus, whereas it is still correct to say that we have both terms in the same key text, it is equally significant that when we look a lit-

---

[42] An exception is an occurrence of the plural in the liturgical part of 1QM in 10:10 where the holy people of the covenant are described as מלומדי חוק משכילי בינ[ה, cf. PTSDSSP 2:116 (Duhaime). It has also been suggested to reconstruct a reference to the Maskil in the lost title of 1QM, cf. Jean Duhaime, *The War Texts: 1QM and Related Manuscripts* (CQS 6; London: T & T Clark, 2004), 53–54 and previous literature referred to there.

[43] For the view that the Maskil's liturgical role was a later development see Christoph Dohmen, 'Zur Gründung der Gemeinde von Qumran (1QS VIII–IX),' *RQ* 11 (1982): 81–96. On this issue see also Newsom, 'Sage in the Literature of Qumran,' 375 and 380 n. 11 where she tentatively proposes, in marked contrast to Dohmen, that the term Maskil might have entered the vocabulary of the sect via the pre-sectarian Songs of the Sabbath Sacrifice.

[44] See, e. g., Davies, 'Scribal School of Daniel,' 259–264.

[45] Cf. Collins, *Daniel*, 73; Henze, *Madness of King Nebuchadnezzar*, 232–233, 241; Koch, *Buch Daniel*, 169; and Mertens, *Buch Daniel*, 64.

[46] On this variant see Robert A. Kugler, 'A Note on 1QS 9:14: the Sons of Righteousness or the Sons of Zadok?,' *DSD* 3 (1996): 315–320.

tle deeper they certainly do not go hand in hand. I will deal with the four most important texts from the Community Rule in turn.

3.1 The Restored Title of the Rule of the Community

It is widely held that the best way to reconstruct the first word of the title of the Community Rule in 1QS 1:1, this part of the title not being attested by any of the 4QS manuscripts, is with למשכיל.[47] On the basis of such a reconstruction it has been argued that the Scroll is best taken as a handbook for the Maskil.[48] This frequently endorsed restoration may or may not be correct, and it seems prudent not to build too much on any reading that is not attested. It is noteworthy, moreover, that the preserved occurrences of Maskil in the Community Rule never associate the official with the term סרך as proposed in the restored title. Instead there is a clear preference for other terms such as חוקים (1QS 9:12//4Q259 [4QS^e] 3 7), תכונים (1QS 9:21//4Q258 [4QS^d] 8 5//4Q259 [4QS^e] 4 2) and once מדרש (4Q258 [4QS^d]1 1//4Q256 [4QS^b] 9 1). The situation is very similar in the Damascus Document where the Maskil is referred to alongside the term חוקים (cf. CD 12:22//4Q266 [4QD^a] 5 i 17). Even if we were to grant limited weight to the restoration, the related point of the importance of the Maskil in the final form, we might say the *Endredaktion*, of 1QS, and certainly of 4Q258 (4QS^d), where the reading Maskil is preserved in the heading,[49] is beyond doubt. On my reading the evidence is best explained if we think of Maskil traditions originally associated with terms such as חוקים and תכונים having been incorporated into larger documents such as the Damascus Document and the Community Rule.

---

[47] So, e. g., DJD 26:32 (Alexander and Vermes); Jean Carmignac, 'Conjecture sur la première ligne de la Règle de la Communauté,' *RQ* 2 (1959): 85–87; Sarianna Metso, *The Textual Development of the Qumran Community Rule* (STDJ 21; Leiden: Brill, 1997), 111–112; and Carol Newsom, *Self as Symbolic Space*, 102. A different view has been put forward by Hartmut Stegemann who considers 1QS a *Sammelhandschrift* rather than a single composition and argues that the title in 1QS 1:1 refers only to 1QS 1:1–3:12, cf. 'Some Remarks to 1QSa, to 1QSb and to Qumran Messianism,' *RQ* 17 (1996): 479–505.

[48] Philip S. Alexander, 'The Redaction-History of Serekh ha-Yaḥad: A Proposal,' *RQ* 17 (1996): 437–456, a view most recently endorsed by Newsom, *Self as Symbolic Space*, 102. Note that Huppenbauer proposed already in 1959 that various parts of S were intended for community leaders rather than the membership at large, cf. Hans Walter Huppenbauer, *Der Mensch zwischen zwei Welten* (ATANT 34; Zürich: Zwingli, 1959), 44 n. 145.

[49] The opening lines of 4Q258 (4QS^d) have been discussed extensively in recent years, see DJD 26:83–98 (Alexander and Vermes) for the text and further literature and section 3.1.3 below.

3.2 The Introduction to the Teaching on the Two Spirits 1QS 3:13–4:26

The title and introduction to the Teaching on the Two Spirits reads as follows,

> For the Maskil to instruct and to teach all the children of light about the biographies of humanity with regard to all the varieties of their spirits as signified by their actions during their lives and with regard to the punishment of their sufferings as well as their happy times.

The value in what follows this heading for our understanding of the Maskil in the Community Rule is limited by three factors. First, since the publication of the Cave 4 manuscripts it has become clear that some manuscripts of the Community Rule did not incorporate the Teaching on the Two Spirits or indeed anything from the first four columns in 1QS and began instead with the equivalent of 1QS 5.[50] Secondly, and not unrelated, is a recent school of thought that considers the Teaching on the Two Spirits as an originally independent composition that was secondarily incorporated into the Serekh.[51] This view stands in marked contrast to the traditional understanding of the treatise as a succinct summary of 'Qumran theology.'[52] And finally, there have been a number of studies making a strong case for the composite character of the treatise.[53] A literary history for the growth of the treatise is further suggested by the presence of a 4QS fragment (4Q255 [4QS^a] frg. 3) containing a small amount of text that is reminiscent of the Teaching on the Two Spirits but does not parallel any portion of it exactly.[54]

---

[50] See DJD 26:85 (Alexander and Vermes).

[51] See Lange, *Weisheit und Prädestination*, chapter 4 and Jörg Frey, 'Different Patterns of Dualistic Thought in the Qumran Library: Reflections on their Background and History,' in *Legal Texts and Legal Issues: Proceedings of the Second Meeting of the International Organization for Qumran Studies Published in Honour of Joseph M. Baumgarten* (ed. Moshe Bernstein, Florentino García Martínez, and John Kampen; STDJ 23; Leiden: Brill, 1997), 275–335. Since this chapter was originally published I have offered a detailed analysis of the place of the Treatise in the Community Rule, see Charlotte Hempel, 'The Teaching on the Two Spirits and the Literary Development of the Rule of the Community,' in *Dualism in Qumran* (ed. Geza Xeravits; LSTS 76; London: T & T Clark, 2010), 102–120.

[52] See, e. g., Helmer Ringgren's description of the Teaching on the Two Spirits, which he incidentally recognized as an originally independent source, as "a short presentation of the theology of the sect," *The Faith of Qumran: Theology of the Dead Sea Scrolls* (rev. and enl. ed.; New York: Crossroad, 1995), 2–3. More recently John Collins has referred to the treatise as "the heart of the sect's theology," 'Apocalypticism and Literary Genre,' 421.

[53] See Jean Duhaime, 'L'instruction sur les deux esprits et les interpolations dualistes à Qumran,' *RB* 84 (1977): 566–594; Peter von der Osten-Sacken, *Gott und Belial: Traditionsgeschichtliche Untersuchungen zum Dualismus in den Texten aus Qumran* (SUNT 6; Göttingen: Vandenhoeck & Ruprecht, 1969), chapters 6–8; Hartmut Stegemann, 'Zu Textbestand und Grundgedanken von 1QS III,13–IV,26,' *RQ* 13 (1988): 95–131.

[54] See DJD 26:36–37 (Alexander and Vermes); Metso, *Textual Development*, 90–91, 137; and Eibert J. C. Tigchelaar, '"These are the names of the spirits of …": A Preliminary Edition of *4QCatalogue of Spirits* (4Q230) and New Manuscript Evidence for the *Two Spirits Treatise* (4Q257 and 1Q29a),' *RQ* 21 (2004): 529–548.

For the purposes of the present enquiry it suffices to note that the association of the Treatise with the Maskil by way of the heading and introduction is best seen as a secondary development and part of the editorial process that shaped 1QS as a whole.[55] I am not denying an association of the teachings contained in this material with the Maskil.[56] I do suggest, however, that this relationship is not as organic as is sometimes assumed.[57] More caution is necessary when we try and make a case for the relevance of this material for evaluating the relationship to Daniel.

3.3 The Introduction to 1QS 5//4Q256 (4QS^b) 9//4Q258 (4QS^d) 1[58]

1QS 5:1–3a	4QS^b 9 and 4QS^d 1 (Composite Text)
⁵¹And this is the rule for the people of the community . who eagerly volunteer to turn back from all evil and to hold fast to all that He has commanded as His wish.	ᵇ¹/ᵈ¹ *Midrash for the Maskil over (or: concerning) the people of the law* who eagerly volunteer to turn back from all evil and to hold fast to all ᵇ²that He has commanded.
They shall keep separate from the congregation of ²the people of injustice to form a community with regard to law and wealth. They shall be accountable to the sons of Zadok, the priests who keep the covenant and to the multitude of the people of ³the community who hold fast to the covenant. On their authority decisions shall be taken regarding any matter pertaining to law, wealth, or justice.	ᵈ²They shall keep separate from the congregation of the people of injustice to form a community with regard to la[w] and wealth. They shall be accountable ᵇ³to the many regarding any matter ᵈ³pertaining to law and wealth.

The opening lines of 1QS 5 and 4Q256/4Q258 have received a fair amount of scholarly attention over the last few years because they preserve a number

---

[55] Here I am in agreement with Metso, *Textual Development*, 139, 145 and Duhaime, 'L'instruction,' 580, 589.

[56] Note the helpful discussion in Metso, *Textual Development*, 135–140, esp. 136–137. See also Catherine Murphy, *Wealth in the Dead Sea Scrolls and in the Qumran Community* (STDJ 40; Leiden: Brill, 2002), 112–114.

[57] In fact, Duhaime ('L'instruction') and Metso (*Textual Development*, 136–137) point to links between parts of the Teaching on the Two Spirits and the Statutes for the Maskil in 1QS 9, and the composite nature of the treatise may hold the answer to the complex question of its relationship both to the Maskil heading and the Maskil section in 1QS 9.

[58] This synoptic translation is taken from Charlotte Hempel, *Rules and Laws I* (ECDSS 1; Grand Rapids, Mich.: Eerdmans, forthcoming). It is based on the editions of the Hebrew text of 1QS in PTSDSSP 1:6–51 (Qimron) and of 4QS in DJD 26 (Alexander and Vermes).

of significant variants between the different manuscripts of the Community Rule. For our present purposes we need to note the presence of the Maskil in the heading of the 4QS manuscripts over against 1QS. In the case of 4Q258 (4QS^d) this passage constitutes the title of the whole document.[59] The most discussed feature of those passages is the authority entrusted in 1QS to the sons of Zadok over against the many (ha-rabbim) in 4Q256/4Q258. When I first looked at the 4QS texts with Daniel in mind it struck me as significant that we have here the Maskil in the heading and the rabbim in the body of the passage occurring alongside one another. I still think this is noteworthy. However, on closer inspection the group immediately associated with the Maskil in 4Q256/4Q258 is called "the people the law" (אנשי התורה) – a *hapax legomenon* in the Scrolls.[60] It is interesting to observe, furthermore, that on the reading of the Cave 4 manuscripts the Maskil is closely associated with admonitions to keep separate from the people of injustice. This group is also linked to the Maskil in 1QS 9 to which I will now turn.

3.4 The Statutes for the Maskil 1QS 9:12–25//4Q256 (4QS^b) 18 1–7// 4Q258 (4QS^d) 8 1–9//4Q259 (4QS^e) 3 6–4 8//4Q260 (4QS^f) 1 1–2[61]

I. 1QS 9:12–21a	I. 4Q259 3
a. 1QS 9:12–14a	**a.**
[12]These are the statutes for the Maskil to walk in them (in his dealings) with all the living according to the rule for each time and according to the weight of each person. [13]He shall execute <u>the will of God</u> according to <u>everything</u> that has been revealed from time to time. He shall acquire every insight which has been found *according to the times* and [14]<u>the statute of time</u>.	[6]These are the sta[tutes] [7]for the Mas[kil to walk in] them (in his dealings) with all the living according to the rule for each [time] [8]and according to the wei[ght of] each person. He shall exe]cute <u>the will of God</u> according to <u>everything</u> that has been revealed [from time to time]. [9]He sh[all acquire every insight] which has been found *before the times* and the [statute] [10]of time.
b. 1QS 9:14b–18a	**b.**
He shall separate and weigh *the sons of Zadok*	[He shall separate and] weigh *the sons of righteousness*

---

[59] Cf. DJD 26:84 and Plate 10 (Alexander and Vermes).

[60] Cf. DJD 26:96 (Alexander and Vermes).

[61] For the sources of the Hebrew texts and translation see note 58 above. The significance of different scripts, the Roman numbers I and II, as well as sections a-c is explained in the analysis that follows.

I. 1QS 9:12–21a

according to their spirit. He shall sustain the chosen ones of the time according to ¹⁵His will <u>according to that which He has commanded</u>. He shall execute judgment on each person according to his spirit. He shall bring near

I. 4Q259 3

according to their sp[i]rit. ¹¹He shall [sustain the chosen ones of the time] <u>according to His will according to that which He has commanded</u>. He shall [execute ¹²judgment on] each person [according to his spirit.] He shall bring near

1QS	4Q256/258^{b/d} (Composite Text)	4Q259
each person according to the cleanness of his hands and ¹⁶according to his insight. <u>And equally his love and his hatred</u>. He shall not rebuke or get into an argument with the <u>people of the pit</u> ¹⁷but <u>conceal the counsel of the law</u>	^{d7:13}[each person] according to the cleanness of [his] ha[nds and] ^{d8:1}according to his insight. <u>And equally his love and his hatred</u>. He shall not rebuke or get into an argument with the <u>people of the pit</u> ^{d2}but <u>conceal</u> his/His counsel	each person according to the cleanness of his hands acc[ording to ¹³his insight. <u>And equally</u>] his [lo]ve and his hatred. He shall not [rebuke] ¹⁴or [get into an argument with the <u>peo]ple of the pit</u> but <u>conceal the coun[sel of] ¹⁵the law</u>
in the midst of the people of injustice. He shall discipline with true knowledge and righteous judgment *those who have chosen ¹⁸the way,* each according to his spirit *according to the rule of time.*	in the midst of the people of injustice. He shall discipline with true knowledge and righteous judgment *the chosen of the way* according to his spirit *and according to ^{b1}the rule of ^{d3}time.*	[in the midst of the people of injustice. He shall] discipline with true knowledge and righteous ¹⁶judgment *the cho[sen of the way,* each] according to his spirit *and according to his rank.*

c. 1QS 9:18b–21a

He shall guide them with knowledge and thus instruct them *in the wonderful and true mysteries in the midst of ¹⁹the people of the community* so that they may conduct themselves perfectly each with *his neighbour* according to all that has been revealed to them. This is the time to prepare the way ²⁰to the wilderness.	**c.** He shall guide them with knowledge and thus instruct them ^{b2}*in the wonderful and true mysteries in the midst of the people of the community* so that they may conduct themselves perfectly each with ^{d4}*his neighbour* according to all ^{b3}that has been revealed to them. This is the time to prepare the way to the wilderness.	**c.** The time (is here) to guide them ¹⁷with knowledge [and thus instruct them in] the *wonderful mysteries. And if the way of the assembly of the community ¹⁸reaches perfection,* so that they may con[duct themselves perfectly each] with *his neighbours* according to all that has been revealed to them. ¹⁹This is [the time to prepare the way] ²⁰to the wilderness.

1QS	4Q256/258^{b/d} (Composite Text)	4Q259
He shall instruct them with all	*He shall instruct them in all*	*He shall make them rulers over all*

1QS	4Q256 (4QS^b) and 4Q258 (4QS^d)	
that has been found to do *at this time, and* they shall keep away from everyone who has not averted his path ²¹from all injustice. Vacat.	that has been found to do. Vacat ^{b4}*At this* ^{d5}*[time* they shall keep away] from everyone who has not averted his path from all injustice. Vacat.	

II. 1QS 9:21b–25
These are the rules of conduct for the Maskil during these times with regard to his love and his hatred. (He shall direct) eternal hatred ²²towards the people of the pit with a spirit of secretiveness. He shall leave to them property and wages like a servant to his master (displaying) humility before ²³his ruler.
He shall be a person who is dedicated to the statute

II.
These are ^{b5}the rules of conduct for the Maskil during [these] ^{d6}tim[es with regard to his love and] his hatred. (He shall direct) eternal hatred towards ^{b6}the people of the pit with a spirit of secretiveness. He shall leave to them property and wa^{d7}[ges like a servant to] his [ma]ster (displaying) humility before ^{b7}his ruler.
He shall be a person who is dedicated to the statute

1QS	4Q256 (S^b) and 4Q258 (S^d)	4Q260 (S^f)
and its time until the day of vengeance. He shall perform the will (of God) in everything he does ²⁴and in everything that is under his control (he) shall comply with that which He has commanded. Everything he encounters	*and ready for* the day of [vengeance.] He shall [perform ^{d8}the will (of God) in everything he does and in] everything that is under his control (he) shall comply with that whi[ch He has commanded. Every]thing he encounters	^{f1}[*and its time* until the day of vengeance. He shall perform the will (of God) in everythi]ng he ^{f2}do[es and in everything that is under his control (he) shall comply with that whi[ch He has commanded.] Everything he encounters

1QS	4QS^b and 4QS^d	
shall readily delight him and he shall derive no pleasure except from the will of God. ²⁵[A]ll His words shall delight him, and he shall not desire anything that He has not comman[ded]. He shall continually look out for God's judgment.	shall readily delight him and [he shall derive no pleasure] ^{d9}except from the will of [God. All His words shall delight him, and he shall not desire anything th]at He has not [commanded. He shall] con[tinually] look out [for] God's [judgme]nt.	

To my mind this passage is the most important one to be discussed here and very probably contains some of the tradition-historically earliest material on the Maskil in S.[62] A good case can be made for the independent origin of this section. Firstly, the same heading as found in 1QS 9:12 ("These are the statutes for the Maskil to walk in them [in his dealings] with all the living ...") occurs in the Damascus Document (CD 12:20–21 // 4Q266 [4QD^a] 5 i 17) without any statutes following it. As I have argued elsewhere, the best way to account for this curious state of affairs in the Damascus Document, is to argue that this piece was an independent tradition which was available to the redactor of the Damascus Document and subsequently became overshadowed by other rules and offices in the Laws, such as the overseer and the camps.[63] The publication of the Cave 4 manuscripts of the Community Rule has provided even stronger pointers towards the originally independent character of this section, since one of the manuscripts lacks a block of material just before this section and continues with a different block of material just after it. I am referring to 4Q259 (4QS^e) which lacks the equivalent of 1QS 8:15b–9:11 up to and including the famous reference to the coming of the prophet and the Messiah of Aaron and Israel immediately before our heading in 1QS 9:12 and continues after it with the calendric text Otot rather than the final psalm.[64] There are no indications to suggest that any of the Cave 4 manuscripts lacked the Maskil section. But if we think of the work of the author(s)/redactor(s) of the Community Rule manuscripts as, at least in some cases, making use of building blocks, it seems that different manuscripts put together the material in different ways just before and after our section. Cumulatively these considerations point towards the originally independent character of this section.

As is so often the case the term Maskil, which occurs twice in this section, is again used in headings. However, in both cases the individual seems to be quite clearly in mind in the material that follows the headings. The statutes that follow are presented as addressed to the Maskil and spell out his duties. It is advisable, therefore, to direct our attention first and foremost to this section in our assessment of the Maskil traditions in the Community Rule and Daniel.

Looking at the text that follows the first heading we noted already the absence of rabbim language. We also observe while there are indications of an incipient communal mentality in parts of this section, it is distinct from the rigidly organ-

---

[62] For a recent treatment of this material see Newsom, *Self as Symbolic Space*, 165 ff.

[63] Charlotte Hempel, *The Laws of the Damascus Document: Sources, Traditions and Redaction* (STDJ 29; Leiden: Brill, 1998), 105–106, 114–121, 189.

[64] See Metso, *Textual Development*, 48–51; DJD 26:50–51 (Alexander and Vermes); Uwe Glessmer, 'Calendars in the Qumran Scrolls,' in *Dead Sea Scrolls After Fifty Years* (ed. VanderKam and Flint), Vol. II, 213–278, esp. 262–268. See also Dohmen, 'Gründung der Gemeinde,' 95 and Knibb, 'Eschatology and Messianism,' 385–386 as well as Chapter 19 section 5.3 below.

ized procedures laid down in most of columns 5–7 of 1QS, and frequently with reference to the rabbim.

We are also in different territory from the one mapped out in the previous column which describes the emerging council of the community in cultic terms as having an atoning function and employs language to describe the community otherwise applied to the sanctuary. Whatever the Maskil might be in other contexts,[65] here we get the impression of an esoterically inclined lay person as opposed to the saturation with cultic and temple imagery we find in 1QS 8.[66] Both passages are idealistic, but the idealism in each one has a different flavour. As far as Daniel is concerned, scholars are divided on the role of priestly concerns in the book.[67] It seems fair to say, however, that in the passages specifically dealing with the Maskilim cultic language is not prominent.

When we look at the whole passage a case can be made for some developments even within this section.[68] This is clear already from a number of differences between the manuscripts which are printed in italics in my translation above. If we focus our attention on the material that follows the first heading I. it seems appropriate to divide this into three sub-sections which I have designated a., b. and c. in the translation above.

As far as the first part of this section is concerned (marked I. a. above: 1QS 9:12–14a//4Q259 [4QSᵉ] 3 6–10), two features are striking. One is the universalistic tone and outlook. Note the reference to the Maskil's dealings with all the living (כול חי) according to the weight of each person (למשקל איש ואיש). He is to acquire every insight that has been found. In these opening lines we do not find any designation for a particular group associated with the Maskil – not even

---

[65] See Metso, *Textual Development*, 136 who argues that the Maskil's role in 1QSb points to a priestly figure. I am not convinced that we should read the evidence of the Community Rule in the light of 1QSb, however.

[66] On the esoteric sphere of influence of the Maskil see Newsom, *Self as Symbolic Space*, 170, who characterizes him as "a figure of mystery." For a recent assessment of the Maskil as a scholarly instructor and role model for community members, though not a priest, see Lawrence H. Schiffman, 'Utopia and Reality: Political Leadership and Organization in the Dead Sea Scrolls Community,' in *Emanuel: Studies in Hebrew Bible, Septuagint, and the Dead Sea Scrolls in Honor of Emanuel Tov* (ed. Shalom M. Paul et al.; VTSup 94; Leiden: Brill, 2003), 413–427, esp. 423; see also section 5.2 of Chapter 19 below.

[67] For a concise overview see Koch, *Buch Daniel*, 169–170. Two diametrically opposed positions are represented by Otto Plöger who advocates anti-hierocratic circles (*Theocracy and Eschatology*) and Jürgen H. C. Lebram who has tried to make a case for priestly authorship ('Apokalyptik und Hellenismus im Buche Daniel,' *VT* 20 [1970]: 503–524). On this topic see also Davies, 'Reading Daniel Sociologically,' 359–361; idem, 'Scribal School of Daniel,' 260; Ernst Haag, 'Die Hasidäer und das Danielbuch,' *TTZ* 102 (1993): 51–63, 53, 61; and Lacocque, 'Socio-Spiritual Formative Milieu,' 335–336.

[68] Christoph Dohmen has argued that a part of this section together with parts of the previous column forms the original Manifesto of an emerging community (i. e. 1QS 8:1–7a+12b–15a and 1QS 9:16–21a). He further holds that 1QS 9:12–16a+21b–26 (i. e. two sections introduced with a Maskil heading, the latter heading being identified as a "redaktionelle Notiz," 88) belong to an originally independent composition that has been inserted here, cf. 'Gründung der Gemeinde.'

a national all-Israel backdrop as in Dan 11:33–35 – but rather a universalistic outlook that is concerned with the Maskil's role vis-à-vis humankind. It is one thing to imagine that this individual's teachings are concerned with all of humanity, but this passage goes much further by referring to his dealings with all the living (להתהלך עם כול חי). This is in marked contrast to a number of other headings, such as 1QS 3:13 (the Maskil is to instruct and teach all the sons of light) or 4Q258 (4QS^d) 1 1 discussed above which speaks of the Maskil and the people of the torah), or outside of the Community Rule we have a text that bears a title resembling its heading: Address of the Maskil to all the Sons of Dawn (4Q298). Unlike the majority of cases reviewed here the present passage does not associate the Maskil with a particular group – quite the opposite: he has dealings with all the living. The repetition of the term 'all' or the use of syntactical features that have a similar meaning such as איש ואיש underlines the all-encompassing universalistic frame of mind.[69] The second feature that strikes us as we read these lines is the persistent emphasis on time (עת).[70] Unlike in Daniel, here the concern with time is not eschatological, but rather of an esoteric, learned, halakhic nature (note the reference to the statute of time and to everything that has been revealed from time to time[71]) and with time in the sense of season, alloted time.[72] It would be worthwhile to explore this universalistic concern expressed here further and see where it comes to the fore in other texts from the corpus of the Scrolls or even in the Community Rule.[73] We certainly observe a universalistic sub-text to the Teaching on the Two Spirits.[74] Although the Maskil is to instruct the sons of light and humankind is divided, the knowledge to be conferred is described in 1QS 3:13–14 as "the biographies of humanity (תולדות כול בני איש) with regard

---

[69] For an insightful discussion of this characteristic, though not with reference to the present passage, see Newsom, *Self as Symbolic Space*, 81.

[70] Note a similar statement in 1QS 8:15. On this emphasis see Albert-Marie Denis, 'Évolution de structures dans la secte de Qumrân,' in *Aux origines de l'église* (ed. Jean Giblet et al.; RechBib 7; Louvain: Desclée de Brouwer, 1965), 23–49, 44–45; Charlotte Hempel, 'The Gems of DJD 36: Reflections on Some Recently Published Texts,' *JJS* 54 (2003): 146–152, esp. 149–150; Newsom, 'Apocalyptic and the Discourse of Qumran,' 143–144; eadem, *Self as Symbolic Space*, 81–83, 169, 174–186. See also Gershon Brin, *The Concept of Time in the Bible and the Dead Sea Scrolls* (STDJ 39; Leiden: Brill, 2001) and Klaus Koch, 'Das Geheimnis der Zeit in Weisheit und Apokalyptik um die Zeitenwende,' in *Wisdom and Apocalyptic in the Dead Sea Scrolls and in the Biblical Tradition* (ed. Florentino García Martínez; BETL 168; Leuven: Peeters, 2003), 35–68.

[71] See Hempel, 'Gems of DJD 36' and Newsom, 'Apocalyptic and the Discourse of Qumran,' 143.

[72] See Johann Maier, 'Zum Begriff יחד in den Texten von Qumran,' *ZAW* 31 (1960): 148–166, esp. 156.

[73] I have recently drawn attention to the close resemblance between 1QS 8:4 and 1QS 9:12, for instance, cf. Charlotte Hempel, 'Emerging Communal Life and Ideology in the S Tradition,' in *Defining Identities: We, You, and the Other in the Dead Sea Scrolls. Proceedings of the Fifth Meeting of the IOQS in Groningen* (ed. Florentino García Martínez and Mladen Popović; STDJ 70; Leiden: Brill, 2008), 43–61, reprinted as Chapter 5 in this volume.

[74] Cf. Newsom, *Self as Symbolic Space*, 88.

to all the varieties of their spirits." See also 1QS 4:15: "All human generations (תולדות כול בני איש) are governed by these (two spirits)." The pronounced dualism that goes hand in hand with the universalistic sub-text of the Teaching on the Two Spirits is not attested in the opening lines of the present text. We do have a reference to the weight of each person in 1QS 9:12 which does point in the direction of dividing humanity, but this emphasis is rather low key here. Turning to Daniel, the vantage point of the Maskilim in chapters 11–12 is fairly and squarely within a national frame of reference. The divisions that matter are those within the people (עם) rather than all of humankind.

In section b of part I (1QS 9:14b–18a//4Q256 [4QS^b] 18 1//4Q258 [4QS^d] 8 1–3//4Q259 [4QS^e] 3 10–16) the infinitive to separate (להבדיל) in 1QS 9:14b does away with this universalistic landscape and introduces the idea of separation which is prominent elsewhere in the Community Rule, cf. the opening lines of 1QS 5//4QS discussed above. Line 14 continues with a reference to weighing the children of righteousness/sons of Zadok depending on which manuscript we follow. On both readings it is clear that the frame of reference has changed from talking about the weight of each person from within all the living, to weighing a particular group. Still in line 14 we are introduced to the unusual designation of the in-group as the chosen ones of the time (בחירי העת), and the time element in this designation provides some continuity with what went before. Lines 15–16 introduce rudimentary community structures reminiscent of more elaborate procedures spelt out elsewhere in the Community Rule such as the use of the verb קרב for admission. Noteworthy are the relatively simple requirements for membership, as well as the absence of references to handing over property or swearing an oath. Lines 17–18 confirm the frame of reference as a particular community, but this time the designation is "the chosen of the way" or "those who have chosen the way", again depending on which manuscript we decide to follow. Not only are we now presented with a separate group, designated with a variety of names and ranked internally by 'weight,' we also have opponents: the people of the pit (אנשי השחת) according to line 16, or the people of injustice (אנשי העול)[75] according to line 17. A number of concerns and terms found in this section resemble the opening lines of 1QS 5//4QS discussed above, such as the notion of a separation and the people of injustice. Whereas the opening lines of the Maskil section were more universalistic and inclusive than the boundaries envisaged in Dan 11–12, lines 14b–18a are closer to the Danielic Maskilim in their focus on a particular group within the nation which has disagreements with other groups. Two important differences are that the larger context of the

---

[75] I have argued elsewhere that the people of injustice stratum is a very early tradition complex attested in various S manuscripts even where the same manuscripts witness radically different readings on other issues, cf. Charlotte Hempel, 'The Community and Its Rivals According to the Community Rule from Caves 1 and 4,' *RQ* 21 (2003): 47–81.

Jewish people as a whole[76] is of no explicit interest in the 1QS passage, and that the structures in place suggesting a community with a system for the formal approval of members goes beyond anything we see in Daniel.

The last section of part I (that is, c. translated above: 1QS 9:18b–21a//4Q256 [4QS^b] 18 1–4//4Q258 [4QS^d] 8 3–5//4Q259 [4QS^e] 3 16–4 2) moves on yet further by presenting the Maskil as someone at work within "the people of the community" (אנשי היחד), thus alluding to and aligning this part of the statutes for the Maskil with other parts of the Community Rule where designations of this kind are common place – here it is out-of-place in light of the designations we came across in the last section. Moreover, the allusion to Isa 40:3 which is dealt with in somewhat greater detail in 1QS 8 further indicates that these lines were written at a time when other parts of the Rule where influencing the author(s)/redactor(s)' choice of words.

Finally, there are good indications, on my reading, to take the second heading and everything that follows it (labelled II. in the translation above) until the end of the passage as a secondary enlargement on what precedes. As I have indicated by way of underlining relevant phrases, almost every issue that is raised in this second part takes up something that was mentioned previously and occasionally elaborates upon it.

4. Conclusion

I hope to have shown that the relationship of the Maskilim of Daniel 11 and 12 to the Rule of the Community is more complex than often portrayed. The assessment of this relationship developed here differs sharply from a recent evaluation by Stefan Beyerle who argues that since the Danielic texts from Qumran do not display sectarian features, they tell us "more about the social setting of the Book of Daniel than about the Qumran community itself."[77] This judgment implies a rigid, and in my view outdated, tendency to compartmentalize our sources. If we de-compartmentalize both our notions of the Qumran community and its heritage and the Book of Daniel and its setting and heritage we may find that both groups are not so different and maybe even overlapped at one point in their history. What I tried to do in the latter half of the study was to offer a fresh assessment of the Maskil traditions in the Community Rule that takes into account the complex literary history of this text. This individual appears in a number of different contexts, some universalistic, others with rudimentary communal requirements, and yet a third group of texts that are quite developed and employ yaḥad terminology. In addition to these texts, the Maskil is also found in

---

[76] See Albertz, 'Social Setting' who rightly emphasizes that the circles behind the 'Hebrew Book of Daniel' (200) 'saw themselves as teachers of the whole people' (201).

[77] 'Daniel and Its Social Setting,' 208.

headings throughout the Community Rule manuscripts and must have been an authority figure both in a number of early traditions as well as at the point of the *Endredaktion* of the manuscripts. It seems likely that the closest points of contact between these traditions and the Danielic Maskilim are found somewhere along this line of development, probably near but not at the beginning. Whereas Matthias Henze has stated rather eloquently that "The covenanters have made Daniel's language their own," I have tried to suggest that, to some extent, it *was* their own.[78] In other words the overlap can be accounted for just as well by the shared roots of these movements as by the influence of Daniel upon Qumran.

---

[78] Henze, *Madness of King Nebuchadnezzar*, 242.

Chapter Sixteen

The Damascus Document and Ezra-Nehemiah[1]

1. Introduction

In any society, ancient or modern, the family is essential in preserving, handing on, and adapting the ethical values of the larger society. This central place of the family is eloquently summarized by Carol Meyers in her essay on the Family in Early Israel,

> Virtually all considerations of human behavior operate under the assumption that there is such a thing as a family in every society. Indeed, the family is empirically ubiquitous. In every corner of the globe and as far back in time as our lenses of historical and anthropological research can peer, a small, kinship-structured unit is visible on the broad landscape of human existence.[2]

Because of this central role of the household and family in laying the ethical foundations of society, a number of political systems have infiltrated, so to speak, the family in an attempt to undermine its sphere of influence. I am thinking, for instance, of the Nazi regime in which parents needed to be wary about talking freely in front of Hitler youth activists in the home as well as communist rule in the former GDR where the *Stasi* (the East German secret police) encouraged children to inform on their families. Much more extreme is the example of child soldiers in Africa who are led to slay members of their own families. Closer to home I can think of numerous examples that were reported in the British press within the last few years that may be cited as examples of a blurring of the borders between the family and the state. There was the extraordinary story of mothers dissatisfied with healthier school meals selling junk food through the

---

[1] This chapter was originally published as 'Family Values in the Second Temple Period,' in *Ethical and Unethical in the Old Testament: God and Humans in Dialogue* (ed. Katherine Dell; LHBOTS 528; London: T & T Clark, 2010), 211–230. I am grateful to Katherine Dell for the invitation to contribute to this project. Earlier versions of this research were presented at the Cambridge Senior Old Testament Seminar, the Biblical Studies Seminar at the University of Birmingham, and the Qumran Section of the Annual Meeting of the Society of Biblical Literature in Boston in 2008. I am grateful to all my colleagues for their comments. I will single out only Prof. Joseph Blenkinsopp of the University of Notre Dame with whom I have enjoyed several illuminating conversations on the matters addressed here.

[2] Carol Meyers, 'The Family in Ancient Israel,' in *Families in Ancient Israel* (ed. Leo Perdue et al.; The Family, Religion, and Culture; Louisville, Ky.: Westminster John Knox, 1997), 1–47, here 1.

fence of the school playground. In an interview with the supplier, the local fish'n chips shop owner, he complained that the parents, and not the state, should be in charge of what their children eat. Then, we had a former British Home Secretary, John Reed, telling Muslim parents to keep an eye on their teenage children and inform the authorities of anything suspicious. And finally, on the other end of the spectrum, we learn about parents of children as young as ten asking the authorities to place an ASBO (Anti-Social Behaviour Order) on their offspring who have grown out of control. Whatever we may make of these individual examples, they do illustrate that the interface of individual households and wider society is a crucial place where the norms and values of society are being thrashed out. This is, of course, why the issue of marriage is such an important one in either maintaining or challenging allegiances in the course of moving on from the family of one's birth.

It must also be borne in mind, however, that the term 'family' refers to much more complex phenomena and interrelationships than at first appears, as has been noted by Miriam Peskowitz.[3] The texts referred to in this chapter, both from Qumran and the Hebrew Bible, offer much scope for further research, and what follows is still mapping the territory especially with regard to the more recently published Qumran texts.[4]

As will become apparent, many of these larger issues are also touched upon in a number of Second Temple Jewish sources, both in the Hebrew Bible and in the Dead Sea Scrolls. The material, both primary and secondary, that might be brought into this discussion is extensive. I will focus in particular on two primary texts: Ezra-Nehemiah and the Damascus Document. In what follows I will first outline a number of areas where correlations between Ezra and Nehemiah and the Damascus Document have been identified as well as add a number of my own examples. In a second section I will focus on the work of Alexei Sivertsev who has made a good case in a recent article as well as a monograph demonstrating the centrality of the household in Second Temple Judaism including in particular Ezra-Nehemiah and the Damascus Document.[5]

---

[3] See Mirjam Peskowitz, 'Family/ies in Antiquity: Evidence from the Tannaitic Literature and Roman Galilean Architecture,' in *The Jewish Family in Antiquity* (ed. Shaye J. D. Cohen; Brown Judaic Studies 289; Atlanta, Ga.: Scholars Press, 1993), 9–36.

[4] See, for instance, the nuanced discussion in Hugh Williamson, 'The Family in Persian Period Judah: Some Textual Reflections,' in *Symbiosis, Symbolism, and the Power of the Past: Canaan, Ancient Israel, and Their Neighbors from the Late Bronze Age through Roman Palaestina* (ed. William G. Dever and Seymour Gitin; Winona Lake, Ind.: Eisenbrauns, 2003), 469–485.

[5] Cf. Alexei Sivertsev, *Households, Sects, and the Origins of Rabbinic Judaism* (JSJSup 102; Leiden: Brill, 2005) and idem, 'Sects and Households: Social Structure of the Proto-Sectarian Movement of Nehemiah 10 and the Dead Sea Sect,' *CBQ* 67 (2005): 59–78.

2. Ezra-Nehemiah and the Damascus Document: Some Common Ground

A number of scholars have suggested at one time or another that the Dead Sea Scrolls, and the Damascus Document in particular, share a great deal with the social realities portrayed in the books of Ezra and Nehemiah.[6] Looking more widely at the Second Temple period, there has been a significant amount of scholarly investigation in recent years of the role and importance of the family and the household in Second Temple Judaism.[7] Most recently the work of Alexei Sivertsev is particularly interesting because of the way in which he argues for a great deal of continuity between the social realities behind Ezra-Nehemiah and the Damascus Document. Finally, Cecilia Wassen's recent book *Women in the Damascus Document*, which is based on her doctoral work supervised by Eileen Schuller, has a great deal of important and relevant discussion on the question of the family in the Damascus Document.[8]

---

[6] Cf., e. g., Joseph Blenkinsopp, 'Interpretation and the Tendency to Sectarianism: An Aspect of Second Temple History,' in *Jewish and Christian Self-Definition* (ed. Ed P. Sanders; Philadelphia, Pa.: Fortress, 1981), Vol. II, 1–26; idem, 'The Qumran Sect in the Context of Second Temple Sectarianism,' in *New Directions in Qumran Studies: Proceedings of the Bristol Colloquium on the Dead Sea Scrolls* (ed. Jonathan G. Campbell, William John Lyons, and Lloyd K. Pietersen; LSTS 52; London: T & T Clark, 2005), 10–25; idem, 'The Development of Jewish Sectarianism from Nehemiah to the Hasidim,' in *Judah and the Judeans in the Fourth Century B. C. E.* (ed. Oded Lipschits, Gary N. Knoppers, and Rainer Albertz; Winona Lake, Ind.: Eisenbrauns, 2007), 385–404; John J. Collins, 'The Nature and Aims of the Sect Known from the Dead Sea Scrolls,' in *Flores Florentino. Dead Sea Scrolls and Other Early Jewish Studies in Honour of Florentino García Martínez* (ed. Anthony Hilhorst, Émile Puech, and Eibert Tigchelaar; JSJSup 122; Leiden: Brill, 2007), 31–52, esp. 38–39; Philip Davies, 'Sect Formation in Early Judaism,' in *Sectarianism in Early Judaism: Sociological Advances* (ed. David Chalcraft; London: Equinox, 2007), 133–155; idem, '"Old" and "New" Israel in the Bible and the Qumran Scrolls: Identity and Difference,' in *Defining Identities: We, You, and the Other in the Dead Sea Scrolls. Proceedings of the Fifth Meeting of the IOQS in Groningen* (ed. Florentino García Martínez and Mladen Popović; STDJ 70; Leiden: Brill, 2008), 33–42; Christine Hayes, *Gentile Impurities and Jewish Identities: Intermarriage and Conversion from the Bible to the Talmud* (Oxford: OUP, 2002); Stephen Hultgren, *From the Damascus Covenant to the Covenant of the Community: Literary, Historical, and Theological Studies in the Dead Sea Scrolls* (STDJ 66; Leiden: Brill, 2007); Morton Smith, 'The Dead Sea Scrolls in Relation to Ancient Judaism,' *NTS* 7 (1960): 347–360; Shemaryahu Talmon, 'The Emergence of Jewish Sectarianism in the Early Second Temple Period,' in *King, Cult, and Calendar in Ancient Israel: Collected Studies* (Leiden: Brill; Jerusalem: Magnes, 1986), 165–201.

[7] See, e. g., Leo Perdue et al. (eds), *Families in Ancient Israel* and Joel Weinberg, *The Citizen-Temple Community* (trans. Daniel L. Smith-Christopher; JSOTSup 151; Sheffield: Sheffield Academic Press, 1992), esp. 49–61.

[8] Cecilia Wassen, *Women in the Damascus Document* (Academia Biblica 21; Atlanta, Ga.: SBL, 2005); see also Jutta Jokiranta and Cecilia Wassen, 'A Brotherhood at Qumran? Metaphorical, Familial Language in the Dead Sea Scrolls,' in *Northern Lights on the Dead Sea Scrolls: Proceedings of the Nordic Qumran Network 2003–2006* (ed. Anders Klostergaard Petersen et al.; STDJ 80; Leiden: Brill, 2009), 173–203.

Let me try to sum up some key areas that point to a relationship between both Ezra-Nehemiah and the Damascus Document under the following three headings: Location – Community – Issues.

2.1 Location

Both Ezra-Nehemiah and the Damascus Document are dealing with a Palestinian background with roots, either historical or theological/ideological, in the exile.[9] More particularly in Ezra-Nehemiah we have towns, on the one hand (cf. Ezra 2:1,70; 3:1; Neh 7:6,72; 11:1–3), while, on the other hand, we have a focus on the city of Jerusalem in particular (cf. Neh 11 and 3:1). Note Blenkinsopp's description of the geographical perspective in Ezra-Nehemiah, "Geographically the field of vision is restricted almost exclusively to Jerusalem and the surrounding region ... ."[10] The focus on Jerusalem needs to be put in perspective, though, if we bear in mind John Collins' observation, "For much of this period, Jerusalem was the only significant Jewish city."[11]

In the Damascus Document we have some rather enigmatic references to towns although the camp structure is clearly the dominant one. A good many references to one's town in the Laws are based on scripture. Thus, the limits laid down for walking about on the sabbath are based on the boundaries of levitical cities in Num 35:4 f.[12] As I argued elsewhere, it is therefore not certain that such references to one's town refer to the actual arrangements reflected in the Damascus Document.[13] We are left with a few references to cities (cf. CD 12:19–20) that are overshadowed by a dominant camp structure behind the document.[14] The Damascus Document also occasionally mentions Jerusalem and includes a prohibition of intercourse in the city of the sanctuary (cf. CD 12:1–2//4Q271 [4QD^f] 5 i 17–18).

---

[9] See Blenkinsopp, 'Qumran Sect in the Context of Second Temple Sectarianism,' 19–20; Davies, '"Old" and "New" Israel,' 34.

[10] Joseph Blenkinsopp, *Ezra-Nehemiah* (OTL; London: SCM, 1989), 60.

[11] John J. Collins, 'Marriage, Divorce, and Family in Second Temple Judaism,' in *Families in Ancient Israel* (ed. Perdue et al.), 104–162, here 104.

[12] See Arie Rubinstein, 'Urban Halakhah and Camp Rules in the "Cairo Fragments of a Damascene Covenant,"' *Sefarad* 12 (1952): 283–296 and Charlotte Hempel, *The Laws of the Damascus Document: Sources, Traditions and Redaction* (STDJ 29; Leiden: Brill, 1990; pb. ed. Atlanta, Ga.: SBL, 2006), 9–12.

[13] Hempel, *Laws of the Damascus Document*, 9–12.

[14] CD 12:19–20 identifies the preceding material as a Serekh/Rule for all the towns of Israel, a note which sits uneasily with the material that comes before, cf. Hempel, *Laws of the Damascus Document*, 160–161.

2.2 Community

In both sets of texts we are dealing with households led by priests and levites as well as lay leadership e. g. the Mebaqqer/overseer in the Damascus Document and Nehemiah.[15] Both texts further share an awareness that priests are not perfect and that others may be superior in skill and ability. Thus according to CD 13:2–7//4Q266 (4QDᵃ) 9 ii first one of the levites and then the overseer are singled out as instrumental in helping the inferior priest do his job.[16] We may compare to this the episode recorded in Nehemiah 13 where Nehemiah corrects the priest Eliaship who had misused a large room in the Temple by making it available to Tobiah and Neh 13:28–29 where Nehemiah deals decisively with the issue of a mixed marriage in a priestly family by chasing the perpetrator away.

Both groups see themselves as the true representative of the people (עם) whereas others are misled particularly relating to a number of halakhic practices.

Both those addressed in the Damascus Document and the people behind Ezra-Nehemiah are well to do with a social conscience and a willingness to assist less fortunate members of the in-group. Thus, according to Neh 5:10,14–18 generosity is recommended within the community, and Nehemiah by his own example tried to encourage "a greater sense of social responsibility among the more wealthy residents of Judah."[17] Similarly the Damascus Document includes a prescription for a collection of two days' wages to support the vulnerable, cf. CD 14:13–18//4Q266 (4QDᵃ) 10 i. 4Q266 apparently refers to a one-off collection as there does not seem to be sufficient space for the words 'every month' (לכל חדש).[18]

Oaths are sworn as a means of holding the in-group together according to Neh 10 and CD 15:8,12//4QD.[19] A difference is that CD 15 seems to envisage a more rigorous assessment of household members on their individual merits than

---

[15] CD 13:5–6 refers to a scenario where the overseer is to instruct a priest who is out of his depth. This would indicate that the overseer is not a priest himself.

[16] See Hempel, *Laws of the Damascus Document*, 107–114.

[17] See Hugh Williamson, *Ezra, Nehemiah* (Word Biblical Commentary 16; Waco, Tex.: Word Books, 1985), 242, see also 241.

[18] For the text of 4Q266 (4QDᵃ) see DJD 18:72–74 (Baumgarten); see also Hempel, *Laws of the Damascus Document*, 131–140.

[19] See Morton Smith, 'The Dead Sea Scrolls in Relation to Ancient Judaism,' 356 and Wassen, *Women in the Damascus Document*, 138. On the admission into the community by swearing an oath see also Charlotte Hempel, 'Community Structures in the Dead Sea Scrolls: Admission, Organization, and Disciplinary Procedures,' in *The Dead Sea Scrolls After Fifty Years: A Comprehensive Assessment* (ed. Peter Flint and James VanderKam; Leiden: Brill, 1999), Vol. II, 67–92, reprinted as Chapter 2 in this volume and Sarianna Metso, 'Creating Community Halakhah,' in *Studies in the Hebrew Bible, Qumran and the Septuagint Presented to Eugene Ulrich* (ed. Peter Flint, Emanuel Tov, and James VanderKam; VTSup 101; Leiden: Brill, 2006), 279–301.

in Nehemiah where we frequently have rather all-inclusive frames of reference, cf. Neh 8:2–3.[20]

Both groups have a penchant for genealogical lists (cf. CD 4:4–6 where a list of names and generations and other details is announced but now lost and Ezra 2 and Neh 7)[21] as well as dividing the community into priests, levites and other groups.[22] CD 14 divides the members of all the camps who are to be mustered and written down by name into 'the priests first, the levites second, the sons of Israel third and the proselytes fourth," cf. CD 14:3–6//4Q267 (4QD^b) 9 v 6–10// 4Q268 (4QD^c) 2.[23] Ezra-Nehemiah allows for a much larger array of cultic specialists (such as gatekeepers and temple-servants). Nevertheless a genealogical ranking system is evident in both texts.

Both texts further refer to the disqualification of some priests. Thus, Ezra 2:61–63 and Neh 7:63–65 refer to priests unable to establish their pedigree and are therefore barred from service and partaking of the sacred food because of possible uncleanness,[24] and Neh 13:28–29 describes how Nehemiah drove away the son of the high priest Eliaship because of his marriage to a foreigner. The Cave 4 fragments of the Damascus Document also deal with the disqualification of certain priests, including priests who had been captive in Gentile lands, at some length.[25] If the late Joseph Baumgarten is correct and the subsequent reference to the curtain in 4Q266 (4QD^a) 5 ii refers to the inner sanctum, this text would ban priests from captivity from becoming high priests.[26] Baumgarten notes the exclusion of certain priests from the consumption of sacred offerings both in the Damascus Document and in Ezra 2:63.[27] Despite the overlapping

---

[20] Wassen aptly describes the ceremony in Neh 10 as 'inclusive' – a long list intent on including everyone.

[21] See Davies, '"Old" and "New" Israel,' 34 and, regarding the biblical witnesses, Williamson, 'The Family in Persian Period Judah,' 471–472 who writes with reference to the early Persian period, "... the position of many individuals in the community was defined by their genealogical affiliation." (471).

[22] Cf. the references to written records of priests and levites in Neh 12:22–23 and the registration in writing of priests, levites, Israelites and proselytes in CD 14:4–6, for instance. Noteworthy also is the reference to the offence of speaking angrily against one of the priests written in the book according to 1QS 7:2.

[23] Only the second of the two references to the proselytes found in CD is preserved in 4Q267 (4QD^b) 9 v, cf. DJD 18:109–110 (Baumgarten) and Hempel, *Laws of the Damascus Document*, 132.

[24] See Williamson, *Ezra, Nehemiah*, 37.

[25] See Hempel, *Laws of the Damascus Document*, 38–43 and eadem, 'Do the Scrolls Suggest Rivalry Between the Sons of Aaron and the Sons of Zadok and If So was it Mutual,' *RQ* 24 (2009): 135–153, reprinted as Chapter 14 in this volume.

[26] On the potentially devastating implications of the unsuitability of captured priests advocated in the Damascus Document, see Maxine L. Grossman, *Reading for History in the Damascus Document: A Methodological Study* (STDJ 45; Leiden: Brill, 2002), 200 cited in Chapter 14 n. 42 above.

[27] See DJD 18:51.

concerns expressed in both texts, the restrictions laid down in the Damascus Document are certainly stricter and more elaborate.

Mass public gatherings play an important part in both texts as rightly noted by Sivertsev who notes that "large public assemblies [...] play a crucial role in controlling and directing activities of individual families within the movement."[28] In this context he refers to Neh 9–10 and the meeting of all the camps in the Damascus Document, cf. CD 14:3 ff. and 4Q266 (4QD^a) 11 17–21 // 4Q270 (4QD^e) 7 ii.

Finally, the fate of excommunication was one that threatened community members or families who stepped out of line, cf. Ezra 7:25–26; 10:8 and Neh 5:13, see also Neh 13:28–29.[29] Banishment and excommunication is also an important disciplinary threat in the Damascus Document, both in the penal code as well as the expulsion ceremony at end of document, cf., e. g. 4Q266 (4QD^a) 10 ii 1–2 and 11 14–16 respectively.

2.3 Issues

Here I am going to be brief although the shared concerns seem to me very significant indeed. We already mentioned some shared economic issues and charity giving in the previous section. Very briefly, other major issues that crop up in both bodies of literature are sabbath obvservance,[30] restrictions on relations with Gentiles of one sort or another,[31] and tithing.[32]

3. Family and Household Structures in Ezra-Nehemiah and D

As far as the Scrolls are concerned, the role of the family in the corpus of non-biblical texts seems to be gaining in importance in the scholarly assessment of this material. A number of factors play a role in this shift in perception. The powerful – and, one might even say, overpowering influence – of the evidence of Josephus and Philo on the Essenes has for a long time made the material on families in the Scrolls seem somewhat peripheral. A common reading of the texts was that the purest and highest level of attainment in the group was achieved by

---

[28] *Households, Sects, and the Origins of Rabbinic Judaism*, 131.
[29] See Blenkinsopp, 'Interpretation and the Tendency to Sectarianism,' 300 n. 11.
[30] Cf. Neh 13:15–22 and CD 10:14–11:18b, cf. Lawrence Schiffman, *The Halakhah at Qumran* (SJLA 16; Leiden: Brill, 1975), 124–125 and Sivertsev, *Households, Sects, and the Origins of Rabbinic Judaism*, 117.
[31] Cf., e. g., the issue of mixed marriages dealt with in Ezra 9–10 and the restrictions laid down on dealings with gentiles in CD 12:6b–11a.
[32] Cf., e. g., the agricultural laws in 4Q266 (4QD^a) 6 iii // 4Q267 (4QD^b) 6 // 4Q270 (4QD^e) 3 iii and Neh 10:36–40 (in the Hebrew numeration, English vv. 35–39).

the celibate members. This understanding of a two-tier system of life forms in the Scrolls was argued for, moreover, on the basis of a passage in the Admonition of the Damascus Document (CD 7:4–10//4Q266 [4QD^a] 3 iii 6) that is often taken to refer to two groups: those who walk in perfect holiness, on the one hand, and those who live in camps and marry and have children, on the other hand. These two groups are commonly understood to refer to the superior celibate lifestyle and the somewhat inferior family life in camps respectively.[33] However, a minority of scholars – most recently Cecilia Wassen – have convincingly shown that a close reading of the passage reveals a contrast between those who walk in perfect holiness (of which the camp residents are a sub-group) with all those who despise.[34] Whereas the former are promised life for a thousand generations, the latter are threatened with the fate of the wicked at the time of the visitation. Moreover, in general, the texts from Cave 4 that were the last to be published do contain a substantial amount of new material that refers to women and family life, cf. especially the wisdom text 4QInstruction[35] and the new legal portions of the Damascus Document attested in the Cave 4 manuscripts.[36] Another text that assigns a prominent position to family structures, the Rule of the Congregation, is customarily taken to refer to the eschaton when, so the argument goes, the celibate community expected to be living in family units again.[37] This view has recently been challenged by the late Hartmut Stegemann and myself. Stegemann proposed that all of the so-called Messianic Rule refers to the present and that even the so-called messianic banquet with which the document ends is to be un-

---

[33] See, e. g., Eisha Qimron, 'Celibacy in the Dead Sea Scrolls and the Two Kinds of Sectarians,' in *The Madrid Qumran Congress: Proceedings of the International Congress on the Dead Sea Scrolls, Madrid 18–21 March 1991* (ed. Julio Trebolle Barrera and Luis Vegas Montaner; STDJ 11; Leiden: Brill, 1992), Vol. I, 286–294 and more recently Alison Schofield, *From Qumran to the Yaḥad: A New Paradigm of Textual Development for the Community Rule* (STDJ 77; Leiden: Brill, 2009), 163–173. Though Collins appears sympathetic to this view, he cautiously notes, "We are given a hint that some members pursue an ideal of perfect holiness, but the document does not describe their way of life or make clear whether it is any different from that of those who live in camps." Collins, 'Nature and Aims of the Sect,' 39.

[34] See Wassen, *Women in the Damascus Document*, 122–128. Cf. also Albert-Marie Denis, *Les thèmes de connaissance dans le Document de Damas* (Studia Hellenistica 15; Louvain: Publications Universitaires, 1967), 135–138. For another recent endorsement of Wassen's reading of the CD passage see now Eyal Regev, 'Cherchez les femmes: Were the Yaḥad Celibates?,' *DSD* 15 (2008): 253–284, esp. 255–259.

[35] For a discussion of women in 4QInstruction see Matthew Goff, *Discerning Wisdom: The Sapiential Literature of the Dead Sea Scrolls* (VTSup 116; Leiden: Brill, 2007), 49–53 and the important commentary published since the original publication of this chapter by John Kampen, *Wisdom Literature* (ECDSS; Grand Rapids, Mich.: Eerdmans, 2011).

[36] For an overview over the contents of the Damascus Document from Cairo and the more recently published Qumran Cave 4 manuscripts see Charlotte Hempel, *The Damascus Texts* (CQS 1; Sheffield: Sheffield Academic Press, 2000), 26–43, esp. 34–36, 41. For a monograph dealing specifically with this material see Wassen, *Women in the Damascus Document*.

[37] Cf., e. g., Lawrence Schiffman, *The Eschatological Community of the Dead Sea Scrolls* (SBLMS 38; Atlanta, Ga.: Scholars Press, 1989).

derstood as an ordinary meal.[38] I have argued for a less radical re-interpretation of this text by emphasizing the lack of eschatological features in the major, central part of this document which comprises instead communal rules very similar to the lifestyle in families attested in the Damascus Document.[39] In other words, here we have a text that although well known for decades, seems to tell us a great deal more about the communities' present arrangements, which included families, than was previously thought.[40] Finally, Eileen Schuller has argued that numerous texts from the Scrolls which employ the third masculine person do in fact include females without explicitly mentioning them.[41] In short, the study of the non-biblical scrolls has witnessed a growing recognition of the importance and centrality of the household and the family.

Looking more widely at the Second Temple period, I mentioned already the volume by Perdue and others on *The Family in Ancient Israel* and two publications by Alexei Sivertsev.[42] Reference should also be made of the work of Joel Weinberg who identified the house of the fathers in Ezra-Nehemiah as a "social institution in the postexilic period" and already referred to the links with some of the Qumran texts such as 1QM and 1QSa which were available when his study first appeared.[43] Sivertsev's recent work argues at much greater length for continuity between the social realities behind Ezra-Nehemiah and the Damascus Document.[44] In a nutshell Sivertsev argues that the household and "traditional kinship groups"[45] were the bearers of holiness and key elements in the structure of Second Temple Jewish society. He sees a shift toward a more individualized disciple model only from the period of Roman rule in the latter half of the first century BCE.[46] In other words, Sivertsev distinguishes two stages in the development of Jewish life:

---

[38] Cf. Hartmut Stegemann, 'Some Remarks to 1QSa, to 1QSb and to Qumran Messianism,' *RQ* 17 (1996): 479–505.

[39] Cf. Charlotte Hempel, 'The Earthly Essene Nucleus of 1QSa,' *DSD* 3 (1996): 253–269, reprinted as Chapter 3 in this volume.

[40] See also Philip Davies and Joan Taylor, 'On the Testimony of Women in 1QSa,' *DSD* 3 (1996): 223–235.

[41] See, e. g., her seminal study, 'Women in the Dead Sea Scrolls,' in *The Dead Sea Scrolls After Fifty Years* (ed. Flint and VanderKam), Vol. II, 117–144.

[42] Cf. Perdue et al. (eds), *Families in Ancient Israel* and Sivertsev, *Households, Sects, and the Origins of Rabbinic Judaism*. Further, Shaye Cohen (ed.), *The Jewish Family in Antiquity*. See also Alexei Sivertsev, *Private Household and Public Politics in 3rd–5th Century Jewish Palestine* (TSAJ 90; Tübingen: Mohr Siebeck, 2002).

[43] Weinberg, *Citizen-Temple Community*, 49–61, quotation at 50.

[44] Note Sivertsev's description of the social building blocks of the community behind both Ezra-Nehemiah and the Damascus Document as "halakhically determined alliances of families," *Households, Sects, and the Origins of Rabbinic Judaism*, 103.

[45] Cf. *Households, Sects, and the Origins of Rabbinic Judaism*, 17.

[46] On this issue see also Dean O. Wenthe, 'The Social Configuration of the Rabbi-Disciple Relationship: Evidence and Implications for First Century Palestine,' in *Studies in the Hebrew Bible, Qumran, and the Septuagint* (ed. Flint, Tov, and VanderKam), 143–174.

a. A first phase extends from ca. the Return in 538 BCE to 63 BCE and is family focused with patriarchal structures: "The Second Temple Jewish Sects that emerged during this time were essentially alliances of individual families bound together by their common understanding of Torah."[47]
b. A second phase extends from ca. 63 BCE to the 2nd and 3rd centuries CE during which the family remained important but gradually became overshadowed by the growing importance of disciple groups.[48]

According to Sivertsev this essential shift is particularly well attested in the Dead Sea Scrolls. Thus, he maintains,

> The first clear example of such a group within Judaism comes from the Dead Sea sect. In fact, the Dead Sea sect may serve as a litmus test for my entire theory since it reflects both stages in the development of Jewish sectarianism ...[49]

Quite apart from the particular topic addressed in this chapter, Sivertsev's analysis of the Dead Sea Scrolls ties in extremely well with some of my own research. On the one hand, Sivertsev's recognition of the existence of family-based life in some texts as opposed to others where family life plays no or a peripheral role is extremely welcome. On the other hand, I entirely disagree with his persistent use, even in the title of his *CBQ* article, of the singular 'Dead Sea sect' in the light of such complex developments reflected in the sources. With others I have tried to make a case for the presence of texts that speak of a parent movement alongside other texts that speak of a more tightly organized Yaḥad.[50] And it is exactly at this point where Sivertsev's interests in the gradual weaning of the importance of households in the Scrolls may enter into meaningful dialogue with some of the work of myself and others on the parent movement. Sivertsev refers

---

[47] *Households, Sects, and the Origins of Rabbinic Judaism*, 20.

[48] Cf. "At the same time I shall argue that the Second Temple period witnessed the gradual emergence of new forms of Jewish sectarianism. This new type of movement encompassed adult male individuals rather than families. It produced a new type of community that tried to surpass and very often replaced natural kinship ties with a new sense of common identity based on the common quest for salvation and commonly recognized unique interpretation of sacred texts." *Households, Sects, and the Origins of Rabbinic Judaism*, 22–23.

[49] *Households, Sects, and the Origins of Rabbinic Judaism*, 22.

[50] Cf., for instance, Florentino García Martínez, 'Qumran Origins and Early History: A Groningen Hypothesis,' *Folia Orientalia* 25 (1988): 113–136 (reprinted in idem, *Qumranica Minora I: Qumran Origins and Apocalypticism* [ed. Eibert J. C. Tigchelaar; STDJ 63; Leiden: Brill, 2007], 3–29). For a recent evaluation of this hypothesis see Gabriele Boccaccini (ed.), *Enoch and Qumran Origins: New Light on a Forgotten Connection* (Grand Rapids, Mich.: Eerdmans, 2005), especially the eleven contributions devoted to the 'Groningen Hypothesis.' For a brief summary of my own position see Charlotte Hempel, 'The Groningen Hypothesis: Strengths and Weaknesses,' ibidem, 249–255; eadem, 'Community Origins in the Damascus Document in the Light of Recent Scholarship,' in *The Provo International Conference on the Dead Sea Scrolls: Technological Innovations, New Texts, and Reformulated Issues* (ed. Donald W. Parry and Eugene Ulrich; STDJ 30; Leiden: Brill, 1999), 316–329, esp. 315–319, reprinted as Chapter 4 in this volume and further literature referred to there; and eadem, 'Qumran Community,' in EDSS 2:746–751.

to this in a single and significant footnote and seems sympathetic. Thus, Sivertsev engages with the pioneering work on the parent movement as reflected in the Admonition of the Damascus Document by Philip Davies and observes, "If we accept this [...] as a working hypothesis, we can talk about the household-based organization of the parent community and its similarity to the organization of the "Congregation of the Exile" in Ezra-Nehemiah."[51] Given that on my reading of a number of texts, especially the Damascus Document and 1QSa, the family setting is one of the characteristics of this parent movement as opposed to the Yaḥad as described in the Community Rule, the work on the importance of the household in Second Temple sources can fruitfully be related to these developments in Qumran studies.

There is a slight inconsistency in Sivertsev's approach which I have just noted: he recognizes complexity and development in the Dead Sea Scrolls (perhaps in the latter stages of the process of writing his book?) but nevertheless talks of a Dead Sea sect in the singular. A similar inconsistency also characterizes his chronological scheme. On the one hand he is very clear about the gradual developments attested in our sources;[52] yet, on the other hand, he is stunningly rigid and firm on identifying a particular year, 63 BCE – the arrival of the Romans on the scene – as a major turning point. Thus, he argues forcefully that, "true internalization of Hellenism by Jewish society began only then [i. e. the time of the arrival of Roman rule in Palestine, C. H.] Prior to that time Jewish Palestine had continued to follow basic social patterns and conventions going all the way back to Achaemenid times."[53] As far as the Scrolls are concerned he specifies an even later date ("by the first century CE") as the backdrop to huge changes in the social make-up of the group.[54] Quite apart from the intrinsic unlikelihood of being able to date a complex process such as the one Sivertsev describes to a single year, historical event, or even decade, there are some factual issues with his treatment of the Dead Sea Scrolls. Although Sivertsev may well be right that the Community Rule reflects a community of like-minded individuals – his post 63 BCE model – he does not deal with the simple fact that three copies of this text were copied before 63 BCE including the most complete copy from Cave 1 which is dated to 100–75 BCE.[55] Given that the Cave 1 copy describes a well established community that has clearly undergone a great deal of challenges

---

[51] See *Households, Sects, and the Origins of Rabbinic Judaism*, 130 n. 115.

[52] Thus, he acknowledges that the lifestyle envisaged in the Damascus Document may well have continued as the sustained copying of the manuscripts of this text indicates, cf. *Households, Sects, and the Origins of Rabbinic Judaism*, 140.

[53] *Households, Sects, and the Origins of Rabbinic Judaism*, 8.

[54] *Households, Sects, and the Origins of Rabbinic Judaism*, 22.

[55] Cf. Sarianna Metso, *The Serekh Texts* (CQS 9/LSTS 62; London: T & T Clark, 2007), 2–3. The oldest manuscript of the Damascus Document (4266 [4QD^a]) also goes back to the first half of the first century BCE, in other words very close to the date of the oldest manuscript of the Community Rule, cf. DJD 18:26–30 (Yardeni).

already – note the provision for someone who turns his back on the community after having been a member for several years in 1QS 7:22–24 – this manuscript almost certainly originated quite some time after the inception of the communities it refers to.[56] It is quite clear that although the overall development outlined by Sivertsev has much to commend it, he severely overstates his case in chronological terms.

In the remainder of this chapter I would like to focus on the role of the family and the household in the Damascus Document and Ezra-Nehemiah, paying particular attention to a certain amount of erosion of its powerbase in these sources. As we will see there is a case to be made that in the Laws of the Damascus Document we can see the household gradually being taken over by the overseer. More interestingly still, these laws preserve legislation on the arrangement of marriages in two quite different contexts. Whereas one passage still has the father of the bride in charge, the other passage allots a key role to the overseer.[57] Sivertsev is inclined to liken the overseer's role to that of Nehemiah.[58] Although it is quite true that both Nehemiah and the overseer have a say in matters of trade and marriage in their respective communities, there does seem to me an important difference. On my reading of the texts it is important to stress that Nehemiah does not lay claim to being consulted in everyday arrangements of marriages, but addresses a particular crisis or a sequence of crises.[59] In the Damascus Document, on the other hand, the overseer demands to be consulted in every act of trade and in every marriage arrangement. There is a significant difference of degree here. Whereas both texts reflect a family-based movement, the Damascus Document testifies to a system where someone else is calling the shots in everyday life – not just in extraordinary cases. Another extreme example of the way in which the authorities are almost literally entering the marital bedroom in the Damascus Document community is the law stipulating expulsion from the community for a man who fornicates with his wife contrary to the law (4Q267 [4QD^b] 9 vi 4–5 // 4Q270 [4QD^e] 7 ii 12–13). Perhaps the most likely explanation of this statement is intercourse with one's wife that is not for the purposes of procreation, although a number of interpretations have been proposed.[60]

---

[56] See also John J. Collins, 'The Time of the Teacher: An Old Debate Renewed,' in *Studies in the Hebrew Bible, Qumran, and the Septuagint* (ed. Flint, Tov, and VanderKam), 212–229, esp. 214.

[57] For some discussion see Sivertsev, *Households, Sects, and the Origins of Rabbinic Judaism*, 110–111. See also Eileen Schuller, *The Dead Sea Scrolls: What Have We Learned 50 Years On* (London: SCM, 2006), 94–95.

[58] Cf. *Households, Sects, and the Origins of Rabbinic Judaism*, 131.

[59] Note the pertinent observation by Hugh Williamson, "... in some matters central to the consideration of family law in this period the texts speak not of the norm, but rather of particular and extraordinary events," 'The Family in Persian Period Judah,' 471.

[60] Cf. DJD 18:162–166 (Baumgarten). Sivertsev's very broad interpretation of this infringement as a reference to any family who does not accept the sectarian interpretation of the law

Whatever its precise meaning, the passage refers to a community taking control of the most intimate parts of family life.[61] The level of control we witness in Ezra-Nehemiah is a soft option by comparison.

Let us look more closely at the two passages from the Laws of the Damascus Document that deal with the arrangement of marriages. These examples are particularly interesting because a strong case can be made to suggest that the Laws preserve traditional arrangements where the father, the head of the household, is in charge, alongside a slightly more developed state of affairs where the overseer is usurping some of the father's responsibilities.[62]

3.1 The Authority of the Father in Arranging Marriages According to the Damascus Document

On the one hand we have a text, preserved in four manuscripts of the Damascus Document from Cave 4 (4Q267 [4QD^b] 7 // 4Q269 [4QD^d] 9 // 4Q270 [4QD^e] 5 // 4Q271 [4QD^f] 3), that firmly places the father in charge of arranging a suitable marriage for his daughter:[63]

---

and would thus automatically fall foul of *zenut* fails to convince, cf. *Households, Sects, and the Origins of Rabbinic Judaism*, 112.

[61] Note Cecilia Wassen's observation that, "In many ways, the D [Damascus Document, C. H.] community has become the extended family of its members, replacing the biological one," *Women in the Damascus Document*, 204. The passage on illicit intercourse with one's wife adds an interesting nuance to the helpful critical discussion of the categories of private and public space in Peskowitz, 'Family/ies in Antiquity,' 26–28. Note also Albert Baumgarten's recourse to Lewis Coser's notion of 'greedy institutions' with reference to the Damascus Document, cf. Albert I. Baumgarten, 'The Perception of the Past in the Damascus Document,' in *The Damascus Document: A Centennial of Discovery. Proceedings of the Third International Symposium of the Orion Center, 4–8 February 1998* (ed. Joseph M. Baumgarten, Esther G. Chazon, and Avital Pinnick; STDJ 34; Leiden: Brill, 2000), 1–15, esp. 6–7. See further the stimulating discussion in Jutta Jokiranta, 'Social Identity in the Qumran Movement: The Case of the Penal Code,' in *Explaining Christian Origins and Early Judaism: Contributions from Cognitive and Social Science* (ed. Petri Luomanen, Ilkka Pyysiäinen, and Risto Uro; BIS 89; Leiden: Brill, 2007), 277–298, esp. 285 on the ongoing and complex process of creating social identity. We appear to be witnessing some of the on-going processes of identity formation in the different pieces of regulation on the arrangement of marriages in the Damascus Document. On the overseer's high level of control see also Eyal Regev, *Sectarianism in Qumran: A Cross-Cultural Perspective* (Religion and Society 45; Berlin: De Gruyter, 2007), 301–333, esp. the section aptly entitled 'Controlling Marriage and Sexuality,' 304–313.

[62] Cf. Eileen Schuller, *The Dead Sea Scrolls*, 94–95.

[63] For the Hebrew text see DSSEL (Baumgarten) with some adjustments, cf. Hempel, *Laws of the Damascus Document*, 65–66 and Eibert Tigchelaar, 'More Identifications of Scraps and Overlaps,' *RQ* 19 (1999): 61–68, esp. 68. For an analysis of this material see Hempel, *Laws of the Damascus Document*, 65–70; Aharon Shemesh, '4Q271.3: A Key to Sectarian Matrimonial Law,' *JJS* 49 (1998): 244–263; Sivertsev, *Households, Sects, and the Origins of Rabbinic Judaism*, 112–114; and Wassen, *Women in the Damascus Document*, 72–89.

The following text is based on 4Q271 [4QD^f] 3 7b–15 with parallels in 4Q267 [4QD^b] 7 13–14 double underlined//4Q269 [4QD^d] 9 1–8 grey background// 4Q270 [4QD^e] 5 14–21; 10 14–15[64] underlined.

7 ואם
8 [את בתו יתן איש לאי]ש את כול מומיה יספר לו למה יביא עליו את משפט
9 [הארדה אשר אמ]ר משגה עור בדרך וגם אל יתנהה לאשר לוא הוכן לה כי
10 [הוא כלאים ש]ור וחמור ולבוש צמר (ו)ופשתים יחדיו vac אל יבא איש
11 [אשה בבריתֿ](?) הקוֿדֿש אשר ידעה לעשות מעשה {מ }־דבר ואשר ידעה
12 [מעשה בבית] אביה או אלמנה אשר נשכבה מאשר התארמלה וכול
13 [אשר עליה ש]ם רע בבתוליה בבית אביה אל יקחה איש כי אם
14 [בראות נשים] נאמנות וידעות ברורות ממאמר המבקר אשר על
15 [המחנה[65] ואח]ר יקחנה ובלוקחו אותה יעשה כמ[ש]פט [ולוא] יגיד עלי[ה]

Translation[66]

7b And if
8 [a man gives his daughter (in marriage) to ano]ther, he shall report to him all her shortcomings lest he bring upon himself the judgment of
9 [the curse as He has sai]d, The one who leads astray the blind from the path. And also he shall not give her to one who is not suitable for her for
10 [that is two kinds (like ploughing with) an o]x and a donkey and to wear wool and linen together. *Vacat.* No one shall bring
11 [a woman into the covenant of holi]ness who has had sexual encounters
12 [while (still living) in the house of] her father or a widow who has had sexual relations since she has been widowed or any (woman)
13 [who had a] bad [repu]tation in her youth in her father's house. No one shall take her unless
14 [on examination by] trustworthy [women] who are knowledgeable and chosen at the word of the overseer who is over
15 [the camp. And afterwar]ds he may take her, and when he takes her he shall act according to the l[a]w [and not] report on [her].

In contrast to the scenario described here, another passage in the same document (CD 13:15–19//4Q266 [4QD^a] 9 iii) preserves a strikingly similar piece of legislation that has the overseer in charge rather than the head of the household.

---

[64] Here I accept the placement and line numbers for 4Q270 (4QD^e) proposed by Tigchelaar, 'More Identifications,' 68. This initially unidentified fragment was published in DJD 18:167 (Baumgarten). Tigchelaar's proposal provides support for Baumgarten's restoration of the opening words of 4Q271 (4QD^f) 3 7 but in the absence of any overlap the placement remains somewhat hypothetical, as Tigchelaar himself pointed out to me in a personal communication in the autumn of 2008. I am grateful to Prof. Tigchelaar for consulting the fragment in question again in the course of a discussion while I was preparing this study.

[65] Baumgarten reads and restores "[the man]y" (ם[הרבי]), cf. DJD 18:132. He is followed by Wassen, *Women in the Damascus Document*, 72. Cf. Hempel, *Laws of the Damascus Document*, 67.

[66] The English translation is my own.

3.2 The Overseer Encroaches on the Father's Role[67]

The following is based on CD 13:7b,15b–19 with parallels in 4Q266 [4QD^a] 9 iii <u>underlined</u>.

7b   וזה סרך המבקר למ֯ח֯נה (...)
15b ואל יע֯ש֯ איש דבר למקח ולממכר <u>כי אם</u> הודיע
16   למבקר <u>אשר במחנה</u> ועשה בעצה <u>ולא ישוגו וכן</u> לו[כ֯ל לו֯ק]ח֯ אש[ה]
17   [ו֯ה֯] [ ]°° [ב֯]עצה וכ֯ן֯[68] <u>לַמגרש והוא יסר את בניהם</u> ובנותיהם [
18   [וטפם ברוח [ענוה ובאהבת חסד <u>אל יטור להם</u>] <u>באף</u> ועברה [
19   פ[שעיהם ואת אשר איננו נקשר בש[   ]

Translation[69]

7b   And this is the rule for the overseer over the camp. (...)
15   No one shall per<u>form</u> an act of trade <u>unless</u> he has informed
16   the overseer <u>of the camp</u> and acted on the advice, <u>and they shall not sin inadvertently.</u> And thus shall be the case for everyone who take<u>s</u> a wife
17   and [ ] °° [with] counsel. And thus (4Q266 [4QD^a] reads in addition: he shall instruct, see note 68 below) shall be the case for one who divorces. And he <u>shall discipline their sons</u> and their daughters]
18   [and their small children in a spirit of] hum<u>ility and with</u> kind <u>love. He shall not bear a grudge towards them</u> [in anger and ra[ge   ]
19   [   ]their [s]<u>ins</u> and th<u>at there may not be</u> any one bound in [

3.3 A Comparative Analysis of the Stipulations Dealing with the Arrangement of Marriages in the Damascus Document

The recent examination of CD 13//4Q266 (4QD^a) by Cecilia Wassen correctly sums up the ways in which this text "highlights the authority of the examiner over the personal lives of community members, both men and women. The major decisions of individual members, such as marriage and divorce, were not personal issues any longer, but belonged to the communal realm."[70] Elsewhere she writes, "These laws show the extraordinary authority the Examiner had over the lives of the members in the community behind D."[71]

Note the role the overseer is given also in the education and raising of members' children.[72] What has not been appropriately recognised and reflected upon

---

[67] For the Hebrew text see DSSEL (Abegg) for CD and DJD 18 (Baumgarten) for 4QD.

[68] 4Q266 (4QD^a) 9 iii 5 includes the additional word יבן after וכן, cf. DJD 18:70–71. Note that Baumgarten does not refer to this variant in his notes, comments, or list of variants, however.

[69] The English translation is again my own.

[70] *Women in the Damascus Document*, 167; see also ibidem, 158–159.

[71] *Women in the Damascus Document*, 164.

[72] See John J. Collins, 'Forms of Community in the Dead Sea Scrolls,' in *Emanuel: Studies in Hebrew Bible, Septuagint, and the Dead Sea Scrolls in Honor of Emanuel Tov* (ed. Shalom

is that the Damascus Document preserves two contrasting sets of stipulations side by side, only one of which could have applied at any given time. Sivertsev quotes both passages without being either troubled or excited by the extent of contradiction they present. Wassen, on the other hand, does try to make sense of this double attestation. She broadly adopts my argument that the Laws of the Damascus Document contain communal rules on the one hand and general halakhah on the other. In my source-critical analysis of the Laws I assigned the first passage to general halakhah, cherished more broadly, and the latter to the communal rules laying down the constitution of the camp movement. Wassen assigns the former to the 'early law code,' as she prefers to call it, and the latter to communal laws.[73]

It seems to me that this clear evidence of development within the Damascus Document is significant and must not be downplayed. We are indeed in the realm of a social make-up similar to Ezra-Nehemiah, but we have also moved beyond it in one and the same text.

Another intriguing question is the relationship of the overseer to the fathers and the mothers of the congregation in the Damascus Document's penal code (4Q270 [4QD^e] 7 i 13–15). What we find there is an offence of murmuring against the fathers of the congregation which is severely punished by expulsion. Then the text goes on to refer to the offence of murmuring against the mothers of the congregation – we almost achieve gender equality until we read on and note the punishment for the latter offence: 10 days' punishment. Quite apart from the difficulty of knowing exactly what the roles of these individuals were, it is interesting to ask ourselves how prominent members who were clearly figures of considerable authority relate to the overseer's role.[74] Did both authority models exist side by side or did one come to replace or dominate the other? On Sivertsev's reading the mothers and fathers of the congregation were members of leading families in the groups, "perhaps founding families related to the priesthood."[75] Conversely, we might be dealing with a phenomenon which

---

M. Paul et al.; VTSup 94; Leiden: Brill, 2003), 97–111, esp. 100–101 where he speaks of the 'intrusive' role of the overseer.

[73] Cf. *Women in the Damascus Document*, 71–89, 156–167; further Cecilia Wassen and Jutta Jokiranta, 'Groups in Tension: Sectarianism in the Damascus Document and the Community Rule,' in *Sectarianism in Early Judaism* (ed. Chalcraft), 205–245, esp. 217–218. I have argued elsewhere, moreover, that the reference to the involvement of the overseer in the selection of qualified women at the very the end of the text quoted in section 2.1 above (cf. 4Q271 [4QD^f] 3 14–15) is a secondary development. This suggestion is supported by the evidence of 4Q159 (4QOrdinances^a) where we have, in fact, a version of a comparable examination by experienced women where the overseer is strikingly absent, cf. 4Q159 2–4 8–10, see Hempel, *Laws of the Damascus Document*, 65–70, esp. 69 and Jeffrey H. Tigay, 'Examination of the Accused Bride in 4Q159: Forensic Medicine at Qumran,' *JANES* 22 (1993): 129–134. See also Shemesh, 'Key to Sectarian Matrimonial Law,' 253–255.

[74] Cf. Jokiranta and Wassen, 'A Brotherhood at Qumran?,' 185.

[75] *Households, Sects, and the Origins of Rabbinic Judaism*, 107.

Joseph Blenkinsopp has referred to as "fictive extended kinship groups" drawing on recent examples such as the Franciscans where fictive kinship language such as brother and father is used.[76] Finally, Jokiranta and Wassen most recently offered the appealing, though somewhat speculative, suggestion that the use of parental language to refer to communal leaders may have been a deliberate mechanism to address some of the tensions resulting from the group's leadership intruding into members' families.[77]

4. Conclusion

In sum, Sivertsev and others have rightly emphasized important elements of continuity between social developments in the early Second Temple period and the literature of the Dead Sea Scrolls. The part where I disagree with Sivertsev in particular, or am inclined to suggest refinements, relates to the gradual points in a sliding scale away from the family towards an individual-based membership. Sivertsev concludes his chapter on the Scrolls by emphasizing the value of these texts as providing "the earliest unambiguous example of gradual transition from the household-based matrix of Jewish sectarianism to a community that encompassed adult male individuals."[78] The question of whether the Scrolls testify to an exclusively adult male environment at any time is hotly debated, and beyond the passing references of recent scholarship on women in the Scrolls here is not the place for a detailed treatement.[79] In general, I agree with the starting point and the end point outlined by Sivertsev but had more to say on the crucial period in the middle. On my reading of the evidence, the Damascus Document reveals a series of stages in the development of social organization starting with the household, or more precisely, a community of like-minded families in the plural, familiar from Ezra-Nehemiah. The text further witnesses the increasing importance of the overseer who usurps some of the roles of the traditional *pater familias* in a much more comprehensive way than is evident in Ezra-Nehemiah. Sivertsev himself appears not unaware of the important role played by the overseer in the Damascus Document, but fails to grasp the full impact of the evidence when he writes,

> The hands-on involvement of the sectarian official (mevaqqer) in what appears to us as private family business indicates the importance of the individual household within the sectarian system of values. The involvement appears to closely resemble the policy

---

[76] Joseph Blenkinsopp, 'The Family in First Temple Israel,' in *Families in Ancient Israel* (ed. Perdue et al.), 48–103, 91–92 and further developed by Jokiranta and Wassen, 'A Brotherhood at Qumran?.'
[77] 'A Brotherhood at Qumran?,' 202.
[78] *Households, Sects, and the Origins of Rabbinic Judaism*, 142
[79] See, e. g., the literature cited in notes 34, 40, and 41 above.

pursued by the leaders of the "congregation of the exiles" in the Books of Ezra and Nehemiah ... .[80]

By contrast, the Damascus Document also illustrates the importance of the overseer in overriding some family business and thus a partial erosion of the importance of the individual household.

Recent research on the household as an important link between early and later Second Temple sources, including the Dead Sea Scrolls, opens up a fruitful avenue for further work. It provides additional grist to the mill that is pointing towards the growing importance of the Scrolls for the wider picture of Second Temple Judaism. I hope to have shown that the multifaceted evidence of the Laws of the Damascus Document dealing with the arrangement of marriages takes us to the nub of some of these extremely important developments.

---

[80] *Households, Sects, and the Origins of Rabbinic Judaism*, 118. Similarly, "Far from denying the religious value of traditional households, supra-familial structures of early Second Temple movements treated families as central for their religious discourse," ibidem, 132.

Chapter Seventeen

The Serekh Tradition in Light of Post-Qumran Perspectives on the Emerging Bible[1]

1. Introduction

The once formidable gap between Hebrew Bible scholarship and the study of the non-biblical Dead Sea Scrolls has been declining in the course of recent years. Regarding matters of date and provenance, for example, we recognize a trend towards dating large parts of the Bible later than once thought.[2] At the same time a growing proportion of the non-biblical material has turned out to be pre-sectarian even if we cannot always agree on where to draw the line in a number of individual cases. It seems to me that both fields – if they may be called that – are also moving closer together on a methodological level. Recent publications have shown that the sectarian texts, such as the Community Rule, were not authored from beginning to end by the charismatic Teacher of Righteousness – as once suggested by some – but rather reflect complex literary developments of the kind frequently proposed with reference to biblical texts.[3] In what follows I would like to use the evidence of the Serekh manuscripts to reflect on the issue of the function of the Rule manuscripts as authoritative works in the community in light of their literary complexity and pluriformity.

Even though the Community Rule will be my main illustrative example, some of the most interesting pieces of evidence on the growth of this and other texts

---

[1] This chapter was originally published in English as, 'Pluralism and Authoritativeness – The Case of the S Tradition,' in *Authoritative Scriptures in Ancient Judaism* (ed. Mladen Popović; JSJSup 141; Leiden: Brill, 2010), 193–208. It was a great pleasure to present this research at a Symposium to honour Prof. Florentino García Martínez' achievements as retiring President of the Qumran Institute in Groningen in 2008. An earlier version of this chapter appeared in German as 'Vielgestaltigkeit und Verbindlichkeit: Serekh ha-Yachad in Qumran,' in *Qumran und der biblische Kanon* (ed. Jörg Frey; Neukirchen Vluyn: Neukirchener Verlag, 2009), 101–112.

[2] See, for instance, the apposite remarks by Carol Newsom, "Suddenly the distance between Hebrew scriptures and Ugarit looks much greater than that between Hebrew scriptures and Qumran." Carol Newsom, 'A Response to George Nickelsburg's "Currents in Qumran Scholarship: The Interplay of Data, Agendas and Methodology,"' in *The Dead Sea Scrolls at Fifty: Proceedings of the 1997 Society of Biblical Literature Qumran Section Meetings* (ed. Robert A. Kugler and Eileen M. Schuller; Atlanta Ga.: Scholars Press, 1999), 115–121, here 116.

[3] See already Peter von der Osten-Sacken, *Gott und Belial: Traditionsgeschichtliche Untersuchungen zum Dualismus in den Texten aus Qumran* (Göttingen: Vandenhoek & Ruprecht, 1969), 11.

are cases where literary developments spill over, so to speak, from one text to another. Steven Fraade has recently described such cases rather well as "synoptic 'intersections".[4] Perhaps the best example of such an overspill is the penal code which is attested in the Community Rule, 11QFragment Related to Serekh ha-Yaḥad, the Damascus Document as well as 4Q265 Miscellaneous Rules.[5] At this point it is interesting merely to note the practice of the editors of the 4QS manuscripts of listing passages from the Damascus Document and 4Q265 as 'parallels' to Serekh text.[6] I have recently dealt with this question elsewhere and will merely note here the improved presentation of the evidence in Eibert Tigchelaar's 'Annotated List of Overlaps and Parallels in the Non-biblical Texts from Qumran and Masada' in the final volume in the DJD Series where he refers to 'overlaps' in the context of multiple copies of the same composition and 'parallels' with reference to material from different compositions.[7]

2. The Literary Panorama of the Rule Manuscripts

In what follows I will be chiefly concerned with the copies of the Community Rule from Caves 1 and 4. Access to the full text of the ten Cave 4 manuscripts of the Rule since the early 1990s has revealed some remarkably complex literary processes in the growth of this text. The scholarly world knew of the existence of several Rule manuscripts from Cave 4 from a number of early reports by Józef Milik, the member of the original editorial team of the Scrolls responsible for

---

[4] See Steven D. Fraade, 'Ancient Jewish Law and Narrative in Comparative Perspective: The Damascus Document and the Mishnah,' in *Dine Israel: Studies in Halakhah and Jewish Law* (ed. Arye Edrei and Suzanne Last Stone; New York: Yeshiva University; Tel-Aviv: Tel-Aviv University, 2007), 65–99, here 93. See also Charlotte Hempel, 'CD Manuscript B and the Community Rule – Reflections on a Literary Relationship,' *DSD* 16 (2009): 370–387, reprinted as Chapter 8 in this volume.

[5] Cf. Joseph M. Baumgarten, 'The Cave 4 Versions of the Qumran Penal Code,' *JJS* 43 (1992): 268–276; Charlotte Hempel, 'The Penal Code Reconsidered,' in *Legal Texts and Legal Issues: Proceedings of the Second Meeting of the International Organization for Qumran Studies, Published in Honour of Joseph M. Baumgarten* (ed. Moshe Bernstein, Florentino García Martínez, and John Kampen; STDJ 23; Leiden: Brill, 1997), 337–348; Jutta Jokiranta, 'Social Identity in the Qumran Movement: The Case of the Penal Code,' in *Explaining Christian Origins and Early Judaism: Contributions from Cognitive and Social Science* (ed. Petri Luomanen, Ilkka Pyysiäinen, and Risto Uro; BIS 89; Leiden: Brill, 2007), 277–298; Sarianna Metso, 'The Relationship Between the Damascus Document and the Community Rule,' in *The Damascus Document: A Centennial of Discovery* (ed. Joseph M. Baumgarten, Esther G. Chazon, and Avital Pinnick; STDJ 34; Leiden: Brill, 2000), 85–93; eadem, 'Methodological Problems in Reconstructing History from Rule Texts Found at Qumran,' *DSD* 11 (2004): 315–335, esp. 317–322; Aharon Shemesh, 'Expulsion and Exclusion in the Community Rule and the Damascus Document,' *DSD* 9 (2002): 44–74.

[6] Compare DJD 26:139 (Alexander and Vermes).

[7] See Eibert J. C. Tigchelaar, 'Annotated List of Overlaps and Parallels in the Non-Biblical Texts from Qumran and Masada,' in DJD 39:285–322.

4QS, who would occasionally refer to a reading in 4QS.[8] It is still a mystery, however, why he never hinted at the remarkable variants between 1QS 5 and 4Q256 (4QS^b) and 4Q258 (4QS^d) in particular.

The official edition of the 4QS manuscripts by Geza Vermes and Philip Alexander appeared in the DJD series in 1998.[9] It should be noted that Alexander and Vermes point out the possibility that two of the Cave 4 manuscripts (4Q262 [4QS^h] and 4Q264 [4QS^j]) are not complete copies of the Rule but may comprise instead parts of collections that also include excerpts from S.[10]

The most important variants between 1QS and 4QS can be summed up as follows:

– None of the 4QS manuscripts attest material from the two annexes to 1QS, i. e. 1QSa (The Rule of the Congregation) and 1QSb (The Rule of Blessings). Because of the fragmentary nature of the manuscripts it is, of course, impossible to say with any certainty that the 4QS manuscripts lacked these additional documents. It is noteworthy, though, that one fragment which was cautiously published as belonging to 4Q256 (4QS^b), does appear to contain the last words of 1QS followed by the remains of a further line, and the latter does not correspond to the opening lines of 1QSa.[11]

Moreover, the only fragment preserved of 4Q264 (4QS^j) contains material from the end of the hymn found in 1QS 11. As noted by the editors and also clearly visible on Plate 21 in DJD 26, remains of stitching are preserved on the left edge of this fragment pointing towards the presence of at least another sheet. As mentioned earlier it is unclear, however, whether or not 4QS^j is part of a fragmentary copy of the Community Rule at all or whether it forms part of a collection of possibly hymnic texts. Vermes and Alexander further observe that this manuscript might have been a *Taschenrolle* or portable scroll. They describe the manuscript as follows, "The tiny writing and the narrow line-spacing are consonant with a very small scroll. 4QS^j may be the remains of a miniature scroll, probably produced in this size as to be easily portable."[12] 4Q298 (Address of the Maskil to the Sons of Dawn) was similarly described as a portable scroll by the editors Stephen Pfann and Menahem Kister.[13] Whatever the case may be, it is not possible for us to ascertain at this point what followed after the stitching and the end of the hymn in 4Q264.

Having said all this, Emanuel Tov has recently mounted a challenge against the widely held view that 1QSa and 1QSb were part of the same scroll as 1QS. In a very important footnote on p. 111 of his *Scribal Practices and Approaches*, a work that is a goldmine of detailed scholarship with important implications for all kinds of questions, he notes, "1QSa was not stitched after 1QS (disproved by the physical evidence): The stitching holes in 1QSa parallel to line 1–8 in that scroll have no counterparts in the well

---

[8] See Józef T. Milik, 'Le travail d'édition de fragments manuscrits de Qumran,' *RB* 63 (1956): 60–62 and idem, 'Texte des varinantes des dix manuscrits de la Règle de la Communauté trouves dans la Grotte 4. Recension de P. Wernberg-Moeller, The Manual of Discipline,' *RB* 67 (1960): 410–416.

[9] DJD 26.

[10] DJD 26:11–12, 190, 201.

[11] See 4Q256 23 frg. 8 in DJD 26:63–64.

[12] DJD 26:201.

[13] See DJD 20:17 (Pfann and Kister).

preserved end of the last sheet of 1QS, and therefore the two texts cannot have been stitched together."[14] Instead Tov, following an early suggestion by Milik, argues that 1QSa may have been rolled up within 1QS. Tov's observations present the lack of evidence for 1QSa and 1QSb in the 4QS manuscripts in a new, and perhaps dimmer, light.

- 4Q256 (4QS[b]) is the only 4QS manuscript to contain the full spectrum of material found in 1QS. This manuscript comprises, therefore, parts of the first four columns of 1QS, material attested in 1QS's central section, as well the final hymn found in 1QS 10–11. However, the material containing text corresponding to the central section of 1QS (1QS 5–9), displays significant variants. Here, 4Q256 (4QS[b]) is close to 4Q258 (4QS[d]) as frequently noted.[15] If the hypothesis put forward by the late Hartmut Stegemann were correct and 1QS was a Sammelhandschrift rather than a single composition,[16] then presumably we would have an alternative version of such a Sammelhandschrift in the form of 4Q256.

- 4Q258 (4QS[d]) does not include any material found in the first four columns of 1QS and begins instead with what I have been referring to as the central portion of 1QS starting in 1QS 5. 4Q258 does, however, have a dramatically different text of this material in many places. Firstly, 4Q258 attests a different heading in 4Q258 1 1. Thus, 1QS 5:1 begins with the words "This is the rule for the men of the community" (וזה הסרך לאנשי היחד) whereas 4Q258 1 1 begins with the title "Midrash for the Maskil over the men of the law" (מדרש למשכיל על אנשי התורה). In 1QS 5:1 we may be dealing with a sub-heading or, with Stegemann, with the title of a new document within a Sammelhandschrift. As far as 4Q258 1 1 is concerned, there is little doubt that we are dealing with the title of the manuscript.[17] Secondly, 1QS 5 and 4Q256 (4QS[b])/4Q258 (4QS[d]) display important variants in their descriptions of leading authorities in the community. Whereas 1QS 5 assigns a key role to "the sons of Zadok and the multitude of the men of the community," 4Q256/4Q258 speak at this very point much more simply of "the many" (ha-rabbim).

These substantial divergences between 1QS and 4Q256/4Q258 have been the subject of a series of articles and a monograph since 1991. Thus, Vermes argued, convincingly in my view, that 4Q258 represents an earlier tradition that predates 1QS's account which gives prominence to the sons of Zadok.[18] It is true that the sons of Zadok are said to operate a kind of power-sharing system with the multitude of the people of the community (רוב אנשי היחד) in 1QS.[19] It seems clear, however, that given the way this group is singled out and referred to before the multitude, they were more than a partner in power-sharing – at least in the literary version of events represented by 1QS. In a different context (namely the Jerusalem priests Zadok and Abiathar in the Hebrew

---

[14] See Emanuel Tov, *Scribal Practices and Approaches Reflected in the Texts Found in the Judean Desert* (STDJ 54; Leiden: Brill, 2004), 111.

[15] Cf., e. g., Sarianna Metso, *The Textual Development of the Qumran Community Rule* (STDJ 21; Leiden: Brill, 1997), 74–90 and DJD 26:46 (Alexander and Vermes).

[16] Hartmut Stegemann, 'Some Remarks to 1QSa, to 1QSb, and to Qumran Messianism,' *RQ* 17 (1996): 479–505 and idem, *The Library of Qumran: On the Essenes, Qumran, John the Baptist, and Jesus* (Grand Rapids, Mich.: Eerdmans; Leiden: Brill, 1998), 108–116.

[17] See Metso, *Textual Development*, 37 and DJD 36:85.

[18] Geza Vermes, 'Preliminary Remarks on Unpublished Fragments of the Community Rule from Qumran Cave 4,' *JJS* 42 (1991): 250–255.

[19] So Metso, *Textual Development*, 122.

Bible) Heinz-Josef Fabry has similarly emphasized the phenomenon of, as he puts it, "Vorordnung bei Gleichrangigkeit" and observes that in literary terms such passages are commonly an indication of latent developments in the background ("literarisch immer ein Signal für latente Vorgänge im Hintergrund").[20] It has further been argued that such a 'Zadokite redaction' left its mark elsewhere in 1QS[21] as well as in 1QSa as I tried to argue elsewhere.[22]

Vermes's initial proposals concerning the literary developments reflected in 1QS and 4Q256 (4QS[b]) and 4Q258 (4QS[d]) where soon confirmed on a much larger scale by the detailed and much cited monograph of Metso.[23] The Vermes/Metso position found favour with a fair number of subsequent scholars. A significant alternative was proposed by Vermes's former pupil and collaborator on DJD 26, Philip Alexander.[24] The key element of Alexander's argument is his stress on the palaeographically earlier date of the 1QS manuscript copy (ca. 100–75 BCE). This he takes as vital evidence against the view that 1QS contains a literarily earlier account. The crucial question raised by Alexander runs as follows: why would the community produce and preserve a carefully executed and good quality copy of an earlier and now obsolete text of the Community Rule such as 4Q258 (4QS[d]) in around 30–1 BCE? Alexander's position has recently

---

[20] Heinz-Josef Fabry, 'Zadokiden und Aaroniden in Qumran,' in *Das Manna fällt auch heute noch: Beiträge zur Geschichte und Theologie des Alten, Ersten Testaments. FS E. Zenger* (ed. Frank-Lothar Hossfeld and Ludger Schwienhorst-Schönberger; Freiburg: Herder, 2004), 201–217, esp. 202.

[21] Cf. the reference to "the sons of Zadok" (בני הצדוק) in 1QS 9:14 where 4Q259 (S[e]) reads "the sons of righteousness" (בני הצדק). It has been suggested that the *waw* was added in 1QS as part of a Zadokite recension, see Robert A. Kugler, 'Priesthood at Qumran,' in *The Dead Sea Scrolls After Fifty Years: A Comprehensive Assessment* (ed. Peter W. Flint and James C. VanderKam; Leiden: Brill, 1999), Vol. II, 93–116, esp. 98–99.

[22] Charlotte Hempel, 'The Earthly Essene Nucleus of 1QSa,' *DSD* 3 (1996): 253–267, reprinted as Chapter 3 in this volume. See also Robert A. Kugler, 'A Note on 1QS 9: 14: The Sons of Righteousness or the Sons of Zadok,' *DSD* 3 (1996): 315–320; Geza Vermes, 'The Leadership of the Qumran Community: Sons of Zadok – Priests – Congregation,' in *Geschichte – Tradition – Reflexion: Festschrift für Martin Hengel zum 70. Geburtstag* (ed. Hubert Cancik, Hermann Lichtenberger, and Peter Schäfer; Tübingen: Mohr Siebeck, 1996), 375–384. On 1QS, 1QSa und 1QSb see DJD 26:10 (Alexander and Vermes). Further contributions on the evidence on the priests in the Rule texts which include further bibliographical items are reprinted in Chapters 6, 13 and 14 of this volume.

[23] Metso, *Textual Development*. Further, Philip S. Alexander, 'The Redaction-History of Serekh ha-Yaḥad: A Proposal,' *RQ* 17 (1996): 437–453; Albert I. Baumgarten, 'The Zadokite Priests at Qumran: A Reconsideration,' *DSD* 4 (1997): 137–156; Markus Bockmuehl, 'Redaction and Ideology in the Rule of the Community (1QS/4QS),' *RQ* 18 (1998): 541–560; James H. Charlesworth and Brent A. Strawn, 'Reflections on the Text of Serek ha-Yaḥad Found in Cave IV,' *RQ* 17 (1996): 403–435; Paul Garnet, 'Cave 4 MS Parallels to 1QS 5:1–7: Towards a Serek Text History,' *JSP* 15 (1997): 67–78; Charlotte Hempel, 'Comments on the Translation of 4QS[d] I,1,' *JJS* 44 (1993): 127–128; and Michael A. Knibb, 'Rule of the Community,' in EDSS 2:793–797. See also the contributions of John Collins ('Forms of Community in the Dead Sea Scrolls') and Eibert J. C. Tigchelaar ('The Scribe of 1QS') in *Emanuel: Studies in Hebrew Bible, Septuagint, and the Dead Sea Scrolls in Honor of Emanuel Tov* (ed. Shalom M. Paul et al.; VTSup 94; Leiden: Brill, 2003), 97–112 and 439–452 and Fabry, 'Zadokiden und Aaroniden.' For further contributions on these issues see Chapters 1, 7, and 18 in this volume and references to more recent literature referred to there.

[24] Cf. Alexander, 'Redaction-History.'

been endorsed by Emanuel Tov and Devorah Dimant.[25] Moreover, Michael Knibb, though clearly sympathetic to the Metso/Vermes hypothesis, stresses the importance of the arguments put forward by Alexander.[26]

My own most recent contribution to the debate about the literary priority of 1QS or 4Q256 (4QS^b)/4Q258 (4QS^d) has tried to steer the argument into a new direction.[27] Even though I aligned myself previously with the position of Vermes and Metso, my recent contribution on the literary development reflected in the Rule manuscripts can stand entirely independently from this debate. In an article published in *Revue de Qumran* in 2006 [and reprinted as Chapter 7 in this volume], I attempted to look beyond the variants between 1QS and 4QS. I made the point that it was inevitable scholars would be drawn to the 4QS variants as soon as they became known, given this new and crucial textual evidence was not available to most of us for decades. A central question since 1991 has been: which manuscript contains the more original form of the text – as if each manuscript, especially the manuscripts from Cave 4, could be seen as solid building blocks in the growth of the S tradition. A close reading of 1QS and the 4QS manuscripts reveals, however, a significant degree of unevenness, contradictions almost, within one and the same manuscript. A good example of manuscript-internal inconsistency in 1QS is the term 'the many' (הרבים) which abounds in 1QS 6–7 despite its noticeable absence from 1QS 5.

We noted already the interest generated by the variant between 1QS 5 which alots a leading role to the sons of Zadok over against 4Q256/4Q258 which speak instead of the many. It is particularly striking to observe, therefore, the preponderance of references to the many in 1QS 6–7 where we find more than thirty occurrences of the term. Especially remarkable is the evidence of 1QS 8:26 where 1QS refers to the authority of the many, a reference that is absent from 4Q258 at this point.[28] The complexity of the evidence paints a picture of fluid traditions within and between different manuscripts. I proposed therefore, that the quest for the earliest form of the text of the Rule is best identified in the common material shared by the manuscripts rather than in the earlier of two variants where the manuscripts diverge. I identified such common ground in the material on the separation from the people of injustice (אנשי העול) shared by 1QS 5 and 4Q256/4Q258 in spite of major differences in the surrounding material.[29] Another example is the shared reference to the sons of Aaron and the multitude of Israel in 1QS 5:20–22 and 4Q258 (4QS^d) 2 1–2.[30] Both manuscripts share this terminology here in remarkable contrast to the language they employ earlier. Both 1QS and 4Q258 are here contradicting their own statements elsewhere (i. e. in 1QS 5:2–3 und 4Q258 1 2).

---

[25] Cf. Tov, *Scribal Practices* and Dimant, 'The Composite Character of the Qumran Sectarian Literature as an Indication of Its Date and Provenance,' *RQ* 22 (2006): 615–630, esp. 619.

[26] Knibb, 'Rule of the Community.'

[27] 'The Literary Development of the S-Tradition: A New Paradigm,' *RQ* 22 (2006): 389–401, reprinted as Chapter 7 in this volume.

[28] For a fuller discussion of this passage cf. Hempel, 'Literary Development of the S-Tradition,' reprinted as Chapter 7 in this volume. See also DJD 26:112 (Alexander and Vermes).

[29] On this material see Charlotte Hempel, 'The Community and Its Rivals According to the Community Rule from Qumran Caves 1 and 4,' *RQ* 21 (2003): 47–81.

[30] See Charlotte Hempel, 'The Sons of Aaron in the Dead Sea Scrolls,' in *Flores Florentino: Dead Sea Scrolls and Other Early Jewish Studies in Honour of Florentino García Martínez* (ed. Albert Hilhorst, Émile Puech, and Eibert Tigchelaar; JSJSup 122; Leiden: Brill, 2008), 207–224, reprinted as Chapter 13 in this volume.

- Almost a whole column of text found in 1QS 8:15–9:11 is lacking from 4Q259 (S^e). The missing material includes inter alia the famous reference to the expectation of the prophet and the Messiahs of Aaron and Israel (1QS 9:11).

- Finally, 4Q259 (4QS^e) closes with the calendrical text Otot instead of the final hymn found in 1QS.[31]

All this leaves us in little doubt that the Rule of the Community manuscripts testify to a long and complicated literary history of this text. Scholars disagree on the direction of this development: from long to short, from (palaeographically) earlier manuscripts to later ones, from "the many" to "the sons of Zadok" or *vice versa*. What seems difficult to deny, however, is the complex literary developments *per se*. The significance of this apparently modest conclusion – what we might call the minimalist position on S – for the study of ancient texts in a wider sense should not be underestimated.[32]

A further twist in this already complex tale are the very close literary relationships, at times even *verbatim* correspondences, between parts of the Community Rule and other texts, such as the Damascus Document.[33] One may think of the relationship between the Rule of the Community and the Damascus Document as the literary equivalent of Siamese twins. We may add to this the evidence of 4Q265 Miscellaneous Rules, a text containing material reminiscent of both S and D.[34] Finally, this web of textual connections should now also include the textual witnesses of Two Spirits material recently identified by Eibert Tigchelaar.[35] In short, the literary developments we witness within and between the individual manuscripts of the Community Rule occasionally spill over into other texts. Put

---

[31] Cf. James C. VanderKam, *Calendars in the Dead Sea Scrolls: Measuring Time* (London: Routledge, 1998), 80–84 and Chapter 19 below which includes some discussion on the relationship of 4Q259 and 4Q319 (Otot) as well as further bibliography. All divergences between the different manuscripts of S are also presented and analyzed in detail in Metso, *Textual Development* and eadem, *The Serekh Texts* (CQS 9/LSTS 62; London: T & T Clark, 2007).

[32] On the wider implications of the complex literary developments reflected in the S manuscripts see George J. Brooke, 'The Qumran Scrolls and the Demise of the Distinction Between Higher and Lower Criticism,' in *New Directions in Qumran Studies* (ed. Jonathan G. Campbell, William J. Lyons, and Lloyd K. Pietersen; London: T&T Clark, 2005), 26–42; Charlotte Hempel, 'Sources and Redaction in the Dead Sea Scrolls – The Growth of Ancient Texts,' in *Rediscovering the Dead Sea Scrolls* (ed. Maxine L. Grossman; Grand Rapids, Mich.: Eerdmans 2010), 162–181; and Geza Vermes, *The Dead Sea Scrolls: Qumran in Perspective* (3d ed.; London: SCM, 1994), 23; idem, *The Dead Sea Scrolls Forty Years On: The Fourteenth Sacks Lecture* (Oxford: Oxford Centre for Postgraduate Hebrew Studies, 1987).

[33] See Charlotte Hempel, 'CD Manuscript B and the Community Rule,' reprinted as Chapter 8 in this volume.

[34] Cf. Charlotte Hempel, *The Damascus Texts* (CQS 1; Sheffield: Sheffield Academic Press, 2000), 89–104 and further literature referred to there.

[35] Eibert J. C. Tigchelaar, '"These are the Names of the Spirits of ...:" A Preliminary Edition of *4QCatalogue of Spirits* (4Q230) and New Manuscript Evidence for the *Two Spirits Treatise* (4Q257 and 1Q29a),' *RQ* 21 (2004): 529–547.

differently, the literary phenomena we observe burst the boundaries of individual manuscripts and at times even compositions.

3. The Authority of Changing Texts: The Emerging Bible and the Serekh

The complex literary evidence provided by the Community Rule manuscripts reviewed above presents scholars with two rather different questions,

1. How did this literary situation arise? What was the direction of the development and which is the most original text?
2. What is the significance of the preservation and production of different texts of the same composition over a prolonged period? Which text was the authoritative one that was referred to by a community at any given time?

In recent years my own thinking and writing has focused very much on the first of these questions, and I have indicated at least briefly where I stand on some of the issues arising from question 1. In the remainder of this chapter I would like to address the second question raised above.

Two different attempts at answering this second question have been offered by Philip Davies and Sarianna Metso. Philip Davies highlights that 1QS is "incoherent, unsystematic and contradictory" and concludes that it comprises a largely utopian work with little basis in an existing community even though he is not opposed to the notion that a historical community of some kind did exist.[36]

Metso, on the other hand, was able to draw on her extensive study of the literary development of the S tradition when raising the question of the of *Sitz im Leben* of the Rule. She finds an answer in "the very nature of halakhic literature" in the Second Temple Period.[37] She argues that the Community Rule should not be conceived of as a written law code or constitution where one might look up cases before taking the appropriate action. Instead she envisages an environment where decisions are taken orally on the part of often priestly authorities that were recorded in writing only after the event.[38]

---

[36] Philip R. Davies, 'Redaction and Sectarianism in the Qumran Scrolls,' in *The Scriptures and the Scrolls: Studies in Honour of A. S. van der Woude on the Occasion of his 65th Birthday* (ed. Florentino García Martínez, Albert Hilhorst, and Casper J. Labuschagne; Leiden: Brill, 1992), 152–163 (reprinted in idem, *Sects and Scrolls: Essays on Qumran and Related Topics* [South Florida Studies in the History of Judaism 134; Atlanta, Ga.: Scholars Press], 151–161).

[37] Sarianna Metso, 'In Search of the Sitz im Leben of the Community Rule,' in *The Provo International Conference on the Dead Sea Scrolls: Technological Innovations, New Texts, and Reformulated Issues* (ed. Donald W. Parry and Eugene Ulrich; STDJ 30; Leiden: Brill, 1999), 306–315, here 312; eadem, 'Methodological Problems;' and eadem, *Serekh Texts*, 63–70.

[38] Alison Schofield has recently proposed that the different manuscripts of the Community Rule reflect a number of diverse communities, cf. Alison Schofield, 'Rereading S: A New Model of Textual Development in Light of the Cave 4 Serekh Copies,' *DSD* 15 (2008): 96–120.

My own response to these questions is sympathetic to Metso. However, I would like to suggest broadening the context beyond the confines of Second Temple *halakhic* literature to include Second Temple texts more broadly, especially also biblical or less anachronistically with George Brooke "pre-biblical texts."[39]

4. The Emerging Bible and the S Tradition: Inconsistencies Welcome!

It seems timely and valuable to me to stimulate more intellectual dialogue between the scholarly debates on the nature of the pre-Bible and the emerging canon in light of the Dead Sea Scrolls[40] and the scholarly debate on the fluidity and complexity of the S manuscripts. The relative neglect of such a dialogue may be based on the surely equally anachronistic and regrettable common-place distinction between "biblical" and "non-biblical" manuscripts in Qumran studies. Such a tendency has recently and laudably been lamented also by Jim VanderKam.[41] This sharp distinction would not have occurred to the occupants of the site although they would, of course, have had an idea about which writings carried particular authority. Much of the scholarship of recent decades has demolished the notion of a Bible at this time. It seems to me that both groups of texts, biblical and non-biblical, and the questions they raise in the minds of scholars share a great deal, and I would like to campaign for less *Apartheid* in treating them and thinking about them than is sometimes, maybe even frequently, the case.[42]

---

[39] Cf., e. g., George J. Brooke, 'The Rewritten Law, Prophets, and Psalms: Issues for Understanding the Text of the Bible,' in *The Bible as Book: The Hebrew Bible and the Judaean Desert Discoveries* (ed. Edward D. Herbert and Emanuel Tov; London: The British Library, 2002), 31–40; and idem, 'Qumran Scrolls and the Demise.' See also Eugene Ulrich, *The Dead Sea Scrolls and the Origins of the Bible* (Studies in the Dead Sea Scrolls and Related Literature; Grand Rapids, Mich.: Eerdmans, 1999).

[40] See, for instance, Brooke, 'Rewritten Law;' Shemaryahu Talmon, 'The Crystallization of the "Canon of Hebrew Scriptures" in the Light of Biblical Scrolls from Qumran,' in *The Bible as Book* (ed. Herbert and Tov), 5–20; idem, 'The Old Testament Text,' in *The Cambridge History of the Bible. Volume* 1 (ed. Peter R. Ackroyd and Christopher F. Evans; Cambridge: CUP, 1970), 159–199; Emanuel Tov, 'Hebrew Biblical Manuscripts from the Judaean Desert: Their Contribution to Textual Criticism,' *JJS* 39 (1988): 5–37; idem, 'Scriptures: Text,' in EDSS 2:832–836; Ulrich, *Dead Sea Scrolls and the Origins of the Bible*; and idem, 'The Bible in the Making: The Scriptures Found at Qumran,' in *The Bible at Qumran: Text, Shape, and Interpretation* (ed. Peter W. Flint; Studies in the Dead Sea Scrolls and Related Literature; Grand Rapids, Mich.: Eerdmans, 2001), 51–66.

[41] Cf. James C. VanderKam, 'Questions of Canon Viewed Through the Dead Sea Scrolls,' in *The Canon Debate* (ed. Lee M. McDonald and James A. Sanders; Peabody, Mass.: Hendrickson, 2002), 91–109, here 95–96.

[42] Alison Schofield has recently independently drawn on some analogies with the scholarly issues addressed by students of the text of the Hebrew Bible in the light of the Dead Sea Scrolls, 'Rereading S,' 105 n. 19. Schofield sketches what one may call a scenario of local text types

I should clarify that by bemoaning the sharp separation on the part of most scholars between biblical and non-biblical Scrolls, I am not implying that I doubt that some kind of distinction can be made. I am not concerned here with the important debates on the authoritative status of a number of fringe compositions such as 'Reworked Pentateuch.'[43] I am rather concerned with broader issues. Even if we did see the day when all of us are agreed on which texts are scriptural and which are not, I am concerned about not keeping these entities cut off from one another in the scholarly questions we bring to them. We seem to witness high levels of specialisation even within an already highly specialised field.

I am thinking here particularly of the relaxed attitude witnessed by the Qumran collection towards a plurality of what will become biblical texts[44] and the equally relaxed and surprising attitude towards a complex and pluralistic S tradition.[45] Inconsistencies between manuscripts did not trouble the owners of these texts – be they scriptural manuscripts or not. As far as the Qumran biblical scrolls are concerned the striking absence of evidence indicating any desire towards promoting a standard text has long and often been noted by scholars. Let me quote one of the pioneers in this field, Shemaryahu Talmon, who writes in his contribution to Volume 1 of *The Cambridge History of the Bible*:

> The co-existence of diverse text-types in the numerically, geographically and temporally restricted covenanters' community, the fact that [...] no obvious attempts at the suppression of divergent manuscripts or of individual variants can be discovered in that voluminous literature, proves beyond doubt that the very notion of an exclusive textus receptus had not yet taken root at Qumran.[46]

It may be time now to acknowledge and recognize that the situation Talmon and others have observed in the realm of the biblical manuscripts appears to apply also to the Rule manuscripts. By asking the question which of the S manuscripts is the current and most authoritative one, we may be bringing questions to the material that did not occur to the tradents and/or authors of these ancient texts. Instead, the textual fluidity of a broad section of the Qumran library indicates that some – maybe all? – Jews of this period were happy to tolerate inconsistencies in and pluralities of texts.

If a group approaches the plurality of scriptural texts with such a "liberal attitude" (to use a phrase employed by Talmon in this context[47]), it is not altogether

---

for S whereas I am stressing the co-existence of multiple witnesses of S testifying to a lack of concern for final texts in the transmission of both the biblical texts and the S manuscripts.

[43] On this issue see Florentino García Martínez and Julio Trebolle Barrera, *The People of the Dead Sea Scrolls* (Leiden: Brill, 1995), 123–138.

[44] Recently Paul Heger speaks of a "laissez-faire attitude," see *Cult as the Catalyst for Division: Cult Disputes as the Motive for Schism in the Pre-70 Pluralistic Environment* (STDJ 65; Leiden: Brill, 2007), 104 ff.

[45] Heger notes a connection between Bible and S, *Cult as the Catalyst for Division*, 115.

[46] Talmon, 'The Old Testament Text,' 185.

[47] Talmon, 'The Old Testament Text,' 185.

surprising that they should handle their own affairs in a comparable manner. Such a relaxed attitude to texts may have several reasons:

It seems possible, maybe even probable, that the liberal attitude to non-standardized texts was shared widely by Jews at this period, a point also raised by García Martínez and Talmon with reference to the biblical scrolls.[48] The question deserves further thought. One may ask, for instance, why the relatively large number of copies of the Damascus Document from Cairo and Qumran display a much more stable text – if you like – than the *Serekh*, and that despite the fact that the dates of the ancient and mediaeval copies span a millennium not to speak of the geographical distance of their discovery. One way to account for this discrepancy in the level of variation is almost certainly the recognition that some texts or parts of texts became fixed more readily and earlier than others – for a variety of reasons. The most topical texts such as the Rule, for instance, would then contain material that was still evolving.

The plurality of texts further indicates that the manuscripts as we have them frequently preserve snapshots of growing, living, or evolving texts. They do not bear witness to a desire to produce a systematic final and/or authoritative document. In a different context (i. e. Milik's identification of proto-Esther at Qumran) García Martínez speaks of the "organic growth of a literary text" and, he continues, "we are right inside this organic fabric of traditions which emerge as 'texts' and end up being 'bible'."[49] The 'bible' element apart, the same applies to the Community Rule. From our standpoint the lack of stability in texts and traditions is always an *interim* state, a stage in a development. The question needs to be asked whether the author(s)/editor(s)/scribe(s) behind S ever intended – or even conceived of the need – for this development to end. Maybe change was a permanent fixture.

Shemaryahu Talmon speaks of the "living Bible' at Qumran.[50] George Brooke has noted the way in which rewriting scripture signals respect for authoritative traditions,

> They show how seriously the Qumran community and its forebears took their inherited authoritative traditions. These works were not to be left untouched on the shelf, but to be used and studied.[51]

---

[48] García Martínez and Trebolle Barrera, *People of the Dead Sea Scrolls*, 123; similarly Talmon, 'The Old Testament Text,' 185.
[49] García Martínez and Trebolle Barrera, *People of the Dead Sea Scrolls*, 136.
[50] Cf. Talmon, 'Crystallization of the "Canon,"' 11.
[51] George J. Brooke, 'Between Authority and Canon: The Significance of Reworking the Bible for Understanding the Canonical Process,' in *Reworking the Bible: Apocryphal and Related Texts at Qumran* (ed. Esther G. Chazon, Devorah Dimant, and Ruth A. Clements; STDJ 58; Leiden: Brill, 2005), 85–104, here 99. See also Anders Klostergaard Petersen, 'Rewritten Bible as a Borderline Phenomenon – Genre, Textual Strategy, or Canonical Anachronism?,' in *Flores Florentino* (ed. Hilhorst, Puech, and Tigchelaar), 285–306, here 285–286 notes 2–3.

These observations may be broadened to include also texts such as the Community Rule. The growth of the Rule points towards a cumulative and successive process or even processes.

Such a pluralistic picture can already be found in the Hebrew Bible which includes its fair share of repetition and contradiction happily existing side by side and helping to provide bread and butter to scholars from ancient times to this day. On the one hand the books of Chronicles offer an alternative version of events recorded also in Samuel and Kings. On the other hand, Deutero-nomy addresses legal issues also dealt with in Exodus[52] extending even to central texts such as the ten commandments. This point is highlighted convincingly by Leiman who argues, "the authorities responsible for its [i. e. scripture's] canonization were not troubled by apparent or real inconsistencies."[53] Later Jewish legal works such as Mishnah and Talmud are also cumulative, and this commonality was noted already by Metso.[54] Adin Steinsaltz observes, moreover, "a new formulation occasionally rendered previous mishnayot superfluous, but since it was the rule that 'a mishnah does not move from its place,' both statements were retained."[55] Comparable to my own assessment of the reasons for different levels of stability in the texts, Steinsaltz writes with reference to rabbinic traditions,

> Halakhah pertaining to biological or ritual matters may be preserved unchanged for long periods because of the stability of the objects under discussion, but this is not so in the case of civil law.[56]

I came to a similar conclusion in my study of the Laws of the Damascus Document noting that the communal rules display more updating than the non-community specific general halakha.[57] Finally, Menahem Kister has noted the shared fluidity between the S manuscripts and talmudic literature.[58]

---

[52] Cf. Petersen, 'Rewritten Bible as a Borderline Phenomenon,' 300, 302 and Brooke, 'Rewritten Law,' 32.

[53] Sid Z. Leiman, 'Inspiration and Canonicity: Reflections on the Formation of the Biblical Canon,' in *Jewish and Christian Self-Definition. Volume Two: Aspects of Judaism in the Graeco-Roman Period* (ed. Ed P. Sanders; London: SCM, 1981), 56–63, here 60.

[54] 'In Search of the *Sitz im Leben*.'

[55] Adin Steinsaltz, *The Essential Talmud* (London: Weidenfeld and Nicolson, 1976), 38–39.

[56] *Essential Talmud*, 145.

[57] Charlotte Hempel, *The Laws of the Damascus Document: Sources, Traditions, and Redaction* (Leiden: Brill, 1998; SBL Paperback 2006), esp. 188–191. There I argue in favour of distinguishing between 'general halakhah' and 'communal rules' in the Laws of the Damascus Document. I further observe that in contrast to the 'communal rules' the 'general halakhah' (on topics such as the sabbath) has been transmitted faithfully and displays few indications of updating.

[58] 'The Development of the Early Recensions of the Damascus Document,' *DSD* 14 (2007): 61–76, esp. 76 n. 40.

5. A Farewell to the End-Serekh

The relationship between 'lower criticism' und 'higher criticism' has been the subject of renewed debate in recent years. Especially noteworthy here are two articles by George Brooke and and Emanuel Tov respectively.[59] Qumran has shown that the search for uncovering an *Urtext* in its pristine purity is obsolete at this period of Jewish history. A remarkably similar picture has been painted by David Parker with reference to the emergence of the New Testament.[60]

Closely related to this is our understanding of the role of scribes and, to use Tov's phrase, "their role in the transmission process."[61] Talmon writes astutely on this topic,

> We can now observe at close range, so to say in situ, scribal techniques of the Second Temple period which left their impression on the text in subsequent stages of its history.[62]

And observe we can, now with Tov's reference book on these processes to hand.[63] A crucial question that arises with reference to the Rule manuscripts is: Are scribes merely responsible for corrections within one manuscript such as attested particularly frequently in 1QS 7–8 or are the same professionals also behind the diverse developments of different manuscripts of S with all their numerous significant variants?

6. Conclusion

In trying to sum up, we note that the search for the original text of the Hebrew Bible has gone out of fashion in light of the evidence of the Dead Sea Scrolls. Brooke speaks of "the abandoned quest."[64] It seems timely, therefore, to refrain from insisting on establishing the final, authoritative *Endtext* of the Rule. Just

---

[59] See esp. Brooke, 'Qumran Scrolls and the Demise;' and Emanuel Tov, 'The Writing of Early Scrolls: Implications for the Literary Analysis of Hebrew Scripture,' in *L'écrit et l'ésprit: Etudes d'histoire du texte et de théologie biblique en hommage à Adrian Schenker* (ed. Dieter Böhler, Innocent Himbaza, and Philippe Hugo; Göttingen: Vandenhoeck & Ruprecht, 2005), 355-371.

[60] See David C. Parker, *The Living Text of the Gospels* (Cambidge: CUP, 1997). Note also his illuminating references to analogies with the study of the development of the text of Shakespeare's plays or the poetry of Wordsworth, cf. *Living Text*, 4–6.

[61] *Scribal Practices*, 25 and chapter 2. See also Brooke, 'Qumran Scrolls and the Demise,' 37–38; Martin Goodman, 'Texts, Scribes and Power in Roman Judaea,' in *Literacy and Power in the Ancient World* (ed. Alan K. Bowman and Greg Woolf; Cambridge: CUP, 1994), 99–108; and Tigchelaar, 'Scribe of 1QS.'

[62] 'The Old Testament Text,' 184.

[63] *Scribal Practices*.

[64] 'Rewritten Law,' 36.

as Emanuel Tov can powerfully speak of a "changing biblical text,"[65] we may also want to accept a "changing Serekh text." Why does it surprise us that the Rule texts witness a considerable degree of plurality, while we have come to acknowledge a remarkable degree of flexibility and plurality with reference to the emerging scriptures?

Given that the notion of a Bible is anachronistic for this period, it may well be that Jewish attitudes to texts were rather relaxed and laid back in the late Second Temple period – surprising and unexpected as this may seem to us.[66] This clearly also applies to cherished and authoritative texts. No text could have been more revered and cherished than the emerging Bible in a movement such as the one behind the Qumran library whose members were steeped in the scriptures. The scriptures gave them the terms of reference for their literary outputs and inspired their identity and self-understanding. The lack of a canon of scriptures and a Rule canon is equally surprising and comparable.[67] The ancient manuscripts found in the vicinity of Qumran testify to an unexpected degree of literary and textual complexity and plurality, and it seems to me that the issues faced by scholars of the Rule texts can be fruitfully and constructively related to the challenges faced by experts on the canon and the text of the Hebrew Bible. The fluidity of these ancient texts appears to cross the boundaries created by customary categories such as biblical and non-biblical Dead Sea Scrolls.

---

[65] Emanuel Tov, *Textual Criticism of the Hebrew Bible* (2d ed.; Minneapolis, Minn.: Fortress; Assen: van Gorcum, 2001), 1; cf. also Brooke, 'Rewritten Law,' 36.

[66] See Heger, *Cult as the Catalyst for Division*, 115.

[67] In a different context Albert Baumgarten eloquently speaks of the "inelegance" of the picture painted by the texts and observes astutely, "reality is regularly much more disorderly than elegant human attempts to organize and then understand it." 'Zadokite Priests at Qumran,' 155.

Chapter Eighteen

The Emerging Bible and the Dead Sea Scrolls: A Common Milieu[1]

1. Introduction

Let me begin by outlining a paradox in Dead Sea Scrolls research. On the one hand, scholars have long recognized and emphasized that the 'Bible' did not exist at the period attested by the Scrolls. The term, we are frequently told, is anachronistic at this point in Jewish history.[2] Scholars sensitive to this recognition use different terms, such as scriptures (with lower or upper case s), authoritative texts, and even pre-Bible.[3] Yet, on the other hand, at several levels of scholarly perception of and methodological approach to the ancient Jewish sources at our disposal, this widely recognized anachronism wields considerable power in all sorts of subtle ways. In short, we are all very capable of reflecting with great subtlety when considering a particular conundrum, or question of definition, only to succumb to a rather unreconstructed approach to a related issue, almost as if caught off-guard after a period of intense scrutiny. One clear example of this is the mainly unselfconsciously anachronistic distinction between the study of biblical and non-biblical texts from Qumran. I am less concerned here with the issue of fringe compositions that are considered scriptural

---

[1] This chapter was originally published in a *Festschrift* for Prof. Robert Gordon as 'The Social Matrix that Shaped the Hebrew Bible and Gave us the Dead Sea Scrolls,' in *Studies on the Text and Versions of the Hebrew Bible in Honour of Robert Gordon* (ed. Geoffrey Khan and Diana Lipton; VTSup 149; Leiden: Brill, 2012), 221–237. Earlier versions of the chapter were presented to the Old Testament Seminar at the University of Oxford and the 20th Congress of the *International Organization for the Study of the Old Testament* (IOSOT) in Helsinki in 2010. I am grateful to Profs. John Barton and Raija Sollamo for their invitations and to the distinguished members of both audiences for their contributions in the ensuing discussion. I would like to single out Prof. Emanuel Tov (Jerusalem), a visitor to Oxford at the time, and Prof. Reinhard Kratz (Göttingen) for their constructive responses. Any remaining shortcomings are to be laid at my feet.

[2] Cf. Jonathan Campbell, '"Rewritten Bible" and "Parabiblical Texts:" A Terminological and Ideological Critique,' in *New Directions in Qumran Studies* (ed. Jonathan G. Campbell, William J. Lyons, and Lloyd K. Pietersen; LSTS 52; London: T & T Clark, 2005), 43–68 and Eugene Ulrich, *The Dead Sea Scrolls and the Origins of the Bible* (Studies in the Dead Sea Scrolls and Related Literature; Grand Rapids, Mich.: Eerdmans, 1999).

[3] See George J. Brooke, 'The Rewritten Law, Prophets, and Psalms: Issues for Understanding the Text of the Bible,' in *The Bible as Book: The Hebrew Bible and the Judaean Desert Discoveries* (ed. Edward D. Herbert and Emanuel Tov; London: The British Library, 2002), 31–40.

by some and para-scriptural by others, e. g. 4Q(Reworked)Pentateuch.[4] Rather, I am keen to stress the lack of dialogue and conceptual overlap in our approaches to Qumran texts that would later become Bible and non-biblical material. For the most part, different scholars plough these apparently different fields. Even if the same scholar ploughs both fields, he or she will often do a quick change-over of mental tools. There are commendable exceptions, such as two excellent treatments of these issues by Brooke and Kratz, the former taking a theoretical approach whereas the latter exemplifies the fluidity of interpretation both within and outside the Hebrew Bible in the Abraham tradition.[5] To give a more specific example, we have long understood that the so-called biblical texts from Qumran attest a perhaps surprising degree of pluriformity. Yet, when faced with the pluriform textual tradition of the Community Rule since the early 1990s, we are troubled by these multiple textual manifestations of the Rule as if faced with such a pluriform picture for the first time.[6] I recently argued that the pluriformity of the texts of the emerging scriptures and the pluriformity of the Rule texts are two sides of the same coin and point towards the likelihood that textual fluidity was a hallmark of ancient Jewish texts preserved mid-way through their crystallization.[7] Readers may disagree with my conclusion on this particular issue, but I am convinced that it is high time to look at the evidence across the board without letting anachronistic labels set the agenda – even if only implicitly.

> In light of the evident literary creativity witnessed by the Damascus Document and the Community Rule it is worthwhile to encourage more dialogue with the current debates on how to understand the phenomena often referred to with the term 'rewritten scripture.' Different ancient Jewish texts are fluid and influencing each other, and as scholars we are caught in the difficult position of trying to trace how the influence operated. It seems certain that comparable processes and activities can be witnessed in the realm of D (the Damascus Document), S (the Community Rule) and the literature dubbed

---

[4] Cf. Sidnie White Crawford, *Rewriting Scripture in Second Temple Times* (Studies in the Dead Sea Scrolls and Related Literature; Grand Rapids, Mich.: Eerdmans, 2008), 39–59.

[5] George J. Brooke, 'New Perspectives on the Bible and Its Interpretation in the Dead Sea Scrolls,' in *The Dynamics of Language and Exegesis at Qumran* (ed. Devorah Dimant and Reinhard G. Kratz; FAT 2.35; Tübingen: Mohr Siebeck, 2009), 19–37 and Reinhard G. Kratz, 'Friend of God, Brother of Sarah, and Father of Isaac: Abraham in the Hebrew Bible and in Qumran,' in *Dynamics of Language and Exegesis at Qumran* (ed. Dimant and Kratz), 79–105; see also idem, *Das Judentum im Zeitalter des Zweiten Tempels* (FAT 42; Tübingen: Mohr Siebeck, 2004), 123–156 and James C. VanderKam, 'Questions of Canon Viewed Through the Dead Sea Scrolls,' in *The Canon Debate* (ed. Lee M. McDonald and James A. Sanders; Peabody, Mass.: Hendrickson, 2002), 91–109, 95–96.

[6] On the evidence of the Rule manuscripts see Sarianna Metso, *The Serekh Texts* (CQS 9/ LSTS 62; London: T & T Clark, 2007).

[7] 'Pluralism and Authoritativeness – The Case of the S Tradition,' in *The Authoritativeness of Scriptures in Ancient Judaism* (ed. Mladen Popović; JSJSup 141; Leiden: Brill), 193–208, reprinted as Chapter 17 in this volume.

'rewritten scripture.'[8] This should not be unexpected since the constituency of people performing such complex learned processes are almost certainly genetically related to one another. If we think of the community or at least its scribal component as learned and engaged in sophisticated dealings with texts and traditions, it is unlikely that they would have made a conscious distinction in their approach to re-writing scripture and re-writing Serekh/D-type-traditions when going about their business.[9]

In other words, the fluidity and creativity we witness in so-called biblical and para-biblical texts from the late Second Temple Period is mirrored by the fluidity and creativity evident in the creation and transmission of non-biblical texts. Moreover, this shared creative approach to texts is most fully appreciated if we disregard the anachronistic distinction between biblical and non-biblical texts in this period.

Now that all the texts from Qumran are available, it is essential that we allow ourselves the intellectual space to stand back and resist the temptation of simply fitting new pieces of evidence into an existing framework. This is particularly necessary since much of the framework we are working with goes back to the initial phase of the discoveries when pioneering scholars needed to make sense of a huge amount of new data: the most natural sifting mechanism was to reach for labels such as biblical/non-biblical and sectarian/non-sectarian. Following the publication of the contents of Cave 4, many more texts emerged that seem to defy straightforward categorisation in one way or another. This in turn poses something of a challenge to the nature of the dominant categories themselves.

2. The Scrolls as Case Studies of the Ancient Jewish Literary Craft

A particularly fruitful area of investigation is the light the Scrolls can shed on the processes of ancient Jewish literary activity.[10] Qumran provides us with more than nine hundred ancient manuscripts from a time when both the text of the

---

[8] I began to develop this line of reflection at a conference held at the University of Toronto in 2010, see 'Shared Traditions: Points of Contact between D and S,' in *The Transmission of Traditions and the Production of Texts as They Emerge from the Dead Sea Scrolls* (ed. Sarianna Metso, Hindy Najman and Eileen Schuller; STDJ 92; Leiden: Brill), 115–131, reprinted as Chapter 9 in this volume. For such an analogy see also Reinhard G. Kratz, 'Der *Penal Code* und das Verhältnis von *Serekh ha-Yachad* (S) und Damaskusschrift (D),' *RQ* 25 (2011): 199–227.

[9] See Hempel, 'Shared Traditions,' 131, reprinted in Chapter 9 above.

[10] Cf. George J. Brooke, 'The Qumran Scrolls and the Demise of the Distinction Between Higher and Lower Criticism,' in *New Directions in Qumran Studies* (ed. Campbell, Lyons, and Pietersen), 26–42; David M. Carr, *Writing on the Tablet of the Heart: Origins of Scripture and Literature* (Oxford: OUP, 2005); Martin Jaffe, *Torah in the Mouth: Writing and Oral Tradition in Palestinian Judaism, 200 BCE–400 CE* (Oxford: OUP, 2001); Karel van der Toorn, *Scribal Culture and the Making of the Hebrew Bible* (Cambridge: Harvard University Press, 2007); Emanuel Tov, *Scribal Practices and Approaches Reflected in the Texts Found in the Judean Desert* (STDJ 54; Leiden: Brill, 2004); and Geza Vermes, *The Dead Sea Scrolls: Qumran in Perspective* (3d ed.; London: SCM, 1994), 23.

Hebrew Bible and the canon were still fluid. Similarly, critical biblical scholarship has worked for centuries in the knowledge that the Hebrew Bible evolved in complex and creative ways. Here again, the evidence of the Scrolls is invaluable in shedding light on the kinds of processes we have long suspected of having left their mark on the final form of the Hebrew Bible.[11]

3. The Scrolls and the Emergence of Jewish Sectarianism in the Persian Period

Moving from texts to social realities behind them, Morton Smith argued already in 1960 that the covenant in Nehemiah 10 involves the first Jewish sect attested. He further emphasized the way in which this sect was defined by "particular legal interpretations, and consequently to peculiar practices."[12] Morton Smith's suggestion that biblical interpretation lies at the heart of early Jewish sectarianism was further developed by Joseph Blenkinsopp in a number of publications.[13] Similarly Shemaryahu Talmon maintained that Jewish sectarianism goes back to the fifth and sixth centuries.[14]

Turning to the Dead Sea Scrolls, we observe a growing retrospective relevance of much this material. Thus, recent scholarship has demonstrated the importance of this cache of manuscripts for our understanding of Second Temple Judaism much beyond the confines of a small, dissident sect. Alison Schofield has recently referred to earlier models of the Qumran community as 'isolationist.'[15] Since we have been able to estimate the full extent of the corpus of Qurman manuscripts the sectarian component emerges as no more than around one

---

[11] See Brooke, 'Demise of the Distinction Between Higher and Lower Criticism' and Emanuel Tov, 'The Writing of Early Scrolls: Implications for the Literary Analysis of Hebrew Scripture,' *DSD* 13 (2006): 339–347.

[12] Morton Smith, 'The Dead Sea Scrolls in Relation to Ancient Judaism,' *NTS* 7 (1960): 347–360, 356.

[13] See Joseph Blenkinsopp, 'Interpretation and the Tendency to Sectarianism: An Aspect of Second Temple History,' in *Jewish and Christian Self-Definition* (ed. Ed P. Sanders; Philadelphia, Pa.: Fortress, 1981), Vol. II, 1–26 and idem, *Judaism the First Phase: The Place of Ezra and Nehemiah in the Origins of Judaism* (Grand Rapids, Mich.: Eerdmans, 2009).

[14] Shemaryahu Talmon, 'The Emergence of Jewish Sectarianism in the Early Second Temple Period,' in *King, Cult, and Calendar in Ancient Israel: Collected Studies* (Leiden: Brill; Jerusalem: Magnes, 1986), 165–201; see also Philip R. Davies, '"Old" and "New" Israel in the Bible and the Qumran Scrolls: Identity and Difference,' in *Defining Identities: We, You, and the Other in the Dead Sea Scrolls. Proceedings of the Fifth Meeting of the IOQS in Groningen* (ed. Florentino García Martínez and Mladen Popović; STDJ 70; Leiden: Brill, 2008), 33–42 and Stephen Hultgren, *From the Damascus Covenant to the Covenant of the Community: Literary, Historical, and Theological Studies in the Dead Sea Scrolls* (STDJ 66; Leiden: Brill, 2007).

[15] *From Qumran to the Yaḥad: A New Paradigm of Textual Development for the Community Rule* (STDJ 77; Leiden: Brill, 2009), 48.

third of the collection.[16] Even with respect to clearly sectarian texts, a number of scholars now advocate a wider view. On the basis of close study of the rich evidence of the Community Rule both Schofield and Collins now prefer to speak of a Yaḥad that goes beyond Qumran.[17] The title of Collins's recent monograph encapsulates his view: *Beyond the Qumran Community: The Sectarian Movement of the Dead Sea Scrolls*, and Jutta Jokiranta likewise speaks of the 'Qumran movement' in her doctoral dissertation.[18]

4. The Shared Scribal Milieu Behind the Emerging Scriptures and the Scrolls

A fascinating next step in tracing the significance of the Qumran Scrolls is the much discussed issue of the social background of the material from a broader perspective. The Scrolls testify to a learned group of Jews engaged in composing, shaping and collecting a very large amount of literature. We know that there were similarly learned Jews engaged in shaping, collecting, and editing another very large amount of literature: the emerging Hebrew scriptures. Since both social spheres share a considerable amount of overlapping material, interests, and skills, the connections between both become even more tangible. Thus, Talmon notes with reference to the Scrolls, "they were written when biblical literary activity was still ongoing" and refers to their "partial chronological overlap with the end phase of the biblical era."[19] Since literacy, and especially learning at the level required to deal with the material at issue here, was the preserve of a small elite in the Second Temple Period (as elsewhere in the ancient world), it is likely that the same limited stratum of highly educated scribes is the pool responsible for collecting and shaping the emerging Hebrew scriptures *and* the corpus of the Scrolls. The job description of both groups is captured exceedingly well by Kratz's account of the chief duties of the scribe as consisting of "die Pflege von Wissen und Literatur."[20] The individuals responsible for composing, collecting, redacting, and archiving the material found in the Qumran Caves are every bit as masterful[21] as the circles that gave us the Hebrew Bible. By removing the wedge

---

[16] See the seminal study by Devorah Dimant, 'The Qumran Manuscripts: Contents and Significance,' in *Time To Prepare the Way in the Wilderness* (ed. Devorah Dimant and Lawrence H. Schiffman; STDJ 16; Leiden: Brill), 23–58.

[17] John J. Collins, *Beyond the Qumran Community: The Sectarian Movement of the Dead Sea Scrolls* (Grand Rapids, Mich.: Eerdmans, 2009) and Schofield, *From Qumran to the Yaḥad*.

[18] Jutta Jokiranta, "Identity on a Continuum: Constructing and Expressing Sectarian Social Identity in Qumran Serakhim and Pesharim" (Ph.D. diss., University of Helsinki, 2005), 54.

[19] Shemaryahu Talmon, *The World of Qumran From Within* (Leiden: Brill; Jerusalem: Magnes, 1989), 24–25.

[20] Kratz, *Judentum im Zeitalter des Zweiten Tempels*, 112.

[21] The term 'mastery' is developed by Carr, *Writing on the Tablet of the Heart*, 190.

that accidents of preservation and discovery have placed between both entities the shared literary, cultural, and perhaps also social worlds of both groups can illuminate one another.[22]

I am thinking here less in terms of authorship (a concept somewhat anachronistic for the ancient world) where the chronological gap between the Scrolls and a great deal of the emerging Hebrew Scriptures can be formidable, but rather in terms of the processes of collecting, transmitting, and shaping existing material. In this realm the Scrolls bring us as close as we can get to a priestly Second Temple group. It seems to me extremely unlikely that a dissident group was able to train and establish the highly developed and sophisticated scribal culture we witness in the Dead Sea Scrolls from scratch. It is inevitable that the milieu behind the Scrolls came out of the wider scribal culture, probably associated with the Temple, and a great deal of the cultural background, even if rejected, will have left its mark on the collection. There was a dis-connect not a dis-tinction between both worlds.

5. Tracing Trajectories from Emerging Sectarianism in the Hebrew Bible to Incipient Communal Life Attested in the Scrolls

By stressing the huge potential of paying close attention to what the Scrolls share with their wider Second Temple Jewish background, it would be foolish to deny the distinctive elements within them. The unique and distinctive component of the Qumran collection is often referred to as the sectarian element. Scholars have grappled with defining sectarian pointers and identifying the sectarian component of the collection ever since it was unearthed – and even before if we consider the struggle to place the Damascus Document found some half century prior to the Scrolls in the Cairo Genizah.[23] Many scholars now shy away from speaking of a neat divide between sectarian and non-sectarian material and acknowledge instead a more gradated scenario. Most recently Brooke proposed a spectrum ranging from 'incipient' to 'full-blown' and 'rejuvenated' sectarianism, whereas Florentino García Martínez proposes abandoning the distinctions

---

[22] On the accidental element in our ancient sources see recently Emanuel Tov, 'The Coincidental Textual Nature of the Collections of Ancient Scriptures,' in *Congress Volume Ljubljana 2007* (ed. André Lemaire; VTSup 133; Leiden: Brill, 2010), 153–169.

[23] See Carol Newsom, '"Sectually Explicit" Literature from Qumran,' in *The Hebrew Bible and Its Interpreters* (ed. William H. C. Propp et al.; Biblical & Judaic Studies; Winona Lake, Ind.: Eisenbrauns, 1990), 167–187; Charlotte Hempel, 'Kriterien zur Bestimmung "essenischer Verfasserschaft" von Qumrantexten,' in *Qumran Kontrovers: Beiträge zu den Textfunden vom Toten Meer* (ed. Jörg Frey and Hartmut Stegemann; Paderborn: Bonifatius, 2003), 71–78; and more recently Annette Steudel, 'Dating Exegetical Texts from Qumran,' in *Dynamics of Language and Exegesis at Qumran* (ed. Dimant and Kratz), 39–53.

sectarian/non-sectarian and biblical/non-biblical altogether.[24] In other words, recent scholarship on the Scrolls conceives of the presence of sectarian and distinctive elements in terms of a spectrum rather than a neat divide. An obvious further question that has not received the attention it deserves is: what happens if we go to or approach the end of the spectrum? In other words, how close does the most 'incipient' end of the Qumran material take us to the much debated context of developing sectarianism in the Hebrew scriptures? Whereas emerging sectarianism in the Hebrew Bible has been the subject of scholarly interest for some time,[25] fresh and exciting new areas for reflection open up if we attempt to connect the dots between this latter and well established line of enquiry and some of the most recent developments in Qumran studies.

As far as the incipient end of the Qumran social spectrum is concerned, my own work has recently looked for fossils of more embryonic[26] states of affairs in otherwise highly developed sectarian texts.[27] In this chapter I would like to explore the potentially extremely exciting *rendezvous* of embryonic sectarianism in the Scrolls and emerging sectarianism in the Hebrew Scriptures.

6. The Scrolls and Recent Research on the Development of the Psalter

As far as the Hebrew Bible is concerned, we may draw attention to the great impetus gained by the Qumran discoveries for our understanding of the growth and shape of the Psalter. The debate is well known between those scholars who would argue that 11QPs^a is a secondary liturgical collection[28] rather than

---

[24] See George J. Brooke, 'From Jesus to the Early Christian Communities: Modes of Sectarianism in the Light of the Dead Sea Scrolls,' in *The Dead Sea Scrolls and Contemporary Culture* (ed. Adolfo Roitman, Lawrence H. Schiffman, and Shani Tzoref; STDJ 93; Leiden: Brill, 2011), 413–434 and Florentino García Martínez, '¿Sectario, no-sectario, o qué? Problemas de una taxonomía correcta de los textos qumránicos,' *RQ* 23 (2008): 383–394 and idem, 'Aramaica Qumranica Apocalyptica?,' in *Aramaica Qumranica: The Aix en Provence Colloquium on the Aramaic Dead Sea Scrolls* (ed. Katell Berthelot and Daniel Stökl Ben Ezra; STDJ 94; Leiden: Brill, 2010), 435–449, 446.

[25] Cf. Davies, '"Old" and "New" Israel in the Bible and the Qumran Scrolls;' Hultgren, *From the Damascus Covenant to the Covenant of the Community*; Smith, 'Dead Sea Scrolls in Relation to Ancient Judaism;' and Talmon, 'Emergence of Jewish Sectarianism.'

[26] I owe the helpful terminology 'embryonic' to my colleague Prof. David Chalcraft of the University of Sheffield.

[27] Charlotte Hempel, 'Emerging Communal Life and Ideology in the S Tradition,' in *Defining Identities: We, You, and the Other in the Dead Sea Scrolls. Proceedings of the Fifth Meeting of the IOQS in Groningen* (ed. Florentino García Martínez and Mladen Popović; STDJ 70; Leiden: Brill, 2008), 43–61, reprinted as Chapter 5 in this volume and eadem, '1QS 6:2c–4a – Satellites or Precursors of the Yaḥad?' in *The Dead Sea Scrolls and Contemporary Culture* (ed. Adolfo Roitman, Larry Schiffman, and Shani Tzoref; STDJ 93; Leiden: Brill, 2011), 31–40, reprinted as Chapter 6 in this volume.

[28] So Moshe H. Goshen-Gottstein, 'The Psalms Scroll (11QPs^a): A Problem of Canon and Text,' *Textus* 5 (1966): 22–33; Patrick Skehan, 'A Liturgical Complex in 11QPs^a,' *CBQ* 35

a Psalms Scroll proper, albeit in a form different from what we would have expected.[29] At present the latter camp seems to be winning the argument and to be much more in tune with the wider recognition of variety and pluriformity attested by the Scrolls.

Recent Psalms scholarship has devoted a great deal of attention to the study of the shape and shaping of the Psalter as a whole. The shape of the Psalter as we have it was still in flux in the Second Temple Period, and there are many indications of gradual growth and compilation in the book itself, perhaps the most clear-cut examples being Ps 72:20 ('The prayers of David son of Jesse are ended'), the identification of Ps 151 in the Septuagint as "outside the number," and the presence of a number of duplicate psalms in the collection (Ps 14=53/ Ps 40:13–17 = Ps 70/P. 108 =Ps 57:7–11+60:5–12. Cf. also Ps 18 = 2 Sam 22). Whereas Arthur Weiser's preface to the third edition of his commentary could refer to the Psalms as "pictures without a frame,"[30] recent research has very much emphasized the frame, the whole as much as the parts. Just as the variety of themes present in individual Psalms has long been noted –leading Martin Luther to describe the Psalter as 'eine kleine biblia'[31] – so the shape of the whole cannot be determined with surgical precision. The parts and the whole eloquently promote a variety of agendas and themes. Modern scholars have proposed a variety of perceptive readings of the final shape of the Psalter and have identified a dominant framework, variously stressing the Davidic element, the instructional element, the eschatology, or the Zion theology. It seems to me, that it is precisely the richness of the material, the parts and the whole, and its clearly complex and successive evolution which gives rise to staunchly defended and well argued proposals of such variety. Several different points of view capture some aspects of the bigger truth. It has often been emphasized that ancient Jewish literary activity promoted its literary heritage by means of creative transmission and supplementation. This seems to be evident in the Psalter as well. Thus, if modern scholars are able to uncover a plurality of emphases, this is because our ancient predecessors left us with such a plurality. Sensitive contemporary readers are able to uncover different parts of the ancient creative mosaic of tradition. A fundamental difference in approach is our compulsion to try and find 'the one' central framework or theological direction, whereas to the ancients several valid frames and directions could be explored side by side. Here, I am sympathetic to

---

(1973): 195–205; and Shemaryahu Talmon, 'Pisqah Be'emṣaʿ Pasuq and 11QPsª,' *Textus* 5 (1966): 11–21.

[29] For the latter view see James A. Sanders, *The Psalms Scroll of Qumran Cave 11 (11QPsª)* (Oxford: Clarendon, 1965) and Peter Flint, *The Dead Sea Psalms Scroll and the Book of Psalms* (STDJ 17; Leiden: Brill, 1997).

[30] Arthur Weiser, *The Psalms: A Commentary* (OTL; London: SCM, 1962), 9.

[31] See Reinhard G. Kratz, 'Die Tora Davids: Ps 1 und die doxologische Fünfteilung des Psalters,' *ZTK* 93 (1996): 1–34.

Stuart Weeks's conclusion to his study of the category of Wisdom Psalms in the course of which he reminds us that "all our distinctions and classification are just a poor approximation to a vibrant and complicated literary culture."[32]

7. A Life Dedicated to Torah Scholarship: Ps 1:2, Josh 1:8 and 1QS 6:6b–7a

In the remainder of this chapter I would like to offer some tentative reflections on a passage found in Ps 1:2, Josh 1:8, and the Community Rule from Qumran. A prominent voice in the search for the shape of the Psalter was the monograph by Gerald Wilson in which he highlights the promise of scrutinizing "the 'seams' between the collections where editorial activity should be most evident."[33] Whatever one's position on the relationship of Psalms 1 and 2 to one another, there is no doubt that Ps 1 is a major seam in the Psalter. Within the first Psalm verse 2 stands out for several reasons. Although the Psalm draws a contrast between the righteous and the wicked, much more attention is devoted to the wicked. When speaking of the righteous, most of the space is devoted to describing their preferred fate at the time of judgment in verse 6, and the image of the reliably fecund tree is applied to them in verse 3. As part of this contrast, verse 2 stands out in terms of its concrete language in describing the ideal life of a righteous person: his delight is the law of the Lord which he recites (יֶהְגֶּה) day and night.

Another characteristic of Ps 1:2 is its close relationship to a similar sentiment and formulation in Josh 1:8. The context of Josh 1:8 is a divine address to Joshua in the wake of Moses' death (vv. 1–9). Commentators customarily attribute Joshua 1 to the work of the Deuteronomists.[34] Moreover, several scholars have noted the resumptive nature of v. 8 which repetitively picks up a number of points raised in the previous verse.[35] There is little doubt, then, that in Josh 1:8 we are again dealing with a 'seam' in the Hebrew Bible – to use Gerald Wilson's terminology. Another intriguing connection between Josh 1:8 and Ps 1:2 is what Alexander Rofé describes as the "'structural' correspondence" between both

---

[32] Stuart Weeks, 'Wisdom Psalms,' in *Temple and Worship in Biblical Israel* (ed. John Day; LHBOTS 422; London: T & T Clark, 2007), 292–307, here 305.

[33] Gerald H. Wilson, *The Editing of the Hebrew Psalter* (Chico, Calif.: Scholars Press, 1985), 5.

[34] Trent C. Butler, *Joshua* (WBC 7; Waco, Tex.: Word Books, 1983), xxi, 6; Martin Noth, *Das Buch Josua* (2d ed.; HAT 1.7; Tübingen: Mohr Siebeck, 1952), 9, 27; J. Maxwell Miller and Gene M. Tucker, *The Book of Joshua* (CBC; Cambridge: CUP, 1974), 7, 21; and Jan A. Soggin, *Joshua: A Commentary* (trans. R. A. Wilson; OTL; London: SCM, 1972), 27.

[35] E. g., Miller and Tucker, *Book of Joshua*, 24.

passages in the opening lines of a collection of material and intended to direct the reading of what ensues.[36]

The close resemblance between Josh 1:8 and Ps 1:2 is well known,[37] and Boling has described the relationship of both passages in terms of "the same subject with some of the same vocabulary."[38] Moreover, Rudolf Smend has observed, "Zwischen unserer Stelle [Josh 18, C. H.] und der Psalmstelle muss ein direkter Zusammenhang bestehen."[39] Joshua is often considered the earlier of the two. Smend further assigns Josh 1:7–9 to a nomistic redaction (Dtr N) that left its mark on the Deuteronomistic history (Dtr H).[40] The rather forced ("etwas gezwungen") introduction of Torah piety in an address offering encouragement in military matters was noted by Martin Noth.[41]

On the basis of the correspondences between Ps 1:2, Josh 1:8, and Isa 59:21 Alexander Rofé has developed a fuller argument than his predecessors.[42] In particular, the secondary nature of Josh 1:8 and its close affinities with Ps 1:2 and Isa 59:21 led Rofé to relate all three passages to "a later Jewish ideal" to be associated with "the final stages of the compilation of the Canon."[43] Rofé is able to draw out connections in terms of message and terminology between all three passages and speaks eloquently of their "cognate origin".[44] In what follows I will focus on Josh 1:8 and Ps 1:2 because of their close relationship to a particular passage in the Scrolls which I would like to incorporate into the stimulating discussion set in motion by Rofé and others.

Returning for a moment to Smend's analysis of Josh 1:7–9, he notes the layered or successive nature of the work of the Deuteronomistic redactor(s) at this point and helpfully draws on Hans Wilhelm Hertzberg's concept of 'Nachgeschichte.'[45] In the remainder of this chapter, I will explore a more prolonged *Nachgeschichte* of this biblical passage in the Scrolls. In two different

---

[36] Alexander Rofé, 'The Piety of the Torah-Disciples at the Winding-Up of the Hebrew Bible: Josh. 1:8; Ps. 1:2; Isa. 59:21,' in *Bibel in jüdischer und christlicher Tradition: Festschrift für Johann Maier zum 60. Geburtstag* (ed. Helmut Merklein, Karlheinz Müller, and Günter Stemberger; Frankfurt a. M.: Hain, 1993), 78–85, 82.

[37] See John Gray, *Joshua, Judges and Ruth* (NCB; London: T. Nelson and Sons, 1967), 50; Soggin, *Joshua*, 32; and Moshe Weinfeld, *Deuteronomy and the Deuteronomic School* (Oxford: Clarendon, 1972), 280.

[38] Robert G. Boling, *Joshua: A New Translation with Notes and Commentary* (AYBC; Garden City, N. Y.: Doubleday, 1982), 125.

[39] Rudolf Smend, 'Das Gesetz und die Völker,' in *Die Mitte des Alten Testaments: Exegetische Aufsätze* (Tübingen: Mohr Siebeck, 2002), 148–161, 149 n. 9.

[40] 'Gesetz und die Völker.'

[41] Noth, *Buch Josua*, 29. I am grateful to Prof. Reinhard Kratz for drawing my attention to this.

[42] 'The Piety of the Torah-Disciples.'

[43] 'The Piety of the Torah-Disciples,' 80–81.

[44] 'The Piety of the Torah-Disciples,' 83.

[45] Hertzberg, *Beiträge zur Traditionsgeschichte und Theologie des Alten Testaments* (Göttingen: Vandenhoeck & Ruprecht, 1962), 70.

documents from Qumran we have again, as we will see, "the same subject with some of the same vocabulary," to use the phrase coined by Boling.[46]

The thought experiment I would like to conduct in this contribution is whether or not we are able to draw a meaningful comparison between the 'pious conventicles,' to use the old-fashioned phrase, reflected in Josh 1:8 and Ps 1:2, and the lowest end of the spectrum of sectarian cohesion in the Scrolls. The passage resembling the ideal set out in Josh 1:8 and Ps 1:2 is found in 1QS 6:6b–7a,[47]

ואל ימש במקום אשר יהיו שם העשרה איש דורש
בתורה יומם ולילה תמיד על יפות איש לרעהו

And in every place where there are ten there shall be present a person who studies the law continually day and night one replacing the other.[48]

Scholars have frequently pointed to the clear influence of Josh 1:8 and Ps 1:2 on the formulation in 1QS 6:6b–7a.[49] By referring to a person who studies the law permanently day and night the stress here seems to be on the constancy of study rather than the identity of the individual who conducts this activity; this is implied also by the notion of rotation. According to the logic of this passage, the individual is exchangeable and almost dispensable. The passage in 1QS 6:6b–7a forms part of a series of disparate statements that stand somewhat incongruously side by side the material that precedes and follows. This was noted already by Michael Knibb who writes of this part of the Rule of the Community that it is "somewhat miscellaneous in character, and it is plausible to think that material of diverse origin and date has been brought together."[50] The opening lines of column 6 stand apart from the remainder of the Rule by referring to 'all their dwelling places' and by including two directives on how to conduct business in a place where ten come together. It is this distinctive material that has inspired John Collins's recent re-evaluation of the Qumran Yaḥad as an 'umbrella organization' of a plurality of communities and as a movement rather than a single, localised community.[51] Sarianna Metso, on the other hand, has proposed instead that the quorum of ten individuals refers to travelling members of the one Yaḥad

---

[46] Boling, *Joshua*, 125.

[47] None of the Cave 4 manuscripts of the Rule preserve these words. The immediate context has survived in 4Q258 (4QS^d) 2 10b, but all that can be said on the basis of the size of the lacuna is that this manuscript preserved a considerably shorter text than 1QS, cf. DJD 26:99–100 and Plate 12 (Alexander and Vermes).

[48] The rendering "one replacing the other" is based on an emendation of the Hebrew יפות על to read חליפות frequently adopted by commentators.

[49] So already William H. Brownlee, *The Dead Sea Manual of Discipline* (BASORSup 10–12; New Haven: ASOR, 1951), 24.

[50] Michael A. Knibb, *The Qumran Community* (Cambridge Commentaries on Writings of the Jewish and Christian World 200 BC to AD 200 2; Cambridge: CUP, 1987), 113.

[51] Collins, *Beyond the Qumran Community*.

who meet while away from the community centre.⁵² Both views, even though rather different, read the material as indicative of geographic diversity. I have devoted three studies to this part of the Rule where I take a different approach.⁵³ Rather than interpreting this material as indicative of a geographical spread, I have suggested that the diverse statements preserved in the opening lines 1QS 6 give us a flavour of embryonic beginnings of communal life. I have variously stressed,

- The small scale set-up of loosely organized groups of like-minded individuals;
- The grass roots flavour of study as opposed to other passages that advocate much more restricted access to the correct interpretation of scripture from what is described here, cf., e. g. 1QS 5:8–9, where prospective members are enjoined to "take upon themselves a binding oath to return to the law of Moses according to all that He has commanded with all (their) heart and all (their) soul according to all that has been revealed from it to the sons of Zadok the priests who keep the covenant [...] and to the multitude of the people of their covenant." Here the sons of Zadok and the people of their covenant are presented as almost exclusive channels of correct interpretation.
- The pragmatic colour of the description which contrasts with the much more ideologically and theologically fine-tuned account of small scale community origins in 1QS 8:1: "The council of the community shall be made up of twelve (lay) people and three priests, perfect in everything that has been revealed from the whole law." The 1QS 8 description is clearly theologically motivated representing the twelve tribes plus the sons of Levi according to Num 3:17.⁵⁴
- I suggested, moreover, that the reference to the three core activities of meeting to eat together, pray together and exchange council together constitute "a very basic level of social interaction between likeminded Jews."⁵⁵ We note that yaḥad here occurs as an adverb and not yet as the technical self-designation it was to become – a development perhaps based on its initial adverbial usage in passages like the opening lines of 1QS 6.

In sum, the opening lines of column 6 comprise a mixture of heterogenous material, some of which gives the impression of going back to the earliest and simplest beginnings of communal life. 1QS 6:6b–7a, which closely resembles Josh 1:8 and Ps 1:2, portrays continuous study of the law as "a shared grassroots com-

---

⁵² Metso, 'Whom Does the Term Yaḥad Identify?,' in *Biblical Traditions in Transmission: Essays in Honour of Michael A. Knibb* (ed. Charlotte Hempel and Judith M. Lieu; JSJSup 111; Leiden: Brill, 2006), 213–235.

⁵³ Charlotte Hempel, 'Interpretative Authority in the Community Rule Tradition,' *DSD* 10 (2003): 59–80; eadem, 'Emerging Communal Life and Ideology,' reprinted as Chapter 5 above; and eadem, '1QS 6:2c–4a – Satellites or Precursors,' reprinted as Chapter 6 above.

⁵⁴ See already Józef T. Milik, *Ten Years of Discovery in the Wilderness of Judaea* (SBT 26; London: SCM, 1959), 100.

⁵⁵ Hempel, 'Emerging Communal Life and Ideology,' 45 and Chapter 5 above.

modity that characterised the community from its earliest days in small groups."⁵⁶ Elsewhere in the Rule access to the correct interpretation of the law becomes restricted to particular interpreters or groups of leading priests. Whereas Steven Fraade would speak of "'elitist' and 'egalitarian'" Torah ethics" operating side by side in the Qumran community,⁵⁷ I proposed that both approaches go back to different periods in the development of the community.

If we try to approach both the two late passages from the Hebrew Bible and what, on my reading of the evidence, is a glimpse of an embryonic kernel of communal activity in 1QS 6 without immediately assuming that one is simply quoting the other, both sets of agendas are less distant from one another than one might expect. All three passages stress the need to apply oneself to the Torah continually. It is at least worth considering that the Scrolls passage is not merely alluding to or even quoting the biblical sister passages as objectified source texts, but that a shared agenda and maybe even a cognate way of life lies behind all three passages. Here I would like to draw on what Susan Niditch has called 'traditional referentiality,' as opposed to direct quotation, as a way of accounting for recurring phrases in the Hebrew Bible.⁵⁸ If, as seems likely, a group of pious Torah scholars advocate a lifestyle not too removed from what our passages promote, then it is likely that the language that recurs in all three texts became 'formulaic' in Niditch's terms, something like a mantra, in those circles.⁵⁹ The increased recognition of orality in the development of ancient Hebrew literature advocated by Niditch and others should make us hesitate in assuming the work of the ancient scholar was reminiscent of our own endeavours in looking for quotes and turning pages followed – hopefully – by conscientious acknowledgments in the footnotes.

Alongside the possibility of a shared outlook over and above the shared language between the late biblical statements and the Scrolls passage, there are subtle differences also, especially the strong *emphasis on study* (דרש) in the Scrolls as opposed to more straightforward recitation (הגה) in the Bible. Both Joshua 1 and Psalm 1 appear confident that the benefits of Torah are freely accessible to Joshua and the righteous one. In the 1QS 6 passage, by contrast, it is necessary to be more searching. Moreover, elsewhere in the Community Rule we notice a progressive narrowing of access to the privilege of arriving at the correct understanding of the law. The element of immediacy is gradually waning. We are reminded also of Neh 8:7–9 where the simple public reading of the

---

⁵⁶ Hempel, 'Interpretative Authority in the Community Rule Tradition,' 79.
⁵⁷ Steven Fraade, 'Interpretative Authority in the Studying Community at Qumran,' *JJS* 44 (1993): 46–69, 68.
⁵⁸ Susan Niditch, *Oral World and Written Word: Ancient Israelite Literature* (Library of Ancient Israel; Louisville, Ky.: Westminster John Knox, 1996), 18–19.
⁵⁹ See Niditch, *Oral World and Written Word*, 18.

law to the people requires guidance from Ezra and the Levites in order to reach the assembled people.[60]

Moreover, the pragmatic idea of regulating a rotation of individual members who devote themselves to Torah study introduced in 1QS 6:6–7 is absent from Josh 1:8 and Ps 1:2.[61] It is possible also that the activities described by the different verbs (הגה and דרש) are of intrinsically different quality. Lohfink has argued with reference to Ps 1:2 and Deut 6:6–7 that הגה refers to a type of rhythmic, meditative murmuring,

> Dass man meditierte, indem man, im Rhytmus des Atmens, auswendig gewusste Texte murmelte, wird hier als selbstverständlich vorausgesetzt.[62]

In the same context he also speaks of "einem halblauten, rhytmischen Singsang". If Lohfink is right than it is not inconceivable for devoted individuals to perform such an activity almost constantly.[63]

8. Conclusion

Turning back to my opening remarks on the common mind-set and milieu of anthologizing, archiving, and updating evident in the Qumran texts and the emerging Hebrew Scriptures, I have tried to suggest that the circles that ultimately gave rise to the Qumran milieu are the heirs of the Torah-disciples identified by Rofé as lying behind the 'winding up of the Hebrew Bible.' If my reading of the opening lines of 1QS 6 as preserving a flavour of embryonic communal life is correct, then these embryonic styles of social organization that foreshadow

---

[60] Cf. also Niditch, *Oral World and Written Word*, 124.

[61] Cf. also the stipulation for 'the many' to devote a third of the nights to read the book and study the law in 1QS 6:7b and the instruction in Neh 9:3 for the seed of Israel to confess their sins and read from the book of the law for a fourth of the day.

[62] Norbert Lohfink, 'Psalmengebet und Psalterredaktion,' *Archiv für Literaturwissenschaft* 34 (1992): 1–22, here 6.

[63] In contrast to my own analysis some have argued that in 1QS 6:6–7 דרש refers to instruction on the part of an expert, see, e. g., Johann Maier, 'Early Jewish Biblical Interpretation in the Qumran Literature,' in *Hebrew Bible/Old Testament: The History of Its Interpretation. Volume I: From the Beginnings to the Middle Ages (Until 1300)* (ed. Magne Sæbø; Göttingen: Vandenhoeck & Ruprecht, 1996), 108–129, 115 and Jaffe, *Torah in the Mouth*, 33. I suspect that the intriguing statement found in 1QS 6:6–7 is all too often read in light of better known hierarchical passages. This is explicitly the case in a study by Adiel Schremer where the quotation of 1QS 6:6–7 is followed by an emphatic statement stressing the role of the teacher in such endeavours in the Damascus Document, cf. Schremer, '"[T]he[y] Did not Read in the Sealed Book:" Qumran Halakhic Revolution and the Emergence of Torah Study in Second Temple Judaism,' in *Historical Perspectives: From the Hasmoneans to Bar Kokhba in Light of the Dead Sea Scrolls: Proceedings of the Fourth International Symposium of the Orion Center for the Study of the Dead Sea Scrolls and Associated Literature, 27–31 January 1999* (ed. David Goodblatt, Avital Pinnick, and Daniel R. Schwartz; STDJ 37; Leiden: Brill, 2001), 105–126, esp. 112.

the fully-fledged Yaḥad – pre-sectarian or incipit sectarian practices – offer opportunities to bridge the gap back to the circles that shaped the final stages of parts of the Hebrew Bible. Similar suggestions with results compatible with my own have been made by Armin Lange in a pair of studies where he explored the connections of the final redaction of the proto-masoretic Psalter, on the one hand, and of Qohelet, on the other hand, to pre-sectarian Qumran sapiential texts such as Mysteries and 4QInstruction.[64] Similarly Reinhard Kratz has shown that the ideal of Jewish learning advocated already in the Hebrew Bible (singling out Deut 6:4–9; Ps 1; and Sir 38:34–39:11) continues to find expression in the Scrolls and subsequently in rabbinic literature.[65] It is hoped that my own suggestions encourage us to look for such connections even in some less expected places. Finally, Rudolf Smend's former student the late Timo Veijola explored his teacher's Dtr N hypothesis more fully in a study entitled "Schriftgelehrtentum: Die Deuteronomisten als Vorgänger der Schriftgelehrten. Ein Beitrag zur Entstehung des Judentums."[66] In this study Veijola boldly sets out to identify the late Deuteronomists behind Dtr N – groups of learned exegetes and teachers of the Law – as the predecessors of the post-70 sages, "eine Vorform des Standes der Rechtsgelehrten."[67] He rightly questions the predominant, and rather unlikely, neat division between what he terms 'Hebraismus' and 'Judentum/Judaismus' and observes, "Von daher lässt sich nicht sagen, dass es sich bei der Entstehung des klassischen Judentums um einen unvorhergesehenen Betriebsunfall handle ..."[68] I have tried to argue here that there are good reasons to take a close look at the Dead Sea Scrolls along the way.

---

[64] See Armin Lange, 'Die Endgestalt des protomasoretischen Psalters und die Toraweisheit,' in *Der Psalter in Judentum und Christentum* (ed. Erich Zenger; Biblical Studies 18; Freiburg: Herder, 1998), 101–136 and idem, 'Eschatological Wisdom in the Book of Qohelet and the Dead Sea Scrolls,' in *The Dead Sea Scrolls: Fifty Years After Their Discovery 1947–1997* (ed. Lawrence H. Schiffman, Emanuel Tov, and James C. VanderKam; Jerusalem: IES, 2000), 817–825.

[65] Kratz, *Judentum im Zeitalter des Zweiten Tempels*, 154–155; see also 113–118 with reference to the ideal of Ezra.

[66] Timo Veijola, *Moses Erben: Studien zum Dekalog, zum Deuteronomismus, und zum Schriftgelehrtentum* (Stuttgart: Kohlhammer, 2000), 192–240.

[67] Veijola, *Moses Erben*, 224.

[68] Veijola, *Moses Erben*, 239–240.

Part VIII

Does 4Q Equal Qumran?
The Character of Cave 4 Reconsidered

Chapter Nineteen

'Haskalah' at Qumran:
The Eclectic Character of Qumran Cave 4[1]

1. Introduction

As has been forcefully demonstrated by Devorah Dimant already in 1995, Cave 4 constitutes something of a centre piece of the Qumran library with a great many texts represented in this cave also found elsewhere.[2] Dimant's judgment still has a great deal to commend it. While not suggesting an alternative to her groundbreaking early analysis, this chapter is intended to offer a fresh perspective on the profile of Cave 4. In particular I suggest that alongside its centrality there is also considerable evidence for the distinctive character of the texts from Cave 4 many of which represent a learned and eclectic selection of material and data that was almost certainly intended for a more restricted audience than the bulk of the library.[3] The title of this chapter subtly pays homage to Prof. Schiffman's seminal study *Halakhah at Qumran*[4] as well as provocatively summing up the assessment of Cave 4 proposed below as to a large extent characteristic of the inquisitive broad learning associated with a privileged circle of 'Maskil(im)'.

Before elaborating on my own hypothesis on the profile of Cave 4 it will be helpful to begin with a brief survey of the caves as well as a review of a selection of recent attempts by scholars to describe the profile of the Qumran manuscript collection as a whole as well as the profile of individual caves or clusters of caves.[5]

---

[1] I would like to thank Prof. Steven Fraade (Yale), Prof. Florentino García Martínez (Leuven), Prof. Michael Knibb (London), Prof. Reinhard G. Kratz (Göttingen), Prof. Sacha Stern (UCL, London); Prof. Joan Taylor (King's College, London), Prof. Eibert Tigchelaar (Leuven), and Dr. Mladen Popović (Groningen) for several stimulating conversations and generous collegial exchanges about a range of issues touched upon here. Any shortcomings are, of course, my own.

[2] Devorah Dimant, 'The Qumran Manuscripts: Contents and Significance' in *Time to Prepare the Way in the Wilderness: Papers on the Qumran Scrolls by Fellows of the Institute for Advanced Studies of the Hebrew University, Jerusalem, 1989–1990* (ed. Devorah Dimant and Lawrence H. Schiffman; STDJ 16; Leiden: Brill, 1995), 23–58.

[3] Cf. DJD 21:14, 83 (Talmon).

[4] Lawrence H. Schiffman, *The Halakhah at Qumran* (SJLA 16; Leiden: Brill, 1975).

[5] See George J. Brooke, *Qumran and the Jewish Jesus* (Cambridge: Grove Books, 2005), 8–10; Magen Broshi and Hanan Eshel, 'Residential Caves at Qumran,' *DSD* 6 (1999): 328–348; DJD 1:3–38 (Lankester Harding, DeVaux, and Crowfoot); DJD 3:3–36 (De Vaux); DJD 6:3–22

2. The Qumran Scroll Caves

The caves in the vicinity of Qumran fall into two types.[6] On the one hand the limestone cliffs above the Qumran settlement are dotted with a large number of natural caves. A survey of the area from 1952 led by Roland De Vaux identified 270 caves.[7] These caves have been used for centuries to give shelter to shepherds, fugitives, and travellers. Five such natural caves (Qumran Caves, 1, 2, 3, 6, and 11) have revealed manuscripts. Particular care was taken over the manuscripts deposited in Cave 1 which contained both intact cylindrical jars as well as fragments of around fifty jars.[8] Moreover, the well preserved scrolls found in this cave were wrapped in linen, placed in jars and sealed with bitumen leading a series of scholars to consider Cave 1 as a *genizah* for discarded manuscripts.[9] In her recent treatment of this issue Joan Taylor proposes that Qumran Cave 1

(De Vaux); Jean-Baptiste Humbert and Alain Chambon, *The Excavations of Khirbet Qumran and Ain Feshkha: Synthesis of Roland de Vaux's Field Notes* (trans. Stephen Pfann; NTOASA 1B; Fribourg: Vandenhoeck & Ruprecht, 2003), 65–72; Józef T. Milik, *Ten Years of Discovery in the Wilderness of Judaea* (trans. John Strugnell; SBT 26; London: SCM, 1959), 20–21; Joseph Patrich, 'Khirbet Qumran in Light of New Archaeological Explorations in the Qumran Caves,' in *Archaeology and History in the Dead Sea Scrolls: The New York University Conference in Memory of Yigael Yadin* (ed. Lawrence H. Schiffman; JSPSup 8; Sheffield: JSOT Press, 1990), 73–95; Lawrence H. Schiffman, *Reclaiming the Dead Sea Scrolls: The History of Judaism, the Background to Christianity, the Lost Library of Qumran* (Philadelphia, Pa.: JPS, 1994), 53–61; Hartmut Stegemann, *The Library of Qumran: On the Essenes, Qumran, John the Baptist, and Jesus* (Grand Rapids, Mich.: Eerdmans, 1998), 86–115; Roland de Vaux, *Archaeology and the Dead Sea Scrolls: The Schweich Lectures 1959* (Oxford: OUP; The British Academy, 1973), 52–56.

[6] See, e. g., Broshi and Eshel, 'Residential Caves at Qumran.'

[7] DJD 3:5–13 (De Vaux); Milik, *Ten Years of Discovery*, 17; Sidnie White Crawford, 'Qumran: Caves, Scrolls, and Buildings,' in *A Teacher for All Generations: Essays in Honor of James C. VanderKam* (ed. Eric Mason et al.; JSJSup 153; Leiden: Brill, 2012), 253–273, 257.

[8] Jodi Magness, *Debating Qumran: Collected Essays on Its Archaeology* (Interdisciplinary Studies in Ancient Culture and Religion 4; Leuven: Peeters, 2004), 151; Joan E. Taylor, 'Buried Manuscripts and Empty Tombs: The Qumran Genizah Theory Revisited,' in *'Go Out and Study the Land' (Judges 18:2): Archaeological, Historical and Textual Studies in Honor of Hanan Eshel* (ed. Aren M. Maeir, Jodi Magness, and Lawrence H. Schiffman; JSJSup 148; Leiden: Brill, 2011), 269–315.

[9] Brooke, *Qumran and the Jewish Jesus*, 9; Eleazar L. Sukenik, *The Dead Sea Scrolls of the Hebrew University* (Jerusalem: The Hebrew University; Magnes, 1955), 17–24; Taylor, 'Buried Manuscripts and Empty Tombs,' 275–276; for doubts on the genizah hypothesis see Milik, *Ten Years of Discovery*, 20; de Vaux, *Archaeology and the Dead Sea Scrolls*, 103; and most recently Florentino García Martínez, 'Reconsidering the Cave 1 Texts Sixty Years After Their Discovery: An Overview,' in *Qumran Cave 1 Revisited: Proceedings of the Sixth Meeting of the IOQS, Ljubljana 2007* (ed. Daniel Falk, Sarianna Metso, and Eibert Tigchelaar; STDJ 91; Leiden: Brill, 2010), 1–13, 7–9; Mladen Popović, 'Qumran as Scroll Storehouse in Times of Crisis? A Comparative Perspective on Judaean Desert Manuscript Collections,' *JSJ* 43 (2012): 551–594; White Crawford, 'Caves, Scrolls, and Buildings,' 270–271; for the view that Cave 1's contents may have been forgotten see Daniel Stökl Ben Ezra, 'Old Caves and Young Caves: A Statistical Reevaluation of a Qumran Consensus,' *DSD* 14 (2007): 313–33, 328 n. 54.

testifies to the careful burial of sacred texts containing the divine name. While special burial ceremonies of sacred manuscripts is still Jewish practice to this day, the case of Qumran Cave 1 is distinctive in terms of the lengths to which the owners of these texts went to preserve the buried texts for as long as possible.[10] Others prefer to consider Cave 1 as a hiding place where scrolls were hidden in the face of Roman attack in 68 CE.[11] Most recently Popović highlights the widespread context of 'violence and conflict' as the background to most manuscript depositions in the Judaean desert including Qumran.[12] Care was also taken with the disposal of scrolls in Cave 11.[13] Caves 2 and 8 revealed 33 and 5 fragmentary manuscripts respectively.[14] Finally, Cave 3 contained the remains of around fifteen manuscripts as well as the distinctive Copper Scroll.[15]

A second type of cave (Caves 4, 5, 7, 8, 9, and 10) is of the 'man'-made or artificial variety situated in the clay and limestone terraces on top of which the settlement itself is situated.[16] As convincingly argued by Joan Taylor recently, Qumran Caves 4–5 and 7–10 form an intrinsic part of the archaeological remains found at Qumran "if 'Qumran' is defined not only as buildings but as all the occupation areas" including "artificially-created habitation caves."[17] Of these

---

[10] Taylor, 'Buried Manuscripts and Empty Tombs,' 287.

[11] So, e. g., García Martínez, 'Reconsidering the Cave 1 Texts' who argues Qumran Cave 1 represents a 'cross-section' of the library hidden there for safekeeping; Milik, *Ten Years of Discovery*; Schiffman, *Reclaiming the Dead Sea Scrolls*, 53, 56; Stegemann, *Library of Qumran*, 60–63; De Vaux, *Archaeology and the Dead Sea Scrolls*; for an argument in favour of a deposit of the manuscripts in the space of a single generation in the first century BCE see Gregory Doudna, 'The Legacy of an Error in Archaeological Interpretation: The Dating of the Qumran Cave Scroll Deposits,' in *The Site of the Dead Sea Scrolls: Archaeological Interpretations and Debates* (ed. Katharina Galor, Jean-Baptiste Humbert, and Jürgen Zangenberg; STDJ 57; Leiden: Brill, 2006), 147–157.

[12] Mladen Popović, 'Qumran as Scroll Storehouse.'

[13] Taylor, 'Buried Manuscripts and Empty Tombs,' 276; Emanuel Tov, 'The Special Character of the Texts Found in Qumran Cave 11,' in *Things Revealed: Studies in Early Jewish and Christian Literature in Honor of Michael E. Stone* (ed. Esther G. Chazon, David Satran, and Ruth A. Clements; JSJSup 89; Leiden: Brill, 2004), 187–196; see also Florentino García Martínez, 'Cave 11 in Context,' in *The Dead Sea Scrolls: Texts and Context* (ed. Charlotte Hempel; STDJ 90; Leiden: Brill, 2010), 199–209; Daniel Stökl Ben Ezra, 'Further Reflections on Caves 1 and 11: A Response to Florentino García Martínez,' in *Dead Sea Scrolls: Texts and Context* (ed. Hempel), 211–223, 220; idem, 'Wie viele Bibliotheken gab es in Qumran?,' in *Qumran und die Archäologie* (ed. Jörg Frey, Carsten Claussen, and Nadine Kessler; WUNT 1.278; Tübingen: Mohr Siebeck, 2011), 327–346, 330.

[14] Emanuel Tov, *Revised Lists of the Texts from the Judaean Desert* (Leiden: Brill, 2010), 20–21, 66.

[15] See, e. g., Stegemann, *Library of Qumran*, 68–74 and Stephen Weitzman, 'Copper Scroll (3Q15),' in EDEJ: 486–487.

[16] Broshi and Eshel, 'Residential Caves at Qumran' and DJD 3:21 (De Vaux).

[17] Taylor, 'Buried Manuscripts and Empty Tombs,' 274; see also De Vaux, *Archaeology and the Dead Sea Scrolls*, 56; Milik, *Ten Years of Discovery*, 20–21; Stephen Pfann, 'Qumran,' in *Encyclopaedia Judaica* (ed. Michael Berenbaum and Fred Skolnik; 2d. ed.; Detroit, Mich.: Macmillan, 2006), Vol. 16, 768–775, 771–775; Stökl Ben Ezra, 'Old Caves and Young Caves,' 322; and White Crawford, 'Caves, Scrolls, and Buildings,' 260.

artificial caves several exhibit distinctive traits. Cave 6 contained a large proportion of papyri,[18] and Cave 7 revealed exclusively Greek texts and is perhaps best identified as a personal selection or a particular part of the larger library concealed in this cave.[19] Cave 8 contained a large number of leather straps which point to its purpose as a workshop.[20] Around twenty five documents were recovered from Cave 5.[21] Very few literary remains were recovered from Caves 9 and 10. A small papyrus fragment preserving the remains of six letters survives from Cave 9,[22] and Cave 10 contained a lamp, a floor mat, and an ostracon preserving two letters, perhaps the beginning of a personal name as well as dates.[23] Broshi and Eshel estimate that the number of artificial caves in the vicinity of Qumran was once in the region of twenty to forty.[24] Our main concern is with the contents of Cave 4 to which we now turn.

3. Qumran Cave 4

Cave 4 was discovered in 1952, first by Bedouin and soon afterwards by archaeologists, and contains by far the largest number of texts, having revealed the remains of almost 700 documents.[25] This figure compares with less than eighty texts found in Cave 1 and even smaller quantities in the other caves.[26] However, the figure of almost 700 texts needs to be put in perspective. One of the characteristics of Cave 4, and one of the main reasons why the publication of its contents was delayed to such a degree, is that most of the texts found in it are very fragmentary. That is to say, even though Cave 4 revealed around 600 more documents than did Cave 1, this does not mean that it revealed more running text were one to count the completely preserved words and lines of text. In contrast to Cave 4, Caves 1 and 11 produced a number of very well preserved scrolls of

---

[18] Stökl Ben Ezra, 'Old Caves and Young Caves,' 323–324.

[19] See, e. g., Stökl Ben Ezra, 'Old Caves and Young Caves,' 323 and White Crawford, 'Caves, Scrolls, and Buildings,' 265.

[20] See, e. g., Broshi and Eshel, 'Residential Caves at Qumran,' 334 and Taylor, 'Buried Manuscripts and Empty Tombs,' 294, 305.

[21] DJD 3:167–197 (Milik) and Tov, *Revised Lists*, 63.

[22] Broshi and Eshel, 'Residential Caves at Qumran,' 334; see also DJD 3:31 (de Vaux) and 163 (Baillet) and Schiffman, *Reclaiming the Dead Sea Scrolls*, 56.

[23] Broshi and Eshel, 'Residential Caves at Qumran,' 334 and DJD 3:31 (de Vaux) and 164 (Baillet).

[24] Broshi and Eshel, 'Residential Caves at Qumran,' 335.

[25] Brooke, *Qumran and the Jewish Jesus*, 9; Dimant, 'The Qumran Manuscripts;' DJD 3:9–22 (De Vaux); Milik, *Ten Years of Discovery*, 16–18, 20; Mladen Popović, 'The Manuscript Collections: An Overview,' in *The T & T Clark Companion to the Dead Sea Scrolls* (ed. George Brooke and Charlotte Hempel; London: T & T Clark, forthcoming); Schiffman, *Reclaiming the Dead Sea Scrolls*, 54–56; De Vaux, *Archaeology and the Dead Sea Scrolls*, 52; White Crawford, 'Caves, Scrolls, and Buildings,' 266–267.

[26] Milik, *Ten Years of Discovery*, 21 and Tov, *Revised Lists*, 6–20.

many meters in length such as the Community Rule (1QS) and the Great Isaiah Scroll (1QIsa[a]) or the Temple Scroll (11QT[a]). Each of these single documents contains as much text as a very large number of fragmentary documents from Cave 4 taken together.

De Vaux and Milik were both of the view that the contents of Cave 4 came from the main library once housed on the settlement and hurriedly concealed in the marl cave in the face of a Roman onslaught.[27] On the basis of pottery remains Milik also suggested very early on that Cave 4 "had once served as a cell for a hermit."[28] Brooke notes it is "naturally air conditioned by the desert winds which come up the valley", and Broshi and Eshel confirm that it is still the only place to offer ambient shelter in the summer heat to this day.[29] By all accounts, Cave 4 would have offered superior accommodation for what one can only assume to have been elevated members of the resident community.

Scholars have suggested a number of different uses for Cave 4 beyond serving as a comfortable and conveniently located place of habitation: a library[30] or the 'stacks' of a library.[31] Schiffman, in particular, has suggested that the holes found in the main chamber of Cave 4 once served as a means of fixing wooden shelves. Over time the wood would have perished and left the manuscripts scattered over the floor of the cave.[32] Taylor, by contrast, suggests Cave 4 served as part of a temporary storage and workshop facility to prepare manuscripts for preservation elsewhere[33] and attributes the fragments of manuscripts scattered across the floor of the cave to an ancient disturbance.[34] By contrast, Cross suggests a disorderly and hurried deposit rather than a disturbance by outsiders.[35]

---

[27] Milik, *Ten Years of Discovery*, 20 and De Vaux, *Archaeology and the Dead Sea Scrolls*, 105.

[28] Milik, *Ten Years of Discovery*, 20; see also Stökl Ben Ezra, 'Old Caves and Young Caves,' 328–329.

[29] Brooke, *Qumran and the Jewish Jesus*, 9 and Broshi and Eshel, 'Residential Caves at Qumran,' 332.

[30] Dimant, 'The Qumran Manuscripts,' 36; Armin Lange, 'The Qumran Dead Sea Scrolls – Library or Manuscript Collection?,' in *From 4QMMT to Resurrection: Mélanges qumraniens en hommage à Émile Puech* (ed. Florentino García Martínez, Annette Steudel, and Eibert Tigchelaar; STDJ 61; Leiden: Brill, 2006), 177–193, 191; Schiffman, *Reclaiming the Dead Sea Scrolls*, 54–57.

[31] Stegemann, *Library of Qumran*, 74 and Stökl Ben Ezra, 'Old Caves and Young Caves,' 327–329.

[32] Schiffman, *Reclaiming the Dead Sea Scrolls*, 56; see also Jean-Baptiste Humbert, 'L'espace sacré à Qumrân,' *RB* 101 (1994): 161–214, 194–195 who suggests we are dealing with a meticulously planned hidden library complex hollowed out in the marl terrace.

[33] Taylor, 'Buried Manuscripts and Empty Tombs,' 292–295.

[34] Taylor, 'Buried Manuscripts and Empty Tombs,' 299; see also DJD 3:21–22 (De Vaux) and Milik, *Ten Years of Discovery*, 20.

[35] Frank M. Cross, *The Ancient Library of Qumran and Modern Biblical Studies* (Grand Rapids, Mich.: Baker, 1961), 27 followed by White Crawford, 'Caves, Scrolls, and Buildings,' 272; see also Mladen Popović, 'Roman Book Destruction in Qumran Cave 4 and the Roman Destruction of Khirbet Qumran Revisited,' in *Qumran und die Archäologie* (ed. Frey, Claussen

To a significant degree the scandal about the delay in the full publication of the Dead Sea Scrolls that came to a head in the closing decade of the twentieth century was a scandal about the publication of the contents of Cave 4.[36] Since 1991 all qualified scholars have been able to gain a picture of the make-up of the entire library including the rich contents of Cave 4. To be sure, a number of Cave 4 texts had been published already prior to 1991, but this group makes up only a small portion of the contents of that cave.[37]

4. The Profile of the Caves

In the wake of gaining comprehensive access to the contents of Cave 4 a number of scholars have offered competing narratives about the profile of the collection in its entirety as well as of individual caves, especially with reference to the abundant Caves 1, 4 and 11.[38]

Before considering a selection of analyses, a word of caution is in order. Thus, Michael Stone and Joan Taylor in particular have recently stressed that the corpus we have today does not represent a complete picture of the contents of the caves as left in antiquity.[39] Firstly, a number of reports of discoveries of manuscripts in caves near Jericho have come down to us from antiquity.[40] Thus, according to the church father Eusebius (*Ecclesiastical History* 6.16.3) Origen (ca. 185–254 CE) was able to draw on a Greek text of the Psalter that was

---

and Kessler), 239–291 who raises further doubts about Roman interference with the contents of Cave 4.

[36] James C. VanderKam and Peter Flint, *The Meaning of the Dead Sea Scrolls: Their Significance for Understanding the Bible, Judaism, Jesus and Christianity* (London: T & T Clark, 2002), 379–403; see also Weston Fields, *The Dead Sea Scrolls: A Full History* (Leiden: Brill, 2009).

[37] Esp. DJD 5 (Allegro with Anderson), a somewhat controversial volume both in terms of the dynamics between its editor and the other members of the editorial team and with respect to the quality of the editions, see John Strugnell, 'Notes en marge du Volume V des 'Discoveries in the Judaean Desert of Jordan,' *RQ* 7 (1970): 163–276 and most recently George J. Brooke, 'Dead Sea Scrolls Scholarship in the United Kingdom,' in *The Dead Sea Scrolls in Scholarly Perspective: A History of Research* (ed. Devorah Dimant; STDJ 99; Leiden: Brill, 2012), 449–486, 453–458 and the important preliminary studies towards a re-edition of DJD 5 in George J. Brooke and Jesper Høgenhaven, *The Mermaid and the Partridge: Essays from the Copenhagen Conference on Revising Texts from Cave Four* (STDJ 96; Leiden: Brill, 2011).

[38] For recent comprehensive overviews see Popović, 'The Manuscript Collections,' and Tigchelaar 'The Dead Sea Scrolls,' in EDEJ: 163–180.

[39] Michael E. Stone, 'The Scrolls and the Literary Landscape of Second Temple Judaism,' in *The Dead Sea Scrolls: Texts and Context* (ed. Hempel), 15–30 and Taylor, 'Buried Manuscripts and Empty Tombs.'

[40] Popović, 'The Manuscript Collections;' Stegemann, *Library of Qumran*, 67–78; Stone, 'The Scrolls and the Literary Landscape,' 17–18; and Taylor, 'Buried Manuscripts and Empty Tombs, 298, 302, 305–306.

found in a jar near Jericho in preparing his famous Hexapla.⁴¹ Several centuries later, in about 800 CE, an undated letter by the Nestorian Patriarch Timothy I of Seleucia (modern day Baghdad) to the Metropolitan of Elam refers to the discovery of books of the Old Testament in a cave near Jericho.⁴² Such earlier discoveries almost certainly explain how copies of ancient Jewish texts attested in the Qumran caves such as the Damascus Document and the Aramaic Levi Document emerged in the form of mediaeval copies from the riches of the Cairo Genizah.⁴³ Furthermore, the sparse textual remains uncovered in Cave 3 probably preserve the rump of a once much more extensive cache of manuscripts.⁴⁴ As Taylor rightly stresses, we have no idea of the number of ancient discoveries in the caves near Qumran and there is no need to presuppose the few isolated literary reports of such discoveries from antiquity offer a full record. Rather, "… these are instances that just happen to be recorded and survived for posterity within the written record."⁴⁵ Further evidence along these lines was brought to light by Hannah Cotton and Erik Larson in the course of their careful analysis of a rather unusual opisthograph 4Q460/4Q350 from Cave 4.⁴⁶ Cotton and Larson propose a plausible scenario of ancient 'tampering' with the contents of Cave 4 after the Roman siege of Qumran and prior to the discoveries near Jericho which were to benefit Origen.⁴⁷ Uniquely 4Q460/4Q350 attests the remains of a Hebrew literary text on the recto (4Q460) alongside parts of a documentary text in Greek (4Q350) preserving an account of cereal quantities on the verso of 4Q460 fragment 9.⁴⁸ The Greek documentary text is likely of post-68 CE provenance, perhaps the work of a Roman soldier, since it is hard to imagine a Jewish scribe would re-use a religious document which includes the divine name (4Q460 9 i 10) in order to record quantities of cereal.⁴⁹ In summing up their case Cotton and Larson stress that the Greek document 4Q350 represents "the only certain evidence for Roman hands tampering with the contents of the Cave, and for human access to the Cave soon after the destruction of the settlement in Qumran."⁵⁰

---

⁴¹ Cotton and Larson, '4Q460/4Q350 and Tampering with Qumran Texts in Antiquity?,' in *Emanuel: Studies in Hebrew Bible, Septuagint and Dead Sea Scrolls in Honor of Emanuel Tov* (ed. Shalom Paul et al.; VTSup 94; Leiden: Brill, 2003), 113–126; 113; Popović, 'The Manuscript Collections;' Stegemann, *Library of Qumran*, 76–77; and Stone, 'The Scrolls and the Literary Landscape,' 17.

⁴² Cotton and Larson, 'Tampering with Qumran Texts,' 113; Paul E. Kahle, *The Cairo Genizah* (2d ed.; Oxford: Blackwell, 1959), 16–17; Popović, 'The Manuscript Collections;' Stegemann, *Library of Qumran*, 68–72; and Stone, 'The Scrolls and the Literary Landscape,' 17–18.

⁴³ Kahle, *Cairo Genizah*, 17 and Stefan Reif, 'Cairo Genizah,' in EDSS 1:105–108.

⁴⁴ Stegemann, *Library of Qumran*, 68–71.

⁴⁵ Taylor, 'Buried Manuscripts and Empty Tombs,' 300.

⁴⁶ Cotton and Larson, 'Tampering with Qumran Texts.'

⁴⁷ Cotton and Larson, 'Tampering with Qumran Texts,' 114.

⁴⁸ Cotton and Larson, 'Tampering with Qumran Texts,' 116.

⁴⁹ Cotton and Larson, 'Tampering with Qumran Texts,' 122.

⁵⁰ Cotton and Larson, 'Tampering with Qumran Texts,' 125; see also DJD 36:294–205 (Cot-

Moreover, during an exploration of the marl terraces north of Khirbet Qumran Magen Broshi and Hanan Eshel identified several instances where earlier caves have partially or totally eroded and collapsed.[51] Finally, the considerable number of fragments that are as yet unidentified eloquently attest to the loss of a considerable number of further texts.[52] In sum, as Joan Taylor astutely observes,

> All our conclusions about what was in the caves in terms of the manuscript repertoire are based on randomly surviving items. [...] The maximum extent of the scrolls corpus remains unclear ...[53]

Having established the limitations of scholarly efforts to offer a definitive account of the profile of the manuscripts from Qumran the issue has nevertheless provoked a substantial amount of constructive discussion since the early 1990ies.

Pioneering work was undertaken by Devorah Dimant with the publication in 1995 of a seminal paper on the profile of the library as a whole.[54] Dimant's primary interest was in the corpus as a whole from a literary perspective.[55] She paid particular attention also to the issue of provenance advocating a key distinction between non-biblical compositions that attest 'Community Terminology' (CT) and others 'without Community Terminology' (NCT).[56]

Dimant also highlighted the considerable extent to which Cave 4 forms an axis around which the remainder of the collection accumulates since many texts found in Cave 4 are also attested in one or more other cave.[57] The centrality of Cave 4 and its inter-relatedness to the other scroll caves is often taken to indicate that the Qumran scrolls form a coherent collection where principal works are attested in two, three, and sometimes even five caves.[58] More recently scholars have recognized and begun to circumscribe a plurality of perhaps inter-related collections at Qumran.[59]

---

ton); DJD 36:369–386 (Larson). For a recent critical re-assessment of the evidence for Roman interference with the contents of Cave 4 see Popović, 'Roman Book Destruction.'

[51] Broshi and Eshel, 'Residential Caves at Qumran' and Stone, 'The Scrolls and the Literary Landscape,' 18.

[52] Stone, 'The Scrolls and the Literary Landscape,' 16.

[53] Taylor, 'Buried Manuscripts and Empty Tombs,' 298.

[54] Dimant, 'The Qumran Manuscripts.'

[55] Dimant, 'The Qumran Manuscripts,' 25 where she identifies "the need for a comprehensive literary description of the Qumran collection" as the starting point of her own efforts.

[56] Dimant, 'The Qumran Manuscripts,' 26 passim; for a recent refinement of her analysis for determining sectarian provenance see Devorah Dimant, 'The Vocabulary of the Qumran Sectarian Texts,' in *Qumran und die Archäologie* (ed. Jörg Frey, Carsten Claussen, and Nadine Kessler; WUNT 1.278; Tübingen: Mohr Siebeck, 2011), 347–395.

[57] Dimant, 'The Qumran Manuscripts,' 35, 44; Devorah Dimant, 'The Library of Qumran: Its Content and Character,' in *The Dead Sea Scrolls Fifty Years After Their Discovery 1947–1997* (ed. Lawrence H. Schiffman, Emanuel Tov, and James C. VanderKam; Jerusalem: IES, 2000), 170–176; see also Stökl Ben Ezra, 'Old Caves and Young Caves.'

[58] Dimant, 'The Qumran Manuscripts.'

[59] Stephen Pfann, 'Reassessing the Judean Desert Caves: Libraries, Archives, Genizas and Hiding Places,' *Bulletin of the Anglo-Israel Archaeological Society* 25 (2007): 147–170;

In 2007 Daniel Stökl Ben Ezra offered another comprehensive analysis of the Qumran manuscripts based on a close study of the average age of the documents found in each cave. In particular, he stressed that the average age of the manuscripts found in Caves 1 and 4 (labelled 'old caves') differs significantly from the average scroll age of Caves 2, 3, 5, 6, and 11 ('young caves') concluding that while the contents of the Qumran caves go back to one and the same community they were deposited on two main occasions: in the face of an enemy attack in 9/8 BCE and then again in the face of the Roman offensive of 68 CE.[60] Stökl Ben Ezra is concerned with determining the average scroll age for each cave rather than being guided by the earliest or latest manuscript attested in a given cave.[61]

Alongside the studies by Dimant and Stökl Ben Ezra the profile of the collection as a whole as well as of individual caves continues to attract a considerable amount of scholarly attention in recent years.[62]

5. Distinctive Elements in the Profile of Qumran Cave 4

In what follows I will offer my own observations on the character of Cave 4 from a number of different perspectives. Given the fragmentary nature of the manuscripts preserved in this cave particular weight will be attached to quantifiable evidence pointing in a particular direction in the surviving remains. In an effort to avoid arguing from silence attention will be paid to the kind of 'noise' our evidence seems to preserve in spite of its fragmentary quality.

It is undoubtedly true that Cave 4 is intrinsically connected to the contents of the other major scroll caves, especially Caves 1 and 11, and Dimant was the first to demonstrate the centrality of its contents.[63] There is no doubt, moreover, that

---

Popović, 'The Manuscript Collections;' Stökl Ben Ezra, 'Old Caves and Young Caves,' 316 and 322–323 raising the possibility that some caves "reflect a specific library section" or a reader's preferences; see also idem, 'Wie viele Bibliotheken,' 333.

[60] Stökl Ben Ezra, 'Old Caves and Young Caves.' On the archaeological evidence for a brief period of abandonment of the site of Qumran in the wake of an enemy attack in 9/8 BCE see Jodi Magness, *The Archaeology of Qumran and the Dead Sea Scrolls* (Grand Rapids, Mich.: Eerdmans, 2002), 67–68.

[61] Stökl Ben Ezra, 'Old Caves and Young Caves;' see also idem, 'Wie viele Bibliotheken?;' idem, 'Further Reflections on Caves 1 and 11;' and García Martínez, 'Cave 11 in Context.'

[62] See especially Brooke, *Qumran and the Jewish Jesus*, 8–10; Devorah Dimant, 'The Composite Character of the Qumran Sectarian Literature as an Indication of Its Date and Provenance,' *RQ* 22 (2006): 615–630; García Martínez, 'Reconsidering the Cave 1 Texts;' idem, 'Cave 11 in Context;' Lange, 'The Qumran Dead Sea Scrolls;' Pfann, 'Qumran;' idem, 'Reassessing the Judean Desert Caves;' Popović, 'The Manuscript Collections;' idem, 'Qumran as Scroll Storehouse;' Stegemann, *Library of Qumran*, 58–79; Taylor, 'Buried Manuscripts and Empty Tombs;' Tigchelaar 'The Dead Sea Scrolls;' Tov, 'The Special Character of Cave 11;' and White Crawford, 'Caves, Scrolls, and Buildings,' 265–273.

[63] Dimant, 'The Qumran Manuscripts,' 23–24; see also eadem, 'The Library of Qumran;' and White Crawford, 'Caves, Scrolls, and Buildings,' 267.

Caves 1 and 4 are particularly closely connected.[64] This is evident not least on the basis of the same scribe having copied 4QTestimonia (4Q175), 1QS, 1QSa, 1QSb, 4QSam^c and corrected 1QIsa^a[65] and perhaps many more documents.[66]

It is nevertheless illuminating to step back from this assessment of Cave 4 and recognize that its contents are also rather distinctive from the point of view of the sorts of texts found within it and in what numbers. Because of the fragmentary nature of the Cave 4 manuscripts their publication was delayed considerably. A consequence of this delay, which was accompanied by increased anticipation and a heightened sense curiosity, the texts from Cave 4 were for a long time and quite rightly considered the missing pieces of the literary Qumran master-jigsaw.[67] While I do not want to gainsay the connections and compatibilities between Cave 4 and the remainder of the collection it is nevertheless timely to try to account for areas where the Cave 4 cache of manuscripts is also distinctive.

In what follows the intention is to offer some fresh reflections on the overall character of Qumran Cave 4 with particular emphasis on some distinctive features. Given the complexity and the subtlety of our evidence, it is rarely possible to make absolute claims. A case can be made, however, that the evidence indicates, on balance, that the contents of this cave are particularly eclectic and diverse, both in terms of content and the sheer number of manuscripts, in comparison with the profile of the other scroll caves. We will begin with a consideration of the texts written in cryptic script.

5.1 Texts Written in Cryptic Script

One segment of the Qumran library that is attested almost exclusively in Cave 4 is a group of fifty five texts written in cryptic script.[68] These numbers are approximate since most of the cryptic texts are fragmentarily preserved leaving us

---

[64] Dimant, 'Composite Character of the Qumran Sectarian Literature;' Stökl Ben Ezra, 'Old Caves and Young Caves;' also García Martínez, 'Reconsidering the Cave 1 Texts.'

[65] See recently Jonathan Campbell, *The Exegetical Texts* (CQS 4; London: T & T Clark, 2004), 89; and Emanuel Tov, *Scribal Practices and Approaches Reflected in the Texts Found in the Judean Desert* (STDJ 54; Leiden: Brill, 2004), 23.

[66] Ada Yardeni, 'A Note on a Qumran Scribe,' in *New Seals and Inscriptions, Hebrew, Idumean and Cuneiform* (ed. Meir Lubetski; Hebrew Bible Monographs 8; Sheffield: Phoenix, 2007), 287–298; see also White Crawford, 'Caves, Scrolls, and Buildings,' 267.

[67] See Dimant, 'The Qumran Manuscripts,' 30 and Schiffman, *Reclaiming the Dead Sea Scrolls*, 54.

[68] See DJD 20:1–30, esp. 9–13 (Pfann and Kister); DJD 36:524–533 (Pfann); Emanuel Tov, 'Lists of Specific Groups of Texts from the Judaean Desert,' in DJD 39:203–228, 227–228; and idem, *Scribal Practices and Approaches*, 51–52, 259–260.

with a fair number of uncertain identifications of various documents and copies thereof.[69]

There is little doubt, though, that we do have a significant number of cryptic texts at Qumran, and that virtually all of them hail from Cave 4. To be precise, out of fifty five cryptic texts only one was found outside of Cave 4, that is 11Q23 cryptA Unidentified Text (see DJD 23:419–420; for details see Table I below).

Not included in this number – nor in the table below – but entirely pertinent, is the closely related encrypted text 4Q186 Zodiacal Physiognomy.[70] 4Q186 is mostly written in reverse order from left to right using a mixture of square Hebrew script, paleo-Hebrew script, a small number of Greek letters as well as a single preserved letter in cryptic script.[71] This curious document attempts to draw astrological inferences from physiognomic characteristics. Though it is not, as first thought, a horoscope, it has recently been described by Popović as "a text representative of the incipient stages of horoscopic astrology in Second Temple period Judaism."[72]

According to Tov the following cryptic texts proper emerged from the Qumran caves[73] including in addition the only cryptic fragment attested outside Cave 4, i. e. 11Q23.[74]

---

[69] For cautionary remarks see García Martínez, 'Reconsidering the Cave 1 Texts,' 5 and Tov, *Scribal Practices and Approaches*, 44, 48–49.

[70] Philip Alexander, 'Physiognomy, Initiation, and Rank in the Qumran Community,' in *Geschichte – Tradition – Reflexion: Festschrift für Martin Hengel zum 70. Geburtstag* (ed. Hubert Cancik, Hermann Lichtenberger, and Peter Schäfer; Tübingen: Mohr Siebeck, 1996), Vol. I, 385–394; idem, '"Wrestling Against Wickedness in High Places:" Magic in the Worldview of the Qumran Community,' in *The Scrolls and the Scriptures: Qumran Fifty Years After* (ed. Stanley Porter and Craig Evans; JSPSup 26; Sheffield: Sheffield Academic Press, 1997), 318–337, 330–333; DJD 5:88–91 (Allegro); Mladen Popović, *Reading the Human Body: Physiognomics and Astrology in the Dead Sea Scrolls* (STDJ 67; Leiden: Brill, 2007); idem, '4Q186. 4QZodiacal Physiognomy: A Full Edition,' in *The Mermaid and the Partridge: Essays from the Copenhagen Conference on Revising Texts from Cave Four* (ed. George J. Brooke and Jesper Høgenhaven; STDJ 96; Leiden: Brill, 2011), 221–258 with extensive bibliography; see also Stephen Pfann, 'The Mount Zion Inscribed Stone Cup: Preliminary Obervations,' in *New Studies in the Archaeology of Jerusalem and its Region* (ed. David Amit, Orit Peleg-Barkat, and Guy D. Stiebel; Jerusalem: The Hebrew University; IAA, 2010), 44–53; and James C. VanderKam, *Calendars in the Dead Sea Scrolls: Measuring Time* (Literature of the Dead Sea Scrolls; London: Routledge, 1998), 88–89.

[71] Popović, *Reading the Human Body*, 25–28; idem, '4Q186,' 227–230; see also Jonathan Ben-Dov, 'Scientific Writings in Aramaic and Hebrew at Qumran: Translation and Concealment,' in *Aramaica Qumranica: Proceedings of the Conference on the Aramaic Texts from Qumran in Aix-en-Provence, 30 June–2 July 2008* (ed. Katell Berthelot and Daniel Stökl Ben Ezra; STDJ 94; Leiden: Brill, 2010), 379–402, 396.

[72] Popović, '4Q186,' 223.

[73] Tov, 'Lists of Specific Groups of Texts,' 227–228 and idem, *Revised Lists*.

[74] Not listed in Tov, 'Lists of Specific Groups of Texts.'

Table I: The Cryptic Texts from Qumran

	Siglum	Name	Edition and Additional Information
1	4Q249	pap cryptA Midrash Sefer Moshe	recto of 4Q250 below; title in square Hebrew script; DJD 35; DJD 36 (Pfann)
2	4Q249a	pap cryptA Serekh ha-'Edah^a (SE^a)	DJD 36 (Pfann)
3	4Q249b	pap cryptA Serekh ha-'Edah^b (SE^b)	DJD 36 (Pfann)
4	4Q249c	pap cryptA Serekh ha-'Edah^c (SE^c)	DJD 36 (Pfann)
5	4Q249d	pap cryptA Serekh ha-'Edah^d (SE^d)	DJD 36 (Pfann)
6	4Q249e	pap cryptA Serekh ha-'Edah^e (SE^e)	DJD 36 (Pfann)
7	4Q249f	pap cryptA Serekh ha-'Edah^f (SE^f)	DJD 36 (Pfann)
8	4Q249g	pap cryptA Serekh ha-'Edah^g (SE^g)	DJD 36 (Pfann)
9	4Q249h	pap cryptA Serekh ha-'Edah^h (SE^h)	DJD 36 (Pfann)
10	4Q249i	pap cryptA Serekh ha-'Edah^i (SE^i)	DJD 36 (Pfann)
11	4Q249j	pap cryptA Lev^h?	DJD 36 (Pfann)
12	4Q249k	pap cryptA Text Quoting Leviticus A	DJD 36 (Pfann)
13	4Q249l	pap cryptA Text Quoting Leviticus B	DJD 36 (Pfann)
14	4Q249m	pap cryptA Hodayot-likeText E	DJD 36 (Pfann)
15	4Q249n	pap cryptA Liturgical Work E?	DJD 36 (Pfann)
16	4Q249o	pap cryptA Liturgical Work F?	DJD 36 (Pfann)
17	4Q249p	pap cryptA Prophecy?	DJD 36 (Pfann)
18	4Q249q	pap cryptA Fg Mentioning the Planting	DJD 36 (Pfann)
19	4Q249r	pap crypticA Unidentified Text A	DJD 36 (Pfann)
20	4Q249s	pap crypticA Unidentified Text B	DJD 36 (Pfann)
21	4Q249t	pap crypticA Unidentified Text C	DJD 36 (Pfann)
22	4Q249u	pap crypticA Unidentified Text D	DJD 36 (Pfann)
23	4Q249v	pap crypticA Unidentified Text E	DJD 36 (Pfann)
24	4Q249w	pap crypticA Unidentified Text F	DJD 36 (Pfann)
25	4Q249x	pap crypticA Unidentified Text G	DJD 36 (Pfann)
26	4Q249y	pap crypticA Unidentified Text H	DJD 36 (Pfann)
27	4Q249z	pap crypticA Miscellaneous Texts A	DJD 36 (Pfann)
28	4Q250	pap cryptA Text Concerning Cultic Service A	DJD 36 (Pfann)
29	4Q250a	pap cryptA Text Concerning Cultic Service B?	Recto and verso; DJD 36 (Pfann)

	Siglum	Name	Edition and Additional Information
30	4Q250b	pap cryptA Text Related to Isa 11	Recto and verso; DJD 36 (Pfann)
31	4Q250c	pap crypticA Unidentified Text I	Recto of 4Q250d; DJD 36 (Pfann)
32	4Q250d	pap crypticA Unidentified Text J	Verso of 4Q250c; DJD 36 (Pfann)
33	4Q250e	pap crypticA Unidentified Text K	Recto of 4Q250f; DJD 36 (Pfann)
34	4Q250f	pap crypticA Unidentified Text L	Verso of 4Q250e; DJD 36 (Pfann)
35	4Q250g	pap crypticA Unidentified Text M	Recto and verso; DJD 36 (Pfann)
36	4Q250h	pap crypticA Unidentified Text N	Recto and verso; DJD 36 (Pfann)
37	4Q250i	pap crypticA Unidentified Text O	Recto and verso; DJD 36 (Pfann)
38	4Q250j	pap cryptic Miscellaneous Texts B	Recto and verso; DJD 36 (Pfann)
39	4Q298	cryptA Words of the Maskil to all Sons of Dawn	DJD 20:1–30 (Pfann and Kister) Title in square Hebrew script
40	4Q313	cryptAMMT^g?	DJD 36:697 699 and Plate 59 (Pfann); PTSDSSP 3:232–233 (Qimron et al.)
41	4Q313a	cryptA Unidentified Text P	DJD 36 (Pfann)
42	4Q313b	cryptA Unidentified Text Q	DJD 36 (Pfann)
43	4Q313c	cryptA Calendrical Document B	DJD 28 (Pfann) Photograph only
44	4Q317	cryptA Lunisolar Calendar olim AstrCrypt, Phases of the Moon	Milik 1974:68 DJD 28 (Pfann) Photograph only Abegg, DSSR 4:58–71
45	4Q324d	cryptA Liturgical Calendar[a]	DJD 28 (Pfann) Photograph only Abegg, DSSR 4:54–55

Siglum	Name	Edition and Additional Information
46 4Q324e	cryptA Liturgical Calendar[b]	DJD 28 (Pfann) Photograph only Abegg, DSSR 4:55–56
47 4Q324f	cryptA Liturgical Calendar[c]?	DJD 28 (Pfann) Photograph only Abegg, DSSR 4:52
48 4Q324g	cryptA Calendrical Document F?	DJD 28 (Pfann) Abegg, DSSR 4:52
49 4Q324h	cryptA Calendrical Document G?	DJD 28 (Pfann) Photograph only Abegg, DSSR 4:52–53
50 4Q324i	cryptA Mishmarot J	DJD 28 (Pfann) Photograph only Abegg, DSSR 4:14–15
51 4Q362	cryptB papUnidentified Text A	DJD 28 (Pfann) Photograph only
52 4Q363	cryptB papUnidentified Text B	DJD 28 (Pfann) Photograph only
53 4Q363a	cryptC Unidentified Religious Text	Pfann, DJD 28 Photograph only
54 4Q363b	Crypt Miscellaneous Texts	DJD 28 (Pfann) Photograph only
55 11Q23	cryptA Unidentified Text not included in Tov list in DJD 39	DJD 23:419–420 (García Martínez, Tigchelaar and van der Woude)

By definition access to this material would have been highly selective and restrictive.[75] The learned nature of the cryptic material is also indicated by the presence of cryptic signs in the margins, and occasionally between the lines, of other texts.[76] According to Tov the scribal annotations in cryptic script draw attention to "matters of special interest" and may even signal "a sectarian code message of some kind."[77]

---

[75] Cf. DJD 20:17 (Pfann and Kister); see also Ben-Dov, 'Scientific Writings in Aramaic and Hebrew at Qumran,' 379–402, 393.

[76] Stephen Pfann, 'The Maskil's Address to All Sons of Dawn,' *JQR* 85 (1994): 203–235, 233–235 and Emanuel Tov, 'Letters of the Cryptic A Script and Paleo-Hebrew Letters Used as Scribal Marks in Some Qumran Scrolls,' *DSD* 2 (1995): 330–339.

[77] Tov, 'Letters of the Cryptic A Script,' 330–331.

Stephen Pfann has recently published preliminary observations on a limestone cup inscription excavated outside the Zion Gate in Jerusalem which includes in line 6 several words in cryptic script.[78] This instance is the first attestation of the Cryptic A script outside of the Dead Sea Scrolls and may reflect a shared priestly milieu.[79]

A number of scholars have drawn attention to an association of the use of cryptic script with the figure of the Maskil,[80] and it is therefore timely to consider the place of this figure in the context of Cave 4.

5.2 The Maskil and Cave 4

Whereas the Maskil is a figure attested across a wide spectrum of texts from Qumran,[81] closer inspection reveals that Cave 4 is something of a 'Maskil hub'. We have the Songs of the Maskil, a collection of apotropaic hymns to be performed by the Maskil (4Q510 Shir^a; 4Q511 Shir^b),[82] the Address by the Maskil to the Sons of Dawn written mostly in cryptic script referred to above (4Q298),[83] as well as a large number of Songs of the Sabbath Sacrifice frequently introduced with a Maskil heading from Cave 4.[84] In addition, one of the Cave 4 copies of the Community Rule is entitled 'Midrash for the Maskil over the people of the law' (4Q258 [4QS^d] 1 1), and the identical phrase appears in the form of a sub-heading in 4QS^b where 1QS 5:1 has a Serekh heading (4Q256 [4QS^b] 9 1).[85]

---

[78] Pfann, 'The Mount Zion Inscribed Stone Cup.'
[79] Pfann, 'The Mount Zion Inscribed Stone Cup.'
[80] Stephen Pfann, 'The Writings in Esoteric Script from Qumran,' in *The Dead Sea Scrolls Fifty Years After Their Discovery* (ed. Schiffman, Tov, and VanderKam), 177–190; see also Alexander, '"Wrestling Against Wickedness in High Places,"' 333 who argues, "A plausible case can be made out for all the coded texts as representing secret doctrine to be kept within the circle of the Maskil."
[81] Charlotte Hempel, '*Maskil(im)* and *Rabbim*: From Daniel to Qumran,' in *Biblical Traditions in Transmission: Essays in Honour of Michael A. Knibb* (ed. Charlotte Hempel and Judith Lieu; JSJSup 111; Leiden: Brill, 2006), 133–156, reprinted as Chapter 15 in this volume and John Kampen, *Wisdom Literature* (ECDSS; Grand Rapids, Mich.: Eerdmans, 2011), 25–28 both of which include references to earlier literature.
[82] Cf. DJD 7:215–262 and Plates 55–71 (Baillet); Alexander, '"Wrestling Against Wickedness in High Places;"' Joseph Angel, 'Maskil, Community, and Religious Experience in the Songs of the Sage (4Q510- 511),' *DSD* 19 (2011): 1–27; and Bilhah Nitzan, *Qumran Prayer and Religious Poetry* (trans. Jonathan Chapman; STDJ 12; Leiden: Brill, 1994), 236–272.
[83] Cf. DJD 20:1–30 (Pfann and Kister); Matthew Goff, *Discerning Wisdom: The Sapiential Literature of the Dead Sea Scrolls* (VTSup 116; Leiden: Brill, 2007), 146–159; Kampen, *Wisdom Literature*, 270–279; Menahem Kister, 'Commentary to 4Q298,' *JQR* 85 (1994): 237–249; Pfann, 'The Maskil's Address.'
[84] PTSDSSP 4B (Newsom and Charlesworth with Strawn).
[85] See Charlotte Hempel, 'The Literary Development of the S-Tradition: A New Paradigm,' *RQ* 22 (2006): 389–401, reprinted as Chapter 7 in this volume; Sarianna Metso, *The Serekh*

Admittedly, the Maskil is attested also in the building blocks of the Cave 1 copy of the Community Rule (1QS) such as the introduction to the Teaching on the Two Spirits (1QS 3:13)[86] and in 1QS 9:12,21 as well as other Cave 1 texts (1QSb 1:1; 3:22; 5:20 and 1QH^a 5:12; 7:21; 20:7 [restored on the basis of 4QH^a]; 24 34; see also 20 14).[87] However, overall we have 40 occurrences of Maskil, 26 of which from Cave 4 over against 11 from Cave 1 and substantially fewer in other caves.[88]

Table II: Profile of Maskil Occurrences in CD and at Qumran

CD	Cave 1	Cave 4	Cave 11
x 2	x11	x26	x1

Even duly taking account of the fact that the participle maskil is employed in a generic sense rather than with reference to a particular office in 4QInstruction[89] and that a number of references to the Maskil constitute multiple attestations of the same passage in different manuscripts (4Q256 [4QS^b] 9 1 and 4Q258 [4QS^d] 1 1; 4Q258 8 5 and 4Q259 [4QS^e] 4 2), the terminology is doubtlessly particularly prominent in Cave 4.

More importantly, we can identify a number of areas where distinctive features that characterize the contents of Cave 4 display various connections with the figure of the Maskil,
– calendric concerns (see section 5.3 below) are associated with the Maskil in the final hymn of 1QS[90] and 1QH^a 20:4–9.[91] It has even been tentatively suggested that "lunar doctrine at Qumran would have been confined to the circle of the Maskil;"[92]

Texts (CQS 9/LSTS 62; London: T & T Clark, 2007); and Schofield, *From Qumran to the Yaḥad: A New Paradigm of Textual Development for the Community Rule* (STDJ 77; Leiden: Brill, 2009) and earlier literature cited there.

[86] See recently Charlotte Hempel, 'The Teaching on the Two Spirits and the Literary Development of the Rule of the Community,' in *Dualism in Qumran* (ed. Geza Xeravits; LSTS 76; London: T & T Clark, 2010), 102–120 with bibliography.

[87] Cf. DJD 40 (Stegemann and Schuller) and Émile Puech, 'Hodayot,' in EDSS 1:365–369, 366–367; see also 11Q17 ShirShabb 7 9.

[88] Abegg, *Dead Sea Scrolls Concordance*, 489, adjusted in light of DJD 40.

[89] Kampen, *Wisdom Literature*, 26–27, 55.

[90] Cf. DJD 26:152, "Calendrical concerns probably fell within his (the Maskil's) province;" see also Ben-Dov, 'Scientific Writings in Aramaic and Hebrew at Qumran,' 394.

[91] See VanderKam, *Calendars in the Dead Sea Scrolls*, 50–51.

[92] Alexander, "'Wrestling Against Wickedness in High Places,'" 335.

- the propagation of documents in cryptic script.[93] Pfann goes as far as labelling Cryptic A "the personal script of the Maskil."[94] It is rather doubtful that the addressees named in the body of the text (children of dawn, people of understanding, etc.) would have been expected to read cryptic script. It is more likely that 4Q298 is the Maskil's 'crib sheet' which would have been delivered orally on his part (note the preponderance of oral terminology such as 'giving ear,' 'listening,' 'lips,' 'words' in the body of the text);
- the attestation of an additional title (4Q258 [4QS^d] 1 1) and sub-title (4Q256 [4QS^b] 9 1) featuring the Maskil in Cave 4 manuscripts of the Community Rule that are lacking from the Cave 1 manuscipt (cf. 1QS 5:1).

Taking into account both the numerical preponderance of references to Maskil/ maskil in texts from Cave 4 alongside the clear connections that can be established between prominent elements of the Cave 4 corpus and the office of the Maskil, a case can be made for a particularly close, albeit not exclusive, connection between the contents of Cave 4 and the Maskil. We have already noted the Maskil's connection to the timely observance of the festivals which brings us to the substantial amount of calendrical literature attested in Cave 4.

5.3 Technical Learning: The Calendar Texts

Cave 4 revealed a large number of technical compositions relating to calendric matters, and all but one of the calendar texts from Qumran are from Cave 4, including also four copies of the Astronomical Book of Enoch (*1 Enoch* 72–82, cf. 4Q208–211).[95] The only exception is the extremely fragmentarily preserved Calendrical Document 6Q17 published in 1962 by Maurice Baillet which contains just two complete words.[96] 6Q17 is referred to as a papyrus fragment (pap-Calendrical Document) in several recent publications.[97] While the fragment is

---

[93] Cf. 4Q298 (Words of the Maskil to the Sons of Dawn) where the Maskil is associated with the most substantially preserved cryptic text both in the heading and the first person singular statements in the body of the work; Pfann reports and endorses Milik's unpublished research on the various Qumran scripts and notes his contention, arrived at on the basis of 4Q298, that Cryptic A was used particularly by the Maskil, see Pfann, 'Writings in Esoteric Script,' 177; also Alexander, 'Physiognomy, Initiation, and Rank,' 391; idem, '"Wrestling Against Wickedness in High Places,"' 333; and Lange, 'The Qumran Dead Sea Scrolls,' 191.

[94] Pfann, 'Writings in Esoteric Script,' 178.

[95] See now James C. VanderKam, '1 Enoch, Astronomical Book of (1 Enoch 72–82),' in EDEJ: 581–583 and further literature cited there.

[96] DJD 3:132–133.

[97] Cf. DSSR 4:78–79; DSSSE 2:1156–1157 and VanderKam, *Calendars in the Dead Sea Scrolls*, 122 n. 30.

found on a plate with several papyrus fragments (6Q16 and 6Q18) it is clearly written on parchment as unambiguously noted by Baillet.[98]

Even before the availability and publication of an extensive corpus of calendrical texts from Cave 4 the issue of the calendar had played an important role in Qumran research from the very beginning.[99] The earliest texts to be published from the corpus of the Scrolls (including the Damascus Document from Cairo [CD]) included a number of brief, not particularly detailed, but firmly phrased and at times polemical statements on matters of calendar and the correct observance of the festivals.[100] In the Community Rule from Cave 1, for instance, 1QS 1:13–15 admonishes community members to observe religious festivals at the ordained time, neither too late nor too early, a passage that is commonly interpreted as hinting at differences of opinion and practice. This interpretation has recently been challenged by Sacha Stern who denies any underlying calendar polemic in favour of a simple admonition to be careful in one's observance.[101] A concern with the proper observance of sacred times is a Leitmotif in the Maskil's hymn in 1QS 9:26–10:8.[102] In the Damascus Document CD 3:14–15 singles out sabbaths and festivals as an area where Israel had gone astray. Another much discussed passage is 1QpHab 11:4–8 where the pesherist offers an interpretation of Hab 2:15 that appears to describe a hostile visit by the Wicked Priest to the Teacher of Righteousness during the Day of Atonement. This passage is traditionally taken to indicate that the Wicked Priest officiating in Jerusalem followed a different calendar from that adhered to by the Teacher and his community or the former would not have been able to absent himself from his own duties during the holiest day of the Jewish calendar.[103]

Read in the context of calendric polemic attested in long known works such as the Book of Jubilees[104] and 1 Enoch,[105] the early phase of calendar research with reference to the Dead Sea Scrolls painted a relatively straightforward picture of a

---

[98] Cf. DJD 3:132, "Peau assez fine, de teinte café au lait clair," and DJD 3: Plate 27.

[99] See the seminal study by Shemaryahu Talmon, 'The Calendar Reckoning of the Sect from the Judaean Desert,' in *Aspects of the Dead Sea Scrolls* (Jerusalem: Magnes, 1958), 162–199.

[100] VanderKam, *Calendars in the Dead Sea Scrolls*, 43–51.

[101] See Sacha Stern, 'The "Sectarian" Calendar of Qumran,' in *Sects and Sectarianism in Jewish History* (ed. Sacha Stern; IJS Studies in Judaica 12; Leiden: Brill, 2011), 39–62.

[102] Cf. Jonathan Ben-Dov, *Head of All Years: Astronomy and Calendars at Qumran in Their Ancient Context* (STDJ 78; Leiden: Brill, 2008), 44–47; VanderKam, *Calendars in the Dead Sea Scrolls*, 46–47.

[103] Cf. Shemaryahu Talmon, 'Yom Hakkippurim in the Habakkuk Scroll,' *Biblica* 32 (1951): 549–563 and VanderKam, *Calendars in the Dead Sea Scrolls*, 45. This interpretation has recently been questioned, see Sacha Stern, 'Qumran Calendars and Sectarianism,' in *The Oxford Handbook of the Dead Sea Scrolls* (ed. Timothy H. Lim and John J. Collins; Oxford: OUP, 2010), 232–253, 245 who plausibly suggests considering the report "as a polemical and edifying tale, rather than as a factual and 'true' historical account;" see further Stern, 'The "Sectarian" Calendar of Qumran.'

[104] Cf. Ben-Dov, *Head of All Years*, 40–44.

[105] See Ben-Dov, *Head of All Years*, 22–40.

community devoted to a highly schematized solar calendar of 364 days per year which systematically bypassed clashes between major festivals and Sabbaths.

More recently, the post-Cave 4 phase of calendar research has resulted in a more complex and challenging picture characterised by an increasingly diverse and expanded corpus of calendar texts with many finer points of interpretation still very much under review.[106]

As the transient nature of the scholarly designations for the calendric compositions indicates, most texts combine data of various kinds including a 364-day solar year, an annual festival cycle, lunar elements, and the priestly courses of service in the Jerusalem Temple often synchronized with one another.[107] Occasionally liturgical elements or even references to key personalities from secular history are integrated into a calendrical scheme also. Some of the texts take their starting point as far back as the creation of the luminaries in Genesis adding to the overwhelming sense of attempting to achieve a comprehensive and harmonious system of divinely ordained time and history.[108]

The following calendrical and related texts have emerged from Qumran Cave 4,
- 4Q317 (cryptA Lunisolar Calendar olim AstrCrypt, Phases of the Moon)
This text is concerned exclusively with an account of the parts of light and darkness visible on the surface of the moon on different days of the month and is devoid of "any religious or cultic feature."[109]
- 4Q318 Zodiology and Brontology ar[110] comprises two distinct texts:[111] a zodiacal calendar noting the movements of the moon across the zodiacal signs in the course of a year and a divinatory text based on the meteorological feature of thunder occurring in the zodiacal signs (brontologion).[112] The zodiacal

---

[106] Cf. Ben-Dov, *Head of All Years*, 4, 11 referring to "multiple 364-day calendar traditions;" DJD 21:1, 14 (Talmon); VanderKam, *Calendars in the Dead Sea Scrolls*, 69, 86; also Uwe Glessmer, 'Calendars in the Qumran Scrolls,' in *The Dead Sea Scrolls After Fifty Years: A Comprehensive Assessment* (ed. Peter W. Flint and James C. VanderKam Leiden: Brill, 1999), Vol. II, 213–278, 268.

[107] For a concise description see Shemaryahu Talmon and Israel Knohl, 'A Calendar Scroll from a Qumran Cave: Mišmarot Bª, 4Q321,' in *Pomegranates and Golden Bells: Studies in Biblical, Jewish, and Near Eastern Ritual, Law, and Literature in Honor of Jacob Milgrom* (ed. David P. Wright, David N. Freedman, and Avi Hurvitz; Winona Lake, Ind.: Eisenbrauns, 1995), 267–301, 269–270.

[108] See Stern, 'Qumran Calendars and Sectarianism,' 242.

[109] VanderKam, *Calendars in the Dead Sea Scrolls*, 76; see also Ben-Dov *Head of All Years*, 140–146, 221–222 and József T. Milik, *The Books of Enoch: Aramaic Fragments of Qumrân Cave 4* (Oxford: OUP, 1974), 68.

[110] Alexander, "'Wrestling Against Wickedness in High Places,'" 333–335; DJD 36:259–274 (Greenfield and Sokoloff); Helen Jacobus, '4Q318: A Jewish Zodiac Calendar at Qumran?,' in *The Dead Sea Scrolls: Texts and Context* (ed. Hempel), 365–395; and VanderKam, *Calendars in the Dead Sea Scrolls*, 88.

[111] Or perhaps two parts of a single composition, cf. VanderKam, *Calendars in the Dead Sea Scrolls*, 88.

[112] Cf. DJD 36:259.

calendar presupposes thirty days per month which corresponds neither with the Qumran solar year nor the Jewish lunar calendar.[113] The editors refer to a comparable combination of texts in tablet II of MUL.APIN and Byzantine period Greek manuscripts,[114] and the document has rightly been described as "an exceedingly learned text."[115]

– 4Q320 Calendrical Document A or Mishmarot A

4Q320 represents the most extensive calendric document from Qumran which arranges the priestly courses of service in the Temple (cf. 1 Chr 24) within a series of solar years.[116] The resulting list of festivals corresponds better to biblical precedents such as Lev 23 and Num 28–29 than the more comprehensive festival calendar known from the Temple Scroll.[117] Unusually the data are presented within a 'literary' framework that highlights the centrality of creation in the foundation of the calendrical system endorsed (cf., e. g., 4Q320 1 i 2–3).[118] The text also displays evidence for attempts to synchronize lunar phenomena with the solar year.[119]

– 4Q321 Calendrical Document B (olim 4Q321 Calendrical Document B^a)

This text co-ordinates solar and lunar dates with priestly courses.[120]

– 4Q321a Calendrical Document/ Mishmarot C (olim Mishmarot B^b)

This fragmentarily preserved document was once considered a second copy of 4Q321, an identification recently called into question.[121] The editor Talmon notes an emphasis on the "progressive decrease of the moon's light and visibility" in this text which he interprets as indicative of a pre-occupation by the authors with demonstrating the superiority of the solar calendar.[122]

– 4Q324b papCalendrical Document A (olim no siglum)

The only preserved calendrical document written on papyrus contains the remains of a list of sabbaths.[123]

– 4Q325 Calendrical Document/Mishmarot D (olim Mishmarot D)

---

[113] DJD 36:264.

[114] DJD 36:270–271.

[115] Alexander, "'Wrestling Against Wickedness in High Places,'" 335.

[116] Ben-Dov, *Head of All Years*, 198–207, 241–243; DJD 21:2, 13–14, 37–63 (Talmon with Ben-Dov); and VanderKam, *Calendars in the Dead Sea Scrolls*, 77–80.

[117] VanderKam, *Calendars in the Dead Sea Scrolls*, 78.

[118] See Ben-Dov, *Head of All Years*, 200–207 and DJD 21:37, 39 (Talmon with Ben-Dov).

[119] Ben-Dov, *Head of All Years*, 198; VanderKam, *Calendars in the Dead Sea Scrolls*, 80.

[120] Ben-Dov, *Head of All Years*, 207–244; DJD 21:13–14; 65–79 (Talmon with Ben-Dov); Veronique Gillet-Didier, 'Calendrier lunaire, calendrier solaire et gardes sacerdotales: recherches sur 4Q321,' *RQ* 20 (2001): 171–205; Talmon and Knohl, 'A Calendar Scroll from a Qumran Cave,' 270; and VanderKam, *Calendars in the Dead Sea Scrolls*, 84–86.

[121] Ben-Dov, *Head of All Years*, 208; see also DJD 21:2, 81–91 (Talmon with Ben-Dov); and VanderKam, *Calendars in the Dead Sea Scrolls*, 86.

[122] DJD 21:82–83.

[123] DJD 21:2, 113–117 (Talmon with Ben-Dov).

This document co-ordinates cycles of sabbaths with the priestly course on duty and festivals.[124]

- 4Q326 Calendrical Document C (olim Mishmarot E[a])
  Previously identified as a Mishmarot text this composition is characterised by Talmon as a register of holy days arranged over the course of a fifty two week solar year.[125]
- 4Q337 Calendrical Document E? (olim Fragment of Calendar)
  A single poorly preserved fragment makes up this text which has been identified as a calendrical document on the basis of three successive occurrences of the phrase 'on the Sabbath.'[126]
- 4Q394 1–2 Calendrical Document D (olim 4Q327 Mishmarot E[b])
  Although initially correctly identified as a separate composition, this text was subsequently published as belonging to 4QMMT.[127] Recent scholarship has reversed this identification, and 4Q394 1–2 is now generally agreed to constitute a separate calendrical document.[128] This document aligns the cycle of sabbaths across a fifty two week solar year with annual festivals.
- 4Q334 Ordo
  This fragmentary text refers to the recital of nightly and daytime 'songs' and 'words of praise' in a sequence of days.[129]

While several of the calendrical documents from Qumran incorporate the priestly courses of service in their calendrical scheme, a number of texts have continued to be identified and designated as Mishmarot proper in recent scholarship (cf. 1 Chr 24):[130] 4Q322 Mishmarot A (olim 4Q323 Mishmarot C[b] 1);[131] 4Q323 Mishmarot B (olim 4Q323 Mishmarot C[b] 2);[132] 4Q324 Mishmarot C (olim

---

[124] DJD 21:2, 123–131 (Talmon with Ben-Dov) and VanderKam, *Calendars in the Dead Sea Scrolls*, 87.

[125] DJD 21:2, 133–138 (Talmon with Ben-Dov) and VanderKam, *Calendars in the Dead Sea Scrolls*, 87.

[126] DJD 21:2, 155–156 (Talmon with Ben-Dov).

[127] DJD 10:6–9, 44–45 (Qimron and Strugnell).

[128] Ben-Dov, *Head of All Years*, 47–48; DJD 21:2; 157–166 (Talmon with Ben-Dov); VanderKam, *Calendars in the Dead Sea Scrolls*, 75–76 (discussion under earlier siglum 4Q327); idem, 'The Calendar, 4Q327, and 4Q394,' in *Legal Texts and Legal Issues: Proceedings of the Second Meeting of the International Organization for Qumran Studies Published in Honour of Joseph M. Baumgarten* (ed. Moshe Bernstein, Florentino García Martínez, and John Kampen; STDJ 23; Leiden: Brill, 1997), 179–194; Hanne von Weissenberg, *4QMMT: Reevaluating the Text, the Function, and the Meaning of the Epilogue* (STDJ 82; Leiden: Brill, 2009), 33–38, 230.

[129] Ben-Dov, *Head of All Years*, 139–140 and DJD 21:167–194 (Glessmer).

[130] See Jonathan Ben-Dov, 'Mishmarot,' in EDEJ: 958–960.

[131] Cf. DJD 21:93–97.

[132] Cf. DJD 21:2, 99–101.

Mishmarot C^c);[133] 4Q324a Mishmarot D (olim Mishmarot C^d 1);[134] 4Q324c Mishmarot E (olim Mishmarot C^d 3–4);[135] 4Q328 Mishmarot F (olim Mishmarot F^a);[136] 4Q329 Mishmarot G (olim Mishmarot F^b, a list of priestly courses focusing on the Passover service rather than a more comprehensive list of festivals as in 4Q320 and 4Q321 [Calendrical Document A and B]);[137] 4Q329a Mishmarot H (olim Mishmarot G).[138] This last list of priestly courses focuses on the Passover service only rather than co-ordinating the mishmarot with a more comprehensive list of festivals as in 4Q320 and 4Q321;[139] 4Q330 Mishmarot I (olim Mishmarot H).[140]

By contrast, a number of manuscripts previously identified as Mishmarot texts have been renamed 'Historical Texts.'[141] The references in these texts to mishmarot serve "pinpointing the date of the specific event being described."[142] The texts in question are: the fragmentarily preserved composition 4Q322a Historical Text H? (olim 4Q323 Mishmarot C^b 3–5, edited by Tigchelaar);[143] 4Q331 papHistorical Text C (olim 4Q324b Mishmarot C^e, published by Fitzmyer);[144] 4Q332 Historical Text D (olim 4Q322 Mishmarot C^a 1–3).[145] This historical text includes references to Alexandra Salome (Shelomzion), who ruled the Hasmonean state between 76–67 BCE, and her son Hyrcanus II presented within a framework of priestly courses. Finally, 4Q333 Historical Text E (olim 4Q324a Mishmarot C^d 2, 5, edited by Fitzmyer)[146] constitutes another example of a text locating references to a historical figure, this time Aemilius (usually identified with the Roman governor of Syria Aemilius Scaurus appointed after the siege of Jerusalem by Pompey in 63 BCE) within a chronological framework based on priestly courses.

A significant number of calendrical documents have also been identified among the cryptic texts from Qumran Cave 4: 4Q313c (cryptA Calendrical Document B); 4Q317 (cryptA Lunisolar Calendar); 4Q324d (cryptA Liturgical

---

[133] Cf. DJD 21:2, 103–106.
[134] Cf. DJD 21:2, 107–111.
[135] Cf. DJD 21:2, 119–122.
[136] Cf. DJD 21:2, 139–141.
[137] Cf. DJD 21:2, 143–146.
[138] Cf. DJD 21:2, 147–150.
[139] DJD 21:147 and VanderKam, *Calendars in the Dead Sea Scrolls*, 87.
[140] Cf. DJD 21:2, 151–154.
[141] DJD 36:275–289, cf. DJD 21:2; for a vocal endorsement in favour of the earlier terminology see Philip R. Davies, 'Historiography,' in *The T & T Clark Companion to the Dead Sea Scrolls* (ed. George Brooke and Charlotte Hempel; London: T & T Clark, forthcoming).
[142] DJD 21:12, see also 107–108 where Talmon observes, "… dates pertaining to the service schedule of priestly courses play a subsidiary role."
[143] See DJD 28:125–128.
[144] See DJD 36:275–280.
[145] Edition by Fitzmyer in DJD 36:281–286; see also DJD 21:2 and VanderKam, *Calendars in the Dead Sea Scrolls*, 86 (referred to under the earlier siglum 4Q322).
[146] See DJD 36:287–289.

Calendar^a); 4Q324e (cryptA Liturgical Calendar^b); 4Q324f (cryptA Liturgical Calendar^c?); 4Q324g (cryptA Calendrical Document F?); 4Q324h (cryptA Calendrical Document G?); 4Q324i (cryptA Mishmarot J). Editions of most of these texts have been prepared by Martin G. Abegg in DSSR 4, and photographs have been published by Stephen Pfann in DJD 28. Despite the fragmentary nature of this sub-corpus of calendrical texts written in cryptic script the confluence of two major spheres of elevated knowledge from Cave 4 offers additional support for the suggestion advanced here that eclectic learning predominates in Cave 4.

Two particularly fascinating cases are manuscripts of that include a calendrical roster, once at the beginning and once at the end of a manuscript. The significance of such appendices or prefaces was noted by Talmon when he observes, "... calendar-related notations are accorded a place of prominence at the conclusion of Yaḥad works, as in 1QS X, 4QS^e, and 11QPs^a XXVII, or at their beginning, as in 4QMMT."[147] I would modify Talmon's observations slightly by highlighting that only in the two cases from Cave 4 are the 'calendar-related notations' simply adding raw data (4Q259 [4QS^e] and 4Q394 [MMT^a]) with little attempt to integrate the data into the larger framework of the composition in question. In 11QPs^a (David's Compositions), and 1QS 10, by contrast, the references to matters calendrical and liturgical are framed within the context of each larger work. An association of David with the Psalter is evident not only in David's Compositions but also in 11QPs^a 28 (Syriac Psalm 151[148]), and the Maskil-speaker of the final hymn in 1QS 9:26 ff. is the subject of a lengthy treatment immediately preceding the final hymn (1QS 9:12–25). We will briefly look at each of the two examples from Cave 4 where a rather technical calendrical element is attached to a larger work of notably different character.

- The so-called halakhic letter 4QMMT is represented by six manuscripts from Cave 4 (4Q394–399 [4QMMT^{a-f}], published by Qimron and Strugnell in DJD 10).[149] The fragmentary remains of a seventh copy written in cryptic script have also been identified (4Q313 [cryptAMMT^g?).[150] One of the manuscripts of 4QMMT (4Q394 3–7 i 1–3) contains the remains of three closing lines of a longer calendric section followed by a vacat and a heading introducing the extensive halakhic part of the document.[151] It is not obvious how this material relates to the rest of the document. Von Weissenberg observes,

---

[147] DJD 21:1.
[148] Cf. DJD 4:63–64, 92 (Sanders).
[149] See also Qimron et al. in PTSDSSP 3:187–251 and von Weissenberg, *4QMMT: Reevaluating the Text*.
[150] Published by Pfann in DJD 36:697–699, Plate 59; see also Qimron et al. in PTSDSSP 3:232–233.
[151] DJD 21:1 and von Weissenberg, *4QMMT: Reevaluating the Text*, 33–38, 230.

... the calendrical section did not constitute an original component of 4QMMT, and rather was annexed to the document in a similar manner as another kind of calendar was attached to 4Q259 (4QS^e).[152]

The possibility that the calendrical data would have been relevant to the halakhic observance of festivals and tithes touched upon elsewhere in 4QMMT raised by Glessmer goes some way to suggesting a possible rationale for relating calendar and halakhah.[153] We do not know whether a calendric section opened the composition in any of the other manuscripts of 4QMMT since this part of the document is preserved only in 4Q394. Von Weissenberg's reference to the 'analogy' in 4Q259 (4QS^e) brings us to our second example.

– Unique among the eleven manuscripts of the Community Rule (1QS [1Q28]; 4Q255–264 [4QS^{a-j}]), 4Q259 (4QS^e) ends with a calendrical component rather than the Maskil's Hymn attested in 1QS 9:26–11:22 with parallels in 4Q256 (4QS^b), 4Q258 (4QS^d), 4Q260 (4QS^f), and 4Q264 (4QS^j).[154] For historical reasons this integral part of the manuscript 4QS^e was published under the separate siglum 4Q319 (4QOtot).[155] Given the fluidity manifest in the transmission process of the Community Rule, as evident from a comparison of the different manuscripts, the addition of a different concluding section in 4Q259 (4QS^e) is not entirely out of the ordinary.[156] As indicated by the pronounced emphasis on the appropriate times for the Maskil's praise in the Final Hymn (cf. esp. 1QS 9:26–10:8),[157] the issue of chronology is also present in those manuscripts of the Rule that contain parts of the closing hymn. Undoubtedly, however, the highly technical and schematic character of 4Q319 (4QOtot) stands out among the varied textual tradition represented by the Rule. Thus, the editor rightly observes, "Indeed, the variance of subject-matter between the organizational-legal material in Serekh ha-Yaḥad and the technical otot schedule seems conclusive."[158] However, if Ben-Dov has correctly identified traces of the word 'blessed' (barukh) in the introduction to 4Q319 (4QOtot) iv 9,[159] then the doxological framework in which calendrical observations are couched is maintained in 4Q259 (4QS^e) in analogy with the other S manuscripts. The links between hymns of blessing and calendrical observance and the creation of the luminaries is also attested in 4Q408 (4Q408 3+3a 6–11

---

[152] Von Weissenberg, *4QMMT: Reevaluating the Text*, 230.
[153] Glessmer, 'Calendars in the Qumran Scrolls,' 239–240.
[154] See DJD 26:134, 150–152 (Alexander and Vermes).
[155] Cf. DJD 21:195–244, Plates 10–13 (Ben Dov); Glessmer, 'Calendars in the Qumran Scrolls,' 262–268; and VanderKam, *Calendars in the Dead Sea Scrolls*, 80–84.
[156] DJD 26:152.
[157] See DJD 26:152 who refer to this part of the Hymn as "a poetical calendar of the times of prayer."
[158] DJD 21:196 (Ben-Dov).
[159] Cf. DJD 21:200, 214–216.

Apocryphon of Moses^c; edited by Steudel)[160] and 1QH^a 20:7–12, a doxology associated with the Maskil (cf. 4QH^a 20:4, 11; the former reference to the Maskil is reconstructed with support from 4QH^a 8 ii 10 and 4QH^b 12 ii).[161] In both of these texts the doxologies further include a reference to the term 'sign' ('ot) from Gen 1:14 which also forms the background to the use of the terminology in 4QOtot.[162] Against this background, the association of the figure of the Maskil with hymns of praise relating to the observance of festivals and calendrical matters further supports the suggestion that the leap from the maskil's hymn to Otot is not quite as far as one might suspect at first sight.[163] We may witness here an experiment by one of the scholars whose literary wealth is found in Cave 4 inserting one of their calendric documents into a copy of the Community Rule. Testifying further to the somewhat avant-garde and experimental nature of 4Q259 (4QS^e) is the fact that 4QOtot itself comprises an anthology of calendrical texts.[164] Further enhancing the learned character of this particular manuscript of the Community Rule is its use of a mixture of scripts especially in 4Q259 (4QS^e) 3 3–4 where several scholars have identified the words 'Israel' and 'children of' (injustice) as written in cryptic script.[165] In sum, while an associative link between the calendrical data in 4QOtot to the remainder of 4Q259 (4QS^e) can be demonstrated this particular manuscript of the Rule constitutes an eclectic and avant-garde exemplar to have emerged from Cave 4.

Myriad items of detailed interpretation raised by the sizeable and varied calendrical component of the Qumran corpus are certain to occupy scholars for the foreseeable future. For our present purposes it suffices to stress the learned and eclectic nature of the calendrical literature recovered from Qumran Cave 4.[166] Few would doubt an international dimension which presupposes some form of scholarly and cultural contact between Mesopotamia and Palestine including

---

[160] See DJD 36:304–308.
[161] See DJD 40:252–253 (Stegemann and Schuller).
[162] See DJD 21:208–211 (Ben-Dov).
[163] See also DJD 26:152.
[164] See DJD 21:201 (Ben-Dov) who speaks of "a compendium of calendrical information" and observes, "While the placement of one calendrical composition within *Serekh ha-Yaḥad* seems acceptable (…), the presence of a collection of texts raises some questions regarding the coherence of the composition."
[165] See Pfann, 'The Mount Zion Inscribed Stone Cup,' 45–46; Ben Zion Wacholder and Martin Abegg, *A Preliminary Edition of the Unpublished Dead Sea Scrolls, Fascicle 3: The Hebrew and Aramaic Texts from Cave Four* (Washington, D. C.: Biblical Archaeology Society, 1995), 60; recently followed by Qimron in PTSDSSP 1:86. DJD 26:145–146 (Alexander and Vermes) remain unconvinced; see further Metso, *The Serekh Texts*, 53–54.
[166] Note in this context the reference to a "Jewish scholarly tradition" in Ben Dov, *Head of All Years*, 281, see also 245; and the emphasis on the "complexity and sophistication" of this literature in Stern, 'Qumran Calendars and Sectarianism,' 239–240.

Qumran. However, for the time being the precise nature and channels of the contact is much debated and difficult to determine.[167]

The late Shemaryahu Talmon has raised the possibility that the full complexity of calendric lore was intended for a more restricted, probably priestly, segment of the community,

> The pluriformity of calendar-related documents suggests that they were intended to provide relevant information and instructions for the diverse Covenanter echelons. The various mishmarot rosters pertain primarily to the priestly domain […] In contrast, the target audience of the unchanging calendrical schedules was the general membership of the Yaḥad.[168]

Along similar lines Talmon comments on 4Q321a (Calendrical Document/ Mishmarot C),

> The painstaking correlation of these data in several Qumran rosters suggests that the preoccupation with the calendar and the prolific production of calendar-related documents were most probably a priestly prerogative.[169]

The elevated and restricted audience who enjoyed access to calendrical lore is also noted by Ben-Dov,

> It therefore appears that the achievements of the Jewish calendrical-astronomical discipline were so highly appreciated that they were restricted to the perusal of properly initiated scholars.[170]

Alongside likely priestly interests reflected in parts of the calendar corpus, Ben Dov has also drawn attention to the presence of some apparently entirely

---

[167] See, e. g., Philip S. Alexander, 'Enoch and the Beginnings of Interest in Natural Science,' in *The Wisdom Texts from Qumran and the Development of Sapiential Thought* (ed. Charlotte Hempel, Armin Lange, and Hermann Lichtenberger; BETL 159; Leuven: Peeters, 2002), 223–243, 236–242; Ben-Dov, *Head of All Years*, 245–278; Mark Geller, 'New Documents from the Dead Sea: Babylonian Science in Aramaic,' in *Boundaries of the Ancient Near Eastern World: A Tribute to Cyrus H. Gordon* (ed. Meir Lubetski, Claire G. Gottlieb, and Sharon Keller; JSOTSup 273; Sheffield: Sheffield Academic Press, 1998), 224–229; Mladen Popović, 'The Emergence of Aramaic and Hebrew Scholarly Texts: Transmission and Translation of Alien Wisdom,' in *The Dead Sea Scrolls: Transmission of Traditions and Production of Texts* (ed. Sarianna Metso, Hindy Najman, and Eileen Schuller; STDJ 92; Leiden: Brill, 2010), 81–114; idem, 'Networks of Scholars: The Transmission of Astronomical and Astrological Learning Between Babylonians, Greeks and Jews,' in *Ancient Jewish Sciences and the History of Knowledge* (ed. Jonathan Ben-Dov and Seth Sanders; New York: New York University Press, forthcoming); on the issue of Aramaic as the vehicle for some of the international exchange between Mesopotamia and Palestine see Ben-Dov, *Head of All Years*, 287; see also idem, 'Scientific Writings in Aramaic and Hebrew at Qumran;' Popović, 'Aramaic and Hebrew Scholarly Texts;' idem, 'Networks of Scholars;' and Samuel Thomas, 'Esoteric Knowledge in Qumran Aramaic Texts,' in *Aramaica Qumranica* (ed. Berthelot and Stökl Ben Ezra), 403–430.

[168] DJD 21:14.

[169] DJD 21:83; see also Popović, 'Aramaic and Hebrew Scholarly Texts.'

[170] Ben-Dov, *Head of All Years*, 146.

secular schemata (see 4Q317 [cryptA Lunisolar Calendar] above). Thus, secular concerns ("scientific interests rather than religious principles"), also attested in the third century BCE Babylonian text TU 11, have been identified as a driving force behind the emphasis on the last visibility of the moon in 4Q320 and 4Q321 [Calendrical Document A and B].[171] We cannot discount the possibility, however, that secular scientific concerns were ultimately "put [...] to the service of religion."[172]

It is clear that the Cave 4 calendrical documents include a wealth of specialist and technical learning including a variety of at times competing systems. The general sense is they comprise a learned collection of specialist, often priestly, knowledge not necessarily intended for public consumption whatever the shape and size of the Qumran public may have been. As Fraade has rightly noted the authors and tradents of the more recently published Cave 4 calendar compositions reveal a thirst for theory quite apart from its application,

> Where we find multiple calendars, calendrical polemic, at least explicit, is noticeably absent. Such texts display an interest in astronomical and calendrical calculations for, in a sense, their own sake.[173]

There is little doubt, then, that the calendrical lore and learning to have emerged in such profundity from Cave 4 testifies to the predominance of specialist learning and scholarship in this cave. More than any other Qumran Cave, Cave 4 attests not only a variety of at times competing calendrical data, but also an impressive and curious repertoire of multiple copies of many compositions to which we will now turn.

5.4 Multiple Attestation

It is noteworthy that a large number of the manuscripts found in Cave 4 are attested in multiple copies and sometimes in large numbers as the following table indicates.

---

[171] Ben-Dov, *Head of All Years*, 243 arguing against Gillet-Didier, 'Calendrier lunaire, calendrier solaire.'

[172] Alexander, 'Enoch and the Beginnings of Interest in Natural Science,' 239.

[173] Steven Fraade, *Legal Fictions: Studies of Law and Narrative in the Discursive Worlds of Ancient Jewish Sectarians and Sages* (JSJSup 147; Leiden: Brill, 2011), 282.

Table III: Texts Attested in Five or More Copies in Cave 4
(Listed in Alphabetical Order; see Tov 2010)

5–9 copies	10–14 copies	15–19 copies	20 plus copies
Apocryphon Jeremiah C	Community Rule	Isaiah	Deuteronomy
Aramaic Levi	Genesis		Psalms
Barki Nafshi	1 Enoch		
Berakhot	Exodus		
Calendrical Document	Mishmarot		
Daniel			
Damascus Document			
Hodayot			
Instruction			
Jeremiah			
Jubilees			
Minor Prophets			
MMT			
(Reworked) Pentateuch			
Pesher Isaiah			
PseudoEzek			
Serekh ha-Edah (cryptic)			
Songs of the Sabbath Sacrifice			
Tobit			
Visions of Amram			
War Scroll			

The only other representative of significant multiple attestation outside of Cave 4 are the Psalms manuscripts from Cave 11.[174]

According to a hypothesis by the late Hartmut Stegemann the contents of Qumran Cave 4 once made up the bulk of the Qumran collection ('Zentralbibliothek' in the German original) previously housed in the settlement itself which might account for the large number of multiple copies of texts.[175] On Stegemann's hypothesis the bulk of the 'library' was hurriedly deposited in Cave 4 in the face of an imminent approach by the Romans from Jericho in 68 CE after

---

[174] See Peter Flint, *The Dead Sea Psalms Scrolls and the Book of Psalms* (STDJ 17; Leiden: Brill, 1997), 39–43 and DJD 23:29–78 (García Martínez, Tigchelaar, and van der Woude).

[175] Hartmut Stegemann, *Library of Qumran*, 75.

a number of compositions had already been taken to other caves further afield. Stegemann's hypothesis builds on the less developed but compatible scenario portrayed by Roland de Vaux.[176]

Moreover, the late Hanan Eshel is credited by Stökl Ben Ezra with the hypothesis that the contents of Cave 1 may be considered a selection taken from Cave 4, a theory which would account for the significant number of instances where Cave 1 revealed a small number of manuscripts of compositions attested in larger numbers in Cave 4.[177]

On either view it is clear that Cave 4 was home to the most diverse collection of texts, often preserving a variety of representatives of a composition side by side. The multiple attestation of so many documents further corroborates our contention that the contents of Cave 4 served the privileged and studious upper echelons and the leadership of the movement behind the library. While it is no doubt true that the manuscripts found in the eleven Qumran Caves point to a learned group that collected, handed on, transmitted and appropriated a large amount of ancient Jewish literature,[178] this is particularly true of the contents of Cave 4. More than any other cave the contents of Cave 4 represent an eclectic and varied collection of texts. The association of a Cave 4 document with leading communal administrators is especially clear in the following example.

5.5 4Q477 – The Overseer's Bookkeeping

While the topic of rebuke (Lev 19:17) is dealt with in several sectarian texts (cf. 1QS 5:24–6:1; CD 9:2–4, 16–20) 4Q477 appears to be a record kept by the overseer of community members whose wrongdoing has been reported to him.[179] This type of text fits the profile of Cave 4 suggested here as reflecting the interests of the upper echelons and leadership tier of the community. In a final section we will consider the lack of compositional refinement evident in some of the texts from Cave 4 quite independently of their often fragmentary state of preservation.

---

[176] DJD 3:34; De Vaux, *Archaeology and the Dead Sea Scrolls*, 56, 105; Schiffman, *Reclaiming the Dead Sea Scrolls*, 56; and most recently Popović, 'Roman Book Destruction.'

[177] See Stökl Ben Ezra, 'Old Caves and Young Caves,' 331 and idem, 'Wie viele Bibliotheken,' 341.

[178] See Charlotte Hempel, 'The Social Matrix that Shaped the Hebrew Bible and Gave Us the Dead Sea Scrolls,' in *Studies on the Text and Versions of the Hebrew Bible in Honour of Robert Gordon* (ed. Geoffrey Khan and Diana Lipton; VTSup 149; Leiden: Brill, 2012), 221–237, reprinted as Chapter 18 in this volume.

[179] DJD 36:474–483 (E. Eshel); see also Charlotte Hempel, 'Who Rebukes in 4Q477?,' *RQ* 16 (1995): 655–656.

5.6 The 'Workaday Quality' of a Number of Cave 4 Texts

Another feature that characterizes a number of texts from Cave 4 is that they appear less finessed and purposeful in their final shape.

5.6.1 4Q265 Miscellaneous Rules

The designation 4QMiscellaneous Rules chosen by the editor Joseph Baumgarten for 4Q265 already makes this point rather eloquently.[180] Whereas a good case can be made for the independence of the traditions in 4Q265 from closely related material in the Community Rule and the Damascus Document,[181] the miscellaneous nature of 4Q265 seems beyond doubt.

5.6.2 Anthologies and Compilations

A number of texts from Cave 4 are clearly anthological in nature. We already mentioned the anthological nature of 4QOtot and 4Q265. We also note the difficulties faced by scholars attempting to fathom the genre of 4Q159 (Ordinances^a) which has been identified as a "legal anthology" by Lawrence Schiffman.[182] A comparable compositional mix has been identified by Talmon and Knohl for other calendric texts also.[183] Moreover, the remains of 4Q329 (Mishmarot G) are described by the editor as including "at least three discrete rosters of priestly courses."[184] In addition 4Q320 (Calendrical Document A) comprises the remains of a rota of otot, alongside other calendrical calculations, flanked by a list of X dates in a six-year cycle together with references to the names of the mishmarot.[185] Further pointing to the workaday quality of 4Q320 (Calendrical Document A) are Ben-Dov's observations on the "low-quality pieces of parchment" inexpertly cobbled together in 4Q320, the oldest calendrical text from Qumran.[186]

---

[180] DJD 35:57–78; for further discussion and bibliography see also Charlotte Hempel, *The Damascus Texts* (CQS 1; Sheffield: Sheffield Academic Press, 2000), 89–104.

[181] Hempel, *Damascus Texts*, 93–104.

[182] Schiffman, 'Serekh-Damascus,' in EDSS 2:868–869, 868; for perceptive recent discussion see also Moshe Bernstein, '4Q159: Nomenclature, Text, Exegesis, Genre,' in *The Mermaid and the Partridge* (ed. Brooke and Høgenhaven), 33–55, esp. 52–53.

[183] See Talmon and Knohl, 'A Calendar Scroll from a Qumran Cave,' 270, noting "In some instances, several registers of various types and calendrical tables of other categories are combined in one composite scroll."

[184] DJD 21:143 (Talmon).

[185] Frg. 3, see DJD 21:51 (Talmon).

[186] Ben-Dov, *Head of All Years*, 198.

To this we may add further examples such as 4Q175 (4QTestimonia), recently labelled "a scriptural anthology."[187] Annette Steudel proposes on the basis of its content, the more careless hand of the same scribe who copied 1QS, and the fact that 4Q175 is limited to a single sheet of leather that this work served as a personal set of notes on matters eschatological or even as a basis to be drawn on in composing more refined exegetical compositions,

> Das Format des Manuskriptes, die Flüchtigkeit der Schreiberhand, die Art der Schriftverwendung und der Inhalt lassen die Vermutung zu, daß es sich bei 4Q175 um einen privat verwendeten "Handzettel" für die Diskussion eschatologischer Fragen handeln könnte [...]. Denkbar wäre auch, daß dies Zitatensammlung etwa die Grundlage für einen thematischen Midrasch über Endzeit-Gestalten bilden sollte.[188]

Similarly 4QTanḥumim (4Q176) has been portrayed as an "anthology of scriptural texts on the theme of divine comfort"[189] that comprises "liturgical texts of various genres."[190]

With reference to the thematic pesharim as a sub-group of texts Shani Berrin – developing a proposal by Steudel – has observed that the latter (such as 4QFlorilegium [4Q174], and 4QCatena A [4Q177]) represent a less 'developed' stage in the emergence of the pesher genre than the continuous pesharim from Cave 1.[191] Note also Brooke's observation that 4QFlorilegium is "made up of exegetical works of more than one type, though the significance of that has yet to be fully discerned."[192] Further examples could be added such as the varied nature of the compilation that makes up 4Q252 (Commentary on Genesis A).[193]

5.6.3 Raw Data

Unlike references to calendrical matters in narrative or liturgical contexts much of the recently published calendrical material has a raw quality as indicated by

---

[187] Campbell, *The Exegetical Texts*, 90; see also PTSDSSP 6B:308–311 (Cross). Similarly, Annette Steudel considers 4QTestimonia amongst a category of 'Exzerpt-Texte,' see Steudel, *Der Midrasch zur Eschatologie aus der Qumrangemeinde (4QMidrEschat$^{a.b}$): Materielle Rekonstruktion, Textbestand, Gattung, traditionsgeschichtliche Einordnung des durch 4Q174 ("Florilegium") und 4Q177 ("Catena A") repräsentierten Werkes aus den Qumranfunden* (STDJ 13; Leiden: Brill, 1994), 178–181.

[188] Steudel, *Midrasch zur Eschatologie*, 180.

[189] Campbell, *The Exegetical Texts*, 78–87; see also PTSDSSP 6B:329 (Lichtenberger) and Revised Schürer 3.1:448 (Vermes).

[190] Johann Maier, 'Tanḥumin and Apocryphal Lamentations,' in EDSS 2:915.

[191] Shani Berrin, 'Pesharim,' in EDSS 2:644–647, 646; see also George J. Brooke, *Exegesis at Qumran: 4QFlorilegium in Its Jewish Context* (JSOTSup 29; Sheffield: JSOT Press, 1985), 83; Emanuel Tov, 'Excerpted and Abbreviated Biblical Texts from Qumran,' *RQ* 16 (1995): 581–600; and the recent edition in PTSDSSP 6B:248–263 (Milgrom).

[192] George J. Brooke, 'Florilegium (4Q174),' in EDEJ: 646–647, 647.

[193] See DJD 22:187 (Brooke); George J. Brooke, 'The Thematic Content of 4Q252,' *JQR* N. S. 85 (1994): 33–59; and Tigchelaar, 'The Dead Sea Scrolls,' 171–172.

the popularity of terms such as 'registers' and 'rosters' for the data they contain.[194] This is captured in the following observation by editor Shemaryahu Talmon when he observes,

> The remnants of diverse chronometrical registers greatly complement the various details of information pertaining to the Covenanters' ritual timetable, partially preserved in their 'Foundation Documents' (1QS, CD, 1QpHab, 1QH^a, 11QPs^a, and 11QT).[195]

A comparative case has been outlined by Ben-Dov with reference to the physiognomic, astrolological and magical material from Cave 4,

> ... three disciplines (physiognomy, astrology, exorcism) are not associated with any kind of literary of [sic] narrative framework. The difference may be due to pure chance, owing to the fragmentary character of the extant scrolls. But a scroll like 4Q318 is long enough to contain some form of framework, if such framework ever existed.[196]

Finally, Thomas astutely notes the difference between texts preserving a narrative account (often in Aramaic) of the privileged transmission of knowledge over against texts preserving what I would call 'raw data,' and what Thomas refers to as 'the content of esoteric knowledge.'[197] Whereas Cave 4 contains both types of material, the domain of 'raw data' predominates in the learned and eclectic environment of this cave.

5.6.4 Serekh and Refinement in Cave 1

We may observe further that the term serekh, which is arguable a key term in the literary refinement and shaping of complex textual artefacts, is much more commonly attested in Cave 1 than in Cave 4.[198] To give a specific example mentioned already above, the Community Rule tradition attests two instances where the 1QS 5:1 serekh heading is represented by a heading announcing "Midrash for the Maskil over the people of the law" (4Q256 [4QS^b] 9 1; 4Q258 [4QS^d] 1 1). The preponderance of serekh in texts published from Cave 1– with much fewer references in the more recently published material from Cave 4 – is clearly evident from the following table.

---

[194] See DJD 21:7 passim; see also Tigchelaar, 'The Dead Sea Scrolls,' 173 "most of them (the recently published calendrical texts, C. H.) are actually lists."
[195] DJD 21:1.
[196] Ben-Dov, 'Scientific Writings in Aramaic and Hebrew at Qumran,' 387.
[197] Thomas, 'Esoteric Knowledge in Qumran Aramaic Texts,' 414; see also idem, *The "Mysteries" of Qumran: Mystery, Secrecy, and Esotericism in the Dead Sea Scrolls* (EJL 25; Atlanta, Ga.: SBL, 2009).
[198] See Charlotte Hempel, 'סרך,' in *Theologisches Wörterbuch zu den Qumrantexten* (ThWQ) (ed. Heinz-Josef Fabry et al.; Stuttgart: Kohlhammer, forthcoming).

Table IV: Profile of Serekh Occurrences in CD and at Qumran

CD	Cave 1	Cave 4
x 10	x31	x18

This is not to deny that 1QS itself has a complex history with internal inconsistencies and may itself be a Sammelhandschrift or anthology.[199] It is doubtless true however, that the final shaping of this manuscript is extremely finessed and 'purposeful.'[200] With similar vision and expertise evident in the work of the compilers of Proverbs or the Psalter in the Hebrew Bible – the final shaping of 1QS has everything packaged neatly; yet on closer inspection plenty of unevenness can be perceived to underlie the patina of order.

These observations on the carefully shaped text of 1QS correlate well to the physical care bestowed on the manuscripts from Cave 1 which were wrapped in linen and stored in jars.[201] It is as if more efforts were invested in the contents of Cave 1 both in terms of shaping the compositions as well as the physical protection of the manuscripts. Note in this context Emile Puech's remarks on 1QH^a observing the "impeccable material crafting of the scroll, which to our knowledge is unique among the manuscripts that have been found."[202] The literarily developed nature of the Cave 1 manuscripts of the Community Rule, the War Scroll, and the Hodayot has recently been noted also by Devorah Dimant when she makes a case for considering 1QS, 1QH^a and 1QM as the "textually most developed representatives of the works they contain."[203] These observations deserve further reflection in light of Hanan Eshel's proposal that the contents of Cave 1 are made up of a selection of Cave 4 manuscripts.[204] For our present purposes the literary, editorial, and at times material refinement evident in a number of Cave 1 manuscripts further highlights the work-a-day flavour of a considerable number of Cave 4 texts. One almost gains the impression that large parts of Cave 4 constitute the laboratory of a learned group where data, texts, and ideas are collected and experimented with over against the show room quality of Cave 1.

---

[199] See Hartmut Stegemann, 'Some Remarks to *1QSa*, to *1QSb*, and to Qumran Messianism,' *RQ* 17 (1996): 479–505; further, Hempel, 'Literary Development of the S-Tradition,' reprinted as Chapter 7 above; Metso, *The Serekh Texts*; and Schofield, *From Qumran to the Yaḥad*.

[200] For the latter term see Shaye Cohen, *The Synoptic Problem in Rabbinic Literature* (BJS 326; Providence: Brown University, 2000), x.

[201] See recently Taylor, 'Buried Manuscripts and Empty Tombs.'

[202] Puech, 'Hodayot,' 365.

[203] Dimant, 'Composite Character of the Qumran Sectarian Literature,' 617 passim.

[204] Stökl Ben Ezra, 'Old Caves and Young Caves,' 331 and idem, 'Wie viele Bibliotheken,' 341.

5.6.5 A Preponderance of Papyrus in Cave 4 over against Caves 1 and 11

Several scholars have noted the preponderance of papyrus over against parchment for the composition or copying of cryptic documents.[205] It is also noteworthy that in the three large hords found in Caves 1, 4, and 11 the largest number of papyri are attested from Cave 4 (86 including 7 opisthographs) with only three preserved from 1Q and a single one from 11Q.[206] Overall Qumran revealed 131 papyri (138 counting opisthographs as two compositions); their preponderance in Cave 4 sits well with the 'workaday' nature of many texts found in this cave.

6. Conclusion

I hope to have shown that a considered exploration of the profile of Cave 4 in the terms outlined above can shed fresh light on the nature of the collection as a whole. A good case can be made that Cave 4 comprises the most eclectic and scholarly corner of the collection. Thus, when Tigchelaar observes "the rise of a new kind of Jewish scholarship that tried to integrate all available disciplines and fields of knowledge" attested in the Scrolls his remarks are particularly apt with reference to Cave 4.[207]

Scholars have grappled with the diversity of the picture derived from the fully published Qumran corpus for some time. One direction explored by Alison Schofield is a radial model that allows for the different versions of the Community Rule having developed in distinct communities.[208] A comparable model is proposed by Joan Taylor who describes the Qumran scrolls as a,

> corpus that exhibits considerable diversity – for example in different versions of the Serekh and Damascus texts – as well as strong bonds of unity. This is then not one library, as such, though scriptures for all Essene communities might well have been manufactured in one production centre; this is a collection from many communities.[209]

---

[205] Stökl Ben Ezra, 'Old Caves and Young Caves,' 326 n. 51 and Tov, *Scribal Practices and Approaches*, 46, 259; see also DJD 39:204–210 (Tov).

[206] See Tov, *Scribal Practices and Approaches*, 44–53, esp. 46 Table 3.

[207] Tigchelaar, 'The Dead Sea Scrolls,' 176; see also Schiffman, *Reclaiming the Dead Sea Scrolls*, 56 noting the comprehensive scope of Cave 4 which "served a special function as the sect's library."

[208] Alison Schofield, *From Qumran to the Yaḥad*; for a recent endorsement see John J. Collins, *Beyond the Qumran Community: The Sectarian Movement of the Dead Sea Scrolls* (Grand Rapids, Mich.: Eerdmans, 2010), 68 and Carol Newsom, 'Flesh, Spirit, and the Indigenous Psychology of the Hodayot,' in *Prayer and Poetry in the Dead Sea Scrolls and Related Literature: Essays in Honor of Eileen Schuller on the Occasion of her 65th Birthday* (ed. Jeremy Penner, Ken Penner, and Cecila Wassen; STDJ 98; Leiden: Brill, 2011), 339–354, 354.

[209] Taylor, 'Buried Manuscripts and Empty Tombs,' 304–305, see also 306.

A fundamental difficulty with the geographical argument is that the evidence for variety was found all in one place – at Qumran – and, as I tried to show, at Qumran predominantly in Cave 4. The hypothesis put forward here suggests that Cave 4 is the learned hub of the Qumran elite who collected and transmitted a large array of learning and literature including Rule texts that need not necessarily have been practised or shared with the membership at large. There is no need to assume that various copies of the Serekh reflect distinctive practices and geographical provenances rather than a fluid textual tradition not unlike the textual fluidity of the emerging scriptures.[210]

The extent to which the contents of Cave 1 – published before the remainder of the library – have had a pivotal influence on our perception of the Qumran phenomenon is well known. Whereas we may consider Cave 1 to have acted as a forthright 'spokesperson' for the Qumran collection for the first fifty years, more recently Cave 4 has arguably grabbed the limelight and set the tone in rewriting the narrative about the Qumran finds. Once the floodgates of Cave 4 opened to the scholarly world in 1991 we perceived for the first time the full spectrum of the plurality and variety of religious literature to have emerged from Qumran. This inaugurated many a reconsideration of the nature of the collection as a whole that is still characterizing Qumran scholarship today. The heady intellectual climate in the wake of the release of the Cave 4 materials is well captured by Lawrence Schiffman's contemporary observation,

> Of all the caves, Cave 4 has yielded the most valuable finds, which have provided keys to unlocking the entire library.[211]

On closer reflection a great deal of the plurality of types of text and variety of content characterizes Cave 4 in particular rather than the collection as a whole. The often technical, esoteric, and certainly varied offerings to have come out of this particular cave would have been the pinnacle of Qumran's 'hierarchy of knowledge.'[212] The eclectic and scholarly character of the contents of Cave 4 proposed here invites re-directing scholarly efforts from pondering the applicability of multiple texts in favour of appreciating the learned and eclectic aspects of the material more fully. Both particularities and commonalities between the contents of Cave 4 and the remainder of the Qumran finds need to be taken into account more comprehensively as we re-conceive the nature and significance of the literary riches from Qumran.

---

[210] This line of argument is spelled out more fully in Chapters 17 and 18 of this volume.

[211] Schiffman, *Reclaiming the Dead Sea Scrolls*, 54; see also Charlotte Hempel, 'Texts, Scribes and Scholars: Reflections on a Busy Decade in Dead Sea Scrolls Research,' *ExpTim* 120 (2009): 272–276.

[212] For the latter terminology see Ben-Dov, 'Scientific Writings in Aramaic and Hebrew at Qumran,' 398.

Cumulative Bibliography

Abegg, Martin G., *The Dead Sea Scrolls Concordance. Volume One: The Non-Biblical Texts from Qumran [Parts 1–2]* (Leiden: Brill, 2003)

Aitken, James K., 'Apocalyptic, Revelation and Early Jewish Wisdom Literature,' in *New Heaven and New Earth: Prophecy and the Millennium* (ed. C. T. Robert Hayward and Peter J. Harland; VTSup 77; Leiden: Brill, 1999), 181–193

Albertz, Rainer, 'The Social Setting of the Aramaic and Hebrew Book of Daniel,' in *The Book of Daniel* (ed. Collins and Flint), Vol. I, 171–204

Alexander, Philip A., 'Enoch and the Beginnings of Interest in Natural Science,' in *The Wisdom Texts from Qumran and the Development of Sapiential Thought* (ed. Charlotte Hempel, Armin Lange, and Hermann Lichtenberger; BETL 159; Leuven: Peeters, 2002), 223–243

Alexander, Philip A., 'Physiognomy, Initiation, and Rank in the Qumran Community,' in *Geschichte – Tradition – Reflexion: Festschrift für Martin Hengel zum 70. Geburtstag* (ed. Hubert Cancik, Hermann Lichtenberger, and Peter Schäfer; Tübingen: Mohr Siebeck, 1996), Vol. I, 385–394

Alexander, Philip S., 'The Redaction-History of *Serekh ha-Yaḥad*: A Proposal,' *RQ* 17 (1996): 437–453

Alexander, Philip A., '"Wrestling Against Wickedness in High Places:" Magic in the Worldview of the Qumran Community,' in *The Scrolls and the Scriptures: Qumran Fifty Years After* (ed. Stanley Porter and Craig Evans; JSPSup 26; Sheffield: Sheffield Academic Press, 1997), 318–337

Allegro, John M., 'An Unpublished Fragment of Essene Halakhah (4QOrdinances),' *JJS* 6 (1961): 71–73

Anderson, Gary A., 'Aaron,' in EDSS 1:1–2

Angel, Joseph L., 'Maskil, Community, and Religious Experience in the *Songs of the Sage* (4Q510- 511),' *DSD* 19 (2011): 1–27

Avemarie, Friedrich, '"Tohorat Ha-Rabbim" and "Mashqeh Ha-Rabbim:" Jacob Licht Reconsidered,' in *Legal Texts and Legal Issues: Proceedings of the Second Meeting of the International Organization for Qumran Studies Published in Honour of Joseph M. Baumgarten* (ed. Moshe Bernstein, Florentino García Martínez, and John Kampen; STDJ 23; Leiden: Brill, 1997), 215–229

Bar-Adon, Pesah, 'Another Settlement of the Judean Desert Sect at 'Ain el-Guweir on the Dead Sea,' *BASOR* 225 (1977): 2–25

Bar-Asher Siegal, Elitzur A., 'Who Separated from Whom and Why? A Philological Study of 4QMMT, *RQ* 98 (2011): 229–256

Bardtke, Hans, 'Die Rechtsstellung der Qumrangemeinde,' *TLZ* 86 (1961): 93–104

Bar-Nathan, Rachel, 'Qumran and the Hasmonaean and Herodian Winter Palaces of Jericho: The Implication of the Pottery Finds for the Interpretation of the Settlement at

Qumran,' in *The Site of the Dead Sea Scrolls* (ed. Galor, Humbert, and Zangenberg), 263–277

Barton, George A., 'The Composition of the Book of Daniel,' *JBL* 17 (1898): 62–86

Baumgarten, Albert I., *Elias Bickerman as a Historian of the Jews* (TSAJ 131; Tübingen: Mohr Siebeck, 2010)

Baumgarten, Albert I., 'The Perception of the Past in the Damascus Document,' in *The Damascus Document* (ed. Baumgarten, Chazon, and Pinnick), 1–15

Baumgarten, Albert I., 'Rabbinic Literature as a Source for the History of Jewish Sectarianism in the Second Temple Period,' *DSD* 2 (1995): 14–57

Baumgarten, Albert I., 'The Zadokite Priests at Qumran,' *DSD* 4 (1997): 137–156

Baumgarten, Joseph M., 'The 4QZadokite Fragments on Skin Disease,' *JJS* 41 (1990): 153–165

Baumgarten, Joseph M., 'The Cave 4 Versions of the Qumran Penal Code,' *JJS* 43 (1992): 268–276

Baumgarten, Joseph M., 'The Disqualifications of Priests in 4Q Fragments of the "Damascus Document:" A Specimen of the Recovery of Pre-Rabbinic Halakha,' in *The Madrid Qumran Congress* (ed. Trebolle Barrera and Vegas Montaner), Vol. II, 503–513

Baumgarten, Joseph M., 'The Duodecimal Courts of Qumran, Revelation and the Sanhedrin,' *JBL* 95 (1976): 59–78 (reprinted in idem, *Studies in Qumran Law* [SJLA 24; Leiden: Brill, 1977], 145–171)

Baumgarten, Joseph M., 'The Qumran-Essene Restraints on Marriage,' in *Archaeology and History in the Dead Sea Scrolls: The New York University Conference in Memory of Yigael Yadin* (ed. Lawrence H. Schiffman; JSPSup 8; Sheffield: JSOT Press, 1990), 13–24

Baumgarten, Joseph M., 'A Fragment on Fetal Life and Pregnancy in 4Q270,' in *Pomegranates and Bells: Studies in Biblical, Jewish, and Near Eastern Ritual, Law, and Literature in Honor of Jacob Milgrom* (ed. David P. Wright, David N. Freedman, and Avi Hurvitz; Winona Lake, Ind.: Eisenbrauns, 1995), 445–448

Baumgarten, Joseph M., 'The "Halakhah" in Miqṣat Ma'aśe Ha-Torah (MMT),' *JAOS* 116 (1996): 512–516

Baumgarten, Joseph M., 'The Laws about Fluxes in 4QTohora^a (4Q274),' in *Time to Prepare the Way in the Wilderness* (ed. Dimant and Schiffman), 1–8

Baumgarten, Joseph M., 'A Qumran Text With Agrarian Halakhah,' *JQR* 86 (1995): 1–8

Baumgarten, Joseph M., 'The Laws of the Damascus Document – Between Bible and Mishnah,' in *The Damascus Document* (ed. Baumgarten, Chazon, Avital Pinnick), 17–26

Baumgarten, Joseph M., 'The Laws of the *Damascus Document* in Current Research,' in *The Damascus Document Reconsidered* (ed. Broshi), 51–62

Baumgarten, Joseph M., 'The Laws of 'Orlah and First Fruits in the Light of Jubilees, the Qumran Writings, and Targum Ps. Jonathan,' *JJS* 38 (1987): 195–202

Baumgarten, Joseph M., 'Pharisaic-Sadducean Controversies about Purity,' *JJS* 31 (1980): 157–170

Baumgarten, Joseph M., 'The Red Cow Purification Rites in Qumran Texts,' *JJS* 46 (1995): 112–119

Baumgarten, Joseph M., 'Sadducean Elements in Qumran Law,' in *The Community of the Renewed Covenant* (ed. Ulrich and VanderKam), 27–36

Baumgarten, Joseph M., 'Scripture and Law in 4Q265,' in *Biblical Perspectives: Early Use and Interpretation of the Bible in Light of the Dead Sea Scrolls* (ed. Michael E. Stone and Esther G. Chazon; STDJ 28; Leiden: Brill, 1998), 25–33

Baumgarten, Joseph M., 'The "Sons of Dawn" in CDC 13:14–15 and the Ban on Commerce among the Essenes,' *IEJ* 33 (1983): 81–85

Baumgarten, Joseph M., *Studies in Qumran Law* (SJLA 24; Leiden: Brill, 1977)

Baumgarten, Joseph M., 'Zab Impurity in Qumran and Rabbinic Law,' *JJS* 45 (1994): 273–277

Baumgarten, Joseph M., Esther G. Chazon, and Avital Pinnick (eds), *The Damascus Document: A Centennial of Discovery. Proceedings of the Third International Symposium of the Orion Center, 4–8 February 1998* (STDJ 34; Leiden: Brill, 2000)

Beall, Todd S., *Josephus' Description of the Essenes Illustrated by the Dead Sea Scrolls* (SNTSMS 58; Cambridge: CUP, 1988)

Ben-Dov, Jonathan, *Head of All Years: Astronomy and Calendars at Qumran in Their Ancient Context* (STDJ 78; Leiden: Brill, 2008)

Ben-Dov, Jonathan, 'Mishmarot,' in EDEJ: 958–960

Ben-Dov, Jonathan, 'Scientific Writings in Aramaic and Hebrew at Qumran: Translation and Concealment,' in *Aramaica Qumranica* (ed. Berthelot and Stökl Ben Ezra), 379–402

Bergmeier, Roland, *Die Essenerberichte des Flavius Josephus: Quellenstudien zu den Essenertexten im Werk des Jüdischen Historiographen* (Kampen: Kok Pharos, 1993)

Bernstein, Moshe, '4Q159: Nomenclature, Text, Exegesis, Genre,' in *The Mermaid and the Partridge* (ed. Brooke and Høgenhaven), 33–55

Bernstein, Moshe J., 'The Employment and Interpretation of Scripture in 4QMMT: Preliminary Observations,' in *Reading 4QMMT* (ed. Kampen and Bernstein), 29–51

Bernstein, Moshe, 'The Re-Presentation of 'Biblical' Legal Material at Qumran: Three Cases from 4Q159 (Ordinances[a]),' in *Shoshannat Yaakov: Jewish and Iranian Studies in Honor of Yaakov Elman* (ed. Shai Secunda and Steven Fine; Brill Reference Library of Judaism 35; Leiden: Brill, 2012), 1–20

Bernstein, Moshe, Florentino García Martínez, and John Kampen (eds), *Legal Texts and Legal Issues: Proceedings of the Second Meeting of the International Organization for Qumran Studies Published in Honour of Joseph M. Baumgarten* (ed. Moshe Bernstein, Florentino García Martínez, and John Kampen; STDJ 23; Leiden: Brill, 1997)

Berrin, Shani, 'Pesharim,' in EDSS 2:644–647

Berthelot, Katell and Daniel Stökl Ben Ezra (eds), *Aramaica Qumranica: Proceedings of the Conference on the Aramaic Texts from Qumran in Aix-en-Provence, 30 June – 2 July 2008* (STDJ 94; Leiden: Brill, 2010)

Betz, Otto, 'The Qumran Halakhah Text *Miqṣat Ma'aśe ha-Torah* (4QMMT) and Sadducean, Essene, and Early Pharisaic Tradition,' in *The Aramaic Bible: Targums in Their Historical Context* (ed. Derek R. G. Beattie and Martin J. McNamara; JSOTSup 166; Sheffield: JSOT Press, 1994), 176–202

Beyerle, Stefan, 'The Book of Daniel and Its Social Setting,' in *The Book of Daniel: Composition and Reception* (ed. Collins and Flint), Vol. I, 205–228

Blenkinsopp, Joseph, 'Bethel in the Neo-Babylonian Period,' in *Judah and the Judeans in the Neo-Babylonian Period* (ed. Oded Lipschits and Joseph Blenkinsopp; Winona Lake, Ind.: Eisenbrauns, 2003), 93–107

Blenkinsopp, Joseph, 'The Development of Jewish Sectarianism from Nehemiah to the Hasidim,' in *Judah and the Judeans in the Fourth Century B. C. E.* (ed. Oded Lipschits, Gary N. Knoppers, and Rainer Albertz; Winona Lake, Ind.: Eisenbrauns, 2007), 385–404

Blenkinsopp, Joseph, *Ezra-Nehemiah* (OTL; London: SCM, 1989)

Blenkinsopp, Joseph, 'The Family in First Temple Israel,' in *Families in Ancient Israel* (ed. Perdue et al.), 48–103

Blenkinsopp, Joseph, 'Interpretation and the Tendency to Sectarianism: An Aspect of Second Temple History,' in *Jewish and Christian Self-Definition* (ed. Ed P. Sanders; Philadelphia, Pa.: Fortress, 1981), Vol. II, 1–26

Blenkinsopp, Joseph, 'The Judaean Priesthood during the Neo-Babylonian and Achaemenid Periods: A Hypothetical Reconstruction,' *CBQ* 60 (1998): 25–43

Blenkinsopp, Joseph, *Judaism the First Phase: The Place of Ezra and Nehemiah in the Origins of Judaism* (Grand Rapids, Mich.: Eerdmans, 2009)

Blenkinsopp, Joseph, 'The Qumran Sect in the Context of Second Temple Sectarianism,' in *New Directions in Qumran Studies* (ed. Campbell, Lyons, and Pietersen), 10–25

Boccaccini, Gabriele (ed.), *Enoch and Qumran Origins: New Light on a Forgotten Connection* (Grand Rapids, Mich.: Eerdmans, 2005)

Bockmuehl, Markus, 'Redaction and Ideology in the Rule of the Community (1QS/4QS),' *RQ* 18 (1998): 541–560

Boling Robert G., *Joshua: A New Translation with Notes and Commentary* (AYBC; Garden City N. Y.: Doubleday, 1982)

Boyce, Mark, "The Poetry of the Damascus Document" (PhD diss., University of Edinburgh, 1988)

Boyce, Mark, 'The Poetry of the *Damascus Document* and Its Bearing on the Origin of the Qumran Sect,' *RQ* 14 (1990): 615–628

Braun, Herbert, *Qumran und das Neue Testament* (Tübingen: Mohr Siebeck, 1966)

Braun, Herbert, *Spätjüdisch-häretischer und frühchristlicher Radikalismus: Jesus von Nazareth und die essenische Qumransekte* (Tübingen: Mohr Siebeck, 1957)

Brin, Gershon, *The Concept of Time in the Bible and the Dead Sea Scrolls* (STDJ 39; Leiden: Brill, 2001)

Brin, Gershon, 'Studies in 4Q424, Fragment 3,' *VT* 46 (1996): 271–295

Brin, Gershon, 'Wisdom Issues in Qumran: The Types and Status of the Figures in 4Q424 and the Phrases of Rationale in the Document,' *DSD* 4 (1997): 297–311

Brooke, George J., 'The "Apocalyptic" Community, the Matrix of the Teacher and Rewriting Scripture,' in *Authoritative Scriptures in Ancient Judaism* (ed. Mladen Popović; JSJSup 141; Leiden: Brill, 2010), 37–53

Brooke, George J., 'Between Authority and Canon: The Significance of Reworking the Bible for Understanding the Canonical Process,' in *Reworking the Bible: Apocryphal and Related Texts at Qumran* (ed. Esther G. Chazon, Devorah Dimant, and Ruth A. Clements; STDJ 58; Leiden: Brill, 2005), 85–104

Brooke, George J., 'Biblical Interpretation in the Wisdom Texts from Qumran,' in *The Wisdom Texts from Qumran and the Development of Sapiential Thought* (ed. Charlotte Hempel, Armin Lange, and Hermann Lichtenberger; BETL 159; Leuven: Peeters, 2002), 201–220

Brooke, George J., *The Dead Sea Scrolls and the New Testament* (Minneapolis, Minn.: Fortress, 2005)

Brooke, George J., 'Dead Sea Scrolls Scholarship in the United Kingdom,' in *The Dead Sea Scrolls in Scholarly Perspective: A History of Research* (ed. Devorah Dimant; STDJ 99; Leiden: Brill, 2012), 449–486

Brooke, George J., *Exegesis at Qumran: 4QFlorilegium in Its Jewish Context* (JSOTSup 29; Sheffield: JSOT Press, 1985)
Brooke, George J., 'The Explicit Presentation of Scripture in 4QMMT,' in *Legal Texts and Legal Issues* (ed. Bernstein, García Martínez, and Kampen), 67–88
Brooke, George J., 'From "Assembly of Supreme Holiness for Aaron" to "Sanctuary of Adam:" The Laicization of Temple Ideology in the Qumran Scrolls and Its Wider Implications,' *Journal of Semitics* 8 (1996): 119–145
Brooke, George J., 'From Jesus to the Early Christian Communities: Trajectories Towards Sectarianism in the Light of the Dead Sea Scrolls,' in *The Dead Sea Scrolls and Contemporary Culture* (ed. Roitman, Schiffman, and Tzoref), 413–434
Brooke, George J., 'Florilegium (4Q174),' in *EDEJ*: 646–647
Brooke, George J., 'Miqdash Adam, Eden, and the Qumran Community,' in *Gemeinde ohne Tempel* (ed. Ego, Lange, and Pilhofer), 285–301
Brooke, George J., 'New Perspectives on the Bible and Its Interpretation,' in *Dynamics of Language and Exegesis at Qumran* (ed. Dimant and Kratz), 19–37
Brooke, George J., 'Parabiblical Prophetic Narratives,' in *The Dead Sea Scrolls After Fifty Years* (ed. Flint and VanderKam), Vol. I, 271–301
Brooke, George J., 'The Psalms in Early Jewish Literature in the Light of the Dead Sea Scrolls,' in *The Psalms in the New Testament* (ed. Steve Moyise and Maarten J. J. Menken; The New Testament and the Scriptures of Israel; London: T & T Clark, 2004), 5–24
Brooke, George J., *Qumran and the Jewish Jesus* (Cambridge: Grove Books, 2005)
Brooke, George J., 'The Qumran Scrolls and the Demise of the Distinction Between Higher and Lower Criticism,' in *New Directions in Qumran Studies* (ed. Campbell, Lyons, and Pietersen), 26–42
Brooke, George J., 'The Rewritten Law, Prophets, and Psalms: Issues for Understanding the Text of the Bible,' in *The Bible as Book* (ed. Herbert and Tov), 31–40
Brooke, George J., 'Some Comments on Commentary,' *DSD* 19 (2012): 249–266
Brooke, George J., 'The Thematic Content of 4Q252,' *JQR N. S.* 85 (1994): 33–59
Brooke, George and Charlotte Hempel (eds), *The T & T Clark Companion to the Dead Sea Scrolls* (London: T & T Clark, forthcoming)
Brooke, George J. and Jesper Høgenhaven (eds), *The Mermaid and the Partridge: Essays from the Copenhagen Conference on Revising Texts from Cave Four* (STDJ 96; Leiden: Brill, 2011)
Broshi, Magen, 'Anti-Qumranic Polemics in the Talmud,' in *The Madrid Qumran Congress* (ed. Trebolle Barrera and Vegas Montaner), Vol. II, 589–600
Broshi, Magen (ed.), *The Damascus Document Reconsidered* (Jerusalem: IES, 1991)
Broshi, Magen and Hanan Eshel, 'Residential Caves at Qumran,' *DSD* 6 (1999): 328–348
Brownlee, William H., *The Dead Sea Manual of Discipline* (BASORSup 10–12; New Haven: ASOR, 1951)
Bruce, Frederick F., 'The Book of Daniel and the Qumran Community,' in *Neotestamentica et Semitica: Studies in Honour of Matthew Black* (ed. E. Earle Ellis and Max Wilcox; Edinburgh: T & T Clark, 1968), 221–235
Butler, Trent C., *Joshua* (WBC 7; Waco, Tex.: Word Books, 1983)
Burrows, Millar with John C. Trever and William H. Brownlee, *The Dead Sea Scrolls of St. Mark's Monastery. Volume II Fascicle 2: Plates and Transcription of the Manual of Discipline* (New Haven, Conn.: ASOR, 1951)
Burrows, Millar, *The Dead Sea Scrolls* (London: Secker & Warburg, 1956)

Burrows, Millar, *More Light on the Dead Sea Scrolls* (London: Secker & Warburg, 1958)
Callaway, Philip R., '4QMMT and Recent Hypotheses on the Origin of the Qumran Community,' in *Mogilany 1993: Papers on the Dead Sea Scrolls* (ed. Zdzislaw J. Kapera; Kraków: Enigma, 1996), 15–29
Campbell, Jonathan G., 'Qumran-Essene Origins in the Exile: A Scriptural Basis?,' *JJS* 46 (1995): 144–156
Campbell, Jonathan, *The Exegetical Texts* (CQS 4; London: T & T Clark, 2004)
Campbell, Jonathan G., '"Rewritten Bible" and "Parabiblical Texts:" A Terminological and Ideological Critique,' in *New Directions in Qumran Studies* (ed. Campbell, Lyons, and Pietersen), 43–68
Campbell, Jonathan G., William J. Lyons, and Lloyd K. Pietersen (eds), *New Directions in Qumran Studies: Proceedings of the Bristol Colloquium on the Dead Sea Scrolls* (LSTS 52; London: T & T Clark, 2005)
Cancik, Hubert, Hermann Lichtenberger, and Peter Schäfer (eds), *Geschichte – Tradition – Reflexion: Festschrift für Martin Hengel zum 70. Geburtstag* (Tübingen: Mohr Siebeck, 1996)
Carmignac, Jean, 'Conjecture sur la première ligne de la Règle de la Communauté,' *RQ* 2 (1959): 85–87
Carmignac, Jean, 'Ordonnances,' in *Les Textes de Qumran: Traduits et Annotés* (ed. Jean Carmignac, Édouard Cothenet, and Hubert Lignée; Paris: Letouzey et Ané, 1963), Vol. II, 295 – 297
Carr, David M., *Writing on the Tablet of the Heart: Origins of Scripture and Literature* (Oxford: OUP, 2005)
Charlesworth James H. and Brent A. Strawn, 'Reflections on the Text of *Serek ha-Yaḥad* Found in Cave IV,' *RQ* 17 (1996): 403–435
Chalcraft, David (ed.), *Sectarianism in Early Judaism: Sociological Advances* (London: Equinox, 2007)
Chazon, Esther G., 'Is *Divrei Ha-Me'orot* a Sectarian Prayer?,' in *The Dead Sea Scrolls: Forty Years of Research* (ed. Devorah Dimant and Uriel Rappaport; STDJ 10; Leiden: Brill, 1992), 3–17
Cohen, Shaye, *The Synoptic Problem in Rabbinic Literature* (BJS 326; Providence: Brown University, 2000)
Collins John J., *Apocalypticism in the Dead Sea Scrolls* (The Literature of the Dead Sea Scrolls; London: Routledge, 1997)
Collins, John J., 'Apocalypticism and Literary Genre in the Dead Sea Scrolls,' in *The Dead Sea Scrolls After Fifty Years* (ed. Flint and VanderKam), Vol. II, 403–430
Collins, John J., *The Apocalyptic Vision of the Book of Daniel* (HSM 16; Missoula, Mont.: Scholars Press, 1977)
Collins, John J., *Beyond the Qumran Community: The Sectarian Movement of the Dead Sea Scrolls* (Grand Rapids, Mich.: Eerdmans, 2010)
Collins, John J., 'The Construction of Israel in the Sectarian Rule Books,' in *Judaism in Late Antiquity Part 5: The Judaism of Qumran. A Systemic Reading of the Dead Sea Scrolls* (ed. Alan J. Avery-Peck, Jacob Neusner and Bruce D. Chilton; HdO 57; Leiden: Brill, 2001), Vol. I, 25–42
Collins, John J., *Daniel* (Hermeneia; Minneapolis, Minn.: Fortress, 1993)
Collins, John J., 'Daniel and His Social World,' *Interpretation* 39 (1985): 131–143
Collins, John J., 'Daniel, Book of: Pseudo Daniel,' in EDSS 1:176–178

Collins, John J., 'Forms of Community in the Dead Sea Scrolls,' in *Emanuel* (ed. Paul et al.), 97–111
Collins, John J., 'In the Likeness of the Holy Ones: The Creation of Humankind in a Wisdom Text from Qumran,' in *The Provo International Conference on the Dead Sea Scrolls* (ed. Parry and Ulrich), 609–618
Collins, John J., *Jewish Wisdom in the Hellenistic Age* (Edinburgh, T & T Clark, 1998)
Collins, John J., 'The Mythology of Holy War in Daniel and the Qumran War Scroll: A Point of Transition in Jewish Apocalyptic,' *VT* 25 (1975): 596–612
Collins, John J., 'The Nature and Aims of the Sect Known from the Dead Sea Scrolls,' in *Flores Florentino* (ed. Hilhorst, Puech, and Tigchelaar), 31–52
Collins, John J., 'The Origin of the Qumran Community: A Review of the Evidence,' in *To Touch the Text: Biblical and Related Studies in Honor of Joseph A. Fitzmyer* (ed. Maurya P. Horgan and Paul J. Kobelski; New York: Crossroad, 1989), 159–178
Collins, John J., 'Sectarian Communities in the Dead Sea Scrolls,' in *Oxford Handbook of the Dead Sea Scrolls* (ed. Lim and Collins), 151–172
Collins, John J., 'Sectarian Consciousness in the Dead Sea Scrolls,' in *Interpretation, Identity and Tradition in Ancient Judaism* (ed. Lynn LiDonnici and Andrea Lieber; JSJSup 199; Leiden: Brill, 2007), 177–192
Collins, John J., 'The Time of the Teacher: An Old Debate Renewed,' in *Studies in the Hebrew Bible, Qumran, and the Septuagint* (ed. Flint, Tov, and VanderKam), 212–229
Collins, John J., 'The Yaḥad and "The Qumran Community,"' in *Biblical Traditions in Transmission* (ed. Hempel and Lieu), 81–96
Collins, John J. and Peter Flint (eds), *The Book of Daniel: Composition and Reception* (VTSup 83; Leiden: Brill, 2002)
Collins, John J., Gregory E. Sterling, and Ruth A. Clements (eds), *Sapiential Perspectives: Wisdom Literature in Light of the Dead Sea Scrolls* (STDJ 51; Leiden: Brill, 2004)
Coppens, Joseph, 'Le célibat essénien,' in *Qumrân: Sa piété, sa théologie et son milieu* (ed. Mathias Delcor et al.; Paris: Gembloux; Leuven: Leuven University Press, 1978), 295–303
Cothenet, Édouard, 'Le Document de Damas,' in *Les Textes de Qumrân: Traduits et Annotés* (Paris: Letouzey et Ané, 1963)
Cotton, Hannah and Erik Larson, '4Q460/4Q350 and Tampering with Qumran Texts in Antiquity?' in *Emanuel* (ed. Paul et al.), 113–26
Cross, Frank M., *The Ancient Library of Qumran and Modern Biblical Studies* (Grand Rapids, Mich.: Baker, 1961)
Cross, Frank M., *The Ancient Library of Qumran* (3d ed.; Sheffield: Sheffield Academic Press; Minneapolis, Minn.: Fortress, 1995)
Cross Frank M. and Esther Eshel, 'Ostraca from Khirbet Qumrân,' *IEJ* 47 (1997): 17–28
Davidson, Maxwell J., *Angels at Qumran: A Comparative Study of 1Enoch 1–36, 72–108 and Sectarian Writings from Qumran* (JSPSup 11; Sheffield: Sheffield Academic Press, 1992)
Davies, Philip R., *Behind the Essenes: History and Ideology in the Dead Sea Scrolls* (BJS 94; Atlanta, Ga.: Scholars Press, 1987)
Davies, Philip R., 'Communities at Qumran and the Case of the Missing "Teacher,"' *RQ* 15 (1991): 275–286 (reprinted in idem, *Sects and Scrolls*, 139–150)
Davies, Philip R., *The Damascus Covenant: An Interpretation of the "Damascus Document"* (JSOTSup25; Sheffield: JSOT Press, 1983)

Davies, Philip R., 'The "Damascus" Sect and Judaism,' in *Pursuing the Text: Studies in Honor of Ben Zion Wacholder* (ed. John Reeves and John Kampen; JSOTSup 184; Sheffield: Sheffield Academic Press), 70–84 (reprinted in idem, *Sects and Scrolls*, 163–177)

Davies, Philip R., 'Historiography,' in *The T & T Clark Companion to the Dead Sea Scrolls* (ed. Brooke and Hempel)

Davies, Philip R., '"Old" and "New" Israel in the Bible and the Qumran Scrolls: Identity and Difference,' in *Defining Identities* (ed. García Martínez and Popović), 33–342

Davies, Philip R., 'The Prehistory of the Qumran Community,' in *The Dead Sea Scrolls: Forty Years of Research* (ed. Devorah Dimant and Uriel Rappaport; STDJ 10; Leiden: Brill, 1992), 116–125

Davies, Philip R., 'Reading Daniel Sociologically,' in *Daniel in the Light of New Findings* (ed. van der Woude), 345–361

Davies, Philip R., 'Redaction and Sectarianism in the Qumran Scrolls,' in *The Scriptures and the Scrolls: Studies in Honour of A. S. van der Woude on the Occasion of his 65th Birthday* (ed. Florentino García Martínez, Anthony Hilhorst, and Casper J. Labuschagne; VTSup 49; Leiden: Brill, 1992), 152–163 (reprinted in idem, *Sects and Scrolls*, 151–161)

Davies, Philip R., 'The Scribal School of Daniel,' in *Book of Daniel* (ed. Collins and Flint), Vol. I, 247–265

Davies, Philip R., 'Sect Formation in Early Judaism,' in *Sectarianism in Early Judaism* (ed. J. Chalcraft), 132–155

Davies, Philip R., *Sects and Scrolls: Essays on Qumran and Related Topics* (South Florida Studies in the History of Judaism 134; Atlanta, Ga.: Scholars Press, 1996)

Davies, Philip R., 'Who Can Join the "Damascus Covenant"?,' *JJS* 46 (1995): 134–142

Davies, Philip R. and Joan E. Taylor, 'On the Testimony of Women in 1QSa,' *DSD* 3 (1996): 223–235

Day, John (ed.), *Temple and Worship in Biblical Israel* (LHBOTS 422; London: T & T Clark, 2007)

Delcor, Matthias, 'Qumran: La Règle de la Communauté,' *DBSup* 9 (1979): 851–857

Denis, Albert-Marie, 'Évolution de structures dans la secte de Qumrân,' in *Aux origines de l'église* (RechBib 7; Bruges: Desclée de Brouwer, 1965)

Denis, Albert-Marie, *Les thèmes de connaissance dans le Document de Damas* (Studia Hellenistica 15; Louvain: Publications Universitaires, 1967)

Dimant, Devorah, 'The Composite Character of the Qumran Sectarian Literature as an Indication of Its Date and Provenance,' *RQ* 22 (2006): 615–630

Dimant, Devorah, 'The Library of Qumran: Its Content and Character,' in *The Dead Sea Scrolls Fifty Years After Their Discovery 1947–1997* (ed. Lawrence H. Schiffman, Emanuel Tov, and James C. VanderKam; Jerusalem: IES, 2000), 170–176

Dimant, Devorah, 'The Qumran Manuscripts: Contents and Significance,' in *Time to Prepare the Way in the Wilderness* (ed. Dimant and Schiffman), 23–58

Dimant, Devorah, 'Qumran Sectarian Literature,' in *Jewish Writings of the Second Temple Period: Apocrypha, Pseudepigrapha, Qumran Sectarian Writings, Philo, Josephus* (ed. Michael E. Stone; CRINT 2.2; Philadelphia, Pa.: Fortress, 1984), 483–550

Dimant, Devorah, 'The Vocabulary of the Qumran Sectarian Texts,' in *Qumran und die Archäologie* (ed. Jörg Frey, Carsten Claussen, and Nadine Kessler; WUNT 1.278; Tübingen: Mohr Siebeck, 2011), 347–395

Dimant, Devorah (ed.), *The Dead Sea Scrolls in Scholarly Perspective* (STDJ 99; Leiden: Brill, 2012)

Dimant, Devorah and Reinhard G. Kratz (eds), *Dynamics of Language and Exegesis at Qumran* (FAT 35; Tübingen: Mohr Siebeck, 2009)

Dimant, Devorah and Lawrence H. Schiffman (eds), *Time to Prepare the Way in the Wilderness: Papers on the Qumran Scrolls by Fellows of the Institute for Advanced Studies of the Hebrew University, Jerusalem, 1989–1990* (STDJ 16; Leiden: Brill, 1995)

Doering, Lutz, *Schabbat: Sabbathalacha und –Praxis im antiken Judentum und Urchristentum* (TSAJ 78; Tübingen: Mohr Siebeck, 1999)

Dohmen, Christoph, 'Zur Gründung der Gemeinde von Qumran,' *RQ* 11 (1982): 82–96

Doudna, Gregory L., 'The Legacy of an Error in Archaeological Interpretation: The Dating of the Qumran Cave Scroll Deposits,' in *The Site of the Dead Sea Scrolls: Archaeological Interpretations and Debates* (ed. Katharina Galor, Jean-Baptiste Humbert, and Jürgen Zangenberg; STDJ 57; Leiden: Brill, 2006), 147–157

Duhaime, Jean, 'L'instruction sur les deux esprits et les interpolations dualistes à Qumran,' *RB* 84 (1977): 566–594

Duhaime, Jean, 'War Scroll (1QM, 1Q33),' in PTSDSSP 2:80–203

Duhaime, Jean, *The War Texts: 1QM and Related Manuscripts* (CQS 6; London: T & T Clark, 2004)

Dupont-Sommer, André, *The Essene Writings from Qumran* (trans. Geza Vermes; Oxford: Blackwell, 1961)

Ego, Beate, Armin Lange, and Peter Pilhofer (eds), *Gemeinde ohne Tempel* (WUNT 118; Tübingen: Mohr Siebeck, 1999)

Elgvin, Torleif, 'The Mystery to Come: Early Essene Theology of Revelation,' in *Qumran Between the Old and New Testaments* (ed. Fred H. Cryer and Thomas L. Thompson; Copenhagen International Seminar 6/JSOTSup 290; Sheffield: Sheffield Academic Press, 1998), 113–150

Elgvin, Torleif, 'The Reconstruction of Sapiential Work A,' *RQ* 16 (1993–1995): 559–580

Elgvin, Torleif, 'Wisdom in the Yaḥad: 4QWays of Righteousness,' *RQ* 17 (1996): 205–232

Elgvin, Torleif, 'The *Yaḥad* is More than Qumran,' in *Enoch and Qumran Origins: New Light on a Forgotten Connection* (ed. Gabriele Boccaccini et al.; Grand Rapids, Mich.: Eerdmans, 2005), 273–279

Eshel, Esther, '4Q477: The Rebukes by the Overseer,' *JJS* 45 (1994): 111–122

Eshel, Esther, '4QLev^d: A Possible Source for the Temple Scroll and Miqṣat Ma'aśe Ha-Torah,' *DSD* 2 (1995): 1–13

Eshel, Eshel, 'Possible Sources of the Book of Daniel,' in *Book of Daniel* (ed. Collins and Flint), Vol. II, 387–394

Eshel, Hanan, '4QMMT and the History of the Hasmonean Period,' in *Reading 4QMMT* (ed. Kampen and Bernstein), 53–65

Evans Kapfer, Hilary, 'The Relationship Between the Damascus Document and the Community Rule: Attitudes Toward the Temple as a Test Case,' *DSD* 14 (2007): 152–177

Fabry, Heinz-Josef, 'Priests at Qumran – a Reassessment,' in *The Dead Sea Scrolls: Texts and Context* (ed. Charlotte Hempel; STDJ 90; Leiden: Brill, 2010), 243–262

Fabry, Heinz-Josef, 'Zadokiden und Aaroniden in Qumran,' in *Das Manna fällt auch heute noch: Beiträge zur Geschichte und Theologie des Alten, Ersten Testaments. Festschrift für Erich Zenger* (ed. Frank Lothar Hossfeld and Ludger Schwienhorst-Schönberger; Herders biblische Studien 44; Freiburg: Herder, 2004), 201–217

Falk, Daniel, 'Liturgical Texts,' in *The T & T Clark Companion to the Dead Sea Scrolls* (ed. Brooke and Hempel), forthcoming

Fields, Weston, *The Dead Sea Scrolls: A Full History* (Leiden: Brill, 2009)

Fitzmyer, Joseph A., *Prolegomenon* to the Reprint of S. Schechter, *Documents of Jewish Sectaries. Vol. I: Fragments of a Zadokite Work* (New York: Ktav, 1970), 9–37

Flint, Peter, 'The Daniel Tradition at Qumran,' in *Book of Daniel* (ed. Collins and Flint), Vol. II, 329–367

Flint, Peter, *The Dead Sea Psalms Scrolls and the Book of Psalms* (STDJ 17; Leiden: Brill, 1997)

Flint, Peter W. and James C. VanderKam (eds), *The Dead Sea Scrolls After Fifty Years: A Comprehensive Assessment* (Leiden: Brill, 1999)

Flint, Peter W., Emanuel Tov, and James C. VanderKam (eds), *Studies in the Hebrew Bible, Qumran, and the Septuagint Presented to Eugene Ulrich* (VTSup 101; Leiden: Brill, 2006)

Forkman, Göran, *The Limits of the Religious Community: Expulsion from the Religious Community Within the Qumran Sect, Within Rabbinic Judaism, and Within Primitive Christianity* (ConBNT 5; Lund: CWK Gleerup, 1972)

Fraade, Steven D., 'Ancient Jewish Law and Narrative in Comparative Perspective: The Damascus Document and the Mishnah,' *Diné Israel: An Annual of Jewish Law* 24 (2007) 65–99 (reprinted in idem, *Legal Fictions*, 227–254)

Fraade, Steven D., 'Interpretative Authority in the Studying Community at Qumran,' *JJS* 44 (1993): 46–69

Fraade, Steven D., *Legal Fictions: Studies of Law and Narrative in the Discursive Worlds of Ancient Jewish Sectarians and Sages* (JSJSup 147; Leiden: Brill, 2011)

Fraade, Steven, 'Rhetoric and Hermeneutics in *Miqsat Ma'aśe Ha-Torah* (4QMMT): The Case of the Blessings and Curses,' *DSD* 10 (2003): 150–161

Frey, Jörg, 'Different Patterns of Dualistic Thought in the Qumran Library: Reflections on their Background and History,' in *Legal Texts and Legal Issues* (ed. Bernstein, García Martínez, and Kampen), 275–335

Frey, Jörg, Carsten Claussen, and Nadine Kessler (eds), *Qumran und die Archäologie* (WUNT 1.278; Tübingen: Mohr Siebeck, 2011)

Frey, Jörg and Hartmut Stegemann (eds), *Qumran Kontrovers: Beiträge zu den Textfunden vom Toten Meer* (Einblicke; Paderborn: Bonifatius, 2003)

Galor, Katharina, Jean-Baptiste Humbert, and Jürgen Zangenberg (eds), *The Site of the Dead Sea Scrolls: Archaeological Interpretations and Debates* (STDJ 57; Leiden: Brill, 2006)

Gärtner, Bertil, *The Temple and the Community in Qumran and the New Testament* (SNTSMS 1; Cambridge: CUP, 1965)

García Martínez, Florentino, 'Aramaica Qumranica Apocalyptica?,' in *Aramaica Qumranica* (ed. Berthelot and Stökl Ben Ezra), 435–449

García Martínez, Florentino, 'Beyond the Sectarian Divide: The "Voice of the Teacher" as an Authority-Conferring Strategy in Some Qumran Texts,' in *The Dead Sea Scrolls: Transmission of Traditions* (ed. Metso, Najman, and Schuller), 227–244

García Martínez, Florentino, 'Cave 11 in Context,' in *The Dead Sea Scrolls: Texts and Context* (ed. Hempel), 199–209

García Martínez, Florentino, 'Damascus Document: A Bibliography of Studies 1970–1989,' in *The Damascus Document Reconsidered* (ed. Magen Broshi; Jerusalem: IES, 1992), 63–83

García Martínez, Florentino, *The Dead Sea Scrolls Translated: The Qumran Texts in English* (Leiden: Brill, 1994)

García Martínez, Florentino, 'Dos Notas Sobre *4QMMT,*' *RQ* 16 (1993): 293–297

García Martínez, Florentino, 'Priestly Functions in a Community Without Temple,' in *Gemeinde ohne Temple* (ed. Beate Ego, Armin Lange, and Peter Pilhofer; WUNT 118; Tübingen: Mohr Siebeck, 1999), 303–319

García Martínez, Florentino, *Qumran and Apocalyptic: Studies on the Aramaic Texts from Qumran* (STDJ 9; Leiden: Brill, 1992)

García Martínez, Florentino, *Qumranica Minora I: Qumran Origins and Apocalypticism* (ed. Eibert J. C. Tigchelaar; STDJ 63; Leiden: Brill, 2007)

García Martínez, Florentino, 'Qumran Origins and Early History: A Groningen Hypothesis,' *Folia Orientalia* 25 (1988): 113–136 (reprinted in idem, *Qumranica Minora I*, 3–29)

García Martínez, Florentino, 'Reconsidering the Cave 1 Texts Sixty Years After Their Discovery: An Overview,' in *Qumran Cave 1 Revisited: Proceedings of the Sixth Meeting of the IOQS, Ljubljana 2007* (ed. Daniel Falk, Sarianna Metso, and Eibert Tigchelaar; STDJ 91; Leiden: Brill, 2010), 1–13

García Martínez, Florentino, '¿Sectario, no-sectario, o qué? Problemas de una taxonomía correcta de los textos qumránicos,' *RQ* 23 (2008): 383–394

García Martínez, Florentino, 'Temple Scroll,' in EDSS 2:927–933

García Martínez, Florentino and Adam S. van der Woude, 'A "Groningen" Hypothesis of Qumran Origins and Early History,' *RQ* 56 (1990): 521–541

García Martínez, Florentino and Mladen Popović (eds), *Defining Identities: We, You, and the Other in the Dead Sea Scrolls. Proceedings of the Fifth Meeting of the IOQS in Groningen* (STDJ 70; Leiden: Brill, 2008)

García Martínez, Florentino and Julio Trebolle Barrera, *The People of the Dead Sea Scrolls: Their Writings, Beliefs and Practices* (Leiden: Brill, 1995)

Garnet, Paul, 'Cave 4 Ms Parallels to 1QS 5.1 7: Towards a *Serek* Text History,' *JSP* 15 (1997): 67–78

Geller, Mark, 'New Documents from the Dead Sea: Babylonian Science in Aramaic,' in *Boundaries of the Ancient Near Eastern World: A Tribute to Cyrus H. Gordon* (ed. Meir Lubetski, Claire G. Gottlieb, and Sharon Keller; JSOTSup 273; Sheffield: Sheffield Academic Press, 1998), 224–229

Gerrard, Kate, "A Contemporary Look at the Jewish Past in Poland: Traces of Memory and the Galicia Jewish Museum, Kraków (2004–2011)" (Ph.D. diss., University of Birmingham, 2013)

Gillet-Didier, Veronique, 'Calendrier lunaire, calendrier solaire et gardes sacerdotales: recherches sur 4Q321,' *RQ* 20 (2001): 171–205

Gillingham, Susan, 'The Zion Tradition and the Editing of the Hebrew Psalter,' in *Temple and Worship in Biblical Israel* (ed. Day), 308–341

Gillihan, Yonder Moynihan, *Civic Ideology, Organization, and Law in the Rule Scrolls: A Comparative Study of the Covenanters' Sect and Contemporary Voluntary Associations in Political Context* (STDJ 97; Leiden: Brill, 2011)

Ginsberg, Harold L., 'The Oldest Interpretation of the Suffering Servant,' *VT* 3 (1953): 400–404

Ginzberg, Louis, *An Unknown Jewish Sect* (New York: Jewish Theological Seminary of America, 1976)

Glessmer, Uwe, 'Calendars in the Qumran Scrolls,' in *The Dead Sea Scrolls After Fifty Years* (ed. Flint and VanderKam), Vol. II, 213–278

Glessmer, Uwe, 'Der 364-Tage Kalender und die Sabbatstruktur seiner Schaltungen in ihrer Bedeutung für den Kult,' in *Ernten was man sät: Festschrift für Kaus Koch zu seinem 65. Geburtstag* (ed. Dwight R. Daniels, Uwe Gleßmer, and Martin Rösel; Neukirchen-Vluyn: Neukirchener Verlag, 1991), 379–398

Goff, Matthew, *Discerning Wisdom: The Sapiential Literature of the Dead Sea Scrolls* (VTSup 116; Leiden: Brill, 2007)

Goff, Matthew J., *The Worldly and Heavenly Wisdom of 4QInstruction* (STDJ 50; Leiden: Brill, 2003)

Goldman, Liora, 'A Comparison of the Genizah Manuscripts A and B of the Damascus Document in Light of Their Pesher Units,' in *Meghillot: Studies in the Dead Sea Scrolls IV* (ed. Moshe Bar-Asher and Devorah Dimant; Jerusalem: University of Haifa/Bialik Institute, 2006), XIV, 169–189 [Hebrew with English abstract]

Goodman, Martin, *Rome and Jerusalem: A Clash of Ancient Civilizations* (London: Allen Lane, 2007)

Goodman, Martin, 'Texts, Scribes and Power in Roman Judaea,' in *Literacy and Power in the Ancient World* (ed. Alan K. Bowman and Greg Woolf; Cambridge: CUP, 1994), 99–108

Goshen-Gottstein, Moshe H., 'The Psalms Scroll (11QPs^a): A Problem of Canon and Text,' *Textus* 5 (1966): 22–33

Grabbe, Lester L., '4QMMT and Second Temple Jewish Society,' in *Legal Texts and Legal Issues* (ed. Bernstein, García Martínez, and Kampen), 89–108

Grabbe, Lester L., 'A Dan(iel) for all Seasons: For Whom was Daniel Important?,' in *Book of Daniel* (ed. Collins and Flint), Vol. I, 229–246

Gray, John, *Joshua, Judges and Ruth* (NCB; London: T. Nelson and Sons, 1967)

Grossman, Maxine, 'Reading 4QMMT: Genre and History,' *RQ* 20 (2001): 3–22

Grossman, Maxine, 'Reading for Gender in the Damascus Document,' *DSD* 11 (2004): 212–239

Grossman, Maxine, *Reading for History in the Damascus Document: A Methodological Study* (STDJ 45; Leiden: Brill, 2002)

Grossman, Maxine, 'Rethinking Gender in the Community Rule: An Experiment in Sociology,' in *The Dead Sea Scrolls and Contemporary Culture* (ed. Roitman, Schiffman, and Tzoref), 497–512

Grossman, Maxine, 'Roland Barthes and the Teacher of Righteousness: The Death of the Author of the Dead Sea Scrolls,' in *Oxford Handbook of the Dead Sea Scrolls* (ed. Lim and Collins), 709–722

Grossman, Maxine, 'Women and Men in the Rule of the Congregation: A Feminist Critical Assessment,' in *Rediscovering the Dead Sea Scrolls* (ed. Grossman), 229–245

Grossman, Maxine (ed.), *Rediscovering the Dead Sea Scrolls: An Assessment of Old and New Approaches and Methods* (Grand Rapids, Mich.: Eerdmans, 2010)

Guillaumont, Antoine, 'A propos du célibat des esséniens,' in *Hommages à André Dupont-Sommer* (ed. André Caquot and Marc Philonenko; Paris: Libraire Adrien-Maisonneuve, 1971), 395–404

Haag, Ernst, 'Die Hasidäer und das Danielbuch,' *TTZ* 102 (1993): 51–63

Hachlili, Rachel, 'The Qumran Cemetery: A Reconsideration,' in *The Dead Sea Scrolls Fifty Years After Their Discovery 1947–1997* (ed. Lawrence H. Schiffman, Emanuel Tov, and James C. VanderKam; Jerusalem: IES, 2000), 661–672

Harkins, Angela Kim, *Reading with an "I" to the Heavens: Looking at the Qumran Hodayot through the Lens of Visionary Traditions* (Ekstasis 3; Berlin: de Gruyter, 2012)

Harkins, Angela Kim, 'Who is the Teacher of the Teacher Hymns? Re-Examining the Teacher Hymns Hypothesis Fifty Years Later,' in *A Teacher for All Generations: Essays in Honor of James C. VanderKam* (ed. Eric Mason et al.; JSJSup 153; Leiden: Brill, 2012), Vol. I, 449–467

Harrington, Daniel J., 'The RĀZ NIHYEH in a Qumran Wisdom Text (1Q26, 4Q415–418, 423),' *RQ* 17 (1996): 549–553

Harrington, Daniel J., 'Review of T. Elgvin et al. DJD 20,' *DSD* 4 (1997): 357–360

Harrington, Daniel J., 'Ten Reasons Why the Qumran Wisdom Texts are Important,' *DSD* 4 (1997): 246–265

Harrington, Daniel J., 'Two Early Jewish Approaches to Wisdom: Sirach and Qumran Sapiential Work A,' *JSP* 16 (1997): 25–38

Harrington, Daniel J., *Wisdom Texts from Qumran* (The Literature of the Dead Sea Scrolls; London: Routledge, 1996)

Harrington, Hannah K., *The Purity Texts* (CQS 5; London: T & T Clark, 2004)

Hasslberger, Bernhard, *Hoffnung in der Bedrängnis: Eine formkritische Untersuchung zu Dan 8 und 10–12* (ATSAT 4; St. Ottilien: Eos, 1977)

Hayes, Christine, *Gentile Impurities and Jewish Identities: Intermarriage and Conversion from the Bible to the Talmud* (Oxford: OUP, 2002)

Heger, Paul, *Cult as the Catalyst for Division: Cult Disputes as the Motive for Schism in the Pre-70 Pluralistic Environment* (STDJ 65; Leiden: Brill, 2007)

Hempel, Charlotte, 'אהרון,' in *Theologisches Wörterbuch zu den Qumrantexten* (ThWQ) (ed. Heinz-Josef Fabry et al.; Stuttgart: Kohlhammer, 2010), columns 76–81

Hempel, Charlotte, 'סרך,' in *Theologisches Wörterbuch zu den Qumrantexten* (ThWQ) (ed. Heinz-Josef Fabry et al.; Stuttgart: Kohlhammer, forthcoming)

Hempel, Charlotte, '1QS 6:2c–4a – Satellites or Precursors of the Yaḥad?,' in *The Dead Sea Scrolls and Contemporary Culture* (ed. Roitman, Schiffman, and Tzoref), 31–40 [reprinted as Chapter 6 in this volume]

Hempel, Charlotte, '4QOrd[a] (4Q159) and the Laws of the Damascus Document,' in *The Dead Sea Scrolls Fifty Years After Their Discovery 1947–1997* (ed. Lawrence H. Schiffman, Emanuel Tov, and James C. VanderKam; Jerusalem: IES, 2000), 372–376 [reprinted as Chapter 12 in this volume]

Hempel, Charlotte, 'CD Manuscript B and the Community Rule: Reflections on a Literary Relationship,' *DSD* 16 (2009): 370–387 [reprinted as Chapter 8 in this volume]

Hempel, Charlotte, 'Comments on the Translation of 4QS[d] I,1,' *JJS* 44 (1993): 127–128

Hempel, Charlotte, 'The Community and Its Rivals According to the Community Rule from Caves 1 and 4,' *RQ* 21 (2003): 47–81

Hempel, Charlotte, 'Community Origins in the *Damascus Document* in the Light of Recent Scholarship,' in *The Provo International Conference on the Dead Sea Scrolls: Technological Innovations, New Texts, and Reformulated Issues* (ed. Donald W. Parry and Eugene Ulrich; STDJ 30; Leiden: Brill, 1999), 316–329 [reprinted as Chapter 4 in this volume]

Hempel, Charlotte, 'Community Structures in the Dead Sea Scrolls: Admission, Organization, Disciplinary Procedures,' in *The Dead Sea Scrolls After Fifty Years* (ed. Flint and VanderKam), Vol. II, 67–92 [reprinted as Chapter 2 in this volume]

Hempel, Charlotte, 'The Context of 4QMMT and Comfortable Theories,' in *The Dead Sea Scrolls: Texts and Context* (ed. Hempel), 275–292

Hempel, Charlotte, *The Damascus Texts* (CQS 1; Sheffield: Sheffield Academic Press, 2000)

Hempel, Charlotte, 'Do the Scrolls Suggest Rivalry Between the Sons of Aaron and the Sons of Zadok and If So was it Mutual?,' *RQ* 24 (2009): 135–153 [reprinted as Chapter 14 in this volume]

Hempel, Charlotte, 'The Earthly Essene Nucleus of 1QSa,' *DSD* 3 (1996): 253–269 [reprinted as Chapter 3 in this volume]

Hempel, Charlotte, 'Emerging Communal Life and Ideology in the S Tradition,' in *Defining Identities* (ed. García Martínez and Popović), 43–61 [reprinted as Chapter 5 in this volume]

Hempel, Charlotte, 'The Gems of DJD 36: Reflections on Some Recently Published Texts,' *JJS* 54 (2003): 146–152

Hempel, Charlotte, 'The Groningen Hypothesis: Strengths and Weaknesses,' in *Enoch and Qumran Origins* (ed. Boccaccini), 249–255

Hempel, Charlotte, 'Interpretative Authority in the Community Rule Tradition,' *DSD* 10 (2003): 59–80

Hempel, Charlotte, *The Laws of the Damascus Document: Sources, Traditions, and Redaction* (STDJ 29; Leiden: Brill, 1998; pb ed. Atlanta, Ga.: SBL, 2006)

Hempel, Charlotte, 'The Literary Development of the S-Tradition: A New Paradigm,' *RQ* 22 (2006): 389–401 [reprinted as Chapter 7 in this volume]

Hempel, Charlotte, '*Maskil(im)* and *Rabbim*: From Daniel to Qumran,' in *Biblical Traditions in Transmission* (ed. Hempel and Lieu), 133–156 [reprinted as Chapter 15 in this volume]

Hempel, Charlotte 1997, 'The Penal Code Reconsidered,' in *Legal Texts and Legal Issues: Proceedings of the Second Meeting of the International Organization for Qumran Studies Published in Honour of Joseph M. Baumgarten* (ed. Moshe Bernstein, Florentino García Martínez, and John Kampen; STDJ 23; Leiden: Brill, 1997), 337–348

Hempel, Charlotte, 'Qumran Community,' in EDSS 2:746–751

Hempel, Charlotte, 'Qumran Communities: Beyond the Fringes of Second Temple Society,' in *The Scrolls and the Scriptures: Qumran Fifty Years After* (ed. Stanley Porter and Craig Evans; JSPSup 26 Sheffield: Sheffield Academic Press, 2003), 43–53

Hempel, Charlotte, 'The Qumran Sapiential Texts and the Rule Books,' in *The Wisdom Texts from Qumran* (ed. Hempel, Lange, and Lichtenberger), 277–295 [reprinted as Chapter 10 in this volume]

Hempel, Charlotte, 'Rules,' in *The T & T Clark Companion to the Dead Sea Scrolls* (ed. Brooke and Hempel)

Hempel, Charlotte, *Rules and Laws I* (ECDSS 1; Grand Rapids, Mich.: Eerdmans, forthcoming)

Hempel, Charlotte, 'The Social Matrix that Shaped the Hebrew Bible and Gave us the Dead Sea Scrolls,' in *Studies on the Text and Versions of the Hebrew Bible in Honour of Robert Gordon* (ed. Geoffrey Khan and Diana Lipton; VTSup 149; Leiden: Brill, 2012), 221–237 [reprinted as Chapter 18 in this volume]

Hempel, Charlotte, 'The Sons of Aaron in the Dead Sea Scrolls,' in *Flores Florentino* (ed. Hilhorst, Puech, and Tigchelaar), 207–224 [reprinted as Chapter 13 in this volume]

Hempel, Charlotte, 'Sources and Redaction in the Dead Sea Scrolls –The Growth of Ancient Texts,' in *Rediscovering the Dead Sea Scrolls* (ed. Grossman), 162–181

Hempel, Charlotte, 'The Teaching on the Two Spirits and the Literary Development of the Rule of the Community,' in *Dualism in Qumran* (ed. Geza Xeravits; LSTS 76; London: T & T Clark, 2010), 102–120
Hempel, Charlotte, 'Texts, Scribes and Scholars: Reflections on a Busy Decade in Dead Sea Scrolls Research,' *ExpTim* 120 (2009): 272–276
Hempel, Charlotte, 'Vielgestaltigkeit und Verbindlichkeit: Serekh ha-Yachad in Qumran,' in *Qumran und der biblische Kanon* (ed. Jörg Frey; Neukirchen Vluyn: Neukirchener Verlag, 2009), 101–112
Hempel, Charlotte, 'Who is Making Dinner at Qumran?,' *JTS* 63 (2012): 49–65
Hempel, Charlotte, 'Who Rebukes in 4Q477?,' *RQ* 16 (1995): 655–656
Hempel, Charlotte (ed.), *The Dead Sea Scrolls: Texts and Context* (STDJ90; Leiden: Brill, 2010)
Hempel, Charlotte and Judith Lieu (eds), *Biblical Traditions in Transmission: Essays in Honour of Michael A. Knibb* (JSJSup 111; Leiden: Brill, 2006)
Hempel, Charlotte, Armin Lange, and Hermann Lichtenberger (eds), *The Wisdom Texts from Qumran and the Development of Sapiential Thought* (BETL159; Leuven: Peeters, 2002)
Hengel, Martin, 'Qumran und der Hellenismus,' in *Qumrân: Sa piété, sa théologie et son milieu* (ed. Mathias Delcor; BETL 46; Paris-Gembloux: Duculot; Leuven: University Press, 1978), 333–372
Henze, Matthias, *The Madness of King Nebuchadnezzar: The Ancient Near Eastern Origins and Early History of Interpretation of Daniel 4* (JSJSup 61; Leiden: Brill, 1999)
Herbert, Edward D. and Emanuel Tov (eds), *The Bible as Book: The Hebrew Bible and the Judaean Desert Discoveries* (London: The British Library, 2002)
Hertzberg, Hans Wilhelm, *Beiträge zur Traditionsgeschichte und Theologie des Alten Testaments* (Göttingen: Vandenhoeck & Ruprecht, 1962)
Hilhorst, Anthony, Émile Puech, and Eibert Tigchelaar (eds), *Flores Florentino: Dead Sea Scrolls and Other Early Jewish Studies in Honour of Florentino García Martínez* (JSJSup 122; Leiden: Brill, 2008)
Himmelfarb, Martha, 'Levi, Phinehas, and the Problem of Intermarriage at the Time of the Maccabean Revolt,' *JSQ* 6 (1999): 1–24
Hooper-Greenhill, Eileen, *Museums and the Interpretation of Visual Culture* (London: Routledge, 2000)
Horgan, Maurya, *Pesharim: Qumran Interpretations of Biblical Books* (CBQMS 8; Washington, D. C.: CBA, 1979)
Hübner, Hans, 'Zölibat in Qumran?,' *NTS* 17 (1970–1971): 153–167
Hultgren, Stephen, *From the Damascus Covenant to the Covenant of the Community: Historical, and Theological Studies in the Dead Sea Scrolls* (STDJ 66; Leiden: Brill, 2007)
Humbert, Jean-Baptiste, 'L'espace sacré à Qumrân,' *RB* 101 (1994): 161–214
Humbert, Jean-Baptiste and Alain Chambon, *The Excavations of Khirbet Qumran and Ain Feshkha: Synthesis of Roland de Vaux's Field Notes* (trans. Stephen Pfann; NTOASA 1B; Fribourg: Vandenhoeck & Ruprecht, 2003)
Hunzinger, Claus-Hunno, 'Beobachtungen zur Entwicklung der Disziplinarordnung der Gemeinde von Qumrān,' in *Qumran-Probleme* (ed. Hans Bardtke; DAWBSSA 42; Berlin: Akademie-Verlag, 1963), 231–247
Huppenbauer, Hans Walter, *Der Mensch zwischen zwei Welten* (ATANT 34; Zürich: Zwingli, 1959)

Ilan, Tal, 'Women in Qumran and the Dead Sea Scrolls,' in *Oxford Handbook of the Dead Sea Scrolls* (ed. Lim and Collins), 123–147
Isaakson, Abel, *Marriage and Ministry in the New Temple* (Lund: Gleerup, 1965)
Jacobus, Helen, '4Q318: A Jewish Zodiac Calendar at Qumran?,' in *The Dead Sea Scrolls: Texts and Context* (ed. Hempel), 365–395
Jaffe, Martin, *Torah in the Mouth: Writing and Oral Tradition in Palestinian Judaism, 200 BCE-400 CE* (Oxford: OUP, 2001)
Jastram, Nathan, 'Hierarchy at Qumran,' in *Legal Texts and Legal Issues* (ed. Bernstein, García Martínez, and Kampen), 349–376
Jokiranta, Jutta, 'Qumran – The Prototypical Teacher in the Qumran Pesharim: A Social-Identity Approach,' in *Ancient Israel: The Old Testament in Its Social Context* (ed. Philip F. Esler; Minneapolis, Minn.: Fortress, 2006), 254–263
Jokiranta, Jutta, 'Social Identity in the Qumran Movement: The Case of the Penal Code,' in *Explaining Christian Origins and Early Judaism: Contributions from Cognitive and Social Science* (ed. Petri Luomanen, Ilkka Pyysiäinen, and Risto Uro; BIS 89; Leiden: Brill, 2007), 277–298
Jokiranta, Jutta, 'Social-Scientific Approaches to the Dead Sea Scrolls,' in *Rediscovering the Dead Sea Scrolls* (ed. Grossman), 246–263
Jokiranta, Jutta, 'Sociological Approaches to Qumran Sectarianism,' in *Oxford Handbook of the Dead Sea Scrolls* (ed. Lim and Collins), 200–231
Kahle, Paul E., *The Cairo Genizah* (2d. ed.; Oxford: Blackwell, 1959)
Kampen, John, 'The Diverse Aspects of Wisdom in the Qumran Texts,' in *The Dead Sea Scrolls After Fifty Years* (ed. Flint and VanderKam), Vol. I, 211–243
Kampen, John, *Wisdom Literature* (ECDSS; Grand Rapids, Mich.: Eerdmans, 2011)
Kampen, John and Moshe Bernstein (eds), *Reading 4QMMT: New Perspectives on Qumran Law and History* (SBL Symposium Series 2; Atlanta, Ga.: Scholars Press, 1996)
Kister, Menahem, 'Commentary to 4Q298,' *JQR* 85 (1994): 237–249
Kister, Menahem, 'The Development of the Early Recensions of the Damascus Document,' *DSD* 14 (2007): 61–76
Kister, Menahem, 'Some Aspects of Qumranic Halakhah,' in *The Madrid Qumran Congress* (ed. Trebolle Barrera and Vegas Montaner), Vol. II, 571–588
Klauck, Hans-Josef, 'Gütergemeinschaft in der klassischen Antike, in Qumran und im Neuen Testament,' *RQ* 11 (1982): 47–79
Klinghardt, Matthias, *Gemeinschaftsmahl und Mahlgemeinschaft: Soziologie und Liturgie christlicher Mahlfeiern* (Tübingen: Francke, 1996)
Klinghardt Matthias, 'The Manual of Discipline in the Light of Statutes of Hellenistic Associations,' in *Methods of Investigation of the Dead Sea Scrolls and the Khirbet Qumran Site: Present Realities and Future Prospects* (ed. Michael O. Wise et al.; Annals of the New York Academy of Sciences 722; New York: New York Academy of Sciences, 1994), 251–270
Klinzing, Georg, *Die Umdeutung des Kultus in der Qumrangemeinde und im Neuen Testament* (SUNT 7; Göttingen: Vandenhoeck & Ruprecht, 1971)
Knibb, Michael A., 'The Book of Daniel in Its Context,' in *Book of Daniel* (ed. Collins and Flint), Vol. I, 16–35
Knibb, Michael A., 'Eschatology and Messianism in the Dead Sea Scrolls,' in *The Dead Sea Scrolls After Fifty Years* (ed. Flint and VanderKam), Vol. II, 379–402
Knibb, Michael A., 'Exile in the Damascus Document,' *JSOT* 25 (1983): 99–117

Knibb, Michael A., 'The Exile in the Literature of the Intertestamental Period,' *HeyJ* 17 (1976): 249–272

Knibb, Michael A., *Jubilees and the Origins of the Qumran Community: An Inaugural Lecture Delivered on 17 January 1989* (London: King's College London, 1989)

Knibb, Michael A., *The Qumran Community* (Cambridge Commentaries on Writings of the Jewish and Christian World 200 BC to AD 200 2; Cambridge: CUP, 1987)

Knibb, Michael A., 'The Place of the Damascus Document,' in *Methods of Investigation of the Dead Sea Scrolls and the Khirbet Qumran Site: Present Realities and Future Prospects* (ed. Michael O. Wise et al.; Annals of the New York Academy of Sciences 722; New York: New York Academy of Sciences, 1994), 149–162

Knibb, Michael A., 'Rule of the Community,' in EDSS 2:793–797

Knibb, Michael A., 'Teacher of Righteousness,' in EDSS 2:918–921

Knibb, Michael A., '"You are Indeed Wiser than Daniel:" Reflections on the Character of the Book of Daniel,' in *Daniel in the Light of New Findings* (ed. van der Woude), 399–411

Knoppers, Gary N., 'The Relationship of the Priestly Genealogies to the History of the High Priesthood in Jerusalem,' in *Judah and the Judeans in the Neo-Babylonian Period* (ed. Oded Lipschits and Joseph Blenkinsopp; Winona Lake, Ind.: Eisenbrauns, 2003), 109–133

Koch, Klaus, *Das Buch Daniel* (EdF 144; Darmstadt: Wissenschaftliche Buchgesellschaft, 1980)

Koch, Klaus, *Daniel* (BKAT 22.1; Neukirchen-Vluyn: Neukirchener Verlag, 1986)

Koch, Klaus, 'Das Geheimnis der Zeit in Weisheit und Apokalyptik um die Zeitenwende,' in *Wisdom and Apocalyptic in the Dead Sea Scrolls and in the Biblical Tradition* (ed. Florentino García Martínez; BETL 168; Leuven: Peeters, 2003), 35–68

Koch, Klaus, 'Stages in the Canonization of the Book of Daniel,' in *Book of Daniel* (ed. Collins and Flint), Vol. II, 421–446

Kosmala, Hans, 'Maśkîl,' *JANES* 5 (1973): 235–241 (reprinted in idem, *Studies, Essays and Reviews* [Leiden: Brill, 1978], Vol. I, 149–155)

Kratz, Reinhard G., 'Biblical Scholarship and Qumran Studies,' in *The T & T Clark Companion to the Dead Sea Scrolls* (ed. Brooke and Hempel)

Kratz, Reinhard G., 'Friend of God, Brother of Sarah, and Father of Isaac: Abraham in the Hebrew Bible and in Qumran,' in *Dynamics of Language and Exegesis at Qumran* (ed. Dimant and Kratz), 79–105

Kratz, Reinhard G., *Das Judentum im Zeitalter des Zweiten Tempels* (FAT 42; Tübingen: Mohr Siebeck, 2004)

Kratz, Reinhard G., 'Laws of Wisdom: Sapiential Traits in the *Rule of the Community* (1QS V–IX),' in *Hebrew in the Second Temple Period: The Hebrew of the Dead Sea Scrolls and of Other Contemporary Sources. Proceedings of the Twelfth Orion Symposium* (STDJ; Leiden: Brill, forthcoming)

Kratz, Reinhard G., 'Mose und die Prophetie: Zur Interpretation von 4QMMT C,' in *From 4QMMT to Resurrection: Mélanges qumraniens en hommage à Émile Puech* (ed. Florentino García Martínez, Annette Steudel, and Eibert Tigchelaar; STDJ 61; Leiden: Brill, 2006), 151–176

Kratz, Reinhard G., 'Der *Penal Code* und das Verhältnis von *Serekh ha-Yachad* (S) und Damaskusschrift (D),' *RQ* 25 (2011): 199–227

Kratz, Reinhard G., *Prophetenstudien* (FAT 75; Tübingen: Mohr Siebeck, 2011)

Kratz, Reinhard G., 'Die Tora Davids: Ps 1 und die doxologische Fünfteilung des Psalters,' *ZTK* 93 (1996): 1–34

Kruse, Colin G., 'Community Functionaries in the Rule of the Community and the Damascus Document: A Test of Chronological Relationships,' *RQ* 10 (1981): 543–551

Kugler, Robert, 'A Note on 1QS 9:14: The Sons of Righteousness or the Sons of Zadok,' *DSD* 3 (1996): 315–320

Kugler, Robert A., 'Halakic Interpretative Strategies at Qumran: A Case Study,' in *Legal Texts and Legal Issues* (ed. Bernstein, García Martínez, and Kampen), 131–140

Kugler, Robert, 'Priesthood at Qumran,' in *The Dead Sea Scrolls After Fifty Years* (ed. Flint and VanderKam), Vol. II, 93–116

Kugler, Robert A., 'Priests,' in EDSS 2:688–693

Kugler, Robert A., 'Whose Scripture? Whose Community? Reflections on the Dead Sea Scrolls Then and Now, By Way of Aramaic Levi,' *DSD* 15 (2008): 5–23

Kugler, Robert and Esther Chazon, 'Women at Qumran: Introducing the Essays,' *DSD* 11 (2004): 167–173

Kuhn, Karl Georg, *Konkordanz zu den Qumrantexten* (Göttingen: Vandenhoeck & Ruprecht, 1960)

Laato, Antti, 'The Chronology of the *Damascus Document* of Qumran,' *RQ* 15 (1992): 605–607

Lacocque, André, 'Socio-Spiritual Formative Milieu of the Daniel Apocalypse,' in *Daniel in the Light of New Findings* (ed. van der Woude), 315–343

Lange, Armin, 'Die Endgestalt des protomasoretischen Psalters und die Toraweisheit,' in *Der Psalter in Judentum und Christentum* (ed. Erich Zenger; Biblical Studies 18; Freiburg: Herder, 1998), 101–136

Lange, Armin, 'Eschatological Wisdom in the Book of Qohelet and the Dead Sea Scrolls,' in *The Dead Sea Scrolls: Fifty Years After Their Discovery 1947–1997* (ed. Lawrence H. Schiffman, Emanuel Tov, and James C. VanderKam; Jerusalem: IES, 2000), 817–825

Lange, Armin, 'Kriterien essenischer Texte,' in *Qmran Kontrovers* (ed. Frey and Stegemann), 59–69

Lange, Armin, 'Physiognomie oder Gotteslob? 4Q301 3,' *DSD* 4 (1997): 282–296

Lange, Armin, 'The Qumran Dead Sea Scrolls – Library or Manuscript Collection?,' in *From 4QMMT to Resurrection: Mélanges qumraniens en hommage à Émile Puech* (ed. Florentino García Martínez, Annette Steudel, and Eibert Tigchelaar; STDJ 61; Leiden: Brill, 2006), 177–193

Lange, Armin, *Weisheit und Prädestination: Weisheitliche Urordnung und Prädestination in den Textfunden von Qumran* (STDJ 18; Leiden: Brill, 1995)

Lapin, Hayim, 'Dead Sea Scrolls and the Historiography of Ancient Judaism,' in *Rediscovering the Dead Sea Scrolls* (ed. Grossman), 108–127

Leaney, Alfred R. C., *The Rule of Qumran and Its Meaning* (NTL; London: SCM, 1966)

Lebram, Jürgen C. H., 'Apokalyptik und Hellenismus im Buche Daniel,' *VT* 20 (1970): 503–524

Leeuwen, Raymond C. van, 'Scribal Wisdom and a Biblical Proverb at Qumran,' *DSD* 4 (1997): 255–264

Leiman, Sid Z., 'Inspiration and Canonicity: Reflections on the Formation of the Biblical Canon,' in *Jewish and Christian Self-Definition. Volume Two: Aspects of Judaism in the Graeco-Roman Period* (ed. Ed P. Sanders; London: SCM, 1981), 56–63

Levin, Christoph, 'Das Gebetbuch der Gerechten: Literargeschichtliche Beobachtungen am Psalter,' in *Fortschreibungen: Gesammelte Studien zum Alten Testament* (BZAW 316; Berlin: de Gruyter, 2003), 291–313

Lichtenberger, Hermann, *Studien zum Menschenbild in Texten der Qumrangemeinde* (SUNT 15; Göttingen: Vandenhoeck & Ruprecht, 1980)

Lieberman, Saul, 'The Discipline in the So-Called Dead Sea Manual of Discipline,' *JBL* 71 (1952): 199–206

Lim, Timothy H. and John J. Collins (eds), *The Oxford Handbook of the Dead Sea Scrolls* (Oxford: OUP, 2010)

Lipscomb, W. Loundes and James A. Sanders, 'Wisdom at Qumran,' in *Israelite Wisdom: Theological and Literary Essays in Honor of Samuel Terrien* (ed. John G. Gammie et al.; Missoula, Mont.: Scholars Press, 1978), 277–285

Liver, Jacob, 'The Half-Shekel Offering in Biblical and Post-Biblical Literature,' *HTR* 56 (1963): 173–198

Liver, Jacob, 'The "Sons of Zadok the Priests" in the Dead Sea Sect,' *RQ* 6 (1967): 3–30

Lohfink, Norbert, 'Psalmengebet und Psalterredaktion,' *Archiv für Literaturwissenschaft* 34 (1992): 1–22

Mach, Michael, 'Angels,' in EDSS 1:24–27

Magness, Jodi, 'The Chronology of the Settlement at Qumran in the Herodian Period,' *DSD* 2 (1995): 58–65

Magness, Jodi, *The Archaeology of Qumran and the Dead Sea Scrolls* (Grand Rapids, Mich.: Eerdmans, 2002)

Magness, Jodi, *Debating Qumran: Collected Essays on Its Archaeology* (Interdisciplinary Studies in Ancient Culture and Religion 4; Leuven: Peeters, 2004)

Maier, Johann, 'Early Jewish Biblical Interpretation in the Qumran Literature,' in *Hebrew Bible/Old Testament: The History of Its Interpretation. Volume I: From the Beginnings to the Middle Ages (Until 1300)* (ed. Magne Sæbø; Göttingen: Vandenhoeck & Ruprecht, 1996), 108–129

Maier, Johann, *Die Qumran-Essener: Die Texte vom Toten Meer* (UTB; München: Reinhardt, 1995)

Maier, Johann, 'Tanḥumin and Apocryphal Lamentations,' in EDSS 2:915, Maier, Johann, 'Zum Begriff יחד in den Texten von Qumran,' *ZAW* 31 (1960): 148–166

Marcus Ralph, '*Mebaqqer* and *Rabbim* in the Manual of Discipline vi.11–13,' *JBL* 75 (1956): 298–302

McKane, Willam, *Jeremiah* (ICC; Edinburgh: T & T Clark, 1986)

Mealand, David L., 'Community of Goods at Qumran,' *TZ* 31 (1975): 129–139

Mertens, Alfred, *Das Buch Daniel im Lichte der Texte vom Toten Meer* (SBM 12; Stuttgart: Echter KBW, 1971)

Metso, Sarianna, 'Creating Communal Halakhah,' in *Studies in the Hebrew Bible, Qumran, and the Septuagint Presented to Eugene Ulrich* (ed. Peter W. Flint, Emanuel Tov, and James C. VanderKam; VTSup 101; Leiden: Brill, 2006), 279–301

Metso, Sarianna, 'In Search of the Sitz im Leben of the Community Rule,' in *The Provo International Conference on the Dead Sea Scrolls* (ed. Parry and Ulrich), 306–315

Metso, Sarianna, 'Methodological Problems in Reconstructing History from Rule Texts Found at Qumran,' *DSD* 11 (2004): 315–335

Metso, Sarianna, 'The Primary Results of the Reconstruction of 4QS^e,' *JJS* 44 (1993): 303–308

Metso, Sarianna, 'Problems in Reconstructing the Organizational Chart of the Essenes,' *DSD* 16 (2009): 388–415

Metso, Sarianna, 'Qumran Community Structure and Terminology as Theological Statement,' *RQ* 20 (2002): 429–444

Metso, Sarianna, 'The Relationship Between the Damascus Document and the Community Rule,' in *The Damascus Document* (ed. Baumgarten, Chazon and Pinnick), 85–93

Metso, Sarianna, *The Serekh Texts* (CQS 9/LSTS 62; London: T & T Clark, 2007)

Metso, Sarianna, *The Textual Development of the Qumran Community Rule* (STDJ 21; Leiden: Brill, 1997)

Metso, Sarianna, 'Whom Does the Term Yaḥad Identify?,' in *Biblical Traditions in Transmission* (ed. Hempel and Lieu), 213–235

Metso, Sarianna, Hindy Najman, and Eileen Schuller (eds), *The Dead Sea Scrolls: Transmission of Traditions and Production of Texts* (STDJ 92; Leiden: Brill, 2010)

Meyers, Carol, 'The Family in Ancient Israel,' in *Families in Ancient Israel* (ed. Perdue et al.), 1–47

Milgrom, Jacob, '4QTohora^a: An Unpublished Qumran Text on Purities,' in *Time to Prepare the Way in the Wilderness* (ed. Dimant and Schiffman), 59–68

Milgrom, Jacob, *Leviticus 1–16: A New Translation with Introduction and Commentary* (New York: Doubleday, 1991)

Milik, Józef T., *The Books of Enoch: Aramaic Fragments of Qumrân Cave 4* (Oxford: OUP, 1974)

Milik, Józef T., 'Le travail d'édition des fragments manuscrits de Qumrân,' *RB* 63 (1956): 49–67

Milik, Józef T., 'Prière de Nabonide et autres écrits d'un cycle de Daniel,' *RB* 63 (1956): 407–415

Milik, Józef T., *Ten Years of Discovery in the Wilderness of Judaea* (trans. John Strugnell; SBT 26; London: SCM, 1959)

Milik, Józef T., 'Texte des varinantes des dix manuscrits de la Règle de la Communauté trouves dans la Grotte 4: Recension de P. Wernberg-Moeller, The Manual of Discipline,' *RB* 67 (1960): 410–416

Miller, J. Maxwell and Gene M. Tucker, *The Book of Joshua* (CBC; Cambridge: CUP, 1974)

Murphy, Catherine, *Wealth in the Dead Sea Scrolls and in the Qumran Community* (STDJ 40; Leiden: Brill, 2002)

Murphy-O'Connor, Jerome, 'The Essenes and their History,' *RB* 81 (1974): 215–244

Murphy-O'Connor, Jerome, 'An Essene Missionary Document? CD II,14-VI,1,' *RB* 77 (1970): 201–229

Murphy-O'Connor, Jerome, 'La genèse littéraire de la Règle de la Communauté,' *RB* 76 (1969): 528–549

Murphy-O'Connor, Jerome, 'A Literary Analysis of Damascus Document XIX,33-XX,34,' *RB* 79 (1972): 544–564

Najman, Hindy, *Seconding Sinai: The Development of Mosaic Discourse in Second Temple Judaism* (JSJSup 77; Leiden: Brill 2003; pb. ed. Atlanta, Ga.: SBL, 2009)

Newsom, Carol, 'Apocalyptic and the Discourse of the Qumran Community,' *JNES* 49 (1990): 135–144

Newsom, Carol, 'Flesh, Spirit, and the Indigenous Psychology of the Hodayot,' in *Prayer and Poetry in the Dead Sea Scrolls and Related Literature: Essays in Honor of Eileen*

Schuller on the Occasion of her 65th Birthday (ed. Jeremy Penner, Ken Penner, and Cecila Wassen; STDJ 98; Leiden: Brill, 2011), 339–354

Newsom, Carol, 'A Response to George Nickelsburg's "Currents in Qumran Scholarship: The Interplay of Data, Agendas and Methodology,"' in *The Dead Sea Scrolls at Fifty: Proceedings of the 1997 Society of Biblical Literature Qumran Section Meetings* (ed. Robert A. Kugler and Eileen M. Schuller; Atlanta, Ga.: Scholars Press, 1999), 115–121

Newsom, Carol A., 'The Sage in the Literature of Qumran: The Functions of the Maskil,' in *The Sage in Israel and the Ancient Near East* (ed. James G. Gammie and Leo G. Perdue; Winona Lake, Ind.: Eisenbrauns, 1990), 373–382

Newsom, Carol, '"Sectually Explicit" Literature from Qumran,' in *The Hebrew Bible and Its Interpreters* (ed. Baruch Halpern and David Freedman; Winona Lake, Ind.: Eisenbrauns, 1990), 167–187

Newsom, Carol, *The Self as Symbolic Space: Constructing Identity and Community at Qumran* (STDJ 52; Leiden: Brill, 2004)

Nickelsburg, George, 'Aaron,' in *Reallexikon für Antike und Christentum: Supplement-Band I* (Stuttgart: Hiersemann, 2001), cols. 1–11

Nickelsburg, George W., '*1 Enoch* and Qumran Origins: The State of the Question and Some Prospects for Answers,' in *Society of Biblical Literature Seminar Papers* (ed. Kent H. Richards; Atlanta, Ga.: Scholars Press, 1986), 341–360

Niditch, Susan, *Oral World and Written Word: Ancient Israelite Literature* (Library of Ancient Israel; Louisville, Ky.: Westminster John Knox, 1996)

Nitzan, Bilhah, 'The Laws of Reproof in 4QBerakhot (4Q286–290) in Light of their Parallels in the Damascus Document and Other Texts from Qumran,' in *Legal Texts and Legal Issues* (ed. Bernstein, García Martínez, and Kampen), 149–165

Nitzan, Bilhah, *Qumran Prayer and Religious Poetry* (trans. Jonathan Chapman; STDJ 12; Leiden: Brill, 1994)

Noth, Martin, *Das Buch Josua* (2d ed.; HAT 1.7; Tübingen: Mohr Siebeck, 1952)

Osten-Sacken, Peter von der, *Gott und Belial: Traditionsgeschichtliche Untersuchungen zum Dualismus in den Texten aus Qumran* (Göttingen: Vandenhoek & Ruprecht, 1969)

Parker, David C., *The Living Text of the Gospels* (Cambidge: CUP, 1997)

Parry, Donald W. and Eugene Ulrich (eds), *The Provo International Conference on the Dead Sea Scrolls: Technological Innovations, New Texts, and Reformulated Issues* (STDJ 30; Leiden: Brill, 1999)

Patrich, Joseph, 'Khirbet Qumran in Light of New Archaeological Explorations in the Qumran Caves,' in *Archaeology and History in the Dead Sea Scrolls: The New York University Conference in Memory of Yigael Yadin* (ed. Lawrence H. Schiffman; JSPSup 8; Sheffield: JSOT Press, 1990), 73–95

Paul, Shalom M. et al. (eds), *Emanuel: Studies in Hebrew Bible, Septuagint, and the Dead Sea Scrolls in Honor of Emanuel Tov* (VTSup 94; Leiden: Brill, 2003)

Perdue, Leo et al. (eds), *Families in Ancient Israel* (The Family, Religion, and Culture; Louisville, Ky.: Westminster John Knox, 1997)

Peskowitz, Mirjam, 'Family/ies in Antiquity: Evidence from the Tannaitic Literature and Roman Galilean Architecture,' in *The Jewish Family in Antiquity* (ed. Shaye J. D. Cohen; Brown Judaic Studies 289; Atlanta, Ga.: Scholars Press, 1993), 9–36

Petersen, Anders Klostergaard, 'Rewritten Bible as a Borderline Phenomenon – Genre, Textual Strategy, or Canonical Anachronism?' in *Flores Florentino* (ed. Hilhorst, Puech, and Tigchelaar), 285–306

Pfann, Stephen, '4Q298: The Maskil's Address to All Sons of Dawn,' *JQR* 85 (1994): 203–235

Pfann, Stephen, 'The Mount Zion Inscribed Stone Cup: Preliminary Obervations,' in *New Studies in the Archaeology of Jerusalem and its Region* (ed. David Amit, Orit Peleg-Barkat, and Guy D. Stiebel; Jerusalem: The Hebrew University; IAA, 2010), 44–53

Pfann, Stephen, 'Qumran,' in *Encyclopaedia Judaica* (ed. Michael Berenbaum and Fred Skolnik; 2d. ed.; Detroit, Mich.: Macmillan, 2006), Vol. 16, 768–75

Pfann, Stephen, 'Reassessing the Judean Desert Caves: Libraries, Archives, Genizas and Hiding Places,' *Bulletin of the Anglo-Israel Archaeological Society* 25 (2007): 147–170

Pfann, Stephen, 'The Writings in Esoteric Script from Qumran,' in *The Dead Sea Scrolls Fifty Years After Their Discovery 1947–1997* (ed. Lawrence H. Schiffman, Emanuel Tov, and James C. VanderKam; Jerusalem: IES, 2000), 177–190

Philonenko, Marc, 'Sur les expressions "Maison fidèle en Israël," "Maison de vérité en Israël," "Maison de perfection et de vérité en Israël,"' in *From 4QMMT to Resurrection: Mélanges qumraniens en hommage à Émile Puech* (ed. Florentino García Martínez, Annette Steudel, and Eibert Tigchelaar; STDJ 61; Leiden: Brill 2006), 243–246

Ploeg, Johan P. M. van der, *Le rouleau de la guerre* (STDJ 2; Leiden: Brill, 1959)

Ploeg, Johan P. M. van der, 'The Meals of the Essenes,' *JSS* 2 (1957): 163–175

Politis, Konstantinos D., 'The Discovery and Excavation of the Khirbet Qazone Cemetery and Its Significance Relative to Qumran,' in *The Site of the Dead Sea Scrolls* (ed. Galor, Humbert, and Zangenberg), 213–219

Popović, Mladen, '4Q186. 4QZodiacal Physiognomy: A Full Edition,' in *The Mermaid and the Partridge: Essays from the Copenhagen Conference on Revising Texts from Cave Four* (ed. George J. Brooke and Jesper Høgenhaven; STDJ 96; Leiden: Brill, 2011), 221–258

Popović, Mladen, 'The Emergence of Aramaic and Hebrew Scholarly Texts: Transmission and Translation of Alien Wisdom,' in *The Dead Sea Scrolls: Transmission of Traditions* (ed. Metso, Najman, and Schuller), 81–114

Popović, Mladen, 'The Manuscript Collections: An Overview,' in *The T & T Clark Companion to the Dead Sea Scrolls* (ed. Brooke and Hempel)

Popović, Mladen, 'Networks of Scholars: The Transmission of Astronomical and Astrological Learning Between Babylonians, Greeks and Jews,' in *Ancient Jewish Sciences and the History of Knowledge* (ed. Jonathan Ben-Dov and Seth Sanders; New York: New York University Press, forthcoming)

Popović, Mladen, 'Qumran as Scroll Storehouse in Times of Crisis? A Comparative Perspective on Judaean Desert Manuscript Collections,' *JSJ* 43 (2012): 551–594

Popović, Mladen, *Reading the Human Body: Physiognomics and Astrology in the Dead Sea Scrolls* (STDJ 67; Leiden: Brill, 2007)

Popović, Mladen, 'Roman Book Destruction in Qumran Cave 4 and the Roman Destruction of Khirbet Qumran Revisited,' in *Qumran und die Archäologie* (ed. Jörg Frey, Carsten Claussen, and Nadine Kessler; WUNT 1.278; Tübingen: Mohr Siebeck, 2011), 239–291

Pouilly, Jean, *La Règle de la Communauté de Qumrân: Son évolution littéraire* (Cahiers de la Revue Biblique 17; Paris: Gabalda, 1976)

Priest, John F., 'Mebaqqer, Paqid, and the Messiah,' *JBL* 81 (1962): 55–61

Plöger, Otto, *Theocracy and Eschatology* (trans. S. Rudman; Richmond, Va.: John Knox, 1968)

Puech, Émile, 'Hodayot,' in EDSS 1:365–369

Puech, Émile, *La croyance des Esséniens en la vie future: Immortalité, resurrection, et vie éternelle* (Paris: Gabalda, 1993)

Puech, Émile, 'Recension: J. Pouilly, La Règle de la Communauté de Qumrân. Son evolution littéraire,' *RQ* 10 (1979): 103–111

Puech, Émile, 'Remarques sur l'écriture de 1QS VII-VIII,' *RQ* 10 (1979): 35–43

Qimron, Elisha, 'Celibacy in the Dead Sea Scrolls and the Two Kinds of Sectarians,' in *The Madrid Qumran Congress* (ed. Trebolle Barrera and Vegas Montaner), Vol. I, 287–294

Qimron, Elisha, 'Chickens in the Temple Scroll (11QT^c),' *Tarbiz* 64 (1995) 473–476 [Hebrew]

Qimron, Elisha, *The Hebrew of the Dead Sea Scrolls* (HSS 29; Atlanta, Ga.: Scholars Press, 1986)

Qimron, Elisha, 'Notes on the 4QZadokite Fragments on Skin Disease,' *JJS* 42 (1991): 256–259

Qimron, Elisha, 'Review of Philip R. Davies *The Damascus Covenant*,' *JQR* 77 (1986–87): 84–87

Qimron, Elisha, 'Rule of the Community (1QS),' in PTSDSSP 1:6–51

Qimron, Elisha, *The Temple Scroll: A Critical Edition with Extensive Reconstructions. Bibliography by Florentino García Martínez* (Beer Sheva: Ben-Gurion University of the Negev Press; Jerusalem: IES, 1996)

Qimron, Elisha, 'The Text of CDC,' in *The Damascus Document Reconsidered* (ed. Broshi), 9–49

Rabin, Chaim, *Qumran Studies* (Oxford: OUP, 1957)

Rabin, Chaim, *The Zadokite Documents: I. The Admonition II. The Laws* (Oxford: Clarendon, 1954)

Rappaport, Uriel, 'Apocalyptic Vision and Preservation of Historical Memory,' *JSJ* 23 (1992): 217–226

Rajak, Tessa, 'Ciò Che Flavio Gulseppe Vide: Josephus and the Essenes,' in *Josephus and the History of the Greco-Roman Period: Essays in Memory of Morton Smith* (ed. Fausto Parente and Joseph Sievers; StPB 41; Leiden: Brill, 1994), 141–160

Redditt, Paul L., 'Daniel 11 and the Sociological Setting of the Book of Daniel,' *CBQ* 60 (1998): 463–474

Reed, Stephen A., 'Genre, Setting and Title of 4Q477,' *JJS* 47 (1996): 147–148

Reeves, John C., 'What Does Noah Offer in 1QapGen X,15?,' *RQ* 12 (1986): 415–419

Regev, Eyal, 'Between Two Sects: Differentiating the Yaḥad and the Damascus Covenant,' in *The Dead Sea Scrolls: Texts and Context* (ed. Hempel), 431–449

Regev, Eyal, 'Cherchez les femmes: Were the *Yaḥad* Celibates?,' *DSD* 15 (2008): 253–284

Regev, Eyal, *Sectarianism in Qumran: A Cross-Cultural Perspective* (Religion and Society 45; Berlin: de Gruyter, 2007)

Regev, Eyal, 'The *Yaḥad* and the *Damascus Covenant*: Structure, Organization and Relationship,' *RQ* 21 (2003): 233–262

Reif, Stefan, 'Cairo Genizah,' in EDSS 1:105–108

Ringgren, Helmer, *The Faith of Qumran: Theology of the Dead Sea Scrolls* (rev. and enl. ed.; New York: Crossroad, 1995)

Rofé, Alexander, 'A Neglected Meaning of the Verb כול and the Text of 1QS vi:11–13,' in *"Sha'arei Talmon:" Studies in the Bible, Qumran, and the Ancient Near East Presented to Shemaryahu Talmon* (ed. Michael A. Fishbane and Emanuel Tov; Winona Lake, Ind.: Eisenbrauns, 1992), 315–321

Rofé, Alexander, 'The Piety of the Torah-Disciples at the Winding-up of the Hebrew Bible: Josh. 1:8; Ps. 1:2; Isa. 59:21,' in *Bibel in jüdischer und christlicher Tradition: Festschrift für Johann Maier zum 60. Geburtstag* (ed. Helmut Merklein, Karlheinz Müller, and Günter Stemberger; Frankfurt a. M.: Hain, 1993), 78–85

Roitman, Adolfo, Larry Schiffman, and Shani Tzoref (eds), *The Dead Sea Scrolls and Contemporary Culture* (STDJ 93; Leiden: Brill, 2011)

Rowley, Harold H., *The Zadokite Fragments and the Dead Sea Scrolls* (Oxford: Blackwell, 1952)

Rubinstein, Arie, 'Urban Halakhah and Camp Rules in the "Cairo Fragments of a Damascene Covenant,"' *Sefarad* 12 (1952): 283–296

Sanders, Ed P., *Paul and Palestinian Judaism* (St. Albans: SCM, 1977)

Sanders, James A., *The Psalms Scroll of Qumran Cave 11 (11QPsa)* (Oxford: Clarendon, 1965)

Schechter, Solomon, *Documents of Jewish Sectaries. Vol. 1: Fragments of a Zadokite Work* (Cambridge: CUP, 1910)

Schiffman, Lawrence H., 'Communal Meals at Qumran,' *RQ* 10 (1979): 45–56

Schiffman, Lawrence H., 'Community Without Temple: The Qumran Community's Withdrawal from the Jerusalem Temple,' in *Gemeinde ohne Tempel* (ed. Ego, Lange, Pilhofer), 267–84 (reprinted in Lawrence H. Schiffman, *Qumran and Jerusalem: Studies in the Dead Sea Scrolls and the History of Judaism* [Grand Rapids, Mich.: Eerdmans, 2010)], 81–97)

Schiffman, Lawrence H., *The Courtyards of the House of the Lord: Studies on the Temple Scroll* (ed. Florentino García Martínez; STDJ 75; Leiden: Brill: 2008)

Schiffman, Lawrence H., *The Eschatological Community of the Dead Sea Scrolls* (SBLMS 38; Atlanta, Ga.: Scholars Press, 1989)

Schiffman, Lawrence H., 'Exclusion from the Sanctuary and the City of the Sanctuary in the Temple Scroll,' *HAR* 9 (1985) 301–320 (reprinted in idem, *Courtyards of the House of the Lord*, 381–401)

Schiffman, Lawrence H., *The Halakhah at Qumran* (SJLA 16; Leiden: Brill, 1975)

Schiffman, Lawrence H., 'Legislation Concerning Relations with Non-Jews in the *Zadokite Fragments* and in Tannaitic Literature,' *RQ* 11 (1989): 379–389

Schiffman, Lawrence H., '*Miqṣat Ma'aśe ha-Torah* and the Temple Scroll,' *RQ* 14 (1990): 435–457 (reprinted in idem, *Courtyards of the House of the Lord*, 123–147)

Schiffman, Lawrence H., 'The New Halakhic Letter (4QMMT) and the Origins of the Dead Sea Sect,' *BA* 53 (1990): 64–73 (reprinted in idem, *Qumran and Jerusalem: Studies in the Dead Sea Scrolls and the History of Judaism* [Grand Rapids, Mich.: Eerdmans, 2010], 112–122)

Schiffman, Lawrence H., 'New Halakhic Texts from Qumran,' *Hebrew Studies* 34 (1993): 21–33

Schiffman, Lawrence H., 'Pharisaic and Sadducean Halakhah in the Light of the Dead Sea Scrolls: The Case of the Tebul Yom,' *DSD* 1 (1994): 285–299 (reprinted in idem, *Courtyards of the House of the Lord*, 425–439)

Schiffman, Lawrence H., 'The Place of 4QMMT in the Corpus of Qumran Manuscripts,' in *Reading 4QMMT* (ed. Kampen and Bernstein), 81–98 (reprinted in idem, *Qumran and Jerusalem*, 123–139)

Schiffman, Lawrence H., 'Purity and Perfection: Exclusion from the Council of the Community in the Serekh Ha-'Edah,' in *Biblical Archaeology Today: Proceedings of the International Congress on Biblical Archaeology, Jerusalem, April 1984* (ed. Janet Amitai; Jerusalem: IES, 1985), 373–389

Schiffman, Lawrence H., *Reclaiming the Dead Sea Scrolls: The History of Judaism, the Background to Christianity, the Lost Library of Qumran* (Philadelphia, Pa.: JPS, 1994)

Schiffman, Lawrence H., 'Sacral and Non-Sacral Slaughter According to the *Temple Scroll*,' in *Time to Prepare the Way in the Wilderness* (ed. Dimant and Schiffman), 69–84 (reprinted in idem, *Courtyards of the House of the Lord*, 297–313)

Schiffman, Lawrence H., 'The Sadducean Origins of the Dead Sea Scroll Sect,' in *Understanding the Dead Sea Scrolls* (ed. Hershel Shanks; London: SPCK, 1993), 35–49

Schiffman, Lawrence H., *Sectarian Law in the Dead Sea Scrolls: Courts, Testimony and the Penal Code* (BJS 33; Chico, Calif.: Scholars Press, 1983)

Schiffman, Lawrence H., 'Serekh-Damascus,' in EDSS 2:868–869

Schiffman, Lawrence H., 'Some Laws Pertaining to Animals in Temple Scroll Column 52,' in *Legal Texts and Legal Issues* (ed. Bernstein, García Martínez, and Kampen), 167–178

Schiffman, Lawrence H., 'The Temple Scroll and the Systems of Jewish Law of the Second Temple Period,' in *Temple Scroll Studies* (ed. George J. Brooke; JSPSup 7; Sheffield: JSOT Press, 1989), 239–255

Schiffman, Lawrence H., 'Utopia and Reality: Political Leadership and Organization in the Dead Sea Scrolls Community,' in *Emanuel* (ed. Paul et al.), 413–427

Schofield, Alison, 'Rereading S: A New Model of Textual Development in Light of the Cave 4 *Serekh* Copies,' *DSD* 15 (2008): 96–120

Schofield, Alison, *From Qumran to the Yaḥad: A New Paradigm of Textual Development for the Community Rule* (STDJ 77; Leiden: Brill, 2009)

Schremer, Adiel, '"[T]he[y] Did not Read in the Sealed Book:" Qumran Halakhic Revolution and the Emergence of Torah Study in Second Temple Judaism,' in *Historical Perspectives: From the Hasmoneans to Bar Kokhba in Light of the Dead Sea Scrolls: Proceedings of the Fourth International Symposium of the Orion Center for the Study of the Dead Sea Scrolls and Associated Literature, 27–31 January 1999* (ed. David Goodblatt, Avital Pinnick, and Daniel R. Schwartz; STDJ 37; Leiden: Brill, 2001), 105–126

Schuller, Eileen, *The Dead Sea Scrolls: What Have We Learned 50 Years On* (London: SCM, 2006)

Schuller, Eileen, 'Women in the Dead Sea Scrolls,' in *The Dead Sea Scrolls After Fifty Years* (ed. Flint and VanderKam), Vol. II, 117–144

Schuller, Eileen M., 'Women in the Dead Sea Scrolls,' in *Methods of Investigation of the Dead Sea Scrolls and the Khirbet Qumran Site: Present Realities and Future Prospects* (ed. Michael O. Wise et al.; Annals of the New York Academy of Sciences 722; New York: New York Academy of Sciences, 1994), 115–131

Schuller, Eileen, 'Women in the Dead Sea Scrolls: Research in the Past Decade and Future Directions,' in *The Dead Sea Scrolls and Contemporary Culture* (ed. Roitman, Schiffman, and Tzoref), 571–588

Schultz, Brian, *Conquering the World: The War Scroll (1QM) Reconsidered* (STDJ 76; Leiden: Brill, 2009)

Segert, Stanislav, 'Die Sprachenfragen in der Qumrangemeinschaft,' in *Qumran-Probleme* (ed. Hans Bardtke; DAWBSSA 42; Berlin: Akademie Verlag, 1963), 315–339

Shemesh, Aharon, '4Q271.3: A Key to Sectarian Matrimonial Law,' *JJS* 49 (1998): 244–263

Shemesh, Aharon, '"The Holy Angels are in their Council:" The Exclusion of Deformed Persons from Holy Places in Qumranic and Rabbinic Literature,' *DSD* 4 (1997): 179–206

Shemesh, Aharon, 'The Scriptural Background of the Penal Code in the *Rule of the Community* and *Damascus* Document,' *DSD* 15 (2008): 191–224

Sivertsev, Alexei, *Households, Sects, and the Origins of Rabbinic Judaism* (JSJSup 102; Leiden: Brill, 2005)

Sivertsev, Alexei, *Private Household and Public Politics in 3rd – 5th Century Jewish Palestine* (TSAJ 90; Tübingen: Mohr Siebeck, 2002)

Sivertsev, Alexei, 'Sects and Households: Social Structure of the Proto-Sectarian Movement of Nehemiah 10 and the Dead Sea Sect,' *CBQ* 67 (2005): 59–78

Skehan, Patrick, 'A Liturgical Complex in 11QPs[a],' *CBQ* 35 (1973): 195–205

Smend, Rudolf, 'Das Gesetz und die Völker,' in *Die Mitte des Alten Testaments: Exegetische Aufsätze* (Tübingen: Mohr Siebeck, 2002), 148–161

Smith, Morton, 'The Dead Sea Scrolls in Relation to Ancient Judaism,' *NTS* 7 (1960): 347–360

Soggin, Jan A., *Joshua: A Commentary* (trans. R. A. Wilson; OTL; London: SCM, 1972)

Solomon, Avi, 'The Prohibition Against *Xevul Yom* and Defilement of the Daily Whole Offering in the Jerusalem Temple in CD 11:21–12:1: A New Understanding,' *DSD* 4 (1997): 1–20

Stegemann, Hartmut, *Die Entstehung der Qumrangemeinde* (Bonn: Privately Published, 1971)

Stegemann, Hartmut, *The Library of Qumran: On the Essenes, Qumran, John the Baptist, and Jesus* (Grand Rapids, Mich.: Eerdmans, 1998)

Stegemann, Hartmut, 'More Identified Fragments of 4QD[d] (4Q269),' *RQ* 18 (1998): 497–509

Stegemann, Hartmut, 'The Origins of the Temple Scroll,' in *Congress Volume: Jerusalem 1986* (ed. John A. Emerton; VTSup 40; Leiden: Brill, 1988), 235–256

Stegemann, Hartmut, 'The Qumran Essenes – Local Members of the Main Jewish Union in Late Second Temple Times,' in *The Madrid Qumran Congress* (ed. Trebolle Barrera and Vegas Montaner), Vol. I, 83–166

Stegemann, Hartmut, 'Some Remarks to *1QSa*, to *1QSb*, and to Qumran Messianism,' *RQ* 17 (1996): 479–505

Stegemann, Hartmut, 'Towards Physical Reconstructions of the Qumran Damascus Document Scrolls,' in *The Damascus Document* (ed. Baumgarten, Chazon and Pinnick), 177–200

Stegemann, Hartmut, 'Zu Textbestand und Grundgedanken von 1QS III,13-IV,26,' *RQ* 13 (1988): 95–113

Steinmann, Andrew, 'The Chicken and the Egg: A New Proposal for the Relationship Between the *Prayer of Nabonidus* and the *Book of Daniel*,' *RQ* 20 (2002): 558–570

Steinsaltz, Adin, *The Essential Talmud* (London: Weidenfeld and Nicolson, 1976)

Stern, Sacha, 'Qumran Calendars and Sectarianism,' in *Oxford Handbook of the Dead Sea Scrolls* (ed. Lim and Collins), 232–253

Stern, Sacha, 'The "Sectarian" Calendar of Qumran,' in *Sects and Sectarianism in Jewish History* (ed. Stern), 39–62

Stern, Sacha (ed.), *Sects and Sectarianism in Jewish History* (IJS Studies in Judaica 12; Leiden: Brill, 2011)

Steudel, Annette, 'אחרית הימים in the Texts from Qumran,' *RQ* 16 (1993): 225–246

Steudel, Annette, 'Dating Exegetical Texts from Qumran,' in *Dynamics of Language and Exegesis at Qumran* (ed. Dimant and Kratz), 39–53

Steudel, Annette, *Der Midrasch zur Eschatologie aus der Qumrangemeinde (4QMidrEschat*$^{a.b}$*): Materielle Rekonstruktion, Textbestand, Gattung, traditionsgeschichtliche Einordnung des durch 4Q174 ("Florilegium") und 4Q177 ("Catena A") repräsentierten Werkes aus den Qumranfunden* (STDJ 13; Leiden: Brill, 1994)

Stökl Ben Ezra, Daniel, 'Further Reflections on Caves 1 and 11: A Response to Florentino García Martínez,' in *The Dead Sea Scrolls: Texts and Context* (ed. Hempel), 211–223

Stökl Ben Ezra, Daniel, 'Old Caves and Young Caves: A Statistical Reevaluation of a Qumran Consensus,' *DSD* 14 (2007): 313–333

Stökl Ben Ezra, Daniel, 'Wie viele Bibliotheken gab es in Qumran?,' in *Qumran und die Archäologie* (ed. Jörg Frey, Carsten Claussen, and Nadine Kessler; WUNT 1.278; Tübingen: Mohr Siebeck, 2011), 327–346

Stone, Michael E., 'The Scrolls and the Literary Landscape of Second Temple Judaism,' in *The Dead Sea Scrolls: Texts and Context* (ed. Hempel), 15–30

Strugnell, John, 'MMT: Second Thoughts on a Forthcoming Edition,' in *The Community of the Renewed Covenant* (ed. Ulrich and VanderKam), 57–73

Strugnell, John, 'More on Wives and Marriage in the Dead Sea Scrolls: (*4Q416* 2 ii 21 [Cf. *1 Thess* 4:4] and *4QMMT* §B),' *RQ* 17 (1996): 537–547

Strugnell, John, 'Notes en marge du Volume V des "Discoveries in the Judaean Desert of Jordan,"' *RQ* 7 (1970): 163–276

Strugnell, John, 'The Sapiential Work 4Q415ff and Pre-Qumranic Works from Qumran: Lexical Considerations,' in *The Provo International Conference on the Dead Sea Scrolls* (ed. Parry and Ulrich), 595–608

Stuckenbruck, Loren T., 'Daniel and Early Enoch Traditions in the Dead Sea Scrolls,' in *Book of Daniel* (ed. Collins and Flint), Vol. II, 368–386

Stuckenbruck, Loren T., 'The Legacy of the Teacher of Righteousness in the Dead Sea Scrolls,' in *New Perspectives on Old Texts: Proceedings of the Tenth International Symposium of the Orion Center for the Study of the Dead Sea Scrolls and Associated Literature, 9–11 January 2005* (ed. Esther G. Chazon, Betsy Halpern-Amaru, and Ruth A. Clements; STDJ 88; Leiden: Brill, 2010), 23–49

Stuckenbruck, Loren T., 'The Teacher of Righteousness Remembered: From Fragmentary Sources to Collective Memory in the Dead Sea Scrolls,' in *Memory in the Bible and Antiquity: The Fifth Durham-Tübingen Research Symposium (Durham, September 2004)* (ed. Stephen Barton, Loren Stuckenbruck, and Benjamin Wold; WUNT 212; Tübingen: Mohr Siebeck, 2007), 75–94

Sukenik, Eleazar L., *The Dead Sea Scrolls of the Hebrew University* (Jerusalem: The Hebrew University; Magnes, 1955)

Sussman, Yaakov, 'The History of the Halakhah and the Dead Sea Scrolls: Preliminary Talmudic Observations on *Miqṣat Ma'aśe ha-Torah* (4QMMT),' DJD 10:179–20

Sutcliffe, Edmund F. S. J., 'The First Fifteen Members of the Qumran Community: A Note on 1QS 8:1 ff.,' *JSS* 4 (1959): 134–138

Sutcliffe, Edmund F. S. J., 'Sacred Meals at Qumran?,' *HeyJ* 1 (1960): 48–65

Talmon, Shemaryahu, 'The Calendar Reckoning of the Sect from the Judaean Desert,' in *Aspects of the Dead Sea Scrolls* (Jerusalem: Magnes, 1958), 162–199

Talmon, Shemaryahu, 'The Community of the Renewed Covenant: Between Judaism and Christianity' in *The Community of the Renewed Covenant* (ed. Ulrich and VanderKam), 3–24

Talmon, Shemaryahu, 'The Crystallization of the "Canon of Hebrew Scriptures" in the Light of Biblical Scrolls from Qumran,' in *The Bible as Book* (ed. Herbert and Tov), 5–20

Talmon, Shemaryahu, 'The Emergence of Jewish Sectarianism in the Early Second Temple Period,' in *King, Cult, and Calendar in Ancient Israel: Collected Studies* (Leiden: Brill; Jerusalem: Magnes, 1986), 165–201

Talmon, Shemaryahu, 'The Essential "Community of the Renewed Covenant:" How Should Qumran Studies Proceed?,' in *Geschichte – Tradition – Reflexion: Festschrift für Martin Hengel zum 70. Geburtstag* (ed. Hubert Cancik, Hermann Lichtenberger, and Peter Schäfer; Tübingen: Mohr Siebeck, 1996), Vol. I, 323–351

Talmon, Shemaryahu, 'The Old Testament Text,' in *The Cambridge History of the Bible, Volume 1* (ed. Peter R. Ackroyd and Christopher F. Evans; Cambridge: CUP, 1970), 159–199

Talmon, Shemaryahu, 'Pisqah Be'emṣa' Pasuq and 11QPs^a,' *Textus* 5 (1966): 11–21

Talmon, Shemaryahu, 'Qumran Studies: Past, Present, and Future,' *JQR* 85 (1994): 1–31

Talmon, Shemaryahu, *The World of Qumran From Within* (Leiden: Brill; Jerusalem: Magnes, 1989)

Talmon, Shemaryahu, 'Yom Hakkippurim in the Habakkuk Scroll,' *Biblica* 32 (1951): 549–563

Talmon, Shemaryahu and Israel Knohl, 'A Calendar Scroll from a Qumran Cave: Mišmarot B^a, 4Q321,' in *Pomegranates and Golden Bells: Studies in Biblical, Jewish, and Near Eastern Ritual, Law, and Literature in Honor of Jacob Milgrom* (ed. David P. Wright, David N. Freedman, and Avi Hurvitz; Winona Lake, Ind.: Eisenbrauns, 1995), 267–301

Taylor, Joan E., 'Buried Manuscripts and Empty Tombs: The Qumran Genizah Theory Revisited,' in *'Go Out and Study the Land' (Judges 18:2): Archaeological, Historical and Textual Studies in Honor of Hanan Eshel* (ed. Aren M. Maeir, Jodi Magness, and Lawrence H. Schiffman; JSJSup 148; Leiden: Brill, 2011), 269–315

Taylor, Joan E., 'Philo of Alexandria on the Essenes: A Case Study on the Use of Classical Sources in Discussions of the Qumran-Essene Hypothesis,' *Studia Philonica Annual* 19 (2007): 1–28

Taylor, Joan E., 'Women, Children, and Celibate Men in the Serekh Texts,' *HTR* 104 (2011): 171–190

Thomas, Samuel I., 'Esoteric Knowledge in Qumran Aramaic Texts,' in *Aramaica Qumranica* (ed. Berthelot and Stökl Ben Ezra), 403–430

Thomas, Samuel I., *The "Mysteries" of Qumran: Mystery, Secrecy, and Esotericism in the Dead Sea Scrolls* (EJL 25; Atlanta, Ga.: SBL, 2009)

Tigay, Jeffrey H., 'Examination of the Accused Bride in 4Q159: Forensic Medicine at Qumran,' *JANES* 22 (1993): 129–134

Tigchelaar, Eibert J. C., 'Annotated List of Overlaps and Parallels in the Non-biblical Texts from Qumran and Masada,' in DJD 39:285–322

Tigchelaar, Eibert J. C., 'The Dead Sea Scrolls,' in EDEJ: 163–180

Tigchelaar, Eibert J. C., 'More Identifications of Scraps and Overlaps,' *RQ* 19 (1999): 61–68

Tigchelaar, Eibert J. C., 'A Newly Identified 11QSerekh ha-Yaḥad Fragment (11Q29)?,' in *The Dead Sea Scrolls Fifty Years After Their Discovery 1947–1997* (ed. Lawrence H. Schiffman, Emanuel Tov, and James C. VanderKam; Jerusalem: IES, 2000), 285–292

Tigchelaar, Eibert J. C., 'Sabbath Halakha and Worship in 4QWays of Righteousness: 4Q421 11 and 13+2+8 Par 4Q264a 1–2,' *RQ* 18 (1998): 359–372

Tigchelaar, Eibert J. C., 'The Scribe of 1QS,' in *Emanuel* (ed. Paul et al.), 439–452

Tigchelaar, Eibert J. C., '"These are the names of the spirits of ...:" A Preliminary Edition of *4QCatalogue of Spirits (4Q230)* and New Manuscript Evidence for the *Two Spirits Treatise (4Q257* and *1Q29a)*,' *RQ* 84 (2004): 529–547

Tigchelaar, Eibert J. C., *To Increase Learning for the Understanding Ones: Reading and Reconstructing the Early Jewish Sapiential Text 4QInstruction* (STDJ 44; Leiden: Brill, 2001)

Tigchelaar, Eibert J. C., 'Towards a Reconstruction of the Beginning of 4QInstruction,' in *The Wisdom Texts from Qumran* (ed. Hempel, Lange, and Lichtenberger), 99–126

Tiller, Patrick, 'The Eternal Planting in the Dead Sea Scrolls,' *DSD* 4 (1997): 312–335

Toorn, Karel van der, *Scribal Culture and the Making of the Hebrew Bible* (Cambridge: Harvard University Press, 2007)

Tov, Emanuel, 'The Coincidental Textual Nature of the Collections of Ancient Scriptures,' in *Congress Volume Ljubljana 2007* (ed. André Lemaire; VTSup 133; Leiden: Brill, 2010), 153–169

Tov, Emanuel, 'Excerpted and Abbreviated Biblical Texts from Qumran,' *RQ* 16 (1995): 581–600

Tov, Emanuel, 'Hebrew Biblical Manuscripts from the Judaean Desert: Their Contribution to Textual Criticism,' *JJS* 39 (1988): 5–37

Tov, Emanuel, 'Letters of the Cryptic A Script and Paleo-Hebrew Letters Used as Scribal Marks in Some Qumran Scrolls,' *DSD* 2 (1995): 330–339

Tov, Emanuel, 'Lists of Specific Groups of Texts from the Judaean Desert,' in DJD 39: 203–228

Tov, Emanuel, *Revised Lists of the Texts from the Judaean Desert* (Leiden: Brill, 2010)

Tov, Emanuel, *Scribal Practices and Approaches Reflected in the Texts Found in the Judean Desert* (STDJ 54; Leiden: Brill, 2004)

Tov, Emanuel, 'Scriptures: Text,' in EDSS 2:832–836

Tov, Emanuel, 'The Special Character of the Texts Found in Qumran Cave 11,' in *Things Revealed: Studies in Early Jewish and Christian Literature in Honor of Michael E. Stone* (ed. Esther G. Chazon, David Satran, and Ruth A. Clements; JSJSup 89; Leiden: Brill, 2004), 187–196

Tov, Emanuel, *Textual Criticism of the Hebrew Bible* (2d ed.; Minneapolis, Minn.: Fortress; Assen: van Gorcum, 2001)

Tov, Emanuel, 'The Writing of Early Scrolls: Implications for the Literary Analysis of Hebrew Scripture,' in *L'écrit et l'ésprit: Etudes d'histoire du texte et de théologie biblique en hommage à Adrian Schenker* (ed. Dieter Böhler, Innocent Himbaza, and Philippe Hugo; Göttingen: Vandenhoeck & Ruprecht, 2005), 355–371

Tov, Emanuel, 'The Writing of Early Scrolls: Implications for the Literary Analysis of Hebrew Scripture,' *DSD* 13 (2006): 339–347

Trebolle Barrera, Julio and Luis Vegas Montaner (eds), *The Madrid Qumran Congress: Proceedings of the International Congress on the Dead Sea Scrolls, Madrid 18–21 March* 1991 (STDJ 11; Leiden: Brill, 1992)

Ulrich, Eugene, 'The Bible in the Making: The Scriptures Found at Qumran,' in *The Bible at Qumran: Text, Shape, and Interpretation* (ed. Peter W. Flint; Studies in the Dead Sea Scrolls and Related Literature; Grand Rapids, Mich.: Eerdmans, 2001), 51–66.

Ulrich, Eugene, 'Biblical Scrolls Scholarship in North America,' in *The Dead Sea Scrolls in Scholarly Perspective* (ed. Dimant), 49–74

Ulrich, Eugene, *The Dead Sea Scrolls and the Origins of the Bible* (Studies in the Dead Sea Scrolls and Related Literature; Grand Rapids, Mich.: Eerdmans, 1999)

Ulrich, Eugene, 'The Evolutionary Production and Transmission of the Scriptural Books,' in *The Dead Sea Scrolls: Transmission of Traditions* (ed. Metso, Najman, and Schuller), 209–225

Ulrich, Eugene and James C. VanderKam (eds), *The Community of the Renewed Covenant: The Notre Dame Symposium on the Dead Sea Scrolls* (Christianity and Judaism in Antiquity 10; Notre Dame: University of Notre Dame Press, 1994)

VanderKam, James C., '1 Enoch, Astronomical Book of (1 Enoch 72–82),' in EDEJ: 581–583

VanderKam, James C., 'The Calendar, 4Q327, and 4Q394,' in *Legal Texts and Legal Issues* (ed. Bernstein, García Martínez, and Kampen), 179–194

VanderKam, James C., *Calendars in the Dead Sea Scrolls: Measuring Time* (Literature of the Dead Sea Scrolls; London: Routledge, 1998)

VanderKam, James C., 'The Common Ownership of Property in Essene Communities,' in *'Go Out and Study the Land' (Judges 18:2): Archaeological, Historical and Textual Studies in Honor of Hanan Eshel* (ed. Maeir N. Aren, Jodi Magness, and Lawrence H. Schiffman; JSJSup 148; Leiden: Brill, 2011), 359–375

VanderKam, James C., *The Dead Sea Scrolls Today* (London: SPCK, 1994)

VanderKam, James C., 'Messianism in the Scrolls,' in *The Community of the Renewed Covenant* (ed. Ulrich and VanderKam), 211–234

VanderKam, James C., 'The Oath and the Community,' *DSD* 16 (2009): 416–432

VanderKam, James C., 'The People of the Dead Sea Scrolls: Essenes or Sadducees,' in *Understanding the Dead Sea Scrolls* (ed. Hershel Shanks; London: SPCK, 1993), 50–62

VanderKam, James C., 'The Pre-History of the Qumran Community with a Reassessment of CD 1:5–11,' in *The Dead Sea Scrolls and Contemporary Culture* (ed. Roitman, Schiffman, and Tzoref), 59–76

VanderKam, James C., 'Questions of Canon Viewed Through the Dead Sea Scrolls,' in *The Canon Debate* (ed. Lee M. McDonald and James A. Sanders; Peabody, Mass.: Hendrickson, 2002), 91–109

VanderKam, James C. and Peter Flint, *The Meaning of the Dead Sea Scrolls: Their Significance for Understanding the Bible, Judaism, Jesus and Christianity* (London: T & T Clark, 2002)

Vaux, Roland de, *Archaeology and the Dead Sea Scrolls: The Schweich Lectures 1959* (Oxford: OUP; The British Academy, 1973)

Veijola, Timo, *Moses Erben: Studien zum Dekalog, zum Deuteronomismus, und zum Schriftgelehrtentum* (Stuttgart: Kohlhammer, 2000)

Vermes, Geza, *The Complete Dead Sea Scrolls in English* (London: Allen Lane, 1997)

Vermes, Geza, *The Dead Sea Scrolls Forty Years On: The Fourteenth Sacks Lecture* (Oxford: Oxford Centre for Postgraduate Hebrew Studies, 1987)

Vermes, Geza, *The Dead Sea Scrolls in English* (Rev. and enl. 4th ed.; Harmondsworth: Penguin, 1995)

Vermes, Geza, *The Dead Sea Scrolls: Qumran in Perspective* (3d rev. ed.; London: SCM, 1994)

Vermes, Geza, 'The Leadership of the Qumran Community: Sons of Zadok-Priests-Congregation,' in *Geschichte – Tradition – Reflexion: Festschrift für Martin Hengel zum 70. Geburtstag* (ed. Hubert Cancik, Hermann Lichtenberger, and Peter Schäfer; Tübingen: Mohr Siebeck, 1996), Vol. I, 375–384

Vermes, Geza, 'Preliminary Remarks on Unpublished Fragments of the Community Rule from Qumran Cave 4,' *JJS* 42 (1991): 250–255

Vermes, Geza, 'Qumran Forum Miscellanea I,' *JJS* 43 (1992): 300–301

Vermes, Geza and Martin D. Goodman, *The Essenes According to the Classical Sources* (Oxford Centre Textbooks 1; Sheffield: JSOT Press, 1989)

Wacholder, Ben Zion, *The New Damascus Document: The Midrash on the Eschatological Torah of the Dead Sea Scrolls. Reconstruction, Translation and Commentary* (STDJ 56; Leiden: Brill, 2007)

Wacholder, Ben Zion and Martin G. Abegg, *A Preliminary Edition of the Unpublished Dead Sea Scrolls, Fascicle 3: The Hebrew and Aramaic Texts from Cave Four* (Washington, D. C.: Biblical Archaeology Society, 1995)

Wassen, Cecilia, *Women in the Damascus Document* (Academia Biblica 21; Atlanta, Ga.: SBL, 2005)

Wassen, Cecilia and Jutta Jokiranta, 'Groups in Tension: Sectarianism in the Damascus Document and the Community Rule,' in *Sectarianism in Early Judaism* (ed. Chalcraft), 205–245

Weeks, Stuart, 'Wisdom Psalms,' in *Temple and Worship in Biblical Israel* (ed. Day), 292–307

Weinberg, Joel, *The Citizen-Temple Community* (trans. Daniel L. Smith-Christopher; JSOTSup 151; Sheffield: Sheffield Academic Press, 1992)

Weinert, Francis D., '*4Q159*: Legislation for an Essene Community Outside of Qumran?,' *JSJ* 5 (1974): 179–207

Weinert, Francis D., 'A Note on 4Q159 and a New Theory of Essene Origins,' *RQ* 9 (1977–1978): 223–230

Weinfeld, Moshe, *Deuteronomy and the Deuteronomic School* (Oxford: Clarendon, 1972)

Weinfeld, Moshe, *The Organizational Pattern and the Penal Code of the Qumran Sect: A Comparison with Guilds and Religious Associations of the Hellenistic-Roman Period* (NTOA 2; Göttingen: Vandenhoeck & Ruprecht; Fribourg: Éditions Universitaires, 1986)

Weiser, Arthur, *The Psalms: A Commentary* (OTL; London: SCM, 1962)

Weissenberg, Hanne von, *4QMMT: Reevaluating the Text, the Function, and the Meaning of the Epilogue* (STDJ 82; Leiden: Brill, 2009)

Weissenberg, Hanne von, 'The Centrality of the Temple in 4QMMT,' in *The Dead Sea Scrolls: Texts and Context* (ed. Hempel), 293–305

Weitzman, Stephen, 'Copper Scroll (3Q15),' in EDEJ: 486–487

Wenthe, Dean O., 'The Social Configuration of the Rabbi-Disciple Relationship: Evidence and Implications for First Century Palestine,' in *Studies in the Hebrew Bible, Qumran, and the Septuagint* (ed. Flint, Tov, and VanderKam), 143–174

Wernberg-Møller, Preben, 'צדיק, צדק and צדוק in the Zaokite Fragments (CDC), the Manual of Discipline (DSD) and the Habakkuk-Commentary (DSH),' *VT* 3 (1953): 310–315

Wernberg-Møller, Preben, *The Manual of Discipline* (STDJ 1; Leiden: Brill, 1957)

White Crawford, Sidnie, 'Not According to Rule: Women, the Dead Sea Scrolls and Qumran,' in *Emanuel* (ed. Paul et al.), 127–150

White Crawford, Sidnie, 'Qumran: Caves, Scrolls, and Buildings,' in *A Teacher for All Generations: Essays in Honor of James C. VanderKam* (ed. Eric Mason et al.; JSJSup 153; Leiden: Brill, 2012), 253–273

White Crawford, Sidnie, *Rewriting Scripture in Second Temple Times* (Studies in the Dead Sea Scrolls and Related Literature; Grand Rapids, Mich.: Eerdmans, 2008)

White Crawford, Sidnie, *The Temple Scroll and Related Text* (CQS 2; Sheffield: Sheffield Academic Press, 2000)

Williamson, Hugh, *Ezra, Nehemiah* (Word Biblical Commentary 16; Waco, Tex.: Word Books, 1985)

Williamson, Hugh, 'The Family in Persian Period Judah: Some Textual Reflections,' in *Symbiosis, Symbolism, and the Power of the Past: Canaan, Ancient Israel, and Their Neighbors from the Late Bronze Age through Roman Palaestina* (ed. William G. Dever and Seymour Gitin; Winona Lake, Ind.: Eisenbrauns, 2003), 469–485

Wilson, Gerald H., *The Editing of the Hebrew Psalter* (Chico, Calif.: Scholars Press, 1985)

Wilson, Robert R., 'From Prophecy to Apocalyptic: Reflections on the Shape of Israelite Religion,' *Semeia* 21 (1981): 79–95

Wise Michael, Martin Abegg, and Edward Cook, *The Dead Sea Scrolls: A New Translation* (London: HarperCollins, 1996)

Woude, Adam S. van der, 'Die Doppelsprachigkeit des Buches Daniel,' in *Book of Daniel in the Light of New Findings* (ed. van der Woude), 3–12

Woude, Adam S. van der, 'Fünfzehn Jahre Qumranforschung (1974–1988): III. Studien zu früher veröffentlichten Handschriften,' *ThR* 57 (1992): 1–57

Woude, Adam S. van der, 'Wisdom at Qumran,' in *Wisdom in Ancient Israel: Essays in Honour of John A. Emerton* (ed. John Day, Robert P. Gordon, and Hugh G. M. Williamson; Cambridge: CUP, 1995), 244–256

Woude, Adam S. van der (ed.), *Daniel in the Light of New Findings* (BETL 106; Leuven: Peeters, 1993)

Wright, Archie T., 'Angels,' in EDEJ: 328–321

Yadin, Yigael, 'A Note on 4Q159 (Ordinances),' *IEJ* 18 (1968): 250–252

Yadin, Yigael, *The Scroll of the War of the Sons of Light Against the Sons of Darkness* (Oxford: OUP, 1962)

Yadin, Yigael, *The Temple Scroll* (3 vols; Jerusalem: IES, 1983)

Yardeni, Ada, 'A Draft of a Deed on an Ostracon from Khirbet Qumrân,' *IEJ* 47 (1997): 233–237

Yardeni, Ada, 'A Note on a Qumran Scribe,' in *New Seals and Inscriptions, Hebrew, Idumean and Cuneiform* (ed. Meir Lubetski; Hebrew Bible Monographs 8; Sheffield: Phoenix, 2007), 287–298

Zahn, Molly, *Rethinking Rewritten Scripture: Composition and Exegesis in the 4QReworked Pentateuch Manuscripts* (STDJ 95; Leiden: Brill, 2011)

Zissu, Boas, 'Odd Tomb Out: Has Jerusalem's Essene Cemetery Been Found?,' *BAR* 25 (1999): 50–55

Index of References*

Hebrew Bible (Jewish Canon)

Gen	321, 330	31:26	156
1:14	327	31:48	32
		31:52	32
Exod	282, 330	35:4–5	256
19:14–15	58		
30:11–16	188	*Deut*	190, 282, 330
30:12	191	6:4–9	299
38:26	190	6:6–7	298
		17:5–13	188
Lev		22	14, 189, 190
1–16	177	22:5	188, 190
12–15	180	22:13–21	188, 189, 190
12:4	180	23:15	176
17	176	23:25–26	182, 188
17:3	176		
19:17	331	*Josh*	
19:17–18	45	1	297
19:23–24	182	1:1–9	293
19:23–25	182	1:7–9	294
22:16	179	1:8	19, 293, 294, 295, 296, 298
25	14, 188, 190		
25:47–55	188		
27	189	*1 Sam*	282
Num		*2 Sam*	282
1:46	190		
3	205	*1 Kgs*	282
3:17	89, 296		
5	57	*2 Kgs*	282
18:2	213		
18:4	213	*Isa*	330
31:14	32	1:10 ff.	92

---

* Generic references to the documents 1QS and CD are ubiquitous in chapters 1–18 and are, therefore, included for the final chapter 19 (pp. 303–337) only. Full references are given throughout for particular manuscripts other than 1QS and CD and particular passages in the latter.

26:3	90	51:19	87, 90
30:1–5	226	53	292
40:3	251	57:7–11	292
51:1	170	60:5–12	292
53:11	238, 239	70	292
59:20	156	72:20	292
59:21	19, 294	105:15	184
		108	292
Jer	119, 207, 330	151	292
11:9–11	218, 222		
		Prov	335
Ezek	196, 207, 219, 226		
37:23	207, 226	Eccl	299
44	207, 219		
44:15	199, 213, 217, 218, 222	Dan	15, 16, 156, 231–252, 330
45:11	188	1:4	238
		2	236
Amos		2–7	233
5:21–24	92	2:4	232
		4	236
Mic		7	232
6	96	7:28	232
6:6–8	87, 90, 92	8	232, 238
6:8	87, 88, 90, 92, 170	11	237, 238, 239
		11–12	15, 231, 234, 237, 240, 251
Hab		11:32	237
2:15	320	11:33	237, 238
		11:33–35	237, 249
Zeph		11:35	238
2:3	170	12	239
		12:3	238, 239
Mal			
3:16–18	12, 162	Ezra	15, 16, 220, 253–270
		2	258
Ps	146, 240, 291, 292, 299, 330, 335	2:1	256
1	293, 297, 299	2:61–63	258
1:2	19, 293, 295, 296, 298	2:170	256
		3:1	256
1:3	293	7:25–26	259
1:6	293	9–10	259
2	293	10:8	259
14	292		
18	292	Neh	15, 16, 220, 253–270
40:13–17	292	3:1	256
51	90	5:10	257
51:18–19	87	5:13	259

5:14–18	257	11:1–3	256
7	258	12:22–23	258
7:6	256	13	257
7:63–65	258	13:2–7	257
7:72	256	13:15–22	259
8:2–3	258	13:28–29	257, 258, 259
8:7–9	297		
9:3	298	*1 Chr*	196, 220, 240
10	146, 254, 257, 258	24	323
10:28–29	145		
10:36–40	259	*2 Chr*	196, 220, 240
11	256		

Apocrypha and Septuagint

Sir	158, 196	*Tob*	330
38:34–39:11	299		

New Testament

Acts
4:32   102

Old Testament Pseudepigrapha

1 En.	4, 77, 78, 234, 236, 320, 330	*Jub.*	4, 78, 155, 207, 234, 320, 330
72–82	319	7:35–37	182
93:10	4, 78, 234	21:24	4, 78, 234

Dead Sea Scrolls

CD *(Damascus Document)*		1:7–8	94
	320, 332, 336	1:8	94
1	4, 5, 75, 78, 94, 206, 234	1:9	68
		1:9–11	69, 70, 77
1:1	170, 183	1:16	76
1:3	72	2	77
1:3–9	4, 69, 76, 77	2:2	170, 183
1:3–11	68–69	2:2–13	71
1:4	68	2:5	156
1:7	94, 197, 214	2:8	71, 72

2:8–9	4, 72, 76, 77	9:2–8	44, 45, 164
2:8–13	70–71, 72	9:8	191
2:9	71	9:8–10	177
2:9–10	71	9:10	38, 156
2:10	70, 71	9:10–16	31
2:11	70, 72	9:13	36
2:11–13	4, 76, 77	9:16–20	164, 331
2:12	70	9:16–10:10	44
2:12–13	184	9:17–23	45
2:13	70	9:18	37
2:14	170, 183	9:19	37
3–4	94, 95, 199, 209, 214, 218, 219, 226	9:22	37
		10:1	38, 156
3:10	74	10:4	59, 60
3:12 ff.	156	10:4–7	38, 156
3:12–17	4, 74, 76, 77	10:5	59
3:12–4:12	73–75	10:6	11, 60, 161
3:14–15	320	10:8	59
3:17–20	74	10:10	191
3:18	94	10:14	191
3:20–4:4	74, 77, 199, 207	10:14–11:18	177, 259
3:20–4:5	217, 227	11:11	42, 56
4	213, 214, 215, 217, 218, 222, 227	11:12	83
		11:21–12:1	181
4:2	73	12:1–2	42, 56, 58, 256
4:4–6	258	12:6–11	182, 259
4:4–12	74	12:9–10	182
4:6	73	12:10–11	34
4:6–7	94	12:19–20	256
4:9–10	94	12:20–21	216, 247
5:20	75	12:20–22	146, 164
5:20–6:11	75–76, 77	12:21	38
6:1	75	12:22	241
6:2	197, 214	12:22 ff.	102
6:2–3	94	12:22–13:2	32, 33
6:3	75	12:23	198, 214
6:6	75	13	7, 105, 267
6:7	75	13:2	11, 32, 36, 60, 82, 161
6:10–11	27		
7	267	13:2–3	7, 103, 104, 145
7:2	45	13:3–4	40
7:4–5	132	13:4–7	198, 222
7:4–6	58, 132	13:5	36
7:4–10	260	13:5–6	257
7:6	58	13:6	37
7:6–7	58	13:7	16, 37
7:6–9	42, 58	13:7–8	165
9:2–4	331	13:10–11	59

13:12	202	16:1	54
13:13	37, 59	16:10	191
13:14–15	165, 169–170	16:10–12	42, 56, 177
13:15–16	31	16:13	191
13:15–19	16, 266, 267	16:19	38, 156
13:16	37, 42, 56	19–20	9, 123
13:22	38, 165	19:2–5	42
14	34, 258	19:11	197, 214
14:3	33	19:16	76
14:3 ff.	259	19:33–20:34	128
14:3–6	33, 34, 54, 258	20	9, 10, 127, 128, 129, 130, 132, 133, 134, 135, 136, 147, 148
14:3–18	54		
14:4	202		
14:4–6	258	20:1	130, 132, 134, 135, 197, 214
14:6	36, 202		
14:6–7	37	20:1–8	9, 127, 128, 129, 130–131, 132, 133, 134, 135, 147, 148
14:6–8	37		
14:8	161		
14:8–9	37		
14:8–12	33, 34	20:17	156
14:9–10	35	20:31–32	128, 132,
14:10	59	**1QH**[a] (*Hodayot*)	5, 38, 156, 239, 334, 335
14:11–12	33, 37		
14:12–13	31	5:12	318
14:12–16	42, 54, 56	7:21	318
14:13	37, 38, 156	20:4–9	318
14:13–18	256	20:7	318
14:18–22	124, 141	20:7–12	327
14:19	198, 214	**1QIsa**[a] (*Isaiah*[a])	307, 312
14:20	44		
15	2, 28, 117, 168, 180, 257	**1QpHab** (*Pesher Habakkuk*)	15, 235, 239
15–16	29, 30, 31	11:4–8	320, 334
15:4	38, 156	**1QS** (*Community Rule*)	307, 312, 318, 332, 335, 336
15:5	54		
15:5–6	30, 42, 56		
15:5–10	2, 29, 30, 154	1–2	30
15:5–13	145	1–4	116, 124, 147
15:5–16:1	28	1–5	116
15:5–16:6	34	1:1	38, 165, 241
15:6–17	28	1:1–3:12	241
15:7–11	28	1:11	31
15:8	37, 257	1:13–15	320
15:8–9	54	1:16–2:25	30
15:11	37	1:16–3:12	10
15:12	257	2:19	30
15:14	37	2:19–22	34
15:15–17	61, 179	2:19–23	35

2:21–22	32	5:23	202
3:2	31, 60	5:23–24	35
3:13	38, 165, 249, 318	5:24–6:1	44, 45, 164, 331
3:13–14	249	6	2, 6, 7, 19, 28, 29,
3:13–4:26	71, 166, 240,		30, 33, 34, 80, 83,
	242–243, 249, 250		89, 95, 101, 102,
4:6–8	58		103, 105, 117, 118,
4:7	43, 58		295, 296, 297, 298
4:15	250	6–7	116, 276
5	2, 14, 30, 38, 39, 40,	6:1–8	80, 101, 102, 104,
	50, 51, 52, 53, 62,	6:2	35, 40, 95
	67, 87, 88, 92, 94,	6:2–4	6, 7, 79, 80, 81, 82,
	95, 111, 116, 117,		89, 91, 95, 97, 101,
	119, 165, 195, 200,		102, 104, 145, 197,
	201, 212, 214, 223,		209
	242, 243, 273, 274,	6:3	7, 60, 103, 118
	276	6:3–4	32, 82, 89, 118, 161
5–7	9, 102, 135, 138, 248	6:4	35, 36
5–9	55, 57, 58, 59, 113	6:4–6	40, 41
5–11	49	6:5	36
5:1	165, 168, 211, 274,	6:6	82
	317, 319, 334	6:6–7	19, 293, 295, 296,
5:1–2	59		298
5:1–3	50, 51, 54, 110, 243	6:6–8	145
5:2	31, 39, 222, 223	6:7	35, 298
5:2–3	39, 89, 138, 201,	6:8	33, 101
	202, 276	6:8–10	33, 34, 35
5:3–7	88	6:8–13	33, 34, 81, 117
5:4–7	86	6:9	201
5:6	199	6:10	60
5:6–7	44	6:11–13	33
5:7	60	6:12	33, 37
5:7–9	2, 29, 30, 31, 153	6:12–13	60
5:7–10	117, 145	6:13 ff.	168, 169
5:7–13	29	6:13–23	2, 28, 29, 30, 31, 34,
5:8–9	296		41, 81, 117, 145, 153
5:8–10	50	6:14	37, 60
5:9	39, 89, 115, 116,	6:16	60
	117, 222, 223, 225	6:17	31
5:11–12	90	6:19	51
5:13	41	6:19–20	31
5:16	201	6:20	37
5:20	59	6:22	31, 35, 202
5:20–22	115, 138, 276	6:23	81
5:20–24	30	6:24–7:25	44, 141
5:21	89, 200, 201, 209,	6:25	41
	223	6:26	160
5:21–22	39, 114, 224	7–8	93, 283

7:1	81	8:16–9:11	135
7:2	60, 258	8:19	35
7:6–8	31	8:19–21	132
7:8–9	45	8:20	9, 10, 132, 147
7:17–19	135	8:22	60
7:22	60	8:26	116, 133, 276
7:22–24	264	9	128, 165, 168, 243, 244
7:24	60		
7:24–25	31	9:2	35, 133
8	7, 10, 79, 82, 83, 84, 88, 92, 94, 95, 116, 117, 118, 127, 129, 136, 248, 251, 296	9:3–6	85, 86, 91
		9:3–7	129
		9:3–11	85, 91, 129
		9:4–5	91
8–9	9, 10, 85, 86, 128, 129, 130, 133, 134, 135, 136, 147, 148	9:5	86, 250
		9:5–6	167, 199
		9:7	39, 89, 129, 200, 201, 202, 209, 223, 224
8:1	60, 89, 197, 209, 296		
8:1 ff.	35, 91, 118	9:8–11	131–132, 135
8:1–4	35, 86	9:9	86
8:1–7	6, 7, 79, 82, 84, 85, 86, 88, 89, 91, 93, 94, 95, 129, 248	9:9–10	128
		9:11	130, 135, 199, 277
		9:12	38, 90, 146, 164, 165, 167, 216, 241, 247, 249, 250, 318
8:1–10	89		
8:1–9:11	84		
8:2	118		
8:3	90, 94	9:12 ff.	16, 90, 240
8:4	90, 91, 249	9:12–14	38, 244, 248
8:4–7	90	9:12–16	168, 248
8:4–8	86	9:12–21	244, 245
8:4–10	91	9:12–25	244, 325
8:5	60, 88	9:12–26	165, 166, 167
8:6	90, 94, 199	9:14	16, 38, 39, 89, 166, 167, 223, 250, 275
8:7	85, 91		
8:7–8	85	9:14–18	244, 250
8:7–10	85	9:15–16	167, 250
8:8	85	9:16	38, 250
8:8–9	199	9:16–18	45
8:8–10	84, 85, 86, 88, 91, 93	9:16–19	167
8:10	93	9:16–21	85, 248
8:11	86	9:17	250
8:12–13	93	9:17–18	167, 250
8:12–15	85, 248	9:18	38
8:13	86	9:18–19	167
8:15	131, 167, 249	9:18–21	245, 251
8:15–9:11	9, 84, 135, 136, 164, 247, 277	9:21	38, 165, 241, 318
		9:21–25	246
8:16–9:2	45, 85, 128, 131–132, 135	9:21–26	248
		9:23	38

9:26	166	1:7	11, 60, 161
9:26 ff.	325	1:8–11	55
9:26–10:8	320, 326	1:9–11	42
9:26–11:22	326	1:11	44
10	325	1:11–22	49
10–11	274	1:14–15	32
10:9 ff.	166	1:15	38, 156
10:20	156	1:15–16	39, 225
11	161, 273	1:16	204
11–12	250	1:18	35
11:1	87	1:19–22	54
11:3–4	11, 160	1:20	44
11:7–9	88	1:21	55
11:8	60	1:22–25	40, 52
11:21	43, 57	1:23	39, 225
		1:23–24	204
1Q20 (*Genesis Apocryphon*)		1:24	38, 39, 52, 53, 156, 204, 225
	155		
10:15	155	1:24–25	53, 225
12:13–15	182	1:25–2:11	35, 47
		1:27–2:3	52
1Q26 (*Instruction*)		1:29	38, 39, 156
	158	1:29–2:1	32
		2	41
1Q27 (*Mysteries*)	158	2:1–2	53
		2:3	39, 52, 204, 225
1Q28a (*Rule of the Congregation*)		2:4–5	62
	1, 3, 11, 15, 27, 30, 39, 42, 43, 47, 48, 49, 82, 111, 118, 153, 156, 161, 162, 175, 204, 209, 224, 239, 241, 260, 261, 263, 273, 274, 275, 312	2:4–9	179
		2:5–9	60, 61
		2:8–9	62
		2:10	62
		2:11	48
		2:11–22	47, 50
1	30	2:13	225
1:1	47, 48, 49	2:15–17	35
1:1–3	49, 50, 51, 52, 53, 55, 153	2:17–22	40, 41
		2:19	36
1:1–8	273	2:21	35
1:2	39, 51, 204, 225	2:21–22	41, 145
1:2–3	55		
1:3	88	**1Q28b (*Rule of Blessings*)**	
1:4–5	42		15, 38, 49, 111, 162, 225, 239, 241, 248, 273, 274, 275, 312
1:6	47, 54, 62		
1:6–9	30		
1:6–11	49	1:1	318
1:6–25	47	3:22	318
1:6–2:11	3, 47, 50, 52, 53, 54, 55, 58, 59, 60, 62	3:22 ff.	225
		5:20	318

1Q33 (War Scroll) 42, 62, 137, 156, 164, 204, 205, 208, 211, 239, 260, 335
3:12–14 204
5:1 204
7:4 61
7:4–6 180
7:9–9:9 205
10:10 240
17:2 205

3Q15 (Copper Scroll)
305

4Q53 (Samuel^c) 312

4Q114 (Daniel^c) 68

4Q158 (Reworked Pentateuch^a)
280, 286

4Q159 (Ordinances^a)
14, 21, 174, 181, 182, 186, 187–192, 268, 332
1 188
1 ii 2–5 181, 188, 189
1 ii 4 192
1 ii 6 12, 177, 191
1 ii 6–8 189
1 ii 6–12 188
1 ii 13 188
1 ii 17 190
2–4 188
2–4 1–3 188
2–4 2 192
2–4 3 190
2–4 3–6 188
2–4 5 192
2–4 6–7 188, 191
2–4 8 189, 193
2–4 8–10 188, 189, 268
5 188

4Q161–165 (Pesher Isaiah^{a-e})
330
4Q163 (Pesher Isaiah^c)
219
22 3 226

4Q174 (Florilegium)
207, 219, 226, 234, 333
1–2 3–5 61, 180
1–2 i 17 206, 226
3 17 206, 226
5 2 107

4Q175 (Testimonia)
312, 333

4Q176 (Tanḥumin)
333

4Q177 (Catena A) 333

4Q186 (Zodiacal Physiognomy)
313

4Q208–211 (Astronomical Enoch^{a-d})
319

4Q213–214b (see also 1Q21) (Aramaic Levi) 309, 330

4Q242 (Prayer of Nabonidus)
233

4Q243–245 (Pseudo-Daniel^{a-c})
4Q245 (Pseudo-Daniel^c)
2 4 235

4Q249 (Midrash Sefer Moshe)
314

4Q249a–i (Serekh ha-Edah^{a-i})
314, 330
4Q249c (Serekh ha-Edah^c)
5 204

4Q249k–l (Text Quoting Leviticus A–B)
314

4Q249m (Hodayot-Like Text E)
314

4Q249n–o (Liturgical Work E?–F?)
314

4Q249p (Prophecy?)
314

4Q249q (Fragment Mentioning the Planting) 314

4Q249r–y (*Unidentified Text A–H*)	11 11–13	81, 117
314	18 1–4	251
	18 1–7	244–246
4Q249z (*Miscellaneous Texts A*)	18 4–5	165
314	4Q257 (Community Rule^c)	
4Q250–250a (*Text Concerning Cultic Service A–B?*) 314		124, 144, 147, 148, 149, 165
4Q250b (*Text Related to Isaiah 11*)	4Q258 (Community Rule^d)	
315		2, 10, 16, 29, 33, 35, 38, 39, 41, 44,
4Q250c–i (*Unidentified Text I–O*)		50, 51, 59, 67, 85,
315		87, 90, 92, 104, 105, 109, 111, 112, 113,
4Q250j (*Miscellaneous Texts B*)		114, 115, 116, 118,
315		124, 138, 145, 147,
4Q251 (*Halakha A*)		166, 167, 202, 211,
1 7	12, 177	240, 241, 243, 244, 273, 274, 276
4Q252 (*Commentary on Genesis A*)	1	52, 110, 195, 212,
333		223, 243
4Q255–264 (*Community Rule^{a–j}*)	1 i	30
6, 10, 326, 330, 335, 336	1 1	38, 67, 165, 168, 241, 249, 274, 275,
4Q255 (Community Rule^a)		317, 318, 319, 334
124, 147, 148	1 1 ff.	168
3	242	1 1–3	115
4Q256 (Community Rule^b)	1 2	59, 117, 223, 276
2, 29, 38, 39, 41,	1 5	199
44, 50, 51, 59, 87,	1 5–7	115, 117
88, 89, 92, 109, 111,	1 7	223
113, 114, 115, 116,	1 7–8	117, 119
124, 138, 145, 147,	2 1–2	114, 115, 138, 200,
148, 202, 243, 244,		201, 209, 223, 224,
273, 274, 275, 276,		2776
317	2 7–8	79, 81, 161
5 1	38	2 10	145, 295
9	110, 195, 212, 223,	3 1–3	117
	243	5 1	124, 141
9 1	165, 168, 241, 317,	6 1–2	79, 82
	318, 319, 334	6 2–3	199
9 1 ff.	168	6 7	131
9 2	59	6 8	129
9 3	223	6 11–12	129
9 5–6	199	6–7	131, 135
9 7–8	223	7 1	116, 134
9 8	119	7 1–3	129
11 5–8	117	7 6	167
11 8	81, 117	7 6–7	199

Index of References

7 7	130, 200, 201, 209, 223, 224	3 2–4	124, 141
7 7–9	129	4a–b 1–7	124, 141
8 1–9	244–246	5a–c 1–9	124, 141
8 2	167	6 a–e 1–5	124, 141
8 3–5	250	4Q262 (Community Rule[h])	
8 5	241, 318		124, 143, 147, 148, 273
8 5–6	165	4Q263 (Community Rule[i])	
4Q259 (Community Rule[e])			104, 145
	9, 10, 11, 16, 44, 84, 85, 88, 90, 91, 93, 111, 112, 113, 116, 128, 129, 133, 134, 135, 136, 145, 146, 147, 148, 160, 164, 166, 167, 199, 200, 240, 247, 275, 277, 325, 326, 327	1 4–5	161
		3–5	79, 81
		4Q264 (Community Rule[j])	
			143, 273
		4Q264a (Halakhah B)	
			159
		4Q265 (Miscellaneous Rules, olim Serekh Damascus)	
1 iii 10	39		1, 10, 12, 21, 27, 44, 79, 86, 87, 92, 98, 113, 114, 118, 119, 124, 126, 141, 143, 149, 150, 175, 203, 272, 277, 332
1 4–15	124, 141		
2 3–8	124, 141		
2 9–16	79, 82		
2 11	94		
2 14	199		
2 15	94	1 i	41
2 17–18	199	1 ii 6	37
3	128, 244–245	2 ii 7–8	35
3 1	93, 131	4 i 2 – ii 2	124, 141
3 3–4	327	4 ii	118
3 6	128, 167	4 ii 3–4	93
3 6–7	165	4 ii 6	92
3 6–8	164	7	88, 93
3 6–10	248	7 3	203
3 6 – 4 8	244	7 5	83
3 7	241	7 6	82, 83, 84, 203
3 10	166, 223	7 7	83
3 16	167	7 7–10	118
3 16 – 4 2	251	7 8	88
4 2	241, 318	7 10	93
4 2–3	165	7 11	83
4Q260 (Community Rule[f])		7 13	83
1 1–2	244–246	7 15	83
4 10	156	7 84	93
4Q261 (Community Rule[g])		**4Q266–273 (Damascus Document[a–h])**	
	44, 104, 111		11, 12, 104, 141, 330, 335
1 a–b 1–2	224		
2 a–c 2–3	161		
3 1	81, 117		

4Q266 (Damascus Documenta)		6 iv	181
	61, 70, 71, 75, 164,	6 iv 4	182, 185
	181, 218, 219, 221,	7 iii 3	37
	257, 263, 267	8 i	145
1	170	8 i 6–9	60–61
1 a–b	217	8 i 9	60
1 a–b 5	170, 183	8 iii 4	59
2 i 11	196, 214	8 iii 5	161
2 i 11–12	94	9	267
2 i 12	94	9 ii	257
2 i 13	69	9 ii 7–8	146, 164
2 ii 1	59	9 iii	16, 266
2 ii 5	156	9 iii 5	267
2 ii 13	70	10–11	44
3 ii 7	75	10 i	257
3 iii 6	260	10 i–ii	124, 141
5 i	199, 216, 218, 219, 222	10 i 3	59
		10 i 4	60
5 i 4	37	10 i 12	198, 214
5 i 9	218	10 ii 1–2	259
5 i 9–12	218	11	10, 44, 127, 147
5 i 9–19	217–218	11 1–20	123–124
5 i 13–14	219	11 5–6	44
5 i 13–15	218	11 8	36, 37
5 i 15–16	218	11 14–16	259
5 i 16	199, 216, 218	11 16	37
5 i 17	165, 216, 219, 241, 247	11 17–21	259
		11 21	219
5 ii	179, 220, 258	18	56
5 ii 1–2	217	18 iii 9	56
5 ii 1–3	179	4Q267 (Damascus Documentb)	
5 ii 1–4	220		75, 181, 218, 222
5 ii 1–16	178	2 6	75
5 ii 4	220	2 7	75
5 ii 5	198, 220	2 8	197, 214
5 ii 5–6	182	5 ii	199, 216, 217, 218
5 ii 8	198, 220	5 iii 1–7	220
5 ii 9–10	198, 220	5 iii 1–8	178
5 ii 10–11	178	5 iii 6	60
5 ii 12	198, 220	5 iii 8	198, 220
6 i	185	6	181, 259
6 i 13	198, 222	7	16, 265
6 i–iii	180	7 13–14	266
6 ii	42	9 iv 10	59
6 ii 4	180	9 v	258
6 iii	181, 188, 259	9 v 6–10	258
6 iii 3–4	191	9 v 8	33
6 iii a	181	9 v 10	33

9 v 11	37	6 iv 15	59
9 v 12	161	6 iv 16	59
9 vi	44, 124, 141	6 iv 17	161
9 vi 4–5	264	6 iv 18	59
4Q268 (Damascus Document[c])		6 iv 20	191
1 14	197, 214	7	10, 44, 127, 147
1 14–15	94	7 i	44, 124, 141
1 15	94	7 i–ii	124
2	258	7 i 4	60
4Q269 (Damascus Document[d])		7 i 10	202
2 3	59	7 i 12–13	57
7	180	7 i 12–15	42
8 ii 1	183	7 i 13–15	268
8 ii 1–3	182	7 i 14–15	57
8 ii 3–6	181	7 i 16	36, 37
8 ii 6	203	7 ii	259
9	16, 265	7 ii 12–13	264
9 1–7	57	8 1–19	57
9 1–8	266	10 14–15	266
11 i–ii	124, 141	4Q271 (Damascus Document[f])	
11 i 2	198, 214		189
16	124, 127	1 i 14–15	57
4Q270 (Damascus Document[e])		2	188
	183, 186, 266	2 1–5	181
2 i 9 – ii 17	184	2 13	203
2 i 9 – ii 21	13, 183	3	16, 188–189, 265
2 ii 1	191	3 3	191
2 ii 5–9	191	3 3–4	188
2 ii 6	185, 198, 219	3 7	266
2 ii 7–8	185	3 7–15	266
2 ii 9	189	3 12–15	189
2 ii 12	185	3 14	37
2 ii 13	184	3 14–15	268
2 ii 14	184	4 ii 12–13	191
2 ii 15	185	5 i 7	83
2 ii 17–18	183	5 i 17–18	256
2 ii 19	170	4Q272 (Damascus Document[g])	
2 ii 19 -21	183	1 i–ii	180
3 i	181	1 ii 2	198, 222
3 ii	181	4Q273 (Damascus Document[h])	
3 ii 19–21	189	2	220
3 iii	259	2 1–2	178
3 iii 13–15	181	4 i 5–11	178
4	42	4 ii	180
5	16, 265	**4Q274 (*Tohorot A*)**	
5 14–21	42, 57, 266		180
6 ii	61, 145	1 1–4	180
6 iv 13	38, 156		

2 i 2	203	**4Q313 (*MMT^g?*)**	315, 325
4Q277 (*Tohorot B^b*)		**4Q313a–b (*Unidentified Text P–Q*)**	
1 ii 5	181		315
1 ii 5–7	203	**4Q313c (*Calendrical Document B*)**	
4Q279 (*Four Lots*)			315, 324
	202	**4Q317 (*Lunisolar Calendar*)**	
5 4	202		315, 321, 324, 329
4Q285 (*Sefer ha-Milḥamah*)		**4Q318 (*Zodiology and Brontology*)**	
	15, 239		321, 334
4Q286–290 (*Berakhot*)		**4Q319 (*Otot*)**	277, 326, 327, 332
	45, 201, 330	iv 9	326
4Q286 (Berakhot^a)	202		
13	202	**4Q320 (*Calendrical Document/ Mishmarot A*)**	322, 324, 329, 330, 332
14	202		
17 b	202		
17b 1–2	201	**4Q321 (*Calendrical Document B*)**	
20 a, b	202		322, 324, 329, 330
4Q288 (Berakhot^c)	202	**4Q321a (*Calendrical Document/ Mishmarot C*)**	322, 328, 330
4Q298 (*Words of the Sage to the Sons of Dawn*)	27, 38, 163, 164, 169, 170, 171, 183, 239, 249, 273, 315, 317, 319		
		4Q322 (*Mishmarot A*)	
			323, 330
		4Q322a (*Historical Text H?*)	
1–2 i 2	170		324
3–4 ii 3–4	170	**4Q323 (*Mishmarot B*)**	
4Q299–301 (see also 1Q27) (*Mysteries*)	11, 155, 156, 157, 160, 163, 236, 299		323, 330
		4Q324 (*Mishmarot C*)	
4Q299 (Mysteries^a)			323, 330
3c	156	**4Q324a (*Mishmarot D*)**	
6 ii 8	156		324, 330
8 6	155, 156	**4Q324b (*Calendrical Document A*)**	
8 7	170		322, 330
10	156	**4Q324c (*Mishmarot E*)**	
10 3	156		324, 330
10 5	156		
10 7	156	**4Q324d–f (*Liturgical Calendar^{a–c?}*)**	315–316, 324–325
60 4	156		
71 1	156	**4Q324g–h (*Calendrical Document F?–G?*)**	316, 325, 330
76 3	156		
4Q300 (Mysteries^b)			
1 a ii–b	156	**4Q324i (*Mishmarot J*)**	
4Q301 (Mysteries^c?)			316, 325, 330
3a–b 8	156, 157		

4Q325 (*Calendrical Document/ Mishmarot D*)   322, 330

4Q326 (*Calendrical Document C*)
   323, 330

4Q328 (*Mishmarot F*)
   324, 330

4Q329 (*Mishmarot G*)
   324, 330, 332

4Q329a (*Mishmarot H*)
   324, 330

4Q330 (*Mishmarot I*)
   324, 330

4Q331 (*Historical Text C*)
   324

4Q332 (*Historical Text D*)
   324

4Q333 (*Historical Text E*)
   324

4Q334 (*Ordo*)   323

4Q337 (*Calendrical Document E?*)
   323, 330

4Q350 (*Account*)   309

4Q362–363 (*Unidentified Text A–B*)
   316

4Q363a (*Unidentified Religious Text*)
   316

4Q363b (*Miscellaneous Texts*)
   316

4Q364–367 (see also 4Q158) (*Reworked Pentateuch^{b-e}*)   280, 330

4Q385–388, 391 (*Pseudo-Ezekiel^{a-e}*)
   330

4Q385a–390 (*Apocryphon of Jeremiah C*)
   330

4Q390 (Apocryphon of Jeremiah C^e)
   207
1 2–3   208

4Q393 (*Communal Confession*)
1–2 ii 7   87

4Q394–399 (*MMT^{a-f}*)
   12, 13, 14, 21, 42, 95, 96, 137, 173–186, 205, 206, 221, 222, 323, 325, 326, 330
B 11–12
B 17 (ed. Qimron and Strugnell)   205
B 25–27 (ed. Qimron and Strugnell)   205
B 39–54 (ed. Qimron and Strugnell)   61
B 49–54 (ed. Qimron and Strugnell)   221
B79 (ed. Qimron and Strugnell)   205
B 80 (ed. Qimron and Strugnell)   222
4Q394 (MMT^a)

4Q394 1–2 (Calendrical Document D)
   323
4Q394 (MMT^a)   325, 326
3–7 i 1–3   325
3–7 i 6–8   183
3–7 i 11–12   183
3–7 i 16 – ii 1   181
3–7 i 19 – ii 1   178, 205
3–7 ii 13–14   178
3–7 ii 14–19   175
3–7 ii 19   176
8 iii 12–19   180
8 iii 19 – iv 4   179
8 iv 8–12   176
4Q395 (MMT^b)
1 10–11   205
4Q396 (MMT^c)
1–2 i 2–4   185
1–2 i 5–6   180
1–2 iii 2–3   182, 185
1–2 iii 3–4   185
1–2 iii 4–11   185
1–2 iv 1   185
1–2 iv 4–11   178
1–2 iv 8   205
1–2 iv 9–11   179

4Q397 (MMT^d)
3 5	176
14–21 7	13

4Q400–407 (see also 11Q17)
(Songs of the Sabbath Sacrifice)
38, 162, 236, 239, 317, 330

4Q408 (Apocryphon of Moses^c)
3+3a 6–11	327

4Q415–4Q418c, 4Q423
(see also 1Q26) (Instruction)
11, 155, 157, 158, 160, 236, 239, 260, 299, 318, 330

4Q416 (Instruction^b)
2 ii 15	163
2 iii	158
2 iii 18	159
2 iii 20–21	159

4Q417 (Instruction^c)
1 i	163
1 i 13–14	163
1 i 18	163
1 i 25	163
2	162
2 i 15–16	11, 162
2 i 17	162

4Q418 (Instruction^d)
8 15	163
81+81a 17	163
238 1	163

4Q418a (Instruction^e)
19 2	163

4Q420–421 (Ways of Righteousness^{a–b})
11, 155, 159, 163, 164

4Q420 (Ways of Righteousness^a)
	164
1 a ii–b 10	164
1 a ii–b 12	164

4Q421 (Ways of Righteousness^b)
	239

4Q424 (Instruction-Like Composition B)
3 2	170

4Q427 (Hodayot^a)
8 ii 10	327
20 4	327
20 11	327
20 14	318
24 34	318

4Q428 (Hodayot^b)
12 2	327

4Q433a (Hodayot-Like Text)
239

4Q434–438 (Barki Nafshi)
330

4Q460 (Narrative Work and Prayer)
	309
9	309
9 i 10	309

4Q461 (Narrative B)
239

4Q477 (The Overseer's Record of Rebuke) 9, 27, 37, 44, 45, 164, 331

4Q491–496 (War Scroll)
62, 330

4Q493 (War Scroll^c) 205
1–2	205

4Q496 (War Scroll^f) 204
10 4	204

4Q502 (Ritual of Marriage)
16	149
16 1–4	144

4Q510–511 (Songs of the Maskil)
38, 162, 239, 317

4Q513 (Ordinances^b)
	208
10 ii 8	208

4Q543–549 (Visions of Amram^{a–g})
330

4Q550, 550a–e (Proto-Esther^{a–f})
281

5Q11 (*Community Rule*)
27, 149

5Q12 (*Damascus Document*)
27

5Q13 (*Rule*) 27, 143
4 1 37

6Q15 (*Damascus Document*)
27
5 27

6Q16 (*Benediction*) 320

6Q17 (*Calendrical Document*)
319

6Q18 (*Hymn*) 320

11Q1 (*paleo Leviticus*^{a})
59, 69, 203, 206,
208n

11Q5 (*Psalms*^{a}) 291, 325, 334
27 325
28 325

11Q13 (*Melchizedek*)
15, 234, 239

11Q14 (*Sefer ha-Milḥamah*)
15, 239

11Q17 (*Songs of the Sabbath Sacrifice*)
7 9 318

11Q19–21 (*Temple Scroll*$^{a-c}$)
155, 177, 184, 206,
207, 208, 334
11Q19 (Temple Scroll^a)
42, 155, 307
22:4–5 206
34:13–14 206
44:5 206
45–47 58
45:12–14 180, 221
52:5 185
60:3–4 182
64:6–9 184
11Q20 (Temple Scroll^b)
5:25 206
11Q21 (Temple Scroll^c?)
176

11Q23 (*Unidentified Text*)
313, 316

11Q29 (*Fragment Related to the Community Rule*)
44, 124, 141,
143–144, 272

KhQ (Ostracon 1) 32

Josephus and Philo

Josephus	42, 97, 139, 146, 259	2.150	35
		2.160	98, 139
Ant.		2.160–161	42
18.20	32		
18.21	42	Philo	42, 259
J. W.		*Apol.*	
2.120–121	42, 98, 139	II.14–17	42
2.122–123	32		
2.123	36	*Prob.*	
2.129	41	84	32
2.137–138	31	91	32

Early Christian Writings

Eusebius
Hist. eccl.
6.16.3 308

Origen 308, 309

Rabbinic Literature

Mishnah 126
m. Sanh.
1:6 89, 102, 145

Inscriptions

En Gedi Synagogue Inscription
184

Mesopotamian Texts

MUL.APIN 322
TU 11 327

Index of Modern Authors

Abegg, Martin G. 28, 59, 100, 104, 109, 163, 164, 204, 212, 217, 225, 239, 267, 315, 316, 318, 325, 327
Ackroyd, Peter R. 279
Aitken, James K. 158
Albertz, Rainer 231, 232, 233, 237, 251, 255
Alexander, Philip S. 11, 28, 35, 39, 79, 86, 88, 89, 93, 105, 109, 110, 111, 113, 116, 124, 125, 128, 129, 130, 131, 132, 134, 138, 143, 148, 156, 160, 164, 165, 166, 167, 168, 195, 200, 202, 211, 223, 241, 242, 243, 244, 247, 272, 273, 274, 275, 276, 295, 313, 317, 318, 319, 321, 322, 326, 327, 328, 329
Allegro, John M. 187, 190, 207, 308, 313
Amit, David 313
Amitai, Janet 61, 180
Anderson, A. A. 308
Anderson, Gary A. 209, 197
Angel, Joseph 317
Aren, Maeir N. 31
Avemarie, Friedrich 40, 41, 45
Avery-Peck, Alan J. 91, 118

Baillet, Maurice 204, 205, 208, 306, 317, 319
Bar-Adon, Pesah 140
Bar-Asher, Moshe 129, 215
Bar-Asher Siegal, Elitzur 13
Bardtke, Hans 26, 84, 232
Bar-Nathan, Rachel 140
Barthélemy, Dominique 52, 53, 59, 61, 225
Barton, George A. 238
Barton, John 285
Barton, Stephen 5
Baumgarten, Albert I. VII, 39, 89, 97, 99, 101, 109, 179, 195, 265, 275, 284

Baumgarten, Joseph 21, 35, 37, 42, 43, 57, 58, 59, 61, 65, 70, 82, 83, 88, 113, 114, 124, 125, 127, 129, 139, 141, 144, 159, 164, 166, 169, 170, 171, 173, 174, 175, 176, 177, 178, 179, 180, 181, 182, 183, 184, 185, 187, 188, 189, 191, 198, 199, 203, 205, 213, 215, 216, 217, 218, 220, 221, 223, 242, 257, 264, 265, 266, 267, 272, 322, 323
Beall, Todd S. 26, 31
Beattie, Derek R. G. 184
Ben-Dov, Jonathan 313, 316, 317, 320, 321, 322, 323, 326, 327, 328, 329, 332, 334, 337
Berenbaum, Michael 305
Bergmeier, Roland 26
Bernstein, Moshe VII, 8, 14, 21, 32, 40, 45, 83, 109, 113, 124, 166, 173, 174, 175, 176, 178, 186, 190, 215, 242, 272, 323, 332
Berrin, Shani (see also Tzoref) 333
Berthelot, Katell 232, 291, 313, 328
Betz, Otto 184
Beyerle, Stefan 231, 238, 251
Bickerman, Elias 99
Black, Matthew 231
Blenkinsopp, Joseph VII, 146, 209, 253, 255, 256, 259, 269, 288
Boccaccini, Gabriele 9, 101, 140
Bockmuehl, Markus 89, 109, 165, 195, 275
Böhler, Dieter 283
Boling, Robert G. 294, 295
Bowman, Alan K. 283
Boyce, Mark 94, 215
Braun, Herbert 57
Brin, Gershon 170, 249
Brooke, George J. VII, 1, 4, 5, 8, 10, 14, 17, 18, 20, 40, 88, 90, 141, 144, 162,

175, 176, 180, 190, 207, 225, 226, 233, 277, 279, 281, 283, 285, 286, 287, 288, 290, 291, 303, 304, 306, 307, 308, 313, 324, 332, 333
Broshi, Magen 42, 56, 57, 61, 68, 69, 130, 181, 183, 187, 303, 304, 305, 306, 307, 310
Brown, Raymond E. 59
Brownlee, William H. 85, 87, 295
Bruce, Frederick F. 231, 234, 235, 239
Burrows, Millar 25, 33
Butler, Trent C. 293

Callaway, Philip R. 173
Campbell, Jonathan G. 17, 68, 78, 255, 277, 285, 287, 312, 333
Cancik, Hubert 26, 28, 39, 89, 111, 165, 168, 195, 212, 275, 313
Caquot, André 57
Carmignac, Jean 38, 164, 165, 187, 190, 241
Carr, David M. 287, 289
Chalcraft, David VII, 3, 97, 99, 102, 227, 255, 268, 291
Chambon, Alain 304
Chapman, Jonathan 317
Charlesworth, James H. 39, 61, 62, 89, 109, 195, 275, 317
Chazon, Esther G. VII, 2, 5, 25, 43, 67, 83, 114, 124, 127, 142, 171, 173, 177, 184, 215, 216, 221, 265, 272, 281, 305
Chilton, Bruce D. 91, 118
Claussen, Carsten 305, 307, 310
Clements, Ruth A. 5, 236, 281, 305
Cohen, Shaye J. D. 254, 335
Collins, John J. VII, 2, 3, 4, 5, 7, 17, 25, 32, 37, 43, 68, 80, 81, 82, 84, 91, 95, 97, 98, 100, 101, 102, 103, 111, 114, 118, 125, 129, 140, 145, 154, 155, 156, 158, 160, 162, 169, 209, 231, 232, 233, 234, 235, 236, 237, 238, 240, 242, 255, 256, 264, 267, 275, 289, 295, 320, 336
Cook, Edward 28, 100, 164, 225
Coppens, Joseph 57
Coser, Lewis 265
Cothenet, Édouard 33, 187

Cotton, Hannah 309, 310
Cross, Frank More 31, 32, 35, 37, 40, 80, 307, 333
Crowfoot, Grace M. 303
Cryer, Fred H. 158

Daniels, Dwight R. 160
Davidson, Maxwell J. 180
Davies, Philip R. VII, 25, 28, 34, 39, 43, 44, 50, 57, 58, 66, 71, 78, 94, 99, 128, 129, 196, 205, 206, 226, 212, 231, 234, 235, 238, 240, 248, 255, 278, 288, 291, 324
Davis, Michael T. 65
Day, John 293
Dell, Katherine 253
Delcor, Matthias 26, 36, 57, 85
Denis, Albert-Marie 25, 38, 48, 89, 132, 249
Dever, William G. 254
Dimant, Devorah 2, 3, 5, 18, 19, 25, 66, 67, 78, 100, 129, 138, 154, 175, 180, 207, 215, 232, 233, 276, 281, 286, 289, 290, 303, 306, 307, 308, 310, 311, 312, 334
Dines, Jines 97
Doering, Lutz 82, 83, 203
Dohmen, Christoph 35, 85, 89, 92, 240, 247, 248
Doudna, Gregory 305
Duhaime, Jean 137, 204, 205, 240, 241, 243
Dupont-Sommer, André 33, 165

Edrei, Arye 272
Ego, Beate 88, 90, 198
Elgvin, Torleif 100, 140, 155, 158, 159, 160, 166, 169
Ellis, Earle E. 231
Emerton, John A. 177
Eshel, Esther VII, 32, 45, 234, 331
Eshel, Hanan 6, 31, 186, 303, 304, 305, 306, 307, 310, 328, 335
Esler, Philip F. 4
Evan, Christopher F. 279
Evans, Craig 18, 313
Evans Kapfer, Hilary 123, 142

Fabry, Heinz-Josef VII, 1, 14, 138, 196, 197, 201, 204, 205, 206, 208, 210, 211, 212, 215, 216, 219, 224, 275
Falk, Daniel VII, 10, 304
Fields, Weston 308
Fine, Steven 14
Fishbane, Michael A. 33
Fitzmyer, Joseph A. 26, 68, 209, 324
Flint, Peter 25, 43, 89, 111, 139, 145, 146, 154, 162, 164, 195, 212, 233, 234, 235, 239, 231, 247, 275, 279, 292, 308, 309, 321, 330
Forkman, Göran 28, 45
Foucault, Michel 127
Fraade, Steven VII, 4, 8, 13, 21, 103, 123, 126, 147, 148, 272, 297, 303, 329
Freedman, David N. 3, 321
Frey, Jörg VII, 3, 166, 242, 271, 290, 310

Galor, Katharina 140, 305
Gärtner, Bertil 92
Gammie, James G. 38, 154, 162, 239
García Martínez, Florentino VII, 2, 4, 5, 8, 13, 25, 26, 28, 32, 33, 35, 38, 40, 45, 48, 50, 66, 67, 68, 78, 79, 83, 90, 101, 102, 113, 115, 124, 125, 134, 139, 141, 142, 145, 149, 166, 174, 175, 176, 178, 186, 195, 197, 198, 203, 206, 211, 213, 215, 224, 234, 235, 242, 249, 271, 272, 276, 278, 280, 281, 288, 290, 291, 303, 304, 305, 307, 311, 312, 313, 316, 323, 330
Garnet, Paul 39, 89, 109, 195, 275
Geller, Mark 328
Gerrard, Kate 6
Giblet, Jean 48, 249
Gillet-Didier, Veronique 322, 329
Gillihan, Yonder Moynihan 26, 28
Ginsberg, Harold L. 238
Ginzberg, Louis 162, 182
Gitin, Seymour 254
Glessmer, Uwe 160, 247, 321, 323, 326
Goff, Matthew VII, 236, 317
Goldman, Liora 129, 215
Goodblatt, David 298
Goodman, Martin VII, 25, 26, 102, 283
Gordon, Cyrus H. 328
Gordon, Nehemia 225

Gordon, Robert P. 154, 231, 285, 331
Goshen-Gottstein, Moshe H. 291
Gottlieb, Claire G. 328
Grabbe, Lester L. 178, 179, 231, 233
Gray, John 294
Greenfield, Jonas 321
Grossman, Maxine VII, 4, 8, 13, 17, 20, 21, 43, 90, 94, 101, 134, 142, 199, 212, 214, 220, 221, 223, 225, 277
Guillaumont, Antoine 57, 58

Haag, Ernst 248
Hachlili, Rachel 140
Halpern, Baruch 3
Halpern-Amaru, Betsy 5
Harkins, Angela Kim 4, 5
Harland, Peter J. 158
Harrington, Daniel J. 154, 155, 157, 158, 159, 160, 162, 163, 169
Harrington, Hannah K. 203
Hasslberger, Bernhard 237
Hayes, Christine 205
Heger, Paul 280, 284
Hempel, Charlotte 1, 2, 5, 6, 7, 8, 10, 11, 13, 14, 17, 18, 21, 26, 34, 35, 39, 40, 41, 43, 44, 45, 61, 67, 68, 79, 80, 81, 88, 89, 90, 94, 97, 98, 99, 101, 103, 104, 109, 110, 111, 112, 113, 114, 115, 117, 118, 119, 123, 124, 125, 129, 134, 137, 138, 139, 140, 141, 142, 143, 144, 145, 146, 147, 153, 154, 161, 162, 165, 168, 170, 174, 175, 186, 195, 196, 198, 199, 200, 201, 203, 204, 211, 213, 214, 215, 216, 219, 221, 222, 224, 231, 234, 236, 239, 242, 243, 247, 249, 250, 265, 266, 268, 272, 275, 276, 277, 282, 286, 287, 290, 291, 296, 297, 305, 306, 317, 318, 320, 324, 328, 331, 332, 334, 335, 337
Hengel, Martin 26, 111, 165, 195, 212, 213, 275, 313
Henze, Matthias 231, 240, 252
Herbert, Edward D. 279, 285
Hertzberg, Hans Wilhelm 294
Hilhorst, Anthony 90, 102, 139, 195, 213, 276, 278, 281
Himbaza, Innocent 283
Himmelfarb, Martha 205

Høgenhaven, Jasper 8, 14, 190, 308, 313, 332
Hooper-Greenhill, Eileen 6
Horbury, William 109
Horgan, Maurya 68, 209, 226
Hossfeld, Lothar 138, 196, 212, 275
Hübner, Hans 57
Hugo, Philippe 283
Hultgren, Stephen 2, 105, 129, 134, 135, 146, 215, 288, 291
Humbert, Jean-Baptiste 41, 140, 304, 305, 307
Hunzinger, Claus-Hunno 84
Huppenbauer, Hans Walter 241
Hurvitz, Avi 321

Ilan, Tal 43
Isaakson, Abel 57

Jacobus, Helen 321
Jaffe, Martin 17, 287, 298
Jastram, Nathan 32, 35, 36, 39
Jokiranta, Jutta VII, 3, 4, 20, 97, 101, 102, 124, 142, 215, 227, 265, 268, 269, 272, 289

Kahle, Paul E. 309
Kampen, John 32, 35, 40, 45, 66, 83, 113, 124, 142, 162, 164, 166, 169, 173, 174, 176, 178, 186, 215, 236, 239, 242, 272, 317, 318, 323
Kapera, Zdzislaw 173
Keller, Sharon 328
Kessler, Nadine 305, 308, 310
Khan, Geoffrey 285, 331
Kister, Menahem VII, 38, 129, 169, 170, 182, 183, 195, 215, 220, 273, 282, 312, 315, 316, 317
Klauck, Hans-Josef 31
Klinghardt, Matthias 26, 31, 81
Klinzing, Georg 85, 87, 88, 94, 196, 197, 212
Knibb, Michael A. VII, 4, 7, 26, 29, 31, 35, 43, 67, 72, 78, 80, 89, 92, 97, 102, 109, 112, 125, 128, 130, 145, 166, 168, 173, 184, 195, 197, 207, 217, 226, 233, 234, 235, 236, 231, 238, 247, 275, 276, 295, 303, 317

Knohl, Israel 321, 322
Knoppers, Gary N. 209
Kobelski, Paul J. 68, 209
Koch, Klaus 160, 231, 232, 234, 235, 237, 238, 240, 248, 249
Kosmala, Hans 38, 162, 239
Kratz, Reinhard G. VII, 8, 9, 10, 11, 17, 18, 44, 137, 133, 142, 285, 286, 287, 289, 290, 292, 294, 299, 303
Kruse, Colin G. 36, 142
Kugler, Robert A. 16, 17, 39, 43, 89, 103, 111, 166, 178, 195, 209, 212, 223, 240, 271, 275
Kuhn, Karl-Georg 116

Laato, Antti 68
Lacocque, André 236, 248
Lange, Armin 3, 11, 71, 88, 90, 153, 156, 157, 162, 166, 183, 198, 236, 239, 242, 299, 307, 311, 319, 328
Lankester Harding, Gerald 303
Lapin, Hayim 21
Larson, Erik 177, 310
Leaney, Alfred R. C. 34, 35, 37, 40, 85, 102, 197
Lebram, Jürgen H. C. 248
Leeuwen, Raymond C. van 160
Lehman, Manfred R. 177
Leiman, Sid Z. 282
Lemaire, André 290
Levine, Amy-Jill VII
Licht, Jacob 40, 62
Lichtenberger, Hermann 26, 39, 89, 111, 153, 162, 165, 168, 195, 212, 236, 313, 328, 333
LiDonnici, Lynn 7, 98
Lieber, Andrea 7, 98
Lieberman, Saul 41
Lieu, Judith L. VII, 7, 80, 81, 97, 112, 118, 125, 145, 146, 231, 296, 317
Lignée, Hubert 187
Lim, Timothy 3, 4, 43, 320
Lipschits, Oded 209
Lipton, Diana 285, 331
Liver, Jacob 39, 186, 189, 196, 199, 208, 209, 212
Lohfink, Norbert 298
Lowndes Lipscomb, William 154

Lubetski, Meir 312, 328
Luomen, Petri 142, 215, 265, 272
Lyons, William J. 17, 277, 285, 287

Mach, Michael 236
Magness, Jodi VII, 6, 31, 41, 100, 140, 304, 311
Maeir, Aren M. 6, 304
Maier, Johann 33, 35, 84, 91, 95, 100, 118, 164, 249, 298, 333
Marcus, Ralph 33
Mason, Eric 4, 19
McDonald, Lee M. 286
McKane, William 119
McNamara, Martin J. 184
Mealand, David L. 31
Menken, Maarten J. J. 144
Merklein, Helmut 19, 294
Mertens, Afred 231, 238, 240
Metso, Sarianna VII, 4, 5, 7, 8, 9, 11, 17, 28, 29, 30, 33, 35, 36, 37, 38, 40, 41, 44, 80, 81, 82, 84, 85, 89, 90, 91, 95, 97, 98, 100, 101, 102, 103, 104, 105, 109, 112, 113, 116, 117, 118, 124, 125, 128, 129, 133, 134, 137, 138, 142, 143, 145, 146, 147, 148, 149, 164, 165, 166, 167, 168, 195, 200, 215, 241, 242, 243, 247, 248, 272, 274, 275, 276, 277, 278, 279, 282, 286, 287, 295, 296, 317, 327, 328, 335
Milik, Józef T. 28, 35, 36, 37, 39, 40, 82, 83, 84, 89, 109, 183, 208, 233, 272, 273, 274, 281, 296, 304, 305, 306, 307, 319, 321
Milgrom, Jacob 177, 180, 321, 333
Miller, J. Maxwell 293
Mittmann-Richert, Ulrike 11
Moyise, Steve 144
Müller, Karlheinz 19, 294
Murphy, Catherine 31, 87, 110, 243
Murphy-O'Connor, Jerome 7, 29, 30, 35, 67, 78, 85, 91, 92, 101, 109, 128, 187, 234

Najman, Hindy VII, 4, 5, 137, 287, 328
Neusner, Jacob 91, 118
Newman, Judy VII, 124, 132
Newsom, Carol VII, 3, 5, 8, 17, 38, 84, 91, 124, 127, 136, 162, 166, 167, 168, 216, 231, 239, 240, 247, 248, 249, 271, 290, 317, 336
Nickelsburg, George W. E. 17, 77, 78, 209, 271
Niditch, Susan 297, 298
Nitzan, Bilhah 37, 45, 201, 202, 317
Noam, Vered VII
Noth, Martin 293, 294

Osten-Sacken, Peter von der 18, 242, 271

Parente, Fausto 26
Parker, David VII, 109, 283
Parry, Donald W. 26, 65, 94, 112, 157, 162, 214, 278
Paul, Shalom M. 7, 43, 80, 98, 100, 111, 129, 139, 248, 268, 275, 309
Pearce, Sarah VII
Peleg-Barkat, Orit 313
Penner, Jeremy 336
Penner Ken 336
Perdue, Leo 38, 162, 239, 253, 269
Peskowitz, Miriam 254, 265
Peterson, Anders Klostergaard 281, 282
Pfann, Stephen 38, 169, 170, 183, 204, 273, 304, 305, 310, 312–313, 314, 315, 316, 317, 319, 325, 327
Philonenko, Marc 57, 134
Pietersen Lloyd K. 17, 277, 285, 287
Pilhofer, Peter 88, 90, 198
Pinnick, Avital 114, 124, 127, 142, 171, 173, 177, 184, 216, 221, 265, 272, 298
Ploeg, Johan P. M. van der 40, 41, 164
Plöger, Otto 238, 248
Politis, Konstantinos D. 140
Popović, Mladen VII, 4, 79, 101, 115, 125, 145, 197, 249, 271, 286, 288, 291, 303, 304, 305, 306, 307, 308, 309, 310, 311, 313, 328, 331
Porter, Stanley 18
Pouilly, Jean 29, 85, 109
Priest, John F. 37
Propp, William H. C. 290
Puech, Émile 90, 93, 102, 128, 134, 139, 195, 213, 235, 276, 281, 307, 318, 335
Pyysiäinen, Ilkka 124, 142, 215, 265, 272

Qimron, Elisha 29, 33, 42, 43, 56, 57, 58, 61, 69, 70, 73, 75, 79, 110, 116, 130, 131, 132, 174, 175, 176, 178, 179, 180, 181, 182, 205, 206, 221, 222, 243, 315, 323, 325, 327

Rabin, Chaim 28, 31, 33, 35, 37, 40, 56, 75
Rajak, Tessa 26
Rappaport, Uriel 25, 67, 78, 238
Redditt, Paul L. 238
Reed, Annette Y. VII
Reed, Stephen A. 45
Reeves, John C. 66, 155
Regev, Eyal 3, 7, 80, 89, 95, 100, 101, 118, 125, 132, 142, 265
Reif, Stefan 309
Rendsburg, Gary VII
Richards, Kent H. 78
Richter, Hans-Peter 59
Ringgren, Helmer 242
Rösel, Martin 160
Rofé, Alexander 33, 293, 294
Roitman, Adolfo 4, 43, 97, 125, 140, 141, 291
Rowley, Harold H. 27
Rudman, Stanley 238

Sæbø, Magne 298
Sanders, Ed P. 88, 282, 288
Sanders, James A. 154, 279, 286, 292, 325
Sanders, Seth 328
Schäfer, Peter VII, 26, 28, 39, 89, 111, 165, 168, 195, 212, 275, 313
Schechter, Solomon 26, 169, 199, 213
Schenker, Adrian 283
Schiffman, Lawrence H. VII, 2, 4, 6, 19, 21, 25, 27, 30, 31, 35, 36, 38, 40, 41, 42, 43, 44, 48, 57, 61, 66, 82, 83, 90, 97, 105, 125, 140, 141, 154, 156, 160, 170, 173, 174, 175, 177, 179, 180, 181, 182, 184, 185, 186, 187, 188, 189, 190, 204, 232, 248, 260, 289, 291, 299, 303, 304, 306, 307, 310, 312, 317, 331, 332, 336, 337
Schofield, Alison 7, 17, 21, 25, 98, 100, 102, 104, 123, 124, 125, 127, 129, 132, 134, 137, 140, 142, 143, 145, 147, 148, 149, 150, 260, 278, 279, 288, 289, 318, 335, 336
Schremer, Adiel 298
Schürer, Emil 197, 333
Schuller, Eileen VII, 4, 5, 17, 43, 50, 57, 98, 105, 137, 139, 255, 261, 264, 265, 271, 287, 318, 327, 328, 336
Schultz, Brian 137
Schwartz, Daniel R. 70, 298
Schwartz, Seth VII
Schwienhorst-Schönberger, Ludger 138, 196, 212, 275
Secunda, Shay 14
Segert, Stanislav 232
Shanks, Hershel 179
Sharpe, Carolyn J. 205
Shemesh, Aharon VII, 124, 179, 180, 215, 265, 268, 272
Sievers, Joseph 26
Sivertsev, Alexei 255, 261, 262, 263, 264, 265, 268, 269
Skehan, Patrick 291
Skolnik, Fred 305
Smend, Rudolf VII, 294, 299
Smith, Morton 146, 288
Soggin, Alberto 293
Sokoloff, Michael 321
Sollamo, Raija 97, 285
Solomon, Avi 181
Stegemann, Hartmut 3, 28, 29, 30, 31, 35, 37, 40, 41, 43, 48, 49, 57, 66, 80, 100, 124, 127, 154, 166, 169, 175, 177, 184, 204, 216, 241, 242, 260, 274, 290, 304, 305, 307, 308, 309, 311, 318, 327, 330, 331, 335
Steinmann, Andrew 233
Steinsaltz, Adin 282
Stemberger, Günter 19, 294
Sterling, Gregory E. 236
Stern, Sacha VII, 3, 5, 21, 303, 320, 321, 327
Steudel, Annette VII, 13, 49, 134, 137, 207, 214, 226, 290, 307, 327, 333
Stiebel, Guy D. 313
Stökl Ben Ezra 232, 291, 304, 305, 306, 307, 310, 311, 312, 313, 328, 331, 335, 336

Stone, Michael E. VII, 6, 66, 83, 97, 99, 105, 206, 305, 308, 309, 310
Stone, Suzanne Last 272
Stuckenbruck, Loren T. 4, 5, 61, 62, 233, 234
Strawn, Brent A. 39, 89, 109, 195, 275, 317
Strugnell, John 28, 43, 59, 61, 157, 158, 159, 163, 173, 174, 176, 178, 179, 180, 181, 182, 186, 187, 205, 207, 221, 222, 304, 308, 323, 325
Sukenik, Eleazar L. 304
Sussman, Yaakov 174, 179, 186
Sutcliffe, Edmund F. 7, 35, 40, 41, 84, 91, 101

Talmon, Shemaryahu 26, 43, 66, 174, 279, 280, 281, 283, 288, 289, 291, 292, 303, 320, 321, 322, 323, 324, 325, 328, 332, 334
Taylor, Joan E. VII, 6, 31, 43, 44, 98, 139, 303, 304, 305, 306, 307, 308, 309, 310, 311, 335, 336
Terrien, Samuel 154
Thomas, Sam 328, 334
Thompson, Thomas L. 158
Tigay, Jeffrey 189, 268
Tigchelaar, Eibert J. C. VII, 8, 13, 26, 35, 44, 48, 84, 90, 102, 111, 125, 129, 134, 136, 139, 141, 143, 144, 159, 164, 195, 206, 213, 232, 236, 242, 262, 265, 266, 272, 275, 281, 283, 303, 304, 307, 311, 316, 325, 330, 333, 334, 336
Tiller, Patrick 88, 157
Toorn, Karel van der 17, 149, 287
Tov, Emanuel VII, 7, 17, 19, 33, 43, 44, 80, 98, 104, 111, 129, 138, 139, 140, 146, 174, 186, 232, 248, 265, 267, 273, 274, 275, 276, 279 283, 284, 285, 287, 290, 299, 305, 306, 309, 310, 313, 316, 317, 330, 333, 336
Trebolle Barrera, Julio 28, 38, 43, 57, 58, 66, 67, 78, 80, 100, 132, 175, 177, 181, 182, 280, 281
Tucker, Gene M. 293
Tzoref, Shani (see also Berrin) 4, 43, 97, 140, 141, 291

Ulrich, Eugene VII, 5, 26, 43, 65, 66, 94, 112, 129, 157, 162, 173, 179, 214, 262, 278, 279, 285
Uro, Risto 124, 142, 215, 265, 272

VanderKam, James C. VII, 2, 4, 19, 25, 31, 43, 44, 58, 66, 68, 89, 111, 128, 129, 139, 140, 145, 146, 154, 162, 173, 174, 179, 186, 187, 195, 212, 233, 235, 239, 247, 264, 275, 277, 279, 286, 299, 304, 308, 310, 313, 317, 318, 319, 320, 321, 322, 323, 324, 326
Vegas Montaner, Luis 28, 43, 57, 58, 66, 80, 100, 132, 175, 177, 181, 182
Veijola, Timo 299
Vermes, Geza VII, 11, 25, 29, 33, 35, 51, 52, 67, 79, 86, 88, 89, 93, 104, 109, 110, 111, 112, 113, 116, 124, 125, 128, 129, 130, 131, 132, 134, 138, 143, 147, 148, 156, 157, 160, 164, 165, 167, 168, 195, 196, 197, 200, 202, 204, 205, 211, 212, 213, 223, 241, 242, 243, 244, 247, 272, 273, 274, 275, 276, 277, 287, 295, 326, 327, 333
Vaux, Roland De 304, 305, 307

Wacholder, Ben Zion 124, 127, 147, 163, 327
Wassen, Cecilia 43, 101, 132, 216, 219, 227, 265, 266, 267, 268, 269, 336
Weeks, Stuart 293
Weinert, Francis D. 12, 181, 182, 186, 188, 190, 191
Weinfeld, Moshe 26, 35, 36, 38, 44, 45, 184, 294
Weiser, Arthur 292
Weissenberg, Hanne von VII, 97, 136, 323, 325, 326
Weitzman, Stephen 305
Wernberg-Møller, Preben 35, 84, 109, 166, 218, 226, 273
White Crawford, Sidnie VII, 19, 43, 98, 100, 139, 150, 206, 286, 304, 305, 306, 307, 311, 312
Wilcox, Max 231
Williamson, Hugh G. M. 154, 264
Wilson, Gerald 293
Wilson, Robert R. 232

Wise, Michael O. 26, 28, 50, 67, 100, 164, 225
Wold, Benjamin 5
Woude, Adam S. van der 48, 144, 154, 160, 206, 232, 235, 236, 278, 316, 330
Wright, Archie 236
Wright, David P. 321

Yadin, Azzan VII
Yadin, Yigael 32, 57, 180, 204, 205, 206
Yardeni, Ada 32, 312

Xeravits, Geza 5, 89, 211, 242, 318

Zahn, Molly 10
Zangenberg, Jürgen 140
Zenger, Erich 196, 212, 275, 299
Zissu, Boas 140

www.ingramcontent.com/pod-product-compliance
Lightning Source LLC
Chambersburg PA
CBHW030603300426
44111CB00009B/1089